TWO WEEK LOAN

Remember to return on time or renew at
**https://icity.bcu.ac.uk/ or
https://capitadiscovery.co.uk/bcu/account**
Items in demand may not be renewable

DIRE   ARY

DIRECTING THE DOCUMENTARY

Sixth Edition

Michael Rabiger

Focal Press
Taylor & Francis Group

NEW YORK AND LONDON

First published 1987
by Focal Press

This edition published 2015
by Focal Press
70 Blanchard Road, Suite 402, Burlington, MA 01803

and by Focal Press
2 Park Square, Milton Park, Abingdon, Oxon OX14 4RN

Focal Press is an imprint of the Taylor & Francis Group, an informa business

Library of Congress Cataloging in Publication Data
Rabiger, Michael.
Directing the documentary / Michael Rabiger. -- Sixth edition.
pages cm
Includes bibliographical references and index.
1. Documentary films—Production and direction. I. Title.
PN1995.9.D6R33 2014
070.1'8—dc23
2014011982

ISBN: 978-0-415-71930-8 (pbk)
ISBN: 978-1-315-86750-2 (ebk)

Typeset in Sabon LT Std
By MPS Limited, Chennai, India

Printed and bound in the United States of America by Sheridan Books, Inc. (a Sheridan Group Company).

In loving memory of my sister Lindsey

TABLE OF CONTENTS

PART 2: DOCUMENTARIES AND FILM LANGUAGE

PART 5: POSTPRODUCTION

BOOK II: STORYTELLING

PART 6: DOCUMENTARY AESTHETICS

PART 8: WORK

PREFACE TO THE SIXTH EDITION

Today people are shooting actuality as never before, using consumer cameras to shoot friends, children, or pets, and smartphones to cover demonstrations or document the retribution meted out by "security forces." On the front lines of human conflict, courageous men and women risk their lives to document war and natural disasters that turn human life into an atrocious struggle. This they do, I believe, because something noble and brave in them believes that people should not suffer alone. The resulting torrent of documentaries—committed, quirky, funny, outrageous, and sometimes horrific—creates an appetite not only to see films reflecting reality, but to make them.

Which is where this how-to book comes in. Today, anyone can make a documentary, and to save you having to reinvent the wheel, here is my half-century of experience in filmmaking and teaching for you to use. I will talk to you as an equal, and give you a reliable path to follow while you figure out your own esoteric ways of operating. Don't be intimidated—the book is not meant as a survival course, but as a cornucopia of resources from which you choose according to your temperament and current needs. Start filmmaking immediately: you learn filmmaking best from doing it.

DIRECTING THE DOCUMENTARY'S WEBSITE

To keep the book portable (a big complaint with the last edition), many of its suggested projects are now downloadable from www.directingthedocumentary.com. See "Contents of Companion Website" following this preface for what the website offers. You will find analysis, development, shooting, and postproduction projects, as well as short film examples, logs, and forms to help you during production.

PLANNING TO EXCEL

The resources to make nonfiction film are now widely accessible, which means you face stiff competition if you want to make documentary your career. If your films are to cross national and linguistic frontiers, you will need to think originally and in terms of pictorial narrative rather than the "radio with pictures" that television has long given us. A film is really a subtly controlled stream of consciousness for an audience, so I shall often remind you that work which is fresh and personal comes from valuing the primacy of your own life-experience. By learning to notice how you receive and process powerful impressions, you will learn how to use the screen not only personally, but effectively, universally, and accessibly.

If you are lucky and have an experienced mentor, he or she will undoubtedly explain or rationalize some aspects of documentary differently from me. This is because making films is an art, not a science. My way is not "the" way, but a path for you to use as you move toward reliance on your own stock of filmmaking experience—the ultimate and truest authority of all.

As you gain in abilities, please share your skills, ideas, and discoveries with anyone interested. The best way to develop is always to try teaching it to someone else.

This new edition has a top-to-bottom, revised, and clarified structure that aims to put best practice information in your hands. Locate anything quickly using the comprehensive table of Contents at the front, where you see that this book is in fact two books—one for each of the major learning phases it takes to become an accomplished storyteller.

BOOK I: OBSERVING

First, like an aspiring musician, you practice to master today's digital instruments—the camera and the editing program—to document personalities and events that develop spontaneously and outside your control. This relatively self-effacing form of authorship suits many temperaments (mine included), and can produce documentaries of high potential as art and social observation. The Parts include:

Part 1: You and Your Ideas helps you articulate your own most valuable potential—the marks your life has made on you. The aim is to define your own particular thematic material, and to confirm the values and convictions that are your documentarian's wellsprings.

Part 2: Documentaries and Film Language describes how documentary expression evolved in tandem with its technology, and how each new form of documentary sets about making a revised construct of reality. The text demystifies film language by showing that techniques of camerawork and editing in fact mimic human habits of perception and physical adaptation.

Part 3: Preproduction covers the pre-shooting stages when you begin to look for, assess, and develop documentary ideas. To solicit audience feedback at an early stage, you develop a working hypothesis, then research, write a proposal, and *pitch* (make an oral presentation of) the film idea to listeners. From their reactions, you develop your film approach.

Part 4: Production outlines the fundamentals of observational filmmaking, along with the technology and techniques of basic lighting, capturing clear sound, and producing fluid, engaged camerawork. This section also deals with the collaborative practices of film teamwork.

Part 5: Postproduction covers the highly creative processes of editing, and describes the critical viewing sessions of *dailies* (uncut material just as the camera shot it). You then find a structure and proper duration for your film, produce a smooth, well-paced cut, and seek feedback from test audiences.

BOOK II: STORYTELLING

Graduating to longer and more complex films means working hard to attract and hold an audience's attention. Films of all kinds need not just a good subject, but the style, purpose, and "voice" of an entertaining storyteller. This involves self-knowledge as well as planning your film's aesthetics and narrative style. It further means seeking to control all the logistical and technical requirements at a high level of professionalism. Almost certainly you will use a more intercessional style of filmmaking to do this.

Part 6: Documentary Aesthetics deals with the narrative universals of point of view, dramaturgy, form, and style. Bigger projects pose bigger problems of dramatic structure, and clarifying the values, ethics, and choices in your documentary becomes an especially fascinating challenge.

Part 7A: Advanced Preproduction describes techniques necessary for advanced ideation, research, and "casting" for all kinds of nonfiction film. This section emphasizes the importance of finding evidence that is visual and behavioral rather than verbal, and metaphorical as much as literal. An important chapter describes advanced digital technology, the perils of workflow, and its repercussions in budgeting and scheduling. There is how to tackle the more sophisticated promotional writing necessary to approach funds and foundations, and make use of crowdfunding.

Part 7B: Advanced Production outlines the technical choices a director makes that affect the audience's perception of space, depth, and the aesthetic consequences of composition. Larger productions usually take a larger and more specialized crew, with the added complication of sound shot with a separate recorder, sync references, and the appropriate record-keeping. Advanced directing also requires planning the style and amount of coverage. Since you and your crew have the power to make filming enjoyable and natural for participants, there is material on developing a keen understanding of their states of mind while being filmed. An extended chapter deals with interviewing—often crucial to the trust and relationship between you and your human subjects—both on-camera or off-camera during research.

Part 7C: Advanced Postproduction outlines how to build a particular kind of film from transcripts, and ways of creating narration so that it sounds natural and spontaneous. Most important are the principles behind fitting words to images: done well, it can transform your film into a seamless flow of consciousness for the audience. There is working through problems of structure and pacing, and diagnostic procedures to help you. Music, important to today's more lyrical documentary, often depends on your rapport with a composer.

Part 8: Work. Read this early, because it can help you decide how to plan out a career in documentary. While you work to develop a directing reputation, expect to do paid crew work for others. Getting work as a freelancer will mean using the networking and social skills that allow any entrepreneur to prosper, and this section outlines the long-term resources you will rely on.

ACKNOWLEDGMENTS

Of particular help while I prepared this edition were the following important people: Mick Hurbis-Cherrier, my esteemed co-writer for the latest edition of the sister volume to this book, *Directing: Film Techniques and Aesthetics*, fifth edition. With his kind permission I adapted his chapter on technology to documentary needs. Help for the music composition chapter came from my son Paul Rabiger, a film composer in Cologne, Germany. For the career development aspects of the book, I turned to Dirk Matthews, educator, filmmaker, counselor, and co-founder of the Portfolio Center of Columbia College Chicago. For grant-writing and proposal development I sought help from my daughter Joanna Rabiger of Austin, Texas, whose specialty is story development and proposal writing for documentary, and from Tod Lending, long-time friend and Academy-nominated maker of many documentaries shown on Public Broadcasting Service. Any errors, I must add, are wholly my own.

For all her support over the years I would like to thank Eleanor Actipis, my former editor at Focal Press during its publication under the Elsevier imprint. For this edition I would like to thank Dennis McGonagle and Peter Linsley of Taylor and Francis, for their kind support, forbearance, and encouragement.

Lastly, I owe enduring gratitude to my wife Nancy Mattei for her ever-constructive critical acumen, humor, love, and patience with the hermit-crab habits of a writer.

Michael Rabiger
Chicago, 2014

CONTENTS OF COMPANION WEBSITE

(www.directingthedocumentary.com)

Visit this book's website www.directingthedocumentary.com and you will find a variety of essential supplementary information, including projects, online film examples, filmography, forms and logs, and teaching notes.

PROJECTS

Each of the thirty-five or so projects comes with brief instructions, and provides enjoyable and challenging workouts in what a documentary director must know and do. Those with an asterisk also have the appropriate outcome-assessment sheets appended. These allow specialists and non-specialists alike to judge each project for its strengths, weaknesses, inclusions, and omissions.

ONLINE FILM EXAMPLES

Six film quotations represent examples of stories that each set up their characters, situations, and mood. Four are complete beginners' short films. They are shown by courtesy of their directors and by permission of the Maine Media Workshops where they were made during a month-long workshop in August, 2005 (*www.mainemedia.edu*).

a) *Dreaming of Blueberries* (dir. Evan Briggs)
b) *Writing on the Wall* (dir. Melinda Binks)
c) *Blaikie Hines* (dir. Orna Mokady Shavitt)
d) *The Yellow House* (dir. Monica Ahlstrom)

Two further examples are the first 5 minutes of two 90-minute documentary features. These are included by courtesy of their director, Academy Award nominee Tod Lending of Nomadic Pictures (http://nomadicpix.com from whom DVDs are available).

e) *Legacy* (dir. Tod Lending, USA, 1999)
f) *Omar and Pete* (dir. Tod Lending, USA, 2005)

FILMOGRAPHY

Films discussed in *Directing the Documentary* are listed in title order, with country of origin, year of release, and director. Use the Index to locate discussion of them in the book.

PROJECTS

These are in MS Word for easy download and amendment. Those with an asterisk include an outcomes assessment form for easy marking by a teacher or class colleagues.

FORMS AND LOGS

a) Camera Log

b) Sound Log

c) Personal Release Form (from *The American Bar Association's Legal Guide to Independent Filmmaking*) courtesy of Lisa Callif and Michael C. Donaldson (American Bar Association, 2011) who comment that many individuals will not authorize the use of their likeness in your advertising without substantial extra payment. It is generally not worth the extra payment, so you may have to take out that provision.

d) Location Agreement Form (also courtesy of *The American Bar Association's Legal Guide to Independent Filmmaking*).

TEACHING NOTES

These discuss ways in which *Directing the Documentary* can be used in different academic settings. They should be particularly useful to anyone teaching production. Some issues are presented in a FAQ format.

BOOK I

OBSERVING

PART 1

YOU AND YOUR IDEAS

Filmmakers learn from *doing*—dancers must have a floor to dance, swimmers must have water, and filmmakers must shoot and edit. Turn a camera on, and you are straightaway collecting fragments of reality—voices, behavior, landscapes, images, people in action, people talking. With digital software you can begin editing your materials into a narrative.

To tell outstanding stories from the real world, you will need a ferment of ideas about life and living, the courage to go where angels fear to tread, and most of all, personal and inventive ways of using the medium. Do this well, and you will catch people's attention and make them wonder, laugh, become spellbound, or even weep. Your reward is to move hearts and minds—and maybe change the world a little. Filmmaking is a beautiful and involving art form, one that synthesizes practically every other art form invented, and that makes learning a lifelong adventure. Most significantly, making documentary means you are learning about yourself, and becoming a fuller human being.

There are plenty of books about techniques and equipment, so this book concentrates upon what is mostly overlooked: that is, what you must consider, feel, do, know, and strive for in order to emotionally engage audiences. Learning this takes many steps, and two major phases, which is why this volume is divided into two books. Book I, with all its short practical work, aims to turn you into a first-class observational filmmaker. Book II concentrates on the art of telling stories, and encourages you to make yourself into a stylish and masterly storyteller.

CHAPTER 1

YOU AND FILM AUTHORSHIP

Directors who touch us do so from a fascination with the human condition, and a love of using the art of cinema to explore it. Their passion is to entertain, move, and persuade, and their films come not only from them—but *through* them. Each film has a progenitor: someone whose heart and mind starts a project going, and over time brings it to completion. This is the documentary director, who leads a team that often totals no more than two or three people.

THE DIRECTOR'S TEMPERAMENT

Emile Zola said that a work of art is "a corner of Nature seen through a temperament."[1] Certainly a gripping documentary leaves this impression, since the people in it, with their predicaments and objectives, seem imbued with the compassion of an unseen human temperament shaping the life on the screen (Figure 1-1). With this in mind, I shall emphasize throughout this book how important certain kinds of self-knowledge and self-inquiry are to the aspiring director, and will show you how to begin. You have a pleasant and perhaps surprising discovery to make—that you already have a formed and focused inner drive ready to lead your work. I call it your *artistic identity*, and once you know its nature, you will want to use it. This you could do in any expressive form. It would help you write fiction, paint pictures, take photographs, choreograph dance—and, yes, make films. You are probably thinking, can't I function without knowing this artistic identity stuff? The answer is yes, because I directed two dozen films before realizing that my work—maybe my whole life—had a common theme. If only I had known about this earlier in life!

Human beings are by nature seekers, and the quest for meaning is both fundamental and noble. To know what yours is, you have to look for it. The respected actor and New York University directing teacher Marketa Kimbrell used to say, "To put up a tall building you must first dig a very deep hole." All compelling art arises because someone has sought understanding and taken a journey fundamental to human development and wellbeing. The authors of *Art & Fear* say categorically that "the only work really worth doing—the only work you *can* do convincingly—is the work that focuses on the things you care about. To not focus on those issues is to deny the constants in your life."[2] To this I say, Amen.

FIGURE 1-1

A joyful record of modern dance in 3D, and a strongly personal exploration of what leadership can mean in an art form. (Wim Wenders' *Pina*.)

UNFINISHED BUSINESS: HOW YOUR LIFE HAS USEFULLY MARKED YOU

Your documentaries become "corners of nature seen through the lens of a temperament" when you pursue how your life has *marked* you. The highest and lowest points of your life, especially its darker moments, have branded you with special experiences, marks etched in your psyche. Whatever arouses you to strongly partisan feelings is usually connected with these bruises and scars. This is your *unfinished business* talking to you and urging you to pay attention.

The drive to make, express, and discover comes from one's artistic identity, and it is something you can name and characterize, as we shall see. Often it will seem provisional, hazy, incompletely understood, and under construction. No matter, answering its call will always make you feel joyfully alive, as if in love. In love, that is, with a mission and purpose in life rather than with a person (that will come too).

Truly "the unexamined life is not worth living,"[3] and today we own the most superb tool for examining lives—the documentary film form. Make your start with a simple pledge: I will not put anything on the screen unless it reveals something, however small, that *I have discovered for myself* about the human condition.

But, you protest, I have nothing to say! Nothing of importance has happened to me yet!

Not true. Nobody gets through their teens without tasting almost every human experience. Metaphorically speaking you have seen death, been in love, lost a kingdom, fought battles, defied death, been a refugee, and have sacrificed and betrayed. That is the nature of being alive. Left over from this is your unfinished business, and unfinished business is urgent business. When blocked it is an energy source that goes haywire. To have order and purpose in your life, you must attend to it.

This is the particular work that your artistic identity expects of you. It may be science work, arts work, medical work, building work, family reparation work, parental work, teaching work, Girl Scout work, historical reconstruction work, psychological work—work of any kind that involves striving and giving. Since you are reading this book, you are thinking of making documentaries as your work, which means that *my* work is to guide, encourage, and enthuse you with everything I know about it.

Properly attended to, the unfinished business emanating from your artistic identity will change over time. New matters arise to claim your attention, and that is your evolution unfolding—just as it should.

Here are a couple of enjoyable and revealing exercises to help you make a flying start.

PROJECT 1-1: THE SELF-INVENTORY (MARKS AND THEMES)

Privately and non-judgmentally, make notes of the marks you carry. Avoid making anything "positive" or "negative" since that is the inner censor at work, always trying to make you acceptable to other people. Divulge nothing too private. You only need recognize the fundamental truths in your background under general headings. Here's how:

a) **List your key experiences:** Go somewhere quiet and in complete privacy write some rapid, short notations as things come to mind. Make a private, non-judgmental list of your most moving experiences. That is, any *experiences that profoundly moved you* (to joy, rage, panic, fear, disgust, anguish, love, etc.). Keep going until you have ten or a dozen, but the more the better. Some will seem "positive" (accompanied by feelings of joy, relief, discovery, laughter), but most will seem "negative," that is, they carry disturbing emotional connotations of humiliation, shame, or anger. Resist the temptation to suppress anything, because there is no such thing as negative or positive truth. To discriminate is to censor, which is just another way to prolong the endless and wasteful search for acceptability. Truth is *truth*—period!

From making this inner agenda visible, you start to naturally see themes. Any single, deeply felt theme can find expression through many film subjects, each one very close to you, yet none of them autobiographically revealing.

Now start writing notes to help you make a presentation to a class, group, or important individual. The more candid you can be, the better, but *you need disclose nothing too private.*

b) **Arrange them in groupings:** On a large piece of paper, group them in any way pertinent. This important technique is called *clustering* because it helps reveal structures, connections, and hierarchies. Name each group and define any relationships you can find between them.

Then, *in public, and preferably to a class or group, and taking no more than 5 minutes,*

c) **Describe a single, powerfully influential experience, and the mark it left on you.** Keep the description brief.

Example: "Growing up in an area at war, I had an early fear and loathing of uniforms and uniformity. When my father came home after the war, my mother became less accessible, and my father was closer to my older brother, so I came to believe I must do everything alone."

d) In 3–5 minutes, summarize your authorial situation by completing these four sentences:
   - The **theme or themes** that arise from my self-studies are...
   - The **changes** for which I want to work are...
   - The **kinds of subject** for which I feel most passionately are...
   - **Other important goals** I have for my documentaries are...

PROJECT 1-2: WHAT IS THE FAMILY DRAMA?

The family is mostly where we learn the hard lessons of growing up, and the family is the great crucible for drama. Why else would the Greek gods all be related to each other? To a person, group, or class,

a) **Describe in 2–3 minutes the main drama in your family.** If there are several, pick the one that affected you most. (Examples: The impact of the family business going bankrupt, discovering that Uncle Wilfred is a cross-dresser, or the effect of a dictatorial parent wanting all the kids to become musicians.)

b) Say **what you learned** from the way the family drama played out, and what kind of subjects and themes it has qualified you to tackle as a result.

You should now feel you have experience and strong feelings to help focus your directing. Maybe making documentaries will become the work you want to do, in and for the world.

See further self-discovery projects under **Project 1-3 Other Routes to Self-Assessment** at this book's website (www.directingthedocumentary.com). They draw on your dreams, favorite surrogates in film, literature, or public life, and the archetypes they suggest to you.

THE WORK OF THE DIRECTOR

What type of person makes documentaries? Go to a documentary festival, and see what a varied lot they are—old, young, shy, outgoing, haunted, extroverted, straight, gay, men, women, large, small. Most are approachable, friendly, and unassuming, and most are supportive of each other and non-competitive. They will be happy you are thinking of joining the documentary community. They may warn you that it is hard to make a living and that you will have to do other work—crewing, teaching, or something else—to make ends meet.

What is the work really like? Sometimes the director does virtually everything and only intermittently works with a sound recordist and an editor. Other times he or she works with a phalanx of colleagues. Either way, the director's work is leadership that includes:

• Choosing subject matter in which one has an emotional investment and a compelling need to learn.

• Explaining the hypothetical project and getting agreement by people to participate.

• Researching the lives of special people, situations, and topics.

• Helping participants enjoy the experience of making a record of their life.

• Leading the crew and taking decisions about what to film and how.

• Using a camera to ethically record whatever is essential and meaningful.

• Empathically bearing witness, especially for those in difficult or dangerous situations.

• Exposing dramas and injustices in life with a socially critical purpose.

• Drawing stories from real life that are cinematically and dramatically satisfying.

• Supervising (or actually doing) the editing and making the sound track.

• Trying to change the world, one film at a time.

• Working long hours and hardly noticing it.

Each new film project will draw you into a new world, subject you to experiences that press you to decide what's significant, and challenge you to crystallize what matters on the screen as a story. Since artworks mainly emerge from conscious choices and decisions, this means that you must,

- Make yourself highly aware and critical of each unfolding aspect of your film's world and characters.
- Retain not only *what* you learned on your learning-journey, but *how* you learned it.
- Use the screen freshly and inventively so that your audience gets an equal or better learning-journey than your own.
- Suggest stimulating ideas and values concerning the nature and meaning of contemporary life.

Directing takes a multi-layered consciousness, and juggling with so many balls that it may seem like an impossible talent. But anyone can learn how, if they want. It is not a talent but a learned skill. The mistakes and miscalculations you make are all inseparable from learning. The *American Cinematographer*'s standard interview asks famous cinematographers, "Have you made any memorable blunders?" and the answers make reassuring reading because everyone has. Periodically everyone screws up, feels inept and defeated. When it's your turn, punch yourself in the chin and just keep going.

WITNESSING WITH THE FUTURE BOX

People make documentaries to seize and preserve something they cherish before it vanishes. Why does this matter so much? Probably because we know that the great mass of ordinary humanity, your ancestors and mine, left nothing by which we can know them, which is tragic. Only by our forebears' folk music, cautionary sayings, and the marks they left on the landscape can we even guess what kind of lives they led. Unless they tangled with the law or did something remarkable, they sank without trace. I would love to learn more about the branch of my father's people who were village chimneysweeps in Victorian times. I know two things: that the boys had to rub saltpeter into their torn knees and elbows (to toughen them so they could climb the inside of chimneys), and that the family believed itself illegitimately descended from Sir John Cheke.[4]

You and I cannot, *must* not, pass so silently from life, nor must we depend on others to tell our stories. The digital revolution has given us the screen through which to chronicle whatever we see and feel, and now our contemporaries and our descendents can know us. Right now, we can use the screen to examine how and why we are alive.

So, use this book to help you bear witness, reinterpret history, or prophesy the future. It is so much easier than it used to be. In Figure 1-2 the New York veteran documentarian David Hoffman shows the cumbersome and expensive equipment he once carried, and what he now uses for personal filmmaking—a tiny, waterproof, wide-angle $400 plastic sports camera called the GoPro. At a moment's notice he can shoot whatever or whomever he runs into, and his films reflect the sparks generated from human encounter. Originally a musician and coming from the Maysles Brothers tradition of spontaneous filmmaking, Hoffman articulates his outlook quite passionately in "Why I use the GoPro for Documentaries" (youtube.com/watch?v=uptn76M8iDQ). We are all, he says, "reporters, narrators—from behind and in front of the camera. We're talking to each other, to the camera, and to the future." Meeting curious strangers in the street, he tells them, "I'm recording for the future what we're doing, thinking, and feeling in the present—so speak to the future, for this [*tapping the camera*] is your *future box*." In another YouTube film "Best Add-ons for the Hero 3 and Hero 2" (youtube.com/user/allinaday) he shows some of the equipment he has tried, and the minimalist rig he uses now. It does what an iPhone does, only much, much better.

FIGURE 1-2 ———

Lifelong independent documentary-maker David Hoffman equipped for work in 1967 and then 2013. *(Photos courtesy of David Hoffman.)*

ETHNOGRAPHY

Perhaps you are interested in recording a people and their culture. Shows like those given by the Royal Anthropological Institute in London or the Margaret Mead Film Festival in New York exhibit a hundred films in a few days, and the filmmakers are there to discuss their work with the audience. Ethnography is truly the testimony of witnesses, since what they place on record sometimes vanishes before their film is finished. Attend one of these festivals and see how ethnographers try to record a way of life without imposing their own values.

WORKING FOR SOCIAL CHANGE

Documentaries, smartphones, and social media are collecting records of today's grassroots life, from steam fairs at agricultural shows, to the obscenity of shells landing in Middle Eastern apartment buildings. As the Arab Spring upheavals showed, those holding power can no longer ignore or silence the mass of alternative voices. People can now organize and communicate via the Internet, and the consequences—for bloody showdowns, for a more equitable tapestry of cultures, and for the dream of free expression and democracy—are incalculable. Today's documentaries are at the center of this because they investigate, analyze, warn, indict, explore, observe, announce, report, explain, educate, promote, posit, advocate, celebrate, experiment, expound, propagandize, satirize, shock, protest, remember, revise, prophesy, chronicle, conclude, conserve, liberate, lampoon, activate…

Notice that all these are verbs, or "doing" words. "Documentary is an important reality-shaping communication," says Patricia Aufderheide, "because of its claims to truth. Documentaries are always grounded in real life, and make a claim to tell us something worth knowing about it."[5] Documentary not only reveals actuality, it prepares us—whether we know it or not—to take action and live differently.

FIGURE 1-3

In *Darwin's Nightmare* Hubert Sauper demonstrates the surreal nature of African poverty and exploitation.

A REWARDING WAY OF LIFE

Film, including the genre of documentary, is a social art in every stage of its evolution. You work with some behind the camera, and with others in front of it. You direct, shoot, and edit a documentary collectively, and then pass your work over to the audience, that other great collective, for its reactions. In the last century, and now in this, collaborative processes have helped make fiction film preeminently influential among the arts. More recently the documentary has made its way from obscurity to a place of new importance in public consciousness. Today, independent documentary is collecting evidence and showing truths that media corporations hardly dare handle. Often it is the lone, keen, and eloquent voice of individual conscience (Figure 1-3).

The documentarian's reward is to live a full, evolving, and fulfilling life. People treat you and your camera as significant since it is, just as David Hoffman says, a "Future Box" that observes on behalf of those alive now and those yet to come. Your future box, when you appear with it, is a magic passport that opens doors, lowers barriers, and lets you pass where others dare not go. The filmmaking relationship, sincerely and daringly pursued, immerses you in other cultures and other lives. Not only will people want to trust you, but they will take bold new steps because of the attention you pay them. You are first to see aspects of people that not even their closest friends or family have seen. With all this influence comes responsibility.

LEARNING FROM WHAT YOU SHOOT

Making nonfiction cinema gives you a chance to relive segments of your life again, and to discover all that you routinely miss. When you run and rerun the material you shot, you keep seeing further dimensions in your participants and their situations. And then, as you assemble and refine

FIGURE 1-4

Mireia Sallarès shooting in Caracas for her astonishing 5-hour film about Mexican women's sexual lives, *Little Deaths*. *(Photo by Gala Garrido.)*

your film, new truths and correspondences keep surfacing, and the film miraculously develops and strengthens like a growing child.

FILMMAKING DEMOCRATIZED

Today you can make films with little money, position, or influence, as the Catalan artist Mireia Sallarès shows in her astonishing five-hour film about Mexican women's sexual lives, *Little Deaths* (Mexico, 2009, Figure 1-4). You can do significant work, as she has said, using a "way of shooting [that is] direct, humble, [and] alone with no crew or extra hardware." All you need is a camera and computer, the will to discover, and buckets of persistence. Your largest obstacles won't be ones of technique or technology, but of timidity and political correctness. Can you step beyond habits of self-protection and truly explore what it means to be alive? Can you delay gratification for months or years in order to compose the film your subject deserves? All this becomes possible when you come to cherish the language and tools of the cinema. Then, unlike so many trapped in work they hate, you will never have to wonder if you are using wisely your one-and-only life.

THE ORDINARY CAN BE EXTRAORDINARY

Filmmaking is a market commodity that thrives or dies according to audience figures. Complaining about this is futile and unproductive because there are plenty of other obstacles to discourage the fainthearted. Luckily, making a small-canvas documentary no longer requires much of a budget, so now—if you can keep body and soul together—you can simply make the film you believe in, and then see where you stand.

Making the audience notice and value transient moments in obscure lives is normal enough in fiction films, but rarer in documentary. Uncertainty about deserving an audience's attention makes documentarians play safe, so they often resort to exotic or sensational subjects. War, murderers, family violence, urban problems, eccentrics, deviants, demonstrations, revolts, as well as victims, victims, and more victims—all these promise something heightened. Yet the consequence for the viewer is a sense of weariness and *deja vu*.

How refreshing instead to find Ross McElwee's self-mocking search for a wife in *Sherman's March* (USA, 1986, Figure 1-5), or Robb Moss's pained contemplation of his childlessness in *The Tourist* (USA, 1991, Figure 1-6). While he and his wife kept failing to conceive, he was working as a cameraman

FIGURE 1-5

Sherman's March, a road movie of encounters between a man and each of the women he might marry. *(Photo courtesy of the Kobal Collection/McElwee Productions/ Guggenheim Fellowship.)*

FIGURE 1-6

Robb Moss's job as a cameraman in *The Tourist* keeps taking him where people have too many children.

FIGURE 1-7 ——————————————————————

Strength and faith to survive in *The Farmer's Wife.*
*(A David Sutherland Film, photo by John Schaefer ©
WGBH.)*

and regularly shooting in Third World countries where people have too many children. These are original voices intent on breaking the veil of silence that masks unfulfillment. For the small stuff of life—the minutia of small-town life or the anguish in a barely solvent marriage—we more often turn to fiction. But this is not inevitable, as you see in *The Farmer's Wife* (USA, 1998, Figure 1-7) directed by David Sutherland, who makes films from long and patient involvement with his subjects.[6] Of similar intensity is Doug Block's film about his parents' half-century of loneliness in marriage, *51 Birch Street* (USA, 2005, Figure 1-8), and Deborah Hoffman's *Complaints of a Dutiful Daughter* (USA, 1994, Figure 1-9), a bittersweet chronicle of caring for a mother who is sinking into Alzheimer's disease.

Documentarians wanting to buck the trends, as these fine films do, will always face special difficulties, not least with raising money for a film about subjects often considered minor and confined to the personal. Yet their warmth, intensity of regard, and courageous honesty leave much that calls itself documentary looking shallow and perfunctory.

FIGURE 1-8 ——————————————————————

Despite appearances, a half-century of mismatch and loneliness in marriage in *51 Birch Street.*

DOCUMENTARIES THAT CROSS BOUNDARIES AND BUCK TRENDS

Fewer documentaries than fiction films or novels manage to travel beyond the parochial, linguistic, or cultural enclosure of their origins. Often they consciously cater to local interests and local pride, and much funding goes into national navel-gazing. The insular nature of so many documentaries comes ultimately from documentary-makers themselves. Through parochialism they often fail to look for themes of more universal significance in their surroundings. This is why art that transcends boundaries so often comes from immigrants, whose displacement sensitizes them to larger truths. It was immigrants fleeing poverty and totalitarianism, not the locals, that founded Hollywood. And it was immigrants who defined the American Dream—itself the dream of humanity more than of America alone.

FIGURE 1-9

Deborah Hoffman and her mother in *Complaints of a Dutiful Daughter*. *(Photo by Frances Reid, courtesy of Deborah Hoffman.)*

IMPORTANCE OF CREATIVITY

As ever more people make ever more documentaries, finding unique content gets more difficult, with the consequence that creativity in form and style is now at a premium. That is, *how* a film sees may be far more significant to the audience than *what* it sees. Thus you will need to practice generating excellent and original ideas about film form.

So, find out where you stand by blitzing friends and colleagues with project ideas, and encourage them to do the same with you. Argue and promote your ideas so you can fully discover the possibilities, depths, and difficulties ahead. This habit alone will massively speed up your evolution, make you interesting to be around, and it won't cost you a dime.

DOCUMENTARY AS A PRELUDE TO DIRECTING FICTION

A seldom-recognized reason to make documentaries is to prepare yourself to direct fiction films. In the relatively small British fiction industry, it is enlightening to see who first worked in documentary: Lindsay Anderson, Michael Apted, John Boorman, Kevin Brownlow, Ken Loach, Karel Reisz, Sally Potter, Tony Richardson, and John Schlesinger. Is this a stellar list by chance? Now add those coming from painting, theatre, and music, or who espouse improvisational methods, and more distinguished names appear, such as Maureen Blackwood, Mike Figgis, Peter Greenaway, Mike Leigh, Sharon Maguire, and Anthony Minghella. Not all these are household names, but they do suggest that having documentary experience may be important.

In this book's sister volume, *Directing: Film Techniques and Aesthetics*, fifth edition (Focal Press, 2013), Mick Hurbis-Cherrier and I advocate the value of making documentaries for aspiring fiction directors. The advantages are,

- Rapid, voluminous training in finding and telling screen stories.
- Confidence in your ability to use the screen spontaneously and adaptively.

- A proving ground for your intuitive judgments.
- An eye for a focused and truthful human presence.
- A workout in a genre that requires great narrative compression and poses the same narrative problems as fiction.
- Opportunities to show real characters in action as they struggle with real obstacles.
- Immersion in the way a person's identity is not something fixed, but constructed through interactions.
- A laboratory for character-driven drama.
- Catalyzing truth from participants in preparation to do the same with actors.
- A benchmark for knowing when people are *being* rather than acting.
- Shooting in real time, thinking on your feet, and plucking drama from life.
- The risk/confrontation/chemistry of the moment, so central to both documentary and improvisational fiction.

GETTING AN EDUCATION

FILM SCHOOL

How and where you learn to make documentaries depends on your resources, learning style, and how many consuming responsibilities you have acquired. A short summer workshop, such as those at the Maine Media Workshops, can get you hooked or deepen some of your craft skills. Those who need an undergraduate degree may choose a four-year college program for its teachers, structured path, equipment, and filmmaking community. There are however academies that teach only practical filmmaking, such as the London Film School, New York Film Academy, and Tribeca Flashpoint in Chicago. Most film students initially study fiction, and perhaps discover documentary along the way. They may only get a survey course and one or two in basic production. This gets you started but cannot develop your skills and understanding as the excellent two-year MA program does at Stanford University. In the USA, Canada, Europe, and Australia you can find many Masters-level programs listed on the Internet. Be careful: most are expensive, and may be heavy in scholarship and light in professional level skills. Any educational courses you find on the Internet should be crosschecked to see what they promise, who is teaching, and what those who have taken the program say about it. In North American film schools, as elsewhere, there are no recognized standards for teachers or programs, and my intermittent attempts to raise the issue informally with educators have met with a polite silence.

An inexpensive two-year postgraduate program funded by the European Union, taught in English, is called DocNomads (www.docnomads.eu). Each intake migrates through three successive European cities—Lisbon, Budapest, and Brussels—with the idea that,

> students are immersed in different cultures and social environments which make them more sensitive to different documentary practices, ways of communication enhancing their capabilities to work outside their own cultural contexts... The students of this itinerant school explore, via the best Portuguese, Hungarian, Belgian, European and international masterpieces, the history and the new forms of documentary, as well as its outstanding representatives, most of whom are involved in the Master Course. It is a *practice-based training*: particular attention is given to fieldwork and practical courses that deepen the students' theoretical knowledge and encourage them to define their own style.

The workload is high, and competition for places keen, but you may be eligible to become a paying or a scholarship student, depending on your circumstances.

TEACHING YOURSELF

If you have a day job, mortgage, and children to support, you won't have time or money to attend film school. Online courses, sometimes free, are becoming available, especially in using the technology (see www.lynda.com or www.coursera.org). Albert Maysles has been actively involved with passing on his experience and skills, and the Maysles Documentary Center has grown to offer a range of educational and other opportunities (http://maysles.org). If you are self-motivated, it is quite feasible to assemble the teaching you need. Use this book, a camera, a computer, and solicit feedback from intelligent friends who won't hide the truth from you. You can learn documentary simply by lots of doing. If you simply worked through the projects gathered on the website, and used the book to guide your journey, you could become an experienced documentarian in a couple of years of sustained work.

PLANNING YOUR FUTURE

No matter how chance may affect your advance, map out your future intentions. If you want to excel, you cannot plunk yourself down in an educational setting and wait for them to form you. Still less should you expect to naturally attract recognition, since that's another excuse to do nothing much but wait and see. Making entertainment is a highly demanding and entrepreneurial occupation, so you must wring the utmost from your education and earn the respect of those you need. This means that you,

- Use the teaching and facilities to do more than the program demands.
- Work only with people who are committed and constructively critical.
- Read everything about those whose work inspires you, so you become like them.
- Immerse yourself by seeing every film you can, and going to every conference and festival you can afford.
- Read nonfiction, newspapers, and even novels to learn about the subjects that fire your imagination.
- Make working on ideas into an addiction. Only by writing can you discover what's in your mind, examine it, and go farther.
- Pitch (describe in some detail) your ideas for films to anyone who'll listen. They are your film's first audience—even though you haven't yet made it.
- Cram in all the production experience you can handle in addition to your directing.
- Specialize in camerawork, sound recording, or editing so you can expect to earn a living working for others.
- Actively seek your teachers' and contemporaries' help, ideas, and criticism.
- Pay attention to the emerging evidence concerning your strengths and weaknesses, since your best chances of future employment rest on what you do surpassingly well.
- Grow a thicker skin if you are hurt by criticism.
- Compile clips of your best work in each craft. From this you will make "show reels" of your camerawork, sound, editing. These will be vital to your employability.

Working in the film industry is uncertain, and success takes determination, social networking, and persistence. You cannot "learn film first" and expect to make a living later. Do please read Part 8, Work, in particular Chapter 36: Developing a Career. It shows that, to develop a career, you must start building the requisite work habits and social skills from the beginning.

Do not be discouraged by a complete lack of advertised jobs in documentary. It is a branch of the entertainment industry, and the world always has room for the best among its actors, comedians, singers, musicians, journalists, poets, novelists, playwrights, painters, animators ... and documentarians. Talent is not something you "have"; it is something you have to develop using all of yourself.

JOURNALS

Learn to walk the walk, and talk the talk, by reading professional journals and websites. They will draw you into your chosen world by showing where the various jobs and interests lead. *The Independent* (formerly *The Independent Film and Video Monthly*—see www.aivf.org), *International Documentary* (www.documentary.org/magazine), *American Cinematographer* (www.theasc.com/ac_magazine), and *DV Magazine* (www.mydvmag.com) are a mine of professional, critical, and technical information. These sources will help you think, act, and handle yourself like an insider and stay abreast of news, ideas and trends, and new approaches in independent filmmaking, cinematography, postproduction, distribution, and festivals.

INTERNSHIPS AS A STUDENT

Well-established film schools have an internship office that connects their best students (mostly advanced level, but sometimes sophomores and juniors too) with local media employers. At mine (Columbia College Chicago) students get paid and unpaid work as a grip, assistant editor, production assistant, camera assistant, and a great many other positions. Via these internships an employer can, at low risk, try students out in positions where they can't do much harm. An internship may turn into your first paid work, and even if it doesn't, it allows you to try out a career at, say, a postproduction house before you commit to it. Internships also provide the all-important professional references when you need them.

Reputable film schools have an internship office to ensure that students do useful work of educational value to themselves rather than finding themselves doing menial tasks unpaid.

HANDS-ON LEARNING

Most chapters end with a section inviting you to do some practical work from among the projects listed on the book's website www.directingthedocumentary.com. I really believe you learn most from simply doing, not waiting until you feel ready. So if you have any kind of camera and know how to run it, why not do **SP-8 Dramatizing a Location**? It asks you to study the daily rhythms and activities in a place such as a terminus, cafe, or car repair shop, then write a shotlist from your notes, so you can shoot selectively as an observer of life. If you can already edit, so much the better. If you can't yet edit, then simply shoot material, watch it critically, and decide how you will edit them later.

NOTES

1. Émile Zola, *Mes Haines* (1866), French novelist writing in the literary school of naturalism.
2. David Bayles and Ted Orland, *Art & Fear: Observations On the Perils (and Rewards) of Artmaking* (Image Continuum Press, 1993), p. 116.
3. Attributed to Socrates (c. 469 BC–399 BC).
4. Classics scholar and tutor to Queen Elizabeth I, imprisoned for his religious beliefs.
5. Patricia Aufderheide, *Documentary Film: A Very Short Introduction* (Oxford University Press, 2007).
6. See www.davidsutherland.com/bio.html for Sutherland's description of his methods.

CHAPTER 2

THE NATURE OF DOCUMENTARY

BEGINNINGS

The documentary approach has never stopped expanding and changing, which makes it a slippery beast to pin down. It does however always concern real people doing real things in their own real lives. As such, people were filming reality of one sort or another from cinema's very beginnings in the 1890s, and onward through the Edwardian and World War I periods that followed (Figure 2-1). Until the pioneer documentarian Robert Flaherty (Figure 2-2) orchestrated nonfiction material to say something overarching about the human condition, nobody had thought of using factual materials as Flaherty did. Others had used reality to tell a narrative, but Flaherty added thematic and socially critical aspects that lifted nonfiction to a new level of significance.

GRIERSON'S DEFINITION

During the 1920s, the Scottish sociologist John Grierson (1898–1972) used the word "documentary" while viewing some of Flaherty's material. He defined the genre as *"the creative treatment of actuality."* This I take to mean, "If you creatively organize pieces of recorded reality into a narrative, you have made a documentary film." But today this definition is far too baggy, for it embraces nature, science, travelogue, industrial, educational, social, and even factually based promotional films. The documentary long ago separated itself from other nonfiction genres by becoming an art form with an underlying seriousness of purpose. Ready to confront the paradoxes and mystery of human truth, its makers set out to elicit the questions, issues, beauties, absurdities, and mysteries of human life in all its myriad forms.

DOCUMENTARY AS ART

In the last chapter, I quoted Zola's definition of art in order to assert that *documentary is a corner of reality seen through a temperament.* This asks for more than a beginning, middle, and end: it expects you to interpret life with provocative intelligence. This highlights the importance of the seer, whose mind and personality act like a lens. It is the human heart and mind, after all, that cry out, "I exist, I am here"—that noble human protestation arising in even the most repressive and brutal society. It asserts the primacy of humanity, of art, and of critical intelligence by saying, "I am alive; see what I see!"

FIGURE 2-1

Workers outside Pendlebury Colliery in 1901. *(Frame from* The Electric Edwardians *footage by Mitchell and Kenyon.)*

AN ORAL TALE WITH A PURPOSE

In its structure, tone, and purpose the documentary may in fact be descended from the oral tale, which includes the kind of folktales, myths, and legends that audiences customarily consumed at a sitting. The stories' wit, practical application, and cautionary nature made people tell and retell them. They were useful because they entertained the listener while warning of the vagaries of human nature or the implacability of fate. They dramatized how important it was to be wary and to have courage, faith, and persistence. What is "Little Red Riding Hood" if not a warning to the young that wolves lie in bed and say they are your loving relative?

ART FINDS ORDER

Beneath life's chaotic surface lie patterns of deeper truth that the artist seeks to identify. T. S. Eliot said that "*art exists to give us some perception of an order in life, by imposing an order on it.*"[1] The documentary has long been good at digging out the order underlying appearances: Robert Greenwald's *WalMart—The High Cost of Low Price* (USA, 2005, Figure 2-3) argues that the big-box chain, touting itself as the champion of low prices, achieves them by ruthless business and employment practices. Alex Gibney's *Enron: The Smartest Guys in the Room* (USA, 2005, Figure 2-4) reveals how the heads of a giant energy company used trickery and deceptive book-keeping to hoodwink investors, regulators, and customers alike. Morgan Spurlock in his very funny *Supersize Me* (USA, 2004, Figure 2-5) tackles the obesity epidemic by experimenting on his own body. Eating supersize McDonalds for a month, he gains 24 lbs, a fatty accumulation in his liver, and a red-alert cholesterol level. Point made.

FIGURE 2-2

Robert Flaherty with his wife and lifelong collaborator Frances. *(Courtesy of The Robert and Frances Flaherty Study Center, Claremont School of Theology, Claremont CA 91711.)*

CHARACTERS WITH GOALS

As a director, you will need to find central characters who can fascinate an audience. The key is simple: look for people who are *trying to get, do, or accomplish* something (Figure 2-6). Their goal may be admirable, reprehensible, or tragic—it doesn't matter. What matters is that your central character—knowingly or otherwise—is engaged in a struggle of some kind. That struggle may be against inner or outer forces, but a striving subject—whether man, woman, child, or donkey—will always generate larger thematic issues for your film to explore.

FIGURE 2-3 ——

WalMart—The High Cost of Low Price: Mom and pop stores go bust when big-box stores undercut their prices.

If, however, you try to work the other way round—by seeking characters to illustrate a favorite issue—your film will refuse to come alive. This is because you are constructing propaganda, that is, an argument designed to sell an idea, service, or product. No matter how virtuous or well-meaning you are, your argument is convergent and illustrates a foregone conclusion. A true documentary, on the other hand, works at discovering what is organic, uncertain, and spontaneously changing. Often this is untidy and contradictory, but as soon as one cares about the central character(s), their efforts help to generate *identification* in us, and *dramatic tension*. Once we're hooked, we need to know what happens next.

PHILOSOPHIES OF APPROACH

Depending on your temperament, the story you have chosen, and the rules of engagement you set yourself, your film can be primarily observational, like an ethnographic or natural history film, or, as its director, you may decide to intercede and draw the underlying issues out into daylight. Thus there are two main kinds of documentary coverage, the *observational* and the *participatory*, each with their pros and cons.

OBSERVATIONAL MODE

This means observing life by using the camera like an anthropologist, whose discipline demands minimal disturbance to the phenomena under study. Accordingly, observational documentary often shoots by available light and minimizes the interaction between crew and participants. Of course, participants nearly always know you are filming them, especially since you have probably asked them to ignore the camera's presence and continue their normal activities. Customarily, participants

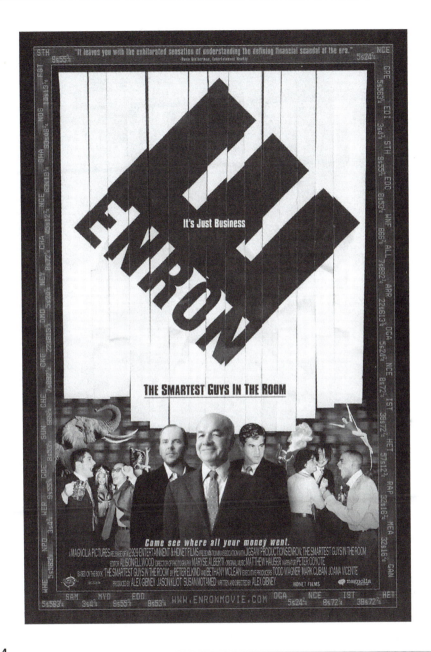

FIGURE 2-4

A house of cards collapses in *Enron: The Smartest Guys in the Room*. *(Photo courtesy of The Kobal Collection/HD Net Films/Jigsaw Films.)*

become used to the camera's presence and find it no more intrusive—yet no more invisible—than having a friend or relative present.

Films whose participants seem unaware they are being filmed are called *transparent* films. This kind of film is a *genre* (type or family of films) that trades on our ability to suspend disbelief,

FIGURE 2-5

Morgan Spurlock taking McDonalds® at their word in *Supersize Me. (Photo courtesy of The Kobal Collection/Roadside Attractions/Samuel Goldwyn Films.)*

FIGURE 2-6

For Nanook and his family, each day is a battle for survival with the elements.

much as in the theatre where we see through the "fourth wall," the transparent boundary between the life onstage and the audience. We can see the characters, but accept that they don't know we are watching them. But actors are very aware of the audience's presence, and so are documentary participants. In the Maysles Brothers' *Gimme Shelter* (USA, 1970, Figure 2-7), Mick Jagger rises from the film-editing machine, and walks away from the evidence of murder at the Rolling Stones Altamont concert. He seems taciturn and cynical, but this might result from his wanting to leave nothing on record that might be used in a liability case. Documentary participants, like theatre actors, are (and must be) affected by the presence of witnesses.

PARTICIPATORY MODE

The alternate philosophy, called *participatory* documentary, permits another range of genres in which the director and crew interact with the participants—off camera, or on—and catalyze or even provoke verbal or physical action (Figure 2-8). At the simplest level, this means questioning, challenging, or even provoking participants, as Nick Broomfield does in *The Leader, his Driver, and the Driver's Wife* (Canada, 1991). In participatory filmmaking, directors can share their thoughts, doubts, and discoveries, and aspects of the filming process, with the audience and/or the participants.

An outstanding film using this approach is Josh Oppenheimer's nightmarish *The Act of Killing* (Denmark/Norway/UK, 2012, Figure 2-9). By offering technical help to a surreally kitsch film they are making to glorify their deeds, the director lures a group of Indonesian thugs into revealing their murderous absurdity. They are the torturers and executioners the military government used to liquidate "communists." The two central characters, who style themselves on Hollywood gangsters, rose from lowly ticket scalping to applying barbaric execution methods in a goon squad. Now parents and grandparents, they live in comfortable impunity, reinventing themselves as they go and claiming due pride for cleansing their society. The surreal, self-aggrandizing musical they are making is meant to celebrate what they did, but instead it becomes a sick, garish advertisement for the psychopathic cruelty of totalitarian regimes everywhere.

FIGURE 2-7

Revealing moment in *Gimme Shelter* when Mick Jagger rises to distance himself from the murder at the Stones' Altamont concert.

FIGURE 2-8

In participatory documentary the director can catalyze or even provoke. In *The Leader, his Driver, and the Driver's Wife*, Nick Broomfield seems close to being whipped by his neo-Nazi subject Eugène Terre'blanche.

FIGURE 2-9

Carefree death-squad in *The Act of Killing. (Photo by Anonymous.)*

Oppenheimer has long experimented with the boundaries between fiction and documentary, and he and his crew launched into this one with extraordinary courage and dedication, since they could easily have been casually murdered. Do not miss the last scene, which shifts everything we know into a different register.

MAKING INCURSIONS

When you begin filmmaking, it is normal and even laudable to doubt your authority. Keep in mind that people regard your attention and your invitation to make a record as a compliment. The documentary process confers recognition, something I suspect that most people privately crave. This allows you to invite a partnership that few ever deny. Your role as director is hard to believe in when you begin, so that you find yourself asking favors with a sense of apology. But soon you find that people mostly welcome your attention. They assist you open-heartedly, and if you press them as you shoot, you discover that making incursions into their lives is not just permitted, it is expected. This makes you feel like a priest taking confessional. Such trust brings high responsibility, but you must resist feeling flattered or obligated, since that will skew your values. Your camera and your profession endow you with certain powers and certain ethical responsibilities, so now you must somehow use them conscientiously. This is a central theme in *The Act of Killing*.

As a participatory director you become assertive and politely demanding in a way that people on the sidelines (wrongly, I think) may deem invasive. For if *your intrusion is morally and ethically justified* and you act unegotistically in belief of your role, people will normally let you inquire. They will journey inward and take you and your camera along to a degree that is surprising and humbling.

GIVING, NOT JUST TAKING

Occasionally filmmaking helps people make changes they never imagined possible. Tod Lending's *Legacy* (USA, 2000, Figure 2-10) followed an Afro-American family for five years after the murder of a beloved family member. In a post-screening discussion, family members said frankly that it was Tod's support and filming that had helped them work their way out of Chicago's notorious Cabrini Green "projects" (public housing set up to warehouse the poor). A film crew that began as witnesses became believers and supporters, and upheld their subjects' sometimes-hesitant progress through an uncaring world. You can see this film's opening at this book's website, www.directingthedocumentary.com.

FIGURE 2-10 ———————————————————

The crew arrives to begin shooting *Legacy*, only to find their young subject has just met his death in the street below.

When you make a documentary, remember you are giving as well as taking. That is, you are conferring recognition, involvement, listening, caring, and giving all the support that those qualities imply.

A WORKHORSE GENRE

Documentaries make human issues palpable in order to exercise the hearts and minds of an audience and raise involvement with other people's lives and predicaments. Each story, however brief and fragmentary, explores its corner of reality in order to reveal what underlies human or other relationships, what motivates couples, families, groups, or corporations, and what sets in motion all their hidden agendas. Do you know what situation your film is challenging? What is at stake? Who cares? Who wins? Who loses? Who grows?

TESTING FOR DOCUMENTARY VALUES

To distinguish a documentary from other nonfiction forms, or to check whether you have strayed beyond the pale, see how you answer these six vital questions:

1. *Does it depict actuality*—that is, real people in a world that exists, or did exist?

2. *Does the film arise from a belief of some kind?* Documentaries nearly always involve beliefs—either those of the participants, or of the filmmakers. A very brief documentary might profile a large beetle trying to climb a stalk in order to take wing. As a kid I once sat with my father watching this happen, and we were both entranced. Its clumsy and laborious climb, and the obstacles making its take-off so uncertain, gave its progress great dramatic tension. When the bug finally went buzzing on its way, it was as if we'd seen a marathon. Something like this could become a complete story about effort and belief, because the beetle assumed it could fly while we doubted its aeronautics—and it proved us wrong.

3. *Is it concerned with raising awareness?* Outstanding documentaries take us into new worlds, or let us see familiar worlds in new ways. They direct and intensify our consciousness of currents, customs, and beliefs in the real world. Examined in depth, a corner of life becomes a strange and profound dream in which we see cause and effect anew, and experience new emotions that encourage us to take action (Figure 2-11).

4. *Does it show a range of human values?* Memorable documentaries usually focus on people struggling with their share of the human predicament, and trying to accommodate or change it. Patricio Guzman's masterly *Nostalgia for the Light* (Chile, 2010, Figure 2-12) compares astronomers at work in the Atacama Desert observatory with lonely, elderly figures digging nearby among the sand dunes. Tragically, their unending search is for the bones of their "disappeared ones," those young idealists whom the Pinochet dictatorship liquidated as enemies of the state, and disposed of like garbage. The film explores the irony of scientists seeking to understand the origins of life while nearby, families try to comprehend the brutality that obliterated their loved ones with neither explanation nor comment.

5. *Does it involve conflict?* Most compelling stories are about people striving to accomplish something that matters to them, which means they are in internal or external conflict. Whether or not they succeed keeps us enthralled. In *Winged Migration* (France, 2001, Figure 2-13) directed by Jacques Perrin, Jacques Cluzaud, and Michel Debats, the "characters" are different species of bird, each compelled to migrate in order to survive. As they wing their way high above the incandescent beauty of Mother Earth, each bird must expend every ounce of energy to overcome the huge distances, treacherous weather, and cold that saps their reserves. Sadly, those weaker or unfortunate do not complete the journey, so the film becomes a haunting metaphor for the transience and brevity of all life, most particularly that which is human.

FIGURE 2-11

An actor faces having a sex change operation in *The Person de Leo N*. Can she dispense with lifelong disguises?

FIGURE 2-12

Memorable documentaries show people struggling with their share of the human predicament, and trying to accommodate or change it. *(Frame from Patricio Guzman's masterly* Nostalgia for the Light.*)*

FIGURE 2-13

The "characters" in *Winged Migration* are birds struggling to survive. *(Photo courtesy of The Kobal Collection/Sony Pictures/Matheiu Simonet.)*

6. *Does it imply social criticism*? Nonfiction genres—such as the travelogue, industrial, info-mentary, and educational films—routinely present a body of information without calling into question any of the human values involved. A factually accurate film that shows how razor blades are manufactured would be an industrial film, but a film showing the effect of repeti-tive precision manufacturing on workers, and *which stimulates the spectator to draw socially critical conclusions*, can only be called a documentary—however accurately it also relays the physical process of manufacturing.

LEARNING FROM YOUR WORK
THE ARTISTIC PROCESS

When you make documentary—or anything in the arts—the work's processes release fresh dimen-sions of understanding. At the beginning, you get clues, then clues lead to discoveries, discoveries lead to movement in your work, and movement leads to new directions. Making documentary is an amazing pathway to acquiring greater social skills and awareness, and pursuing it gives you the sense of growing and of developing your "voice." You will want to work persistently at eliminating each film's imperfections, but eventually something in you signals that you have liberated its best potential. This is the culmination of the *artistic process*.

You are making films, but your films are also making you. They are teaching you and develop-ing your sensibility, a growth inseparable from the artistic process. Your work—whether a piece of writing, a painting, a short story, a film script, or a documentary—is therefore both a laboratory and a motivation to continue. Help comes in mysterious ways: more than once, inexplicably lucky "coincidences" occurred in my filmmaking career as if some higher power had stepped in. Of this, Goethe said, "The moment one definitely commits oneself, then Providence moves too. All sorts of things occur to help one that would never otherwise have occurred."[2] A trenchant saying in the same vein is that *luck favors the prepared mind*.

WHEN YOU LOSE YOUR WAY

You will lose your way—and rediscover it, repeatedly. This is how you find your innate instincts and learn to trust them. Important work and learning usually arise from tension and con-flict, never from comfort and contentment, so don't even ask for better circumstances. Do how-ever choose work partners carefully, since with good ones you can handle anyone and anything. The social nature of filmmaking also holds some risks. In the face of criticism and well-intentioned suggestions, you can lose sight of your intentions. Your best defense against this is an articulate, resilient set of beliefs that help you hold on to the central purpose behind this particular work. Writing down your mission and purpose in a working hypothesis (to be explained later) helps you stay anchored to your central purposes.

Never, ever alter more than small details without first taking time to reflect.

PRIVACY AND COMPETITION ISSUES

If you decide to work in the arts, you cannot remain private—which is a euphemism for "safe and untouched." Opening your inner self to creative partnership is important, for we cannot urge liberation on others without trying to free ourselves first. Within any group you'll see people of courage, often those shy by nature, who even so go out on a limb. Others make a noisy show of self-assurance but prove afraid to reveal themselves. Which person will have the better life? Which will contribute most to the lives of others?

HOSTILE ENVIRONMENTS

Making documentary challenges you to step out of your comfort zone. Some educational environments, however, are hostile. The personal chemistry is wrong, or competitive personalities dominate. Usually this is because someone is operating a patronage system, and steering advantages to favorites. Common and deplorable though this is, regard it as a challenge put there to test your mettle. Sooner or later you'll encounter this in the workaday world, so make a resolution to bloom where you are planted.

HANDS-ON LEARNING

For practical work there is the study project **AP-8 Analyze a Director's Thematic Vision** and among shooting projects there is covering any kind of process in **SP-6 Process Film** or **SP-7 Event Film**. Most documentaries have many sequences of this kind, and showing the stages of something, and making them brief, interesting, and revealing of the people involved is a fascinating challenge. Study the assessment critera supplied with each project since they will help you know what to put in your film.

Among useful books, there are: Patricia Aufderheide, *Documentary Film: A Very Short Introduction* (OUP, 2007), Betsy A. McLane, *A New History of Documentary Film* (Bloomsbury Academic, 2012), and Robert Coles, *Doing Documentary Work* (OUP, 1998).

NOTES

1. Thomas Stearns Eliot (1888–1965), American poet who migrated to England.
2. From John Anster's "rather free" 1835 translation of *Faust* by Johann Wolfgang von Goethe (1749–1842).

PART 2

DOCUMENTARIES AND FILM LANGUAGE

Your film heritage is a language no less evolved and subtle than the mother tongue you use to communicate verbally. Knowing its evolution through film history prepares you to make films that audiences find striking.

CHAPTER 3

DOCUMENTARY HISTORY

TECHNOLOGY AND SCREEN LANGUAGE

A good general information website for technology and film history is Greatest Film Milestones in Film History at AMC's Filmsite, www.filmsite.org/milestones.html. The roots of documentary film lie in two nineteenth-century inventions: photography and sound recording. First came still photography, developing steadily from the 1830s onward (Figure 3-1). It was the first instance of preserving moments in time, and people thought it miraculous. Encountering his first Daguerreotype photograph, a French painter of the day exclaimed, "From today painting is dead."[1] Of course he was wrong. Painters simply had to rethink painting—a radical reconsideration that many artists have to face. Edison's first sound recordings in 1877 also struck people as revolutionary, something you can sense from listening to the first scratchy talking and singing preserved from so long ago.

The first movies in the 1890s were silent and used static camera angles to make single-shot movies of daily life, or staged short improvised scenes (Figure 3-2). Gratified by the reactions of their audiences, the makers learned by experiment what techniques worked best for domestic cameos, newsreel events, or magic shows. In the decades that followed, they developed a host of new tools—cameras, faster film stocks, synchronous sound, and editing equipment—so that film's language, and its ability to move hearts and minds, all developed fast. Because the audience's grasp of screen conventions was in evolution too, filmmakers found they could use an increasingly sophisticated narrative shorthand.

You can see most of the growth in cinema language that fuels today's screen eloquence from little more than a dozen chosen documentaries. Very little technique has been outmoded or superseded: almost every advance in screen language, almost every technical and ethical issue remains vibrantly alive today (Table 3-1).

In the text that follows, key films or film anthologies are in **bold** print. With each groundbreaking film I have tried to pair an example that uses the same film language in a modern context. You can view passages from nearly all the films cited by entering their titles and director's surname in YouTube (www.YouTube.com). Beware "personalized" versions in which someone has mashed up (re-edited) the original. Often you can find interviews with notable directors on the Internet, or films about them. Since some of my own history and that of my family exists as threads in this century-long tapestry, I have taken the liberty of mentioning them. Cinema is a living art spun from intertwined human lives.

FIGURE 3-1

Perhaps the earliest photo of a human being—a Parisian having his shoes polished—taken by Daguerre, spring 1838.

FIGURE 3-2

1904 holiday-makers at Blackpool Victoria Pier in *The Electric Edwardians*.

TABLE 3-1 How film's technology and its language developed

Year	Picture	Sound	Consequences
1820s	First still pictures. Long exposure times necessary. More spontaneous imagery was not possible until more responsive film became available later in the century.		First mechanical preservation of still images from real life now possible. They represent moments in time, miraculously preserved for posterity by the agency of a device instead of laboriously by an artist's hand.
1870s		Wax cylinder recording.	First recordings of voices and music now possible.
1890s	35mm silent film camera (hand cranked, tripod-mounted cameras could shoot fast or slow motion).		Cinema experience invented: magic shows, travelogue, and ethnographic film taken in faraway places, followed quickly by fiction. Screen language using manipulation of time developed rapidly in response to audience reactions.
1910s		Electrical amplification of sound possible but no way yet to sync with film.	Beginnings of radio and entertainment through sound.
1920s	Light, portable 16mm film cameras available for amateurs (inexpensive to run but mainly used for silent home movies).		Home movie footage preserved an invaluable archive of informal life. Low-cost film copies available for home projection.
	35mm sync film camera (camera noise had to be muffled by a bulky soundproof "blimp." Sound shooting was only practicable in a studio setting).	Sync and "wild" (non-sync) sound recording now possible using a massive "sound camera." In use until the 1950s, it recorded photographically on to 35mm sound stock.	Synchronous sound now feasible, making the full theatrical experience in the cinema possible. Action and actors were however subservient to the technology. Until the 1950s documentaries were commonly shot silent, the editor post-constructing a sound track from music, narration, and sound effects.
1960s	Faster film invented, and advent of Eclair NPR 16mm camera (compact, shoulder-mounted, and able to make very rapid magazine changes).	Nagra tape recorder (portable hi-fi sync shooting on to magnetic tape).	A revolution in TV filmmaking: mobile equipment and fast film allowed the crew to capture the tempo of life as it actually happened. High shooting ratios and color film made documentaries extremely expensive to produce, but need for story compression drove documentary editors to make major narrative and stylistic advances. These were adopted by fiction films.

(*Continued*)

TABLE 3-1 (Continued)

Year	Picture	Sound	Consequences
1970s	Black-and-white analog video recording using reel to reel tape recorders (easy playback but very cumbersome to edit).		Low-cost actuality capture under available light, with prospect of low-cost filmmaking getting closer. Diary filmmaking now economically possible.
1980s	Color analog recording using tape cassettes (easy playback but sophisticated editing difficult because of cassette-to-cassette copying, and quality degradation between copies).		Color documentary material now inexpensive to shoot, but editing remains labor-intensive and clumsy. Rising activity among young independent documentary makers, and shift toward more personal subject matter.
1990s	Digital video using smaller cameras (low-cost acquisition, fewer picture flaws, excellent quality copying).		Digital formats and nonlinear computerized editing return editing to the piecemeal flexibility of film, but without the labor of film's handling or film's laboratory costs. Huge increase in independent documentary filmmaking of all kinds. Films often long, wandering, and diffuse since shooting is more accessible than the skills of storytelling.
2000s	High definition [HD] video (picture resolution and low-light capability now allow quality approaching 35mm film. Sophisticated editing and color correction now possible in a laptop computer). DVDs and potential of the Internet promise wide distribution.		Much larger, wide-screen image with quantum leap in quality opens up new range of scenic and other high definition subject matter. Animation and easier picture manipulation permits greater freedom from the tyranny of naturalism.
2010s	Cameras and sound recorders now light, small, and with excellent image resolution (few moving parts, rugged, and solid-state recording. LED lighting means lighter, less power-hungry lighting instruments. Computer programs make the panoply of cinema effects and image manipulation available at low cost).		Miniature cameras can go anywhere, attract little attention, yet produce high quality imagery. Phone cameras make home movies always possible and democratize acquisition in demonstrations, war, or natural disasters. Internet and social media make Arab Spring revolutions possible. Downside for filmmakers is the proliferation of video formats and compression codecs that make workflow a minefield. All the known possibilities of cinema expression are now in the hands of the moderately affluent consumer.

BIRTH OF THE CINEMA

In 1895 the brothers Auguste and Louis Lumière (Figure 3-3) laid the foundations of the cinema in France. During a business trip to New York, their painter and photographer father, who owned a photographic business in Lyon, saw Edison's Kinetoscope (Figure 3-4). He saw a moving image in a box, and thought his sons were inventive enough to get the image up onto a public screen. They fulfilled their dad's expectations by borrowing the intermittent action of the sewing-machine to fashion a hand-cranked camera of wood and brass (Figure 3-5). They filmed nonfiction scenes from the daily lives of those around them and began showing 50-second movies. By ingeniously coupling it to a light source they made their camera double as a projector and contact printer.

By mounting the camera on a tripod and letting the action pass in and out of the frame, their filming technique came direct from still photography. *The Lumière Brothers' First Films* (France, 1896-98, DVD remastered from the originals) shows their work as fresh as in its infancy. The Lumière employees go to lunch in *Workers Leaving the Factory* and in *Arrival of a Train at La Ciotat* (1896, Figure 3-6) we see

Auguste and Louis Lumière. *(Courtesy of Institut Lumière.)*

an everyday scene at a station in which the descending passengers glance at the camera, oblivious that they are making history. Each little narrative lasts the entire run of the camera, is structured around an observed or contrived event, and the brothers have no idea yet of making camera movements or cuts. Participants usually know they are being filmed; in *Feeding the Baby* (1895) Auguste and Marguerite Lumière enjoy showing off their daughter Andrée, and the family gardener becomes the victim of a hosepipe prank in *The Sprinkler Sprinkled* (France, 1895). Plainly he enjoys hamming it up for his employers' camera.

These simple and extraordinarily beautiful works are the world's first home movies. Notice that film is always *now* and in the present. The invention of film brought a new tense to international language, one you might call the present eternal. True, *Train Arriving* took place over a century ago, but we are right there with those passengers alighting on the platform each time the film plays.

Soon Lumière operators swarmed across the world shooting exotic or newsworthy events, and their films founded a new money-making show called the cinema. Somebody broke company policy by taking a moving shot from a Venetian gondola, and others soon followed by shooting *tracking shots* from carriages, automobiles, and trains. The race to develop film language was on. Visit the Lumière Museum online at www.institut-lumiere.org and see a range of early cinema gadgets at www.victorian-cinema.net/machines.htm.

Early footage is still turning up. In the 1990s someone clearing a French sanatorium attic found a biscuit tin containing two unknown Lumière films. They had lain there for a century after a show given for inmates. In England, workmen demolishing a factory found barrels containing 28 hours of wonderful footage from the early 1900s. *The Electric Edwardians—The Lost Films of Mitchell*

FIGURE 3-4

Edison's Kinetoscope—moving images in a box. *(Image courtesy of the Kobal Collection.)*

FIGURE 3-5

The Lumière Brothers' hand-cranked camera. *(Photo courtesy of Institut Lumière.)*

FIGURE 3-6

Passengers in the Lumière Brothers' 1896 film at La Ciotat railway station have no idea they are making history. *(Photo courtesy of the Kobal Collection.)*

FIGURE 3-7

Mineworkers and their families outside a colliery seeing a movie camera for the first time in the BFI's *The Electric Edwardians*.

FIGURE 3-8

Outside a Bioscope traveling cinematograph show. The man on the right is clearly directing a laughing crowd to surge down a staircase. *(Frame from* The Electric Edwardians).

& Kenyon (GB, 2005, Figure 3-7) shows the work of two photographers filming busy street scenes in the north of England. They developed their footage and invited paying customers to see themselves on the screen the same night. Perhaps my great-uncle Sidney Bird, a cinema projectionist in Portsmouth in 1909, projected material like this. Go to YouTube and see tradesmen jogging past in horse-drawn carts, and others idling in the street, mugging at the camera, or running errands by bike. The Mitchell and Kenyon footage contains some of the earliest shots of someone directing staged footage (Figure 3-8).

THE DOCUMENTARY ARRIVES ON THE SCENE

Between 1895 and 1920 cinema audiences saw great quantities of reality footage, particularly that representing the vast, unfolding tragedy of World War I. In spite of so much actuality in the cinemas, it was not until Robert Flaherty's *Nanook of the North* (USA, 1922, Figure 3-9) that audiences saw a nonfiction narrative with a deliberately imposed thematic meaning. Flaherty was an American mining engineer who had spent his boyhood prospecting with his father in northern Canada. There he had learned to love and respect the Inuit people. In 1915, using an early 16mm camera, he began an ethnographic record of an Eskimo family. Editing his film back in Toronto, he discovered that nitrate film stock and chain-smoking make dangerous bedfellows, for his 30,000 feet of negative went up in flames, and he was lucky to escape alive. Afterwards, seeking funding to reshoot, he was compelled to screen his surviving workprint repeatedly. This convinced him that his film was flat and pedestrian, and so he resolved to shoot another that would tell more of a story.

Setting out again with his hand-cranked camera and slow film stock that often needed artificial light, he began shooting in appalling weather conditions. Often he would ask his subjects to

FIGURE 3-10

While they act as though in a fictional story, the participants in *Nanook* collaborate to make the film as authentic as possible.

FIGURE 3-9

Nanook warming his son's hands in Robert Flaherty's *Nanook of the North*. *(The Museum of Modern Art/Film Stills Archive.)*

do their actions in special ways for the camera. Flaherty's Inuit cast were keen to demonstrate an old way of life, and by now his central character Nanook (not his real name) really liked Flaherty. The two felt they were putting on record a vanishing culture, and would watch *dailies* (uncut material) together. Thus Flaherty came to shoot a factual film in real surroundings, but acted like a fictional story (Figure 3-10). His shooting style is basic even by the standards of his day, but his cast is delightful and the Arctic majestically beautiful. His *participants* (as I shall call those who take part in documentaries) came to know and trust him so well that they seem free of all self-consciousness.

To us the film seems ethnographically authentic, but Nanook's clothing and equipment actually come from his grandfather's time. You can't see it, but the igloo has no roof (to allow in light for filming) and the hunting spears are antiques because the Inuit were already using rifles. Flaherty was in fact reconstructing a way of life already swept aside by industrial society and its technologies. Audiences did not know it, but Nanook, shown cheerfully biting a phonograph record after hearing it play, was no ignorant native. He was Flaherty's astute collaborator who transported and assembled their filming equipment, and developed their footage ready for screenings.

Generations of critics have argued over the ethics of Flaherty's artifice, but what lifts *Nanook of the North* above the level of complaint is its noble vision of an Eskimo family surviving in the hostile Arctic. Not only does it respect its subjects, but it builds a larger theme—that of humankind's ancient and deadly struggle for life against the forces of Nature. Flaherty shows a traditional Eskimo family as a tightly interdependent unit whose very survival depends on everyone carrying out assigned functions. Nanook as their leader is a human dynamo; during their increasingly isolated and perilous journey he improvises housing with irrepressible humor. He hunts food, teaches his children, and uses his ingenuity to tackle each new obstacle. The flame of life, the film implies, depends on resourcefulness, cooperation, and endurance. Most tellingly, Flaherty does not return the family to safety at the end of the film, but leaves them huddled in the Arctic wastes with a snowstorm engulfing their long-suffering huskies. Then, while New York audiences lined up

FIGURE 3-11 ——————————————

While audiences lined up to see *Nanook*, its central figure died hungry and in obscurity.

around the block to see the film, its subject died hungry and in obscurity—perhaps at home from disease, or perhaps as a result of a hunting accident. Who can imagine a sadder or more ironic validation of the underlying truth in Flaherty's vision? (Figure 3-11).

Flaherty's hybrid. melding of truth and fiction in the service of a higher purpose did not die with him. It is alive and well this century in *The Story of the Weeping Camel* (Germany, 2003, Figure 3-12) directed by two Munich film students, Luigi Falorni and Byambasuren Davaa. In collaboration with Mongolians living in yurts in the Gobi Desert, the directors have made a partly scripted, partly improvised film about Mongolian family life. It centers on the annual birth of the bactrian camels on which their lives have traditionally depended.

Very little in documentary history has gone out of date or been abandoned. Every approach and technique still has its modern application.

DOCUMENTARY PARADOXES

The word "documentary" surfaced during a mid-1920s conversation between Flaherty and John Grierson, a Scottish social scientist interested in the psychology of propaganda. Commenting on a cut of

FIGURE 3-12 ——

The Story of the Weeping Camel, a modern tale from the Gobi Desert that is directly in the Flaherty tradition. *(Photo courtesy of the Kobal Collection.)*

FIGURE 3-13 ─────────────────────

In *Man of Aran*, Flaherty assembled his own photo-
genic family rather than use an existing one. *(Photo
courtesy of the Kobal Collection/Gainsborough
Pictures.)*

FIGURE 3-14 ─────────────────────

Going a step farther with poetic and emotive performance, Flaherty wrote *Tabu* in 1931 for F. W.
Murnau.

Flaherty's fiction film *Moana* (USA, 1926), Grierson said he thought it was "documentary" in intention.
And so, retrospectively, was *Nanook*—today acknowledged as the nonfiction genre's seminal work.

Laurels never came easily to Flaherty, who came under attack for creating lyrical archetypes.
This is undeniably true, for Flaherty was a romantic who never forgot his wilderness boyhood.
Several of his films even use a boy as their central character. Though his detractors admired his
humanism and poetic photography, they thought it deplorable that he assembled his own photo-
genic families instead of filming authentic ones. In *Man of Aran* (USA, 1934, Figure 3-13) he further incensed his critics by leaving out the large house of the Aran islanders' absentee landlord, the
individual mostly responsible for the islanders' deprivations. It was the Aran Islanders' ancestral
struggle with Nature that excited Flaherty, not their abuse by an extortionate social system.[2]

The charges leveled at Flaherty's romanticism and the resulting volley of questions about the basis
for documentary still reverberate today: What is documentary truth? How objective is the camera?
Can you ever be objective like a social scientist? Must one show literal truth or can it be *the spirit
of the truth*? And whose truth should you show? When you juxtapose material to imply new meanings, what makes your edited version more truthful or less so? When can you use poetic and emotive
means, as Flaherty does, to evoke feeling? And what part does aesthetics play in persuading an audience? Flaherty went a step farther and in collaboration with F. W. Murnau helped initiate a thoroughly spurious fiction film (*Tabu—a Story of the South Seas*, USA, 1931) set in Tahiti (Figure 3-14).

THE CINEMATIC EYE

After the 1917 Russian Revolution, the Bolshevik government found itself administering a vast
federation of nations whose least educated citizens could neither read nor understand each
other's languages. Among those working for the revolution by compiling newsreels for the
Agitprop regional train screenings was the poet, musician, and film editor Dziga Vertov. Seeing
how powerfully affected audiences were by imaginative camerawork and editing, he developed his
Kino-Eye manifesto—meant to be a prescription for recording life without imposing on it.

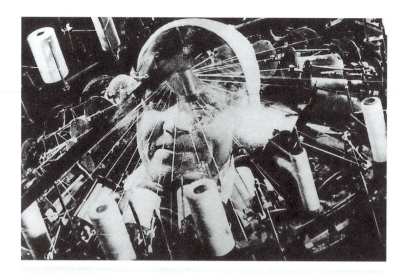

FIGURE 3-15

Dziga Vertov aimed to create a specifically cinema eye in *The Man with the Movie Camera. (Photo courtesy of the Kobal Collection/VUFKU.)*

FIGURE 3-16

The tripod taking a mock bow in *Man with the Movie Camera.*

Vertov's silent masterpiece **Man with the Movie Camera** (USSR, 1929, Figure 3-15) is a visual symphony. It begins in a movie theatre and dashes into the streets to spin many strands of simultaneous narrative—in homes, in the streets among the homeless, in workshops and factories, on the beach—all making up a tumultuous day among the citizens of Moscow and Odessa. The film works virtually without titles, and revels in showing its ubiquitous cameraman mounted on flying trucks, clambering up bridges, or standing astride towering buildings. Vertov includes every form of trick-photography in the film's gallery of playful illusions, and at the end, with its virtuoso performance complete, the camera takes a mock bow on animated, striding tripod legs (Figure 3-16).

The DVD of *Man with the Movie Camera* (significantly enriched by Michael Nyman's obsessive, minimalist score) divides the film into chapters with titles that suggest how ambitiously Vertov has seized the medium: Awakening, Locomotion, Assemblage, Life Goes On, Manual Labor, Recreation, Relaxation, and Cinematic "I" (a play on "Kino-Eye").

With brilliant foresight, Vertov extols film's unending possibilities by making the camera almost humanly aware of its own magic vision. That is, by juxtaposing so much action and so many points of view, Vertov believed he had freed the screen from all viewpoints except that of the all-seeing camera. In reality it is Vertov's mind and personality that deliver what we see. In a virtuoso experiment, he demonstrates how each action, movement, and shot has its own inherent rhythms. From the film's form and content, so creatively edited even though editing machines did not yet exist, we see music for the eye. Today's equivalent is MTV and music videos.

Man with the Movie Camera demonstrates one of the medium's most important capacities— that it can alter our perception of time and space. Notice how its opening shots compress the lacing of a film projector down to a few short, indicative shots. Ordinarily this is quite a lengthy, fiddly process, but Vertov shows a hand mounting a film spool, and then a hand making the first moves to thread the film path. This convention, called Ellipsis, is like shorthand since it allows just a few actions to imply a much longer process, a technique universally used today to abridge time and space.

In its first quarter-century the cinema developed a richly expressive language of action, movement, and imagery. Silent film, accompanied by live music, stimulated the audience's imagination by telling stories and developing ideas visually. In the 1920s, electrically driven cameras freed the operators to use both hands, and become even more mobile and inventive.

SOUND

Sadly, the cinema's tidal wave of visual creativity lost impetus when synchronous sound arrived in the late 1920s. The cinema, including documentary, fell into the grip of a theatrical discourse that relied on narration, music, and sound effects. This was because of the sheer bulk and power requirements of sound equipment, which confined shooting to film studios. I first saw a sound camera (as they were called) in the late 1940s as a nine-year-old making a day visit with my dad, a make-up man at England's Pinewood Studios. He led me off the blindingly bright Technicolor stage to step into the gloom of a darkened truck parked nearby. There sat the Westrex behemoth that recorded sound photographically on to 35mm film. Its unlucky operator sat distant from the hubbub of the set, permanently wearing headphones and awaiting instructions.

A year earlier my father, a recently demobilized sailor, had somehow talked his way into becoming a make-up trainee for David Lean's classic Dickens adaptation, *Oliver Twist* (GB, 1948). His first assignment was to put an ominous black patch over the eye of Bill Sykes' white bull-terrier. One evening at home he tried to get me to play the moment when Oliver faces the orphanage overseers and holds up his bowl, saying "Please sir, can I have some more?" (Figure 3-17). Living as I did in a rural village, and having seen no drama of any kind, I was mystified by what he asked of me. Long after his death I realized he must have been reliving the orphanage youth of which he never spoke.

TRAVELOGUE

Narrated travelogue became common in the 1930s, and in **Land *without* Bread** (Spain, 1932) Luis Buñuel satirizes the genre. As the renegade son of a privileged Spanish family, Buñuel implies that the medieval poverty and suffering he finds in a remote region of Spain results from criminal neglect by his own caste. The ragged, stunted, and inbred villagers that we see know nothing about the water-borne illnesses that are killing them, and Buñuel makes us incredulous that church, state, and landlord could remain indifferent to the human souls in their care.

Using a grandiloquent symphony as musical accompaniment, the film's flat gaze at its catalogue of horrors drives even a modern audience to outrage. By nature, Buñuel is a satirist. He purposely makes us angry by showing a surreally awful situation using the pseudo-scientific cant of the travelogue. Like Flaherty, he was not above rigging the evidence—if you look carefully at the death

FIGURE 3-17 ———

Oliver asking for more in David Lean's grimly realistic *Oliver Twist*.

of the goat when it falls from a ravine, you'll see a tell-tale puff of gun-smoke. Everything else, however, seems authentic enough. One of the crew even steps into the frame to help a sick child that died the next day (Figure 3-18). The dead baby floating down a stream in her little coffin as the grieving family makes its way to the grave-yard is an indelibly tragic image.

ESSAY FILMS

The documentary could seldom afford sync sound in a studio, and anyway its subject matter was supposed to be real life captured as it happened. So its makers continued to shoot silent, the editor creating a sound track afterwards from music, effects, and narration (Figure 3-19).

Harry Watt and Basil Wright's **Night Mail** (Great Britain, 1936, Figure 3-20), made by John Grierson's General Post Office film unit, features

FIGURE 3-18 ————————————————————————————

Poverty, sickness, and death in *Land without Bread* because of a ruling caste's indifference.

a crack postal team sorting letters on an express train for delivery next morning in Edinburgh. The bucolic vision of fields, cows, rabbits, and ancient churches evokes an interlude of tranquility between two grimy industrial heartlands. What you see are metaphors for a society in flux—wealth and poverty, industrial cityscape and rural countryside, night and day, past and present. Through orchestrating the beat of words, images, repetitive work, and the rhythmic beat of the

FIGURE 3-19

Flaherty shooting silent footage for *Louisiana Story* in 1948. Location sync sound would not become practical for documentaries until the 1960s. *(Museum of Modern Art/Film Stills Archive.)*

train wheels, the film creates a driving sense of forward movement. Key to this are two important elements: Benjamin Britten's score and W. H. Auden's striding narration:

> *This is the Night Mail crossing the border,*
> *Bringing the check and the postal order,*
> *Letters for the rich, letters for the poor,*
> *The shop at the corner and the girl next door...*

The brief sync dialogue exchanges in *Night Mail* were probably *post-synchronized*, that is, spoken lines were post-recorded and lip-synced to simulate live dialogue. To accommodate the large 35mm camera, the letter-sorting and dialogue sequences had to be shot in a set with a removable wall. Thus the postmen you see are re-enacting their daily work in a replica sorting carriage that is being rocked by stage-hands to simulate the train's movement.

FIGURE 3-20

Mail sorters re-enacting their work on a set for *Night Mail*. *(Photo courtesy of the Kobal Collection/GPO Film Unit.)*

The film generates tension because the postmen are working against the clock to complete their tasks before the journey's end. Helping this are charged scenes of the high-speed mailbag drops and pick-ups along the line. The film's temporal spine comes from its subject—an epic journey from the smoky metropolis that takes us up through rural England's backbone and arrives just as the sun rises over Edinburgh, its citizens still snoozing in their beds:

They continue their dreams,
And shall wake soon and long for letters,
And none will hear the postman's knock
Without a quickening of the heart,
For who can bear to feel himself forgotten?

The commentary that started out with a quick, sharp, repetitive beat, now ends on a slower, loping beat as the train majestically slows for its arrival. *Night Mail* shows what is possible with a stirring subject, great photography and narration, and first-rate music. It also shows that film *is* music. Incidentally, film industry lore says that no film involving train travel has ever failed.

Color film was expensive and came late to documentary. Alain Resnais' ***Night and Fog*** (1955, France, Figure 3-21) integrates black-and-white with color, and might be the most haunting documentary ever made. In 31 nightmarish minutes the film visits what remained of the World War II Auschwitz extermination camp, and projects us headlong into the terrified daily existence of the prisoner. What, it asks, lies beneath the brackish water in the ponds, now that it's all over? Much of the film's power comes from its restrained and evocative narration by the French poet Jean Cayrol, himself a death camp survivor. Another powerful element is the astringent strings and woodwinds in the atonal score of Hanns Eisler, an Austrian wounded in World War I.

Playing against stereotype, the film never dramatizes or heightens. Instead its questioning narration is spoken in a dry, neutral monotone, while the score counterpoints delicate, playful woodwind themes or spins out high, trilling violin cascades against archival footage of casual horror. Here every mute object speaks, and the film ends by asking: Who among us will step forward next time, ready to torture and kill in exchange for a little power?

Night and Fog is a pinnacle in documentary filmmaking, and after many a screening my classes would sit in shattered silence. Its non-sync shooting, coupled with brilliant writing,

FIGURE 3-21

Resnais' impassioned plea for humane watchfulness in *Night and Fog*. *(Films Inc.)*

composing, and editing shows that a screen essay can deliver a huge impact. Today, this eloquent technique is very little used.

Two of my earliest editing assignments—one concerning international marriage customs, the other, the 1966 soccer World Cup—were shot and cut in this way. It was laborious but satisfying work, because you created an audio composition of narration, music, and sound effects. The highly original films of the photographer, traveler, and filmmaker Chris Marker, such as *Le Mystère Koumiko* (France, 1965) and *Sans Soleil* (France, 1983, Figure 3-22), make him one of the cinema's truly original essayists, whose preoccupations include the fleeting and unstable nature of memory. Anyone who has seen his short, enigmatic sci-fi photomontage *La Jetée* (France, 1962, Figure 3-23) has had an unforgettable cinema experience, though not one that can be called documentary.

FIGURE 3-22

Sans Soleil, directed by the essayist, traveler, and thinker Chris Marker.

FIGURE 3-23

In Marker's *La Jetée*, love is a lost memory from a previous life.

SHOOTING GOES MOBILE

Halfway through the twentieth century, new technologies began to make the film unit light and mobile. First came magnetic tape recording in the 1950s, which allowed sound shooting with a portable audio recorder. The industry favorite was the ultra reliable battery-powered Nagra, which held a steady speed even as its operator broke into a run (Figure 3-24). Faster film stocks allowed cameras to shoot by almost any available light, and 16mm cameras were evolving. The Eclair NPR, with its quiet mechanical movement, low-profile coaxial film magazines, and virtually instant magazine changes, sat comfortably on the operator's shoulder and revolutionized camera design (Figure 3-25). Filmmakers now had the tools to capture actuality as it happened, and this completely transformed every aspect of location

FIGURE 3-24

Portable sync sound from the 1960s onward, thanks to the Nagra III. *(Photo courtesy of Nagra, a Kudelski Group Company.)*

filming, from newsgathering and documentary to fiction film. In the documentary, event-driven or character-driven stories practically replaced scripted and narrated subject-driven ones.

Documentary influenced fiction filmmaking, and I was fortunate to work on Tony Richardson's *A Taste of Honey* (1962, GB, Figure 3-26), shot almost wholly by available light on location. Documentary cameraman Walter Lassally's portrait of sooty, post-industrial Manchester—a city of canals and decaying industrial might—was simply thrilling. The script, about a pregnant working class girl abandoned by her mother, came from the autobiographical play by Shelagh Delaney. Richardson came from the experimental theatre but had participated

FIGURE 3-25

The revolutionary Eclair NPR wielded by the author. *(Photo courtesy of Aran Patinkin.)*

FIGURE 3-26

Tony Richardson's *A Taste of Honey.* a fiction film benefiting from the expertise of documentary cameraman Walter Lassally.

in the Free Cinema Movement, a loose grouping of London residents from several countries who made short, ground-breaking documentaries about British working-class life. Their work sharply challenged the stuffy institutional documentaries and mediocre, studio-dominated feature films of the day, where my cinema life began. Richardson's preference for working fast and informally, and his actor-centered directing, brought a new but short-lived vibrancy to British cinema.

DIRECT CINEMA AND *CINÉMA VÉRITÉ*

The new immediacy generated opposing philosophies about the proper relationship between the documentary camera and its human subjects. The central question was this: Is truth on the screen something you find, or is it something you participate in and help to make?

OBSERVATIONAL DOCUMENTARY

Prominent American and Canadian documentarians of the time favored *transparent* filmmaking, in which participants seemed to live their lives unaware of the camera. Robert Drew, Richard Leacock, D. A. Pennebaker, Fred Wiseman, Allan King, and others favored what they called *direct cinema* (now called *observational cinema*). Like ethnographic filmmakers, they shot unobtrusively and by available light, aiming to capture the spontaneity and uninhibited flow of events as people were living them. In the late 1960s the intrepid Albert and David Maysles and their editor Charlotte Zwerin made the landmark documentary *Salesman* (1968, USA, Figure 3-27). The brothers had taught themselves filmmaking and even cobbled their own equipment together. Their amazing film follows a sales drive by hard-nosed bible salesmen—really a pack of hunters goaded on by corporately generated sales quotas. To complete each sale, a salesman must gain entry, befriend the householder, give a demonstration, and then make a killing by securing a signed order. We see them use all manner of persuasion, but their customers live pitifully narrow, cramped lives and don't need, and can't afford, lavishly illustrated bibles.

Here is the pinched lower middle-class world that Arthur Miller wrote about in his classic play *Death of a Salesman*. The central character is Willy Loman, a salesman based on Miller's own father who is degenerating from exhaustion, misplaced optimism, and worry over supporting his family. In the Maysles Brothers' documentary, Paul is the kindest and funniest of the salesmen, and cannot bring himself to extort the likeable,

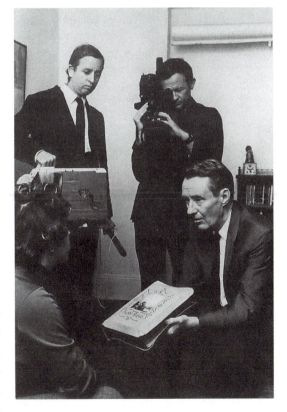

FIGURE 3-27

The Maysles Brothers' 1968 landmark documentary *Salesman* exposes the struggle for survival among door to door salesmen.

struggling homebodies from whom they try to extract orders. Like Miller, the Maysles brothers have put a frame around the man whose kind heart and active conscience doom him to fail in a system of corporate exploitation. No two works expose the cost of the American dream with more deadly wit and accuracy.

PARTICIPATORY DOCUMENTARY

Europeans favored the *participatory* approach to filming documentary, which at the time was called *cinéma vérité*. This approach seeks truth by treating any significant activity, in front of the camera or behind it, as proper subject matter for the documentary record. The idea came from the French ethnographer Jean Rouch who had found, while documenting life in Africa, that filming invariably provoked important off-camera relationships with participants. These he felt should become part of the film record and so

FIGURE 3-28

In *Chronicle of a Summer* Jean Rouch and his team asked ordinary Parisians the deceptively simple question: "Are you happy?"

he included them in his ethnographic films. In ***Chronicle of a Summer*** (France, 1961, Figure 3-28), working with his sociologist co-director Edgar Morin and their Canadian cinematographer Michel Brault, Rouch asked ordinary Parisians the deceptively simple question: "Are you happy?" It releases a torrent of touchingly personal and confessional responses. These the unit filmed as a free interaction between themselves, the crew, and participants. Some people, shown their own replies later on the screen, wanted to extend the dialogue—which Rouch and Morin filmed and included. As a gesture to Vertov, they called their method *cinéma vérité*, since "cinema truth" is a translation of his *kino-pravda*. Afterwards the term *cinéma vérité* degenerated into a catch-all for spontaneous filming of any kind, so *participatory cinema* is the term used today.

By acknowledging documentary as a collaboration with participants, rather than an objective observation of them, the directors of participatory cinema could now catalyze or even provoke events, and probe for truth rather than simply await its appearance. Rouch particularly prized the "privileged moments" when a human truth emerges plainly and miraculously like an egg from a chicken.

An excellent participatory film is Ira Wohl's *Best Boy* (USA, 1979, Figure 3-29), in which a New York family faces a gathering crisis. Pearl and Max are aging, and love their 52-year-old mentally handicapped son Philly so much that they can't let him go. Wohl sets out to film his lovable cousin, and while time remains, presses his uncle and aunt to consider letting Philly move into an appropriate institution. We see Philly being tested by a psychologist, many scenes of him at home doing chores for his mother, and Philly singing "If I were a rich man" from *Fiddler on the Roof*. Max dies, worn out after an operation, and leaves his wife Pearl bereft. How, she asks, can she ever let go of her "best boy" now? But relinquish him she must, and Philly begins to flourish among challenging responsibilities in a residential home. Pearl, always so open, talks with heartbreaking candor about how very alone she now feels. We realize that this is the price she must pay for her son's autonomy. The family was very aware of the filming, but the camera's presence seems to bring out the best in everyone, not least because the director cares so deeply for them. The DVD contains a follow-up film with the ever-cheerful Philly, now aged 70.

FIGURE 3-29

Best Boy, a deeply moving participatory film by Ira Wohl about his mentally handicapped cousin Philly. *(Photo by Ira Wohl.)*

WAITING FOR PRIVILEGED MOMENTS

Best Boy shows that you must often keep the camera running when shooting people under duress, and just wait. People need time to process anything that is emotionally taxing, and impatient film-makers blow such moments by chivvying their subjects onward. Wohl (who went on to become a psychotherapist) is always willing to linger for truth to unfold, and when great tension leads to a major sense of release, his patience is amply rewarded. This barometric rise and fall of pressure is called the *dramatic arc* or *dramatic curve*. Characteristically it builds, intensifies, peaks at a *crisis* point, and then releases (Figure 3-30). To direct well, you will need to develop sharp instincts for how this works—in life as in drama—so we shall give documentary's dramatic components closer attention in the next chapter.

OBJECTIVITY AND SUBJECTIVITY

Some claimed a certain truth and transparency for the "fly on the wall" observational documentary, but unless the camera is actually hidden—ethically dubious at best—participants know it's there and adjust accordingly. In fact, *every* form of observation produces some change in a human situation, whether it's a child visiting a family playing a game of cards, or a crew shooting discreetly at a distance. An observational film may make us feel like privileged observers, but we are seldom seeing life unmediated as such films imply. They appear so because an editor has subtracted everything that would break the illusion, such as people turning to the camera, or visibly adopting special behavior.

For a recent "fly on the wall" observational documentary, see Yoav Shamir's *Checkpoint* (Israel, 2003, Figure 3-31). It is the director's first film, and records without comment what happens at Israel Defense Force (IDF) checkpoints, where Shamir himself once served as a guard. The

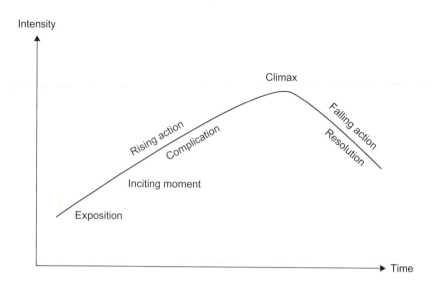

FIGURE 3-30

The dramatic curve, which builds, intensifies, then peaks at a crisis point and releases.

FIGURE 3-31

Yoav Shamir's *Checkpoint* is a recent "fly on the wall" observational documentary.

state of Israel exists because of the atrocities of the Holocaust, which in 1948 impelled Zionists to carve the country out from territory long settled by Palestinian Arabs. Today it is a small, embattled region in which dispossessed Palestinians must constantly pass checkpoints. Some youthful IDF guards carry out their policing function with tolerance and even humor, while others do not. It is always demeaning for the indigenous Palestinians to wait in line—sometimes for hours—to attend a nearby hospital, or to get to their workplace. The IDF scrutinizes every pedestrian, car, truck, bus, and ambulance because each at some time has been a conduit for bombs that killed and maimed Israelis.

Some of the uniformed, gun-toting 19-year-olds "follow orders" with sadistic disregard. Plainly they enjoy subjecting Palestinians to senseless aggravation. Every story Palestinians tell them is suspect, no matter how credible and evident the reason for needing to cross. The cases get worse as the film proceeds, and you feel a growing hopelessness and outrage. The film uses no commentary or interior monologues: its points emerge simply from faces, behavior, body language, and by the way it lingers for minutes on some dignified older man trying in vain to get his sick wife to a medical appointment. You feel a deepening rage and frustration on behalf of the humiliated—which is what this Israeli film wants you to feel. How tragic, you tell yourself, that the scrutiny meant to protect a nation is worsening the conditions that threaten that country's very existence. This is a message the film doesn't ever need to put into words: it gathers like a thunder cloud.

Checkpoint's structure is a series of repeating cycles, each worse than the last. The whole business feels like the advancing screw-thread in a torture device. Ironically, the IDF has since adopted the film as training for its guards in what *not* to do.

WHICH APPROACH IS BEST?

The documentary historian Eric Barnouw neatly summarizes the differences between these two major documentary philosophies:

> The direct cinema documentarist took his camera to a situation of tension and waited hopefully for a crisis; the Rouch version of *cinéma vérité* tried to precipitate one. The direct cinema artist aspired to invisibility; the Rouch cinéma vérité artist was often an avowed participant. The direct cinema artist played the role of uninvolved bystander; the cinéma vérité artist espoused that of provocateur.[3]

To reveal human truth on the screen, documentary-makers of either persuasion must make subjective judgments. The differences between them pale to insignificance when you realize that both depend on editing to abridge, shape, and intensify what is diffused by time and space in real life. Both approaches prize the unpredictably spontaneous and telling moment, and both reject the essentially theatrical process of scripting and re-enactment. Since both need story structure to hold the viewer's attention, both share much with the fiction film.

You need declare no allegiance in your filmmaking to either approach: today's documentaries are eclectic and use whatever approach best serves the needs of the evolving subject matter. Science, nature, or historical documentaries that rely on archive footage or on re-enactment still need scripting, and being able to write a film narration is still a key skill that you should develop, since one day you will need it.

THE ASCENDENCY OF EDITING

Both documentary approaches had similar drawbacks: they used high film shooting ratios (meaning a high amount of footage shot compared with that used) and they were uncertain of outcome. In trying to fashion a gripping narrative from a mass of captured action, editors took on a new burden, and rose to the challenge by inventing new forms of allusion and abbreviation, or ellipsis. Building on the legacy of Dziga Vertov, they found freer and more intuitive ways of counterpointing voice and effects tracks, and used impressionistic, even hallucinatory cutting to abridge time and space. In due course these innovations became an accepted part of feature film language.

THE THREE-ACT STRUCTURE IN DOCUMENTARY

With longer documentaries fashioned out of ever-larger bodies of source material, editors had to create dramatic structures able to sustain an audience through a feature-length film. And so the three-act dramatic structure, first identified in Greek drama several hundred years BC, begins to appear in the documentary as it had long done in fiction cinema. The three-act form is simply a way of classifying the phases of an unfolding story:

Act I   Establishes the *setup* (establishes characters, relationships, and situation and dominant *problem* faced by the central character or characters).

Act II   Escalates the complications in relationships as the central character struggles with the obstacles that prevent him/her solving the main problem.

Act III   Intensifies the situation to a point of *climax or confrontation, when the central character then resolves* it, often in a climactic way that is emotionally satisfying. A resolution isn't necessarily a happy ending: it might be an ageing boxer accepting defeat—sad, but inevitable.

The Maysles brothers' *Salesman* (1968) indeed breaks into the classic three-act structure:

Act I   (Boston, snow) is the exposition that introduces the salesmen and their work, shows their working class origins, and delineates their "problem" (having to hunt for sales to stay alive)

Act II   (Chicago, packed conference hall) is the corporate sales conference that escalates their "problem." Publishing moguls announce their goals, pressures, and values, and put the group on notice. Stragglers, they say menacingly, will be eliminated for "refusing success."

Act III   (Florida, heat) is the extended race for survival during which Paul, the most likeable of the bunch, inexorably falls behind until he confronts defeat and becomes tacitly ostracized. This leaves us conflicted: Paul has failed at predation, has been rejected by his colleagues, and is now suffering. Somehow he will have to reinvent himself elsewhere—a quintessentially American predicament. Will he find a more amenable and constructive way to make a living, or is this all he knows?

Later in **Chapter 18: Dramatic Development, Time, and Story Structure** we shall see how prevalent this three-act structure is, and how useful it can be to your directing as you seek to predict the actions and rhythms at work in everyday life.

VIDEO AND DIGITAL TECHNOLOGY

In the 1970s, reel to reel video recording promised a cheaper and more flexible process. At first it was of poor quality and clumsy to edit, but the advent of cassettes and small format video improved the situation. Compared with editing film, tape-to-tape editing was deathly slow because every editing change required a follow-up ripple of changes throughout the tape. Once nonlinear (computerized) editing arrived in the late 1980s, documentarians began moving gratefully toward the promised land. Digital cameras and computer software handed them the kind of freedoms writers had got from word-processing.

Today with a home computer we can edit, create text and titles, freeze, slow-motion, or reverse our footage, as well as make color and contrast changes. We can not only weave together sound and picture but also apply the full range of contemporary image manipulation. This unshackles the screen from the banality of real time and pictorial realism, and allows us to use a narrative language that is more subjective and impressionistic.

ECLECTIC FILMMAKING

From the 1980s onward, documentary-makers moved toward mixed documentary forms and drew more freely on allied art forms and disciplines. Here are some examples to give a flavor of the genre as it moves toward its second century.

LONGITUDINAL STUDY

Michael Apted's *28 Up* (GB, 1986) is the most famous episode in a series of *longitudinal study* films, the first shot in the early 1960s. At seven-year intervals ever since, Apted has stepped away

FIGURE 3-32

Every seven years Michael Apted steps away from his feature career to shoot another *Up* episode. *(Photo courtesy of The Kobal Collection.)*

from directing feature films to revisit the same fourteen English individuals (Figure 3-32). Begun as *7 Up* when they were seven-year-olds, the series has now reached *56 Up*, with each film drawing upon an ever-growing bank of earlier material. We have the unique privilege of watching them grow from kids through tremulous young adulthood, and on into middle-age. Composed mainly of sensitive, probing interviews, the *Up* series shows both individual stories and the dynamic of groups. The series *premise* (ruling idea) is that family and social class implant profound expectations that are both positive and negative in their consequences, which children go on to realize in their subsequent lives. In chilling support of this, *7 Up* quotes the Jesuit saying, "Give me a child until he is seven, and I will show you the man." At first it comes largely true, and in *28 Up* the most disturbing portrait is of Neil, who blames his home life for making him wind up as a solitary vagabond, plagued with psychological disturbances. For his sake alone you will want to see the rest of the series. Accompanying the DVD for *49 Up* is an illuminating interview with Apted, who seems gloomily resigned to continuing the series until he keels over. Some participants are equally weary of putting their lives on record, but everyone seems to recognize that the series is the most embracing account ever made of people growing up and wrestling with their destinies.

Structurally an *Up* film is like an octopus, each arm a single story, and all joined to the common body of a recorded past. The commanding determinants of class and race persist, but half a century later we see that the suffocating original premise has fractured under the pressure people feel to make life-saving adjustments. Sure, family advantages and disadvantages are alarmingly evident in children's self-image and expectations, but most participants alter their trajectories in maturity, often with startling and hopeful results (Figure 3-33).

BRECHTIAN PROTEST

Through a series of imaginative, elliptical, and disturbingly urgent tellings and performances, Marlon T. Riggs' *Tongues Untied* (USA, 1989, Figure 3-34) conveys what he and others, black and gay like himself, experienced while growing up in a majority white, racist, and homophobic society. A journalist and poet, Riggs has produced a performance art film like Brechtian theatre. Sidestepping all recognizable traditions it hurls us from a finger-popping rap performance to the anguish of losing friends to AIDS; from a sad drag-queen telling of her loneliness, to stories of gay-bashing and of a white gay club that refused a black gay man entry on the grounds of his color. From archives come civil rights marchers and Eddie Murphy telling a homophobic joke.

Called *performative* in style, there is no through-line of argument or assertion, only a volley of forcefully stylish performances—everything from dance and body movement to inner monologue, street talk, and rap. Structuring the film's kaleidoscopic form is a driving, insistent sense of rhythm, as though Riggs is angrily drumming out the remains of his foreshortened life. Because the film received some national arts funding, it caused apoplexy among conservatives over the use of taxpayers' money. Riggs died of AIDS, and sadly the film is his last testament.

FIGURE 3-33

Some *Up* participants maintain their trajectories in maturity, others go off at a creative tangent in this long and most fascinating of documentary sagas. (Frame from *7 Up*.)

FIGURE 3-34

Marlon Riggs and Essex Hemphill defiantly face the camera in *Tongues Untied*. (*Photo courtesy of Signifyin' Works/Frameline.*)

DOCUMENTARY NOIR

Errol Morris' *The Thin Blue Line* (USA, 1989, Figure 3-35), though built traditionally on a foundation of interviews, makes imaginative use of music, re-enactment, and clips from old detective movies. Creating its own trial structure, the film examines the course of Texas justice on behalf of a man who may be falsely imprisoned. Its hypnotic Philip Glass score helps fuse an opiate mix of fact and fiction that gradually undermines the probity of the original trial. The crux of the discussion is contradictory evidence concerning what happened during 30 seconds one night on a Dallas freeway. A police car stopped someone driving on the freeway without lights, and as the cop walked over to tell him to turn on his lights, the car's occupant shot him. Who did the shooting? The film repeatedly re-enacts the encounter, but with key differences according to each witness's account. Morris uses the lawyers, passers-by, drawling Texas policemen, as well as the two men in the car, to subvert each witness's version. With its central characters on death row, and so much of its action taking place at night, Morris jokingly classified his film as a *documentary noir*.

His rock-steady visual style, minimalist score, and obsessive re-examination of key details eventually pays off by eliciting new evidence that points to the actual murderer. Because of Morris' film, Randall Adams not only escaped execution but was released from prison. See the masterly opening on YouTube, which lays out the Adams' feelings about being a hostage to destiny.

DIARY

Agnes Varda, who directed the diary/essay documentary *The Gleaners and I* (France, 2000, Figure 3-36), is an experienced fiction director whose late husband Jacques Demy was France's most imaginative maker of musicals. Varda's

FIGURE 3-35 ⎯⎯⎯⎯⎯⎯⎯

Randall Dale Adams, convicted for a murder he did not commit, in Errol Morris' "documentary noir" *The Thin Blue Line*. *(Photo courtesy of The Kobal Collection/American Playhouse/Channel 4 Films.)*

FIGURE 3-36 ⎯⎯⎯⎯⎯⎯⎯

Agnes Varda, director of the intimate documentary journal *The Gleaners and I*. *(Photo courtesy of The Kobal Collection/Stéphane Fefer.)*

documentary, beginning from the throb of string quartet music and nineteenth-century paintings of gleaners in cornfields, develops the theme of picking up and using what others have thrown away—a green habit by which she has furnished her cosy home. Armed with a small handicam she journeys to different regions of France in search of junk and more junk. Along the way, she meets a rich array of characters gleaning for food, art materials, or, as some relate with passion, simply out of ecological principle. Like a road movie the film goes from one encounter to the next. Varda makes what she films into state-of-mind representations so that we see her vanished childhood, her love for Jacques, and that she too will be discarded—by life itself. Her journey in this tender, good-natured film becomes metaphysical, so that denotation becomes connotation. By the end, this highly circular autobiography conveys a rare sense of intimacy.

AMBUSH AND ADVOCACY

In *Sicko* (USA, 2007, Figure 3-37) Michael Moore produces a damning satire on American business methods. The film trains its cross-hairs on the US health system where it exposes an appalling litany of failure. At the time, 50 million men, women, and children had no medical coverage, and privatized insurance was excluding anyone with a "pre-existing condition" (now, who doesn't have one of *those*?). Moore builds a series of surreal comparisons of other countries' health systems that make you guffaw in disbelief. After exposing the denial of healthcare to 9/11 first-responders sick from their heroic rescue efforts, Moore loads them into a boat and cruises to Guantanamo Bay in Cuba. Calling up through a megaphone at some scary-looking US Army fortifications, he asks if his patients might get some of the free medical care available to the "evildoers" imprisoned within. The reply, a warning siren blast, sends Moore scuttling off to Havana with his sad cargo. There they get free medical care, since Cubans, it seems, have better health and life statistics than Americans, and all for a fraction of the cost.

As always, Moore combines ambush journalism, hilarious satire, and leftist sympathy for the ordinary working stiff. His films' preferred form is the Everyman quest, for which he dresses in his signature baseball hat and baggy tee shirt (Figure 3-38). His first-person narration starts from

FIGURE 3-37

Just a regular guy—Michael Moore in *Sicko* asking a few simple questions. *(Photo courtesy of The Kobal Collection/Dog Eat Dog Films/Weinstein Company.)*

FIGURE 3-38 ───

Moore's preferred form is the Everyman quest, for which he dresses in his signature baseball hat and baggy tee shirt. *(Frame from* Bowling for Columbine.*)*

a central question, and then proceeds to alternate between reasonable question and astonished discovery. Simple disbelief propels him from one anomaly to the next until, and like some latter-day Candide, he can only acknowledge that the American health system is *not* the best of all possible worlds. Moore sees healthcare in America as a theatre of the absurd. Using stunts that juxtapose victims and perpetrators, he projects an appalling vision of how the profit motive distorts what elsewhere is a basic human right.

ARCHIVE-BASED FILMMAKING

The San Francisco experimental filmmaker Jay Rosenblatt often plucks his archetypal homemaker moms, pipe-smoking businessman dads, and rigid, emotionally beleaguered kids from a trove of mid-twentieth-century "informational" films that he found on a dump. He makes them

FIGURE 3-39 ───

Jay Rosenblatt behind his ill-fated brother Eliot in *Phantom Limb. (Frame from their father's 8mm film, courtesy of the filmmaker.)*

represent the suffocating roles his family endured while he was growing up. In **Phantom Limb** (USA, 2005, Figure 3-39) Rosenblatt uses interviews and a range of found materials to fashion a 12-chapter confrontation with a domestic tragedy—his own and his family's unexpressed guilt and anguish following the death of his younger brother. Rosenblatt's work, and this film in particular, often feels like the strangled inner scream of a generation marching in lockstep with the received wisdom of its time. Seeing his body of work, however, you see a vital rebalancing taking place. In *I Used to Be a Filmmaker* (USA, 2003, Figure 3-40) Rosenblatt celebrates filmmaking and fatherhood, clearly the two great salvations in his emotional life.

FIGURE 3-40

I Used to Be a Filmmaker brings together filmmaking and fatherhood. *(Photo courtesy of Jay Rosenblatt.)*

Archive footage is a staple for History Channel and Discovery Channel productions, which specialize in expositions of historical and scientific matter. A fine combination of testimony and archives underpins Ken Burns and Lynn Novick's impassioned series for PBS, *The War* (USA, 2007). There World War II participants do what battlefield veterans seldom do, that is, speak about the atrocious suffering they inflicted or witnessed, and about the resulting pain they will carry to their graves. Equally good is *The Central Park Five* (USA, 2012) directed by Ken Burns, Sarah Burns, and David McMahon. It reveals what the five New York black teenagers suffered when falsely indicted for raping and half-murdering the young woman known as the Central Park jogger. Based on interviews, archives, and contemporary footage, the film makes imaginative use of surreal montage techniques which convey the nightmare of being alone and powerless in the coils of a justice system convinced you must be guilty. Harried into making false confessions ("so you can go home") prior to their trials by cynical police, the five got long prison sentences in response to a media frenzy and a public eager to blame poor, black youths.

3D DOCUMENTARIES

Two films that amply repay the somewhat unnerving assault of 3D on the viewer are Werner Herzog's *Cave of Forgotten Dreams* (France, 2010, Figure 3-41) and Wim Wenders' *Pina* (Germany, 2011). Both subjects use the new technology justifiably, since each has a particular need for the third dimension. Herzog's treatment of man's earliest known artworks in a cave near Chauvet in Southern France shows how the artists of 32,000 years ago integrated the rock-face undulations in their depictions of animals. Though the film was a box-office success, it left Herzog uninspired about using 3D again.

Wenders' film is about the late modern-dance choreographer Pina Bausch, whose Wuppertal company perform her most acclaimed works. Of all artforms treated by the screen, dance has always seemed to suffer worst, so the addition of depth makes a critical difference. The film however is really about Pina herself who, rather than drill her company to a standard, took a personal and supportive interest in developing each of her dancers in their own way. She then drew on what

FIGURE 3-41

Werner Herzog's *Cave of Forgotten Dreams*, in which 3D reveals how the artists of thousands of years ago made use of the cave-surface irregularities.

FIGURE 3-42

Wim Wenders' *Pina*, which uses 3D to make dance happen in space on the screen.

each could uniquely contribute, notably in her dances about male–female relationship. Thus the film is about the wise leadership of an unegotistic, enlightened creator, remembered by her dancers with great love (Figure 3-42).

THE INTERACTIVE DOCUMENTARY

Rather like the 1958 William Burroughs novel *Naked Lunch* that came looseleaf in a box for the reader to arrange, the interactive documentary makes a set of documentary resources available on the Internet for the postmodern viewer to explore at will. The writer and interactivity author-ity Sandra Gaudenzi (www.interactivedocumentary.net) divides the interactive documentary into four modes—the hypertext, the conversational, the participatory, and the experiential.[4] Unlike traditional media that "hardwires" documentary materials into a unique structure that blurs their separate identities, hypermedia keeps the elements and structure separated, leaving users free to create their own relationships and meaning from source materials. The interactive movement's search is for a commendable openness that permits "the participator to enter in the creative process" and thus have greater agency. Not since Gutenberg introduced moveable-type printing have people felt such excitement about exchanging ideas and knowledge, so the influence of the Internet, of offering open access to (someone's choice of) documentary materials, holds unknown potential. Meanwhile, those who know what's best for us are racing to invent better censorship, so democratic choice may become moot anyway.

Quite separately, I wrote a keynote article for the Australian film journal *Lumina*[5] about the Arab Spring rebellions, and the action that followed Middle East social media users viewing and exchanging what were essentially documentary materials. Their governments had been unable to suppress the exchange of opinions, experiences, essays, cartoons, jokes, reality footage of all kinds, underground political writings, historical parallels, and whatever else. Yet social media users, without necessarily making or seeing special documentaries, had ingested source materials and concluded they must protest their regimes. I speculated action came from a collective-unconscious conclusion made from years of having internalized documentary forms and arguments. Probably it will take decades to unravel what really happened.

Interactive literature did not catch on with the public, and interactive documentary may not either, unless made into an artfully structured game, which weakens the cause of free exploration. Most prefer the more tainted process of watching a narrative and pondering the construct of relationship between cause and effect. Perhaps we best find our own way through encountering the propositions and interpretations of others. Through the very ancient medium of stories we resonate to different sensibilities and worldviews, identify our affinities and antipathies, and decide who and what we must push against. It is a viable but unscientific way of being curious. Maybe the interactive documentary will change documentary as web forms have changed so much else.

HANDS-ON LEARNING

Why not make an analysis of a few minutes in a favorite documentary of yours using **AP-1 Making a Split-Page Script**? Also known as TV script format, you use it to lay out images and action in the left-hand column, and the corresponding words and sound against them in the right-hand. Its merit is that it allows an exact transcription of the relationship between words, music, sound effects, and imagery, which is often highly revealing, and something you cannot precisely appreciate in a viewing. The split-page script-form also makes an excellent planning medium if you intend to make, say, a historical film involving archival footage and voice-over. Another form of film you could try is the diary form, using the **SP-14 Diary Film** project. You could make use of family video footage and still photos, and record your inner thoughts and feelings at the time, or now in retrospect, as voice-over.

NOTES

1. Paul Delaroche, circa 1839.
2. Included with the DVD of *Man of Aran* is George Stoney and Jim Brown's *How the Myth Was Made* (1978) which returns to Aran and investigates Flaherty's processes with some of the film's surviving cast.
3. *Documentary: A History of the Non-Fiction Film* (Oxford University Press, 1974), pp. 254–55.
4. See Sandra Gaudenzi, "The Interactive Documentary as a Living Documentary" at the documentary website Doc Online, www.doc.ubi.pt, an especially rich source to those who can read Spanish and Portuguese.
5. Rabiger, "Synaptic Documentary," *Lumina*, July 2011, Australian Film and Television School.

CHAPTER 4

CONSTRUCTING REALITY

THE "CONTRACT" AND EXPOSITION

Opening any dramatic work takes art and verve, or you lose your audience. The *exposition* (background or scene-setting information) is part of the opening *contract* you offer your audience. This implies a promise by the maker to the audience about the film's purview, style, and purpose. It tries to set up the world of its central characters as economically and appealingly as possible. At this book's website www.directingthedocumentary.com you can run 12 minutes from *Legacy* (USA, 2000) and *Omar and Pete* (USA, 2005), two documentaries by the Academy Award nominee Tod Lending, and see how each implies its purview and intentions. You can also see four 5-minute student documentaries in their entirety.

Whether an audience goes on watching your film depends on how you set up its dramatic purview, and how attractive it finds the discourse you mean to use. I see three main types:

Propaganda: Wants the audience to buy the premise and produces only the evidence to support a predetermined conclusion.

Binary: Likes to give "equal coverage to both sides," as if truth is like a coin which only has two sides, while remaining neutral and shadowy as a narrative voice. Sees the audience paternalistically as empty vessels that need filling.

Dialogical: Sees the audience-member as willing to sift through contradictions and make thoughtful judgments. Aims neither to condition nor distract the viewer but to share the contradictions and mystery of real human situations whose outcome may remain unknown.

Only the last treats its audience as mature equals, so how you signal your film's language as well as its nature and purpose within the first minute will matter greatly. Like a restaurant handing out an inviting menu as customers arrive, the astute storyteller sets terms in the opening moments that make the audience anticipate something worthwhile.

How much should you lay out? How much factual material can the audience absorb before meeting the characters and absorbing their predicament? Should you start the action (a lesson, an arrest, or, in the case of *Legacy*, a death) to give momentum during the initial exposition of the film? How much information should you hold back to enhance dramatic tension? What kind of evidence should the audience expect?

FIGURE 4-1

Ari Folman's *Waltz with Bashir*, an animated documentary developed from a recurring dream.

The answers to these questions can never be standardized; they emerge from the experience of watching each film on its own terms.

ACTUALITY AND EVIDENCE

TYPES OF ACTUALITY

The reality everyone can point to, agree on, and defend in court is what the documentary theorist Bill Nichols calls *historical reality*. Films about political or scientific subjects fall into this camp, though facts and other evidence can be contradictory—and even more interesting because of it. No less real, and a lot harder to convey, is what people think, feel, fear, hope for, or dream about—which is their inner, *subjective reality*. This, especially when it involves extreme situations, can be fascinating.

Ari Folman's *Waltz with Bashir* (Israel, 2008, Figure 4-1) is an animated documentary that developed from a recurring dream of the director's. It arose from emotional trauma during the 1982 assault on Beirut, in which the director participated as a 19-year-old soldier. Now Folman contacts friends one by one to ask about their nightmares and lost memories. He uses a form of animation invented by his group which greatly helps the film achieve its dreamlike intensity. At the core of his friends' faulty recall is the massacre of over 700 refugee Palestinians, mostly women and children, at the refugee camp of Shatila, near Beirut. Though perpetrated by a Lebanese Christian militia, it happened under the eyes of Israeli Defence Forces, including Folman's friends. The experience has left an indelible stain of guilt that numbs these former boy soldiers, and leaves them with recurring nightmares. The last 10 minutes of the film leave you overwhelmed with sorrow for humankind.

OBJECTIVITY, BALANCED REPORTING, AND PROPAGANDA

Because the camera is a mechanical recording device, people often assume the documentary is objective. But can a camera really record anything objectively? What, for instance, is an objective camera position, when someone must decide where to place the camera? How can you turn a camera on and off objectively, or decide objectively what to select from your recorded material? Closely examined, every step in filmmaking takes judgment and subjective decisions.

FIGURE 4-2

Robert Greenwald's exposé of right-wing political outreach, *Outfoxed: Rupert Murdoch's War on Journalism.*

It is true that much news reporting and some documentaries—particularly older ones—appear objective because they balance opposing points of view. So-called "balanced reporting" is an old newspaper strategy developed to evade charges of political bias. It is a strategy that can fail its readership in spectacular ways. Reputable British newspapers in the late 1930s depicted the trouble brewing in Germany as a contemptible squabble between equally culpable Communists and Nazis. In the war that followed, millions lost their lives, and Britain was dangerously unprepared to defend itself since the mainstream press had failed to foresee what had been building.

The "balanced perspective" is a convenient posture that lets journalists present the opinions and judgments of others in a false counterpoise. It makes a convenient cover for conditioning the reader. When reporting, however, leads to preordained conclusions, it becomes the convergent information of *propaganda*, which aims to indoctrinate rather than open its audience to the open-ended complexities of real-life issues. Robert Greenwald's *Outfoxed: Rupert Murdoch's War on Journalism* (USA, 2004, Figure 4-2) levels this charge to great effect against the Fox News Channel, which likes to advertise itself as "fair and balanced."

FAIRNESS

If you cannot be objective, you can be fair. That means not stacking the evidence and including evidence that may be contradictory. If your film is about a medical malpractice accusation, for instance, it would be prudent to give careful, sympathetic coverage to the allegations of both surgeon and aggrieved patient.

Like any good journalist or detective, the documentarian crosschecks everything independently verifiable, since people and their issues are seldom what they seem. The accused is not always guilty, the accuser not always innocent, and the bystander is not always disinterested. Counterpoising opinions and impressions helps protect your interests by acknowledging that most truth is complex, and one can only assess it like a juror—in the light of human experience.

FIGURE 4-3 ⎯⎯⎯⎯⎯⎯⎯⎯⎯⎯⎯⎯⎯⎯⎯⎯⎯⎯⎯

Soldier Girls takes a disquieting look at how the US Army trains its women soldiers. *(Photo courtesy of The Kobal Collection/First Run Pictures.)*

There is good reason for this cautiousness. Films that say something make enemies, so you must be ready to defend your work—possibly in court. If they find a single error, your opponents will use it to destroy your credibility. Michael Moore's critics took some questionable chronology in his first film, *Roger and Me* (USA, 1989) and did their utmost to discredit him. Documentary must often lead its audience through a maze of conflicting facts and evidence, so that audiences can arrive at their own conclusions. Interestingly enough, this is how courts put evidence before a jury of ordinary people—still, after thousands of years, the preferred test of truth in a democracy.

EVIDENCE THEN AND NOW

The modern documentary differs from its earlier, more scripted and premeditated forms whose clumsy technology required the action to be choreographed for the camera. Earlier audiences were more trusting of authority and more ready to accept what they were told, but today's audiences have learned to be skeptical. Happily, light and mobile equipment allows you to record events as they unfold, so we are accustomed to seeing people dealing spontaneously with heightened moments in their lives. As we watch, we make character and motive judgments much as we do in life.

In Nicholas Broomfield and Joan Churchill's *Soldier Girls* (UK, 1981, Figure 4-3), we see how the US Army trains its women soldiers. Through formal and informal moments, including sadistic training and ritual humiliations, we come to question some of the army's most basic assumptions. How is it, we ask, that authoritarian white male sergeants are allowed to routinely humiliate black or Hispanic female recruits?

The film delays confronting a central paradox: warfare is brutal and unfair, so caring instructors cannot kindly train soldiers of either gender to survive. However, the army's arguments wear thin after what we have seen, and leave us disturbed by larger questions about military traditions and training—just as the film's makers intended. Though we share what moved or disturbed Broomfield and Churchill, they never tell us what to feel or think. Instead, by exposing us to contradictory and provocative evidence they draw us into realization and inner debate. We become a jury arbitrating not right versus wrong—which is easy to decide—but right versus right, which is not. Humanity's more interesting problems are usually of this order.

DOCUMENTARY IS NOT REALITY, BUT A CONSTRUCT

You cannot show events themselves, only a *construct* of selected shots and viewpoints that sketch in the key facts, action, and emphases—all subjectively determined by you, the filmmaker. Doing it fairly will face you with ethical dilemmas over which you will sometimes lose sleep. But if your film can show a broad factual grasp of its subject, evidence that is persuasive and self-evidently reliable, and the courage and insight to make interpretive judgments, then it is worthy of our trust. That is the best anyone can do.

DRAMA

A good documentary is a drama drawn from lived reality, with all its moral and social implications made visible by the enhancement of astute storytelling. Analyze most documentaries, and they have dramatic ingredients similar to fiction stories. That is, they contain characters, situations, pressures, choice, conflict, tests, reconciliation—everything we are used to seeing in drama.

Your documentary must reveal characters and their situations; show what is at issue, and what the central characters are trying to get, do, or accomplish. To satisfy your audience you will probably have to reveal the obstacles that prevent them, one by one, and ultimately include a *confrontation* between the forces in conflict. You will need to show how the ultimate conflict is resolved and what the consequences are. Include all these, and you will entertain your audience members and exercise their judgment to the full.

AUTHORED CONSTRUCTS

Transparent documentary tries to create the feeling that you are seeing unmediated reality, but close analysis soon reveals that though the illusion may be skillfully sustained, it does so by using proven fictional techniques of juxtaposed shots and artfully compressed time and space. We have said that documentaries, like the fiction films they resemble, are *authored constructs*. There is nothing inherently dishonest in this: they are directors' attempts to pass over the spirit of truth, rather than its letter.

Each film is a vehicle—conscious or otherwise—for the values of its makers. How and why the director tells the tale proceeds from convictions that you draft in the *working hypothesis*. This merely states, formally and concisely, intentions you might otherwise carry out less thoroughly and consciously by instinct.

The simple fact is that, as a purposeful entertainer, you make a film in order to *act upon* your audience, and your film is a bridge connecting your audience to your chosen "corner of nature" by way of your "temperament."

CONFLICT

Think of those you have known longest and best—your parents, perhaps. Try naming their long-term, major conflicts. Easy, or difficult? Everyone is engaged in struggle of some kind, but few know their own deepest goals and demons. As a documentary author, you must be able to see them in those around you. Particularly when you plan a *character-driven story*, you must press yourself to define, as best you can, what your central character is trying to *get, do, or accomplish*, and therefore *what obstacles block his or her path*. As you learn ever more about your characters, revise and refine these judgments, for they strongly influence what story you can tell, what issues are at stake, and what you can do as a storyteller to structure and maintain dramatic tension.

Your main job as a director is to characterize what your central character is really striving for—short term and long term. This is the secret to vibrant storytelling, and though it sounds simple, its implementation is not. Your research will demand penetrating and dedicated observation, and much careful thought as to how to show what you find.

CHARACTER-DRIVEN OR PLOT-DRIVEN STORIES

All stories can be preliminarily divided into two kinds: one is energized by a character or characters, the other takes its energy from predominating events. To decide which you are dealing with, simply decide the source of the film's driving energy. A film about the effect of a tornado on a sleepy little town would be a *plot-driven story* because its energy comes from a huge, life-changing event that affects many people and in many different ways. They are the puppets of Fate.

Other stories may be *character-driven*, since life is full of strange and wonderful personalities. If you are intrigued by the saying, "character is fate," you will see how often people enact events that, quite unconsciously, they have made happen. Werner Herzog's *Grizzly Man* (USA, 2005, Figure 4-4) tells the story of Timothy Treadwell's life and death using his own footage of the wild bears that he loved and unwisely trusted—until they literally ate him. Errol Morris's *The Fog of War: Eleven Lessons from the Life of Robert S. McNamara* (USA, 2003, Figure 4-5) is

FIGURE 4-4

Grizzly Man, a cautionary tale about a man who thinks bears reciprocate his feelings for them. *(Photo courtesy of The Kobal Collection/Discovery Docs.)*

FIGURE 4-5

The Fog of War: Eleven Lessons from the Life of Robert S. McNamara. (Photo courtesy of Fourth Floor Productions.)

another character-driven film in which the former US secretary of defense tells, in his own unreliable words, how he was a hawk during the Vietnam War but later heard his conscience and now shares the anti-war position.

DRAMATIC TENSION

In life, everyone pushes against obstacles while trying to realize their needs and goals. Often these are none too visible to themselves or to anyone else. McNamara in *Fog of War* is the high government official who wants to get on the right side of history. He tells us he was deluded into supporting policies that killed thousands during the Vietnam War. The film is a chilling character study, since it shows someone who supported government policies that killed thousands, and who now tries to justify what he did while seeking public absolution. Its *dramatic tension* lies in watching a man struggle to rescue his place in history. His main *conflict* appears to be the fear of going down in history as evil when he wants to be seen as good.

DEVELOPMENT

In a world convulsed with evil and pain, many stories are designed to tell the grim truth while nonetheless leaving us with a little hope. If we see nobody learn something and grow, even just a little, then their struggles give us that all-too-familiar mood of despondency and resentment. Because this discourages us from taking any action ourselves, many tales try to incorporate *development*, or growth in the central character, no matter how minimal and symbolic.

When you work at an idea for a documentary, it will be important to predict *who or what is likely to develop* during your film's time span. Can the son break away from the father? Will the rain finally come and answer the farm cooperative's prayers? Can the immigrant couple learn enough of the new language to find employment? Will the child learn the identity of her father from her mother (Figure 4-6)? What sustenance, what hope, what truths can the audience draw from any of the likely changes?

FIGURE 4-6

The mother who won't reveal her daughter's paternity in *The German Secret*.

FILM LANGUAGE

It has been said that "a documentary film is shot with three cameras: 1) the camera in the technical sense; 2) the filmmaker's mind; and 3) the generic patterns of the documentary film, which are founded on the expectations of the audience that patronizes it."[1] This third "camera" refers to the audience's frame of mind as they interpret the film according to the culture of film as they know it.

You hope to use the film medium justly and persuasively, and for your audience to understand what you mean. Historically, television documentary has favored *monological discourse*, that is, actuality delivered in a linear way by specialists and authority figures who interpret, assign meanings, and signal what's important to the rest of us. Except for specialized nature and science films, audiences have grown to distrust this relationship, so that many documentaries now use a *dialogical discourse*—that is, voices in conversation with each other, multiple voices spinning a tapestry of diverse impressions and opinions. Dialogical films, rejecting the stance of settled, paternalistic lecture, opt to reveal instead a more charged, conflicted, and multifaceted reality.

Viewers actively assess these conflicting impressions, perceptions, and voices against their own knowledge of life. Under extreme conditions, human perception turns surreal and hallucinatory, as you see so memorably in Errol Morris's *The Thin Blue Line* (USA, 1988, Figure 4-7). Exceptional documentaries convey not just the outward, historical reality of those they film, but also a strong sense of the way that outward actions come from inner conflict.

Our thoughts, memories, dreams, and nightmares should also count as actuality since they are the interior dimension of outward actions. Writers have always been able to portray interior realities, sometimes including the storyteller's perceptions as part of the narrative. At a certain point in John Fowles' postmodern novel *The French Lieutenant's Woman*, the narrator wryly admits he has lost control of his characters, and gets into a Victorian train to brood on his main character Charles sitting across the carriage. Film, the newborn among the arts family, is gradually learning to claim such imaginative freedoms.

Today's documentaries use every imaginable storytelling method to hold our attention: they can magnify a tiny backwater, explore intimate and unlikely relationships, chronicle large historical events, or rattle the teeth of a nation by speaking truth to power. Whatever you intend for your

FIGURE 4-7 ——

Under extreme conditions, human perception turns surreal and hallucinatory, as in *The Thin Blue Line*.

audience, the medium is also part of the message, and only by doubting how that message arrives, and testing exhaustively what impressions your film actually conveys, can you be confident that your construct ultimately delivers all you intended. The more intricate the issues, the more work it will take to strike a balance between clarity and simplicity on the one hand, and fidelity to the murkiness and complexities of actual life on the other.

FORM AND STYLE

A documentary's *form* is the way a film presents its story, and this usually hinges partly on the need to maintain dramatic tension, but on clarity and practicality too. With the architect Louis Sullivan's famous advice in mind, "Form follows function," decide how you want to act upon your audience. Your film's life-materials strongly determine your film's form, but what you are trying to accomplish should order and organize its form too.

How best to handle time often leads you to your film's most effective form, and this helps us decide whose particular stream of consciousness the film wants us to share. A film may present time chronologically, in retrograde motion, or as a set of imperfectly grasped, randomly accruing memories, as in *Waltz with Bashir* mentioned earlier. Its viewpoint may belong to the storyteller, the narrator, one of the participants, or to someone else more peripheral.

Style refers to visual and other characteristics that let us relate a film to works like it—whether by the same director, or by others working in the same period, "school," or subject matter. This is because every work of art or science grows out of all the others that preceded it. "If I have seen further," wrote Isaac Newton to a colleague, "it is by standing on the shoulders of giants."[2] A film's references are full of particular language and precedent that the audience can place in our common film and cultural vocabulary.

Form and style are thus closely related, and can together produce a film that is controlled and premeditated, spontaneous and unpredictable, lyrical and impressionistic, starkly observational, satirical, or even farcical. A documentary can use commentary or no speech at all, interrogate or ambush its subjects, catalyze change, or muse aloud about its own unsatisfactory progress. It can narrate using words, images, music, or human behavior. It can employ literary, theatrical, or oral traditions and borrow from painting, music, song, essay, or choreography.

For examples of inventive form and style, look to the other arts. Film is cousin to them all. Your task will always be to find a form and a style uniquely suited to your film's purpose, and your ability to do this will set you apart like nothing else.

HANDS-ON LEARNING

Since the great challenge in making documentary is to tell a story visually, rather than fitting pictures to a narration, why not make your own silent film? That is, one that can have music and inter-titles, but no *diagetic sound* (sound that is inherent to the situation being filmed). Music that you add would be non-diagetic because it has been added authorially and the characters in your film cannot hear it. Try **SP-4 Flaherty-style Film** which allows you to choreograph your cast as if shooting fiction, or **SP-5 Vertov-style Film** which builds its action and atmosphere by *montage* (action shots cut together to supply information, and build atmosphere and process).

NOTES

1. Trinh T. Minh-ha, "The Totalizing Quest of Meaning," in Michael Renov, ed., *Theorizing Documentary* (Routledge, 1993), p. 98.
2. Sir Isaac Newton (1642–1727), English physicist and mathematician.

CHAPTER 5

STORY ELEMENTS AND FILM GRAMMAR

PERCEPTION AND MAKING STORIES

Filmmaking follows the processes we adopt when turning an experience into a story that we can tell to others. This chapter aims to help you found your shooting and editing in human perception.

It begins from the way we naturally sense the world around us. Go and stand in a busy street and notice how your senses function. Your eyes flicker after moving objects such as vehicles and people; your ears pick up particular sounds and tell your eyes where to look; or you see something that makes your ears search for the sound it is making. Always on the lookout for danger, your ears and eyes monitor the environment, and as people or vehicles come toward you, you adapt by moving, or by looking warily around before crossing the road. At the same time, you register a woman in a striking red dress, and notice an acquaintance going into a coffee shop with whom you might stop and chat. While this is happening, your memory fills any vacant spaces with visual and aural associations, and your imagination is visualizing what you might do with some time you have spare later in the day.

Note down everything you can remember from 5 minutes of observation. The memory is a wonderful story editor, because it remembers what is significant, and jettisons everything else. With some prodding, your memory will disgorge a Virginia Woolf stream of consciousness, which soon looks like a short but rich documentary script. If you work at the potential in your piece of writing, you will discern some quite serious preoccupations and a theme.

Thus there is a strong parallel between what we do in life (seeing, hearing, experiencing, remembering, and retelling the events of a morning, say) and the steps one takes in making a piece of cinema. Each has three parallel stages:

TABLE 5-1 Turning everyday experiences into an anecdote, and making a documentary film

Life	Cinema
(a) Living various experiences and storing the highlights in memory.	**Shooting** events on to a memory medium (using the camera's eyes, ears, and memory like a human being under particular pressures).
(b) Inwardly reviewing the main points, and fashioning them into a narrative with a meaning.	**Editing** (using a computer to help you replay, shape, structure, and abbreviate the story materials into something significant).
(c) Telling the story to different audiences—to entertain, gauge its effect, and validate one's feelings at the time.	**Screening** the story (for audience reaction, feedback on what it conveys, and to gauge whether the film acted upon the audience as intended).

Everyday awareness involves faculties we use constantly and unconsciously, like our leg muscles when we decide to start walking. Try now to dig into your awareness and notice how your stream of consciousness actually functions. It will take a second "observer you" who stands back and studies how the "normal you" imbibes experiences and stores them as impressions. You will need high concentration, so be prepared to learn in small snippets. The good thing here is that you can practice just about anywhere and under any circumstances. Keep trying, even though your whole being screams to go back to the comfort of normal unconsciousness.

We turn now to how you tell an incident. One that happened to me one winter night came out something like this:

Tramp, tramp through the icy dark of a Chicago winter with Cleo padding along on her lead. Suddenly, the ominous scraping sound of my booted foot sliding, a momentary vision of whirling horizon, then the sound of teeth rattling in my head, and the thump and clatter of forehead and eyeglasses hitting icy concrete. Lifting nose from gritty ice, I lumber onto all fours, suffused with rage at the neighbor who doesn't shovel after snowfalls. Surprisingly, my hand is still clutching the dog lead. Cleo is shocked but excited that I have plummeted to her level. From the direction I'm now facing I realize that I must have spun round in mid air before landing on forehead and knee-caps. I get up and move off, one knee and both hands aching fiercely.

From under a street-light a man watches. He stands mute, expressionless, and unknowable like destiny.

Each sound, image, or event here is like a movie shot or sound effect, and more importantly, it suggests a meaning. Telling it to friends, we see how they react, and with repeated tellings we improve the story so that it now carries a *subtext* (that is, an underlying meaning). Usually we structure a telling chronologically (in the order that things happened), but maybe some other priority will predominate if it enhances the underlying meaning. Mine was "disaster that can kill you happens faster than you imagine."

HOW SCREEN LANGUAGE MIMICS CONSCIOUSNESS

To see how someone's consciousness permeates the handling of a camera, imagine you go to your high school reunion and find a little camcorder that someone has left behind. Hoping to guess whose it is, you view its footage and see that someone has naively used the camera like his eyes and ears. From the off-camera voice you know the owner is male. The recorded events tell you not only whom he was drawn to, but how his mind worked and how he spent his evening. Though he says little from behind the camera, his material gives you such a strong idea of his tastes, reactions, and personality that you can infer his heart and mind from his material.

Often a stretch of film—cut or uncut—produces the thrilling sensation of being in the presence of a questioning, guiding human intelligence. This is the effect of a director's interests and sympathies working hand in glove with all the potential of the cinema. Such a film is Alberto Vendemmiati's *The Person de Leo N* (Italy, 2006, Figure 5-1), about a 40-year-old actor born in a male body but who has felt like a woman all her life. Her central problem is whether to get a sex change operation, and stopping her is the fear that her beloved mother

FIGURE 5-1

A warmly questioning empathy guides *The Person de Leo N* throughout.

will reject her. Masterfully shot in Venice and Bologna, the film's empathic and highly intimate camera handling, emotional music, and taut, glancing editing style creates an unparalleled closeness to Nico, and makes us feel keenly the ultimate mystery of gender and self-identity.

Cinema of the highest order like this leaves us feeling we have lived through the events ourselves. Engaged, intimate camerawork (by the director), allied with impressionistic editing, makes us feel intimately involved with the recorded events and personalities. Afterwards we feel we have somehow experienced these events ourselves. Misused professionalism, on the other hand, produces the soulless efficiency familiar from hack TV series and corporate video. One form is based on hyper-conscious human responses behind the camera, and the other on strategies of audience manipulation.

DOCUMENTARY INGREDIENTS AND HUMAN CONSCIOUSNESS

Throughout this book I shall stress that film language at its most effective simply makes the screen reproduce human interior processes of thought and emotion. The eyes are the camera, the ears are sound recording, and movements of the camera and editing together signify the reactions, expectations, and decisions that take place in our stream of consciousness as it guides us bodily through the stream of life-events around us.

ELEMENTS

All documentaries are composed of remarkably few elements, and their recombinant possibilities, though endless, are limited like any language by the conventions of the cinema and its audience. First, here are the basic ingredients with which every documentarian cooks.

How films combine these elements is already familiar, but you will need to internalize the groundwork of film language for yourself if you are ultimately to use the screen in your own way. You will have to decide from your audience's reactions "what works" and figure out why it works. This is how one arrives at one's own "voice" when practicing any of the arts.

A GUIDING THEORY

Some theoretical guidance may help, so we will draw parallels between types of shot and everyday human experience, and then work toward greater complexity by looking at the building blocks of cinema language.

TABLE 5-2 Picture and sound elements from which all documentaries are fabricated

Picture	
Action • People • Creatures • Landscapes • Inanimate things	**People talking** • Unaware of camera and spontaneous • Aware of camera and its portrayal
Graphics • Photographs • Documents, titles, headlines • Line art, cartoons, or other graphics	**Interviews** • Interviewer present in frame • Interviewer present but off-camera • Interviewer absent and questions edited out
Archive material • Library material • Material recycled from other films	**Re-enactments,** factually accurate, of situations that, • Were not filmed, or could not be • Are suppositional or hypothetical
	Blank screen—makes us think over what we have been seeing, or gives heightened attention to existing sound.

Sound	
Diagetic sound (synchronous sound shot while filming) • Dialogue • Accompanying sound, especially of sound events	**Sound effects** • Wild (non-sync) sound effects • Spot (sync) sound effects • Wild atmospheres • Location ambience
Narration (non-synchronous) • Narrator • Voice of the author • Voice of a participant	**Non-diagetic sound** (composed or added in order to comment on scene)
Voice-over • Audio-only interview • Drawn from interview, but picture discarded	**Silence**—a temporary absence of sound creating a mood change, or causing us to look critically at the picture.
Music • Diagetic (audible to participants) • Non-diagetic, added to comment on scenes	

SHOTS ARE LIKE THE HUMAN GAZE

Shots with a camera reproduce aspects of human regard, which can be short or long, casual or intense. With thoughtful framing, composition, and context you can inflect each shot with special meaning, because *a particular shot often implies the thoughts and feelings of whoever is doing the seeing.*

TABLE 5-3 Film terms and their equivalency in everyday perception

Film term and definition		In daily life, equivalent to
Shot	Framed view	Long or short period of watching, staring, expecting, enjoying, confronting—either close or at some distance.
Pan (Shot inflection)	Camera pivots horizontally	Taking in one's surroundings; comprehending; discovering; revealing; escaping; assessing; fearing, expecting.
Tilt (Shot inflection)	Camera pivots vertically	Assessing height or depth; looking up to; looking down upon. Threatening or feeling threatened. Admiring, assessing.
Crane (Shot inflection)	Camera travels vertically	Traveling up with; down with; getting up; sitting down; looking up at; looking down on.
Dolly, track (Shot inflection)	Camera travels horizontally	Physically moving toward or away from something or someone; traveling alongside, behind, or in front of someone. Attraction; repulsion; advance; retreat (perspective changes).
Zoom (Shot inflection)	Objects grow bigger or smaller	Looking more closely or retreating (but more psychologically than physically since perspective relationships remain unchanging during a zoom).

If film equipment functions like human eyes and ears, the mind that interprets their input functions as the seeking, reacting, physically guiding human intelligence. This makes the camera a mobile, thinking, and feeling participant in what it records—a stream of consciousness and movements with which the audience tends to *identify* (feel in sympathy).

CUTS

Putting two shots together, one after another in *juxtaposition*, implies a meaning much as your thought patterns do when you glance from a bread recipe to the temperature gauge on your kitchen stove. Cut any two images together and you lead us to infer meaning from their relationship. The famous Lev Kuleshov "bowl of soup" experiment used the same reaction shot in three different contexts and demonstrated how an audience thought it was seeing three different reaction shots. The shot is of a man looking out of frame, and associating him with a bowl of soup, a dead child, and a seductively dressed girl, Kuleshov discovered that the audience inferred successively that he was (a) hungry, (b) grieving, then (c) feeling desire. Clearly, shots in juxtaposition not only imply relationship, but encourage us to bring our own subjective interpretations to what our eyes see.

Early experiments with film, and early film theories, were developed in Russia. Two theorists of editing, Vsevolod Pudovkin (1893–1953) and Sergei Eisenstein (1898–1948), came up with differing ideas about the technique of montage, as editing was then called. To Pudovkin, editing shots together was a structural activity that built information, relationship, and meaning. Eisenstein was interested by the awareness one could stir in the viewer by the clash of the dissimilar and antithetical. Here are examples of their principles:

TABLE 5-4 In Examples 1 to 5, Pudovkin's *categories of juxtaposition* supply expository details
for the narrative. They establish the location's geography, the characters, and the central character's
"problem"—whatever he or she is trying to get, do, or accomplish. Examples 6 to 13, Eisenstein's
categories of dialectic editing, confront us with juxtapositions that argue as much as they inform

	Shot A	Shot B	B in relation to A	Type of cut and its function
Examples 1–5 PUDOVKIN'S CATEGORIES OF JUXTAPOSITION				
1	Woman descends interior stairway	Same woman walking in street	Narrates her progress	Structural (builds scene)
2	Man runs across busy street	Close shot of his shoelace coming undone	Makes us anticipate his falling in front of a vehicle	Structural (directs our attention to significant detail)
3	Hungry street person begging from doorway	Wealthy man eating oysters in expensive restaurant	Places one person's fate next to another's	Relational (creates contrast)
4	Bath filling up	Teenager in bathrobe on phone in bedroom	Shows two events happening at the same time	Relational (parallelism)
5	Exhausted boxer takes knockout punch	Bullock killed with stun-gun in an abattoir	Suggests boxer is a sacrificial victim	Relational (symbolism)
Examples 6–13 EISENSTEIN'S CATEGORIES OF DIALECTIC EDITING				
6	Police waiting at road block	Shabby van driving erratically at high speed	Driver doesn't know what he's soon going to meet	Conflictual (still vs. the dynamic)
7	Giant earth-moving machine at work	Ant moving between blades of grass	Microcosm and macrocosm coexist	Conflictual (conflict of scale)
8	Geese flying across frame	Water plummeting at Niagara Falls	Forces flowing in different directions	Conflictual (conflict of graphic direction)
9	Screen-filling close-up of face, teeth clenched	Huge Olympic stadium, line of runners poised for pistol start	The one among the many	Conflictual (conflict of scale)
10	Dark moth resting on white curtains	Flashlight emerging out of dark forest	Opposite elements	Conflictual (dark vs. light)
11	Girl walks into carnival	Distorted face appears in carnival mirror	The original and its reflection	Conflictual (original vs. distorted version)
12	Driver sees cyclist in his path	In slow motion driver screams and swings steering wheel	Event and its perception	Conflictual (real time vs. perceived time)
13	Driver gets out of disabled car	Same image, car in foreground, driver walking as a tiny figure in distance	Transition—some time has gone by	Jump cut

Like a spoken language, film language is in slow but constant evolution, so use it according to its potential for expression in your daily life rather than just according to cinema convention.

CAMERA MOVEMENT

The camera's physical actions (moving aside, coming closer, reframing, backing away, altering focus, craning up) also imply the emotional connotations that accompany human movement of any kind. A camera move can communicate anticipation, curiosity, appreciation, surprise, apprehension, intuition, dread, affection, and anger—all depending on the context. Imagine the camera equivalency to each of these actions:

- A voice behind you in a crowd makes you turn around to see who it is.
- While you are writing, footsteps approach. You lift your head to look at the door, anticipating who will enter.
- Someone enters whom you find tedious, so you turn back to your writing.
- In a ski lodge you open an outside door and find yourself facing a mountainside. You tilt your head back to see the peak.
- Your eyeline is obstructed by a tree, so you move sideways to see past it.

Whatever the camera pursues, avoids, or finds exciting will color that "corner of nature seen through a temperament." We will feel the vibrancy of a heart and mind at work, one that sees opportunity, enigma, threat, obstruction, beauty, or surprise as each new situation takes shape. Sometimes the camera is tired or drained, and reacts passively. Other times it draws us along with hectic ideas and agendas. If it has a living temperament, it also has changes in its moods.

To see all this in action, run any of direct cinema's seminal works, such as *The Man with the Movie Camera*, or the more recent *Primary* (USA, 1960) by Robert Drew, Terry Filgate, Richard Leacock, Albert Maysles, and D. A. Pennebaker, which chronicles the process by which John Kennedy sought the presidency. You can clearly sense the moment-to-moment reactions and decision-making during the filming, just as you can in Vendemmiati's *The Person de Leo N*, mentioned earlier in the chapter.

Finding patterns and implying explanations—what T. S. Eliot called "imposing order"—is an important function of authorship that we fulfill unconsciously all the time. Now your job is to hold a camera and microphone and use them to express your own changing states of attention. You, after all, are a surrogate for the audience and exploring life on their behalf. How well can you do it?

MOTIVATED CAMERA MOVEMENTS AND CUTS

Every edit and camera movement must feel motivated because in life something always initiates our mental and physical actions. We either act from an internal signal, such as a thought ("I wonder when the crossing-light will change?"), or from an external stimulus, such as an approaching vehicle, rain beginning, or someone waving from across the road. In your cinema work, as in life, there must be a constant flow of cause and effect.

DENOTATION AND CONNOTATION

A shot's content is what it *denotes* (what it "is") but the associations the shot can awaken are called *connotation*. Imagine calm shots of a flower or a hand lighting a candle. The shots denote what their subjects "are," that is, a flower and a candle. But depending on its context each shot can *connote* or suggest "natural beauty," "devotion," or a host of other associations. You encourage these associations when you want to lead your audience toward the contemplative and philosophic, which is the domain of mature life. To practice for this, adopt the editor's habit of assessing everything on film—images, sounds, words—as a potential symbol or metaphor. You can also practice this in everyday life as the poet does. You are looking for the spirit of things beneath their physical substance. Iranian cinema is powerful because it comes from a culture immersed in poetic thinking. Even a humble shepherd can recite poetry by heart and is trained by the poetry in his religion to recognize matters of the spirit in symbols and metaphysical imagery. This way of seeing is something you can cultivate and make your own.

THE CAMERA IN RELATION TO ACTION

PREPARING TO SHOOT WITH FEELING

Using a camera with sophistication goes far beyond framing and shooting a subject with care, since this can seem devoid of warmth or meaning. In fact, an audience often feels that the camera is informed by feelings—most often curiosity, identification, and empathy. Recognizing when this happens is not difficult; but for a camera operator or director to infuse an inanimate camera with feeling seems on the face of it impossible. Is it all down to editing? No, because editing can seldom create what is absent from the footage.

To film with feeling, we must first reverse the idea that we are mainly passive and acted upon by others. Then we must see what we frame and film analytically, while retaining our emotional investment in what we see. Following are some practical ideas about how we react—emotionally and physically—to different human circumstances. They begin with how we think of human inter-action itself.

THE ACTOR AND THE ACTED-UPON

In interchanges we seldom feel we have much effect, but the dramatic theorist Stanislavski proposed we are *acting upon those around us all the time*—even when adopting the strategy of passivity. Everyone has an agenda, so those we act upon, act back upon us. You see this most obviously in par-ent/child relationships, so often bristling with frustrations. A documentarian's job is always to seek the subtext of relationships, and to film them as they unfold with deliberate, timely camera framings and movements. This can give more psychic revelation than anyone was able to see at the time.

OBSERVING A CONVERSATION

Choose two people deep in discussion, and listen to their conversation. Most importantly, watch how your onlooker's perceptions move around. At first you probably look only at whoever speaks. Naive camera operators will cover a whole conversation like this, and they produce what I think of as Dog Television. Man's best friend, lacking powers of interpretation, can only look hopefully at the speaker. Walk? Dinner? Play with Charlie?

As a human interchange intensifies, notice how your involvement changes too. You look at each speaker as she begins, but then in mid-sentence switch to the listener. You have begun antici-pating something. What is it?

You must think in terms of *actor* and *acted-upon*. Recall watching a tennis game when, at any given moment, one player will *act* (hit the ball), while the other is about to be *acted upon* (receive the shot). When Player A launches an aggressive serve, your eye jumps ahead of the ball to see how B handles the onslaught. She runs, jumps, swings her racquet, and the moment you know she's successfully intercepted, your eye flicks ahead of the ball again to see if A can handle the return.

HUNTING SUBTEXTS

We follow the actions and reactions in human relationship like this because we know that people are always *trying to get*, *do*, or *accomplish* something. A tennis game is openly a competition for points, but a human interchange is also playing for goals, and we want to know their nature. Notice while you observe an interchange, how your eyes spontaneously *judge where to look*, moment to moment? Without you consciously directing them, they probe according to action and reaction, changes of eyeline by the speakers, and meanings flowing in the conversation.

Notice how your eyes know when to leave a speaker in mid-sentence to monitor the listener? Why? Because you were subconsciously *looking for evidence of developing feelings*. Notice how fast the "actor" and the "acted upon" switch roles. Your eyeline is probing their motivations while your mind is unconsciously building hypotheses about who wants what.

Apply these ideas about mental probing to camera handling, and you now have the golden key to techniques of camera coverage and editing. Of course, you can't swing a camera around as fast as the changing human gaze, so you will have to simplify the core of what is happening. Can you pinpoint the moments of realization that prompt—or should prompt—each cut or camera pan?

All this has immense practical significance, because editing closely replicates how we investigate behavioral evidence, which exposes clues to volition and motive. Run any distinguished feature film, and you will see that the editing reproduces the observing, assessing, questing that we do as we *watch an action closely and inwardly debate its meaning*. We humans are empathic beings: we identify, live with, and live through those around us. We have been doing this for millions of years as we developed from tribal creatures, whose survival depended on astute relationships with the given power structure. This is in our DNA, and is such a constant in our daily lives that we do not even register we are doing it. As a director, however, you are now in the human relations business, so you must become wholly conscious. Once you begin seeing this principle forever at work in human life, the shooting and editing decisions that mimic it fall into place as logical and satisfying. However, your decisions about motives also depend on one more principle, mentioned earlier.

HIDDEN AGENDAS AND SUBTEXTS

Beneath what is visible in any human situation are *hidden agendas*—that is, the participants' hidden, often half-conscious drives that provide much of the situation's tension. A married couple's argument isn't really about who should take their child to the doctor. You sense there's a *subtext* (an underlying explanation). You eavesdrop until you realize it comes from his feelings of hurt and jealousy because she had lunch with an old boyfriend. The acrimony is not really about their car arrangements. It's about his possessiveness and her need for autonomy, or maybe in her insecurity she needs to make him jealous to prove her own worth. You will have to keep watching and hypothesizing until everything falls in place.

In fiction cinema, actors, directors, and editors put a vast amount of work into developing subtexts like these, because they fuel the tensions that animate real life. In documentary you can only imply the subtexts you think are present by astute camerawork and editing that makes the subliminal more visible. Obviously you can't rehearse and direct the participants to evidence their subtexts. Instead you encourage the audience to,

- Look for hidden agendas and subtexts. (Is he delivering an insult, and if so, how should she react?)
- Formulate a subtext. (I don't trust that smile of his. What's he driving at?)
- Test the information. (Can this be true? What does it remind me of?)
- Commit something significant to memory. (I'll need to think about that later.)

- Imagine consequences or alternatives. (If … supposing … then …)
- Decide what is hidden and what is visible. (Can he show that knowledge or will he hide it?)

Framing, camera movement, and associative editing help the audience develop particular thoughts and feelings about the participants, or become aware of crucial contradictions. Such techniques convey a living human heart, intelligence, and soul at work.

ATTENTION AND FOCUS

Sometimes while operating the camera your mind goes ahead of, or away from, the task in hand. You are admiring or doubting the value of a composition, guessing the source of a shadow, or thinking associatively about something else. You are no longer in the present and the audience may sense it. Actors call this "losing focus."

Camera operators lose focus when they should maintain an unbroken interior life on behalf of the camera, or continue to move, react, search, retreat, evade, or go closer in the way that a focused human intelligence should. This motivation and reactivity is very obvious in handheld, spontaneous coverage, but is still present in a tripod-mounted camera that produces a more settled, formal coverage.

By the way, work from a tripod whenever you use a long lens and want shots to remain steady instead of wobbly like a telescope. An unsteady camera during an interview, for instance, is simply a distraction unless the participants are riding in the back of a truck in a war zone. In that case, the improvised nature of the exchange would be manifestly justified.

EYE CONTACT AND EYELINES

When you observe two people in earnest conversation, you'll see that, contrary to the fixed notions we hold, neither makes eye contact more than fleetingly. Eye-to-eye exchange is intense, draining, and reserved for special moments. Why is this?

Recall that each is either *acting on* the other person, or *being acted upon*. In either mode, each glances only occasionally at the other, either for enlightenment, or to judge the effect of something just said or done. The rest of the time each was looking inward, and their eyes hopped around, or rested on some convenient object.

Now, what made *your* eyeline shift around while observing them? Often, changes in their eyelines made you shift yours. Each blink and eyeline-shift alerts you to significance elsewhere, and your eye goes hunting for it. Watch two people like this long enough, and you'll detect a rhythm and motivation in their eyeline-changes that is being orchestrated by the shifting contours of the conversation itself. This can only be fully rendered in fiction film since conversations in documentary cannot be repeated and are seldom covered by more than one camera.

LOOKING AT, AND LOOKING THROUGH

In the fiction film *Five Easy Pieces* (Bob Rafelson, USA, 1970, Figure 5-2), the poignant two-person exchanges between the failed pianist and his sad waitress girlfriend relay three points of view: one each for the two characters and a

FIGURE 5-2 —————————————————

Depending on the drift and intensity of a conversation, the audience can identify with either character at different points. (*Frame from Five Easy Pieces.*)

third more detached one that is both ours and that of the Observer. Bobby and Rayette's perspective on each other is intimate, while the Observer's is outside their enclosed consciousness and looks upon them from a more analytic vantage. Depending on the drift and intensity of the conversation, the audience identifies with each character at different points. While Bobby talks, for instance, the observing camera (through whose eyes and mind we see) looks through Rayette's eyes at Bobby in search of clues to his inner feelings. At other moments we see Rayette through Bobby's more sardonic vantage. The third, authorial viewpoint comes via cooler, more detached two-shots in which we see them as a couple—mismatched and drowning.

In a two-person documentary scene, the camera does not quite have this freedom of coverage, but uses on-the-spot camerawork to capture and convey all those interpretive reactions by the characters that *both accompany and direct* human observation. The implications are complicated to grasp, but you'll understand best from watching yourself during an intense exchange and discovering how you first (passively) observe and then (actively) decide what action to take. There are many nonverbal signs to help you—in body language, eyeline shifts, rhythmic changes, voice inflections, and particular actions—all in their context implying particular meanings. Being responsive like this is what makes film language truly universal.

SCENE GEOGRAPHY AND AXES

Filming a scene well depends on *inhabiting* that scene with your empathy and consciousness. Figure 5-3 represents A and B under observation by O, the Observer who is their child. He makes a good example because children are highly observant, have vivid emotions, and often go unseen. As you imagine how O's eyeline moves back and forth between his parents as they talk, we can now name some of the "axis" components.

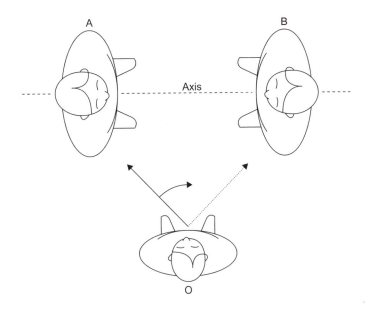

FIGURE 5-3

The Observer watching a conversation.

SCENE AXIS

O's awareness is drawn to the *line of tension* between his parents, an invisible, active pathway of words, looks, awareness, and volition between them. This is the *scene axis*, or *subject-to-subject axis*. If the scene contained four people, there would be multiple lines of tension and at different parts of the scene you would have to decide which was dominant.

CAMERA AXIS

Every scene also has an *observer-to-subject axis*, which O would think of as the "me to them" relationship. My example shows this at right angles to the axis between A and B. That is the *camera-to-subject axis*, often called the *camera axis*.

This may all sound rather technical but it's really quite human. From O's point of view, he has strong relationships (a) along his axis to each of his parents, (b) to the invisible connection (their axis, sometimes called the *scene axis*) between them, and (c) to the consequences upon him of whatever emotions pass along these axes. It is the human tribal-survival situation mentioned earlier, never more urgent than during our perilous apprenticeship as a dependent child. This sense of self versus others stays with us lifelong—often tinged with apprehension, but freighted with other emotions too, such as love and trust.

PANNING AND CUTTING

In turning to look from person to person, the camera mimics the Observer's actions by a *panning* movement between the two speakers (that is, the frame moves horizontally as when scanning a panorama). In Figure 5-4, O has moved closer to A and B's axis and, to avoid missing any of the action, must swerve his attention quickly between A and B. Under this circumstance, humans blink their eyes to avoid the unpleasant blur between widely separated subjects (try it for yourself). The brain, however, reads this as *two static images with no intervening period of black*. Cinema reproduces this by cutting between two subjects, each taken from the same camera position. Historically this solution must have emerged when some nameless person cut out a failed pan between two characters. It "worked" because its counterpart is embedded in human physical and psychological experience.

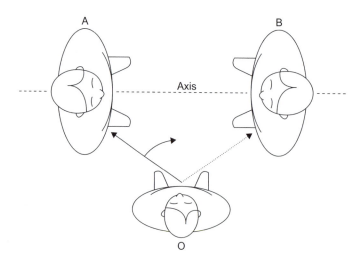

FIGURE 5-4

The Observer moves closer to the characters' axis.

SCREEN DIRECTION

A subject's direction of gaze, or movement through a composition, is called his *screen direction*, and this is described as "screen left to right," "screen right to left," and "up screen" or "down screen" (Figure 5-5). Where a subject's movement flows across several shots, as in a sequence of shots showing someone in a procession, this becomes rather important. All the action in successive shots should use the same screen direction (Figure 5-6). As a practical matter, this requires

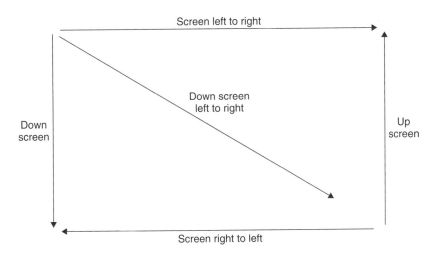

FIGURE 5-5

A range of screen directions and their descriptions.

FIGURE 5-6

Series of shots all maintaining right to left movement.

that you remember to shoot *characters and their movements from only one side of the scene axis*. Imagine instead that you take shots of a parade then run ahead so you can shoot it filing past a landmark. To get a better background, you cross the parade's path to shoot from the other side, something that feels quite unremarkable. However, when you try to intercut the R-L material with the L-R close-ups shot earlier, things go awry. The audience presumes there must be two factions marching toward each other. Cutting to the new camera position causes confusion because we see only the "before" and "after," and *not the transition where you crossed the scene axis*.

CHANGING SCREEN DIRECTION

You can in fact change the screen direction of a parade, chase, or character's path, but you *must show crossing the scene axis* on-screen. Two ways to do it are:

- By filming at an angle to a corner as in Figure 5-7. The marchers enter in the background going L-R, turn the corner in the foreground, and exit R-L. In essence they change screen direction during the shot. Subsequent shots must maintain their screen direction as R-L.

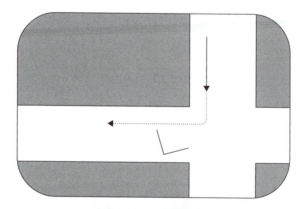

FIGURE 5-7

By shooting at a corner, a parade or moving object can be made to change screen direction.

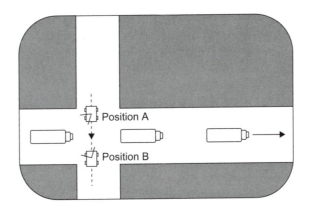

FIGURE 5-8

Dollying sideways between floats in a parade changes the parade's effective screen direction, but the dollying movement must be shown.

- By dollying *visibly* during a gap in the parade so that you cross the subject's axis of movement (Figure 5-8). The audience sees and understands the change in screen direction. In subsequent shots the action must maintain the new screen direction.

SHOT DURATION, RHYTHM, AND DEMAND ON THE AUDIENCE

GENERATING OPTIONS

Whenever you shoot a static shot, hold it longer than necessary, "just in case." When you pan over a landscape, add a longish "hold" at the beginning and end, so your editor can use the shot in multiple ways. Generating multiple options like this is standard practice in filmmaking.

If, however, you shoot a composite panning shot—a hold, a pan to a new composition, a second hold, then a pan on to a third composition—you will need a guiding principle to judge the "hold" between pans, and another to get the panning speed right. If possible, you shoot several takes incorporating different rhythms, so there's a version for different eventualities.

SHOT DURATION

As an editor, you hold a shot onscreen according to how long the viewer needs to absorb it. An analogy is to an advertisement on the side of a bus: if it's a simple image with four words of text the bus can drive past quickly and you'll get the ad. But if there are four lines of text and a complicated diagram, the bus must go slower, or the message is lost. We hold a shot on the screen long enough for the audience to absorb what matters, no longer. But shoot more than necessary, "just in case."

VISUAL RHYTHM

In a *montage* of shots, dissimilar shots edited together will be of different lengths yet feel similar in duration because the editor has timed them to require a similar level of scrutiny by the audience. When each is present for the right duration needed to "read" it, their *visual rhythm* feels similar even if their temporal spans vary.

Film language makes use of many speeds and rhythms that are native to the human mind and body. Our breathing and heart rate provide rhythms. We tap our feet to music, or jump up to dance when the music takes us. The rhythms, duration, and capacity of our minds and bodies determine everything we do. The optimal length of a feature film is said to be determined by the capacity of the human bladder!

RHYTHMS HELP US CONCENTRATE

Anything on the screen with a strong rhythmic component helps us to maintain concentration and remember what we saw. This is surely why the minstrels of antiquity performed their epic stories as songs or poems. Film makes use of every possible rhythm. Many sounds from everyday life—bird song, traffic, the sounds from a carpenter's shop, or the wheels of a train—imply rhythms that help the sequence find its particular rhythmic characteristics. Even pictorial compositions contain visual rhythms such as symmetry, balance, repetition, and opposition—all patterns that occupy, entertain, and intrigue the eye.

SPEECH RHYTHMS

When you shoot long dialogue exchanges, you'll become very aware of individuals' rhythms of speech, body language, and the development of subtexts. You will want to move your camera (and later edit) within this rhythmic framework.

Pacing and cutting mimic the rhythms of a bystander's consciousness as it probes a situation from different psychological or physical vantage points. One character's long pause before reacting might suggest "she's uncertain how to answer." Cut the reaction quicker, and now it implies "she's been waiting for him to say that." It is astonishing how varying reaction times can suggest quite different subtexts.

Charged dialogue scenes are exquisitely demanding to get right, either when moving with the camera during handheld coverage, or later when you edit together complementary angles. You can enhance subtexts by orchestrating the delicate nuances of behavior and coverage, and this is wonderfully challenging work.

SEQUENCES AS BUILDING BLOCKS

In the unending flow of events in a life, only a few are significant. A short biographical film might reduce a lifetime to 30 minutes by depicting just its significant moments—highs and lows—bridged together. You might think of these as: the hero's visit to the hospital emergency room after a road accident; the long moments of exalted realization during his residency in Rome; and three stages in building his own home while his wife became increasingly exasperated.

ELISION

Each of these narrative building blocks is a sequence that depends on *elision* (abbreviation to essentials). Imagine recounting a significant event in your life such as a first visit abroad. Make it into a waveform with some high points and some low (Figure 5-9). When you narrate only the highs and lows, not the middling stuff, your listener assumes you are using the *elision* principle to limit your story to the significant. Film naturally does the same. If you shoot someone's fearful visit to the dentist, you would aim to capture the intense moments of fear and anticipated pain. Most importantly, you would be sure to shoot the *transitions between stages* in the dreaded dental

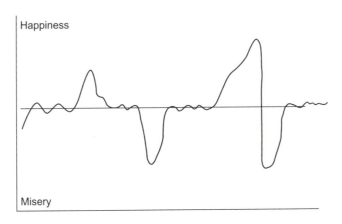

FIGURE 5-9

A period—of a day, maybe a month—during which someone's happiness fluctuates. By focusing on the extremes, biography condenses portraiture to what is significant.

chair, so your edited version can sketch in the recognizable steps in the progression from arrival, examination, X-ray, anaesthetic, drilling, and filling—and ending on a grateful escape into the sunny street. You do documentary research to prepare for what to film—and, just as importantly, what to ignore.

TRANSITIONS AND TRANSITIONAL DEVICES

PICTURE TRANSITIONS

The transitions between the building blocks (sequences) of a story are junctures that you can either hide or show, as the story demands. You would show those important to understanding a process, such as the stages in milking a herd of cows. But many of the physical transitions we make through life—from place to place, or time to time—are imperceptible because we are at ease and preoccupied. Film narratives replicate this by minimizing the seams between sequences.

An *action match* cut between a woman drinking her morning fruit juice and a beer drinker raising his glass in a smoky dive minimizes the scene shift by focusing attention on the act of drinking. A *dissolve* from one scene to the other indicates (in outdated screen language) "and time passed." A simple *jump cut* from a sunny morning to a rainy one signals (a) an elision of time, and (b) that the audience must imagine what is missing. For example, at a university department meeting we see a bored committee member suddenly wake up, and rise with a look of shock. We cut to him in the street, out of breath and swiping his credit card at a parking meter. The viewer infers that (a) he must have visualized getting a hefty parking ticket, (b) that he ran all the way to the car, and (c) that avoiding a parking fine is more important than attending the meeting.

When a transition should surprise or shock the audience, we emphasize the junctures between sequences rather than minimize them. A teenager singing along to the car radio during a long, boring drive, followed by flash images of a truck, screeching tires, and the driver yanking the steering wheel is intentionally a series of shock transitions. It replicates the violent changes someone goes through when taken nastily by surprise.

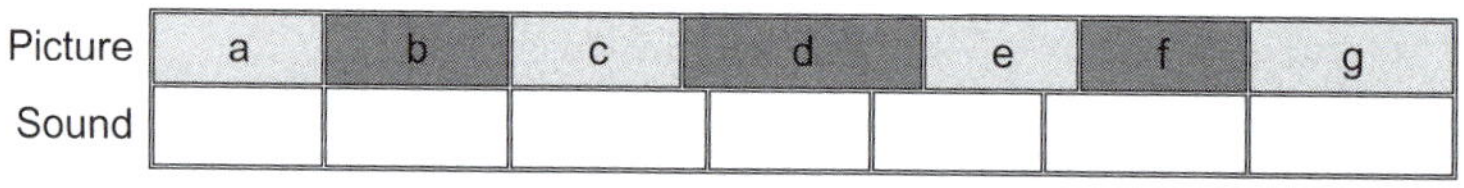

Picture	a	b	c	d	e	f	g
Sound							

FIGURE 5-10

Diagram of a sequence containing three level cuts and three overlap cuts. "Lap" cuts mimic the disjunctive way our eyes and ears absorb a conversation.

SOUND TRANSITIONS

Sound can also function as a transitional device. Hearing a conversation over an empty landscape draws us forward into the next scene (of two campers in their tent). Cutting to a shot of a cityscape while the birdsong from the campsite is still fading out gives the feeling of having moved to the city while the mind and heart lag behind in the woodland. Both examples imply an emotional point of view.

OVERLAP CUTS

When picture and sound cuts are staggered like this rather than level, we call them *overlap cuts*, *L cuts*, or *lap cuts*, as in the sequence diagrammed in Figure 5-10. Because our eyes and ears seldom shift their focus in tandem, film editing makes extensive use of overlap cutting to reproduce the disjunctive shifts of attention we make under intense circumstances. **Chapter 15: Editing for Refinement** looks at this principle in detail.

YOUR DUAL ROLES: OBSERVER AND STORYTELLER

Above I described the three stages we go through when telling stories from life—whether as next-door neighbor, gossip columnist, or stand-up comedian. They are:

- Acquiring and memorizing particular experiences.
- Selecting highlights and compressing them into a purposefully inflected narrative.
- Performing the story to get reaction and feedback.

Most discussion of documentary concerns only what happens in the first stage—as the observer finds, captures, or initiates material. The last two stages of filmmaking, in which the Storyteller takes over from Observer, get little attention. Yet the Storyteller's concern is with interpreting "what happened" and telling a good story, which means thinking from inception how to abbreviate, intensify, and inflect the contents in order to maximize their meaning and impact.

Generally storytelling gets rolled into documentary's long editing period, as if it were applied afterwards, and goes unnamed. To separate and dramatize the importance of these two roles, I capitalize them as the Observer and Storyteller.

The Observer role is concerned with,

- Creating a hypothesis.
- Seeking and interpreting significant events and evidence.
- Noting the patterns, cycles, and structure in actuality.
- Learning the clues to individual behavior that substantiate temperament, intention, and action.

- Respecting the integrity of "what is."
- Waiting for actuality to yield its intrinsic meanings.

The Observer, fascinated by the profundity and mystery of the actual, is a tireless witness who compulsively records and interprets. It is an ideal role for a documentary camera operator, sociologist, anthropologist, detective, or observational documentary director.

The Storyteller role exists to fascinate, challenge, and entertain the spectator. To frame and intensify the story, and make it connect with the greatest number of people, the Storyteller should be ready to draw on any of the associations and conventions in narrative art's long history. He or she goes about it by,

- Creating a hypothesis.
- Interceding during production to catalyze movement and truth when it does not emerge spontaneously.
- Finding a tale's implied meanings, philosophy, and point of view.
- Transforming relatively uninflected records into the heightened and purposeful intensity of artful narrative.
- Using all the tools of traditional form to intensify, dramatize, and contextualize the tale.

This is an ideal role for an actor, comedian, teacher, dedicated popularizer of history or science, or the participatory documentary director.

CONFLICTS BETWEEN THE TWO

Ideally the Storyteller-self is active from the outset, and works hand in glove with the Observer-self. Less ideally, the two may seem in opposition. If you shoot magazine material for television, for instance, you will have to withstand tight scheduling, and pressure to subordinate the spirit of truth for a more sensational film. This distorts and compromises the integrity of the original events, and storytelling runs amok. However, in less desperate circumstances you need some drive to stylize your shooting in the service of the story, or your film will emerge as humdrum realism. Much institutional documentary is like this because television long ago entrenched "objective" journalism. Nowadays, with huge and high quality screens to fill, documentary again needs to be effective cinema.

This makes documentary directors into split beings, which, let us say quickly, is nothing unusual. The director simply accepts the competing roles of faithful Observer on the one hand, and scintillating Storyteller on the other, and finds a balance.

RESOLVING TENSIONS

The Storyteller and Observer can liberate hidden truths through intelligent stylistic and narrative strategies. During this process, you will have important collaborators. For observation and interpretation you have your DP (director of photography), and for interpreting and storytelling, there is your editor. For now, while you are a one-man band making short trial projects, it is enough to be aware of these interesting issues.

HANDS-ON LEARNING

For the work in this chapter you might use the **AP-1 Making a Split-Page Script** analysis format to transcribe and analyze the shooting axes of an intricate dialogue scene in a favorite feature film.

Because of the degree of control, directors use far more deliberate *blocking* (scene organization) in fiction, and use a number of complementary angles arranged around the scene axis, or axes. A good follow-on would be to shoot a documentary dialogue scene with a handheld camera as in **SP-12 Observational Film.** As with all the shooting projects, be sure to apprise yourself of the assessment criteria beforehand. You can set up the scene between two colleagues or family members, telling them not to look at or act for the camera. The object is to practice camera handling and staying to one side of the scene axis. Editing the scene down to a shorter length (an operation called *ellipsis*) will be both interesting and revealing. Ordinary life contains a great deal of repetition, so ellipsis is both possible and desirable. See if you can do it.

PART 3

PREPRODUCTION

Memorable films go beyond the neutrality of merely reflecting the actual. Rather, they see the world they present in an engaged and critical light. A documentary idea begins in the *ideation* stage that is based on a conviction of some sort. You then conduct research to decide how and what to film. Some films seem researched and premeditated, while others appear to spring fully armed from the moment. But this is seldom so, for even seasoned filmmakers can seldom rely on spontaneous inspiration. For one thing, the pace and intensity of filming usually take all of one's attention, a point Werner Herzog once made when questioned after a screening about "the intellectual challenge during shooting." He replied caustically that, "Filmmaking is athletic, not aesthetic." It is so grueling, he told a startled Chicago Art Institute audience, that rarefied thought is all but impossible. In *Day for Night* (France, 1973) Truffaut uses fiction to make a similar point when its central character, a director played by Truffaut himself, is collapsing under a raft of problems and compromises. He confides that he always expects each film to be his best, then halfway through shooting can only think about surviving to the finish. My own fantasy was to escape by miraculously turning into the owner of a rural grocery.

For a productive and trouble-free shoot, you must plan and problem-shoot extensively in order to attune yourself to all you may meet. You must also assemble the people, permissions, and resources to carry out the project. You want your work to have a backbone and an individual stamp, so you develop a *working hypothesis*—a core definition of intentions. This helps you rise above the enclosing immediacy of your work so that you can survey, refine, and sharpen your intentions. This alone can raise a film above the parochial and conventional.

CHAPTER 6

DEVELOPING STORY IDEAS

IDEATION

Choosing and developing ideas can be haphazard and by luck and impulse, or you can tackle it in the more sustained and deliberate process known as *ideation*. This helps make a work's foundations solid, but even in fiction work this stage receives scant attention. Look through all the books on screenwriting, and there is virtually nothing to help you develop and sift initial story ideas. For this reason I wrote *Developing Story Ideas* (Focal Press, 2005) which gives a great many sources and methods for heightening story materials for fiction and documentary.

BEGINNING THE WRITING PROCESS

Potential film ideas are all around you. By taking notice, writing them down, and testing their merits and possibilities, you raise critical awareness of your surroundings and hone your ability to find core ideas. This, more than technological mastery alone, is most likely to make you into an interesting film artist. Ideation is an aspect of composition, and not something to put off or dismiss. There are right and wrong ways to do this work and you should know that productive writers routinely change hats. That is, they use different parts of their psyche for different aspects of the job:

- *Discovery mode* uses free-ranging play, imagination, and intuition as you search for the subjects or topics that bring you the "shock of recognition." This means that you keep searching around until your intuitive recognition says, "Yes, *yes*!"
- *Story development and editing mode* uses logic, analysis, and dramaturgical principles to structure and organize the material you've generated. The intellect is good at shaping and improving what tale is possible on the screen.

During the discovery stage, allow your mind to behave associatively so that it can play with all the possibilities. Trying to wrench it into productive order simply shuts down its powers of invention at this stage. Teaching that insists you start from an outline cripples many people early in life, and writer's block is the result. This comes from the logical mind barging into the play area, censoring and belittling what it finds. Logic, intellect, order, and control will all have their place later.

STORY SOURCES

You may already be using some of these ways to collect and sift material for a story, *the* story you need to tell. Be ready to try different methods because each person finds their own most productive methods, and you must experiment to find yours. Collecting and categorizing is creative busy-work because it helps you to recognize your fascinations and the underlying structures in your tastes.

MAKING AN IDEA DATABASE

Story ideas arise simply from juxtaposing material in new ways. If you are a dab hand with a database, consider using FilemakerPro or similar software to store and sort your material (Figure 6-1). By adding thematic or other keys, you can call up idea material, and then group and sort it by priorities. Making entries and reading over your bank of observations will in any case spark ideas. A computer isn't inherently better than, say, handwritten index cards, except that it's easier to sort and print your collection, and to experiment with different structures.

At a simpler level you can list material in a word processor table, and then by highlighting one particular column, and using "Sort" (under "Home" in Microsoft Word), you can rearrange the whole table by date, location, or other priority.

Read over your growing files every so often, and look for the shadowy collector, the self that is implacably assembling examples of its hidden preoccupations. Nowhere is this more evident than in your journal.

KEEPING A JOURNAL

Carry a notebook and note down whatever strikes you (Figure 6-2). Transfer your best materials to a computer, and the act of copying gives you time to consider and explore. By using a speech-to-text program like Dragon, your dictation can appear immediately in print. Be warned that you have to train such programs or put up with many comical misunderstandings.

A whole film arose from my journal notes from attending a lecture during a birdwatching trip in Central America. It led to co-writing a proposal with a Costa Rican friend, who went on to shoot *Discovering Eden* (Juan Manuel Fernandez, Costa Rica, 2012, Figure 6-3).

Date	12/09/2009	**Place**	Savegre Valley, Costa Rica
Observations	Son of the founder gave excellent & spirited lecture in English about the way his father and uncle got lost, fifty years or more ago, and discovered the hidden valley by accident. Returned, camped in damp cave, nearly starved as they created a habitation. Brought their families, met American who helped them populate river with trout, created access road over several years. Fishermen came at first, developed eco-tourism center for birdwatchers & other nature-lovers like ourselves.		
Idea	"Discovering Eden" -- film about long, difficult building of an eco-center in contrast with the wide-scale destruction elsewhere in Costa Rica in order to build holiday homes		

FIGURE 6-1

Using a customized database to store and sort your research material and ideas.

To reread your journal is to make a repeatable journey through favorite ideas and associations. The more you note what catches your eye, the closer you get to your current themes and underlying preoccupations. Think you know them already? Nobody ever does—that's the fascination of the artistic process. Each of us has someone within who is more intelligent, purposeful, and creative.

FIGURE 6-2

A journal is a log of everything you find significant. Later, by clustering the groupings, you find the underlying patterns in your preoccupations.

FIGURE 6-3

Research photo that led to *Discovering Eden*.

NEWSPAPERS AND MAGAZINES

You are always looking for situations that align with your particular interests. Newspapers are a cornucopia of the human condition at every level, from the trivial to the global, and real life is always where you find the really outlandish tales. Keep clippings and transcribe anything that catches your interest, and classify them by idea or theme. Local papers—where they survive—are particularly useful because the characters and settings you read about are accessible and reflect the local economy, conditions, and idiosyncrasies. The agony columns, the personals, and even the ads for lost animals can all suggest subjects and characters. With every source, you have possible characters, situations, plots, and clues to underlying meanings.

ONLINE

The Internet is a fount of possibility but you'll need some inventiveness to find situations that are local and accessible. By looking up my own locality in the community website www.craigslist.com, I quickly found these samples. I could have approached any of the writers (whose names I have removed) about doing a film. Notice that each involves a situation that somebody wants to solve. Each, in dramatic terms, has a "problem":

Peace Corps: My Daughter just informed me that she has been accepted, Medical and FBI part left to do. For god's sake how safe is it really? She wants to go to Africa and work on Aids/HIV education. Seriously, why do I feel like my child is going off to war? Is this a normal reaction? Don't get me wrong...I am very proud of her but scared as well.

Documentary Filmmakers Wanted: "InnerViews" is a series of short films being created at L---- Geriatric Centre in S---- to document the life stories of our residents. Each of these films will chronicle the life of a resident from infancy to childhood to adulthood and through his or her senior years. The only prerequisites to volunteering for this project are computer literacy and an interest in documentaries and filmmaking.

Stop Smoking/Volunteer to be Hypnotized: Hypnotists in training seeking volunteers to be hypnotized. You can have a free session! Contact instructor L---- W----- to schedule your session! Indicate the issue you are seeking help with when calling or emailing.

   Peace Corps might lead to a film about an anxious mother/daughter relationship; *Documentary Filmmakers Wanted* could show beginning filmmakers struggling to make their first films with old people; and *Stop Smoking/Volunteer to be Hypnotized* could investigate the mystery of hypnosis and of smokers trying to master their addiction. Good films could come from any of these.

HISTORY

Historians, they say, find what they look for, which means that history is all about point of view. It involves not objective truth, but an angle on a vast pool of available facts. Most localities have their historians passionately exploring the past, so you might make a film about enthusiastic amateurs, or about some feature in your locality with stories attached to it. Two hours from my home is Starved Rock on the Illinois River. Legend has it that in the late eighteenth century a group of Illini Indians, pursued by Ottawa and Potawotami tribesmen, took refuge on the butte and died of starvation rather than give in. A short film might explore what such a fate really involved, and whether the legend is apocryphal.

   You will also find people re-enacting history, that is, playing parts in some real-life drama that took place long ago in a particular place. Whole families re-enact historic events wearing authentic costumes and according to the best historical knowledge.

FIGURE 6-4

Yesterday's protesters in *Prisoners of Conscience*, guaranteed to dispel one's fear of aging.

If you find archeology fascinating, the PBS series *The History Detectives* shows people reconstructing the past in an admirably stylish and unacademic way (www.pbs.org/opb/histo-rydetectives). Usually they take a handed down artifact or piece of information and research its significance or authenticity. Here are three documentary "teasers" from their website:

- *Bonnie & Clyde Bullets: Could five .45 caliber bullets owned by a woman in a small Wisconsin town be responsible for the demise of the notorious Bonnie Parker and Clyde Barrow?*
- *Movie Palace: Is it possible that a theater in the small town of Baraboo, Wisconsin, could have been the country's first great movie palace?*
- *Sears Home: Might an Ohio couple's residence be a long-forgotten Sears home? (After World War I many homes were built to designs provided through the Sears Roebuck catalogue)*

Notice that each is phrased as a question, which is very common with dramatic issues of all kinds. If history thrills you, your job may be to pose questions, and disinter stories that answer them, with force and political meaning. Earlier in my life I made a series of oral history films for the BBC that involved finding out how people experienced important events. Elderly activists were proud of having used their lives well, were great to work with, and dispelled my young person's dread of ageing (Figure 6-4).

LEGENDS

Legends are defined as "inauthentic history." Every culture, locality, community, and family develops iconic stories that reflect its sense of saints, fools, and demons. Find or resurrect them, and they can make powerfully emblematic film subjects. By comparing the facts in relation to the legend, you can explore how and why humankind rewrites the past. Mark Rappoport does this in his hybrid production, *From the Journals of Jean Seberg* (USA, 1995, Figure 6-5), which uses a look-alike actress to play the unfortunate Jean Seberg who was hounded by the FBI for supporting the Black Panthers. Instead of allowing Seberg to die tragically young as actually happened, Rappoport imagines her living on to critically review the parts she played during her short life, and to figure out how she had been used.

MYTHS

Myths express the kind of conflicts that humans cannot solve, and that we must somehow accommodate. The human truths in Greek mythology do not lead to easy or happy resolution, but instead leave the bittersweet aftertaste of unalterable fate and are for some reason strangely uplifting. Nemesis, the goddess of revenge, played a trick on the beautiful youth Narcissus, whose pride made him disdain those who loved him. She made him fall in love with his own image in a pool, in which he drowned, rather than relinquish his image. Many a beauty has fallen on hard times when their attractions fade, and has awoken to the hard dawn of isolation, the just consequence of self-involvement.

FIGURE 6-5

The iconic actress Jean Seberg, around whose roles and life Mark Rappoport wove an improvised fiction film. *(Photo courtesy of The Kobal Collection/ Columbia Pictures.)*

Yes, we think of a situation redolent of mythology: *that's* how it is! In Martin Doblmeier's *Bonhoeffer* (USA, 2001, Figure 6-6) we meet the intriguing young German theologian who worked his way around from nonviolence to justifying an assassination attempt on Hitler. When the attempt failed, Hitler had him executed in a ghastly mimicry of the crucifixion. Bonhoeffer's courage as a pacifist, weighing the evil of assassination against the larger evil of Hitler's regime, makes him into a mythical figure, a Christ as well as a David heroically losing the battle to Goliath. Myths and legends are always available to help us penetrate the full resonance of any particular tale from the real.

FAMILY STORIES

All families have favorite stories that define special members. Those about my grandmothers belong in a magic realism novel. Of Granny Bird the family said that she "found things before people had lost them." Conventional in most ways, she had mild kleptomania, especially where fruit and flowers were concerned. At an advanced age, during breaks in long car journeys, she would hop over garden walls to borrow a few strawberries or liberate a fistful of chrysanthemums.

How a family explains and accommodates such eccentricities illuminates how it defines itself. My other grandmother, Granny Rabiger, began life as a rebel in an English village and married an alcoholic German photo-engraver. He took her abroad, beat her until she nearly lost an eye,

FIGURE 6-6

Martin Doblmeier shooting *Bonhoeffer* in the jail that once held the dissident pastor. *(Photo courtesy of Journey Films.)*

and then left her in France, where she stayed the rest of her life. Her story and those of her three children would make quite a documentary, were any of the primary witnesses still alive. The tale involves life in an orphanage, ballet dancing, orchestral conducting, inept spying for the Allies, and the white slave trade in Argentina. These are lives so far-fetched that no self-respecting novelist would try to use them. Family tales can be heroic or very dark, but they make vivid oral history. Often they influence descendants by suggesting who we may be ourselves.

CHILDHOOD STORIES

Most people stumble out of childhood as if from a war zone. If you tackled the creative identity exercises in the previous chapter, you surely wrote down traumatic events that now seem pivotal. One of mine is from when I was a 17-year-old apprentice in a film studio, and overheard a casually misogynistic comment on the set about my editor. I naively repeated it to her as something absurd. She flushed scarlet and sped out of the room to find him—leaving me to die several deaths while waiting for her to return. What a lesson in discretion!

The question the incident poses is this: when life hands you unforeseen power, should you use it, and if so, how? My choice, had I realized it, was between spy, guardian, or defender. All the childhood stories lodged in your memory undoubtedly have special meaning for you. Do you know what they are?

SOCIAL SCIENCE AND SOCIAL HISTORY

If you are moved to rage by the exploitation of the poor and powerless, you can find excellent social science studies to support your sense of what happens, say, to farm, factory, domestic, or other workers. Social scientists and historians are disciplined chroniclers who interpret from large, methodically compiled knowledge bases. Their studies are not only fascinating, they are a vital resource for the documentarian. Usually they contain bibliographies, and the more modern the work, the bigger the bibliography.

Case histories contain trenchant detail when you need to be certain what is typical or atypical. Usually they include both observation and interpretation, so you can check how your own instincts compare with those making informed surveys. A potent source of documentary work is to partner with a social scientist once you have developed your filmmaking skills.

FICTION

Don't disregard fiction because you are working with actuality. Novels, short stories, and fiction films can be superbly observed and give inspirational guidance in a highly concentrated form. Jane Smiley's *A Thousand Acres* is not just a reinterpretation of *King Lear* in the rural Midwest; it is also a superbly knowledgeable evocation of farmers and farming. If you were making a work on, say, the depopulation of the land while agribusiness swallows up family farms, Smiley's novel would prime you with important reminders of what to show.

SELECTING A SUBJECT

Making art is a way to contribute useful work to the world. Anyone marked by intense experience (of being an immigrant, say, or of living homeless in the streets) has little difficulty finding a subject, but for those of us with less dramatic lives, identifying our mission can be baffling. For your documentaries to be original and authentic you will need to recognize your hot issues, or you can't do your best work. The key is already within you, but will require some honest self-examination. Use the projects that follow to make a self-profile—candidly and in private—so that your likely artistic identity will emerge. Depending on the degree of your self-knowledge, it may confirm what you expect, or it may take you by surprise (as mine did) and reveal what you have somehow overlooked for years.

Once you have workable ideas, push them out into the public arena. Most of us are shy and cautious, but film is an audience medium, so you must get people to listen to your ideas and react to them. Self-promotion is an unpalatable but necessary business, but you can lower the discomfort by being generous and supportive in partnership with colleagues. Promote development in those around you, and then what goes around, comes around.

TESTING A SUBJECT

You test a subject idea by researching to discover its potential. Cinema technology is not an alchemy that will aggrandize and ennoble whatever you put before the camera. It is more a magnifier, which means that what is profound and moving will be memorable, and what is superficial and banal will become even more so. Tough self-questioning can help ensure that you are not deceiving yourself, and that you are the right person to handle it. Most important is to ask, "Do I *really* want to make a film about this?" Silly question? Beginners routinely dive into worthy subjects when making a documentary is a long, slow process; a moderate initial enthusiasm will not carry you through the long haul. So try answering these questions:

- In what area am I most knowledgeable and even opinionated?
- What is the underlying significance of this subject to me?
- Do I have a drive to learn more about this subject? (This is particularly revealing.)
- Can I do justice to the subject, and what single aspect could I cover really well?

- Do I feel a strong and emotional connection to doing it—more so than to any other?
- What would I most like to discover about this?

These questions, answered candidly, will help flush out where your idea needs more work. The aim is not to block or dim your engagement, but to keep you digging until you unearth a subject and an approach that feel so right that they energize you. Clarifying your personal feelings about a subject should take you down a new and exciting road. Ask also,

- What do most people already know, and not know?
- What is unusual and significant?
- Where is this specialness truly visible?
- What can I *show* (as opposed to verbally narrate)?

Set down on paper anything you intend to show, and also what you want to avoid. Defining what you *don't* want is important to creativity, because it forces you into new areas.

DON'T BITE OFF MORE THAN YOU CAN CHEW

Initially everyone, absolutely everyone, takes on too much out of fear that their subject will be undernourished. You shouldn't, for instance, consider topics only open to large companies. A biographical study of a movie actor, for example, would be impossible without corporate backing because the actor's work is only visible in heavily copyrighted works. Why not instead consider profiling a community theatre actor, and make your film about acting instead of fame?

An institution might make a fascinating film topic, but you would have to secure high-level approval to get access. Most have nothing to gain from letting you in, since you may dig up (or worse, manufacture) sensational and damaging evidence. For this reason, even an animal shelter may be hedged with politics and suspicion. In fact most institutions prove unremarkable—they do what you'd expect them to do, so a film merely reiterates the obvious. And what's the use of that?

Pick manageable subjects that match your capabilities and budget. Not for a moment need this confine you to small or insignificant issues. If the wars in the Middle East fascinate you, and you cannot afford combat footage, you might find that a local plumber is a military veteran with a fascinating and representative experience. Further, he has a network of friends with snapshots, video footage, and mementos. Now you've found a way to show how Everyman went to war believing he was defending freedom, only to discover—what? Good ideas always emerge from circling round unanswerable questions.

NARROW THE FRAME

Much development work consists of paring away everything extraneous to one's central purpose, a focusing activity called *narrowing the frame*. It is part of articulating what your film is really about, which often proves amazingly difficult. With each degree of success, you'll feel yourself penetrate deeper into what remains. Let's say you want to chronicle inner-city life. Commonly people make a shopping list of everything they could show, but this leads to scatter-shot generalizations with no sense of focus. Instead, think small and think local. Any number of great films exist within a mile of where you live. Ask,

- How narrowly (and therefore how deeply) can I focus my film's attention?
- What single aspect of my subject area most grips my interest?
- Where is that most visible?
- What could I jettison, to leave only what most concerns me?

Often people think that to be "fair" they must make a survey, and this leads to a photomontage approach that lacks focus or point. The audience learns nothing of value, sees nothing develop, and can enjoy no penetrating intelligence leading the project. However, were you to choose a barber saloon with a regular clientele of local men, you can capture their jokes, political interests, and running jokes so that we get to know them. We learn how they are convinced that "the neighborhood is changing, and changing fast." Through voice recordings, you could develop an interior monologue of fears and regrets. It can become penetrating and touching, an intimate core sample of a time and place.

FIGURE 6-7

Peter Thompson's father in *Anything Else*: loneliness and stubborn self-sufficiency in a hollow marriage.

CHOOSING A CENTRAL CHARACTER

In every story, something should be at stake for the central character or characters. If intuition tells you that you have a fine central character, then you must decide what, at the most profound level, is he or she *trying to get, do, or accomplish*? Is it to win acceptance by a mother or father? Win recognition for a skill? Get clear of an accusation? Obtain forgiveness for a betrayal?

Naming what most profoundly drives someone will take a lot of quiet, highly focused observation, and a willingness to keep on digging for the most embracing portrait. Why not *ask* what drives him or her? The simple fact is that none of us has much idea of our own deepest drives. That's for you the Storyteller to see and delineate. My late and much loved colleague Peter Thompson does this unforgettably in *Two Portraits*. His short film about his stoic father's life and suicide, *Anything Else* (USA, 1987, Figure 6-7), is deceptively simple and terribly moving. Nobody has drawn a more profound picture of loneliness and stubborn self-sufficiency in a hollow marriage.

CHARACTER IS DESTINY

As a dramatic portraitist your job is always to decide what motivates someone who interests you. "Character is destiny," said the Greek philosopher Heraclitus, remarking on how each person shapes his own fate. Consider your own parents, or anyone you have long known. What formed their paths before and after they met? How did they complement each other, play into each other's strengths and weaknesses? You can only answer this by thinking like a dramatist and a psychologist.

LOCATING AND RAISING THE STAKES

Whenever you plan to direct, keep asking what is *at stake* for the central characters. What do they have at risk? "Raising the stakes" is a screenwriter's expression, derived from gambling. It means asking what would make matters more challenging for your central character(s). Here are some examples:

Subject	Stakes go up if...
During her 20-year quest to find her husband, Isabel Godin des Odonais makes the long journey from Western Peru to the mouth of the Amazon.	Her boat enters a stretch where the piranha-infested river narrows and the water runs ever faster and more dangerously.
Rookie climbers take a new route up a steep rock face.	Rain begins to fall—a very dangerous situation.
Founders of a real estate company get ready to repay their capital loan.	A stock-market plunge means their business is now in danger of going broke.
Nanook in *Nanook of the North* starts making the igloo for the night.	The snowstorm begins, leaving people and dogs clinging to life itself.

You get the idea. The more anyone risks, the more important it becomes to succeed, and the more compelling and significant their struggle. The coalminers who strike to establish their right to unionize in Barbara Kopple's *Harlan County, USA* (USA, 1976, Figure 6-8) do so in order to secure more humane conditions. The stakes rise dramatically when company thugs shoot at the film crew in the dark, and eventually kill one of the dissident miners.

New circumstances provide greater pressure, more hazards, and more "tests" that the hero in the folk story must always face while he—or she, of course—undertakes the epic journey. Consider:

FIGURE 6-8

Harlan County, USA: real-life violence in the making. *(Photo courtesy of Krypton International Corp.)*

- What further obstacles your protagonist(s) might face.
- Whether this will happen spontaneously.
- Whether you can legitimately rearrange matters to help raise the stakes.
- How to get your camera in the right place at the right time.
- How to film appropriately and with the greatest credibility.

MANIPULATION DANGERS

Contriving what typically happens rather than catching it happening spontaneously can get you into trouble. John Schlesinger's "city symphony" documentary *Terminus* (UK, 1961) is about the events and rhythms in a great London train terminus. A small boy's mother leaves him with their suitcase and then fails to return (Figure 6-9). This is every child's nightmare, and when a policeman takes him to the stationmaster's office, his fright and misery are palpable. Schlesinger had contrived this with the mother's agreement, and was lambasted by critics for improving his film at the cost of a child's misery. By coincidence *Terminus'* camera assistant Nick Hale met the boy later in life. He was amused that people had worried on his behalf and said that the experience had done him no harm. I wonder.

To raise the dramatic temperature, and make your audience care about your characters,

- Make sure you clearly establish what pressure each character is experiencing.
- Be sure you cover each step in the escalation of detail of their journey.
- Be ready to help things happen when expected situations fail to develop or resolve, but only if it's ethically justified.
- Raise the stakes if you have the permission of those involved, or can obtain their agreement afterwards that your intercession was justified.
- Don't risk losing your participants' trust by injecting what is false. There may be no way back into favor.

FIGURE 6-9

Rigged moment at a train station: a small boy realizes he has lost his mother in *Terminus*.

- By all means set ethical lines that you won't cross, but do not forgo all experiment. You don't have to show everything you shoot.

USING THE MEDIUM TO STIR FEELINGS

SHOCK VALUE

My late BBC producer Stephen Peet thought that the best documentaries deliver an emotional shock. This might occur in a single memorable scene, as in *Bowling for Columbine* (USA, 2002) when Michael Moore brings a wheelchair-bound shooting victim to confront Kmart and ask for a refund on the bullets still lodged in his body (Figure 6-10). Shocks can occur once or twice in a film, or consist of several small, quiet events rather than big, shattering ones. Paul Watson's *Malcolm and Barbara: A Love Story* (GB, 1999) concerns a wife inexorably losing her pianist husband to Alzheimer's Disease (Figure 6-11). There are many poignant and harrowing moments in Malcolm Pointon's decline, but the emotional shocks lie in the frankness of gaze with which the film shows what is normally private.

PRIMARY EVIDENCE

Because the screen isn't like other forms of communication, "What can I show?" is the key issue. We want visible evidence, because documentary grips us most when it shows real people and real situations taking place in the here and now. Doing and feeling are more interesting and more inherently credible than any amount of talk about doing and feeling. Talk is in the past tense because it concerns what has already concluded. A story that is open-ended is inherently more gripping than one already over.

Can you position yourself so that your camera witnesses primary evidence in the here and now? Can you show us your participants in pressing, unfolding situations? Can you film actions and show us a story with minimal speech? The fewer the words in a film, the more important are those that remain.

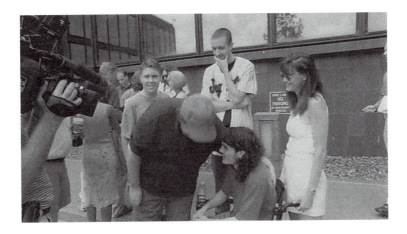

FIGURE 6-10

Shock tactics *in Bowling for Columbine*: Michael Moore brings a shooting victim to Kmart, who sold the ammunition.

TESTING FOR CINEMATIC QUALITIES

Are you still thinking like a journalist, who writes dialogue, and then illustrates it with pictures? Or are you thinking like a dramatist who gives us chunks of dynamic life, action, and imagery? Please show us behavior, action, and interaction; then we'll feel fully alive from thinking, feeling, and making judgments as we watch.

You can test any film idea's strength by imagining it as action and music alone. Is it conceived visually and behaviorally? Can the onlooker follow the story and understand the characters? Or is it so speech-dependent that without dialogue it loses meaning?

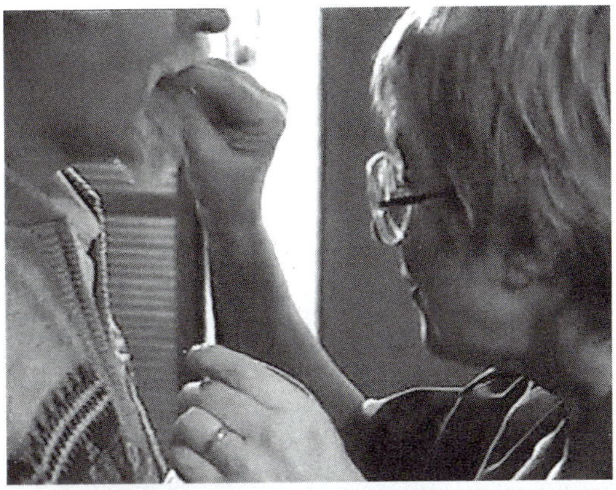

MOOD MATTERS

When good cinematography and strong action create a powerful mood, viewers enter your

FIGURE 6-11

Caring for a husband suffering from Alzheimers in *Malcolm and Barbara: A Love Story*.

movie with their hearts open to your film's thematic intentions. Plan therefore to give us atmospheres, interesting lighting, and eloquent detail, since these all build a world that viewers can enter with delight from personal experience. In his masterpiece about national amnesia, *Nostalgia for the Light* (Chile, 2010, Figure 6-12), Patricio Guzman devotes much screen time to building the imposing presence of the Atacama Desert and its telescopes. They are searching for clues to the origin of the universe among starlight that has taken millions of years to arrive. All the more shocking, therefore, to learn that the older people rummaging in the desert sands nearby are searching for the bones of their lost children (Figure 6-13). Their loved ones are *los desaparecidos*, "the disappeared ones" murdered by the Pinochet regime and hastily dumped in the sand when the government saw its power ending.

FIGURE 6-12 ——

Telescopes searching for the origins of the universe in Guzman's *Nostalgia for the Light*.

FIGURE 6-13 ——

Nearby, relatives in an endless search for the remains of their loved ones in the Atacama Desert.

Guzman confronts us with the irony of scientists searching for the key to the universe while heartbroken relatives search endlessly for those they will never stop missing. Through Guzman's meticulous building of time, place, and atmosphere, he brings home the aching tragedy of searching for anything at all that remains of a beloved child, spouse, or sibling. We feel the engulfing catastrophe of a nation that prefers to pardon murderers rather than acknowledge how they worked. *Nostalgia* draws out the irony in scientific curiosity coexisting with purposeful amnesia.

LOCAL CAN BE LARGE

Aim to make small films that are thematically large. Do this by taking local material, making your eye wise, and finding the truths that can make an audience across the globe nod in recognition.

FIGURE 6-14

Arguing passionately to save the lives of children in *The Interrupters*.

To find this, you will have to vacate your comfort zone, push your imagination to the limit, and use everyone around you as sounding boards.

SUBJECT-DRIVEN, CHARACTER-DRIVEN, AND PLOT-DRIVEN FILMS

One way to avoid journalistic argument, which illustrates concepts like a PowerPoint lecture, is to jettison any idea of a message as a starting point. Sam Goldwyn is supposed to have told a producer, "If you want to send a message, use Western Union." Look for a character of spirit and energy who is trying to get, do, or accomplish something. That will make your film a *character-driven* tale rather than a *subject-driven* polemic.

FIGURE 6-15

In *My Architect*, Nathaniel Kahn searches for the truth about the enigmatic, aloof father he hardly knew. *(Frame from film.)*

In Steve James' *The Interrupters* (USA, 2011, Figure 6-14) Ameena Matthews argues passionately for young gang members to foreswear violence and rethink their lives while they still have time. The irony is that she once ran with the Chicago gangs herself and her father is the uncrowned (now jailed) king of gang-bangers. Matthews brings her expertise in gang relations to nonviolent conflict resolution, and commands the respect of those whom she seeks to save.

Many seekers are traveling a less visible road. In his extended essay *My Architect* (USA, 2003, Figure 6-15), Nathaniel Kahn's pained search for the truth about his enigmatic, aloof father is dominated by the spirit of the great architect who, sadly for his son, was far from a great human being. To escape the unassuaged longing he has always had for the father he never knew, the son must try to find what drove his father, and made him so remote and obsessive. Can this even be done?

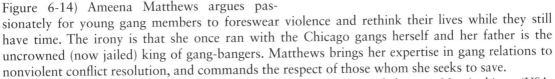

SUBJECT-DRIVEN FILMS

To become fully human, *everyone needs something to push against*. A documentary becomes compelling when we see meaningful effort expended against opposition. Those making waves always have issues: they may be connected with blood relations, giving, regaining something, revenge, justice, redemption, letting go, taking back … anything in the spectrum of ardently emotional human endeavor. You become attractive as a teller of tales when you find and convey something fundamental in the human spirit. To do this best, find central characters laboring in the same vineyard as yourself. This is why it matters so much to confront your own artistic identity. For me that would mean anyone struggling with feelings of imprisonment (such as in the military, in a societally determined sexual orientation, or in a soul-destroying role). Uncovering what your main character's issues are, and showing them in action, will hold great metaphoric meaning for you, your subject, and your audience.

With enough imagination, you can get a compelling film from any special character, even that of a household pet. Our dog, for instance, maintains a close and adversarial relationship with the vacuum cleaner. She feels obliged to confront it, snarl at its advances, nip at its windpipe, and challenge its every twist and turn. It's a domestic comedy, of course, but also an echo of the survival imperatives of the wolf from which all dogs descend.

Plot-driven films are those whose events are more important and coherent than the lives of their characters. A plot-driven film usually needs a strong structure with an inevitable forward momentum through time. A film about a hurricane, plague, flood, drought, circus visiting a small town, or factory closing is one whose characters, even though they animate the film's events and processes, are not the film's major focus. To understand this, see Pare Lorentz's two magnificent New Deal epics about the rape of the environment, *The Plow that Broke the Plain* (USA, 1936) and *The River* (USA, 1938, Figure 6-16). Each uses a symphonic form and stunning imagery to indict humankind for its blind abuse of mother earth. Today, catastrophic winds and flooding make these early environmental films prophetic.

FIGURE 6-16

Stark imagery and ironic montage set up a haunting vision of the rape of the land in Pare Lorentz's two magnificent New Deal epics, *The Plow that Broke the Plain* and *The River*. (*Photos courtesy of the Museum of Modern Art Film Stills Archive.*)

WHAT TO AVOID

You are wise to stay away from,

- Worlds you haven't experienced and cannot closely observe.
- Any ongoing, inhibiting problem in your own life (see a good therapist—you won't find relief while directing a film).
- Anything or anyone typical (nothing real is typical, so nothing typical will seem real).
- Preaching or moral instruction of any kind.
- Problems for which you already have the answer (so does your audience).

DISPLACE AND TRANSFORM

As we have said, each of us carries marks, each is deeply motivated by just a few particular issues. A colleague once said that underlying all his films was the search for a father (his own died when he was young). Most documentarians find direct autobiography inhibiting or even abhorrent, but *pursuing situations analogous to one's own* is liberating and energizing. Every film I have ever made has been about trying to escape captivity, but it was many years before I realized it. A single theme can have a thousand passionate incarnations.

HANDS-ON LEARNING

To penetrate the mind of someone whose documentaries you admire, try **AP-8 Analyze a Director's Thematic Vision**. Initiate several film ideas of your own by making a brief working hypothesis for each, using **DP-3 Brief Working Hypothesis**. Writing your ideas down always helps your mind go further than merely thinking about them.

CHAPTER 7

RESEARCH

Conducting research for initial ideas means immersing yourself, keeping notes, and thinking creatively. This can be slow and uncertain of outcome, so the wise keep more than one documentary pot on the stove. Not only do ideas seem to cross-pollinate, but having back-ups can get you out of a jam. I once had a subject set in Paris collapse a week before the crew arrived. Instead, I hastily developed a topic I noted in a magazine I had read on the plane.

DEVELOPING A PROPOSAL

On finding a subject, novices often feel they must start shooting *immediately*. And so, without preparation or planning, they shoot…and shoot, and shoot. The problem is that when you run the camera, everything looks equally significant, so you shoot everything that moves. Later, sitting at the computer and facing hours of random footage, you are dismayed to find neither common denominators nor viewpoint.

To direct, rather than merely shoot a film, you must *focus your ideas ahead of time, so you shoot with a set of intentions.* But, you protest, this is documentary! Don't I shoot with an open mind, rather than decide what's going to happen?

Yes, and no. What you need is a plan to narrow and deepen your quest. Then as you shoot you'll either see what you logically expected, or you'll see new aspects developing that alter your idea's center of gravity. With a plan in hand, you can decide whether to incorporate the new, discard it, or change the plan.

The major preparation steps are:

1. Write a *working hypothesis* (a statement that crystallizes your intentions for the filming but which remains flexible so that you can amend and develop it as you go).

2. Make a *pitch*, a brief oral presentation of your film to an individual, or to a small audience, so you get feedback that can help you go farther.

3. Develop a *proposal* (a written description of what you expect to film, to help raise the financial or material support you need, and even to start filming).

A NOTE ON FILM WRITING

To produce writing with the immediacy of the viewing experience, filmmakers write in a particular way. While literature or journalism usually speaks in the past tense, writing for film is in the present tense, active voice. This is because we experience film in the here and now.

At first you'll probably write, "He will be shown digging his garden." Then, realizing this is in the future tense, passive voice, you change it to the present tense, active voice: "He is digging his garden." Better yet would be, "He digs his garden." The original seven words have come down to four compact, purposeful ones. To write like this means fighting the habits of a lifetime and Microsoft Word can be set to help you by underlining passive sentence constructions.[1]

RESEARCH OVERVIEW

Below are common steps during research, but don't fret if you have to take them out of order. Real life is messy and circular while proposals have to present ideas in logical sequence. "Art exists," said T. S. Eliot, "to give us some perception of an order in life, by imposing an order upon it."

Remember, you are looking for *visual evidence* so that your camera shoots material with shape, atmosphere, progression, and meaning. The research phase usually goes like this:

1. *Test your documentary idea* by developing a working hypothesis
2. *Meet people*, do a lot of watching and listening, and
   a. *Explain your interests*, so you become known and trusted
   b. *Decide provisionally whom you might film*
   c. *Decide what roles* people have adopted
   d. *Decide who represents what* in the scenario you can see developing
3. *Note characteristic activities* so you can,
   a. Shoot each one comprehensively, briefly, and with visual panache
   b. Recognize when something unusual or dramatic starts happening
4. *Break shooting into scenes* and,
   a. *Assign a functional purpose for each in your narrative*
   b. *Analyze how best to film them*
   c. *List basic information* (exposition) that you must establish for each
   d. *Consider possible outcomes* so you are ready for changes and upsets

MAKE A WORKING HYPOTHESIS

A director's point of view does not materialize with time; it is something you must actively seek and decide, and what helps is to start making a working hypothesis straight away. Probably you are thinking, "But I haven't done any research! I don't know anything yet!" Ah, but you do. No matter how provisional your ideas, the working hypothesis begins to expand and arrange them along the through-line spine of a narrative. Invariably it shows that you *do* know quite a bit already. To do this, take any film idea, no matter how preliminary, and complete the prompts in Table 7-1. Ignore those italicized—we shall use them in Book II.

The working hypothesis in fact functions like a delivery system. It begins from your conviction in relation to the subject (Prompt 1), and delivers the particular thoughts and feelings of a total experience to your audience (Prompts 13 and 14). In between come the body of ideas, purposes, and concepts that make your film dynamic, dramatic, and persuasive.

TABLE 7-1 Prompts for a Brief Working Hypothesis (Project DP-3 on the book's website, www.directingthedocumentary.com)

DP-3 BRIEF WORKING HYPOTHESIS
(The italicized prompts will be explored in Book II)

Steps
 1. In life I believe that... (your life-principle concerning this subject)
 2. My film will show this in action by exploring... (situations)
 3. My central character is... (name, role, characteristics, etc.)
 4. What he/she/they are trying to get, do, or accomplish is...
 5. The main conflict in my film is between... and...
 6. *My film's point of view, or its POV character, will be...*
 7. I expect my film's structure will be determined by...
 8. *The subject and POV suggest a style that is...*
 9. The theme my film explores is...
10. *The premise of my film is...*
11. *The Storyteller's characteristics are...*
12. Possible resolutions to my film are...
13. Ultimately I want my audience to feel...
14. ...and to understand that...

PROJECT 7-1: DEVELOPING A BRIEF WORKING HYPOTHESIS

If prompts in Table 7-1 are a little cryptic, here is some guidance:

1. **In life I believe that...**
   a) Your convictions that make this topic so attractive.
   b) Any truths or "laws of the universe" that affect your central person or subject.

2. **My film will show this in action by exploring...**
   a) Brief description of the "corner of nature" in which your conviction will come to life and the events we shall see. Your film's exposition must establish basic facts and situations so we can follow the story.

3. **My central character is...**
   a) This can be a person, creature, or thing. Some films portray multiple central characters or a group, which is more complicated.

4. **What he/she/they are trying to get, do, or accomplish is...**
   a) You must decide to your own satisfaction what he/she is trying to accomplish, in each sequence, and also long-term, possibly lifelong. This is the key to showing an active character developing through time.
   b) Show the obstacles that stand in your main character's way, and adaptations he/she makes.
   c) Show whether he/she overcomes (or fails to overcome) the impediments.
   d) Your main character usually cannot tell you more than a fraction of his/her goals: you must use your intuition and confirm it through your powers of observation.

5. **My film's main conflict is between... and...**
   a) This refers to the main competing forces that your film wants us to consider. Usually these involve the main characters and are highly related to your answers in #4.

b) Be really careful; it's easy to designate conflict superficially and then to discover that deeper levels exist when it is too late.

6. *Ignore (Prompts 6, 8, 10, and 11 will be explored later in Book II Storytelling, **Chapter 22: Advanced Research**).*

7. **I expect my film's structure will be determined by...**

a) To generate a strong storytelling momentum, decide what is organic to the story that can help its development through time. Is it a journey or an event? A process that someone must go through? A rite, ritual, or test of stamina or skills?

8. *Ignore*

9. **The theme my film explores is...**

a) A theme is an idea or concept central to the story, such as rebirth, nostalgia, family conflict, identity conflict, and so on.

b) You should be able to express it in one or two words only.

10. *Ignore*

11. *Ignore*

12. **Possible resolutions to my film are...**

a) Documentaries are improvisations that often conclude in unexpected ways—a chance filmmakers and their audiences take. Try to anticipate different outcomes (resolutions) and assign whatever different meanings they may yield, so that you can have different shooting strategies ready.

13. **Ultimately I want my audience to feel...**

a) This is the prevailing mood (or succession of moods) that you want your audience to experience since hearts and minds change because of feelings, not facts.

14. **... and to understand that...**

a) Here you define what you want your audience to realize during and after your film.

Sharpen and compress your hypothesis statements until each is brief but comprehensive. If anything appears twice under different headings, sort out the confusion. Do discuss your ideas with collaborators, but do not share your conceptual infrastructure with participants. They will probably find such ideas alien and even manipulative.

The working hypothesis is of long-term usefulness, since it hands you a work-in-progress checklist to periodically update. As such, it becomes a navigator's compass all through research, shooting, and editing.

Table 7-2 Is a typical working hypothesis (see next page).

FIELD RESEARCH

Everyone fears rejection or the stinging rebuke, so beginning to research means facing one's inbuilt barriers of shyness. You can limber up wherever you find yourself by opening a conversation to find what makes people tick. Such encounters are the documentarian's push-ups, and Al Maysles, the doyen of American documentary, was still doing them in his 80s when we traveled on a Mexican bus together.

Research usually brings home how welcoming and helpful most people are. After all, you and your camera do bring a little glamour, a little immortality. Don't be afraid to exploit it.

TABLE 7-2 Specimen Brief Working Hypothesis for *The Foreign Boy*

WORKING HYPOTHESIS *THE FOREIGN BOY*

1. In life I believe *that you can avoid failure by not trying, but life keeps facing you with tests. Overcome even something minor, and you feel great.*

2. My film will show this in action by exploring *a grade school swimming lesson full of alienating noise, activity, and boisterous kids.*

3. My central character is *a timid Iranian boy still learning the language and culture of his American peers.*

4. What he is trying to get, do, or accomplish is *to learn to swim like the other kids, and gain their approval and acceptance.*

5. The film's main conflict is *between the struggling individual and the incipient tribal cruelty of young children.*

6.

7. I expect my film's structure will be determined by *the events in preparation for the process of a school swimming lesson, and its aftermath—all mostly seen from the frightened child's perspective.*

8.

9. The theme my film explores is *that courage usually finds helpers (the caring swimming instructor)*

10.

11.

12. Possible resolutions *are that, (a) the boy has a bad time and can't swim, (b) he manages a little swimming and feels hopeful about it, or (c) he does poorly but someone (a friend or teacher?) encourages him to continue.*

13. Ultimately I want my audience to feel *the boy's relief at being recognized or accepted after his heightened fear and loneliness.*

14. ... and to understand that ... *the boy's ordeal epitomizes the immigrant experience; and that everybody faces trials like it one time or other.*

NARROWING THE FRAME

You research not only to decide on people and situations to film, but to decide the restrictions you want to apply. To say "I want to shoot an intimate observational character portrait, not a talking head interview film" is part of deciding the aspects you like, and the strategies that will do them justice. The clay on the potter's wheel is a shapeless lump until the potter's hands begin containing and squeezing it.

TAKING NOTES

It seldom feels right to use a camera or sound recorder on first meeting people. Better is to ask questions and take notes of what you see and hear. Writing serves multiple purposes: it relieves you from having to maintain eye contact, allows you to listen for *subtexts* (underlying meanings), and lets you keep a record that will be vital for crosschecking if you wind up seeing many people. For some reason the act of writing also helps one better absorb and remember.

RESEARCH METHODS ARE SUBJECT-DRIVEN

The subject and type of documentary you intend making naturally determine how you should research. Good films usually require exploring blind alleys as well as those more fruitful, in order to be sure what you need.

Example 1. You want to make an observational film about a street gang, so you use *networking* to make contact, to convey your interests to those who are suspicious, and to clear you to make your first visit. It will be easier to approach the gang through the recommendation of someone they know, and this applies in every walk of life. A London journalist friend used to say, "Anyone can get to anyone else in the world in five or less phone calls."

Once the gang shows interest you may need to hang out with them over a period of weeks or even months until they come to thoroughly know your motives and trust them. This is how the modest, kindly Hubert Sauper made *Darwin's Nightmare* (2004, Austria, Figure 7-1), a grimly absurd tale about sick, starving Tanzanians trapped in a toxic ring of exploitative commerce. Lake Victoria's fishermen catch a predatory fish, then foreign merchants and middle-men sell it to European gastronomes. The local people get the rotting heads. Guess what the Russian transport planes bring in unmarked boxes on their way back to Africa? Guns.

Sauper stayed around for months and local people came to accept that he truly wanted to know them. The result is a series of amazingly candid, inwardly searching conversations that he held with street urchins, weary Russian pilots, prostitutes who dream of education and a good job, and the security guard of a research facility whose only weapon is a bow and poisoned arrows. Their frankness makes this occasionally funny, often shocking film very special.

FIGURE 7-1

Darwin's Nightmare, Hubert Sauper's ghoulish tale of starving Tanzanians trapped in a toxic ring of exploitative commerce.

Example 2. You want to make a tightly argued film about a group of scientists, so you must research using books, libraries, interviews, and the Internet to master intricate patterns of scientific cause and effect. Choose someone knowledgeable as an adviser and mentor, so you don't get the science wrong. You'll want to profile the personalities and workplaces of the scientists themselves so they come off as full human beings. Find out how they relax, what their family life is like, what they fear, and what they hope for.

Example 3. You want to make a film about how children visit a zoo. Again, you must hang out, ask questions, and observe the regular, cyclical patterns by which each day follows the last. Wittily and economically your film should establish how everyone catches their breath at the stink when they enter the lion-house, how grandparents and babies doze off after lunch, or how gaggles of boys taunt the unfortunate chimpanzees. These are obligatory scenes that will make your audience smile in recognition.

By the time you are ready to shoot, you need to know everything typical (so you can film necessary steps), and everything unusual. There's that kid lying on his side so he can look the armadillo in its beady black eye! There's that depressed man in a raincoat and red woolen hat sitting with his back to a depressed baboon. Quick, shoot it!

FINDING THE PARADIGM

Directors often fail to define the *paradigm* for their film—that is, the central and irreducible purpose of their story. Your most potent skill will be learning to analyze an idea, locate its true purpose, and construct your shooting plans around this center. With the paradigm undefined, a story will stay unfocussed and blurred. To complicate the task, the paradigm will keep shifting or dissolving, each time challenging you to nail it again.

SHOOTABLE EVIDENCE

Human situations may involve learning, dependency, humor, control, imitation, power relationships, obedience, revolt—anything in the vast spectrum of human aspiration. You will need to develop a good eye for what is major in people's lives. To prepare for shooting, note evidence of whatever meaning you intend to highlight, and note exactly *how* your mind was persuaded by it. If your character is "comfortably placed in life," note the fine objects and tasteful layout of their dining room, say, because these can be filmed. Stop yourself from jumping directly to ideas and conclusions, because a camera can only record what is concrete and tangible, it cannot record abstractions. Look for meaningful objects, words, actions, and behavior that you can shoot.

MAKING AN INVENTORY

From research and forming a film in your head, make an inventory of materials you'll need to shoot. Your shopping list might look like this:

"Immigrants" (10 minutes)

Action Sequences
- *Garage Sequence - Kenny at work*
- *School Sequence - Jean in the gym*
- *Clinic - Maria getting an X-ray*
- *Home - Family dinner, Jean doing homework*

- *Letter carrier on rounds, delivers envelope to McPhersons*
- *Maria interviewing for the new job*

Archive

- *Parents' 8mm film of Maria as child (beach, Christmas, Easter)*
- *Parents' tape of Jean as a child (beach, soccer, birthday parties)*
- *Maria's tape of her parents Jorge and Ana visiting from Mexico*

Interviews

- *Jean re mother's ambitions*
- *Kenny re money troubles*
- *Maria concerning low expectations of her parents, and changes she's trying to make in her own outlook*

Sound only

- *Chihuahua folksong sung by Jorge*
- *Playground atmosphere*
- *Hospital atmosphere with announcements*
- *Repair shop atmosphere*
- *Christmas carols at local church*

PROJECT 7-2: DRAMATIC CONTENT WORKSHEET

Drama takes particular people and events, and arranges their doings to suggest an underlying meaning. For any film idea you have in mind, the Dramatic Content Worksheet in Table 7-3 will help you dig out what is humanly significant. You may not be able to answer all its questions, but trying will stimulate your imagination and creativity.

HOW TO FILM IT: STYLE AND CONTENT

You can lay out your ideas for shooting style by using a simple Style and Content Worksheet as in Table 7-4. Aim to name each sequence and give it a distinct mood, purpose, and meaning. Aim also to accentuate the intrinsic identities and contributions of each part of the material, and keep in mind that even a simple interview will benefit from a deliberate setting and mood.

Don't worry about the material's order since that will be dictated by the logistics of shooting, and won't be settled until you finish editing. Remember to include archive footage. Even though its style and content are largely given, its pictorial quality can be somewhat altered in postproduction (hue, contrast, color saturation and balance, etc.).

If this resembles a fictional approach, remember that film proposals are works of imagination: to communicate your authorial ideas to a producer, fund, or other interested party they have to be idealistic and visionary. The imaginative proposal helps you find material that you will only properly encounter once you start organizing it for editing.

HANDS-ON LEARNING

For any documentary idea you have in hand, try using **DP-1 Dramatic Content Helper**. Its purpose is to help you turn a probably static-seeming life situation into something that is essentially dynamic and where something significant is at stake. The aim is not to falsify, but to release the underlying principles and make them visible.

TABLE 7-3 Dramatic Content Helper (Project DP-1 on the book's website, www.
directingthedocumentary.com)

DP-1 Dramatic Content Worksheet

For each intended scene…

1. **Who/What/When/Where/Why** (Exposition)

a) **Who** are the main characters?	Their types, personalities, and backgrounds? Which is the main character and why?
b) **What** is their situation?	What is it, what led to it, where will it go next?
c) **When** is this happening?	Era, season, month, time of day or night?
d) **Where** is this taking place?	War-torn Sierra Leone or sleepy Nebraska; city or village; in a train, car, mansion or slum; kitchen or bedroom; upstairs or down?

2.

a) What is **routine and characteristic**?	What's necessary and normal in this activity? How little can I show to establish what is happening? What's especially revealing in each main character's actions or temperament?
b) What is **surprising or special**?	What's beneath the surface and goes unnoticed by the casual onlooker?
c) What **patterns** lie in the situation?	What characteristic movement and cycles of repetition does the place or situation have (by people, traffic, machines, animals, natural phenomena, etc.)? What obstructs or conflicts with these patterns?

3. **Will and Conflict** (Worthwhile drama depends on active, aspiring characters)

a) **Volition** What's the main character trying to get, do, or accomplish?	In life generally? In this scene?
b) **Obstructions.** What in general stops him/her/it?	Overall? In this scene?
c) **Conflict**	What conflicts will occur in the film? What's the single, central conflict in my film?
d) **Strategies.** How might he/she/it deal with each new obstruction?	By reflex and without thought? Creatively? In panic, surprise, disbelief (you name it)?
e) **Resolution**	What do you see as possible outcomes for the scene? Which is most likely? How will you go forward with shooting if a change becomes necessary?

For the film as a whole…

4. **Structure** (A well-structured story gives a sense of movement and purpose)

a) The hook: How will you engage your audience?	How will you seize your audience's attention? How to signify the "contract" (what your film is going to deal with and how it will do this)?

(Continued)

TABLE 7-3 (Continued)

DP-1 Dramatic Content Worksheet

b) **Momentum.** What will structure your sequences and drive your film forward from beginning to its end?	The steps of a process, event, or journey? The emotional order of memory (in retrospect)? The needs of a character (character-driven movies)? A series of orchestrated contrasts? A series of graduated moods? Other_____?
c) **Time.** How will you order it?	According to the chronology of the original events? As someone remembers the events? According to a storytelling logic for telling the events (for instance showing a court case conclusion before reconstructing all the steps to get there)? Other_____?
d) Apex or **Crisis.**	What is the pivotal event, moment, scene, or situation that makes your film's likely high point? (You may not know yet.)

5. **Change, growth, and resolution** (A satisfying story reflects change and growth)

a) Who has the potential for **change?**	Who or what is under pressure? Who is taking risks? Who or what needs to change? What is really stopping that change?
b) **Confrontation**	How will your audience see the main, conflicting forces the film deals with meet and collide? How to ensure this happens onscreen?
c) **Growth**	Who or what might grow? Can you legitimately help that growth (by positive intercession)? What mistakes must you avoid if you intercede?
d) **Resolution**	What outcomes to the film seem possible? Which is most likely? How to handle each so your film can end meaningfully?

6. **Audience, Impact, and Theme**

a) **Target audience.** Who in particular are you addressing? (Don't say "Everyone!")	A type of person shown in the film? An authority or institution? A section of the public, and if so, which? Other_____?
b) My **audience must feel** ...	What emotions must you awaken in your audience?
c) My **audience must think about** ...	What issue, idea, contradiction, conflict, etc. should your audience be left thinking about?
d) The **theme** of my film will be ...	Recall your "In life I believe that..." statement and restate the theme your film will establish.

TABLE 7-4 Specimen Style and Content Questionnaire for three sequences of a documentary about a child visiting grandparents (Project DP-2 on the book's website, www.directingthedocumentary.com)

DP-2 Style and Content Worksheet

Sequence name & content	What it should convey	Coverage style
Bus station: Parents put Ellen on bus and wave goodbye.	Ellen is fearful about traveling alone. The experience is troubling.	Handheld camera, emphasizing movement, instability, weird faces, disconnection, noise.
Small town bus-stop: Ellen gets off, looks for grandparents. She is surprised to find only Grandpa there. She asks where Grandma is.	Small figure in a big world; anxiety, then relief at arriving. But where is Grandma?	Tripod and long lens as bus arrives and a small Ellen gets off. Then handheld as she searches for her grandparents and finds only Grandpa.
Hospital. Grandma is in bed after a stroke; asleep but could be dead. Ellen is scared until Grandma awakes and greets her. She seems tired but alright.	The hospital room has scary equipment, plastic tubes, electronic metering. Grandma looks very vulnerable until she awakes and smiles. By intercutting Ellen we get a strong sense of her concern, then of her relief.	Tripod-mounted camera, wide-angle shots to give unpleasant distortion. Perspectives stabilize as Ellen realizes that Grandma is going to be OK. Do POV close shots of the dials, read-outs, tube clamps as well as record all the sounds, especially Grandma's labored breathing.

NOTE

1. Click the Office Button in the document top left-hand corner > Word Options > Proofing > Spelling & Grammar > Grammar Settings, and under Style, check Passive Sentences.

CHAPTER 8

DEVELOPING AND PITCHING
A SHORT DOCUMENTARY

TURNING DRAMATIC CONTENT INTO AN OUTLINE

Now you can expand your preparatory writing into a brief story outline. This is a narrative using the present tense, active voice. It walks the reader through the experience of seeing and hearing the intended film, and uses one paragraph per *sequence* (a setting or block of time). You will need to establish the characters, the main character's situation, and his/her *problem* (whatever he or she is trying to accomplish, overcome, solve and whatever obstructs this). Describe how you imagine the film develops, and what the likely outcome will be. Most important is to say why you and nobody else should make it. If you have significant imponderables and alternative possible endings, write about them. The reader needs to know you are ready to handle alternative outcomes.

Avoid promising to "investigate" anything while filming: this raises red flags because a proposal should demonstrate a thorough understanding of its subject, and the word "investigate" is a euphemism for "I haven't researched this yet." Try to bring vision and enthusiasm to what you expect to film, and to disperse all notion that you expect to float along passively with whatever happens.

PITCHING

The next step is to take your attractive documentary idea and *pitch* it to an audience. The term, derived from baseball, means giving a brief, orally delivered, colorful description from which listeners can easily visualize your film. From this, paradoxically enough, you can collect audience feedback and start shaping a better film—even when you haven't shot a frame.

Pitching is salesmanship and acting, so at first it won't be easy or comfortable. In professional situations you may get no more than 3–5 minutes for a 5–20 minute film and perhaps 10 minutes to pitch a 90-minute feature-length documentary. There is no set formula, and part of the challenge is to present your idea in whatever narrative steps best serve its nature. Use colorful and evocative language, and let your passion and belief in the special qualities of the story show. Here are some guidelines, which you should restructure to best serve your idea:

WHO/WHAT/WHEN/WHERE/WHY

Supply the following in whatever order works best:

- **Title**, and **background** to the topic.
- **Character or characters**, and what makes them special.
- **Problem** or situation that makes the main character(s) active and interesting.
- **Point of view.** Through whose eyes and feelings will we mostly see?
- **Style.** The kind of camera and editing treatment you'll give the events you've described.
- **Resolution.** Describe any changes or growth you expect during the filming and what **outcome(s)** you expect.
- Why this film must get made, and **why you are the person to make it**.

It may help to put prompts on a postcard as a reminder. Do not read from a script—it's deadly. Look your listeners in the eye and talk to them. Once you improvise from memory, your speech will become lively and spontaneous.

A TYPICAL PITCH

The representative pitch below is developed from the working hypothesis in Table 7-2 for *The Foreign Boy* in the previous chapter. I have bolded the key concepts to show how I worked them in.

This 6-minute documentary is called The Foreign Boy, *and deals with the lonely terrors of being foreign and trying to win the acceptance of one's peers. Nine year-old Mohsen is a sheltered and introverted Iranian boy whose English is still limited. The* **setting** *is a rough-and-tumble urban grade school in an all-white district. The buildings are old and run down, and the kids are hard to discipline. Mohsen's* **problem** *is that he is new to the school, new to the country, and speaks little English. Life at school is overpoweringly confusing.*

In **style**, *the observational camerawork and editing will give us a strongly subjective feeling of the way he sees and feels. There will be little dialogue and no interior monologue—everything we learn, we learn from watching, as Mohsen the foreign boy must do in his new surroundings. In the early classroom sequence, his raucous and lively classmates seem distant, distorted, and almost jeering at him. His experienced, overworked 50-year-old home-room teacher Mrs. Mullen notices his shyness and the way he watches the other kids, and imitates what they do. He has a strong* **drive** *to fit in with the other kids, to be accepted, and not to feel different.*

The children go by bus to the local swimming baths. Mohsen hates taking his clothes off and shivers in the cold air. The staff separate the kids into those who can swim, and those who can't. Mohsen now faces the **ordeal** *of learning to swim. The pool is at first hellishly deafening and confusing. His sympathetic teacher Terry, a dedicated African American swimming instructor in his 30s, acts as if Mohsen can succeed. The camera will follow Mohsen underwater when he panics. Gradually as Terry calms him and gets him to concentrate, the noise recedes. He finds that the other kids are now aware of him and are encouraging him. Terry is likeable and treats all the kids considerately and sympathetically. The film concentrates on the relationship between Terry and Mohsen as the teacher aims to get the boy's trust, and to get him to take a few strokes with his foot off the floor.*

Sooner or later Mohsen will **develop** *by making the advance that means so very much to him. If Mohsen takes his first strokes, the film's* **resolution** *is Mohsen's sense of accomplishment. If it* *doesn't happen, we will keep shooting until Terry coaxes him into succeeding just a little—which Terry is sure will happen.*

The film's **theme** *is that taking first steps in something frightening is the key to earning other people's respect, and that it helps greatly to have someone who believes in you.*

This film matters greatly to me *because I went to four different schools between the ages of 9 and 11, and never felt I could fit in. My stomach still gets knotted up at the sound of a school yard. I want to exorcize these memories by revisiting the situation as an adult, and making a film sympathetic to a boy in a predicament I know only too well myself.*

From this you can "show" your as-yet unmade film to an audience, and seek early responses. Like a theatre actor you can sense from moment to moment whether you are holding your audience's interest. Make notes of any comments afterwards, and say as little as possible. Change your approach in subsequent pitches until every aspect works for every audience.

Try pitching a new five-minute documentary idea every week. You will be amazed at how many good ideas you can come up with, and how much you learn from pitching them. Afraid someone will steal your ideas? If you have plenty, you won't be.

CRITIQUING A PITCH

When a friend pitches a film to you, use the criteria in Table 8-1 to help you give practical feedback. This type of outcomes-oriented assessment is useful to any endeavor, and listing multiple goals helps you not forget any of them.

Question F concerning "Form" asks whether the way you intend telling the story looks promising, while question H on "Style" wants to know whether the film fits into a recognizable type of documentary, and makes use of what the audience expects of that genre.

TABLE 8-1 Criteria for a Good Pitch (Project DP-10 on the book's website, www. directingthedocumentary.com)

	Criteria for a good pitch	0	1	2	3	4	5
A	**Situation:** Clear and dramatically promising						
B	**Characters:** Clearly differentiated, inherently interesting						
C	**POV character(s):** Trying to get, do, or accomplish something tangible						
D	**Stakes:** Main character has a lot at stake						
E	**Development** and change in a main character seem likely						
F	**Form:** Inventive and cinematic, fits the subject						
G	**Structure** of the story is logical and organic to the events						
H	**Style:** Type of documentary is clear and appropriate						
I	**Metaphor** will be used productively in the film						
J	**Socially critical attitude** implied by the film toward its subject is evident and appropriate						
K	**Commitment** strongly demonstrated by filmmaker						
L	**Strong audience appeal** seems likely						

EXPANDING THE PITCH TO A PROPOSAL

Here are two more ideas expanded into proposals, limited here to content and meaning, although you can add comments on style and production if you wish. Each film now suggests a distinct area of endeavor in the human or natural worlds:

The Smallest in the Litter

We see a breeding kennel in the distance. Unseen dogs of every age bark maniacally in every register. The owner carries food from pen to pen talking freely to us about the dogs and their puppies. Most litters, he explains, have a runt—a puppy that somehow got less in the womb and enters the world undersized and under-equipped to compete. The owner exits, leaving us alone with a litter of puppies. In extended observation and montage, we see that every puppy fights for a teat, feeds aggressively, goes wandering, gets tired and sleeps, then awakens to fight for a teat again in a repeating cycle. The poor little runt has a bad time, getting elbowed out of competition and having neither the energy nor curiosity of the larger pups to go exploring their pen. It's a sad business until a human hand in close-up disconnects the most aggressively successful feeder and replaces him with the runt. In equally large close-up we see a concerned human face (is it the owner? someone else?) who is ready to mediate if the smallest is threatened.

Bobcat

Urban building site, sun rising. Concentrated together; huge cranes, cement delivery trucks, bulldozers, giant hole-borers all furiously at work with construction people yelling or talking into walkie-talkies. Uproar changes to orchestral music in which the larger, heavier instruments of the orchestra accompany the action of the larger, heavier machines in an extended ballet. Bobbing and weaving at the feet of all the huge machines is a small four-wheeled Bobcat earth pusher. It changes its direction not by steering but by skidding one set of wheels. This gives it crazy, jerky, frenzied movements that are quite different from all the other machines. The music has a fast, high, repeating melody that syncs comically with the Bobcat, which has to constantly defer to, or avoid, its more ponderous brethren. As the sun sinks, the machines all come to a halt and drivers leave their cabs. The Bobcat is the last to stop. Its driver gets out and joins the other men. As the music resolves to a harmonious close, the construction men joking with each other and picking up their lunch pails all look the same. End on a montage of heroic, static machines, including the Bobcat, framed to make it look as large as the other machines.

The Foreign Boy was a drama, *The Smallest in the Litter* a tragedy, and *Bobcat* a Chaplinesque comedy realized through machines, yet all three started from the same conviction in their working hypotheses. From any passionately held conviction you can generate a hundred good films.

SCHEDULING

To schedule a short film, break your material into intended sequences then allot reasonable time to shoot each, as well as time to travel between locations. Minimize time lost traveling by doing all your shooting at once in each location.

Expect to cover perhaps two lengthy sequences in a day of work, provided you can get from one to the other without too long a journey. Setting up lights not only gives novice participants the jitters, it greatly slows progress compared with shooting under available light. If you have exteriors that depend on a particular kind of weather, schedule them early and have interior shooting on standby in case you need it. If your film hinges on the success of a particular scene or situation, shoot it early in case failure renders the rest of the film moot.

More about scheduling appears in **Chapter 24: Advanced Technology and Budgeting**.

SIGNED AGREEMENTS

LOCATION AGREEMENT

For each privately owned location you will need a signed permission called a location agreement *before* you shoot (see this book's website, www.directingthedocumentary.com). You will need one to shoot in any building or on any piece of land that is not a public thoroughfare. No matter whether it's an empty church, public park, or city transportation, each comes under the jurisdiction of a guardian body to which you must apply. This lets owners regulate shooting on their property, protects them against liability suits, and protects you against legal action too. When things go wrong it works like this: You shoot without permission on a bus with someone in the background, and he just *happens* to be running away with someone else's wife. Their shot just *happens* to appear on national television, so he sues the bus company for allowing you to invade his privacy. Guess whom the bus company sues?

PERSONAL RELEASE

For an individual you obtain a signature on a release form *after* shooting. A brief one suitable for student productions appears in **Chapter 13: Directing**, under "Securing the Personal Release." Fuller, more legally binding, and downloadable forms for location and individual release can be found in the book's website, www.directingthedocumentary.com. These come by permission from Lisa Allif and Michael C. Donaldson's excellent *The American Bar Association's Legal Guide to Independent Filmmaking* (American Bar Association, 2011).

BUDGET

As an eye-opener, add up what your film would cost if you rented equipment and paid everyone, including yourself. Use the Internet to find approximate daily rates for professionals and their equipment, and budget a day of editing for every 2 minutes of final screen time. Allow a *shooting ratio* of 24:1, which means that the *stock* on which you shoot (hard disk or solid-state memory cards) has 24 times the capacity of your intended screen length. Thus for a screen time of 10 minutes you will need $24 \times 10 = 240$ minutes, or 4 hours of recording capacity.

Shocked at your budget grand total? Films cost big money, which is why surviving as a professional takes astute business skills.

PROJECT 8-1: A SHORT OBSERVATIONAL DOCUMENTARY

You learn filmmaking best from doing it, so use your preparation thus far to propose and shoot a 5-minute documentary. Find *a process* or *event* that you can shoot in the observational mode (no directing action, no interviews, no lighting). Try to ensure you have a reliable beginning and ending. Some suggestions to stimulate your own ideas:

For typical *processes* show someone making and testing a kite; mixing, kneading, and baking their first loaf of bread; taking their driving test, full of fears.

For typical *events*, try using the camera to follow: a contestant in a sports meeting; someone taking shots for a photography competition; or an actor auditioning for a part in a play.

With a central character trying to get, do, or accomplish something, you will have some ready-made dramatic tension, always present when people deal with obstacles, difficulties, or resistance.

Give your work front and end titles, and incorporate the following camerawork:

- Some shots from a tripod and some handheld (think of what different situations call for a stationary or a moving camera).
- Some shots in which the camera stays abreast of someone on the move.
- Close-ups of salient detail and wide shots which establish the geography of each location.

Once you make short films, start planning to travel the festival circuit with a film of winning caliber so you can initiate relationships with distributors, make contact with other filmmakers, and start leveraging new projects.

SOME SHORT FILM PROPOSALS AND THEIR FILMS

At this book's website (www.directingthedocumentary.com) you can see short film proposals and the actual films they became. These are good beginners' films made during a month-long workshop at the summer school now called the Maine Media Workshops+College (www.mainemedia.edu).

HANDS-ON LEARNING

For this chapter, **DP-5 Basic Proposal** can help you develop and present the essentials of a documentary idea for anyone you are seeking to persuade. Often this is a funder or granting committee. Persuasive writing is the prerequisite to persuasive filmmaking! You will also find **BP-1 Basic Budget** a good place to start if you are developing a budget for your proposed film. Since you will be pitching your films, try getting your audience to fill in **DP-10 Criteria for a Good Pitch,** so you can see how people think you are doing.

CHAPTER 9

THE CREW

You "develop" rather than "choose" or "hire" a crew because it is wise to do some exploratory work first. Documentary seldom allows rehearsal or repeats, so everyone has to understand each other's values, signals, and terminology, especially if doing "run and gun" shooting. One operator's close-up is another's medium shot, so they won't make the subject-selection, framing, composition, speed of camera movements, or microphone positioning you want unless you first discuss your language and values. For your part, you will need to understand their signaled alerts when there are sound problems, or shadow difficulties, say.

From trial footage expect to find wide variance in taste and skill levels. Look, too, for variations in responses, technical vocabulary, and interpretation of standard jargon. It is the director's responsibility to unify the crew so it becomes like a many-armed individual.

DEVELOPING YOUR OWN CREW

In the worst-case scenario you live remote from centers of filmmaking, and must train your own crew. Let's say you have access to a camera, microphone, and computer. How many and what kinds of people will you need? What are their responsibilities?

Certainly ascertain technical expertise and experience, but ask about their feelings and ideas concerning documentary, books, plays, music, hobbies, and interests. Technical acumen matters, but maturity and values matter more. You can negotiate many changes, but not with someone who is indifferent to your choice of subject or approach.

WHY CREWMEMBERS' TEMPERAMENTS MATTER

Today documentary crews are smaller than ever—two, maybe three persons upon whom you depend utterly. They must have personalities that support not only the project and each other, but those in front of the camera. Why? Most participants have never been in a film before, and feel weird at first. The crew's interest and support are vital, especially when shooting extends over days or weeks. The BBC usually assigned me wonderful crews, but occasionally I encountered problems. Typically it was wholly forgivable lapses in mental focus, but more than once I got people who were actively subversive. Being under pressure and away from home seems to exacerbate some personality's latent insecurities and jealousies. This is hard to foresee, and becomes an appalling liability in any work where good relationships are so important. Participants doing new and unfamiliar work are often highly susceptible to bad atmospheres.

Whenever potential crewmembers have done other film or teamwork, speak confidentially with their coworkers. Silences on certain aspects of their performance, or lukewarm enthusiasm, are red flags. Filming is intense, so work partners quickly learn each other's temperamental strengths and weaknesses. Assess new teammates according to,

- Realism
- Reliability
- Ability to sustain effort and concentration over long periods and in discomfort or danger
- Commitment to the processes and purposes of making documentaries
- Knowledge and appreciation of films or filmmakers that you respect

In all film crew positions, beware of those who

- Fail to deliver on what they've promised
- Forget or modify verbal commitments
- Habitually overestimate their own abilities
- Let their attention wander beyond their own field of responsibility
- Have only one working speed (it's usually medium slow; faced with a crisis these people slow up in confusion or go to pieces)
- See you as a stepping-stone

As leader, be sure to name everyone's areas of responsibility. In a minimal crew each person ends up with multiple roles, and someone usually takes on those such as prophet, visionary, scribe, or fixer. Someone is always the jester and every unit develops its own special in-jokes. The pleasure from working well together is the best intoxicant you can imagine. It becomes headiest under pressure and there's no hangover the morning after. Carefully selected partners make anything possible, because determined friends are unstoppable.

SMALL CREW ROLES AND RESPONSIBILITIES

Here is an outline of each crewmember's responsibilities in the kind of minimal crew you will probably use for your first films, and the strengths and weaknesses you might look for. Of course, in real life many of the best practitioners are the exceptions, so this list is fallible. For editors and their work see "Editing Personnel, Process, and Procedures" under **Chapter 14: Creating the First Assembly.** For producers, production managers, gaffers, and grips found working on larger projects look under **Chapter 29: Organization, Crew, and Procedures for the Larger Production.**

DIRECTOR

The director, who is responsible for the quality and meaning of the final film, must:

- Assemble funding.
- Conduct or supervise research.
- Decide on content.
- Assemble a crew.

- Schedule shooting.
- Lead the crew.
- Direct participants during shooting.
- Supervise editing.
- Hustle distribution.

A good director has a lively fascination with the causes and effects behind the way real people live. He or she is social, loves delving into people's stories, and is always searching for links and explanations. Outwardly informal and easygoing, he or she is methodical and organized but quite able to throw away prior work when early assumptions prove obsolete. An ideal director has: endless patience in stalking the truth; strong ambitions in doing it justice in cinematic terms; is articulate and succinct; knows his or her own mind without being dictatorial; can speak on terms of respectful equality with other film craftspeople; can understand their problems and co-opt their efforts into realizing his or her authorial intentions.

Directors are often however all too human. Many are obstinate, private, awkward, and even shy beings who do not explain themselves well, change their minds, or are disorganized and visceral. Most can be intimidated by bellicose technicians, have difficulty in balancing attention between crew and participants, and are apt to desert one for the other under pressure. During shooting, sensory overload catapults many into a state of acute doubt and anxiety in which all choice becomes painful. Some cannot relinquish their original intentions and go catatonic or act like the captain sinking at the wheel of the ship. Directing can change normal people into manic-depressives chasing the Holy Grail, and if that is not enough, the director's overheated mental state can generate superhuman energy that tests crewmembers' patience to the limit.

Like mountaineers with precipices, directors are apt to become addicted to the adrenaline rush during the cinematic chase, and suffer fear and anxiety.

DIRECTOR OF PHOTOGRAPHY (DP), AND/OR CAMERA OPERATOR

In the minimal crew, the DP,

- Orders the camera equipment if it's hired.
- Tests and adjusts it.
- Masters all its needs and working principles.
- Answers to the director, but takes initiative when shooting handheld action footage.

The DP is also responsible for:

- Scouting locations to assess light and electricity supplies.
- Lighting aesthetics.
- Setting up lighting instruments.
- Deciding camera positioning in collaboration with the director.
- Camera handling and making all camera movements.

Handheld camerawork is a talent that all operators think they have, but which few do. Work on it by shooting test footage and analyzing the results together. A good operator is:

- Highly image-conscious, preferably from training in photography and fine art.
- Has a highly developed sense of composition and design.

- Has an eye for the sociologically telling details that show in people's surroundings.
- Sensitive to the behavioral nuances that reveal so much about character.
- Interested in people, not just photography.
- Rhythmically keyed to physical movements by participants or other moving determinants.

Experienced camera personnel sometimes hide in the mechanics of their craft at the expense of the director's deeper quest for themes and meanings. One such answered a question of mine with "I'm just here to make pretty pictures." He might have added, "and not get involved."

You can only direct someone handholding a camera up to a point; usually you have to rely very much on the operator's sensibilities, though you can tell much from their movements. Some appear deaf and judge pictorial elements as if nothing else were happening. Some are intermittently attuned to the unfolding interpersonal drama in a verbal exchange, and a few have a highly developed sense of drama and use the camera surefootedly to capture the heart and soul of drama.

For all these reasons a camera operator must be decisive, and physically and mentally dexterous. The best are low-key, practical, and inventive types who don't ruffle in crises and enjoy improvising solutions to intransigent logistical, lighting, or electrical problems. A "tech" mentality is never good enough: crewmembers must comprehend both the details and the totality of a project, and see how to make the best contribution at any given moment. Look for the perfectionist who will cheerfully find the best and simplest solution when time is running out.

SOUND RECORDIST

Capturing clear, clean, and consistent sound is highly specialized, but students often consider it unglamorous and unimportant, and the director is left using anyone willing. Poorly recorded sound, however, fatally disconnects the audience.

The recordist is responsible for:

- Checking equipment in advance.
- Choosing the right equipment for the situation.
- Not causing shadows or letting the mike creep into frame.
- Keeping the microphone(s) close to the sound source even during handheld shooting.
- Hearing sound inequities and curing them whenever possible.
- Shooting atmospheres and sound effects on his/her own initiative.

The camera position and lighting (if there is any) come first, so the sound recordist must hide mikes, cause no shadows, and yet deliver first-rate sound. For some, shooting becomes a series of aggravating compromises, and many professionals end up bitter mutterers who feel that "good standards" are getting trampled. Maybe so, but it's the disconnected craftsperson, not the whole filmmaker, who gags on necessary compromise.

With a camera that is handheld and on the move, sound work takes skill, awareness, and quietly agile footwork. The recordist must wear soft shoes, ear-enclosing headphones, and when handling a mike must be able to hear differences (Figure 9-1). For this, musical interests and training are best. For a trial run, shoot some material together, edit it, and *then* you will begin hearing the inequities.

PUT COMMITMENTS IN WRITING

Whenever you agree on an area of responsibility, a period of commitment, or an amount of remuneration, *write it down*. Partnerships regularly go on the rocks because people recall agreements

FIGURE 9-1

Wearing high quality headphones is the only sure way to monitor sound quality. *(Jason Longo and Byron Smith shooting for David Sutherland Productions.)*

differently and have neglected to make a record. It can be something as simple as an exchange of emails, so long as expectations are spelled out, exchanged, and agreed. As soon as real money is involved, each person should receive and sign a letter of engagement, a model of which can be found in Richard Gates' *Production Management for Film and Video* (Focal Press, 1999).

PART 4

PRODUCTION

The eyes and ears of your documentary work are the camera and microphone. To make your work with each accomplished, you will need to understand their basic principles and techniques, and prepare for your first experiences of directing participants. A measure of inside knowledge will help you enjoy your work and make you an enjoyable and reassuring colleague.

CHAPTER 10

CAPTURING SOUND

Sound is the neglected step-sister in film, yet it is so important to drama of all kinds that I have placed it first among production concerns. The eye sees, but the ear imagines.[1] Well-designed film sound creates its own emotively loaded reality, and even though the audience may not consciously be aware of this, it greatly affects them.

In early life, beginning an apprenticeship at England's Pinewood Studios, my guide to music and to the wider significance of sound was my friend Brian Neal, who was not connected with the film industry at all. He had slowly lost his sight as a child and was declared legally blind in his early teens. At first it felt like a death sentence, but music became his great love, and from being a piano-tuner he rose to singing in Windsor Chapel Royal choir. He had a keenly humorous appreciation of the everyday world whose anomalies he would delight in sharing. He was a mimic as talented as Billy Crystal, and could tell you about his morning's work by impersonating a running argument, complete with interruptions, between an old Polish couple whose upright he had just tuned. Afterwards you felt you had been there yourself, and had even tasted the little pastries they served.

So, yes, the eye sees, but the ear imagines.

HEADPHONES TO MONITOR YOUR WORK

Whoever shoots sound must continuously assess their recording quality through professional, ear-enclosing headphones (Figure 10-1). Not doing so always proves costly. Unless you are a musician, you will have to learn how to analyze the elements in film sound, and hear what makes it acceptable or otherwise. This means becoming an analytic and critical listener, which has its own rewards and pleasures.

SOUND DESIGN AND SOUNDSCAPES

In a highly stylized documentary such as Errol Morris' dreamlike *The Thin Blue Line* (USA, 1988), or in Alberto Vendemmiati's lyrical *The Person de Leo N* (2006, Figure 10-2), the imaginative canvas claimed by both filmmakers gives them great latitude for operatic or surreal soundscapes.

Memorable sound does not come from slavishly reproducing life's complexity, but from concentrating and heightening a few selected sounds, as so memorably established during the French New Wave (see François Truffaut's *Jules and Jim*, France, 1962 for its sound treatment). Particular sounds trigger particular associations and flights of imagination, a central assumption of *psycho-acoustics*, the term describing how sound makes our minds perceive and interpret. The expert here is Michel Chion, whose *Audio-Vision—Sound on Screen* (New York: Columbia University Press, 1994) explains principles he developed over three decades. These are not simple, and require you to master a specialized vocabulary.

When you can visualize how sound behaves, your ear starts to discriminate. The sound terms below begin with the recordist's main priority, and then move through the various obstacles and compromises that make sound work such a fascinating challenge. From a recordist's point of view, every place and indeed every room in a house has its own soundscape, and only a highly attentive ear can pick out what makes it individual. We carry out a lot of this interpretation subconsciously, and perhaps this is what motivated the World Soundscape Project, begun in 1975, which is researching the acoustic ecology of six European villages. Sponsored by Tampere Polytechnic Institute in Finland, the goal is to record their changing acoustic environments over many decades (www.6villages.tpu.fi).

FIGURE 10-1

A sound recordist must continuously assess recording quality through professional, ear-enclosing headphones.

FIGURE 10-2

Through imaginative soundscapes and lyrical photography, Vendemmiati's *The Person de Leo N* enlarges its story to operatic proportions. The film culminates in a reunion between Nico and her mother, who cannot see her as a daughter.

Any movie sound track has the potential to become orchestral in nature, something you can design from the outset to further the aims of your film. As you develop your documentary proposal, ask,

- What kind of world are you showing?
- What are its special sound features?
- What will you need to record, and how?
- What kind of impact should the sound track make at different junctures on the audience?

SOUND TERMS

Sound terminology describes not only what sound is and how it behaves, but also what we feel about it—since sound and emotion are intimately related. First there is an assessment procedure.

ACOUSTICS AND THE HAND-CLAP TEST

To assess the *acoustics* of the sound environment at a location, a sound recordist gives a single loud hand-clap and listens intently (Figure 10-3). That brief, sharp sound is a *transient* that takes only fractions of a second to move through the air. It starts with a sharp *attack*, has almost no *sustain* (unlike a violin or piano note), but unlike the example in Figure 10-3 may have an audible *decay* if it *reverberates* between sound-reflective surfaces. A hand-clap in a tiled kitchen will sound *live* because it has a long and highly reverberant decay. This is quite different from one made in an upholstered parlor, where it will sound relatively *dead*.

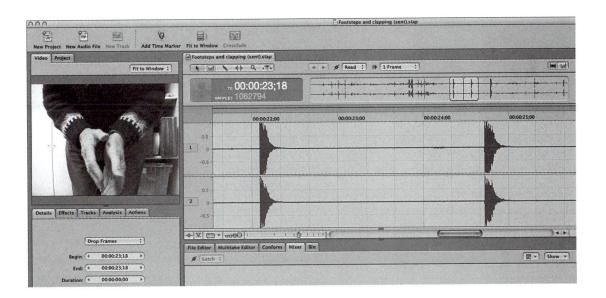

FIGURE 10-3

Two hand-claps with virtually no reverberation seen as modulations on a timeline.

SIGNAL, NOISE, AND SIGNAL-TO-NOISE RATIO

The recordist always aims to make a clean recording—whether a speaker's voice, three cicadas chirping on a tree branch, or orange juice pouring onto cracking ice cubes. The sound you want is called *signal*. Everything that impedes it—interference such as wind noise, traffic, a distant playground, a gravel quarry, or aircraft overhead—is called *noise*. Using modern recording systems, appropriate microphone choices, and intelligent mike placement, you can achieve a good *signal-to-noise ratio* (abbreviated as S:N). The hissing in historic recordings, called *system noise*, was inherent to their primitive recording methods. The genius of Ray Dolby (1933–2013) eliminated it from the cinema experience, and digital electronics have done the rest.

AMBIENCE

Every location whether interior or exterior has its characteristic accompanying *ambience*, *background*, or *atmosphere*. This might be distant traffic, playground voices, the hum of a passing aircraft, or the nearby buzz of a fluorescent light fixture. The aim is to have it present in the completed film, consistent in level, and not intrusive. Creative recordists in their downtime collect all sorts of potentially useful *"atmos"* recordings. It might be the rustle of trees in a forest, the babble of voices in a canteen, or the hum of machinery in a power station. Atmospheres allow the editor not only to fill holes in dialogue tracks but to build a film's tracks into an evocative sound composition.

RESONANCE AND ECHO

A resonant space is one having a special note at which it *resonates*. You'll know this from singing in your shower, and finding a frequency at which the room augments the note of your voice with its own sympathetically resonating frequency. An *echo* is caused by reflected sound traveling by a longer path, and arriving whole, but later than the signal.

PRESENCE

Every room has its own atmosphere. Its components vary according to the season and time of day. No scene is complete until everyone goes rock still while the recordist makes a few minutes of *presence* track recording. This is also called *buzz track*, *room tone*, or *ambience*.

MICROPHONES

TRANSDUCTION

Like the human ear, a microphone employs a diaphragm. It is classed as a *transducer* because it transforms sound vibrations detected as varying air pressures into tiny electrical signals, which are then amplified. A loudspeaker is another kind of transducer because it changes electrical signals back into the air pressure variations by which sound travels.

MICROPHONE AXIS AND DIRECTIONALITY

Mikes classed as *omni-directional* pick up sound equally from all directions, but a *directional* mike picks up sound best from its most receptive axis. This is called *on-axis* or *on-mike* sound. Other arriving sound is classed as *off-axis* or *off-mike* sound. Since directional mikes are designed to suppress off-axis sound, this sound records at a lower level. Thus directional mikes do not somehow zoom in and grab sound, they simply discriminate with varying degrees of effectiveness against off-axis sound (Figure 10-4). The ultra-directional microphone does this to the highest degree, but at some cost to the mike's warmth and fidelity.

SOUND PERSPECTIVE

This is the sensation of changing sound direction and distance when a person walks away, a helicopter takes off, or a mechanical street-sweeper goes past. From sound alone we sense from the evidence of *sound perspective* whether a speaker is near, far, stationary, or moving. Without sound perspective, recordings lack something important. Though body mikes make a person's voice pleasant and highly intelligible, they always have a certain deadness. It is because they are fixed to the speaker's clothing, and remain unnaturally close and stationary.

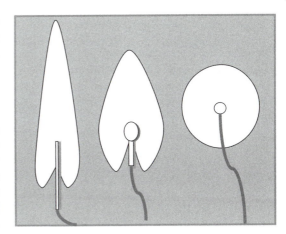

FIGURE 10-4 ───────────────

Diagram indicating pick-up pattern differences between (1) shotgun, (2) cardioid, and (3) omni-directional microphones.

HOW SOUND BEHAVES

Imagine hitting a bunch of billiard balls and seeing one go into the intended pocket, while the others ricochet randomly off the cushions before slowing to rest. The sound made by a hand-clap behaves like this in a moderately sound-reflective space. It is the *signal* that ricochets off sound-reflective surfaces, which reflect *reverberant sound* as a mass of disorganized, decaying reflections that arrive at the ear (microphone) after differing degrees of delay. *Echo* on the other hand is the kind of crisply organized sound reflection that, after a short delay, returns your voice intact across a valley.

Figure 10-5 represents the sound components a sound recordist deals with while recording an interview situation next to a busy street. Ideal dialogue recordings have lots of signal (what you want) and very little "noise" (everything else).

Direct sound, also called *signal*, is that percentage of the speaker's voice that travels direct to the microphone.

Reverberant sound is that which radiates outward and bounces off the floor, ceiling, walls, and table surface in front of the speaker before arriving at the mike fractionally later. By making longer journeys, reverb sound then combines with signal at the microphone to muddy the signal's clarity. Once combined, signal and reverb are no more separable than the eggs in an omelet.

Ambient sound, or *presence*, is that which is native to the environment such as distant traffic, the hum of a refrigerator, a dog barking, or the whirr of air conditioning in summer.

Notice that sound in Figure 10-5 is being shot with a *deck* mike (one fixed to the camera), and is of necessity distant from the speaker. This has profound consequences on dialogue recording quality.

SIGNAL DECAY OVER DISTANCE

A nasty little secret awaits the rookie recordist: a sound's *amplitude* (loudness) changes radically as you move a mike toward or away from its source. This is because sound, like light, decays over distance in a logarithmic, not linear fashion. The dotted line in Figure 10-6 is what most of us think is the loudness-to-distance relationship, but the curved solid line is the dismal actuality. As you see, the last few feet in mike-to-subject distance make a big difference to the *amplitude* (effective volume) of the recording. A sound recordist therefore must work hard to keep the mike close to the sound source, but out of frame.

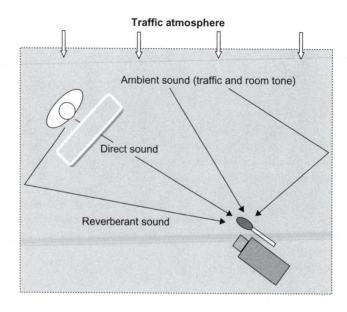

FIGURE 10-5

Diagram representing a film interview and the three types of sound present in any recording situation: direct, reverberant, and ambient.

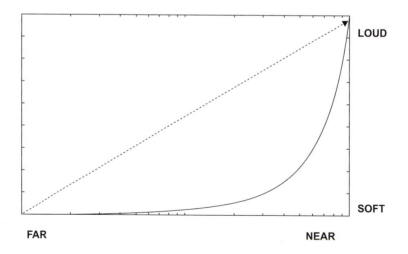

FIGURE 10-6

The dotted line is how one imagines a microphone behaving as you move it closer to a sound source, but the solid line—a logarithmic curve—is the actuality.

FIGURE 10-7

A microphone on a fishpole can reach over people and get close to the sound source. *(Photo courtesy of Nomadic Pictures, Inc.)*

DEFENSIVE MEASURES

The sound recordist's world has its dragons, but they can be tamed. By angling the axis of a directional mike at the speaker (as in Figure 10-5), one can lower some of the reverb and ambience, most of which arrives from off-axis directions. Importantly, one could move that mike much closer to the speaker. This barely changes ambience or reverb levels, but it produces a much higher signal level. An independently movable mike is thus essential, since any mike mounted on the camera,

- Is always at the camera's distance and seldom proximate to the signal source.
- Only ever points along the camera-to-subject axis. New speakers in a discussion, for instance, will remain annoyingly off-mike until the camera turns to them.
- Is ideally situated to record the whine of the camera's zoom and focus motors, and the bumping sound of your hands fumbling for the camera controls.

It is thus vital to position a mike closer using a *boom* or *fishpole* (Figure 10-7). We'll look at boom handling techniques a little later. In a really noisy situation you would instead use a body mike, which also has its pros and cons. Remember that in postproduction you can always *add* atmosphere or reverb to a clean recording, but you can seldom subtract noise that is commingled with signal.

SOUND ENVIRONMENTS AND SIGNAL-TO-NOISE RATIO

If you record a speaker in a large, sound insulated, carpeted room with heavy drapery over the windows, you will have an excellent signal-to-noise ratio because there's a minimum of reverb and ambient noise. Now follow him when he walks into that tiled kitchen with the washing machine going, and you'll have a dreadful S:N ratio and barely intelligible speech. Recordists therefore aim to,

- Choose the microphone with the best pickup pattern for the circumstances.
- Get a high ratio of signal-to-noise by placing each mike as close as practicable to its intended signal (the speaker/s).
- Procure on-mike sound by pointing the mike's reception axis at the sound source and away from a source of noise.

These noble aims are often frustrated by documentary's improvised nature. Imagine your difficulties when your main character chooses to confess what's breaking his heart while working out in a noisy health club or driving his rattly old pickup truck. So much to go wrong!

WHY SOUND CONSISTENCY IS SO IMPORTANT

Viewing a moving handheld shot, one can tell from the camera movements why the mike is moving in relation to the subject, and hear the sound quality change. However, in an edited sequence, the recordist has been forced to make mike position-changes in order to stay out of shot. Material may edit together beautifully for picture and narrative continuity, but each sound cut produces a distressingly obvious change in sound quality, level, and S:N ratio. True, you make adjustments in the speaker's voice level from angle to angle, but that varies the admixture of ambience illogically at each sound cut. In postproduction you can reduce these disparities by adding ambience to the quieter tracks, but this is piling noise upon noise—all of which competes with signal.

Shooting sound will always be a series of compromises, so:

- Try to shoot in the quietest, least reverberant surroundings—seldom an option in observational documentary.
- Optimize S:N ratio by
  - Choosing the right mike for the job.
  - Placing the mike close to the signal source.
  - Pan the directional mike so its axis always points at the signal source.
  - Be ready to alter the scene axis during setup, if possible, so location noise comes from off-axis to the mike.
- Reduce reverb where possible by
  - Making wise choices of location.
  - Damping sound-reflective surfaces by laying carpet or blankets out of camera sight on hard surfaces such as the floor. To be fully effective on walls, these must hang several inches away from the offending wall, not be hard against it.

SOUND AND THE CAMCORDER

BALANCED AND UNBALANCED INPUTS

Professional mikes use *balanced line* cables, always recognizable from their sturdy XLR locking connectors, and noise-canceling three-wire connections (Figure 10-8). This allows long cable runs that are free of electrical interference pickup. Consumer equipment uses two-wire *unbalanced* sound connections identifiable by their two-contact jack plugs (Figure 10-9). Cable runs are

FIGURE 10-8

XLR plug on three-wire balanced line cable and the locking socket it goes into.

restricted to a few feet, beyond which you should expect electrostatic interference.

STRAIN RELIEF

Cables most often break down at the point where they enter a plug, so provide *strain relief* by anchoring cables to the body of their devices (Figure 10-10). This protects both plug and socket when inevitably someone trips on the cable. Mini-jack sockets are particularly vulnerable, especially those mounted direct on circuit boards. A single yank can do untold damage.

AUTOMATIC SOUND LEVEL

Using automatic sound-level spares you from overload distortion, but during long silences in an oral memoir, for example, the recording level will often "hunt." That is, during silences it records ambience at ever-louder levels until your subject resumes speaking. This is because the circuitry is slavishly doing its job strictly according to sound input. Auto-level sound may also vary from one part of a scene to another, and the two edit together badly. So, unless you face a chaotic

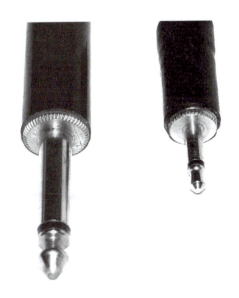

FIGURE 10-9

Phone jack and mini-jack plugs. Two-connector unbalanced lines like these are vulnerable to hum and other electrical interference.

recording situation—soft sound punctuated by door slams and screaming revelers, say—help the editor by setting and maintaining audio levels manually.

MANUAL SOUND LEVEL

Aim to set one level in advance so you don't have to *ride gain* (adjust volume) during a scene. First make a representative sound test to see how levels register on the volume units meter (averaging *VU meter*) or *peak reading bar graph*. Peaks should not exceed, say, −6 decibels (check camcorder recommendations). Be sure to test-record and play back loud *transient* sounds such as door slams, engine roaring sounds, or billiard ball impacts so you can pinpoint the level at which distortion sets in. When shooting mono sound, there is a neat way to use the camera's second sound channel as a safety backup. See "Averaging and Peaking" below.

VOLUME UNIT (VU) METERS

Note that VU meter scales run counter-intuitively (Figure 10-11). Low sound levels register as high *minus* decibel (dB) numbers, and then as amplitude rises, they diminish to the safe or *sound saturation* point of 0 dB. Unless the recorder literature says otherwise, VU meters are averaging meters: they have a slight lag as well as an insensitivity to transient peaks, a combination useful to the recordist because it approximates human perception of sound.

AVERAGING AND PEAKING

Digital sound recorded beyond 0 dB produces such spectacular distortion that the sound is often unusable. A trap awaits the unwary here, because unless your equipment has a *peak reading* facility, it is probably averaging incoming signals and masking the truth about extremes. A red LED light blinking on sound peaks usually signifies that peaks of unknown amplitude have already happened, leaving a raggedly distorted section.

FIGURE 10-10

Cable anchored to camera body to provide strain relief.

Guard against overloading (a) by setting averaging record levels to peak at −6 dB or so, and (b) as a safety backup, split a mono mike signal across the two stereo channels, setting Track 2 to record at a lower level. You can sometimes accomplish this using a microphone input box.

THE MICROPHONE INPUT BOX

If you are using a consumer camera with a single mini-jack mike input, consider adding a proprietary input box. That shown in Figure 10-12 takes two mike inputs and can route each to a different channel, or spread a single mike's output to both channels. The box's output is via a stereo (three-connector) mini-plug on a short lead, which plugs into the camera's mike input. Clamped under the camera body, the box and its beefy XLR sockets safely absorb cable-handling stresses, protect your camera, and let you adjust levels for two balanced-line microphones.

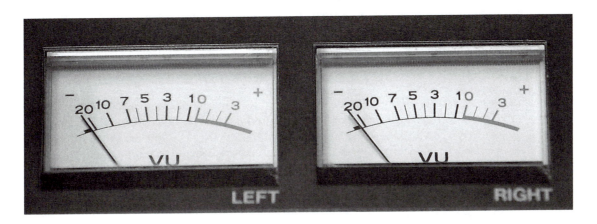

FIGURE 10-11

Typical stereo sound volume units (VU) meter layout. Camcorders usually allow you to see a moving bar-graph in the viewfinder.

FIGURE 10-12

Two-channel input box that can handle input from either microphone or amplifier (line). (*Photo courtesy of Beach-TEK, Inc.*)

MAKING USE OF STEREO INPUTS

Virtually all camcorders have stereo (two-track) recording capability. Not only can you record a mono mike with a lower-level safety backup (see in "Averaging and Peaking" above), but using a microphone input box or multichannel mixer your camcorder can record two entirely different mono inputs. These might be two people wearing *lavalier* (chest) microphones, or a mother and son phone conversation using a lavalier on the mom and a *telephone attachment* to pick up her son. Since they are on discrete tracks, you can adjust their relative levels later in the sound mix.

MICROPHONE TYPES AND PICKUP PATTERNS

Film recording uses a variety of microphones made by a host of manufacturers such as Sennheiser, Schoeps, Audio Technica, and Shure. With microphones, as with hot dinners, you mostly get what you pay for. You get better or worse performance depending on your knowledge of mike strengths and weaknesses. A friend who teaches sound says, "There is no such thing as a bad microphone, only bad users."

POWER SUPPLIES

Many mikes use an internal battery, so carry spares. Use only the alkaline variety, since they do not excrete a corrosive mess into the mike body after running down. Note that condenser microphones—particularly *shotgun* mikes—either run on inbuilt batteries, or draw current from *phantom power* supplied by some (but by no means all) cameras and a few input adapter boxes. Phantom power is 48 volts supplied at a tiny current to the mike through two legs of its three-wire cable. If a mike should mysteriously refuse to function, suspect it of needing phantom power.

PICKUP PATTERNS

Most important is to understand sound pickup patterns for several microphone types. The representation earlier of three different mike pickup patterns in Figure 10-4 indicated where you would have to place a noise emitter, if you circled around each type of mike with a tame cicada, to maintain an equal level recording.

   The omni-directional mike is easy to understand: it picks up sound equally from all around, so you'd place your cicada at the same distance all around it. Other types of mike achieve good on-axis sound by discriminating against that which is off-axis. Here are some performance generalizations:

   Omni-directional mikes give the most pleasing voice reproduction, but indiscriminately pick up unwanted sound reflected by surrounding surfaces.

   Directional mikes (also called *cardioids* because of their heart-shaped pickup pattern) help reduce off-axis reverberant and background noise. In practical terms this means that pointing the mike's axis at a speaker improves his S:N ratio. By the way, directional mikes intentionally have poor sensitivity at the rear end of the mike's axis (Figure 10-13).

   Hypercardioid or *shotgun* mikes (so-called owing to their shape and menacing appearance (Figure 10-14) do the best job of discrimination. During the Vietnam War a BBC news crew using a shotgun mike in the jungle was astonished to find it had taken a Viet Cong prisoner. A favorite in documentary and electronic newsgathering (ENG) work, the shotgun is especially practical in noisy situations. Its drawback is a slight loss of sound warmth and fidelity. More than most mikes, it needs astute handling so it stays out of shot, doesn't cast shadows, and points at the right speaker in a group.

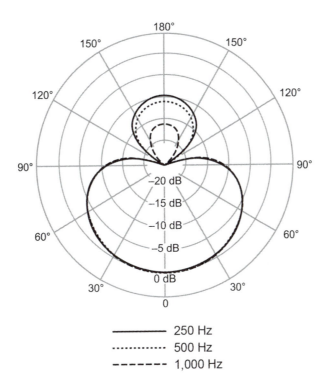

```
         250 Hz
......... 500 Hz
------- 1,000 Hz
```

FIGURE 10-13

Shure VP89S microphone polar pattern, showing that directional mikes are least sensitive at the rear end of the mike's axis. *(Courtesy of Shure, Inc.)*

Lavalier, lapel, or body mikes are favored for interviews or speech recording in noisy surroundings (Figure 10-15). Participants wear these tiny, omni-directional mikes under upper clothing so they stay exceptionally close to the signal (speech) source. Place them under clothing out of sight, and at least a hand's breadth away from a speaker's chin, or sound levels will vary too much when the speaker's head swivels.

FIGURE 10-14

Shure VP89S hypercardioid or shotgun mike, good for off-axis discrimination. *(Photo courtesy of Shure, Inc.)*

Clip the mike in place, anchoring its cord as in the photo, leaving a free loop under the mike as strain relief. Then if the cord is touched or yanked, handling noise or damage won't reach the mike. You'll need one lavalier per speaker, and a location mixer for multiple speakers (see **Chapter 28: Advanced Location Sound**). Lavaliers give lovely voice quality but are weirdly devoid of *sound perspective*. This is because movements toward and away from the camera remain in unnaturally constant relation to their sound source. We only hear our own voice with that kind of constancy.

BODY MIKE PRECAUTIONS

Lavaliers pick up clothing rustles and body movements—especially if the user wears man-made fibers. These generate thunderous static electricity noises. Warn participants to wear natural fibers,

FIGURE 10-15

Wire looped under lavalier clip as strain protection for a delicate mike.

but if they forget, place adhesive tape between the mike and the offending surface. Lavaliers excel at amplifying loose dentures and the intestinal activity that follows dining.

ROLL-OFF

Many larger mikes have small switches that allow you to *roll off* (attenuate, reduce) a particular band of frequencies. A "lo-cut" is commonest, and useful to reduce traffic rumble during street dialogue scenes. Many sound mixing boards have a low cut switch for each mike circuit.

WIRELESS MIKES

Like mobile phones, radio mikes are wonderful when they work. Connect a lavalier mike to a personal radio transmitter, clip a small radio receiver to the camera, and hey presto, everyone has complete mobility. Alas, they have occasional dead spots. Be warned, too, that participants forget they are wearing them and may, without your intervention, broadcast their visit to the bathroom. A court used a recording made inadvertently by some of my students as evidence to indict a duplicitous police chief at a Native American demonstration.

WIRED MIKES

A wired lavalier, though limiting to your subject's mobility, is trouble-free compared with its wireless brethren. Hide the cable in the participant's clothing so it emerges from a pants leg or skirt bottom. People usually forget they're wearing them and walk away until they quite literally reach the end of their tether.

SPARES AND ACCESSORIES

Breakdowns happen mostly where cables enter connectors, so carry spares. Mikes and mixers need batteries, so carry the right alkaline spares. A basic toolkit of solder, soldering iron, pliers, plain

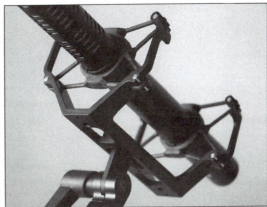

FIGURE 10-16

Two types of mike shock mount. The rubber-band type (left) is common but liable to introduce noise of its own. On the right is the more reliable design. *(Photo courtesy of K-TEK.)*

and Phillips-head screwdrivers, Q-tips, adjustable wrench, Allen keys, can of compressed air (for cleaning), flashlight, and an electrical multi-meter can often get you out of trouble in the field.

MICROPHONE HANDLING

HANDLING THE FISHPOLE

One shoots much location sound with a directional mike mounted on a fishpole and angled at the subject. Keep your hands in position: that is, don't slide them or tap the pole, since handling noises reverberate through the pole to the mike. Be sure to monitor all sound you shoot through professional level, ear-enclosing headphones. Listen for sound quality, not meaning!

Position the mike above, below, or from either side of the frame. Miking from above is preferable because a voice will be louder than the speaker's footsteps and body movements. Should the fishpole cause shadow problems, try coming in from the side of the frame. When all else fails, point the mike upwards from below frame, remembering that this may privilege footsteps and body movements over voice levels.

WINDSCREENS AND SHOCK MOUNTS

When working alone, you can minimize camera handling noises by mounting a separate mike in a flexible cradle called a *shock mount* on the camera body. This helps minimize camera handling sounds traveling via conduction to the mike. Figure 10-16 shows a common rubber-band model on the left, but the right-hand design works better.

You are always better off with the mike handled by someone operating a *fishpole* (Figure 10-17). It means that an autonomous mike is independently seeking the best sound, wherever that might be in relation to the camera.

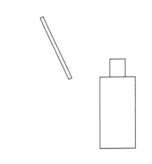

FIGURE 10-17

The camera shoots a reaction shot while the mike covers an off-camera speaker. In everyday life, our eyes and ears often unconsciously separate like this.

FIGURE 10-18

A rigid zeppelin wind guard. *(Photo courtesy of K-TEK.)*

Shield the mike from air current interference, even indoors, with a *windscreen* (Figure 10-18). This is a rigid zeppelin wind guard, with a fuzzy fur miniscreen, or *windsock* added to defeat larger volumes of air movement (Figure 10-19). Without such shielding, air currents shake the mike's diaphragm and produce earthquake quantities of wind rumble.

WHEN SOUND AND PICTURE SUBJECTS DIVERGE

Frequently the sound source originates in the camera frame but then moves elsewhere. In a group scene, for instance, the camera may dwell on someone's telling reaction long after someone new starts speaking. The mike cannot stay with the (now silent) camera subject but must turn immediately toward the new sound subject, as diagrammed earlier in Figure 10-17. Novice sound recordists have to train themselves to prioritize listening above looking—quite counter-intuitive at first.

THE RECORDIST AND THE CAMERA

Getting on-mike sound without causing shadows takes close coordination between recordist, camera operator, and director. Miking from a safe distance is never an option because signal-to-noise ratios and voice quality decline so precipitously. The goal is to position the mike as close as possible, and pointed at each new speaker, while staying just out of frame. Handheld sequences are always the most challenging because the mike must not edge into the frame. Usually the recordist stands a little ahead and to the left of the camera, staying in the camera operator's left-eye sightline (Figure 10-20). Experienced, on-the-ball recordists constantly glance between the subject, the likely edge of frame, and the camera operator for telling facial expressions or hand signals. These might signify, "Watch out, I'm going to swing in your direction," or the more agitated "Back off—mike's edging into frame." Staying close to moving participants' sound axes, yet keeping the mike from drifting into frame, requires the recordist to guess who, between camera and participants, will move next, and what direction they may take.

Sometimes the operator makes a hand signal to warn of a coming pan to the left, or of intending to back away for a wide shot. The recordist may lift the mike over the camera and cross the shooting axis behind the camera in order to position the mike temporarily over the camera from the right (Figure 10-21).

SAFETY COVER

In a two-person crew when the camera starts to track backward, the recordist or the director will lightly touch the operator's back with a free hand to signal, "I'm here and I'm watching for your safety." This touch includes gentle steering—gentle because over-zealous handling would rock the camera. The aim is to help the camera operator go in reverse, clearing kerbs, doorways, or furniture without looking backward.

VIRTUOSO PERFORMANCES

It's quite marvelous to watch the precision and confidence with which an experienced crew negotiates such obstacles. The ultimate challenge to the mobile documentary unit is a rapidly moving subject who whirls through a street market then jumps into a taxi, all the while chatting to the camera. Keeping all this nicely framed on the screen, and with no sign of the unit's frantic adaptations, will stretch a crew to its limits, particularly when two people silently cram

FIGURE 10-19

Fuzzy fur miniscreen or windsock covering zeppelin guard. *(Photo courtesy of K-TEK.)*

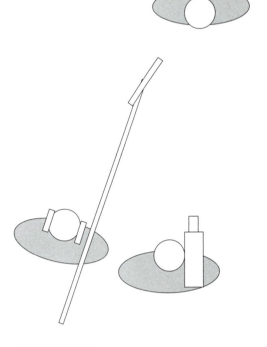

FIGURE 10-20

Typical sound recordist's positioning during mobile shooting.

themselves and their equipment around a surprised taxi driver. With experience, crews learn
to work in perfect balletic harmony—and even
to exchange hand or eye signals during the take.
It's a joy to watch.

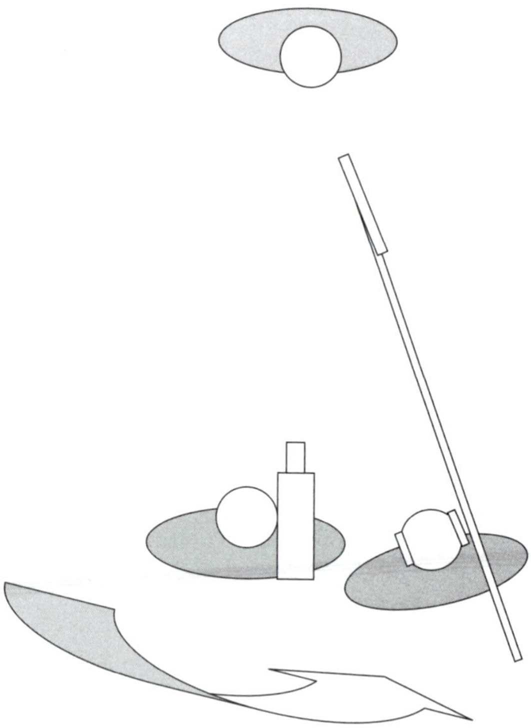

SHOOTING

LOCATION SPOTTING AND AMBIENT NOISE

Every shooting situation comes with problems,
of which you take careful note while scouting
the location. Overhead wires can turn into aeo-
lian harps, dogs bark maniacally, garbage trucks
mysteriously convene for bottle crushing competitions, and somebody starts practicing scales on
the trumpet. The astute location spotter can only
anticipate some of these sonic disasters.

INTERIORS

While the camera is running, close all doors
and windows to block exterior sounds, no matter how hot the room. Also temporarily disable anything liable to run intermittently like
air conditioning or a refrigerator. Leave your car
keys with any appliance you must remember to
switch back on.

Ambient sound is most noticeable during
relative silences, but each location, and each
mike position within that location, has its own

FIGURE 10-21

The recordist must sometimes cross behind the
camera, mike still in place, to angle in from the
right of frame. The camera now blocks eyeline
exchanges with the camera operator.

characteristic "presence." One may not cut well with another. In each case, choice of mike, the axis
of directional mikes, and getting the mike in close to the desired signal all help toward consistency.

SOUNDS ON THE SET

During takes, the crew and any onlookers must be stationary and silent, and the camera must
make no sound that the mike can pick up. Fluorescents like to buzz, filament lamps can hum, and
pets come joyously to life at inopportune moments. Mike cables placed in parallel with power
cables may produce electrical interference through induction, and sometimes very long mike cables
pull in cheery DJ's via radio frequency (RF) interference. Elevator equipment can generate alternating current magnetic fields, and the most mysterious hum sometimes proves to come from
something on the floor above or below. Every situation has some degree of remedy once you have
located the cause.

PRESENCE TRACK RECORDING

Before calling for a wrap at any location, whether interior or exterior, let the crew record a *presence track* (also known as *atmosphere*, *room tone*, or *buzz track*). Do this in *every* location, *every*

shooting day, because each occasion has its own changing ambience. The procedure is simple. The recordist,

- Calls "Everyone freeze for a presence track!" and everyone stands silent.
- Records ambient sound, using the current mike position.
- Calls "Cut," when everyone jumps into action, wrapping up that location's equipment ready for the next.

SOUND WITH EDITING IN MIND

HOW THE EDITOR USES PRESENCE TRACKS

The 2 minutes of presence recorded on the set, duplicated if necessary, becomes the vital filler for any dead spaces in edited dialogue tracks. These might occur when, for example, you use a cutaway that was shot silent, or remove an off-camera expletive. Because postproduction can only add, never remove, background atmosphere in dialogue tracks, the editor must work to make every angle's background sound consistent. Tracks with quiet presence must match those in the angle having the loudest, if all angles are to end up with the same ambience.

AMBIENCE INCONSISTENCIES

Watching a finished film, the audience expects each new sequence to sound as it does in life. The ear identifies its nature, then screens it out while concentrating on the foreground signal. This natural adaptation fails, however, when irritating and intrusive changes in "atmos" occur from angle to angle. To cure this, background atmospheres and presence tracks must be added and level-adjusted to create a seamless auditory experience. This is our experience of ambience in life—so we expect no less in films.

WILD TRACKS

Any voice or atmosphere track shot asynchronously and independent of picture is called a *wild track*. When a participant flubs a sentence, or some extraneous sound intrudes on dialogue, the alert sound recordist asks to make a wild, voice-only recording immediately after the director calls "Cut." The participant repeats the previous words just as he or she spoke them during the take. Because it's recorded in the same acoustic situation, the words can be seamlessly edited in. Be sure to verbally identify the section of wild track, so the editor can locate it.

SOUND EFFECTS

A non-synchronous recording of a sound useful to a sequence's sound track is called an *effects* (FX) or *atmosphere track*. The recordist might carry a small recorder to get tracks of that early-morning rooster, or distant church bells to help create a composite atmosphere. In a woodland location this might include daybreak bird calls, river sounds of water gurgling, ducks dabbling, and wind rustling in reeds. A woodpecker echoing evocatively through the trees is probably best found in a wildlife library, since getting near them is hard and background noise normally is too high. A sound recordist needs initiative, imagination, and a naturalist's tolerance for frustration.

SOUNDSCAPE CONSTRUCTION

Films often provide sound that liberates the imagination rather than sound literally present in the location. To be true in spirit, you might wholly construct a soundscape in postproduction. At the exquisite nature center near my home in Chicago there are deer, wild flowers, some prairie, a lake with a heron or two, and lots of wild birds. I have daydreamed about filming a yearlong cycle of life there, but vehicles roar past only two blocks away, and it's under the flight path of the world's busiest airport. I would need to reconstruct every atmosphere and sync sound because no audience could concentrate on lyrically backlit meadow grasses to the ominous whine of sinking jetliners.

HANDS-ON LEARNING

An interesting exercise is to make a sound montage that tells a story without any narrating. You might, for instance, make a short montage of your morning, telling it through the characteristic sounds of each phase. Do you have pets at home? See what you can do with the different ambiences and spaces. Shoot music where it is part of the natural circumstances (listening to the radio for the news to begin, for instance). This is a good subject to observe and take notes before you shoot sound. There is no special project for this, but perhaps there should be!

NOTE

1. Previously I credited this saying to Robert Bresson, only to discover after rereading his *Notes on Cinematography* (Urizen Books, 1977) that it was my summation of his ideas, not his words.

CHAPTER 11

LIGHTING

Comprehensive lighting instructions are beyond the scope of this book, but here is some essential information, including a simple and reliable lighting setup, to help you function when you need lighting. Supplemental to what follows below, you'll find at this book's website (www.directingthedocumentary.com) under project **AP-3 Lighting Analysis**, a brief description of lighting terms with illustrations. You can also see part of the film from which illustrations were drawn.

Today's camera viewfinder gives a good idea of what your lighting looks like, so digital technology is very much on your side, and makes working in dicey lighting situations easier. For tripod camera situations, especially in high ambient light situations when a viewfinder can be hard to see, a quality monitor attached to the camera video output multiplies this help many times over.

The best way to learn about lighting is to analyze fiction material for its lighting. Do also study observational documentaries shot by available light, since they show all the deficiencies that lighting seeks to rectify. Let's first consider light as a physical phenomenon.

LIGHT QUALITY

Hard or **specular light** comes from relatively small, bright sources such as the sun, or a spotlight, and is recognizable by the sharp-edged shadows it makes (Figure 11-1). Such shadows are the product of light traveling as organized, parallel rays. Paradoxically, a candle, in spite of its low power, creates hard light, the result of it being an effectively small light source that casts distinct, hard-edged shadows.

SOFT LIGHT

Light is *diffused* or *soft* when it creates soft-edged shadows (Figure 11-2). Diffused, disorganized light rays have the same effect as scattered light arriving from a broad source. Soft light throws shadows, but so soft that they are hardly noticeable.

FIGURE 11-1

FIGURE 11-2

Hard or specular light produces sharp-edged shadows and a high contrast between highlight and shadow areas.

Soft light is diffused and either creates soft-edged shadows or no shadows at all.

LIGHTING INSTRUMENTS

LIGHT QUALITY AND LIGHTING INSTRUMENTS

Figure 11-3 shows the kind of portable lighting kit that documentarians use. You can do acceptable interior work armed only with a 750 watt quartz *soft light* (Figure 11-4). You can produce soft light from one of the stand-mounted quartz open-face lamps in Figure 11-3 by (a) bouncing its light off a white wall or ceiling, (b) off the aluminized umbrella provided, or (c) by diffusing its output through a large square of silk or fiberglass. If instead you want the kind of hard light associated with sunlight, you will need a *focusing lamp* or *spotlight* (Figure 11-5).

Open-face quartz lamps are light and compact for travel. Quartz bulbs have a long life, remain stable in color temperature, and have tungsten filament bulbs small enough to cast a moderately hard light. Their disadvantage is that light pours uncontrollably in every direction, making lighting a rather rudimentary exercise unless you have *barn doors* (adjustable flaps at the sides, top, and bottom as in Figure 11-3) to stop light spilling in unwanted directions. Useable, low-cost quartz worklights can be found at hardware stores, but check the color-temperature rating on the bulb body.

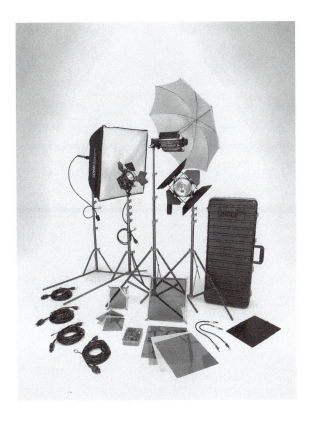

FIGURE 11-3 ———

Lowel® DV Creator lighting kit. *(Image courtesy of Lowel-Light Mfg, Inc.)*

FIGURE 11-4 ———

Tod Lending shooting an interview using only a soft light.

LIGHT EMITTING DIODES (LEDS)

Banks of LEDs are now quite powerful (Figure 11-6) and can be bought with adjustable color temperature and light output. They are low voltage, create no heat, draw very little current, and are safe and easy to use. The Litepanels LP Micro panel clips to the top of the camera and is useful for fill light while shooting inside a car (Figure 11-7, and see www.litepanels. com). You can mount a circle of LEDs around the lens (Figure 11-8) for traveling shots that require some fill light, but this can be painfully distracting for participants, as with any camera-mounted lighting. Find out what it feels like by becoming a camera subject yourself.

HMI LAMPS

An HMI is a small, high-intensity light source enclosed in a quartz envelope. They use mercury vapor and metal halides, and two tungsten electrodes generate light like a miniature arc light. Their color temperature is approximately that of sunlight, but changes as the bulb ages. They combine a high light output with economy of consumption, require an electrical ballast, and are expensive unless you rent them.

FIGURE 11-5

Molequartz® 650 watt Tweenie II Solarspot Fresnel spot lamp. *(Courtesy of Mole-Richardson Co.)*

FIGURE 11-6

A 1 x 1 Litepanels™ LED bank. *(Photo courtesy of Litepanels, Inc.)*

FIGURE 11-7

Litepanels™ LP Micro LED panel on top of a camera. *(Photo courtesy of Litepanels, Inc.)*

FIGURE 11-8

Litepanels™ Ringlite™ Mini, with LEDs surrounding a camera lens. *(Photo courtesy of Litepanels, Inc.)*

FLUORESCENTS

Fluorescent tubes produce soft light in a broken spectrum, but if you need to make a fluorescent-lit area consistent, you can get tubes and CFL (compact fluorescent lamps) rated by Kelvin temperature. They divide into warm white (3000 K or less), white or bright white (3500 K), cool white (4000 K), or daylight (upward of 5000 K).

COLOR TEMPERATURE

There is a good article on color temperature in Wikipedia, with color illustrations. Your main preoccupation will be with two standards: studio interior lighting color temperature of 3200 K, and a nominal exterior color temperature of 5600 K. Actual K of exterior light—whether sunlight, mountain light, overcast sky daylight—will vary according to the situation, but this is a cinematographer's special concern. In Chapter 12 there is a section on shooting under mixed color temperature circumstances.

SAFETY

As a rule, high consumption *luminaires* (lighting instruments) run extremely hot and require prudence. So,

- Let lamps cool before you disassemble them after shooting.
- Never touch quartz bulbs. Use a wadded tissue to hold them since oil in your skin bakes into the quartz envelope, causing the bulb to discolor or even explode when next turned on.
- Never switch on an open-face lamp if anyone is within range. Bulbs most often explode at this moment, sending out razor-sharp fragments.
- Never let rain get to hot bulbs. Sudden cooling by water droplets can cause them to explode.

POWER SUPPLIES

POWER REQUIREMENTS VARY BY INSTRUMENT

The amount and type of lighting you will need depends on the size and reflectivity of the location space, the amount and color temperature of available light, and the kind of lighting look that you want. LED lamps are very energy-efficient, but for harder, more *specular* (hard-edged, shadow-producing) light you will need tungsten spotlamps or quartz movie lights which are power-hungry, run hot, and consume anywhere between 500 and 2000 watts each. A 2 kW (2 kilowatts, or 2000 watts) soft light running from a 110 volt supply consumes 9.5 amps (or 4.5 amps if the supply is 220 volts). The basic North American domestic household circuit (110V at 15A) is unable to power a 2 kW lamp, so you must locate a supply of 20A or better.

CALCULATING CONSUMPTION

Lamps are rated in watts of energy consumption. To calculate their power consumption in *amps* (rate of flow), divide your total desired *watts* (amount of energy consumption) by the *volts* (pressure) of the supply voltage. If you know any two, you can calculate the third.

Assuming you are using a working supply of 111 volts,

Amperes (A): $W \div V = A$ (Example: 2,000W $\div$ 110V = 18.18A)

Watts (W): $A \times V = W$ (Example: 25A $\times$ 110V = 2750W)

Volts (V): $W \div A = V$ (Example: 4,000W $\div$ 36.36A = 110V)

SCOUTING LOCATIONS

Survey the electrical supply, keeping high current requirements in mind. Locate the building's power breaker-box: inside will be a number of circuit-breakers (or in old buildings, fuses), one for each of the building's circuits. They will carry a rating of 15 A, 20 A, 50 A, etc. on the fuse or breaker. Do not replace with a fuse or breaker of higher rating as this can start a fire in the wiring.

Map your supply by powering up one circuit at a time and tracing its outlets with a plug-in handlamp. By numbering or color-coding each circuit's outlets, you can now plan to power your lighting, if necessary, by spreading the load over multiple circuits. Make a note to bring the necessary lengths of heavy-duty extension cable, and spare fuses. Circuit breakers are reset-table because they pop open when the load exceeds their rating. Slo-blow breakers, designed for air-conditioning and refrigerator motors with a high initial current, tolerate a second or two of higher current.

An expensive mistake is to tap into a 220 V supply and blow one's lamps. Arm yourself with a cheap little multimeter (combining voltage, resistance, and current) from an electronics store so you can check supply voltages. Use it also to measure voltages at a heavy-consumption lamp that is getting its power via an extension cord. Any reduced voltage can markedly lower color temperatures.

At each location, determine whether any intermittent appliance (refrigerator or air condi-tioner, say) is going to kick in during shooting and either make noise or trigger a circuit overload. When you turn anything off while shooting, leave your car keys there to remind you to turn it back on when you leave.

LIGHTING

Lighting in fiction films pays little attention to actors' comfort since it's their job to adapt. Lighting in documentaries, however, can strongly affect ordinary people's sense of normality. Old boxers, actors, or conjurors may like it, but for others normally out of the public eye, lighting can induce an overwhelming self-consciousness. Even they can get used to it, if you occupy them well.

DEFINING SHADOWS (HARD AND SOFT LIGHT)

Light is defined not only by its strength but by its shadow-casting properties. A *hard light* source casts organized, parallel light rays that cast hard-edged shadows. The rays of *soft light* are disor-ganized and cast soft-edged, less perceptible shadows. Do not however confuse hard and soft light with the strength of the source, since sunlight and the light of a candle, although wildly differ-ent in strength, both cast hard-edged shadows and count as hard light sources. Sunlight coming through a cloud layer, however, is diffused light that arrives via an effectively large source. A soft-light source this large can cast virtually no shadows.

WHY YOU MAY NEED LIGHTING

Digital cameras can register good images by candlelight, so you would think lighting was unneces-sary. However,

- An interior lit by daylight has bright highlight areas and impossibly dark shadow areas.
  - *Problem*: Contrast ratio of key to fill light is too high.
  - *Solution*: Cut highlight illumination—difficult with sunlight—or boost shadow area lighting.

- An interior lit by daylight with pools of artificial light does strange things to skin hues when people move around.
  - *Problem*: they are passing through mixed color temperature lighting.
  - *Solution*: See next chapter's advice on shooting under mixed color temperatures. Essentially you filter one source to make it consistent with others.
- An exterior where you must shoot in heavy shadow has a sunlit background that burns out.
  - *Problem*: There's a huge contrast ratio disparity between sunlit and shadow areas.
  - *Solution*: Use lighting or reflectors to raise light level in shadow area, or angle camera differently to incorporate a less "hot" background.

Other conditions that may call for supplementary lighting:

- Shadow area is too dark to get an exposure on detail where you need it.
- A scene or an object does not look its best under available light.
- Available light is too contrasty, creating "hot" (overbright) highlights and impenetrably murky shadow areas.
- You are working under mixed color-temperature sources, that is, light sources having a mix of color biases.

CURING CONTRAST PROBLEMS

No camera can handle a *contrast ratio* (range of brightnesses) like the human eye, so lighting work must often squeeze that range into whatever the imaging technology can handle. In practical terms, reducing contrast often means raising light levels in the shadow areas, which you do with *fill light* (from a soft light or by using *bounce light*, that is, light diffused by reflecting it off a white card, silver reflector, or white walls and ceiling). Once you lower the lighting ratio to a range your imaging system can handle, your screen reproduces the picture you wanted—now with adequate detail in both highlight and deep shadow areas, detail otherwise lost (Figure 11-9).

FIGURE 11-9 ———

A subject with side key-light, and the same subject with fill-light lowering contrast.

A low overall light level may be impractical for quite another reason: it forces you to shoot at a wide lens aperture, and thus at the much-reduced depth of field (DOF) that wide aperture produces. Focusing also becomes impractically critical if the camera must follow any spontaneous action. However, by adding more overall light, you can reduce the lens *aperture*, and now, using less area of the lens, you have a greater DOF and less critical focusing is necessary.

AVOIDING THE OVERBRIGHT BACKGROUND

In light-toned spaces, light thrown into the lens by the walls can overpower that reflected by your subjects. At its worst this gives dark humanoid outlines against a blinding white background. The solution is to *cheat* (imperceptibly separate) furniture and subjects away from walls, and raise lighting levels on the foreground subject while lowering it on background walls. You do this best by sending light downward from instruments raised high. This helps keep light from spilling on to the background and also casts shadows low and out of the camera's line of vision.

LIGHTING METHODOLOGY

When you light a set or an object, you are usually trying to make your subject look interesting and credible while counteracting various problems endemic to photography. To this end, you deal with hard light and soft light, each fulfilling a different purpose, as you try to erase all artificiality from the scene. You are using the art that hides art.

KEY LIGHT DIRECTION

The key light is a relatively hard source that creates the highlight and shadow areas from whose direction we sense the time of day, season, lighting environment, and so on. Resist the folklore about taking photos with your back to the sun. Interesting lighting begins when the key light's angle of throw is to the side of the subject or even relatively behind it. This ensures some shadow area in the subject, which provides *modeling*, that is, evidence of the subject's third dimension—depth.

When shooting by available light you can often produce interesting lighting simply by reorienting the proposed action in relation to the ambient lighting, or by altering the camera placement

Fill light is often a soft light source close to the camera-to-subject axis. It provides enough light to see fill shadow areas so we can see detail there. Being close to the camera, the soft-edged light casts its shadows directly behind the subject, and they go largely unseen.

Backlight creates a rim of light separating subject from background, gives highlights to hair, and texture to smoke or vapor (Figure 11-10). Achieving subject/background separation is important in black-and-white photography but less so in color, where varying hues help define and separate the different planes of a composition.

PRACTICAL

A light source that appears in picture is called a *practical* but it seldom functions to provide any of the lighting (Figure 11-11). Cut its light output if needed by putting layers of paper or neutral-density (ND) filter around the inside of its shade.

CHEATING

Providing you stay within the bounds of the credible, you can *cheat* (creatively adjust) the angle of the key for convenience, artistic effect, or to minimize ugly background shadows. You can also cheat furniture and participants away from walls, and, by using a key light on a tall stand, project

FIGURE 11-10

Backlight creates a rim of light round the subject, and makes vapor or smoke visible.

people's shadows low and out of sight instead of visibly behind them on to walls. To help with framing you can also cheat participants closer to each other than usual—always providing you don't compromise their sense of normality.

TWO BASIC LIGHTING METHODS

ADDING TO A BASE AND USING A KEY

In documentary when you often have to work fast, there is a simple and reliable solution to lighting interiors called *adding to a base*. First you provide enough ambient soft light for an adequate exposure, then you add *modeling* by using a harder light source as a shadow-producing key. Here's what to do:

Baselight

If there is insufficient baselight, provide your own by bouncing hard light off a reflective wall or ceiling. This provides a good overall illumination, but used alone will give a rather dull and *flat*

FIGURE 11-11 ───

A light source appearing in picture is called a *practical*. Often it provides no light useful to photography.

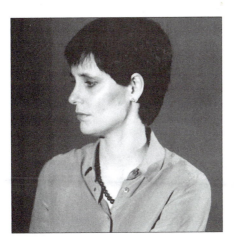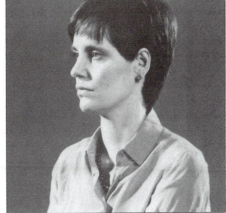

FIGURE 11-12 ───

A flat-lit subject and the same subject side-lit.

(that is, comparatively shadowless) look (Figure 11-12). This may be just right for some dull, flat situations (hospital, classroom, office, etc.).

Key Light

The light that provides highlights and casts telltale shadows is called the *key* light. From its pattern of light and shadow the audience unconsciously infers time of day, mood, and even time of year.

Key light should be "motivated," that is, it must appear to come from a logical source. In a bedroom scene, for instance, you would position the key low and out of frame to produce the characteristic shadow pattern cast by a bedside lamp. For a warehouse scene lit by a bare overhead bulb hanging into the frame, the additional key light would come from above. In a pathology lab where the source is a light table, the key would have to strike the subject from a low angle.

Using multiple key lights is a skilled business and without a lot of practice can lead to the dread trademark of amateur lighting—ugly, multiple shadows. When in doubt, keep it simple.

THREE-POINT LIGHTING

This is the standard setup for lit interviews and you can find good tutorials on YouTube. It uses fill light for an overall exposure in the shadow area, with modeling provided by adding a key light and backlight, sometimes called a hair light or rim light.

LIGHTING TESTS AND REHEARSALS

To assess lighting, shoot tests and critically assess the results. If lighting is at all elaborate, a lighting rehearsal ahead of time, with a series of representative digital stills, can obviate embarrassingly protracted location lighting sessions—or worse, costly electrical failures.

BACKGROUNDS

Shoot when possible against dark or book-covered walls, since they absorb reflected light that would otherwise overpower that reflected by your subjects. When this is impossible, keep light off the background walls by (a) angling light from high down, and (b) using flags or barn-doors to keep illumination from falling on backgrounds, and (c) cheating participants away from walls so you can better control background illumination problems as well as your subjects' propensity for casting shadows. Distancing participants from sound-reflective surfaces has the double advantage of reducing sound reverberation problems.

HANDS-ON LEARNING

Take a feature film you like and study some sequences for their lighting using **AP-3 Lighting Analysis**. Be sure not to miss the several pages of text and illustrations that accompany this project. Try planning for a shoot using **AP-2 Making a Floor Plan.** This sketch method is good for working out the fewest necessary camera angles in relation to the expected action, for planning lighting in addition to any natural light available, and also for mapping out power supplies.

CHAPTER 12

CAMERA

This chapter outlines what will be most helpful—theoretically and practically—to make your first shooting experiences truly productive. Normally a director works with one or more other people as crew, but for a fast learning curve when you begin, it is fine to shoot and edit solo. You can certainly acquire high quality imagery with a small camera and little else (Figure 12-1). To see the latest consumer camera features and capabilities, see "best HD camcorder reviews" at http://camcorders.toptenreviews.com/hdv. Otherwise go to the B&H Photo and Video website, www.bhphototovideo.com, for a full spectrum of amateur and professional equipment.

CODECS AND WORKFLOW

To work with the least tech complications, make sure your editing program input can handle your camera's file output, or *codec*. This (short for code/decode) is a way of electronically compressing and decompressing the digital files that a camera and sound recorder generate. MPEG-4 and H.264 are two common codecs, and their function is to produce manageably smaller files. "Lossy"

FIGURE 12-1

You can do excellent work with the Sony FDR-AX100/B digital camera. (*Photo courtesy of Sony Corp.*)

codecs however show signs of the codec's economies, especially during image movement. The codec in use may restrict the amount of color correction and image manipulation you can do. At the other end of the scale are RAW files generated by top-of-the line digital equipment, which are uncompressed imaging or audio information. RAW files are enormous, and only very advanced editing and color correction equipment can handle them.

Cameras at consumer and *prosumer* (between professional and consumer) levels use standard codecs that an up-to-date editing program should handle without problem, but prove compatibility by running a test. To incorporate materials from archival sources, you must ensure compatibility between all devices, programs, and files in your intended production workflow. Book I covers the basics to get you shooting, and you will see from it why directors place camera, sound, and editing in the hands of specialized colleagues. A director must eventually concentrate on directing, but for now, you can learn a lot from shooting a short observational documentary alone.

EQUIPMENT CHECKOUT

Whoever collects equipment should arrive early, and assemble and test every piece there and then, before leaving checkout.

GOLDEN RULE #1, TEST IT FIRST

Make "test and test again" your true religion. Never assume that everything will be all right because the supplier is reputable. If you do, Murphy of Murphy's Law is waiting to get you. ("Everything that can go wrong will go wrong.") Expect him to sabotage everything that should fit together, slide, turn, lock, roll, light up, make a noise, or work in silence. The whole Murphy clan lurks in every wire, plug, box, lens, battery, and alarm clock. Make no mistake; they mean to ruin you. Make lists, then lists of lists. Pray.

GOLDEN RULE #2, PREPARE FOR THE WORST

Hopefulness and film production do not belong together. One blithe optimist left the sound tapes of a just-completed feature film overnight in his car trunk. The car happened to be stolen, and a vast amount of fiction work turned into so much silent footage overnight.

Your imagination expended in darkly imagining the worst will impel you to carry spares, special tools, manuals, emergency information, First Aid kits, and three kinds of diarrhea medicine. As a pessimist constantly foreseeing the worst, you will be tranquilly productive compared with the optimist, because you don't dice with fate.

CAMERA

For information on any specific camera see the website of B&H Photo-Video, New York at www.bhphotovideo.com/c/shop/1881/Cameras. B&H must have the best selection of digital filmmaking equipment anywhere, and their website is a mine of helpful and impartial production information.

CAVEAT CONCERNING DSLR CAMERAS AND TIMECODE

Be aware that a DSLR (digital single-lens reflex camera designed for stills), though it may shoot beautiful video, probably does not write *timecode*. TC is the time signature (in hours, minutes, seconds, and frames) assigned by dedicated video cameras that postproduction software depends on to manage your footage. You will find software discussed on the Internet that adds TC to

FIGURE 12-2

For handheld work the ideal camera has a side-mounted eyepiece and a body balanced to sit on the user's shoulder. Essentially the camera becomes part of the user's head and shoulders. (*Photo courtesy of Nomadic Pictures, Inc.*)

DSLR files, but it takes time, planning, and management. Some editing programs automatically add TC when you import video files that lack it. However, should you need to reimport anything (at higher resolution, say), the new TC will not match the old, with dire consequences to your editing. Further aspects of TC are discussed under "Settings and Options" in **Chapter 27: Advanced Cameras and Equipment.**

BODY DESIGN

In documentary you often shoot material handheld, so the professional electronic newsgathering (ENG) camera has a side-mounted eyepiece and a body balanced to sit on the user's shoulder. This allows the camera to become part of the operator's head and shoulders (Figure 12-2). DSLR and small digital video cameras often record amazing sound and picture, but having their eyepiece or liquid crystal display (LCD) at the rear makes the camera a free-floating appendage that you must hold ahead of your face (Figure 12-3). The absence of bodily contact soon produces distress in your arms, wrists, and hands when you hold shots steady for minutes at a time. A shoulder brace may help, but will sometimes obstruct adapting to the action.

VIEWFINDER

Usually a pivoted liquid crystal display (LCD) unfolds from the side of a small camera so you can look into it from any angle. For low angle shots you can look down into it. You can even point it forward so you frame yourself up as you talk to your own camera. LCD screens work fine until you try shooting in strong daylight, and the image becomes washed out. That's when a viewfinder eyepiece becomes a necessity.

FIGURE 12-3

Handholding a small camcorder becomes stressful because you can't brace it against your face or body.

CAMERA CONTROLS

On small cameras controls are miniaturized, fiddly, and not always placed where you want them. You set the variables in video and audio menus through tiny switches or thumbwheels. Familiarize yourself with what they offer, and run through all the options until you've set and reset every one. Your most frequent adjustments will be to focus, exposure, and sound level. Ideally these should be manually controlled, but this may not be feasible while operating handheld. The options you choose show up in the viewfinder as icons, so you must recognize these too—or discover later that all your participants have yellow jaundice because the winking saucer was trying to tell you, "Set white balance."

The key to these riches lies in cramped manuals, so download a PDF version from the manufacturer's website and print it large so you can make annotations. To absorb the manual painlessly, turn it into flash cards so that you and your colleagues can test each other. Tossing on the high seas in a trawler is no place to start looking for the sound level control.

Practice all your camera's functions until it's second nature. This is your concert instrument: practice till you play like a pro. Never doubt that your camera is capable of serious work, once you've learned to work within its limitations (Figure 12-4).

PROFESSIONAL OPTIONS

Professional equipment, being rugged and physically large, provides visible, easy to set controls. Expect professional and prosumer cameras to have multiple sound channels, a black level control, a gamma (color linearity) control, and manual settings for exposure, focusing, sound level, and a lot else. Professional equipment has one unwelcome aspect: it may draw attention to you in the street and trigger exaggerated expectations in some participants. A camera that captures well but looks like a holiday accessory may be a necessity in situations where you want to look like a tourist, not a broadcast journalist.

FIGURE 12-4 ——

Many cameras are capable of serious work, if you work within their limitations. These, damaged in conflict, produced *Five Broken Cameras*. One blocked a bullet, saving Emad Burnat's life.

COLOR BALANCING THE CAMERA

WHITE BALANCE OPTIONS

To make flesh tones look natural in color work, the camera must have a correct "white balance." This adjustment allows the camera to shoot white objects under a particular light source, and to reproduce them as white, not pale pink, green, or orange. The reason is this: though white light contains the whole spectrum, real-life light sources—even different kinds of skylight such as overcast, blue sky, mountain sky—are in reality mixes of light in which particular colors predominate. The human eye compensates effortlessly for this state of affairs, but electronic image-recording is nowhere so efficient. Sadly, it records what is scientifically present. Thus, each illumination source is said to have its own *color temperature,* and to compensate for this, you must set your camera's "white balance" control for shooting under *that particular light source*. If you don't, everyone under those supermarket fluorescents will become a bilious green. On your camera, expect these white balance options:

Automatic—not good for all situations but a necessity for some. When you first shoot, you'll probably set everything in your camera to automatic (white balance, exposure, focus, and sound level) so you can concentrate on filming. This is fine while you grapple with the human content of your filmmaking, which will take quite a while. Automatic white balance is almost a necessity if you must follow someone through several lighting zones. The auto white balance and exposure will probably make all the necessary adjustments with wonderful efficiency.

Manual—preferable under stable lighting situations. A custom white setting means that color remains stable as you pan across differently lighted areas. Set the camera to "manual white balance," frame a white surface under the given source light, and press the button that initiates white balancing. After a few seconds the camera lets you know it has locked on to the new setting.

Options you often get:

Preset white balance. These are factory settings offering typical sunlight (which has a blue bias), typical tungsten-filament bulb light (orange bias), and typical fluorescent light (green bias). Since no light is typical, presets are approximations that you should only use in emergency.

Manually set white balance. Using this to adjust for an actual, rather than nominal, light source is always best.

White balance memory retains your settings while the camera is turned off or while you change its battery. Keeping settings in memory allows you to shoot matching material days or months later under similar lighting conditions.

SHOOTING UNDER MIXED COLOR TEMPERATURES

Setting a white balance allows the camera to respond accurately under a given light source, but it cannot handle the mixed color temperature sources that may prevail in, say, a restaurant partially illuminated by interior lighting and daylight. This is because outdoor and indoor color temperatures vary. If you use indoor lighting of between 2800 K to 3200 K (Kelvin), and you white-balance for this source, then outdoor light seen through a window will look cold (blue-biased) because skylight may be 5600 K. Conversely, if you white-balance for the outdoor light, the folks indoors turn orange. So that's no solution. Watch documentaries for their lighting and you'll see all sorts of variations.

For an interior with mixed color temperature, three common approaches are:

Solution A: Tape gel filter #85 (orange) over windows. Color filter lets pass its own color, and holds back other colors of light. #85 filter is reddish and holds back the excess blue in the daylight, the remainder of which now matches your interior lighting. By white-balancing to the interior color temperature, colors inside and outside the window will all look normal.

Solution B: Place #80A filters (blue) over your 3200 K halogen movie lights. This holds back excess orange content so their light output now matches daylight color temperature. This, however, halves the output from your lights—so they may not remain adequate. Unless you use LED lights, lighting fixtures get very hot, gels melt, and only heatproof glass filters will stand up to the punishment.

Solution C: Do nothing. If the view through the window is incidental and unimportant, just let it go blue. Conversely, when an evening exterior includes a building with a lighted room, let it go orange. Audiences accept both as a convention of movies.

Can't I fix color in postproduction? Yes and no. Digital color correction in postproduction is remarkable. It lets you warm an overall cold color cast, or change contrast and brightness, but changing only a single shade (a human face, for instance) without altering everything else takes advanced software and the skills of a trained colorist. Moral: cure everything you can during the shoot.

EXPOSURE

AUTOMATIC EXPOSURE

Many cameras set auto exposure by averaging light in the whole frame. This works well in a desert-scape, where everything is similarly exposed. But shoot a chef in a glaring, white-tiled kitchen, and his face will be severely underexposed. Even when the camera samples chosen areas

FIGURE 12-5

Sunset silhouette shot enhanced by underexposure.

of the frame, you can get undesirable effects, so don't get used to relying on auto exposure. Use it, however, in circumstances of rapidly changing light, since this may be the only way to get acceptable results. Imagine following someone out of a car at night and into a roadside café. You pass through a maze of lighting and color temperature situations that only auto exposure and auto white balance can handle.

MANUAL EXPOSURE

Most cameras permit manual exposure control, so that exposure does not float up and down whenever the picture composition changes. By locking exposure you can now underexpose to simulate a sunset (Figure 12-5), or overexpose to see the features of someone who is backlit (Figure 12-6). The type and accessibility of control (lever, knob, thumb-wheel) is as important as its responsiveness. Positive and immediate control is good; floating and sluggish is not. The link may be electronic or, in more expensive cameras, a physical *lens aperture* (or *f-stop*) control.

BACKLIGHT CONTROL

This is a one-size-fits-all compensation for situations when light is coming toward the camera, and your subject's face is backlit and in relative darkness. To adequately expose for facial detail, you must over-expose the background, but to get the exact effect, you will need to set exposure manually.

PICTURE GAIN

This, calibrated in decibels, amplifies the camera's response so you can shoot in really low-light situations. Useful, but expect to pay with increased *picture noise* (electronic picture "grain").

FIGURE 12-6 ───

Detail in features of backlit subject achieved by increasing exposure. The consequence is a "hot" (overexposed) background.

When you increase picture gain, wear a rubber band on your wrist to remind you to return gain to normal.

FILTERING

NEUTRAL DENSITY

Many cameras have an inbuilt *neutral density* (ND) *filter*. This acts like sunglasses, lowering the amount of light reaching the imaging chip while remaining color-neutral. A one-stop reduction is .3 rating, two stops is .6, and so on. Avoid overexposure by using ND filtering, or use it to force your lens into using a larger aperture, which then lets you work at a shorter depth of field (DOF—see below). This is useful when you want to throw planes other than the subject-plane out of focus.

OTHER FILTERS

With the addition of a *matte box* (Figure 12-7) to hold filters in place, you can:

- Use a color correction filter.
- Cool a hot (overbright) sky with a graduated ND filter.
- Use a fog filter to simulate fog or mist.
- Use a diffusion filter to throw light into shadow areas and reduce picture contrast.
- Create sparkles on highlights or a star effect.
- Use a polarizing filter to reduce the glare from water and certain metal surfaces.

FIGURE 12-7

Matte box attachment for a Sony camera. *(Photo courtesy of Chrosziel GmbH.)*

LENSES

Unless designed for DSLR (digital single lens reflex) cameras, video camera lenses often lack external calibration, but you can get basic tech specifications in order to make comparisons through the B&H website (www.bhphotovideo.com), whose camcorder section has a wealth of information on products and production methods.

The prime lens is one of fixed focal length and excellent optical characteristics since primes have few lens elements. Expect a wide maximum aperture (large light-transmitting ability) with little distortion and minimal interior halation (light reflecting between lens elements). The prime lens's superiority won't show up unless your camera has a superior imaging system.

The normal lens is one whose focal length makes perspective look normal onscreen. "Normal" means that familiar objects at different distances from the camera appear onscreen in the same relative proportions as they do to the human eye. Digital cameras incorporate differing imaging receptors, and each size demands its own particular focal length lens to render perspective normally.

The telephoto lens is one of high magnification like a telescope, and requires the camera to be tripod-mounted to produce a steady image. A telephoto brings distant objects close; has a shallow DOF (good for isolating a single plane and throwing other planes out of focus); makes objects at different distances look closer than reality; has a limited maximum aperture (that is, a restricted usefulness in low light).

The wide-angle lens is one of low magnification that makes close objects look more distant, exaggerates the distances between planes, and distorts perspective markedly. It has a large DOF, and a large maximum aperture (that is, a good ability to function in low light). It makes moving shots look steadier, and lets you cover the action in a confined space such as a courtyard, car interior, or cramped apartment.

The zoom lens is a multi-element lens of continuously variable focal length between two extremes. A lens whose longest (telephoto) setting is 180 mm and widest (widest-angle) setting is 18 mm has a ratio of 10:1, which represents a ten times (10×) magnification power.

To manually focus a zoom lens (a) zoom in close so focusing becomes critical, (b) find focus, then (c) zoom back to preferred frame size. Unless you are filming wildlife, a zoom with a long telephoto won't be as generally useful as one with a truly wide wide-angle.

INTERCHANGEABLE LENSES

A camera body that accepts interchangeable 35 mm stills-camera lenses is a wonderful idea, but make sure the imaging chip is commensurately large—that is, approaching 35 mm film dimensions—or much of the image gets wasted and the advantages of lens choice are largely illusory.

LENSES AND PERSPECTIVE

Note that zooming in or out *does not alter image perspective.* Try it for yourself. Sure, magnification changes, but the proportion of foreground objects in relation to those in the background remains the same. No matter what lenses you use, *you can only alter perspective by changing the camera-to-subject distance.*

Here is a typical table of lens information, with the information explained:

TABLE 12-1 Typical lens information—this is for the lens of a Canon XA-20 camera

Information	Explanation
Zoom Range: 20× Optical/ 400× Digital 35 mm Equivalent: 26.8 to 576 mm	26.8 mm (35 mm camera equivalent) focal length is the wide end of the zoom range, 576 mm is telephoto. This is an impressive 20:1 zoom (dividing larger focal length by the smaller). Digital magnification has limited usefulness: it magnifies the pixels and gives a grainy image.
Focal Length: 3.67 to 73.4 mm Max Aperture: f1.8–2.8	Focal length describes the distances from the lens optical center to the imaging plane, depending on zoom setting in use. Aperture size describes the lens's maximum light-gathering ability. At the wide-angle end of the zoom it opens to f/1.8, but only to f/2.8 in telephoto mode— about 1½ stops less. Each stop-change halves or doubles light, so f/2.8 admits rather less than half the light of f/1.8—quite a difference.
Minimum Focus Wide: 0.8" (20 mm)	By using the macro adjustment, this is how close you can focus on an object.
Minimum Focus Throughout Zoom Range: 23.6" (60 cm)	If you want to zoom in or out, you must be no closer than about 2 feet.
Zoom Speed Settings: Variable, Constant (16 levels), Fast, Normal, Slow	The zoom has a wide variety of speeds.
Filter Ring Size: 58 mm	58 mm is the size of any filter you screw directly on the front element of the lens.

LENS PROTECTION

For everyday use, keep an *ultraviolet* (UV) *filter* on the front element of your lenses. It protects the lens from damage and inhibits the UV light, invisible to the naked eye, which collects in large landscape shots and registers onscreen as mist. Always use a *lens hood* to shield the front lens element from stray shafts of strong light. Light coming from outside the lens's field of view will strike the lens's front element at an angle and cause *lens halation* (light bouncing internally between lens elements). This will degrade the overall picture with an admixture of white light.

ASPECT RATIO

Aspect ratio refers to the width of a screen image in relation to its height. In the early days the cinema screen standard was the relatively square 4:3 or 1.33:1, a ratio copied when the first black-and-white television sets appeared. Attempting to distance itself from TV, the 1950s cinema offered color and wide-screen images of various aspect ratios. Today the high definition (HD) TV standard aspect ratio is 16:9 internationally, or 1.77:1, close to the cinema's standard 1.85:1 (Figure 12-8). In this era of rapidly evolving standards, integrating 4:3 archive footage in a 16:9 HD documentary is just one of the workflow problems you face, but History Channel programs, or any professional film using archive footage, will demonstrate how various formats are commonly integrated together.

FOCUS AND DEPTH OF FIELD

The camera operator must often adjust focus, especially during handheld coverage. In well-lit surroundings, focus is deep and non-critical with cameras that use small imaging chips. However, if you are using 35 mm type DSLR optics or similar, DOF can be very shallow and focusing during a handheld take can become maddeningly critical. Automatic focus, properly set up, will pull focus for you, provided the critical part of your subject is identifiable to the camera. A professional camera's large viewfinder, and its mechanically positive lens control, makes adjusting focus by eye much easier. Expect most cameras to offer the following focus options:

Automatic focusing (AF) is fast and accurate but depends entirely on which part of the image the optics are set to scan. Usually it's a small area in the center of frame but if there are options, see if you can maximize your chance of maintaining proper focus. Some *DSLR* (digital single-lens reflex) cameras incorporate face recognition in their focusing, but have a disconcerting habit of locking focus to a face in a street advertisement instead of your subject. Check how to disengage auto focus so the camera doesn't go hunting for focus every time picture composition changes. Autofocus won't usually work through glass. It either hunts, or focuses on the glass rather than the subject.

Manual focusing is preferable, but without a large, light-proof eyepiece, focusing can be hit or miss. High definition (HD) video raises the stakes—which is why you often see mis-focused footage on the nightly news. To find manual focus, zoom in quickly, run back and forth through focus to find what's visibly best, then quickly zoom back to the preferred image size. Try to confine this procedure to unimportant action, such as a question during an interview.

Macro focusing allows you a short focus range that often permits focusing within inches of the lens—useful when shooting small objects or images.

1.33:1 or 4:3 ratio (Early cinema and standard definition TV format)

1.85:1 or 16:9 ratio (High definition television format)

2.4:1 ratio (35 mm anamorphic cinema format)

FIGURE 12-8

Three common picture aspect ratios.

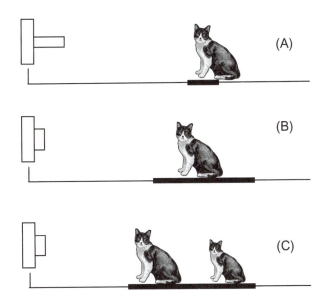

FIGURE 12-9

Every optimal point of focus has further areas in acceptable focus. In A (telephoto lens) depth of field is shallow, deeper in B (wide angle), and adjusted in C to include foreground and middle-ground subjects both in focus.

PRACTICALITIES OF FOCUS AND DEPTH OF FIELD

Focus is a relative term since you aim for focus acceptable to the eye, rather than an absolute. Every optimal point of focus has some additional depth, both nearer and farther, in which objects are acceptably in focus (Figure 12-9A). The amount of DOF available changes according to the lens in use, and the aperture (f-stop) you choose to work at.

To restrict DOF use a telephoto lens, or shoot with a wide lens aperture. This, for instance, can allow you by focal plane alone to isolate a notice in a crowded street. A shallow DOF does however make focus very hard to maintain when subject or camera are on the move.

To enlarge depth of field, use wider-angle lenses, more light, and smaller lens apertures (Figure 12-9B). Wide-angle lenses have an inherently larger DOF than normal or telephoto lenses, and so are always easier to keep in focus. By creating deep DOF you can expect to adjust the point of focus to *bracket* within acceptable focus two subjects widely separated in distance from the camera (Figure 12-9C).

Hyperfocal distance is a lens focus setting that yields the deepest DOF to include infinity, which for practical purposes is any plane more than a hundred feet distant. Hyperfocal distance varies according to the focal length of the lens and the *f-stop* (iris setting) in use. In bright daylight everything may be in good focus from, say, 4 feet to infinity (Figure 12-10). This is the principle behind the *deep focus* photography that Greg Toland made famous in Orson Welles' *Citizen Kane* (USA, 1941). In the wrong circumstances, however, deep focus deluges the eye with detail, and sends you hurrying to create the selectiveness of *shallow focus*.

FIGURE 12-10

A lens's hyperfocal distance is a focus-setting made at a particular f-stop that produces the deepest focus to include infinity.

POWER SUPPLIES

For mobility, camera and recording equipment runs off rechargeable batteries, but if you have a handy AC supply available, chargers can double as power converters, and you can run stationary equipment indefinitely. Seldom do rechargeable batteries run equipment as long as you want, especially if incorrectly charged. Estimate generously how many batteries you should take on location, and try to work each battery to its useable limit before completely recharging it, which may take between 6 and 10 hours. Read manuals carefully in relation to conserving battery life, since wrong handling can shorten a battery's "memory."

FIGURE 12-11

Tripod and spreader. (*Photo courtesy of Vinten, a Vitec Group brand.*)

CAMERA SUPPORT SYSTEMS

TRIPOD AND ACCESSORIES

There's cold comfort here for the under-funded since the budget *tripod* and *tilt head* are a dismal substitute for the real deal. They work fine for static shots, but try to pan or tilt, and wobbly movements reveal why professionals use heavy tripods and hydraulically damped tilt heads. Turning on the camera's *image stabilization* may smooth your movements, and all camera movements look better when you use a wide-angle lens. A *baby legs* is a very short tripod for low-angle shots, and a *high hat* is a hat-shaped support for placing the camera on the ground or other solid surface. A serviceable alternative here is a sandbag, which you pat into shape to allow the degree of angling you want. A *spreader* or *spider* is a folding three-arm bracket that goes under the spike legs of a professional tripod (Figure 12-11). Remember to lock the tripod legs to the spreader so they don't splay and collapse. A spreader guards against scratching or denting a floor, and lets you pick up the camera, tripod, and spreader as a single unit so you can rapidly plunk it down elsewhere.

FIGURE 12-12

Ball-mounted tripod heads make fast leveling easy.

PAN/TILT HEAD SETUP

At each new setup check that the *pan/tilt head* is level by using the inbuilt spirit-level bubble and altering tripod leg lengths. If you forget, you'll make a pan only to end up with a shot whose horizontals are skewed. Better tripods allow rapid leveling through a ball and cup system (Figure 12-12).

When you prepare to pan or tilt, adjust the head to give some drag. This helps smooth out your movements. If your pan/tilt head permits, position the camera's center of gravity to balance its weight equally over the pivoting point. If you don't, it will try to roll forward or back when you momentarily let go of the *pan handle*. In documentary it is wise to never lock the tilt head while the camera is running in any situation where you might need to reframe.

QUICK-RELEASE PLATE

This bolts to the base of the camera, allowing the camera to mate instantly with the pan/tilt head (Figure 12-13). Later, when you decide to go handheld, pulling a single lever instantly frees the camera. Take care: some quick-releases are dangerously sensitive if your sleeve catches the lever. I once caught my camera in mid-air.

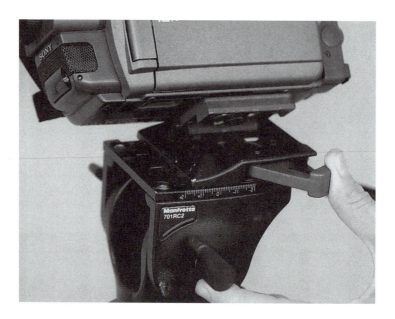

FIGURE 12-13

A quick-release plate bolted to the base of the camera. It allows you to mount the camera quickly on the pan/tilt head, or to detach it instantly for a handheld shot.

MOBILE SUPPORT SYSTEMS

A practiced and well-coordinated human being makes an excellent mobile camera support. During long-take shooting you may need a *shoulder brace* (Figure 12-14). For more ambitious work involving movement, consider one of the Glidecam (Figure 12-15, www.glidecam.com), Varizoom (www.varizoom.com), or Steadicam (www.steadicam.com) systems. Heidi Ewing and Rachel Grady make good use of one in *Jesus Camp* (USA, 2006), their frightening film about the religious conditioning of young children. Fundamentalist preachers groom them with a mixture of inspiration and fear, and whip them up into a fervor in a session of "taking back America for Christ." The gliding, swooping camera complements the kids' agitation as they reach a weeping, speaking-in-tongues torment (Figure 12-16).

For a *dolly* (wheeled camera support) use a wheelchair with its tires a little underinflated. Professional dollies run on tracks like a miniature railroad, but your production must fully justify the outlay since they are heavy to transport, expensive to rent, and labor-intensive to use. If your film is a historical reconstruction, for example, you may need all the equipment and expertise of a feature film crew. Before you reach this point, you can shoot perfectly good tracking shots,

- Backwards out of a car trunk or station wagon.
- Forward or sideways off a tripod tied down inside a car with bungee cords and shooting through any window aperture.
- Forward from a camera securely roped to the car hood with a towel under it to protect the car surface.

FIGURE 12-14

During long-take shooting you may need a shoulder brace. (*Photo courtesy of the Ikan Corporation.*)

FIGURE 12-15

For ambitious work involving movement consider the Glidecam X10. Such systems need much practice. (*Photo courtesy of Glidecam.*)

FIGURE 12-16

Highly mobile camerawork used to capture children's agitation in *Jesus Camp*.

As always, shoot using a wide-angle lens to minimize undue movement and road vibration. You can also smooth a tracking shot during postproduction by applying a degree of slow-motion.

MONITORS AND VIEWFINDERS

Reliable color and framing come only with a properly adjusted field monitor, which can double as a jumbo viewfinder when you are shooting off a tripod. This is your guarantee of color fidelity while shooting, and a double-check on viewfinder framing, which is occasionally misaligned. If you must make do with a domestic TV set, use the highest quality video input. Monitors and TVs have abysmal sound quality, so during viewings run sound through a stereo system.

COMPOSING THE SHOT

When you set up a shot, and particularly when action is taking place, make a habit of scanning the entire frame, moving your eye around the edges and consciously noting the arrangement of visual elements. If you don't do this, you will lapse into the mental state of an assassin staring fixedly at his target. Unpracticed camera operators set up the shot, then stare contentedly at the subject, immune to changes that might be taking place to the composition as people and vehicles move about in the background.

RULE OF THIRDS

The least satisfactory way to frame a human subject is to plunk them bang in the middle of frame. If you divide the screen up into three bands horizontally and three bands vertically, the commonest points for the focus of interest in the frame are the four places where the lines intersect (Figure 12-17).

FIGURE 12-17

Rule of Thirds: Divide the screen into three bands horizontally and three vertically. The recommended focus of interest is where the lines intersect. (*Photo of Helena by Stella von Malapert.*)

FIGURE 12-18

Three sizes of image. If you want any two compositions to cut together well, the compositional center—here the subject's eyes—must occupy the same part of the frame.

MATCHING SHOTS

If you shoot an interview conventionally off a tripod in a wide shot, medium shot, and close shot, the three angles will not cut well together unless you place the focus of interest (usually the eyes of the interviewee) proportionally in the same place in the frame in all three angles (Figure 12-18). That means that the close shot may crop the top of a head and bottom of a chin.

LEAD SPACE

When a human subject faces across the screen, either sitting in conversation, or walking, we leave *lead space* in front of them (Figure 12-19). If you shoot a conversation off a tripod between two people on a couch, the person on the left will have lead space to their right, and the person on the right will have lead space to their left. The two shots will cut very nicely together if you make these two *complementary shots* (shots designed to cut together) of similar size, with the figures at a similar height.

FIGURE 12-19 ——

Lead space in front of a subject who faces across the screen, as here in *The Interrupters*.

HANDHELD COMPOSING

The same guidelines apply when you are mobile, except that you must continuously monitor the design of your frame, and make adjustments to accommodate movements by you, your subjects, and the changing background elements.

Do not be surprised if, at the end of a 10 minute shot, you can barely remember what you shot. When the mind works overtime designing the frame in real-time, this is normal.

COVERING TWO PEOPLE STANDING IN CONVERSATION

When you shoot two people walking or standing in conversation in the street, it is often a good idea to be close to the scene axis (the invisible line between them—see **Chapter 5: Story Elements and Film Grammar**, "Scene Geography and Axes"). That way, you can hold both Person A and Person B in the same frame, and the action takes place more dynamically in the frame's depth rather than flattened and across the frame. Showing both in two-shots lets us see their relationship in space, and the body language of each. The diagram in Figure 12-20 shows how, using a mobile camera and your lens set wide-angle, you can keep the frame continuously occupied, produce five basic shots, and even use the handheld transitions from one to the next. In editing you can often eliminate some of the camera movements if the shots are composed to cut together. Here is the full sequence:

1. Start with an *establishing two-shot* containing Person A and Person B.
2. Move in to take an *overshoulder shot* on A (that includes B's head and shoulder in the foreground) and hold.
3. Move forward to isolate A in close-up, and hold.
4. Then, by pivoting around A, transition to a complementary over-shoulder shot onto B (meaning it will cut well with its *complementary* over-shoulder shot on A).
5. Move forward to take a close shot on B.
6. By pivoting around B, you arrive back at the over-shoulder on A, or pull out to the establishing two-shot.

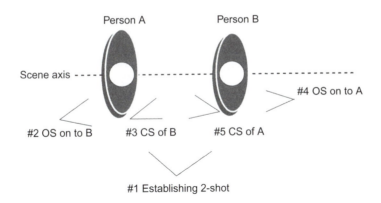

FIGURE 12-20

How to cover a conversation handheld, moving between five basic shots. The frame is continuously occupied, and the movements can all be usable.

Notice that *you must stay to one side of the scene axis* (the imaginary line between the two characters), or your succession of shots will not cut together logically.

For further ideas on camerawork and composition, see **Chapter 26: Optics**, in particular "Composition."

CAMERA OPERATING

Tripod or handheld? Decide what sort of experience you want the audience to have. At a young children's party, you'd get the handheld camera down to kid level. That height and handheld camera movement would complement the children's experience of each other. The point of view of an amused uncle standing apart, being more stable and grounded, might be shot high-down from a tripod. The camera is tripod-mounted in the kind of interview you see in Figure 12-21 where Nancy Schiesari is directing *Tattooed under Fire* (USA, 2008).

Broadly speaking, there is secure and insecure camerawork, objective and subjective, and a place for either—depending on the experience you are documenting, and what you want us to feel about it. If your subject—a kid on roller skates, say—calls for complete camera mobility, sacrifice stability for nimbleness and go handheld. Otherwise you might use a telephoto lens from a tripod-mounted camera, paying close attention to focusing since with long lenses it is always critical.

CHECK AND RECHECK COMPOSITION

While you are operating camera, make a habit of constantly scanning the whole image, looking for improvements, or changes demanded by the changing content of your screen. As we have said, the inexperienced operator gazes mesmerized at the subject (speaking, walking, cleaning his shoes, etc.) instead of looking critically at the composition as a pictorial construct. Remember the Rule of Thirds. Any of its points of intersection are generally preferred over placing the composition's center of interest at the dead center of the screen.

CAMERA OPERATOR'S INTERIOR MONOLOGUE

While you shoot, it helps to maintain an *interior monologue* that articulates how you are composing and what composition you should transition to next. Then concentrate on executing it as

FIGURE 12-21

Typical setup using tripod-mounted camera for off-axis interviewing in *Tattooed under Fire*. Note boom operator's positioning in a tight space. (Photo by Rebecca Adams, courtesy of Nancy Schiesari.)

smoothly and naturally as possible. A focused stream of consciousness helps you stay hyper-aware of what you are doing, and locked into executing each precious moment perfectly.

OPERATOR'S BODY MECHANICS

Try always to,

- Position yourself during pans so you turn from an uncomfortable to a comfortable holding position.
- Halt during a tracking shot in a bodily position that lets you smoothly resume movement onward to the next composition.
- If you must kneel, sink on one knee only, or you'll be unable to rise without jerking the camera.
- If you sit down, place one or both feet under you, so you can rise without rolling forward.

REFOCUSING DURING A SHOT

Having to find or reset focus while the camera is running is an accepted part of actuality filming. To do this:

- Zoom in close.
- Run the focus ring quickly back and forth to find where focus is sharpest.
- Zoom back to the size of shot you want.

The editor may take the opportunity to edit out this procedure and instead cut from, say, your wide shot to your close shot. If you think this likely, choose a dead spot in the action to carry out the focus check, and zoom back and reframe as quickly as possible.

HANDHELD SHOTS

Very important: treat handheld shooting *as a series of static compositions linked by efficient and tasteful movements*. Each should take its movement cue, where possible, from subject movement within the frame. When you want to pan from looking one direction along a road to another, wait for a passing vehicle to "carry" or motivate the pan movement. If you want to track through guests at a party, find someone to follow, who will serve as apparent motivation for the movement.

The worst misuse of a handheld camera is to make wobbly shots of buildings or landscapes. Our perception of such things, unless we are inebriated or staggering during an earthquake, is invariably that they are solid and secure. Commonsense dictates that the camera sees similarly, and that you place the camera on a stable support.

Long lenses always prove too unsteady for mobile handheld material, so use only your widest zoom setting, and create all necessary image size-changes by physically moving the camera toward or away from your subjects. Shooting handheld with a small camera often means holding it in front of your face, so your steadiness deteriorates as your arms get tired. For long-take work, consider a shoulder brace as in Figure 12-16.

WALKING A HANDHELD CAMERA

To make any handheld tracking shot, put all thoughts of dignity aside, and learn to walk like Groucho Marx. That is,

- Bend your knees a little so you glide, and don't bob up and down.
- Turn your feet a little outwards, duck fashion, then walk placing your feet in a straight line so you don't sway from side to side.
- Draw (don't lift) each foot over the floor surface, in order to,
  - Make an imperceptible weight transfer from foot to foot, and avoid any stomping or rocking
- Feel any bump or stair ahead with your foot before having to deal with it

Use the camerawork exercises to develop your skills (see Shooting Projects **SP-1–SP-3**).

CHECKING YOUR HANDHELD TRACKING SKILLS

With the camera angled toward a brick wall at around 3 feet distance, execute a 1 minute walking track, parallel with the wall. On playback, ask,

- Does the camera keep a fixed distance from the wall?
- Does the brickwork slide by level or is the camera swaying and bouncing?
- Is the movement speed-consistent?
- Did you remember to hold on a static shot of the wall before starting the movement, then hold on another static after you stopped?

Practice until you are using your body properly to execute steady tracking shots. Few camera operators do this really well.

TRIPOD PREPARATION

Always check horizontality of the tripod head using its spirit level. Set a degree of drag on both pan and tilt axes, and hold the pan-handle lightly with two fingers when you perform camera moves. Give the editor options by holding the shot for, say, 5 seconds *before* and *after* each movement. Novices move the camera too readily and overuse the zoom (yes, it's called "firehosing"). Poorly judged camera movements must often be edited out, while long, slow, uncertain camera movements make editing difficult or even impossible.

ERROR RECOVERY

Occasionally when making a camera movement, you will alight on an incorrect framing. If so, hold the erroneous composition for a few seconds and then imperceptibly "creep" the frame to its optimal proportions. If you recover too quickly and obviously, the audience will notice the error and henceforth feel insecure.

OPERATING WITH EDITING IN MIND

Whether you shoot off a tripod or handheld, make bold differences in image size. That is, make a clearly differentiated wide shot (WS), medium shot (MS), and close shot (CS). For a special moment there's also big closeup (BCU), also known as an ECU or extra close up.

Why do bold image size differences matter? Because only large size differences cut well together. When the size-change is insufficient, two shots of a statue (for instance) will cut together poorly, looking tentative or even like an ugly jump-cut.

INSERTS AND CUTAWAYS

Before allowing the crew to *wrap* (finish the day's shoot), cast your mind back over events just filmed and itemize what special shots you might need to enable ellipsis- or cross-cutting.

Your editing can nearly always benefit from *cutaway shots* or *inserts* (sometimes called *cut-ins*). How are cutaways and insert shots different? An *insert* shot is an enlargement of something already visible in the main frame, such as a page of the book that someone is reading. A *cutaway* is a shot of something outside the frame, such as the wall clock that somebody looks out of frame at. Shoot it from her eyeline as safety coverage.

During a scene I once directed of a carpenter in his workshop talking to camera, he was folding and unfolding something below frame that made a clicking noise while he spoke (*A Remnant of a Feudal Society*, GB, 1970, Figure 12-22). The cutaway we took of his hands folding and

FIGURE 12-22

(A) A carpenter talking to camera, and (B) the cutaway of his hands audibly clicking his ruler outside the close-up frame.

unfolding his carpenter's ruler enabled me to visually explain the offscreen noises, and also conceal that we cut to another section of interview.

CAMERA OPERATOR'S CHECKLIST

Among the Checklists at this book's website (www.directingthedocumentary.com) is a lengthy one for anyone operating a camera.

HANDS-ON LEARNING

For composition study, try **AP-4 Picture Composition Analysis**, and perhaps try a piece like *Inside Llewyn Davis* (Coen Brothers, USA, 2013) for its celebrated cinematography, or Alexander Payne's *Nebraska* (USA, 2013). Both films have many scenes of vernacular realism and represent a very high level of film craft. As handheld camera practice, try **SP-1 Skills: Handheld Camera Track on Static Subject, SP-2 Skills: Handheld Tracking Moving Subject,** and **SP-3 Skills: Handheld Back-Tracking with Moving Subject.** They will start getting you acclimatized to integrating your camerawork with a world that moves in its own way.

CHAPTER 13

DIRECTING

Directing for the first time is a lonely and exposed experience. For other people's experiences in every aspect of making contemporary documentary, go to The D-Word website at www.d-word.com and search their voluminous archives for your own needs and interests. It is a wonderful resource, and a great place to go online to seek specialized advice.

DIRECTING PARTICIPANTS

CREATING TRUST

Normally you develop relationships of trust during the research period, but sometimes you will shoot a particular scene or topic with someone you have just encountered. You will have to convince them that something about their lives is valuable for other people to see or know about. You can for instance film an old man feeding his dog, and talking to it, because he senses you know it's a special part of a special life. A taxi driver will happily chat to the camera while cruising for a fare because that is his daily reality and it pleases him to share it. You may even discreetly film a woman relaxing in her morning bath because it was in this very bath that she took the momentous decision to visit Egypt.

People will let you and your camera explore their lives whenever they sense that you and your crew personally accept, like, and value them.

A DOCUMENTARY IS A RECORD OF RELATIONSHIPS

Your success at making documentaries often depends on what took place before the camera was ever switched on. For this reason I have always avoided topics or participants for which I feel little interest or empathy. Not always, though. I once embarked with very mixed feelings on a BBC film *The Battle of Cable Street* (GB, 1969, Figure 13-1) in which the central figure was the renegade aristocrat Sir Oswald Mosley, leader of the 1930s British Union of Fascists. I was shocked that while I grew up, my parents and their generation had said not a word about fascism existing in Britain. My researcher Jane Oliver and I set about finding people who had taken part in the decisive anti-Semitic street confrontation, in particular those among Mosley's followers. They turned out to be shockingly ordinary; no horns or cloven feet to be seen. They wanted to present their case, which even made sense in a specious way. Jane and I meanwhile played the part of innocent

FIGURE 13-1

The British Fascist leader Sir Oswald Mosley. *(Frame from* The Battle of Cable Street.*)*

youngsters learning history from its protagonists. In the end I interviewed Mosley himself. His reputation was that of an urbane, upper-crust swaggerer with an egomaniacal sense of importance about everything connected with himself. I felt apprehensive—less over his followers' reputation for violence, or by revulsion for their values, than from fear of his reputation for squashing interviewers. So, instead of trying to trick or expose him, I simply encouraged him to explain the events for which his published accounts seemed farthest from reality.

During the lengthy editing period afterwards, the editor and I grew fascinated and repelled. To relay Mosley's version of the 1936 events, yet show its delusional nature, we juxtaposed his account with those of other witnesses and participants. Metaphorically speaking, he hanged himself on the rope we gave him. The film pleased the Left, which opposed the freedom Mosley had been given by the police to organize racial hatred, and it pleased Mosley, who had expected to have his account distorted.

IN SEARCH OF NATURALNESS

People often ask, "How do you get people to look so natural in documentaries?" Of course, you want to shake your head and imply long years spent learning professional secrets. Actually, this is much easier to achieve than, say, a satisfactory dramatic structure, but it still takes some basic directorial skills. The key lies in the way you brief your participants, as we shall see.

Interviewing is a way to give direction to a documentary, and gripping films by Errol Morris, Michael Apted, or Werner Herzog sometimes contain little else. In an oral history piece, little other than the grizzled survivors may exist, so talking heads may be all you can really show. Most directors, intent on sparing the audience from the hypnotic intensity of being talked at for long periods, take pains to show people active in their own settings, doing what they normally do. The audience prefers, I think, to judge character and motivation from what people do, rather than from what they say. Film can capture behavior beautifully, so documentary directors try to *make sure that participants have familiar things to do*, things that set them at ease.

So you decide to shoot your subject in three ways: relaxing with his family at home, collaborating with a fractious employee at work, and playing pool with cronies in a neighborhood bar. These situations won't get beyond stereotype unless you can make them yield something unusual and striking. There is also a slight hitch: your subject feels most normal when nobody is watching him. Once he's under scrutiny by your camera, his sense of self goes to pieces. This happened once to me. Filming in a glass-door factory, we turned our camera on a lady who had spent years passing frames through a machine. To her intense embarrassment, the frames began to jam or miss the jet of rubber sealer solution. It happened because she was now *thinking* about her actions and watching herself do them, instead of just doing them automatically. Feeling she must "act," she lost automatic harmony with her machine, and all I could do was reassure her that this sometimes happens. We simply waited until she managed a few rounds in her old rhythm.

GIVING PARTICIPANTS WORK

Make sure your participants have familiar tasks to do, even while they talk to your camera. For every action sequence, have some suggestions lined up in case you sense self-consciousness. I should have asked the lady in the factory to mentally count backward in sevens, or to discuss her shift with a colleague, to help move her mind away from the disturbing idea that she was being filmed.

INTERVIEWING IN BRIEF

Interviewing is a highly productive skill, and **Chapter 31: Conducting and Shooting Interviews** in Book II is devoted to the subject. For this, your early work, here are some commonsense reminders:

Preparation

- Know what you want to explore or find out.
- Make a list of questions on an index card.

Before you roll camera

- Let your interviewee know in general what specially interests you.
- Try *not* to use your question list since working from a list will seem formal.
- Instead, keep it handy on your knee in case your mind goes blank.

Beginning the interview

- Stay relaxed and natural, so tension in you does not affect your interviewee.
- Maintain supportive eye contact throughout.
- React and interact facially but not vocally (see "Avoiding Voice Overlaps" below).
- Using stimulating questions, evoke answers on everything you want explored.

Ending

- Glance at your question list to ensure you overlooked nothing important.
- Before calling "Cut," ask interviewee if there is anything he/she wants to add.

AVOIDING VOICE OVERLAPS

If you mean to edit out your questions, it will be *important that your voices never overlap*. Each new answer from the interviewee must have a clean start with no voice overlaps, and no beginning that depends on your question. You can try asking interviewees to incorporate your question's information in their answer, but they nearly always forget.

If, for instance, you ask "Tell me about your first job" you might get an answer that starts, "Well, it was in a school bus company, and I had to…" Without your question, this is incomprehensible. So you ask him to start again, suggesting he begin with, "My first job was…" As the interviewer you must listen for comprehensive, clean starts to each answer, and to interrupt and restart the interviewee as necessary. It's also your job not to trample on their outgoing words, since this too is an overlap.

SILENCE IS GOLDEN

Very important—as the interviewer, *do not be afraid of silences*. Stay with each issue until you are certain the interviewee has said all she is willing to say. If you suspect there's more to come, *wait*. You can sometimes prompt by saying "And…?" Using digital media means that waiting costs nothing, and you're going to edit the material anyway. A pause is not a failure—it's being considerate, and often by waiting you get gold.

WINDING UP GRACEFULLY

It is good manners and good policy to ask at the end, "Did we cover everything you wanted to say?" This signifies openness and an attitude of shared control. It also leaves on record that you gave the interviewee full opportunity to supplement or modify all that went before.

FILMING IN INSTITUTIONS OR ORGANIZATIONS

Organizations, especially those operating in extreme situations, may be more paranoid than individuals. At any time they may want you to explain in writing why you are filming this topic or that scene, or say they "must see your script." Keep any explanations general, simple, and uncontroversial, especially written ones. You should be consistent (because participants compare notes) but not so specific that you box yourself into a corner.

DIRECTING THE CREW

COMMUNICATION

Day-to-day direction while shooting should begin from a comprehensive printed schedule with timely updates in cases of change. Include travel directions and everyone's cell phone number, in case vehicles get separated. Put everything in writing since shooting is no time to test people's powers of recall.

Ideally you involve the crew in developing the film's approach, but if you shoot for television you may get an assigned crew. If so, outline the intended filming for the day, and keep the crew abreast of developments—something I sometimes forgot when pressure mounted.

WHO IS RESPONSIBLE FOR WHAT

Be formal about the chain of responsibility at first, and relax the traditional structure only when things are running well. If instead you start informally then find you must tighten up, you will meet with great resentment.

Once the crew assembles at the location, privately reiterate the immediate goals. You might for instance want a store to look shadowy and fusty, or to emphasize a child's view of the squalor in a trailer park. Confirm the first setup, so the crew can get the equipment ready. A clear working relationship with your director of photography (DP) will relieve you from deciding a myriad of details. Never forget that your main responsibility is toward participants and the authorial coherence of the film.

WORKING ATMOSPHERE

The transition to shooting should hide the excitement and tension you may feel and instead be a time of relaxed, professionally focused attention. You and your crew, incidentally, should all wear soft shoes that let you move noiselessly. Shooting should take place in as calm an atmosphere as possible, and the crew should convey warnings or questions to you by discreet whispers or through agreed hand signals. The sound recordist may hold up three fingers to indicate that only 3 minutes of memory remain, or the camera operator may make a throat-cutting gesture with eyebrows raised (meaning, "Shall I cut the camera?").

CREW UNITY

Many situations—with the public or with participants—are potentially divisive, so only the director should give out information or make policy decisions. The crew preserves outward unity at all costs, and makes no comment that could undermine anyone's authority or sow the seeds of discord. They should be scrupulous about keeping disagreements from the participants, whose concentration depends on a calm and professional atmosphere.

When student crews break down it is often because somebody considers himself more competent than the director. As difficulties arise, well-meaning but contradictory advice alights on the director, creating alarm and despondency among participants and crew alike.

CHECK THE SHOT

Whenever the camera is on a tripod, make a habit of checking the cinematographer's compositions before you shoot, because afterwards it will be too late. At the end of the shot, look through the viewfinder again to check the ending composition. Some camera operators may imply you don't trust them because of this. Insist, since it is you who will be responsible, not them. After a while you'll find checking is seldom necessary.

RUN-UP

Each time you give the command "Roll camera," allow a few seconds of equipment run-up time before saying the magic word "Action" to your participants. Today's cameras reach speed almost instantaneously, but during action immediately following a startup the camera may have problems of color or picture instability, so wait a few seconds. Under "The Countdown to Shooting" in **Chapter 29: Organization, Crew, and Procedures for the Larger Production** is the more elaborate procedure you need when you start up separate camera and sound recorder in a "double system" recording.

POSITIONING YOURSELF

Whether the camera is tripod-mounted, or handheld, position yourself just to its left so you can see what it sees, and also be close enough to whisper to the operator. Be ready to move quickly, should the camera wheel around.

CREW ETIQUETTE

To avoid distracting participants while shooting, each crew member makes no unnecessary movements, maintains a professionally neutral expression, and stays away from participants' eyelines. Even when something funny happens, the crew tries to remain silent and expressionless. If instead you react like an audience, participants will quickly take their cue and henceforth try to entertain you.

COMMUNICATING WITH THE CAMERA OPERATOR

Ahead of a shot, tell the operator briefly what you expect to happen and how you want it to look. Rather than micromanage, make your overall intention clear so that he or she can adapt to the unexpected. Once the camera is running, whisper any necessary further instructions into the camera operator's ear, being careful that your voice does not spoil a recording. Give brief, concrete instructions: "Go to John in medium shot," "Pull back to a wide shot of all three," or "If he goes into the kitchen again, walk with him and follow what he does." Often you must trust the operator's judgment, or risk sowing confusion.

COMMUNICATING WITH THE SOUND RECORDIST

Whenever the camera is running you communicate with sound personnel using hand or facial signals. If the camera is handheld, the recordist already has much to do—adapting to the action, covering what the camera needs, and staying out of frame. She will shoot you meaningful glances now and then, growing noticeably agitated at the approach of a plane or the rumble of a refrigerator turning itself on in the next room. Wearing headphones, she won't know what direction the interference is coming from.

  Once, shooting a former policeman in a raucous London pub, an incredulous look stole over the recordist's face as a drinker in the next bar lost his investment, followed by the clank of cleanup operations with a mop and bucket. The interviewee was still talking, having noticed nothing, but the recordist was peering around apprehensively. It took great self-control not to howl with laughter. In circumstances like this, the recordist normally draws a finger across his throat, and mimes whether to call "Cut!" What should you do?

SENSORY OVERLOAD

You have many immediate decisions to make, and your head pounds from stress. You are supposed to be keenly aware of ongoing content and yet must resolve through glances and hand signals problems of sound, shadows, escaped pets, or other versions of the unexpected. At such times you are half-blind from sensory overload and can only stagger onward.

BREAKS

When you direct, you are fully involved all the time and tend to overlook mere bodily interruptions like hunger, cold, fatigue, and bathroom breaks. If you want a keen and happy crew, stick to 8-hour days, and build meals and breaks predictably into the schedule. On long shoots away from home, allow the crew time off to buy presents as peace offerings to their loved ones.

WHO ELSE CAN CALL "CUT!"

Nobody but the director can call "Cut!" unless you've agreed the right to do so beforehand. The camera operator, for instance, might abort the scene if some condition that only she can see makes it pointless to continue. An arbitrary halt, however, may damage a participant's confidence, so it's nearly always best to keep rolling. Sometimes a participant, unhappy with something said or done, may call "Cut!" and you then have no option but to comply. Do not however encourage participants to take over your role.

SOUND PRESENCE

Warn participants that you have to shoot *presence tracks*. When the time comes, everyone stands in eerie silence for a couple of minutes. You are uncomfortably aware of your own breathing and all the little sounds in the room until the recordist calls "Cut!"

Record a minute or two of presence at each location and for each mike position. Called variously *presence*, *buzz track*, *room tone*, or *ambience*, this is background atmosphere inherent to the location. All locations, even those indoors, have their own characteristic presence, and you must shoot one per scene. Collecting some from every location and every mike setup ensures that the editor can always fill in spaces or make other track adjustments. For more information, see **Chapter 10: Capturing Sound** and **Chapter 28: Advanced Location Sound**.

SECURING THE PERSONAL RELEASE

Once you finish shooting with anyone, ask them straightaway to sign a personal release document. You won't have legal problems unless people think you have tricked them, or you get involved with those who nurture the (not unknown) fantasy that you are going to make a lot of money selling their footage. Cast participants with this in mind! There are various approaches to getting clearance.

(a) Some documentarians carry a release statement in a notebook and each new participant signs under previous signatures. As door-to-door canvassers know, people sign more willingly when they see friends or neighbors have signed before them. A signature gives you the right to make public use of the material in return for a purely symbolic sum of money, such as $1. It does not however immunize you against legal action should you misuse the material or libel the signatory.

(b) Some documentarians get a *verbal release* by asking participants to say on camera that they are willing to be filmed and that their name and address is such-and-such. This certainly guards against claims later that they "didn't know they were being filmed." A verbal release does not however explicitly release you in all the ways that a lawyer would want, nor does it guard against people deciding later they don't want to participate—thus rendering months of work void.

(c) A signature on the brief release version in Table 13-1 will suffice for your first productions, but any work for broadcasting will require a form whose pages of legalese send ordinary mortals pale with alarm. For full-length location and personal release forms, see this book's website (www.directingthedocumentary.com).

"IT'S A WRAP"

Once you have shot the scene, and all necessary materials are "in the can," it is time to strike (dismantle) the set or otherwise move on (Figure 13-2). Be sure you shot presence track, then call "It's a wrap!" Everyone starts their winding-up responsibilities:

• Lower the lights and roll up cables while any hot lighting fixtures cool off.
• Strike the set, collect clamps, stands, and boxes.
• Take the camera off its support, dismantle it, stow it in its protective travel boxes.
• Stow sound and lighting equipment in their own travel boxes.
• Replace furniture and household goods exactly as you found them.
• Confirm the schedule for the next day's shooting.

Before you leave,

- Check the location is undamaged and everything is clean and tidy.
- Thank each participant and each person in the unit for a good day's work.

TABLE 13-1 Short Personal Release Form suitable for student productions.
See the website (www.directingthedocumentary.com) for a professional-level
equivalent—its legalese can intimidate those contributing to modest productions

Personal Release Form
For the sum of $_____ consideration received, I give _____ Productions, its successors and assigns, my unrestricted permission to distribute and sell all still photographs, motion-picture film, video recordings and sound recordings taken of me for the screen production tentatively entitled _____ Signed _____ Name (Please print) _____ Address _____ _____ Date _____ Signature of parent or guardian _____ Name (Please print) _____ Witnessed by _____ Date _____

FIGURE 13-2

Fully equipped documentary crew moving on to the next location. *(Photo Camille Zurcher/Colectivo Nomada.)*

ASSURING QUALITY

FEEDBACK

When participants are out of earshot, encourage the crew to freely discuss the production, because you often learn things from them. Don't be shocked if they lack a holistic grasp. The cause is simple: fully engaged crew members each have particular areas to monitor.

Camera operator watches for lighting, focus, compositions, framing, movements, and whether the mike is edging into shot.

Sound recordist listens for unwanted reverb or echo; ambient noise; mike handling sounds; sound consistency from shot to shot; voice quality; and the relativity of sound levels.

Director monitors the scene for content, subtext, and emotional intensity. What does this add up to, so far? What meanings are taking shape under the surface as *subtext*? Where is the scene going? Is this what I expected? Does it deliver what I hoped, or is this something new?

Neither camera nor sound personnel can possibly have a balanced awareness of film content, so don't expect it of them. They will, however, have noticed all sorts of things that have escaped you.

REINFORCING THE PURPOSE OF THE SHOOT

Crewmembers at work monitor a restricted area of *quality*, so you should periodically reconnect them to the project as a conceptual entity. Not everyone will appreciate your efforts. In "the industry" there is sometimes a veiled hostility by which "tekkies" separate themselves from "arty types" and vice versa. Your crew may never have had their opinions sought outside their own area of expertise. From being treated like factory hands they may not have considered filmmaking from a directing standpoint, so be ready to meet hesitant or even hostile reactions to your efforts. Persist. If you want a crew whose eyes, ears, and minds extend your own, share your thinking with them.

Acknowledge crew feedback gratefully—even when it's embarrassingly off target. Make mental adjustment for any skewed valuations and be diplomatic with advice you can't use. Above all, encourage involvement, and don't retreat from communicating.

HANDS-ON LEARNING

If you haven't yet done **AP-2 Making a Floor Plan,** this is a good time to try it. You might also use **DP-8 Dramatic Form** to bring out any latent dramatic elements in your subject. This would be a good time to start interviewing with **SP-10 Interview, Basic, Camera on Tripod.**

PART 5

POSTPRODUCTION

Postproduction is the extremely creative phase in documentary-making during which you transform the sound and picture dailies, along with any graphics, text, captions, photographs, or animation, into a stream of consciousness for consumption by an audience. Editing a documentary is normally a long, experimental procedure, and represents your second chance to direct. The major challenge usually lies in finding a strong, logical narrative structure. Some films have their temporal spine usefully predetermined because their subjects follow a well-defined process, such as rescuing miners after a mining accident, or a youthful oboe player taking an all-important music exam. Other, less process-oriented films—about researching traditional weaving processes, say, or climate changes resulting from coal-fired generating plants—may have no obvious, inbuilt time progression as a narrative backbone, and so you have to look for an alternative. Life can prove very random, and films you shoot about it can be very ad hoc. Several times I have finished shooting with no clear idea of how to assemble my film, because shooting turned out so unlike what I anticipated. Editing is then like making a collage from found objects. These, placed experimentally in juxtaposition, eventually suggest what film narrative is possible and desirable.

This part of the book describes tried and tested operations that will help you find the wood among the trees. Your film's identity and purpose will assuredly emerge as you work on it—a truly fascinating experience.

CHAPTER 14

CREATING THE FIRST ASSEMBLY

Newcomers to editing usually do well, once they have mastered the editing software. Editing a documentary is similar no matter whether the film is long or short. Longer films require more complex structuring and of course a more extensive filing system.

Most operations described in this chapter are the small-unit editor's responsibility.

EDITING PERSONNEL, PROCESS, AND PROCEDURES

DIRECTOR-EDITORS

Under the rubric of economics, the director often becomes the editor. By all means edit your own work in the early stages, but when you move on to longer and more complicated projects, a one-man band can be folly. Every film benefits from the independently questioning viewpoint of an editor, and this is not a challenge for control, but a collaboration in which the editor is consciously a proxy for the audience. Having no prior investment in research and shooting, editors can often see ideas and solutions that surprise the director, who is often depressed from a sense of failed intentions while shooting. One of my most fruitful working relationships as a director was with an editor whose politics were quite different, and even opposed to my own. We liked and respected each other, so the creative tension between us kept me in useful proxy dialogue with those in my audience skeptical of my political and social outlook.

EQUIPMENT

Editing with nonlinear editing (NLE) software by Avid, Final Cut Pro, or Adobe Premiere is now ubiquitous and accessible. The early-established Avid system (Figure 14-1) is the front-runner in performance and user friendliness, but can prove costly in updates. It is the industry standard, so knowing it will be a large feather in your professional cap. Many documentarians however use Final Cut Pro (Figure 14-2) or Adobe Premiere Pro because of their lower cost (Figure 14-3).

USING TRANSCRIPTS

MAKING THEM

If you have much speech in your film, transcribing your participants' every word will be invaluable to grasping all that is there. It sounds tedious, but is never as laborious or unrewarding as people

FIGURE 14-1

What the Avid® user sees.

FIGURE 14-2

The main window of Final Cut Pro®.

fear: it has its own fascinations, saves work later, and ensures you miss few opportunities. If your film involves court testimony, the actual words people use will be paramount, and transcribing them unavoidable. **Chapter 32: From Transcript to Assembly** describes how to make a whole first assembly from edited transcripts.

FIGURE 14-3

The Adobe Premiere Pro® interface.

A WORKAROUND SOLUTION TO TRANSCRIBING

Instead of verbatim transcripts, you can log stretches of discussion or interview by *topic categories*. You summarize topics covered during each scene or interview, and log these by approximate time-code in- and out-points. That will give quick access to any given subject, but you will then need to make decisions by ear during editing, which is hard labor of a different stripe.

TRANSCRIPTS CAN BE MISLEADING

Using transcripts too literally has some dangers: words that look significant on paper sometimes prove anemic on the screen, and vice versa. The act of transcribing always invites a degree of literary organization—the more so if the original scene took place impulsively and chaotically. When voices overlap, or people use special nuances or body language, transcripts mislead by interpreting reality. Also, *how* somebody says something can be more telling than *what* is said, since we qualify what we say with our faces and bodies. A transcription never conveys all the subtext.

POSTPRODUCTION OVERVIEW

Videomaker (www.videomaker.com) has excellent articles and reviews on everything for digital production and postproduction, and through its website one can find very helpful filmmaking videos. Try Google "Groups" to locate users of your particular software; often this yields answers at dead of night when you're ready to tear your hair out. Likewise, entering a problem or procedure in YouTube.com often brings up a medley of instructional or demonstration videos.

The work of the editor and editing crew includes the following:

- Digitizing from the camera storage medium to the computer hard drives.
- Synchronizing sound with action (necessary if sound acquisition was via a separate "double system" recording).
- Screening dailies for the director and producer's choices and comments.
- Logging material in preparation for editing.
- Making an editing script, unless the director and/or writer makes one.

Making a first assembly.

- Evolving the first assembly to a rough cut.
- Evolving the rough cut to a fine cut.
- Supervising, with the director, the recording of narration (if there is one).
- Locking picture in preparation for any narration and music recording.
- Preparing for and supervising, with the director, any original music recording.
- Laying sound tracks (finding, recording, and laying components of multi-track sound such as atmospheres, backgrounds, and sync effects in preparation for the sound mix).
- Supervising, with the director, the sound engineer's mix-down of these tracks into one smooth final track.
- Obtaining titles and graphics.
- Supervising color correction with the cinematographer.
- Finalizing postproduction and supervising the making of release copies, safety masters, etc.

On a large project, postproduction is handled by specialists, but on low-budget projects the editor wears several hats. Such intensive exposure to the bone and muscle of screen creation can quickly turn you into a first rate editor, especially if you become good at solving the structural and dramatic problems that documentaries always pose. Such experience is the finest preparation for directing them.

FORESTALLING WORKFLOW PROBLEMS

The first step will be to transfer all selected material to the editing computer's hard drive. Check assiduously that your editing software can handle not only the camera format, but also those archive sources such as analogue video, photographic files, and scanned film of various formats. Older material will be in antiquated screen aspect ratios, and older editing software may need modification to handle a newer camera codec.

Watch out! Your *workflow* can easily get complicated and very expensive if you decide to integrate, for instance, NTSC (American standard video) at 30 frames per second (fps), with film scanned from 25 fps PAL (European) video, as well as stills in JPEG file format and others in Windows BMP (bitmap) format. Add to this that your main footage is in 24p HD (24 frames per second progressive scan high definition) and that you would like the opportunity to distribute on Blu-Ray, and your workflow has now turned into a minefield. You will be courting disaster if you kick the can down the road and deal with problems as they arise.

The solution is to first research other people's advice and experience thoroughly. For now, especially if you have little experience, treat yourself kindly by keeping your technological pathway simple. Follow whatever experienced users recommend. For more on this see **Chapter 35: Editing Refinements and Structural Solutions.**

LOW RESOLUTION EDITING

It may be an advantage when editing HD material to edit in "lo res" (low resolution) since this permits much faster computer operations. Later, use the edit decision list (EDL) to re-digitize only the material used in the cut. The computer will then reassemble the edit at high resolution.

DIGITIZING

Your dailies will probably be shot by one camera and therefore in a common digital format. This should easily transfer into your NLE program without any file conversions. Material shot in other formats, or with other picture or sound codecs, may require *transcoding* before it will integrate with the bulk of your material. Organize the material by digital folders called *bins*, each containing a major sequence or classification of material (Figure 14-4). Logging the material by shots or sections helps you memorize all the materials available, and puts the material at your fingertips.

SYNCHRONIZING SOUND

If you shot "double system" (shot sound with an additional and separate audio recorder) then you will have used a clapper or timecode marking system while shooting. This is mandatory in order to identify each sound segment. Then during postproduction you synchronize each shot with its appropriate track, putting each take in sync by lining up the crack of the clapper bar with the first picture frame in which it is visibly closed. Over long takes, keep a weather eye open for creeping sync (drifting out of sync).

During doublesystem recording, camera operators often leave the deck mike open, thus recording a *scratch track*, a back-up useful when shooting conditions left separately recorded sound materials chaotic and without announcements or clapper sync points.

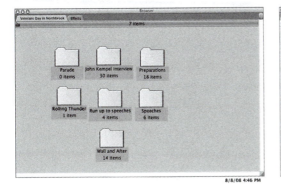 

FIGURE 14-4

FCP project bins and the shots in one of them.

LOGGING AND CATEGORIZING THE MATERIAL

We call the unique, time-related number assigned by the camera to each video frame *timecode*; it is the ID by which the editing program handles all that goes into compiling its *edit decision list* or EDL.

Log each scene, important action, or event, so you can find it later. Keep descriptions brief—they only need remind you what to expect. For example,

01:00:00	WS (wide shot) man at tall loom.
01:00:30	MS (medium shot) same man seen through weaving threads.
01:00:49	CS (close shot) man's hands with shuttle.
01:01:07	MS as he works. Stops, rubs eyes.
01:01:41	His POV (point of view) of his hands & shuttle.
01:02:09	CS feet on treadles (MOS).

The figures are hours: minutes: seconds. Timecode ends with a frame count, but in a content log you don't need hair-splitting accuracy. The example explains standard shot abbreviations except the last. In Britain the expression for "shot without sound" is "mute," but America still enshrines its German immigrant directors' call of, "Mit out sound!"—abbreviated to MOS.

Logs, bins, and shot descriptions should help you locate material quickly, so it is good to design divisions, indexes, or color codes that assist the eye. The housekeeping you set up for a short production need not be as detailed as those for one longer, where the chance of being unable to find material becomes an employment hazard. Nothing is more humiliating than searching for a shot while your director, sponsor, or employer stares at their fingernails. Inadequate filing always exacts revenge because Murphy (of Murphy's Law) loves to lurk in sloppy filing systems.

VIEWINGS BEFORE YOU BEGIN THE ASSEMBY

Viewings during the editing process are an important forum for the exchange of impressions, ideas, and postmortem realizations. The processes below may seem like overkill for a short documentary, but become vital for anything more complex.

Screenings include various people and have various purposes. At any viewing you will learn much from sitting at the back and watching viewers' body language. It will prepare you for the thoughts, feelings, and observations soon to be articulated by your trial audiences.

CREW DAILIES-VIEWING SESSION

Even when crewmembers have seen dailies piecemeal, they should also see the entire dailies at a sitting or two after shooting ends. Everyone should see their patterns, limitations, and mistakes—not just the successful material in the final edit. The editor might attend this viewing, but discussion is likely to be a crew-centered postmortem that is not relevant to editing.

CREW REACTIONS

When the crew sees dailies, there will be useful debates over the effectiveness, meaning, or importance of different aspects of the material. Be ready for crewmembers to be partisan over filming situations and particular participants, and to harbor specific feelings about participants' credibility and motivations. Listen and don't argue, since similar thoughts may well occur to your future audience.

Keep in mind that the crew are less objective than you are. Until they see a cut, they don't see the film holistically from an audience perspective, but from the subjective immersion of their work. Not only have they developed feelings of relationship to the participants, they are deeply involved in their own discipline, and will often overestimate its positive or negative effects. That said, their insights do often include valuable revelations.

EDITOR AND DIRECTOR'S VIEWING SESSION

To find and agree on the general thrust of the material, you and your editor see all the dailies together. As you face the problems in the piece, your mind working overtime to find ways out, this is a stressful time, especially as you probably feel oppressed by failed goals. Maybe you see irritating mannerisms in one of the participants that you must cut around if he is not to appear shifty. Or, one of your two main characters is more interesting and articulate, and you must shift your original premise.

Listen to what your editor sees in the material, because a newcomer not involved with acquiring the material sees it with an objectivity and sense of possibility that a director simply cannot have.

View all the material again, scene by scene. Stop whenever necessary to thrash out each scene's problems and possibilities.

TAKING NOTES

During showings, the editor or an assistant keeps notes of the director's choices, comments, and any special cutting requests. If you must write notes, make large, scribbled notes on many pages of paper, so that your eyes almost never leave the screen. If you look away, you will undoubtedly miss important moments and nuances. The sum of the dailies viewing is a *dailies notebook* full of the director's and editor's choices and observations, as well as many glancing impressions of the movie's potential and deficiencies.

GUT FEELINGS MATTER

Note all emotional high points or unexpected outcomes, since these probably contain important clues whose meaning may not emerge until you work out later where they come from, and what they signify. Almost certainly they will be mainstays in the future film.

Note any unexpected moods or feelings. If you find yourself reacting with, "She seems unusually sincere here" or "I can't believe that really happened," then note it down. Afterwards one can easily doubt that your gut feelings really matter, and so you are apt to ignore and forget them. But seldom are these isolated personal reactions, since whatever triggered them lies embedded in the material, and will also strike first-time audiences. Later, when inspiration lags from over-familiarity, all your early perceptions will become useful navigation stars.

BEGINNING THE ASSEMBLY

Choose segments and lay them as a first loose assembly along the program's *timeline* (the horizontal line across the software screen that represents the advance of time, Figure 14-5). You will be able to lay the corresponding sound track opposite its picture, and to predetermine sound levels so you can hear a relatively layered and sophisticated track as you edit. Unlike film editing, in which the editor physically altered a workprint, a digital editing program stores versions as an Edit Decision List or EDL. This is a set of internally generated access instructions to the bank of shot materials. The pool of material itself remains pristine throughout editing, like a library consulted

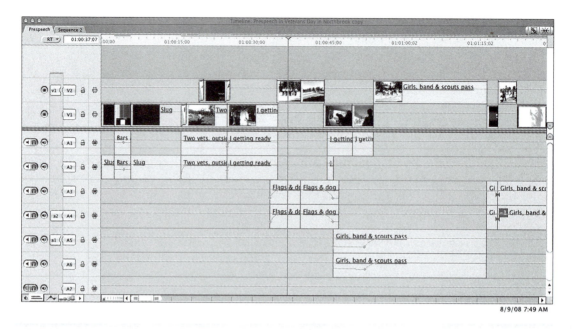

8/9/08 7:49 AM

FIGURE 14-5

FCP timeline with segments of picture and their sound track sections laid below.

but never emptied. Date each new version, and when the draft is complete, make a newly dated copy as the basis for starting the next draft. This will leave a trail of versions to which you (or your biographer…) may revert at any time. If you prefer an earlier sequence, it is straightforward to copy it from the earlier version of the timeline and paste it wholesale into the new version.

SEEKING A VISUALLY DRIVEN FILM

Now the director changes hats. No longer are you the instigator of the material: instead, you and your editor are surrogates for the audience. Every time you view parts of the film, or the whole in its entirety, you must try to *see it as if for the first time*.

If your film has sufficient imagery, and you first assemble all the film's usable visual and behavioral material, something rather exciting happens because you are starting from the strength of the cinema (imagery) rather than its weakness (talking heads). By choosing a likely time-structure and arranging the material in a loosely assembled flow, you are building a rough narrative out of behavior, action, imagery, and atmosphere. The more they lead your story, the more cinematic and memorable it will become.

At some point you will almost certainly need to draw on language, but you'll use it to supplement your visually established structure. How you do this depends on how you approached directing the subject, what you were able to shoot, how you organize the editing, and ultimately what Storyteller role you decide to play in relation to your audience.

Building a film from transcripts, however, leads to one stuffed with wall-to-wall talking. For movies based on hosts, performers, and interviews, no other kind of film is possible, and this includes any historical film for which little imagery is available. Some people telling stories are simply fascinating, but if you conceptualize a film starting with words and ideas, it will always

FIGURE 14-6 ——

Al Gore delivers an extended lecture in *An Inconvenient Truth*.

lead to illustrating them, which means taking the path of journalism, and privileging language over the visual. The difference is starkly apparent if you compare Godfrey Reggio's *Koyaanisqatsi* (USA, 1982) with Al Gore's *An Inconvenient Truth* (Davis Guggenheim, USA, 2006, Figure 14-6). Both deal with the rape of the environment, but while Reggio's film is a visual tragedy of operatic proportions, Gore's is a one-man performance piece, as passionate as any revivalist meeting, but afterwards utterly forgettable. Reggio's film lives on in memory, Guggenheim's does not.

THE ONLY FILM IS IN THE DAILIES

Your whole filmmaking world, for the time being, exists within those dailies that you shot. So, purge yourself of prior knowledge and intentions, since the audience's whole understanding and feeling must arise from the screen. Besides, nobody wants to hear your war stories about what you intended, or what you could have produced.

RENDERING

This is the process in which the computer pauses, sometimes for unimaginably long periods, to knit its brows over making new files for shots that combine elements in some way, such as titling, or optical effects like fades and dissolves. Have other things ready to do!

FINDING A STRUCTURE

WHY STRUCTURE MATTERS

A gripping narrative feels charged with forward momentum because, one way or another, it promises a meaningful experience of some kind. Michael Angus and Murray Fredericks' *Salt* (Australia, 2009, Figure 14-7) does it visually. It fills us with curiosity as a waterscape reflecting the sky slowly yields a tiny figure riding a bike towards us through a vast salt lake only inches deep. Who is he? Where is he? Why does he return year after year to live in a tiny tent under the dome of the heavens and photograph the phenomena of nature? It proves to be an anguished spiritual quest

FIGURE 14-7

Mystery and a driven man in *Salt*.

and not just one of curiosity, and it leaves him on the mobile phone, struggling to explain his absences to his wife, angry that he leaves her with their family every summer.

If you managed to realize your directorial goals while shooting, structuring the assembly may be straightforward. More often, your intentions were frustrated by the unexpected, and now you must pick yourself up and make something of what you actually filmed. Editing is your chance to regain control.

TIME AND STRUCTURAL ALTERNATIVES

Identifying a structure for your footage begins with deciding how it should handle time, since temporal progression is an all-important organizing feature in any narrative. To develop a structure for your film, try asking yourself:

- What makes the best overall story from your dailies?
- What different ways could you tell it?
- Whose story is it?
- In what order should you show cause and effect?
- What advantage lies in altering the natural or chronological sequence of events?
- Should you use *parallel storytelling* to run two narratives concurrently?

FINDING AN ACTION-DETERMINED STRUCTURE

If you have plenty of action and visual sequences, put a rough assembly together of observational material alone, and then view it without stopping. Then ask yourself,

- What is the thrust of this material? Does it, for instance, tell a story, convey a mood, introduce a society, or set an epoch?
- What memorable interchanges or developments did I capture on-camera? This, of course, will probably take pride of place because it's your strongest and most persuasive "evidence."

- What period does my material span, and how well does the assembly convey this? (It's often helpful to a narrative if its events are pressurized by happening in a set time period.)
- What would your film convey if it were a silent film? (This is the acid test by which to recognize whether your material can be made cinematic rather than literary, theatrical, or journalistic.)
- How many phases or chapters does the material fall into, and what characterizes each?

Once you have revised and considered your rough assembly of visual and behavioral material, you can ask:

- What verbal material, as yet unused, could I employ to bring further dimensions to the "silent film" assembly so far made?
- What new dimensions does the original action- and behaviorally based film acquire? (Make a new working hypothesis.)
- How little speech material do I need to shift the film farther toward something articulate?

Beginning from visual and behavioral evidence lets imagery suggest the story. By bringing a few words to your behavioral assembly, and perhaps by using voice-over rather than "talking heads," you can portray characters who seem to be speaking from their interior lives rather than interacting conventionally with an interviewer.

USING A SPEECH-BASED NARRATIVE STRUCTURE

If your film is a historical retrospective, or one that scans many people's viewpoints, you will probably start by assembling interviews. Your best word-driven structure will likely develop during the intensive process of making a paper edit from transcripts (see **Chapter 32: From Transcript to Assembly**).

THE CONTRACT

Whatever story structure you find affects the *contract* you must strike with your audience. Yes, your audience expects a contract—an indication in the film's first moments of its premise, genre, and goals. This is your promise to keep up the *dramatic tension* that comes from having a good tale to tell. This, as we shall say in **Chapter 17: Point of View and Storytelling**, is part of your Ancient Mariner's skill at detaining the Wedding Guest. You may signal the contract in the film's title, spell it out in narration, imply it in the logic of the film's opening minute or two in a *prequel*, or otherwise as a *hook* by something shown, said, or done at the outset. Leo Tolstoy in his tale of the unhappily married woman Anna Karenina does it famously by beginning with, "Happy families are all alike; every unhappy family is unhappy in its own way." All good stories engage their audience, and your work must grab their attention right away since viewers can kill off your film with a single prod at the TV remote.

You'll find longer film structural types with examples in **Chapter 18: Dramatic Development, Time, and Story Structure**. The examples and discussion there may further help you decide what limitations or potential lie in your dailies. Ways to analyze your film and find alternative structures appear in **Chapter 35: Editing Refinements and Structural Solutions**.

STORIES NEED DRAMATIC TENSION

A story which is going somewhere, and which manifestly has a purpose, holds our attention from sequence to sequence if it is at all skillful, for *dramatic tension* is at the core of all effective

FIGURE 14-8

Michael Apted's classic *Up* series, a longitudinal study over decades that began in its subjects' childhood.

storytelling. With each sequence you should aim to create a question in the audience's mind—what will she do next? Will the check really be in the mail? Can the detachment hold out until the reserves arrive? Did he decide to stay or go?

STORIES NEED DEVELOPMENT

An important element in any story is that somebody in it should learn, grow, or develop—however minimally or symbolically. This, called the story's *development*, may take less obvious and even "negative" forms. In *Grizzly Man*, Treadwell's love of bears prevents him from protecting himself, a failure that leads to his destruction by them. Treadwell is opposing the rules of the universe, as the filmmaker and philosopher Michael Roemer would say (see "Plot and the Rules of the Universe" in **Chapter 18: Dramatic Development, Time, and Story Structure**). Such heroes are the norm in tragedy: their development lies in the central character's drive for a trial of strength and a showdown.

   A problem for many documentaries is that human change is often too slow to happen within an affordable shooting schedule, so development has to be implied rather than shown. Other films become *longitudinal studies* and chronicle their subjects' progress over years or decades. Michael Apted's *Up* series (GB, 1964–present, Figure 14-8) takes a group who were seven-year-olds in the early 1960s and revisits them every seven years, in each film intercutting their present most poignantly with their past, and showing the serpentine unfurling of destiny for each. Robb Moss's *The Same River Twice* (USA, 2003, Figure 14-9) takes a film about his friends in the late 1970s, who once rafted nude down the Colorado river together, and revisits five of them a quarter century later to see what they have done with their lives. How satisfying to see people exploring hopes, dreams, and betrayals over a such large chunk of their lives!

FIGURE 14-9

Where are they now? Robb Moss revisits companions of a youthful journey in *The Same River Twice*.

Longitudinal films are more feasible now filmmakers can own equipment of their own and start filming at the drop of a hat. Paradoxically, intermittent filming is easier for independents than for corporations—so often tied to industrial schedules and the need for immediate viewing figures.

- How will your film imply that someone has grown or changed, or has been defeated by fate?
- Who in your film needs to change, and who or what does change?
- Take advantage of literary, poetic, theatrical, musical, and other disciplines with parallel stories that can help you spot what is inherent in the story you are developing.

MICROCOSM AND MACROCOSM

To tackle a large, diffuse subject like industry polluting the water table, you must often find an example, a microcosm that will imply the macrocosm. Back when the UK was joining the European Common Market, I worked on a BBC series whose intention was to introduce aspects of French life to the British TV audience. Since we could not even begin to show all the different regions, we soon decided to confine ourselves to the capital. "Faces of Paris" thus showed aspects of France and French culture by showing the lives of interesting Parisians. You look for the particular to represent the universal, yet how typical is any Parisian? Whoever you choose only demonstrates how triumphantly atypical all examples really are.

In the relentlessly specific medium of film, making abstract generalizations is problematic. Writers solved similar problems in previous centuries. John Bunyan's *Pilgrim's Progress* (1678) is a journey of adventure, but it functions also as an allegory for the journey of the human spirit. The Maysles Brothers' superb *Salesman* (USA, 1969, Figure 14-10) does something similar by showing that a share in the American dream comes at the price of humiliation and moral surrender.

FIGURE 14-10

Humiliation and moral surrender in *Salesman*.

It achieves this by showing how every phase of door-to-door selling is driven by corporately dictated sales figures, something the Maysles Brothers had endured themselves when selling encyclopedias. Don't imagine that today's technology has simplified a storyteller's apprenticeship. Your models for strong narratives lie in expertise developed over centuries in all the time arts. Understand how they solved particular narrative problems, and you won't have to reinvent the wheel.

Fred Wiseman likes to use an observational camera and an allegorical "container" structure. That is, he films an institution and treats it as a complete and functioning microcosm of the larger society. The emergency room doors in *Hospital* (USA, 1970, Figure 14-11) admit the hurt, the wounded, the drug-overdosed, and the dying in a frightful vision of the violence, despair, and self-destruction stalking American urban society. Yet the same "institution as walled city" idea applied in the less obviously crisis-ridden *High School* (USA, 1968, Figure 14-12) seems diffuse and directionless. The relationship Wiseman wants us to notice between teachers and the taught is too low key, repetitive, and unremarkable to build much momentum or sense of development. I have a similar problem with Wiseman's *At Berkeley* (USA, 2013), made nearly a half-century later. His non-interventional approach and lack of guiding narration leaves him with few tools to focus, develop, and intensify the vital issues. He would probably retort that it's my job to work that out. And this is true.[1]

ASSEMBLING

Whether you found a structure by using a visual, behavioral approach, or a verbal one through transcripts, you can now roughly assemble the useable material. Don't agonize over the consequences of what you are doing. Leave everything long and expect repetition. You have two different accounts of how the dam broke? Slap both in, and decide which seems best onscreen.

Making the first assembly is the most exciting part of editing, because it is like a birth. Don't worry at this stage about length or balance. You should *see a whole assembly as soon as possible*

FIGURE 14-11 ——

The institution as window on urban violence, despair, and self-destruction in *Hospital*.

FIGURE 14-12 ——

High School——no place to learn democracy. *(Photo courtesy of Zipporah Films, Inc.)*

before doing detailed work on any sections. Only then can you make far-reaching resolutions about its future development. Of course, you will want to polish a favorite sequence, but fixing details is often a way to evade a confrontation with your film's lack of overall identity and purpose.

FACING THE FIRST ASSEMBLY

RETURN TO INNOCENCE

To judge a first assembly, try to purge all foreknowledge from your mind so you can see with the eyes of a first-time viewer. This unobstructed, audience-like way of viewing is a hard discipline to maintain, but one utterly necessary *every* time you run your film. What always helps is to have anyone present for whom the movie is new. Sit behind them and absorb their body language for clues. Even if they never utter a word, the presence of a newcomer somehow gives you fresh eyes.

After viewing the first assembly, your material will start telling you where and how to cut. This signals a welcome and slightly mysterious change in your role from proactive to reactive. Formerly you had to expend energy to get anything done, and now the energy starts to surge from the film itself, and you must struggle to keep up.

RECOGNIZING YOUR FILM'S IDEAL LENGTH

As your creation comes to life, early viewings begin to reveal its nature, dramatic shape, and optimal length. Look to the content of your film for guidance on length. Spend any time sitting on a festival jury and you will know that most documentaries are at least 30–50% too long. The director is the worst judge of length, and a film's natural span depends on the richness and significance of its content, as well as where an audience sees it. Audiences for television, cable, community cable, cinema, or YouTube all bring different expectations. Where does your project really belong? If your advisers can persuade you to recognize that your film has a 10-minute content, then you can get tough with that earnest 25-minute assembly and shape it for its most likely audience.

Where your film might be shown helps determine its length and structure:

* Classroom films are normally 10 to 20 minutes.
* Television uses 30-, 40- (in Europe), 60-, and 90-minute slots.
* Festivals, where reputations are made, love short films that say a lot: the shorter the better.
* Internet videos on YouTube, etc. have been limited to 10 minutes, but are getting longer.

As the Internet moves toward delivering full fidelity, longer and more substantial pieces will inevitably join the mercifully short ones. Nobody, however, will watch a longer film unless it exhibits the storytelling flair and craft sophistication that a general audience demands.

DIAGNOSTIC QUESTIONING

Immediately after this viewing, scribble a list of material making the most impact—you're going to use this list later. Facing your film in its crudest form, you must now elicit your own dominant reactions. Flush them out by asking:

Exposition:

* How much setup information should I give, and how soon?
* Who should give it?

- Does the audience presently get too much or too little? (A sequence may fail if its context is inadequately explained.)
- Can some be delayed? (Too much exposition too early can deluge viewers in information about people and issues they have not yet learned to care about.)
- Is it too clumped? (Consider thinning or holding back expository material until it's really needed. Make the audience work—they enjoy it.)

Characters and their point of view:

- Which participants held your attention, and which didn't? (Some may be more congenial or just better on camera than others.)
- Who is the story really about?
- Whose point of view should we mainly share? (The main character's? The director's? That of a secondary character?)

Content and meaning:

- What kinds of metaphysical allusions could my material make?
- Could I make use of connotation and metaphor?
- Are my film's values and beliefs emerging? (Use open rather than leading questions.)

Dramatic shape:

- Which parts of the film seem to work, which drag, and why? (This helps to assess whether the film's development is even, and to spot impediments in the film's momentum.)
- Was there a satisfying alternation of types of material? (Was similar material clumped indigestibly together? Where did you get effective contrasts and juxtapositions? Can you make more? Variety is as important to storytelling as to dining.)
- Does the film feel dramatically balanced? (That moving and exciting sequence in the film's middle may be making all that follows seem anticlimactic.)
- Were there any forces in opposition, and did they come into confrontation?
- When does the story move, and when does it hang?

WHAT WORKS AND WHAT DOESN'T

The human memory is a great editor because it discards whatever lacks meaning. From a screening, compare what left a strong impression against a full sequence list. What you "forgot" is failing to deliver for some reason. This does not mean it will never deliver, only that it's not doing so yet. Common reasons for material to misfire:

- Two or more sequences are making the same point (Repetition does not advance an argument unless there is escalation, so make choices and ditch what's redundant.)
- A climax is in the wrong place (If your stronger material peaks early, the remainder of the film becomes anticlimactic.)
- Tension builds then slackens (Plot your movie's rising and falling emotional temperatures: if it inadvertently cools before an intended peak, the viewer's response is seriously impaired. Sometimes transposing a couple of sequences can work wonders.)

- The film raises false expectations (A film, or part thereof, fails when you don't deliver what the viewer has been led to expect.)
- Good material is somehow lost on the audience (We read into film according to the context. A misleading setup, or a failure to direct attention to the right places, can make material fall flat.)
- Multiple endings (Decide what your film is really about and kill your darlings.)

If this list resembles traditional dramatic analysis, you are right. Like a playwright watching a first performance, your lifelong diet of drama sensitizes you to your assembly's faults and weaknesses. This is tricky ground because there are no objective measurements. All you can do is assess what you *feel* about your material's dramatic effectiveness.

THE DOCUMENTARIAN AS DRAMATIST

Where does the instinct for drama come from? Certainly we learn from all the entertainment we consume, beginning with nursery stories. Probably we have been hard-wired for drama since antiquity. Think of the Greek myths, Aesop's Fables, or Arthurian legends from the Middle Ages—they are still being adapted and updated after hundreds or even thousands of years, still giving new meaning and pleasure to people's lives. The nameless folk who shaped them are the giants upon whose shoulders we all stand, and the enduring presence of folk art—in plays, poetry, music, architecture, and traditional tales—should alert us to how many of our tastes are ancestral and shared with each other.

PLEASING YOUR AUDIENCE

Since the documentary is a tale about the actual that is consumed at a sitting, it probably carries on the oral tradition. Whenever it connects with the audience's emotional and imaginative life, it succeeds. One must concern oneself, therefore, with more than self-expression, which can be narcissistic. Instead, one must learn how best to entertain and enlighten an audience. Like other strolling players, the filmmaker has a precarious economic existence, and pleases the audience or goes hungry.

WHAT NEXT, WHEN THE DUST SETTLES?

After the first assembly, fundamental issues emerge. Maybe you see your worst fears: your film has no less than three endings. Your favorite character makes no impact at all beside others who seem more spontaneous and alive. You have to concede that a sequence in a dance hall, which was hell to shoot, has only one good minute in it. A woman you interviewed for a minor opinion actually says some striking things and is upstaging a contributor whom you considered more important.

Avoid trying to fix everything you now see wrong in one grandiose swipe. Also, forswear the pleasures of fine-tuning or you soon won't see the forest for the trees. Wait some days and think things over. Soon you'll be ready to tackle the major needs of the film.

HANDS-ON LEARNING

If you don't have a current working hypothesis, why not practice with **DP-3 Brief Working Hypothesis**? Then try using **DP-1 Dramatic Content Helper** to help put your ideas under dramatic expectation.

NOTE

1. See Matt Zoller Seitz's excellent and illuminating review, www.rogerebert.com/reviews/at-berkeley-2013.

CHAPTER 15

EDITING FOR REFINEMENT

Documentaries are largely created through intelligent editing, an alchemy that works magic and miracles. Few understand this until they take its long, exploratory journey for themselves.

Editing techniques are hard to grasp from a book, but you can see their results from films you admire. Work out for yourself how editing suggests eyes, ears, and the warmth of human intelligence working together, all guiding your attention toward hidden meanings. This elevated state is seldom even visible in early cuts of most documentaries. More often you seem stuck with a hopeless cause. Do not despair. The curse of the first assembly is its length and slowness, and we need to look at techniques that will move the story along faster.

COMPRESSING AND JUXTAPOSING

ELISION

Cutting from action to action, or sequence to sequence, parallels the way we mentally register our movement through a day, a vacation, or a visit to a new town. This principle called *elision* has the same effect as a photo album in which the owner has made a construct by compressing the essence of a wedding or holiday into a photomontage.

CUTTING BETWEEN SEQUENCES

If you are cutting from event to event, see if you can remove the front and end of each sequence, retaining only the heart of what counts in the emerging narrative. Try to enter the sequence when it is already in action, and leave before it concludes. The test is to ask whether the audience can (a) imagine how the sequence began and thus not need to see it, and (b) imagine how the sequence will end, and therefore need not see that either. Cutting from a man eating breakfast at home to him at the wheel of a truck is a way to elide (shorten) all the unimportant material and show only his relations with his family and what he does for a living.

CUTTING WITHIN A SEQUENCE

The breakfast can be compressed to essentials too. If you have handheld coverage of the whole 30-minute meal, and have moved the camera from angle to angle, you might only want to show that he has a wife and two daughters, is a fond parent who jokes with his children, and a husband who does the cooking. This you can do in perhaps four or five shots lasting a minute. Cut to interior truck!

ACTION-MATCH CUTTING

Much of human activity is repetitive, and if you shoot the breakfast in different angles and different-sized shots, you will find coffee pouring in wide shot and coffee pouring in a close shot. You can bridge the two shots together, and eliminate some time, providing:

- The action and settings match between the shots (both girls are still in their chairs).
- There is a good difference between the shots in size and/or in angle.
- You have a defined movement (beginning to pour coffee, say) to act as the *bridging action* between the two shots.

The perfect moment to make a match cut always comes at the psychological moment when the spectator mentally identifies the action to come:

- You see a coffee pot lifted and see it *just* begin tilting (ah, he's pouring coffee).
- You see someone cross a room, turn, and *just* begin bending their legs (ah, she's sitting down).
- You see a boxer stumble, turn, draw back his right arm, and *just* begin a thrust (ah, he's going for the other guy's jaw).

The precise moment when the action's purpose becomes evident is the precise moment to cut and *complete* the expected action in the new shot, whether it goes long to close shot, or close to long shot. Because the eye does not register a new shot's first frames, you must *repeat the action by two–three frames* if the action is to appear continuous. If instead you scientifically match the action, it will look jerky, as though frames are missing from the incoming shot. Try it for yourself.

So the match-cut rule is: Let the action initiate (that is, until we *just* recognize what's coming), then complete the action in the new shot. Repeat some frames in the incoming action to make the action across the cut appear smoothly continuous.

JUMP CUTTING

When a continuous shot has a stretch of time cut out, we call it a jump cut. If you cut from a kid first in his underwear, then wearing shirt, then adding pants, and finally a winter jacket all in the same shot, you have dressed your kid in three jump cuts for a winter journey to school, and the whole thing happens in a sprightly 10 seconds. For this we have the TV commercial to thank.

USING FAST OR SLOW MOTION

You can also use your editing software to complement the narrative by showing an action in fast or slow motion. Use fast motion to humorously speed up the banal, and slow motion to show us something significant in detail, such as a humming bird approaching a flower, or a train derailing on a bend. Again, these modes parallel the way our attention waxes and wanes according to the significance or otherwise of the action.

PARALLEL CUTTING

A useful way to abridge time is to take two simultaneous activities and cut back and forth between the two storylines, paring each down to essence by intercutting. In *Roger and Me* (USA, 1989) Michael Moore famously intercuts the GM choir singing sycophantically to chairman

FIGURE 15-1

While a choir serenades the GM chairman in *Roger and Me*, the sheriff evicts his laid off workers.

Roger Smith, "Santa Claus is coming to town," while a sheriff disconsolately evicts a former GM worker's family. Smith reads from Dickens' *Christmas Carol* while the sheriff's men pile the family's pathetic goods on the sidewalk, including their Christmas tree (Figure 15-1). It is a heartbreaking, maddening comparison, and Roger Ebert is right to call the film a revenge comedy.

CUTTING TO A RHYTHM

If you want a series of cuts to hit the beat of a jazz piece, or to happen on the rhythmic sounds of someone using an axe, you must position the cuts two–three frames *before* the actual "beat" frame. This is because human vision takes about 1/8th of a second to register a new image.

UNIFYING MATERIAL INTO A FLOW

After running your first assembly two or three times, it seems like clunky blocks of material with no flow. First you may have some illustrative stuff, then several blocks of interview, then a montage of shots, then another block of something else, and so on. Sequences go past like floats in a parade, each separate from its fellows. How to orchestrate sound and action, and create the effortless flow seen in other people's films?

This often means bringing together the sound from one shot with the image from another, but you cannot really work out counterpoint editing in a paper edit since it depends too much on the nuances of the material, but you can easily decide which materials should intercut well. The specifics emerge from the materials themselves, as we shall see when we come to overlap cutting.

THE AUDIENCE AS ACTIVE PARTICIPANTS

Notice that a demanding texture of word and image places the spectator in a more critical relationship to the "evidence." It expects an active rather than passive participation, and the implied contract is not to sit and be instructed, but to *interpret and weigh what you see and hear*. Sometimes the film uses action to illustrate, other times to contradict, what has seemed true. The teacher is a good man, but also an *unreliable narrator* whose words you cannot take at face value. However, whatever makes someone an unreliable narrator is going to be something intriguingly human.

There are other ways to stimulate the audience's imagination through changing the conventional coupling of sound and picture. For instance, in a street shot you might show a young couple we presume are lovers go into a café. They sit at a window table, but the camera remains outside near an elderly couple discussing the price of fish. The camera moves in close to show the couple talking affectionately to each other, but what we hear is the older couple bemoaning the price of cod. The result is ironic: in two states of intimacy, we see courtship, but hear the concerns of later life. With great economy of means, and not a little humor, a cynical idea about marriage is set afloat—one that the film might go on to dispel with more hopeful alternatives.

By juxtaposing materials and demanding that the audience interpret them, film can counterpoint antithetical ideas and moods, and kindle the audience's involvement with the dialectical nature of life itself.

THE OVERLAP CUT

A very useful editing trick is to change *straight cuts* (sound and picture cutting at the same moment) to *overlap cuts* (sound and picture cuts each staggered for a particular reason or effect). This mimics something we do all the time unawares.

MONO- AND BI-DIRECTIONAL ATTENTION

In life, if you notice, we often probe our surroundings mono-directionally (eyes and ears directed at the same information source) and sometimes bi-directionally (eyes and ears directed at different sources—watching a bird high in the air while hearing kids shrieking in a nearby swimming pool, say).

Our attention can also move about in imaginary time—forward (anticipation and imagination) or backward (memory). Look for these facets particularly in fiction films you like, and you will see how the editing functions to suggest eyes, ears, and intelligence working together. As such, they form the kind of probing coalition our eyes, ears, and intelligence use to extract meaning from layers of impression. The overlap cut is an important editing technique because you can use it to suggest the shift of mono- or bi-directional attention, especially in dialogue sequences.

DIALOGUE SEQUENCES

The *overlap cut* (aka *lap cut* or *L cut*) breaks the level-cut convention (sound and picture cut at the same moment) by bringing in sound ahead of picture, or picture ahead of sound. If, say, you set out to show that a likeable teacher has a superb theory but a poor teaching performance, you would shoot two sets of materials, one of him describing how he teaches, and the other of him droning away in class. Editing these materials in juxtaposition, one uses the conservative, first-assembly method that alternates segments as in Figure 15-2A: a block of the man explaining his ideas, then a block of teaching, then another block of explanation, then another of teaching, and so on until you've made the point with a sledgehammer. When technique and message become predictable, the audience tunes out.

Imagine instead integrating the two sets of materials, as in Figure 15-2B. The teacher begins to describe his philosophy of teaching. He is a nice man, and while he speaks, we cut to the classroom sequence with its sound low and the teacher's explanation continuing over it (this is called *voice-over*, abbreviated as VO). When the voice has finished its sentence, we bring up the sound of

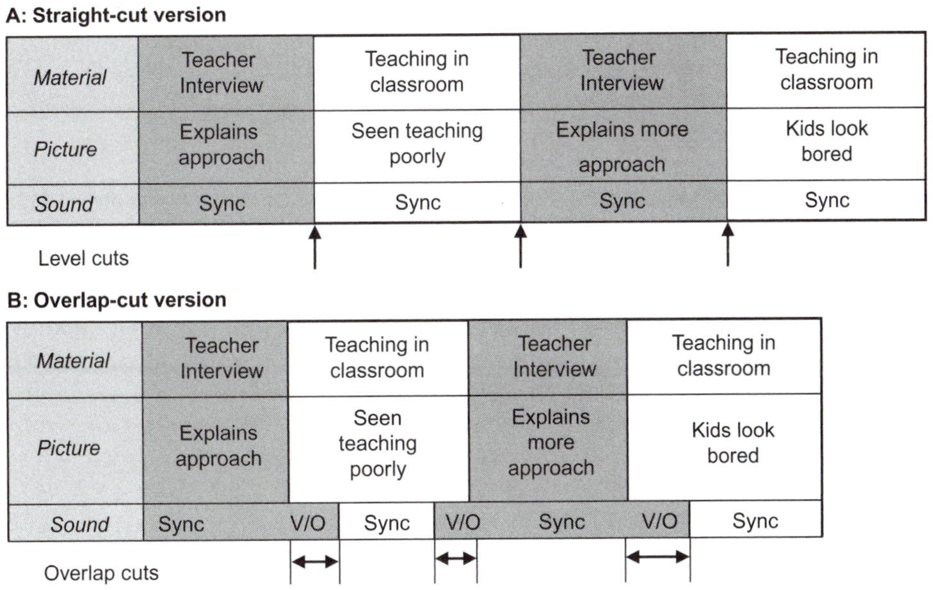

A: Straight-cut version

Material	Teacher Interview	Teaching in classroom	Teacher Interview	Teaching in classroom
Picture	Explains approach	Seen teaching poorly	Explains more approach	Kids look bored
Sound	Sync	Sync	Sync	Sync

Level cuts

B: Overlap-cut version

Material	Teacher Interview	Teaching in classroom	Teacher Interview	Teaching in classroom
Picture	Explains approach	Seen teaching poorly	Explains more approach	Kids look bored
Sound	Sync	V/O	Sync	V/O	Sync	V/O	Sync

Overlap cuts

FIGURE 15-2

In A, the first-assembly method of alternating segments. In B the two sets of materials have been edited in counterpoint.

the classroom sequence and play the classroom at full level. Then we lower the classroom atmosphere and bring in the teacher's interview voice again. At the end of the classroom action, as the teacher gets interesting, we cut to him in sync (that means including his picture to go with his voice). At the end of the third block we continue his voice, but cut—in picture only—back to the classroom, where we see the bored and mystified kids of Block 4.

Now, instead of having description and practice in separate blocks of material, you lay description against practice, ideas against reality, in a harder-hitting counterpoint that demands interpretation by the audience. There are multiple benefits: the total sequence is shorter and sprightlier; talking-head material has been pared to a minimum; and the behavioral material—the classroom evidence against which we measure the teacher's sense of himself—is now in the majority.

In dialogue exchanges the lap cut circumvents the jarring effect of the level cut, and mimics the way our eyes and ears move around, separately detecting packages of information for our brain to synthesize.

OVERLAP CUT THEORY

Usually L cuts are a refinement of later editing, but we need a guiding theory. Think of how our ever-reliable model for editing—human consciousness—handles these experiences. Think of witnessing a conversation: you turn your head from one person to the other, but seldom do you turn at the exact moment to catch the next speaker beginning—only an omniscient being could be so accurate. In reality you cannot know when another speaker will break in. Instead, a new voice intrudes and you turn your eyes to locate the speaker.

To make conversation seem spontaneous, the editor should mimic the way that eye attention and ear attention move, either by making picture cuts lag behind sound cuts, or sometimes by making them anticipate them. This replicates the disjunctive shifts we unconsciously make as eyes follow hearing, or hearing tunes in late to something just seen. This is quite simple in principle, but it will put your editing in a new league.

SUBTEXTS

Effective cutting mimics the needs and reactions of a *concerned Observer* watching keenly for evidence of *subtexts* (hidden meanings and emotion developing in one or both characters). As a speaker begins a new point, we often switch ahead in search of its effect on her listener. Even as we ponder, the listener begins to reply. A hint of forcefulness causes us to switch attention over to the other person, now listening. The line of her mouth hardens, and we guess that she is disturbed.

Often the concerned Observer watching a conversation is processing complementary impressions—the speaker through hearing, but the listener through vision. We *listen to the person who acts*, but often *scrutinize the person being acted-upon*. When that situation reverses and the person acted-upon begins his reply, we glance back to see how the original speaker is reacting.

Human beings are forever searching out visual and aural clues—in facial expressions, body language, or vocal tone—that might unlock the protagonists' hidden agenda. Good editing replicates this habitual searching process. By catching key moments of action, reaction, or subjective vision, it engages us in *interpreting what is going on inside each protagonist*. In dramatic terms, this is the *search for subtext*, for what is going on beneath the surface. Much of human life is spent doing this, and good cinema replicates this.

For the ambitious editor the message is clear: Be true to life by conveying the developing sensations of a concerned Observer. When you do this, sound and picture changeover points are seldom level cuts. Overlap cuts achieve this important disjunction by allowing the film to cut from shot to shot independently of the "his turn, her turn, his turn" speech alternations in the sound track.

TRANSITIONS BETWEEN SEQUENCES

Sometimes you want to bring a scene to a slow closure, perhaps with a fade-out, and then gently and slowly begin another, perhaps with a fade-in. But *opticals* (such as fades and dissolves) insert a rest period between scenes and usually you cannot afford to lose narrative momentum. Here is a transition between two scenes handled in three different ways:

Straight Cut

A boy and girl are discussing going out together but the boy is worried that her mother will stop them. The girl says, "Oh don't worry, I can convince her." CUT TO the next scene, mother closes refrigerator with a bang and says firmly, "Absolutely not!" to the aggrieved daughter.

Picture Anticipates Sound

In this version, the girl says "Oh don't worry," and CUT TO the mother standing at the refrigerator as the girl's voice-over ends, "I can convince her." The mother slams the fridge door (which carries some metaphorical force) and says, "Absolutely not!"

Sound Anticipates Picture

Another way to merge one scene into the next would be to hold on the two after the girl speaks her line, and place the mother's angry voice saying "Absolutely not!" over the tail end of their scene, then CUT TO the mother slamming the fridge door.

The first version makes the "joint" between sequences like a scene shift in the theatre. The second is something of a shock cut that emphasizes the mother's determined opposition, while the third seems gentler and sympathetic to the difficulties of their romance.

ANTICIPATORY AND HOLDOVER SOUND

You have also seen the lap cut carried out with sound effects: The factory worker rolls reluctantly out of bed, then as he shaves and dresses, we hear the increasingly loud sound of machinery until we CUT TO him working on the production line. Here *anticipatory sound* drags our attention forward to the next sequence. We do not find the location switch arbitrary since our curiosity demands an answer to the riddle of machine sounds in a bedroom. Alternatively we could see the man on the assembly line and CUT TO him putting food together in his kitchen at night. *Holdover sound* of factory uproar continues over the cut and slowly subsides as he wearily eats leftovers at his kitchen table.

In the first example, the aggressive factory sound draws him forward out of his bedroom; in the second, it lingers even after he has got home. Each lap cut implies a psychological narrative because each suggests that the sound exists in his head. From it we gather how unpleasant and omnipresent he finds his workplace. At home he thinks of it and is sucked up by it; after work the din follows him home to haunt him.

Overlap cuts soften transitions between locations, or suggest subtext and point of view through implying the inner consciousness of a central character. You could play it the other way, and let the silence of the home trail out into the workplace, so that he is seen at work, and the bedroom radio continues to play softly before being swamped by the rising uproar of the factory. At the end of the day, the sounds of laughter on the television set could displace the factory noise and make us CUT TO him sitting at home, relaxing with a sitcom.

Use sound and picture transitions creatively, and you transport the viewer forward with none of the ponderousness of optical effects like dissolves, fades, or (god help us) wipes. You can also scatter important clues to your characters' inner lives and imaginations.

EDITING PITFALLS

Here are some traps you'll want to avoid that emerge during editing:

- *Mis-identified sources*: Allowing re-enacted or reconstructed material to stand unidentified in a film that is otherwise made of original and authentic materials can get you into trouble. Identify the material's origin by narration or subtitle. Identify speakers too, if they need it, with subtitles.

- *Mis-identified people*: If you start an interior monologue voice-over (VO) on Person A and then reveal through a talking-head that it is actually Person B speaking, your audience will be irritated that you misled them. Make a practice of identifying VO by starting it over a shot of the speaker (doing his laundry, feeding the cat, etc.). Then you can continue the VO during other shots.

- *Spatial errors*: Check you are being true to essential geography, or your editing can suggest the kitchen is next to the bathroom, and London south of Madrid.

- *Temporal mistakes*: Show events in a chronology that is demonstrably wrong, and your detractors will seize it to discredit your whole film, as happened to Michael Moore with *Roger and Me* (USA, 1989).

- *Elision distortions*: Documentary editing involves compression: statements that serve the film but misrepresent the speaker's original pronouncement may boomerang in court.

- *Bogus truth*: By juxtaposing unrelated events or statements, you manufacture meaning. Even though something may be invisible and insignificant to you and even to a general audience, participants can be scandalized. They cannot believe that you have compressed the nine months it took to buy their house into three shots. Be ready to defend and justify what you have done with other film examples.

- *Participant fears*: Sometimes you face a participant's fear-fantasy when, after weeks of anguish, she wants to retract an innocuous statement that is vital to your film's sense. She signed a release giving you the legal right to use it, and you know it can cause her no harm. Can you, *should* you, go ahead and override her wish? Your good name and career may suffer, and at the very least your conscience will prick you for violating her trust. Then again, you may have a lot of time or money invested. Perhaps a trusted third party can talk her out of her apprehension? A screening with a number of people she respects may also help.

- *Informed consent*: If you work for a media company, they will have an explicit consent policy designed to protect the integrity of the organization. When participants sign this *informed consent form* they are, in effect, declaring they understand you will use their material according to your own judgment, and that they understand the consequences. Though this permits you to imply a critical view of someone's behavior or function, do you also have the moral right to deceive them and cause them harm? Public figures may be fair game, but private people usually deserve your diligent protection. Listening to your conscience is good, but getting the opinions of responsible friends and colleagues, and consulting a lawyer, are usually better. You may need to level with your participant, to see what he or she feels, but you must also make it clear that audiences watch documentaries because they are critical. They are not made to be flattering.

Ethical dilemmas seldom pose you a choice between right and wrong, but more often a choice between right versus right. So seek advice—and don't feel that ethical dilemmas are ever something you must solve alone.

REGAINING SOME DISTANCE

After considerable editing, a debilitating familiarity sets in and you lose confidence in your ability to make judgments. This is a particular hazard for director-editors who have long lived obsessively with the intentions for their footage. Soon every alternative version looks similar, and all seem too long. Be careful: this is a dangerous situation since you can begin inadvertently destroying your work. You need a technique to help objectify your judgments, and get some distance. Here are two steps I take. The first is to make a flow chart of your film so you can see its ideas and intentions in an alternative light. The other is to show the working cut to a trial audience of a chosen few.

MAKE A DIAGNOSTIC FLOW CHART

Film is an illusionary medium and deceives its makers even more than its audience. New understanding is hard to come by during editing, so it helps to translate something over-familiar into another form, as statisticians do by turning their figures into graphs and pie charts. The Narrative Diagnostic Worksheet (Table 15-1) will help you achieve an overview of your film's contents, no matter how short or long it is. It works by producing a sort of annotated flow chart, from which you can make a functional analysis of your film and achieve a fresh perspective.

TABLE 15-1 Turning a film into an annotated flow chart—helpful when you face intractable problems

---

Project AP-5 Narrative Diagnostic Worksheet	
Production title_____ Length_____	
Editor_____Date_____ Page #_____	
Sequence Content Tag-Title	Contribution to Film's "Argument"
_____ _____ _____ Seq #_____ Ends at TC ___:___:___	_____ _____ _____ Impact ★ ★ ★ ★ Length ___:___:___
_____ _____ _____ Seq#_____ Ends at TC ___:___:____	_____ _____ _____ Impact ★ ★ ★ ★ Length ___:___:___
_____ _____ _____ Seq #_____ Ends at TC ___:___:____	_____ _____ _____ Impact ★ ★ ★ ★ Length ___:___:___
_____ _____ _____ Seq #_____ Ends at TC ___:___:____	_____ _____ _____ Impact ★ ★ ★ ★ Length ___:___:___

Project **AP-5 Diagnosing a Narrative** in the book's website www.directingthedocumentary.com.

To use the worksheet,

1. Stop your film after each sequence and briefly describe its content in the box. It might simply convey a special mood or feeling, but more likely develops exposition, a new situation, or a new thematic strand. Perhaps it introduces a location or relationship that is developed later in the film.
2. Note what the sequence contributes to the film's development as a whole.

3. Add timings (optional, but helpful for making decisions about the value of each sequence and the work's overall length).

4. Award each sequence an impact rating of 1–5 stars (this helps you assess how well the strong and weak materials are distributed).

Your film has become a flow chart that shows you what is subconsciously present for any audience. How does its progression stack up? Here are some likely problems:

*   Lack of early impact or a pedestrian opening that makes the film a late starter (fatal to TV or Internet viewings).
*   Redundancy, especially of expository information.
*   Necessary information inconsistently supplied.
*   Holes or backtracking apparent in progression.
*   Type and frequency of impact poorly distributed over the film's length (resulting in uneven dramatic intensity and progression).
*   Similar thematic contributions made several ways; choose the best and dump (or reposition) the rest.
*   Material you like that fails to advance the film. Be brave and kill your darlings.
*   The film's conclusion emerges early, leaving the remainder an unnecessary recapitulation.
*   Multiple endings—three is not uncommon. Decide what your film is really about, choose the most appropriate, and discard the rest.

As you can give each ailment a name, it suggests its own cure. Put these into effect, and you can feel rather than quantify the improvement.

After housecleaning, expect a new round of problems to surface, so *make a new flow chart*, however unconvinced you are of its necessity. Almost certainly you'll find more anomalies.

This formal process will become second nature during your career, and will occur spontaneously. Even so, filmmakers of long standing invariably profit from subjecting their work to some such formal scrutiny. Work that hasn't been rigorously critiqued looks sloppy and indulgent, and audiences have no patience for it.

A TRIAL SHOWING

Knowing what every brick in your movie's edifice must accomplish, you are ready to test out your movie on a small audience. In a media organization this may be the people you work for—producers, senior editors, or a sponsor—so the experience will be grueling. Better is to first show the film to half a dozen whose tastes and interests you respect. The less they know about your film and your aims, the better. Warn them that it is a *work in progress*, and still technically raw, with materials missing—music, graphics, sound effects, end titles, whatever. Do place a working title at the front because it helps signal the film's identity and purpose.

SOUND CHECK

Before each public showing, run the film purely for *sound levels*. Even experienced filmmakers will misjudge a film whose sound varies between inaudible and overbearing. Present your film at its best, or be ready for misleadingly negative responses.

Working with the flow chart should have helped you decide what to explore with your first audience. You suspect which are the strong and weak points, and now you can find out.

SURVIVING YOUR CRITICS AND USING WHAT THEY SAY

After the viewing, ask first for impressions of the film as a whole. You are about to test the film's working hypothesis and prove the "what it contributes" part of your analysis form. Don't be afraid to focus and direct your viewers' attention, or someone may lead off at a tangent.

Following is a typical order of inquiry. It starts with large impressions and issues, and moves down to the component parts:

- What do audience members think is the film's theme, or themes?
- What are the major issues in the film?
- Did the film feel the right length or was it too long?
- Which parts were unclear or puzzling?
- Which parts felt slow?
- Which parts were moving or otherwise successful?
- What did they feel about … (name of character)?
- What did they end up knowing about … (situation or issue)?

Listen carefully, take notes, and retain your bearings toward the piece as a whole. Say no more than strictly necessary; never *explain* the film or *explain* what you intended, since that compromises your audience's perceptions and suggests they are dumb. A film must stand alone without explication from its authors, so imbibe what your critics are saying. If these are your employers, all the more reason to be quietly receptive.

Depending on how interested your trial audience became in the discussion, you may get useful feedback on most of your film's parts and intentions. Make allowance for the biases and subjectivity that emerge in your critics, and expect the occasional person who talks about the film *he* would have made, rather than the one you have just shown. When this happens (and it will), diplomatically redirect the discussion. If two or three people report the same difficulty, wait. Their feedback may elicit other comments canceling theirs out, in which case no action may be required.

This kind of listening takes great self-discipline since hearing negative reactions and criticism of your work is emotionally battering. Keep this in mind: when you ask for criticism, people look for possible changes—if only to make a contributory mark on your work. Expect to feel threatened, slighted, misunderstood, and unappreciated, and to come away with a raging headache. Handcuff yourself for three or four days so you do nothing to the film.

After one of these sessions it's quite normal to feel that you have failed, that your film is junk, and that all is vanity. The fact is, works-in-progress always look fairly awful. Audiences are disproportionately affected by a wrong sound balance here, a shot or two that needs clipping, or a sequence that belongs earlier. What matters above all is that you *hold on to your central intentions*. Never revise these without strong and positive reasons to do so. For the time being, *act only on those suggestions that support and further your central intentions*. This is a dangerous time for the filmmaker, and indeed for any artist, since trying to please everyone makes it fatally easy to abandon your work's underlying identity.

So, wait two or three days for your passions to cool. Run your film again, and you will see it with the eyes of the three people who failed to realize that the boy was the woman's son. Yes, their relationship is twice implied, but you see a way to insert an extra line where the boy calls her "Mom." Problem solved. You move on to the next one, and solve that too. This is the meat and potatoes of the artistic process.

PARTICIPANT VIEWINGS

When should a participant have the right to see and veto a cut? This seems like an easy and natural thing to agree, but in reality it is a minefield. Your work, like that of a journalist, counts as free speech, and you have a right to uncensored self-expression that you never relinquish without good cause. Keep in mind that participants seeing themselves on the screen, particularly for the first time, do so with great subjectivity. Most absolutely hate how they appear on the screen. To overcompensate in the hope of pleasing them is to abandon documentary for public relations.

So if you,

- Have made a film that might land you or your participants in legal trouble, get legal advice. Keep in mind that lawyers look on the dark side, look for snags, and err on the side of caution.
- Agreed at the outset that you would solicit participants' feedback, then this is their right.
- Did *not* work out a consultative agreement with your subjects, then it's a bad idea to embark on one now without very strong cause.
- Agree to show a work-in-progress cut to participants, then only do so after clearly explaining that their rights are limited to expressing preferences.
- Think a participant may feel upset or betrayed by something in your film, then prepare him or her in advance so he does not feel humiliated in the presence of family and friends. Fail, and that person may see you as a traitor and all film people as frauds.

Sticky situations at public showings usually go best if you have general audience members *and* the person's friends and family present. The enjoyment and approval by the majority usually relieves the subject's heightened sensitivities, and leaves him or her feeling good about the film as a whole.

THE USES OF PROCRASTINATION

Whether you are pleased or depressed about your film, it is always good to cease work for a while and do something else. You might take a week away from the film, or, if you are under deadline, go to a birthday party instead of working all night.

If this anxiety is new to you, take comfort: You are deep in the throes of the creative experience. This is the long, painful labor before giving birth. When you pick up the film again after a judicious lapse, your fatigue and defeatism will have gone away and the film's problems and their solutions will seem manageable again.

TRY, TRY AGAIN

A film of substance often requires an editing evolution of many months, and several new trial audiences. Show it again to the earliest audience at some point to see what progress they think you've made.

HANDS-ON LEARNING

Try **AP-5 Diagnosing a Narrative.** It is a deceptively simple way of getting an overview on your film, but it usually springs some pleasant surprises and discoveries. It is particularly useful when you are getting to the end of your tether, and nearly always leads to making some important and very positive changes.

CHAPTER 16

EDITING FROM FINE CUT TO FESTIVAL

AIMING FOR A FINE CUT

Cautious filmmakers do not call the last editing stage "the final cut," but the *fine cut* since it usually still needs minor changes and accommodations. Most of these arise from laying music, after which comes *picture lock*, when the film is deemed ready for tracklaying in preparation for the *sound mix*. If you are commissioning original music, the picture lock stage is when you should work with your composer (see the description of that process in **Chapter 34: Using Music and Working with a Composer**).

CHECK ALL SOURCE MATERIAL

As you near fine cut, review all your dailies to make sure you've overlooked nothing useful. Time consuming though this is, you will surely have one or two "Eureka!" discoveries that make the long viewing worthwhile.

LOOKING AHEAD TO THE SOUND MIX

For your first films, you can use the audio suite supplied with your editing program to do a decent job of mixing sound. For more advanced work you will need a specialist equipped with a sound suite program like Pro Tools (Figure 16-1). A sound mix uses a first-rate amplifier and speakers to replicate the best cinema sound. Few cinemas approach the state of the art, yet good sound, as Dolby cinemas know, is good business. Sound may yet get its day.

SOUND DESIGN

Sound is an incomparable stimulant to the audience's imagination, but only rarely does it get designed into the film from the early stages. Usually sound is really dialogue tracks that languish on the back burner until the "audio sweetening" session, an expression I dislike for its rescue connotations. Better terms are sound design, sound editing, and sound mix.

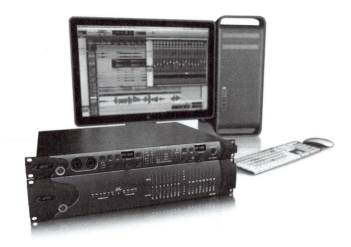

FIGURE 16-1

Pro Tools® interface.

If you had a sound design from the inception of the film, this part of the process is now one of finalizing. More often, film sound just evolves, so an overview discussion now, near the end of editing, is a good way to ensure you are stepping back to take in the big picture.

THE SOUND DESIGN DISCUSSION

The components of film sound are dialogue, atmospheres, effects, and music, but since they combine like a composition in the listener, one should try to consider sound design holistically. How and why you intend using music, and what music rights may complicate your choice, also needs careful discussion.

Decide an overall sound strategy for the entire film before the editor goes to work reorganizing dialogue tracks and laying in missing sound effects. Try to assign a particular sound identity to each sequence. This might be loud and noisy, mysterious, lyrical, building from quiet to a crescendo—all sorts of patterns and moods might apply. You should also agree on how to tackle known sound problems. This is a priority since dialogue reconstruction—if it's needed—is an expensive, specialized, and time consuming business, and no film can survive having it done poorly (see **Post-synchronizing dialogue** below).

Though documentary leads the way in narrative inventiveness, feature films use far more resources to develop their sound tracks, and documentarians can learn much from them. Walter Murch, the doyen of editors and sound designers, makes a practice of watching any film he is editing with the sound turned off, to allow himself space in which to imagine what the sound composition might be. Other functions of sound, listed in Randy Thom's important article "Designing a Movie for Sound" (www.filmsound.org/articles/designing_for_sound.htm), are to,

- Indicate a historical period.
- Indicate changes in time or geographical locale.
- Connect otherwise unconnected ideas, characters, places, images, or moments.

- Heighten ambiguity or diminish it.
- Startle or soothe.

It's not the quantity or complexity of sound that makes a memorable sound experience, but the psychological journey it leads you on. This is the art of *psychoacoustics*. A strong, simple sound track does this more effectively than one that's dense and naturalistic. Often this requires you to simplify the numbing panoply of sounds in a contemporary location, and replace them with those few that have a strongly subjective meaning to the point of view (POV) character.

SOUND CLICHÉS

If you load up your film with naturalistic sounds instead of responding creatively to the narrative needs of the movie, your film will sound clichéd. A shot of a cat walking across a kitchen does not need a cat meow, unless said cat is visibly demanding its breakfast. This is a sound cliché. For a hilarious list of them, look up www.filmsound.org/cliche. Here all bicycles have bells; car tires always squeal when a car pulls away, turns, or stops; storms start instantaneously; wind always whistles; doors always squeak; and so on.

Post-synchronizing dialogue (aka "automatic dialogue replacement" or ADR): Rarely used in documentary, post-sync is used to remedy poor dialogue tracks and requires making participants lip-sync what they said in an existing shot. Variously called dubbing, looping, or ADR, you have seen its full horrors in low budget films where actors have watched a screen and spoken a couple of lines to picture. Long dialogue exchanges are broken into multiple small increments, and recorded voices invariably sound flat and dead in contrast with live location recordings. This is not because they lack background presence (which can always be added) or even because sound perspective and location acoustics are missing. What kills ADR is the artificiality of the situation itself. The poor actor, laboring to reconstitute 10 seconds of dialogue, is flying blind and completely in the hands of whoever signs off on each few sentences.

Dialogue replacement invariably degrades actors' performances, so they hate it with a passion. If actors feel that way, imagine what you are asking of a chef, auctioneer, or hospice nurse. In documentary, there is really no need, since audiences understand that this is the trade-off for capturing reality and will tolerate patches of poor sound recording. The moral? Never consider ADR unless the original is utterly incomprehensible. Even then, first try adding subtitles, which is the usual solution in documentary.

RECREATING SOUND EFFECTS (SFX)

You can however shoot and fit sound effects to your film, and greatly improve it. These may come from a sound library, be shot on location, or generated in a Foley studio. The Foley process got its name from its intrepid inventor, one Jack Foley, who realized back in the 1940s that with the right resources you could mime all the right sounds to picture. He used a sound studio equipped with a range of resources, materials, and props. Often what a film needs is an authentic-sounding mass of footsteps, so a Foley studio has a variety of surfaces—concrete, heavy wood, light wood, carpet, linoleum, gravel, and so on. To this, Foley artists may add sand, paper, or cloth to modify footsteps so they suit what's on the screen. My job in an appalling Jayne Mansfield comedy (*The Sheriff of Fractured Jaw*, Raoul Walsh, GB, 1959) was to *post-sync* horse footsteps with coconuts, and simulate steam engine noises with a modified motorcycle engine. It was great fun. We also shot all the footsteps, body movements, horse harnesses jangling, and I don't know what else.

It takes some ingenuity to create the right sound for a particular shot. Baking powder under compression in a sturdy plastic bag, for instance, makes the right scrunching noise for footsteps

FIGURE 16-2 ——

Like many films involving nature, *The Story of the Weeping Camel* had to reconstruct some of its sound.

in snow, and you might have to experiment with punching a cabbage or thumping a sandbag to get a decent range of body blows for a film about boxing. The art of sound lies in making sound authentic to the ear. Paradoxically, one must contrive many effects because the genuine article sounds phoney. A door-close that sounds like someone kicking a cardboard box destroys the illusion of authenticity on which film depends.

You can create sounds to fit a repetitive action such as knocking on a door, shoveling snow, or feet going up stairs by recording their action a little slower, and then, on the computer, removing some frames before each impact's attack. More complex sync effects (two people walking through a quadrangle) will have to be post-synced to picture, paying attention to the different surfaces that their feet pass over (grass, gravel, concrete, etc.)

A grueling post-sync session makes you understand two things: that location recordists who procure good original recordings are worth their weight in gold, and that feature sound and editing crews are often phenomenal craftspeople.

There is much Foley work in Luigi Falorni and Byambasuren Davva's documentary, *The Story of the Weeping Camel* (Germany, 2003, Figure 16-2). They shot important action with the camels using long lenses, so usable sound was not possible with the unit so distant. Recreating sound was unavoidable, as in so many nature subjects.

SOUND LIBRARIES

Appropriate sound effects can often be found in a good sound library, but never assume anything will work until proved against picture. Googling "sound effects library" turns up many, some of which let you listen and download. Try Sound Ideas at www.sound-ideas.com/bbc.html. Sometimes libraries hold material shot long ago and their SFX may come with a heavy ambience or system hiss. This is no problem with loud or exotic sounds such as helicopters, Bofors guns, or elephants rampaging through an Indian jungle. It's nitty-gritty noises like footsteps on grass,

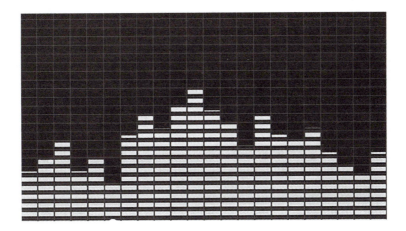

FIGURE 16-3

Equalizer display. Each column represents the loudness of a band of sound frequencies. By using selective equalization, each column can be made more or less loud in relation to the others.

doorbells, or "small dog growling" that may be tough to get right. At one time only *six* different gunshots were in use throughout the film industry. I heard attempts at recording new ones, and they sounded like a ruptured air hose.

EQUALIZATION (EQ) AND WHAT THE SOUND MIX CAN DO

The culmination of the editing process is the *mix*, in which you combine sound components together in their final proportions. Balancing sound tracks is more than adjusting levels, it also requires adjustments in *equalization* (EQ).

Each sound track contains a variety of frequencies, and each group of frequencies is adjustable by level relative to other groups (Figure 16-3). For instance, in a busy street we see two people talking, but their conversation is on the margin of intelligibility owing to a heavy traffic background. Their voices are in the frequency range of 500–3,000 Hz (Herz, or cycles per second), but most of the traffic is below 200 Hz. By *rolling off* or *attenuating* frequencies in the low frequency band, you effectively lower the volume of that band of frequencies. Since traffic rumble is below the range of human speech, you can filter some of it out and leave voices unaffected. With less low frequency competition they now seem louder and clearer (Figure 16-4).

EQ has other uses. A voice recorded from two mike positions often doesn't match when you cut the tracks together, but by "tweaking" the different bands of component frequencies, they can often be made indistinguishable. This work in skilled hands lets your film achieve the seamlessness that moviegoers take for granted.

You can also use EQ to make sound effects either easier on the ear, or more striking, and EQ adjustments can prevent sounds meant to be background on one track from competing with those intended as foreground on another, which might be speech or music. Sound and sound mixing deserves a very large book all to itself, so what follows is a list of essentials along with some tips.

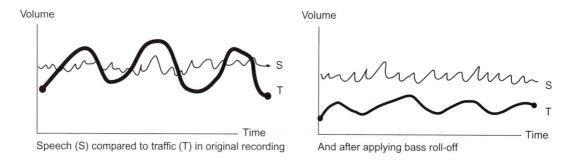

Volume   Volume

Time   Time

Speech (S) compared to traffic (T) in original recording   And after applying bass roll-off

FIGURE 16-4

Graph representing speech and traffic sound levels during a street conversation. Original levels are on the left, and on the right, the bass traffic has been "rolled off" using EQ. It no longer fights speech frequencies for attention.

You are ready to mix down tracks into one master track when you have,

- *Locked* the picture content of your film.
- Fitted *music*, making any necessary picture or cutting point adjustments.
- Split *dialogue* into multiple tracks, grouping them to require the fewest EQ changes:
  - a separate track for each mike position used in dialogue recording.
  - sometimes a different track for each speaker, depending on how much EQ is necessary for each mike position on each character.
- Filled in *backgrounds* (missing sections of background *ambience*, so there are no dead spaces or abrupt background changes).
- Recorded and laid *narration* or *voice-over* (if there is any).
- Recorded and laid *sound effects* and mood setting *atmospheres*.
- Finalized sound timeline contents and layout.

The mix procedure determines the following, described in detail later:

- Balance of *sound levels* (say, between a dialogue foreground voice against a background of noisy factory sounds if, and only if, they are on separate tracks).
- *EQ* adjusted for sound quality consistency.
- *Level changes* (fade up, fade down, sound dissolves, and level adjustments to accommodate sound perspective and to facilitate entry of new track elements such as narration, music, or interior monologue).
- *Sound processing* (adding echo, reverberation, telephone effect, etc.).
- *Dynamic range* (a compressor squeezes the broad dynamic range of a movie into the narrow range favored in TV transmission; a limiter leaves the main range alone but limits peaks to a preset maximum).
- *Perspective* (to some degree, EQ and level manipulation can mimic perspective changes, thus helping create a sense of space and dimensionality through sound).
- *Multichannel sound distribution* (if you are developing a stereo track or 5.1 surround sound treatment, a sound specialist will send different elements to each sound channel to create a sense of horizontal spread and sound space).

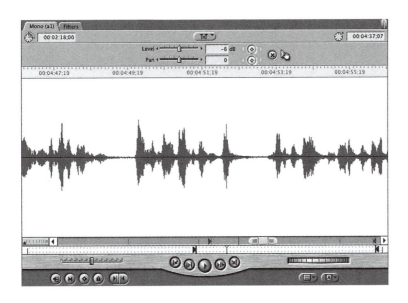

FIGURE 16-5

As you cut and lay sound tracks, use the program's audio waveforms display to see what you are doing.

SOUND MIX PREPARATION

Place sound track elements in different groups according to their hierarchy, which conventionally favors holding back control of dialogue over SFX and music. That order may vary: you might want music to occupy the foreground and make dialogue scarcely audible. To cut and lay sound tracks, consider using the program's audio waveforms option (Figure 16-5). It displays sound *modulations* (waveform) and saves you from clipping a sound's *attack* (its inception) or from cutting off its barely audible *decay* (tail). Laying tracks using Pro Tools, or any waveform display, means you can edit with surgical precision, even within a syllable. You can see the "mods" you are cutting, and hear your work immediately. Sound editing should be done at moderately high volume, so you can hear what is (or isn't) present.

NARRATION OR VOICE-OVER

When laying narration or interior monologue, fill gaps between dialogue or narration sections with room tone, so the intervening track remains "live." This is vital during a quiet sequence, but less necessary in a street scene having lots of ambient noise. If you need to write narration, see **Chapter 33: Creating Narration.**

DIALOGUE TRACKS AND PROBLEMS OF INCONSISTENCY

Digital editing systems can handle many tracks, but it is usually prudent to premix tracks in groups, holding back control over the most essential until last, so dialogue remains intelligible over music or effects.

Begin by dividing up the dialogue tracks. This is necessary because different camera positions occasion different mike positions. Played "as is," they will vary disturbingly in level and room acoustics from shot to shot. This strains the audience's patience and prevents them concentrating.

Intelligent EQ adjustment during the mix, plus work on background tracks, can greatly improve the feeling of consistency. First rate sound editing produces the seamless sound continuity familiar from feature films, but it requires painstaking, labor-intensive sound work:

- *Split the dialogue tracks,* that is,
  - Lay them on separate tracks according to speaker, mike positioning, or other sound determinant. (In a scene shot from two angles and having two mike positions, all close shot sound goes on one track, and all the medium shot sound goes on the other. You can now minimize EQ setup labor by using a blanket EQ setting for each track.)
  - With four or five mike positions, expect to lay at least four or five tracks.
  - Tracks may need subdividing according to character, who may also need different EQ and level settings, especially if one is louder than the other.
  - Determine EQ settings roughly during tracklaying, but leave final settings until the mix. Aim to make all voices consistent and to bring all tracks into acceptable compatibility. The viewer usually expects sound perspective to match the different camera distances.
- *Clean up background tracks.*
  - Remove extraneous noises, creaks, and mike handling sounds—anything that doesn't overlap dialogue and can be removed.
  - Fill any resulting gaps with authentic room tone or you will have audible drop-out.
- *Inconsistent backgrounds*: Frequently when you cut between two speakers in the same location, the background to each is different in level or quality. The microphone may have been angled differently, or background traffic or other activities perhaps changed over time. The cure is to,
  - Use the location presence track to augment the lighter track so it matches its heavier counterpart.
  - Consider using a graphic equalizer to filter out an intrusive background sound. Any intruding sound, such as a high-pitched whine, or the rumble of traffic, can be made less intrusive. Graphic EQ lets you tune out the offending frequency, but in so doing you may lose that band of frequencies in your characters' voices.
  - The worst place to make an ugly atmosphere or ambience change is in the clear. Try to do it as a quick dissolve behind a commanding foreground sound, which distracts the audience's attention from noticing the change.
- *Inconsistent voice qualities*: When speakers' voice qualities vary, your audience experiences strain and irritation from having to adjust to irrational changes. The causes can be,
  - Varying acoustical environments in the location.
  - Different mikes.
  - Different mike working distances.

LAYING MUSIC TRACKS

Laying music is not difficult, but acquiring it legally may be excruciating (see **Chapter 34: Using Music and Working with a Composer**). To make library music conclude at a certain point, back-lay it from the known ending point, then see if you can fade it up at the start point. If the music is only a little too long, you can commonly find repeated sections and cut one or two out. Conversely, if it's a little short, consider copying a section and repeating it.

In and Out Points

Cut in music or any pre-recorded sound just before the first sound attack so we don't first hear studio atmosphere. Arrow A in Figure 16-6 represents the ideal cut-in point; to its left is unwanted

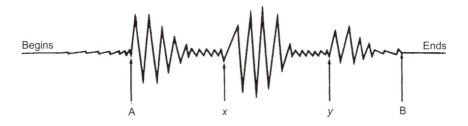

FIGURE 16-6

Diagram of sound attack and decay for a recording of three footsteps. Points A and B are ideal in and out cutting points. Points *x* and *y* are alternative in points.

presence. To the right of A are three attacks in succession that lead to a decay down to silence at arrow B.

Attack-Sustain-Decay Cutting

The sound profile in Figure 16-6 reappears in many repetitive sounds such as footsteps, hammering on a building site, or a clock ticking. By removing sound between x and y we could reduce three footfalls to two. One can also remove some of the quiet before the attack to make footsteps faster. These editing strategies have many applications.

SPOT SOUND EFFECTS

These are the effects that sync to something onscreen—like a car door closing, a coin placed on a table, or someone picking up a house-phone. *Sound effects* (SFX) are often necessary because the location recording is unavoidably poor. The click of a door in a peaceful chapel interior may, for instance, be marred by the drone of trucks passing from outside. So you have to use a new atmosphere and record the few footsteps, then add the dramatic clicking, which must be synchronized and have an acceptable perspective.

USING ATMOSPHERES

You lay atmospheres to create a mood, which might be morning birdsong over a valley, or singing and tire irons jangling from within a garage. Notes:

- Obey screen logic by laying atmospheres to cover the entire sequence, not just a part of it.
- When a door opens during an interior scene, the atmosphere outside (playground, for instance) will rise while the door is open.
- When you intend a sound dissolve, check there is enough extra to allow for the sound overlap.
- Check sound overlaps for inequities, such as the recordist quietly calling "Cut."

When you face an ugly background change, mask it by placing a commanding foreground effect over the transition, such as a doorbell ringing, or even dialogue. Bring any new background sound in or out by fading up or down, because the *ear registers a gradual sound transition far less acutely* than one that is a cut, and sudden.

SOUND MIX STRATEGY

PREMIXING

A battle sequence in a feature-length documentary might need 40 or more sound tracks, so you must group tracks ready for premixing. Too often, documentary location sound is only marginally intelligible, so plan therefore to mix down your elements *in an order that leaves control over the most important until last*. Usually this means determining dialogue-to-background levels in the last stage.

TAILORING

Many tracks, played as laid, enter and exit abruptly, leaving an unpleasantly jagged impression. So, unless you are deliberately disrupting attention, aim for a seamless effect. Use short sound dissolves rather than cuts, and cut from quiet to noisy, or vice versa, by tailoring: that is, by building in a fade-up or fade-down of a few frames so the louder track meets the quieter on its own terms. The effect onscreen is still that of a cut, but not one that assaults the ear (Figure 16-7).

BE CAUTIOUS WITH COMPARATIVE LEVELS

Mix studios use first-rate speakers but with misleading results, since many will hear your documentary through the dismal little speaker in their domestic TV. These make the foreground and background, so nicely separate in the sound mix, merge into a confusing mush. Be conservative, therefore, and ask the sound mixer to keep foregrounds and backgrounds well separated. A mix suite can usually replay through a TV set if you ask, so you can check what the home viewer will hear.

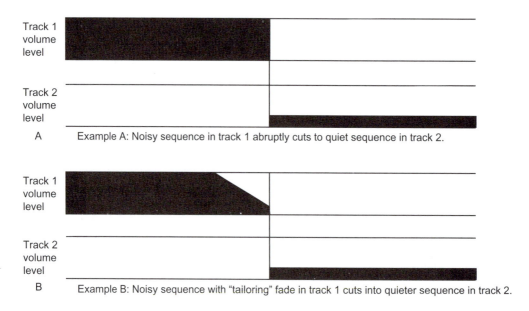

FIGURE 16-7

An abrupt sound cut tailored by making a quick fade of the outgoing track so it matches the level of the incoming track.

REHEARSE, THEN RECORD

You and your editor must approve each stage of the mix and feel sure that each sequence meets your expectations. The mix engineer will offer alternatives according to latitude and alternatives provided by the sound editor in the tracks. Mixing is best accomplished one section at a time, building sequence by sequence from convenient stopping points.

At the end, *listen to the whole mix without stopping*, just as the audience will. There is nearly always an anomaly or two needing correction.

SAFETY COPIES

A sound mix being a long and painstaking process, professionals immediately make backup copies on a durable medium to be stored in multiple buildings in case of loss or theft. Follow the same backup principle for picture: that is, keep media masters and safety copies in different places so all trace of your work doesn't vanish. An unlucky Chicago group suffered irreparable losses in a fire, and a friend in New Orleans had the agony of finding ten years of work wiped out by the waters of Hurricane Katrina. More often it's thieves walking off with a computer.

MUSIC AND EFFECTS (M & E) TRACKS

Some foreign purchasers require a separate M & E track. A foreign-language crew makes their own voice dub and uses your atmosphere, effects, and music tracks in their sound mix. They will also need you to supply a dialogue transcript (see below under "Transcript and Subtitling").

TITLES

Every film has a working title, but its makers must often choose the final in an agony of indecision. TV listings and festival programs rarely have space to describe their offerings, so the title you choose may be your sole means of drawing an audience. Your title should be short, snappy, and descriptive of the film's main allure.

STYLE

Form follows function, so documentary titles are usually plain and unfussy. Check examples in other documentaries and note that some of the most artistically ambitious films use brief and classically simple white lettering on a black background. You could do a lot worse.

TITLING

Professional quality titles are easy to generate in digital postproduction, but you may need a plug-in program for refinements. All lettering, and especially that for subtitles, is more legible when you choose a black outline to the lettering, which makes the characters stand out no matter whether the background is light or dark.

FONT, LAYOUT, AND SIZE

Choose font for clarity and size. Probably you have a large array of typefaces with drop shadow, movement, crawl, and other exotic behaviors. Unless your film's topic and treatment call for something special, resist temptation and keep titling classically simple. Anything too small or fancy disappears on home screen where most people see documentaries. Keep titling well within a safe area of the screen, especially subtitles.

OVERLADEN TITLES

A sure sign of amateurism is a film loaded with a long and egocentric welter of credits. Keep acknowledgments brief, and the director's name should not crop up in multiple capacities.

SPELLING

Check titles and subtitles scrupulously for spelling and use at least two highly literate, eagle-eyed checkers. The proper spelling for people's names should receive special care since a mistake indicates for all time that you cared too little to get someone's name right.

TITLE DURATIONS

See box for title length calculations. Long *crawl titles* (titles that slide up or across the screen) must run fast, or TV stations chop them. Check the speed of other people's.

COPYRIGHT MARK

At the very end of the titles, remember to include your name and the © symbol, with the year you claimed copyright protection of your material. To file for copyright in the United States, look up the US Copyright Office at www.loc.gov/copyright. For other countries, check out copyright procedure with professionals.

TRANSCRIPT AND SUBTITLING

If your film makes an international sale, or is exhibited in a film festival, you will probably be asked for a dialogue transcript of the whole film for simultaneous translation during projection. If your film is in a minority language, they will also expect a subtitled version, usually in English. You can plan subtitling using the typed transcript, but,

- Compress dialogue exchanges down to minimal essentials and eliminate anything not strictly necessary—your audience can't be too busy reading to see your film.
- Have the text translated by a *literate, native speaker* and typed up with all the appropriate accents.
- Make sure that two or more other literate native speakers approve every detail of the text.
- Make a copy of your film on which to superimpose subtitles.
- Pick a plain typeface in yellow with black edging, so your subtitles are clearly legible no matter how light or dark the background. Use a size of font that is easy to read on a small TV screen and keep subtitles well in the TV safe area (that is, not near image edges).
- Place every sentence within a continuous shot (when titles persist over two shots, we read the whole title a second time, which is annoying).
- To accomplish this, break long sentences into short sections as you are placing each subtitle, indicating anything that is run-on with triple periods (...) as in this example, spread over four shots:

How are you?	Shot 1
I feel OK just now...	Shot 2
...but I'm hoping you can...	Shot 3
...give me some advice.	Shot 4

ACKNOWLEDGMENTS

Participants or location owners often grant favors in return for an acknowledgment in the titles, so be sure to honor your debts to the letter. Double-check every such agreement before you lock down titles. Funding sources or other contracts may require you to use particular wording for credits and acknowledgments, and ask you to supply text for closed captioning.

LEGAL OMISSIONS

No television channel will transmit your film unless you have documentary proof that all contents are legal for them to transmit. Be sure you have secured legal rights to use everything your film contains, especially contributions by participants, and all music that is not legitimately part of a location's diagetic (inherent to the location) sound. Legal omissions can be costly or even paralyzing when you come to sell your film.

WEBSITE AND PRESS KIT

Now your film is complete, you can enter it in festivals. People who like your work will look for your website, expecting to reach you and buy copies. Plan to build a website or blog (try Wordpress.com) and through it begin compiling a list of supporters whom you can alert to screenings, keep abreast of developments, make funding appeals, etc.

To help market your work at festivals, carry copies of a *press kit* to give out. This might be a folder containing

- A leaflet promoting the film's subject and main characters.
- Quotations from any reviews it has received.
- Brief details on the careers of the makers.
- Good quality press photographs.
- Social media contacts for the film.

Everything printed should include all desirable contact details such as email and website, and your street address and email.

FESTIVALS

Find festivals via the websites cited in **Chapter 36: Developing a Career**. At last you experience the ultimate rite of passage—seeing your film with a paying audience. This can be thrilling—or chastening. Whichever comes your way, it's the final reckoning, and closes the loop of learning all you can about the artform from your present project. Go to all the festivals you can afford, and go armed with press kits and business cards. You will be surprised what develops from serendipitous encounters at screenings and conferences.

Now what film will you make next?

BOOK II

STORYTELLING

PART 6

DOCUMENTARY AESTHETICS

Book I: Observing led you through the stages of observing with the camera and then of editing footage into a narrative. Observational films usually fall into the realist tradition of transparent documentary that took off in the 1960s. The *cinema verité* movement, profiting from the first truly mobile sync film equipment, set about further pursuing Dziga Vertov's manifesto on the camera's ability to capture reality.[1] Purists however found observational filmmakers' claims to truth spurious, arguing that transparent filming got its appearance of objectivity from questionable practices: one was to ignore the subjectivity inseparable from every step of filmmaking; another lay in editing out all signs that subjects knew they were being filmed. Participatory documentary, on the other hand, could include filmmakers' modes of interceding and instigating events, and it allowed the makers to acknowledge the ambiguities, even the impossibility, of representing unmediated reality on the screen. This, however, shifts a documentary's focus away from its subject and on to its means and makers. A way to hold the elements in balance lies in the "voice" a film acquires, the voice of its storyteller.

ENTER THE STORYTELLER

We turn now to the range of thinking and techniques that can help you augment your role as a Storyteller. This means drawing on available aesthetic options to design your narrative with a distinct storytelling voice and purpose. From the screen we always hope for stories with significance, humor, and style—stories that

FIGURE 17-1 ——

Michael Moore as amazed naif in *Roger and Me*, a film that breathed new life into the American documentary.

reverberate with meaning and have something to say. Anyone can hold up a mirror and show its reflections, but as Henri Cartier-Bresson says, "Facts are not interesting. It's a point of view on facts which is important."[2] Nobody can give you the Ancient Mariner's power to detain the Wedding Guest. Rather, it is something you must ponder, seize, and develop. Power to do or be anything is seldom given, it must be grasped and taken.

Today's documentarians have a plethora of storytelling models, but common to them all is finding a purpose and style that stands consciously between subject and audience, bridging the two together. Michael Moore does this boldly in his Emmy Award winning first film *Roger and Me* (USA, 1989, Figure 17-1). As its narrator he plays the part of an amazed local whose simple and humane mission is to have a little talk with the head of General Motors. It is a brilliant strategy that justly made him famous; indeed, his film inaugurated the renaissance of the American documentary.

For your Storyteller you could adopt a filmic voice that is grave, saucy, brazen, nonplussed, sarcastic, resigned, pleading—whatever the nexus between story and audience calls for. Moore's force surely lies in the playful charm and sardonic quality of his storytelling voice, while Werner Herzog's imprimatur might come from his sustained, mesmerized gaze at the sheer range and depth of human conduct. What seems to drive directors like Kim Longinotto, Jill Godmilow, and Chris Choy is a justified outrage that women remain an underclass. Most people's storytelling voice is probably molded early in life by their most pressing circumstances of conflict.

An authorial voice in documentary, and the particular screen language needed to frame it, seems to arise from *an individual grappling with the particularity of a human predicament, and who uses heart and mind to articulate the process*. That is, while the Storyteller witnesses characters wrestling with their situation, he or she shares with the audience the empathic process of finding the story's wider implications.

GIVE YOURSELF A STORYTELLING ROLE TO PLAY

Choose the Storyteller role your film needs to adopt, and play it to the hilt. As though you were an actor looking at a fictional character's backstory, start by examining the marks you carry. What kind of documentaries must this Storyteller make? Your job is not to psychoanalyze yourself or to find ultimate truth (which is impossible) but to fashion a role you can play with all your heart. Don't hesitate to be brash and bold, indeed push your mission to the point of caricature, because it's an experimental role, not a straitjacket. You will change and evolve it as you go.

This Part is about documentary aesthetics, a phrase that implies the luxury of choice when often one feels handcuffed by one's documentary situation. An intended film about a primary school, for instance, may seem to offer only classroom material, teacher and children interviews, and visuals of kids in class or play-ground. But those limitations arise from our television conditioning in a medium hobbled by schedules, bud-gets, and ratings.

Imagine instead that you are Vietnamese or Lithuanian, and arrive to shoot in an English-speaking school. To your foreigner's eyes, everything strikes you as different: the children's faces, clothes, schoolbooks, even the sound of their language. Everything feels particular, significant, and special. What you hear is not the meaning of their words but a vocal composition mixed with the birdsong from an open window. You are feverish to record this new world's textures and imagery. Later, when the school sees your film, they are astonished at the lyrical otherness you found in their lives.

How to find this freshness and sensitivity toward one's own tribe? Picasso said he spent three years as a child learning to draw like Raphael, then many, many years learning how to see and draw again with a child's eyes. Radical insight like this begins from refusing the obvious, default options. That means de-programming oneself of all that is stale and stereotyped—which is not easy. The resources to do this, however, lie within you.

NOTES

1. See Brian Winston, "The Documentary Film as Scientific Inscription," in Michael Renov, ed., *Theorizing Documentary* (Routledge, 1993).
2. From a 1971 interview with Cartier-Bresson by Sheila Turner-Seed, *New York Times*, June 20, 2013 (http://lens.blogs.nytimes.com/2013/06/20/henri-cartier-bresson-living-and-looking) with thanks to Ana Lucia Jimenez Hine for bringing it to my attention.

CHAPTER 17

POINT OF VIEW AND STORYTELLING

MONOLOGICAL VERSUS DIALOGICAL FILMS

The early sound documentaries did a good deal of lecturing and nowadays strike us as authoritarian. Old habits of disseminating improving tracts to the unwashed masses die hard, of course, but documentary is now less *monological* and more *dialogical*. That is, today's makers are using the complexities of language, thought, and purpose once the province of older art forms like literature and theatre. Today's documentaries plumb people's inmost thoughts and feelings, and are open to the contradictory elements of human identity. They do this by sharing evidence with, rather than lecturing conclusions at, their audience. The benevolently authoritarian narrator—a legacy of comfortably colonial power structures—has given ground to a contrapuntal chorus of experience from the grassroots, where we all truly belong. This multiplicity of viewpoints has made the documentary far more richly textured, nuanced, and human.

POINT OF VIEW

The expression *point of view* (POV) suggests tools of political or psychological analysis, but in literature or cinema it implies feelings and perceptions that draw us into empathic relationship. A mature film tries to convey not just a perception *of* its characters, but perceptions *by* them too. This draws us into a feeling of emotional fellowship, so that we *identify* with them. You surely know that exciting feeling, in a book or film, of temporarily vacating your own existence and entering someone else's emotional and psychological experience. You sense the author's involvement with the characters, and share in it, yet its nature is evasive and its workings nearly impossible to pinpoint.

Filmmakers able to convey POV seem to do so viscerally rather than consciously. Inevitably, some of this chapter is about your state of mind as you shoot, but don't expect to feel you have any control over POV during the mechanics of a shoot. Point of view is about human vantage, and mostly what you need is a lively one as you shoot, and the faith that it will somehow translate into the film.

FILM, LITERATURE, AND GRAPHIC ART

A human vantage is present in humankind's oldest artworks. Twenty thousand years ago the Paleolithic cave painters at Lascaux painted bulls, stags, horses, and a single dying man. Each portrait suggests a viewpoint that is tangibly human, though not easy to interpret. Is this how a hunter sees his prey? Or is it the mind and emotions of a devotee picturing spiritual meanings? And what about the fallen man?

Through the painters' visions you sense their preoccupations and the intricacies of their spiritual cosmos, but mainly what you sense is vast and unfathomable. You confront something similar in Homer when he conjures up his brave but vulnerable heroes as they sail before the winds over the "wine dark" seas of temptation and danger in the ancient Mediterranean.

Art reveals not only *what* is seen (the subject's denotation), but also *how* it is seen, and *by whom* (form and meaning as human connotation). Painting and literature are significantly different from cinema: they initiate a pensive, contemplative inner activity within which the meanings assemble in your mind. Film on the other hand is an onslaught of here-and-now happenings. Literature can direct the reader into the past or the future, but film—like life itself—embraces the spectator within its relentless, advancing torrent of the present. A flashback or flash-forward, though it can transport us temporarily in time, soon swallows us up in a new present-tense cascade. Watching an engrossing film is thus like dreaming. What a difficult medium for its authors to control! Yet control of a kind is possible, and here is how I think it happens.

WILL AND EMPATHY

When you direct a documentary, you use your storehouse of experience to guess at your participants' agendas and infer their inner lives. You look for evidence of their *will* as you try to determine what they are trying to get, do, or accomplish. At the same time, you are conscious of changing levels of *empathy* in yourself as you ask, with whom do I identify? What situations, feelings, and motives can I sense at work, in myself and in this person? A director has to become conscious and articulate about sensations that normally develop half-consciously and by instinct. The aim is to use the medium's "point of view" capacity to sensitize us toward what characters perceive and feel about each other. Where the writer can take us directly inside a character's mind, and reveal their thoughts and feelings, the cinema usually makes us read characters from their outward verbal and physical actions. As in life itself, we face the mystery of other people's motives and actions. We try to read what they feel and want, so we can anticipate what they may do next.

USING YOUR EMOTIONAL SELF

Film techniques, we have often said, are modeled on the psychic and physical actions we take while negotiating the tensions between perception and emotion. Thus, to connect us with the hearts and minds of your participants, your own heart will have to rule over the tools of your trade. I do not mean you must inject sentimentality, only that you will have to recognize, share in, and record whatever emotion is present. You are not a scientist who demonstrates, weighs, and measures at a distance: you are immersed in a living artform, and are present and active within the very process you are recording.

Is this a problem? Yes, because everyone has armed himself against vulnerability while growing up. We learn to master our emotions, to distance ourselves—to hide them from others and ultimately from ourselves. Making documentary helps undo this numbing process, and each of your films will chart your progress. For fully evolved filmmaking, see the Maysles Brothers' *Grey Gardens* (USA, 1975, Figure 17-2), a work that fully accepts its highly eccentric mother and daughter. Never does it patronize or mock them, as would be so easy. Rather, it embodies the faith that "nothing human is alien," and, like a Samuel Beckett play, brings us two people in the act of endlessly sounding out the margins between memory and imagination.

Shifting points of view begin to emerge spontaneously when the filmmaking,

- Is fully mature in its embrace of others, however different they seem.

- Has a clear guiding purpose for telling the tale.

- Relates empathically and not just intellectually to the characters and their story.

- Knows at every point what it wants the audience to notice and feel.

POV IN SCREEN DRAMA

Film can convey a range of points of view, and how the camera embraces them is highly influential. In the diagrams that follow, the camera outline symbolizes a recording eye and ear, but it transcends the mechanical because it is directed by a heart and mind resonating to each new situation. The diagrammatic lines connecting the camera, director, and participants represent their awareness of, and complex relationships to, each other. These you can think of as *lines of tension*, pathways of significant danger to which you and your camera are instinctively drawn. However, see any of the accompanying film examples, and you will understand that each diagram is a simplified view of a subtle and complex range of possibilities.

FIGURE 17-2

Grey Gardens—eccentric characters taken on their own terms. *(Photo courtesy of The Kobal Collection/Portrait Films.)*

OBSERVATIONAL OR PARTICIPATORY APPROACH

In **Chapter 3: Documentary History** we said that filmmakers found themselves having to choose between *observational* and *participatory* modes. Figure 17-3 represents filmmakers collecting evidence with an observational camera, and doing their utmost as onlookers to exert minimal effect on the proceedings.

Figure 17-4 represents participatory cinema, in which camera and crew are avowedly present and inquiring, and ready to catalyze as necessary an interaction between participants, or between participants and themselves. Few documentaries in fact take a purist attitude, and most use whatever strategy best serves each situation. If 15 fire engines are hard at work putting out a fire, you probably won't need to intervene and apply any formative pressures. But if a naked environmentalist has chained himself to the Department of the Interior railings, you will have to interact with him, or the filming won't transcend a single enigmatic image.

The distinguished American documentarian Fred Wiseman, a former lawyer, only ever uses observational cinema. To minimize any compromise with his ethnographic intentions he shuns artificial lighting or questioning and directing his participants. He shoots massive amounts of footage and fashions his films without narration from the evidence he collects.

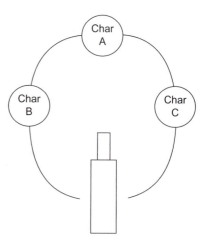

FIGURE 17-4

Diagram representing participatory cinema, first called *cinéma vérité*. The camera and crew may be discreet onlookers or step in to precipitate responses and situations.

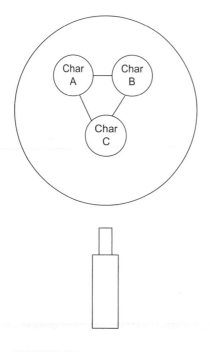

FIGURE 17-3

Diagram representing direct or observational cinema, in which the camera records life by interceding as little as possible.

If you have similar convictions about learning from life, then you may well choose subjects suitable for this approach. But asking a single interview question means you've catalyzed the record—even though you may subsequently edit out every sign of your input. A fairly recent purely observational film is Yoav Shamir's *Checkpoint* (Israel, 2004), discussed in **Chapter 5: Story Elements and Film Grammar**. It has no central characters and observes without comment the social process of one set of human beings filtering another at arbitrary boundary points.

OVERVIEW OF GENERATING POVs

You begin discerning likely points of view during *ideation* (the process of elaborating the central idea), and they solidify during the film's creation (researching, writing, shooting, and editing). Maintaining your empathic involvement will help you withstand the endless distractions that come with making films. Novelists and painters are lucky: they work alone in silence with a brush, pencil, or computer. You however must work in a hubbub of equipment, lights, and onlookers. No wonder that inspired cinema is rare.

Points of view will strengthen during editing as you crystallize your film's identity and purpose. The clearer and stronger your inner attitudes are—both toward your participants and to the film's function, the more your film acquires heart and soul, and the better it finds and serves its authorial purposes. This is the reason that this book reiterates the idea of self-knowledge as the bedrock of creative identity, and creative identity as the springboard to purposeful and inspired filmmaking.

RANGE OF POV ON THE SCREEN

SINGLE POV (CHARACTER IN THE FILM)

Figure 17-5 represents filming that is channeled through (and perhaps narrated by) a single main character. This person—observing, recounting, participating in, or re-enacting an event—may be a bystander or major protagonist. This type of film is often a biography or autobiography, with a critical tension developed between biographer and subject.

The seminal, single point of view documentary is Flaherty's *Nanook of the North* (USA, 1922), with its heroic central figure struggling to uphold his family unit's survival. Though the film is silent, it nonetheless creates a strong sense of intimacy with the father of the family. It establishes that *POV emanates from what a person does and feels*, and that actions are often more eloquent than anything a person might say.

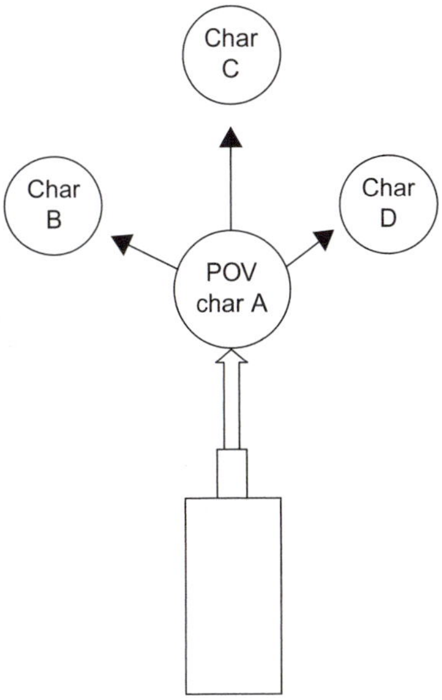

Vesting a film's point of view in a leading character does however restrict its scope. We only experience what that person can legitimately know, understand, and represent. By making Nanook represent the Inuit nation, Flaherty places a heavy onus on a single nominee, who must enact Flaherty's vision of the heroic, unspoiled native fighting on behalf of an endangered people. The man who played Nanook (real name, Allakariallak), and the two women who played his wives, had a strong historical sense of their people, and assuredly agreed

FIGURE 17-5

Diagram representing a single point of view (seeing through a character in the film).

to represent their survival prowess. Paired with one DVD version of *Nanook* is George Stoney and Jim Brown's sympathetic documentary *How the Myth Was Made* (USA, 1978), which revisits the scene of the film, talks with some of Flaherty's surviving participants, and makes clear the apolitical selectivity of Flaherty's gaze. From *Man of Aran* (USA, 1934) onwards, Flaherty's "noble savage" idealizations became more uncomfortably visible, and in his later work, Flaherty declined to collaborate. By *Louisiana Story* (USA, 1948) the passion in his storytelling has become sentimentality, and his dramatizing, manipulation.

A rather different biographical documentary is Werner Herzog's *Land of Silence and Darkness* (Germany, 1971, Figure 17-6), which follows the deaf-blind Fini Straubinger, who lay cut off from humanity in an institution for 30 years until someone taught her the deaf-blind tactile language. We see her journey around Germany in search of others as isolated and despairing as she once was herself. Their world is one of such cruel and complete isolation that Herzog's film needs only to observe while Fini, with her restricted communication, travels from encounter to encounter. Even so, it includes a few interviews, but Fini's eerie, prophetic simplicity as the film progresses gives you the shivers. Before our eyes she becomes a gauche angel personifying the love and nobility latent in the human spirit. Because of her, you realize how profoundly we take human contact for granted, and how devastating its absence must be for those whose senses have shut down. This situation reaches its nadir among those never awoken by social contact, like Vladimir who has mental handicap added cruelly to his deaf-blind condition.

Though Pernilla Rose Grønkjær's *The Monastery: Mr. Vig and the Nun* (Denmark, 2006) chronicles the interaction between two central characters, the main POV comes through the director's evident fondness for, and fascination with, the eccentric old Mr. Vig. He owns a dilapidated castle, and has always wanted to start a monastery. Now nearing the end of his life, he offers it to

FIGURE 17-6

Through its character-within-the-film point of view, Werner Herzog's *Land of Silence and Darkness* shows that for the deaf–blind, contact with the rest of the world is by touch alone. *(Photo courtesy of New Yorker Films.)*

FIGURE 17-7

The Monastery: Mr. Vig and the Nun—an austere and unlikely love story.

the Russian Orthodox Church, who send a graceful but very businesslike nun from Moscow who will soon set about organizing the project and the exhausted Mr. Vig (Figure 17-7). This delicately beautiful film is set in a huge, crumbling building that is returning to Nature, just as Mr. Vig himself will soon do. It tells the contradictory story of friction but growing respect between these two very unusual people. Grønkjær mostly observes with her camera, but sometimes interacts with her subjects from behind it.

MULTIPLE CHARACTERS' POVs WITHIN THE FILM

The viewpoints represented in Figure 17-8 are of multiple characters, in which none need predominate. The combination of camera and editing may look *at* the other characters, or *through* each individual's consciousness of the others. Through what each sees, we intuit what he or she is conscious of, and feeling. The Maysles Brothers' *Salesman* (USA, 1969) is such a film, and so are Michael Apted's longitudinal study films in the *Up* series (GB, one every seven years from 1964–present).

Barbara Kopple's classic *Harlan County, USA* (USA, 1976, Figure 17-9) chronicles a protracted strike by impoverished Kentucky coal miners. Since the central issues are the exploitation and class conflict between workers and big business, the film has prominent characters but no ruling point of view. Ironic protest songs often carry the narrative forward—timeless laments that create a powerful aura of ballad and folktale, making the film live on powerfully in memory afterward like a Berthold Brecht play. Shot mostly as observational cinema, there are moments when the filmmakers become participants in the events—most memorably one night when company goons shoot at the crew.

Andrew Jarecki's *Capturing the Friedmans* (USA, 2003) and Doug Block's *51 Birch Street* (USA, 2005, Figure 17-10) are each about the extraordinary dynamics within a family. The first concentrates on the closet homosexuality of the father, and the second on the unfulfilled love life of the mother. By exploring their family's multiplicity of views and allegiances, each film looks for the underlying sources for the "questionable" and atypical behavior. *51 Birch Street* must be one of the most revealing journeys yet made into the hidden pain of an outwardly normal, comfortably middle-class family. Block's diary style creates an intimate portrait of his family while he was growing up, and of himself uneasily forming in its crucible of mysterious pressures. We come to understand the intolerable role that women had to play in the mid-twentieth century, and the cost to them in terms of stunted personal fulfillment. Surprisingly, the film's outcome is constructive and positive. Here is the emotional liberation that making an intelligent documentary can bring its participants, and which becomes the ultimate posthumous tribute to Block's mother.

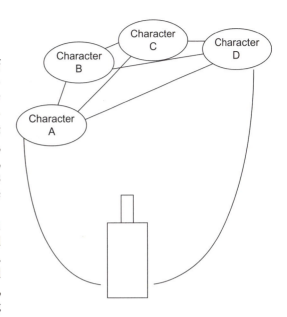

FIGURE 17-8 ——————————————

Diagram representing multiple points of view. We may "see" anyone by way of anyone else's perspective.

FIGURE 17-9 ——————————————

In *Harlan County, USA*, music adds expression to the multiple characters' viewpoints. *(Krypton International Corporation.)*

FIGURE 17-10

The Block family during the 1970s in *51 Birch Street*—concealing their stresses like any normal family. *(Photo courtesy of Doug Block.)*

OMNISCIENT POV

Typically narrated in the third person, the omniscient documentary often expresses a collective rather than personal viewpoint. Omniscience works well for complex and far-reaching subjects such as war or race relations: there an individualized point of view would seem egocentric or parochial. The omniscient POV may be institutional, corporate, or that of the filmmaker, who as Storyteller need make no apology or explanation. Omniscience is sometimes likened to the eye of God, who is said to be everywhere, and knows everything. The limitations of my diagramming (Figure 17-11) suggest that omniscience is mostly free camera movement. Certainly the POV is no longer limited to what one character can see or know, and the eye of the omniscient Storyteller moves freely in time and space. Much favored by corporations and governments, omniscience can be veneer for authoritarian instruction, but in subtler hands, the Storyteller can speak for a nation or generation, and convey a distinct outlook and moral purpose.

The early documentary seems to have acquired its stance of omniscience from the nineteenth-century gentleman's scientific slide lecture. By modestly presenting his travels as science or ethnography, he (rarely she) could avoid speaking egotistically in the first person. Older documentaries that adopt this stance sometimes skip the humility. Leni Riefenstahl's *Triumph of the Will* (Germany, 1935, Figure 17-12) and *Olympia* (Germany, 1938) use an omniscient camera to camouflage a proudly partisan view of Hitler and Nazi Germany. Her masterly use of narrationless documentary serves to ascribe power and inevitability to her subject, but the exercise warns us that "art for art's sake" can be dangerously deceptive.

Pare Lorentz's *The Plow That Broke the Plains* (USA, 1936, Figure 17-13) and *The River* (USA, 1937) use poetic narrations that turn each film into a long, elegiac ballad—a folk form that legitimizes the films' omniscient eye and seemingly egoless passion. Their powerfully aesthetized imagery and ironic montage establish a grim vision of a land plundered through ignorance and political opportunism. This is propaganda at its best, though my late friend and mentor Robert Edmonds, author of *Anthropology on Film* (Pflaum, 1974), contended that since all documentaries seek to persuade, all are propaganda. He liked to be provocative: all documentaries argue for

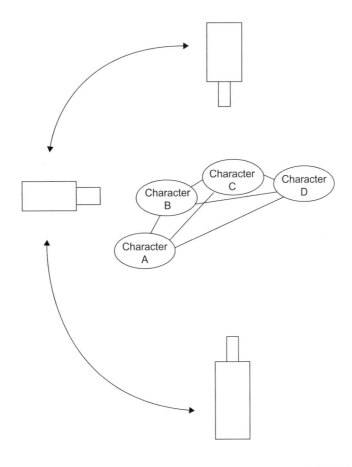

FIGURE 17-11

Diagram representing the omniscient point of view, in which the camera moves freely. Since POV comes from the storyteller, not a particular character, it's free to roam in time and space.

something, but one that simplifies the evidence to make its conclusions unavoidable is seeking to condition, not educate. To propagandize is to condition.

Few documentaries are set in the future, but Peter Watkins' *The War Game* (GB, 1966, Figure 17-14) appropriates a breaking news style to posit the nuclear bombing of London. Here the omniscient POV, appropriating the authoritarian voice of the newsreel, relocates the facts of nuclear bombing in Japan, and the fire-bombing of Dresden, to a hypothetical but highly credible present. With grim impartiality, it constructs an infernal, incontestable vision of nuclear war, one made mesmerizing by its ferocious social breakdown. Passionately seeking to persuade, the film shuns the resourcefully heroic central character that routinely provides reassurance in disaster movies. The absence of any reassurance makes us include ourselves and our loved ones with the doomed. Seeing the film as a new parent made the experience nearly unbearable.

PERSONAL POV

The personal point of view is unashamedly and subjectively that of the director (Figure 17-15), who will sometimes narrate the film, as happens in *The Tourist* (USA, 1986, Figure 17-16). In it, Robb

FIGURE 17-12

A Hitler mass rally in Leni Riefensthahl's *Triumph of the Will*. *(The Museum of Modern Art/Film Stills Archive.)*

FIGURE 17-13

In his omniscient classic *The Plow That Broke the Plains*, Pare Lorentz uses stark imagery and ironic montage to convey a haunting vision of implacable Nature. *(Museum of Modern Art.)*

FIGURE 17-14

Peter Watkins' *The War Game*, a frightening view of nuclear disaster that broadcasting kept from the public. *(Films Inc.)*

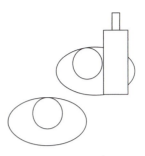

FIGURE 17-15

Diagram representing the personal point of view, in which the author/story-teller becomes the point of view character.

FIGURE 17-16

A happy couple in *The Tourist* whose marriage seems set to be childless.

FIGURE 17-17 ⎯⎯

A hall of mirrors: the director Banksy's alter ego Thierry in *Exit through the Gift Shop*.

Moss ruefully looks back over his still-childless marriage at a time when his job requires him to film huge families in Third World countries. A limit to the personal point of view is that the film cannot credibly venture outside what the author/storyteller can demonstrably see and know. This becomes interesting, however, when a story is guided by an *unreliable narrator*. We quickly realize, for instance, that Timothy Treadwell in *Grizzly Man* has a fatally skewed perception of his beloved bears.

A double POV emerges, mirror fashion, in the controversial *Exit through the Gift Shop* (Banksy, USA/UK, 2010, Figure 17-17). Thierry Guetta shows us his addiction to documenting everything in his Los Angeles life, an obsession with preservation whose poignant roots lie in childhood with the death of his mother. Ever since, he has recorded anything whose memory might be snatched away. Fascinated by the nocturnal sorties by graffiti artists, he gathers a vast footage of them, culminating in a relationship with the reclusive genius Banksy, who is visiting from Britain to give a show. Thierry accumulates thousands of hours of footage but proves incapable of making a film, so Banksy takes over. The result is a highly articulate account of turning Thierry into Mr Brainwash, a conceptual artist whose highly publicized show becomes a runaway social and commercial success.

Critics claim that creating Mr Brainwash was just another brilliant Banksy hoax, but the film deliberately raises questions about the relationship between art, money, and marketing. By the film's end you can hear spectral applause from Marcel Duchamp, who in 1917 outraged the New York art world by entering a urinal in a show and titling it "Fountain." By caricaturing art that is eye-pleasure, *Exit through the Gift Shop* makes art serve the cause of caustic, radical questioning so that it belongs with the Dada movement. Thierry becomes Banksy's alter ego, and the documentary becomes Banksy's displaced autobiography—all of which augments my private theory (don't tell anyone) that much documentary is displaced autobiography.

REFLEXIVITY AND REPRESENTATION

Reflexive documentaries are those that acknowledge and even investigate the effects of filmmaking. In Figure 17-18 the filming can now reflect the directing, shooting, and editing of the filmmaking process itself. Jay Rosenblatt is an experimental filmmaker whose mastery of the medium's subtleties and history shows in his *I Used to Be a Filmmaker* (USA, 2003, Figure 17-19).

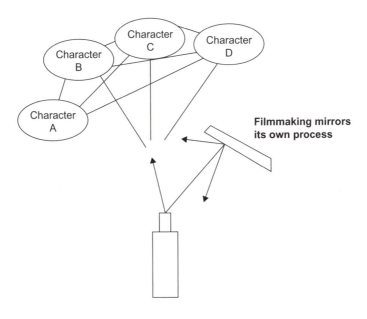

FIGURE 17-18

Diagram representing the reflexive point of view, one able to reveal salient aspects of the filmmaking process itself with the audience.

FIGURE 17-19

Jay Rosenblatt faces the new force in his life in *I Used to Be a Filmmaker*. *(Courtesy of the filmmaker.)*

Ostensibly about film practice and terminology, it yields to the joy of discovering his infant daughter Ella. Playfully the film bridges two essential and synergistic relationships—between Rosenblatt's child and his art. In the interplay, Rosenblatt compares the development of a medium with the development of a human being—even the development of a new love.

I have symbolized reflexivity—perhaps too simplistically—by a mirror. According to anthropologist Jay Ruby, who specializes in assessing the cultural content of public imagery, reflexivity means that you,

> structure a product in such a way that the audience assumes that the producer, the process of making, and the product are a coherent whole. Not only is the audience made aware of these relationships, but it is made to realize the necessity of that knowledge.[1]

A film that exposes the paradoxes of its own evolution can expose issues that have dogged documentary from the beginning. For instance,

- How often are we really seeing spontaneous life rather than something instigated by or for filmmaking itself?
- Does the film reflect reality or serve to manufacture it?
- How much of a film's purview is inhibited by ethical concerns for its participants?
- Do the participants realize how we may judge them?

By dispensing with the figment that we are watching unmediated life, reflexive films can acknowledge how screen works are "created, structured articulations of the filmmaker and not authentic, truthful, objective records."[2] Ruby points out that the investigation of documentary language began with Vertov in the 1920s, particularly his *Man with the Movie Camera* (Russia, 1929). Vertov aspired to show "life as it is," but was fascinated by the mysterious processes of cinema. He believed that the dynamics of camera and montage transcended human agency, and though we often see shots of the cameraman, he is portrayed more as the camera's servant than its master. Downplaying personal authorship, Vertov invested the apparatus with the power of finding truth—an ebullient mystification that he didn't quite pull off. Though Vertov's life-embracing Kino Eye manifesto met with incomprehension and disapproval by the Russian authorities at the time, it prepared the ground for *cinéma vérité* in France 40 years later. Today, reflexivity allows the filmmaker to focus on any of the art's ambiguities. Ethnographic filmmaking, supposed to be uncontaminated by the filmmaker's own cultural assumptions, is a prime candidate.

Aside from investigating film's boundaries, distortions, or subjectivity, there are further issues to concern us:

- Under what circumstances do we as an audience suspend, or resist suspending, disbelief?
- When does the medium deceive its makers?
- What are the ethical ramifications to reflexive filmmaking—and when are we exploiting people?

SELF-REFLEXIVITY

The ultimate in reflexivity is the self-reflexive form, which reflects its authors' thoughts, doubts, and self-examination while filming (Figure 17-20). This threatens to become the snake eating its own tail, or the pool in which a certain young man drowned. Though treacherously difficult to pull off, it can prove wonderfully rich in the right hands. Alan Berliner in *Nobody's*

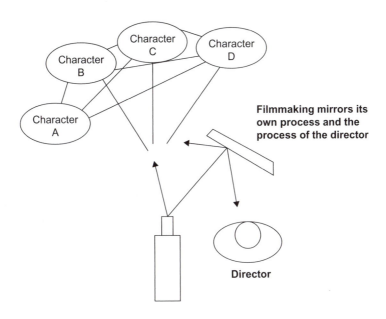

FIGURE 17-20

Diagram representing the self-reflexive point of view. A film can now reflect not only its own process but those of its maker(s) too. Handle with caution since little separates self-reflexivity from self-indulgence.

Business (USA, 1996, Figure 17-21) uses the documentary process as a means of approaching his crabby father. He hopes to achieve a better understanding, but is roundly repulsed—hence the film's title. The older man is adamant that he is an ordinary man with nothing to say. This, a challenge to any documentarian, sends the son to home movies, photographs, and letters in search of the father he hardly knows. Since his dad is the son of an immigrant Jew, the quest broadens by association to include ethnicity, ethnic identity, and even America as the melting pot that failed (thank goodness) to dissolve its citizens into a common culture. What emerges more than justifies the intrusion it takes to get there. Like all films that really illuminate family life, this one shows how the important doors never open until the director pushes and pushes. Power (that is, vital information that tells you who you are) is never given. You take it when you decide to grow up.

FILM LANGUAGE AND THE AUTHORIAL VOICE

The range of more confident, authorial voices now available confirms that documentarians no longer have to pretend they are making objective social science or have to suppress the ambiguities and contradictions they encounter in real life. Subjectivity is not just allowable, it is positively welcome, and today's technology allows you to subtitle, freeze, or interject in ways that all help disrupt the illusion of objective realism. You can slow the image, play it fast or backwards, filter it, superimpose or interweave texts at will, and thus invite us to question, doubt, and reflect on the fugitive nature of that waking dream we call actuality.

FINDING FRESH LANGUAGE

Your greatest challenge as a filmmaker will always be to find film language not tarnished by over-familiarity. You will always do this best, I contend, by looking inward for the exact texture of your own emotional and psychic experience, and then seeking its equivalency in the cinema palette so you can put its spirit on the screen. Only this way can you connect us convincingly with other realities—yours and those of your subjects. Perhaps someone will see your work and repeat something said about Louis-Ferdinand Céline—that he wrote "not about reality, but about the hallucinations raised by reality."[3]

Documentary is a young genre in the young art of cinema; it has only scratched the surface of its potential. You come on the scene when documentaries have an expanding canvas and their only restraints remain productive ones— that anything is documentary if it (a) presents aspects of actuality (past, present, or future) and (b) implies a critical relationship to the fabric of social life.

FIGURE 17-21

STORYTELLER AND POV QUESTION CHECKLIST

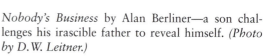

Nobody's Business by Alan Berliner—a son challenges his irascible father to reveal himself. *(Photo by D. W. Leitner.)*

Each possible POV offers a different way of entering the people and their world. Switching POV creates a vital contrast between what each character sees and feels while navigating human predicaments. Seeing through other eyes, we retain our values and have a double experience, one that *helps us realize both ourselves and others*. Of your film, ask:

- How many POVs are possible in my film?
- Which POV should predominate
  - Throughout?
  - Through different parts of the documentary?
  - Through one or two parts?
- What is my brief description of each POV in relation to the
  - Character's agenda?
  - Character's limitations and blind spots?
  - Overall development of the story?
- What must I shoot to serve each necessary POV?
- How should I shoot each so I complement the character's nature and biases?
- How do I, as the Storyteller, want to color the story?
- What role does my Storyteller play in order to further the nature of the story?

- What should I shoot to show the Storyteller's POV?
- How should I shoot to imply the Storyteller's POV, so I build the storytelling atmosphere and emphases?
- Should my audience be able to take into account
  - Aspects of the filmmaking that surfaced during production?
  - My/our experience during the filmmaking that might affect what the audience will think and feel?

HANDS-ON LEARNING

For analyzing the means that filmmakers use to tell their tales, make an analysis of a representative few minutes of a favorite work with **AP-1 Making a Split-Page Script.** The reason for imagery used against language, of language overlapping picture cuts, and the use of voice-overs emerges in all its subtlety when you log it out on paper.

NOTES

1. Jay Ruby, "The Image Mirrored: Reflexivity and the Documentary Film," in Alan Rosenthal, ed., *New Challenges for Documentary* (University of California Press, 1988), p. 65.
2. Ibid., pp. 717–75. See Ruby's long essay "Exposing Yourself: Reflexivity, Anthropology, and Film" at http://astro.temple.edu/~ruby/ruby/exposing.html.
3. André Malraux's comment on *Journey to the End of the Night* by the visionary novelist Louis-Ferdinand Céline (1894–1961). Quoted from memory—I have been unable to trace the origin.

CHAPTER 18

DRAMATIC DEVELOPMENT, TIME, AND STORY STRUCTURE

Documentaries are stories that aim to change our hearts and minds by organizing their characters, situations, and pressures toward a revelatory purpose. They mean to expand our knowledge and alter our emotional frame of reference.

This chapter looks at the relationship between the chronology of documented events, their organization into a satisfying dramatic form, and the way in which a story's dramatic needs may require reorganizing a story's events for maximum impact.

PLOTS AND THEIR CENTRAL CHARACTERS

PLOT AND THE RULES OF THE UNIVERSE

The filmmaker and philosopher Michael Roemer suggests intriguingly that plot in fiction is really about the rules of the universe at work, and that the most absorbing characters are those who contest—heroically, and often unsuccessfully—the way things are.[1] This holds true for documentary, since a central character refusing to accept his fate can be either funny or tragic. Some contest the status quo set by society and win; others are unable to accept the workings of a much darker fate. Josh Oppenheimer's *Act of Killing* (Denmark/UK/Norway, 2012, Figure 18-1) deals with an intractable kind of human cruelty—by those sponsored by the authorities to wreak unimaginable brutality on those protesting their grip on power. That "might makes right" or that the ends justify the means is one of the ugliest among human delusions, and its grip on rulers is virtually universal. Anyone who follows world news sees the cost in blood, torture, and death everywhere.

ACTIVE AND PASSIVE

Why do we so often think of central characters in documentary as people *to whom things happen*? Maybe, being the hero of our own story, we notice how people act on us, but not how we act on others. Is this a survival mechanism, or a mindset left over from the vulnerability of childhood?

Ingrained passivity when directing documentaries will blind you to all the ways that participants fashion their own destiny and make you keep seeing victims. Surely this is why so many

FIGURE 18-1

In Josh Oppenheimer's *Act of Killing*, former killers model their lives on Hollywood gangsters. *(Photo by Carlos Arango de Montis—framegrab.)*

documentaries enshrine the "tradition of the victim."[2] There is something dangerously patronizing about this. How you think of your central character largely determines what reaches the screen.

HEROES AND HEROINES

What makes a hero, and do they mainly exist because we have need of them? The archetypal hero is one writ large, a character of magnitude who faces outsize challenges. This was hardly Rosa Parks, who in 1955 challenged the status quo in the South by refusing to yield her bus seat to a white person. Her action of refusal was a timely symbolism that helped precipitate the American civil rights movement. In the late 1960s I filmed World War I conscientious objectors who had faced imprisonment, torture, and execution for refusing to put on uniform and kill men like themselves. At first they were "cowards," but soldiers returning broken from the obscenity of trench warfare said they too would have been "conchies," had they known what war was really about. So which are the heroes?

The dramatic tension a film generates from such situations comes from getting us involved with people and their issues, and making us care that they prevail. In a way, delineating such people is easy because their accomplishments are so tangible. How do you involve us with someone less extraordinary?

"CHARACTER IS FATE"[3]

Apply this to anyone you know well to see how closely character and destiny are related. Use this when making a character-driven film to see how much your subject has forged their own destiny. Simply revealing this can often make a very satisfying biographical film, especially as ordinary lives often have something heroic about them—the spouse who cares selflessly for a partner whose Alzheimer's disease prevents the sufferer from even recognizing the carer.

WHETHER THE HERO DEVELOPS

Effective stories nearly always have a central character who develops because of their struggles. In Steve James's *Hoop Dreams* (USA, 1994, Figure 18-2) the two black basketball players William

FIGURE 18-2

The two central characters in *Hoop Dreams* find they are pawns in a white-controlled sports circuit.

FIGURE 18-3

Philippe Petit walking between the doomed World Trade Center buildings in *Man on Wire*.

Gates and Arthur Agee grow up, but their development is disillusioning because they find they are just pawns in a system. The development in *Grizzly Man* (USA, 2005) is particularly ghastly since the special relationship Timothy Treadwell imagined he had with bears was a prescription for death. Philippe Petit's heart-stopping high wire walk between the ill-fated World Trade Center towers in James Marsh's *Man on Wire* (UK, 2008, Figure 18-3) successfully demonstrates Petit's extreme skills and courage, and although he does not change, it is enough to see him survive.

FIGURE 18-4 ——

In *Stevie*, a director returns to his hometown in search of the troubled child he once befriended.

THE ANTIHERO

In the history of literature, some writers reacted with such nausea to the moral exhortation implicit in "good" characters that they invented the antihero. Fielding's Tom Jones, Thackeray's Becky Sharp, and Camus's Meursault are all stigmatized, humanly flawed characters trying to make their mark as they negotiate an amoral world. In documentary, the confused, petty criminal who is the title character in *Stevie* (USA, 2002) is also an antihero. When he was a troubled child in a dysfunctional family, the director Steve James had been his "Advocate Big Brother," and is now returning to his small town roots to find out where Stevie is now (Figure 18-4). The young man's problems have only grown, and he is in trouble with the law. By the end of the film, Stevie goes to prison for sexually molesting an eight-year-old relative. A heinous crime, certainly, yet the film makes one compassionate toward him. Failed on all sides, he is never less than pitiably human, and this leaves James wondering whether he might have done more.

Whatever the antihero may be, he or she is not a victim. Too much television ennobles victims or glorifies those who overcome horrific injuries "against all the odds." It seems cynically facile to "celebrate the human spirit" of some poor young man rendered legless and impotent. Lured into the military on the promise of going to college, he goes instead into combat—something his political masters assiduously avoid when it comes to their own offspring.

As protagonists, antiheroes are complex, contradictory, and hostile to convention. Often their special qualities emerge in unexpected ways as they negotiate the hand dealt by fate. Some important questions:

- What do you want your audience to make of your central figures?
- What are you trying to say through them?
- What do you want to say about human nature, folly, vulnerability, or aspiration?

DRAMA AND THE THREE-ACT STRUCTURE

Analyze a few dramatic plots—fiction or nonfiction—and you soon find common denominators in their organization. To explain this, the ancient Greeks devised the *three-act structure*, touched upon earlier in **Chapter 3: Documentary History** in relation to the Maysles Brothers' *Salesman*

FIGURE 18-5

The rise and fall of Paul Brennan in *Salesman* makes a perfect three-act tragedy.

(USA, 1961, Figure 18-5). The three-act structure is still an invaluable tool for understanding and organizing story elements. See it not as a formulaic strait-jacket, but as an aid to the clarity of your thinking as a dramatist. To recapitulate:

Act I   Establishes the *setup* (establishes characters, relationships, and situation and dominant *problem* faced by the central character or characters).

Act II   Escalates the *complications* as the central character struggles with the obstacles that prevent him/her solving his main problem.

Act III Intensifies the situation to a point of *climax* or *confrontation*, at which point the situation is *resolved*, often by the central character and in a climactic way that is emotionally satisfying. A resolution doesn't necessarily have to be happy: it might be an ageing boxer accepting defeat—sad, but inevitable.

This archetypal organization of a story is probably rooted in the way early humans narrated their hunting journeys and battles with rival tribes. Without lighting, they must have spent much time in winter recalling stories around a fire, and narrative form as we know it must have evolved from the way they evolved storytelling for the best audience response.

The three-act structure is plainly visible in a "reality" survival type of program, *Pioneer Quest: A Year in the Real West* (Canada, 2003). A group sets out to discover what life was like on the prairie for pioneers. Winter is coming and they must race to build a shelter. They work through all the obstacles that made hand-building a cabin from local materials slow and difficult, and the resolution is a viable (if draughty) cabin, in which the volunteer "immigrants" struggle to keep warm during the coldest winter for 120 years.

By trying to imagine our ancestors' lives, "how would I manage as a prairie settler?" is a central type of question. It is especially poignant if you realize how little you really know about your

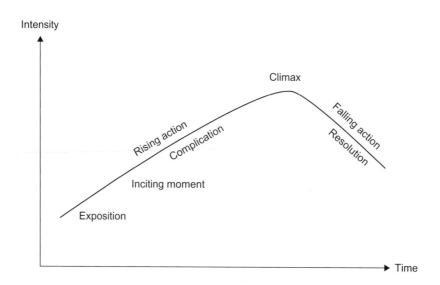

FIGURE 18-6 ———————————————————————————————————————

The arc of changing pressures fundamental to all drama.

own parents' lives, because you never thought to question them. Social experiments are a wonderful way to discover someone else's key predicaments, and make superb projects for documentary-makers. The situations revolve around the fundamentals of character, obstacles, inventiveness, and struggle, all of which determine the outcome (or *resolution*).

THE DRAMATIC ARC

Cycles of character/problem/escalation/crisis/resolution form units that dramatists represent through a *dramatic curve* or *dramatic arc*, whose build-up, peaking, and downturn look rather like a fever patient's temperature chart (Figure 18-6). The concept comes from ancient Greek dramatic theory by graphing each story-unit (scene, act, or entire drama) as rising pressure. It states the central character's *problem*, and maintains *dramatic tension* through events of increasing intensity and *complication*, until arriving at an *apex* or *crisis*. Following this comes the *resolution*—though not, let me emphasize, one that is necessarily happy or peaceful.

You seldom know how a documentary shoot will turn out, but even in research it is good to imagine where you might place available materials along the film's imagined dramatic arc. You can apply it as a template for an entire story, or use it to help you identify the changing dramatic pressures in a single scene. Knowledge of the concept helps you to decide, as you shoot a scene, where you are, dramatically speaking, during an argument between two children in a playground, or in a dispute over the validity of a discount coupon. When it comes to postproduction, the dramatic arc, like the three-act structure with which it is closely associated, provides superb guidance for how to orchestrate the story's rising and falling pressures.

DEFINING THE CRISIS

To begin deciding a scene's dramatic shape, first nail down its pivotal point, or *crisis*. This is the turning point of maximum pressure, struggle, and change. In Nicholas Broomfield and Joan

FIGURE 18-7

Paul Brennan in *Salesman* staring failure in the eye.

Churchill's *Soldier Girls* (USA/GB, 1981), it is probably where Private Johnson, after a series of increasingly stressful scenes of conflict with authority, leaves the army dishonorably but in a spirit of relieved gaiety. After this major character leaves the stage, the film's resolution is to examine more closely what soldiers need during training to survive battle conditions.

In the Maysles Brothers' *Salesman* (USA, 1969), discussed in **Chapter 3: Documentary History**, most people consider the story's apex to be the moment when Paul Brennan, the salesman falling behind the pack like a wounded animal, sabotages a colleague's sale. In the film's coda, his partners have distanced themselves as if from contagion, and the film's resolution is a shot of Paul gazing offscreen into a void, as if staring mesmerized at his oncoming fate (Figure 18-7).

No matter what unit of drama you analyze—whether a dramatic unit in a scene, or an entire movie—the whole cycle emerges once you have pinpointed the apex or crisis. Commonly, around two-thirds of the drama precedes the crisis, and a third follows it. By taking *Soldier Girls* we can examine the three-act structure so you can make use of them:

Act I   The *exposition* establishes the *setup* by laying out main characters and their situation, and giving enough *necessary exposition* (time, place, period, and so on) to get the story moving. *Soldier Girls* aims to secure the audience's interest for the duration by signaling the scope and focus of the film to come. The story usually quickly establishes the main *conflict*, or struggle between opposing forces, as part of the documentarian's implied *contract* with the audience. The *inciting moment* is whatever sets in motion the opposition of interests. Film, often consumed at home, cannot afford to delay the major *committing action* since the viewer can easily switch to something else.

During military training, boot camp is the battleground for the struggle between the homogenizing goals of the army and the self-protecting individualism of the recruit. In *Soldier Girls* the *committing action* is Private Johnson smirking after Sergeant Abing has rebuked her, and getting caught. This sets off a long and unequal struggle between them. The army aims to break the individual's resistance and replace it with a psyche trained to obey unthinkingly. Here, because white males are imposing their will on minority females, the situation abounds with disquieting overtones of slavery and colonialism.

Act II   *Rising action* or *complication* usually shows the basic conflicts being played out at escalating intensity—here as variations involving surprise, suspense, and reversal. The army expressing its will, and the misfits acting out their cowed resistance, repeatedly raises the tension a notch toward ever more serious and offensive levels. Seeing *protagonists* and *antagonists* engaged in such a revealing struggle, we come to understand the motivations, goals, and background of each, and choose whom to identify with. In the face of ambiguity, our sympathies sometimes vacillate.

Act III   In the final *confrontation* comes the *climax* or apex of the curve, a point of irreversible change. The *resolution* or *falling action* is what the piece establishes as the consequences. This includes not only what befalls the characters but also what interpretation for the whole is suggested by the last scenes. How the audience last sees your characters—in a documentary as in other story forms—can alter the impact of an entire film.

Hollywood uses the three-act formula with awful fervor, and some screenwriting manuals even prescribe a page count per act, with actual page numbers at which *plot points* should occur (a plot point takes the story off at an unexpected tangent). Documentary is far too wayward to permit such iron control, but it must give its audience dramatic satisfaction too. The same dramatic form remains true for essay, montage, or other forms of documentary, not just those featuring physical struggle.

Indeed, you can find this dramatic form—escalation of pressure up to a crisis, then a lowering pressure after the resolution—expressed in songs, symphonies, opera, dance, mime, and traditional tales—all the time arts, in fact. It is as fundamental to human existence as breathing or sex.

SCENES ARE DRAMAS IN MICROCOSM

A successful documentary scene will often reproduce in microcosm a similar dramatic curve of pressures that you see on a large scale in a whole work. A scene is thus a drama in miniature. Even compilation montage films about nature that lack any foreground characters, such as Pare Lorentz's *The River* (USA, 1937), or Godrey Reggio's *Koyaanisqatsi* (USA, 1982), use the same cyclic building and then release of pressure. The documentary director orchestrates this—either in the cutting room, or from behind the camera at the time of shooting.

In real life things are not so tidy. For every human interaction that spontaneously fulfills the dramatic arc, ten others suffer delays, paralysis, or regression. In observational documentary, you are left frustrated and impotent, but in participatory documentary you can do something about it.

THE DIRECTOR INTERCEDES

When a scene develops, spin its wheels, and refuses to go anywhere, some judicious *side coaching* (verbal inquiry or prompts by the director from off-camera) can help the characters work at an

FIGURE 18-8

Steve James questioning Stevie Fielding, now in prison.

issue differently and produce a significant change. Skillful editing can now make the scene function without looking assisted in any way. But, you protest, that isn't true to life or honest! You can argue with some justice that, providing your side-coaching helps the participants reach their own solution, the results on film serve the spirit of truth if not its literal word.

When the director feels responsible for the main character's progress, as Steve James does in *Stevie* (USA, 2002, Figure 18-8), he cannot avoid becoming a player in Stevie Fielding's struggle with himself. James can pose questions, suggest options, ask for memories or ideas that Stevie might think of for himself, were he less beset by demons.

In such a situation, the participatory director becomes a surrogate for the audience, pursuing what the audience wants elucidated, and applying pressures the audience might apply were it, rather than James, confronting Stevie. Becoming the film's interlocutor in this way carries responsibilities, since the director can misuse his weight to exert moral censure, judgmental righteousness, or to claim that what Stevie has done wrong is justified. If so, the director's values and sensibility are now out in the open for the audience to assess. To acquit him- or herself well, the director must work carefully from clues manifest by the person under scrutiny. In fact, once you become attuned, you can develop strong intuitions, and do all you can—verbally and nonverbally—to midwife new stages into being. How can this be? And how is this connected with dramatic form? We must now look at another important moment in drama which you should recognize.

BEATS AND DRAMATIC UNITS

In dramaturgy an important moment of change in a character's consciousness is called a *beat*. Let's be quite clear that this has nothing to do with music, rhythm, or a moment of delay (as fiction screenplays sometimes demand). A dramatic beat is *a fulcrum point, a moment of irrevocable change*. Well-trained actors know beats as turning points in each of the dramatic units that make up a well-written scene. You might have a touching moment when a mother realizes for the first time that her daughter loves her: well, that turning-point moment is a beat! It might be a pickpocket realizing he is trapped in a subway train. Another beat.

In neither scenes do other characters notice anything, but the character under scrutiny (along with us, the audience, of course) recognizes that the character has (a) gone through a moment of irreversible change, and (b) must now act differently.

The documentary director busy shooting life must understand this principle, and learn to see beats forming and happening before his or her camera. Two friends maneuvering a new fridge through a narrow hallway might yield a series of beats:

They puff and pant getting the fridge to the doorway

Obstacle A: They realize it's too big to go through the doorway (*Failure*, **beat**).

Strategy: They confer, measure it, realize it'll go through if they remove the door (delay while they find tools). Remove fridge door and interior shelves.

Try again: it's lighter (*Success*, **beat**). Rejoicing: it goes through the doorway.

Obstacle B: Now it won't go under a rigid light fixture.

Strategy: Too complicated to dismantle fixture, so must lie fridge down lengthways.

They back it into doorway, roll it forward, get under the fixture and (*success*, **beat**) move forward

Obstacle C: The fridge is too long to get past the bottom of a protruding staircase.

Strategy: They must roll the fridge upright again. They are getting tired and irritable with each other.

They try this and it works (*success*, **beat**). With difficulty they can maneuver the fridge into the kitchen (*resolution.*) Mission accomplished, weary high-fives.

Finding the solution to each *obstacle* requires a *strategy*. Whether it fails or succeeds, it's probably a beat, the proof being that they have to change tactics. If another approach works, the problem is solved, and so another beat, a new problem, and new strategies. Solving one problem usually leads onward to a new one, and so on. Thus when two people try to accomplish something, each *dramatic unit* normally includes:

- Realizing there is a *problem* and agreeing or not agreeing on what it is.
- Pursuing an *agenda* which may be mutual or not.
- *Complication*s arise to *raise the stakes* (which makes success all the more imperative).
- They approach the *crisis* (apex of their efforts).
- Their final make-or-break strategy either works or doesn't, leading to a *beat* that is the *crisis*—the highest point of struggle and change.
- *Resolution* (outcome) leads on to a new issue or problem.

In dramatic tradition there are three main types of conflict—two external, one internal:

- Man against man.
- Man against nature.
- Man against himself.

MISIDENTIFYING CONFLICTS

It is fatally easy, indeed strangely universal, to define a situational conflict inadequately or downright wrongly, which will distort or even destroy the course of your film. A woman who tries to rescue family photos during a flood is not in conflict *with* the photos, or *over* the photos, but with the overwhelming forces of nature that threaten to destroy her history. A young actor struggling to overcome her sheer terror at going onstage for the first time is not in conflict with the play, or with the situation: she is in conflict with her own fear of failing, which makes it "woman vs. herself."

Always *doubt you've properly located the conflict* in whatever you are witnessing or shooting—it's a very slippery and deceptive concept and worth double-checking. In the refrigerator example above, the conflict is not men vs. fridge, because the fridge is not putting up a fight. It is simply being its awkward, lumpen self. Surely the conflict is "man vs. man" since the action is two individuals arguing their way through the difficulties of teamwork. The fridge is the catalyst for difficulties which cause them to try to cooperate. Define the locus of conflict properly, and you can shoot it well. Misidentify it, and you'll shoot the scene wrongly.

A SCENE MAY HAVE ONE DRAMATIC UNIT OR SEVERAL

Make a practice of recognizing beats taking place around you in daily life. Count the beats in each scene, and imagine how you'd film them. For the fridge scene, how much attention should your camera give to the fridge? How do you show the obstacles? How much should you dwell on one or other of the two men? What character traits do they manifest during their struggle, and how can you bring them out?

INHALATION AND EXHALATION

When dramatic units follow one after another, your film is breathing, in and out. Recognizing dramatic units in life, covering them sensitively with the camera as they take place, and editing to expose their essential nature is a skill supremely important to your directing, no matter whether in fiction or documentary. Very few people master this, so if you can teach yourself such awareness, and capture it on film, your work will register immediately as somehow superior.

A successful progression of beats hikes the *dramatic tension*. It sets up questions, anticipations, even fears in your audience. Never be afraid when editing to make your audience wait and guess what comes next. "Make them laugh, make them cry" said the father of the mystery story, "but make them wait." [4]

THE DIRECTOR AS DRAMATIST

From now on, think of yourself as a *dramatist*, someone who specializes in profiling character, development, and destiny. Many times, as you shoot a situation's progression, the scene stalls instead of resolving into the change you anticipated. Perhaps somebody's aspiration leads to failure or flies off at a tangent (in dramaturgy this is a *plot point*). Now you see an entirely new cycle of problem, complications and escalation. Or maybe you see that the scene is simply hanging. If you are shooting participatory rather than observational documentary, you can try breaking the log-jam with a well-considered question, or by suggesting an action of some kind. Alternatively you might cut the camera and confer with the participants before proceeding.

Once you can recognize where any moment of an unfolding scene lies on the dramatic arc, you can direct more intuitively. To get there, work on your insight during the everyday activities around you—in the post office line, say, as a grumpy clerk tries to persuade an obtuse customer to step aside and fill up a different form. Often you will see scenes of tension in which someone grapples with obstacles, handling them from the entrenched perspective of their own agenda. Scan along the dramatic arc by asking yourself:

- The *main character* is…
- His/her *problem* is…
- The *inciting moment* was…
- The *agendas* for each of the characters are…
- The *complications* in the situation are…
- The *crisis* came when…
- And the *resolution* or outcome was…

Seeing ahead of the participants in a human interchange, you are forewarned and ready for what they might do. Even more important is that your camera operator be so too.

No matter what kind of cinema you are making, your responsibility is to see, understand, and shoot *dramatic units* because they are the piston strokes of powerful drama.

TIME AND STRUCTURE

Satisfying stories generally have *momentum* (forward-moving energy). The key lies not only in *givens* (who/what/when/where) and the characters' agendas, but in the obstacles that build up an energy field by providing resistance. To depict this in his teaching, my Australian friend Russell Porter uses his Dead Fish Analogy (Figure 18-9). The head is the beginning of the film, the tail is its end. Any story with momentum has a strong backbone leading surely from head to tail. This is usually indicated in the Hook, or "Contract," which indicates the direction and purpose of the story in the film's first minute or so. Once the momentum and reliability of the spine is established, you can afford to have ribs, each representing a sidebar excursion.

Imagine applying this to a hypothetical project about walking the medieval pilgrim's trail from the Pyrenees to Santiago de Compostela in Spain. Once the pilgrimage is established and begun, you can leave the trail along the way to visit Pamplona, Burgos, Leon, and even small villages. The spine represents the goal of traversing the pilgrim's way, and the tail is the magnificent cathedral of Saint James, always there as the film's goal.

Any strong idea is like this. It might be a man's quest for the father he hardly knew, as in Nathaniel Kahn's *My Architect* (USA, 2003, Figure 18-10). Having established the primacy of his mission, Nathaniel can take time to visit Louis Kahn's buildings around the world, talk with the women in his father's life, and question the architects he knew and influenced.

In their ethnographic study *Sifinja—the Iron Bride* (2009, Sudan/Germany, Figure 18-11) Valerie Hänsch and Kurt Beck study an extended family in Sudan who renovate a classic brand of

FIGURE 18-9 ———

Russell Porter's dead fish analogy for dramatic structure.

FIGURE 18-10

In *My Architect*, the boy is emblematic of Nathaniel Kahn searching for his father in his father's work.

FIGURE 18-11

The spine of *Sifinja* is not a journey or a stretch of time, nor even a process. It is the desert craftsmen's proud declaration that they can keep elderly Bedford trucks going forever.

British truck. The spine of the film is not a journey or a stretch of time, but a proud declaration by the desert craftsmen that they can keep these Bedford trucks going forever. The film proves this by showing their resourcefulness at using basic tools and techniques to rebuild engines and transmissions, and repurpose suspensions and bodies to accommodate local needs. This is a process film whose development is the truck's rebirth as a brightly painted, bedecked galleon of the desert, piled high with goods, people, and clucking chickens.

The sidebar excursions deal with the ingenious though primitive resources by which they solve mechanical problems, the customs and humor of the country, and competition looming on the horizon as customers desert the Bedford for a larger, newer truck. The film implies that when human beings have skills, pride, and a social system valuing humor, they can be endlessly creative.

PREPARING FOR THE PREDICTABLE

Many life situations have foreseeable elements. Imagine you are going out with a fire engine company to document the impact of a fire on a family. What can you predict? As research, you question the engine crew on typical fires—and they will have much to tell you. You learn that every event has a predictable course with inevitable givens (in this case, causes and effects), and so with some forethought you can be fairly sure your story will include:

- How the fire started.
- How people tried to stop it.
- How it spread.
- What neighbors did—heroic or otherwise—to save the victims.
- How far the fire got before coming under control by firefighters.
- What the family lost that mattered to them.
- What the consequences are for their lives thereafter.

You can even see where each element might belong in the three-act structure. Now you can collect material and come away with coverage that practically guarantees the elements of a full story. Most importantly, you have envisioned what outcomes to expect, since any one of them provides the all-important *development* that saves your film from getting no farther than stating the obvious. Even though everyone escapes without physical harm, there is a great deal of mental suffering, and you become the witness to this. You might even follow your family for months or years afterwards.

Most narratives tell the chapters of their tale in chronological order, but you can do otherwise if (a) there is a compelling reason to organize them differently, or (b) because basic chronology is weak, absent, or unimportant to the *angle* (storytelling purpose or emphasis) of the story.

STORIES NEED DEVELOPMENT

In plenty of reports on extreme situations like refugee camps and hunger, nothing changes, leaving the viewer feeling impotent and hopeless about humanity. It's the kind of portrayal that has stereotyped Africa as a continent of passive victims, when much today is positive and constructive there—socially and economically. My own feeling is that narrative art is an indulgence if it does not find evidence of growth and change somewhere. The problem is that most human growth is very slow, and the documentarian cannot always stay around to show it.

If you can't afford a long shooting period, choose your subject carefully. When long-ago I worked on a BBC series called *Breakaway*, we skirted "non-event films" by building a series around people undergoing major changes. My two films were about people choosing to migrate abroad,[5] but another followed an elderly person into a retirement home, and a third chronicled an apprentice ladies hairdresser deciding to join "a man's world" in the Army. Each film had a clear "before" and "after"—and a major, assured turning point as the apex of the dramatic arc.

The list that follows, not meant to be definitive, is of common documentary types that each imply structures.

CHRONOLOGICAL TIME

THE EVENT-CENTERED FILM

An event, especially one that is familiar, often provides a strong, clear structure. Its stages become the vertebrae in the film's temporal spine, and provide a strong sensation of forward movement. Once the event is under way, its momentum lets you plug in sidebars (the ribs along the spine) knowing that the audience is always ready for the story to revert to the temporal spine's next stage. These digressions might be sections of interview, pieces of relevant past, or even pieces of the imagined future.

Some events, such as a marathon race or a political rally, move fast or have many unfolding facets. Leni Riefenstahl's dark classic, *Olympia* (Germany, 1938, Figure 18-12), presents the 1936 Berlin Olympic Games in this way and places Hitler and the German contestants with seductive virtuosity at the center of a mass of events that Riefenstahl references to the heroic deeds of antiquity.

FIGURE 18-12 ───────────────────────────────

The beauty of sports seen through National Socialist eyes in *Olympia*. *(The Kobal Collection/Olympia-Film.)*

When multiple strands of narrative are happening simultaneously, you may need multiple camera units. I directed one such unit in a series called "All in a Day": the film was about an aristocratic pheasant shoot, and my unit tracked the gamekeeper. Any situation having multiple actors that runs its course in a predictable span, such as a court trial, spelling bee, or rodeo, is likely to have just as predictable a shape and structure. Its "unknowns" will be who or what predominates in the welter of action. To cover one like this, divide the activities into stages, and carefully brief each unit to cover particular aspects of each stage, since your film must be able to indicate what is expected by the audience. Plan carefully or the units wander into each other's fields of vision by mistake. Knowing you have what is vital pinned down, your units are freed to record the unexpected along the way.

THE PROCESS FILM

A process is any sequence of events that produces or accomplishes something. Building a shed, taking a journey, or getting married can transcend the banal and become fascinating if you can reveal them as atypical, archetypal, or metaphorical. Like event films, process films are modular, each stage having its own arc containing beginning, middle, and end. Usually you show them in chronological sequencing, but you can use *parallel storytelling* to intercut multiple events or processes by weaving together the multiple story strands pioneered by Dickens in his novels. A father may be at work in a factory, for instance, while his daughter is in school getting the education that allows her *not* to work in a factory. As each sequence advances by steps, the characters and their predicaments develop in a linear fashion, and, most importantly, you can imply meanings and create dramatic tension by juxtaposing particular actions. By allowing you to make only minimal references, parallel storytelling permits brevity and a potent form of authorial comment.

A three-year longitudinal study like David Sutherland's *The Farmer's Wife* (USA, 1998, Figure 18-13) chronicles the effects of relentlessly growing economic pressure. The process in question—shocking in the world's wealthiest nation—is slow starvation for a Nebraska farming

FIGURE 18-13

Longitudinal study of a farming family under extreme duress in *The Farmer's Wife. (Photo courtesy of David Sutherland Productions.)*

family. Blow by blow, and in extraordinary intimacy, we see Darrel and Juanita Buschkoetter struggling to stave off bankruptcy. Culled from 200 hours of footage, the film shows many poignant, lonely episodes that play out as sustained husband/wife interactions. Each is filled with tension, and many become the kind of dramatic experience you could only hope for in a strong theatre production. During the six one-hour episodes, Darrel doggedly works multiple jobs while she holds the family together and finishes college. Eventually it is her strength of character that pulls them through—hence the series title. Over the three-year span, Juanita matures from girl to woman, but their marriage suffers badly.

Les Blank's *Burden of Dreams* (USA, 1982, Figure 18-14) chronicles the making of Werner Herzog's *Fitzcarraldo*, a fiction feature about a real-life opera impresario who contrived to drag a river steamer over the Andes. Blank documents Herzog's own struggle to get a steamer up a jungle mountainside, and reveals how a cherished project can become more important to its director than the physical dangers faced by his workers. Herzog's objectives and values revealed by the process become metaphors for the ruthlessness that often lurks under the guise of making art.

FIGURE 18-14

Werner Herzog and the boat he hauls up a hillside in Les Blank's *Burden of Dreams*. *(Photo by Maureen Gosling.)*

THE JOURNEY FILM

Journeys promise change and development. Luc Jacquet's *March of the Penguins* (France, 2005, Figure 18-15) shows the epic journey that Emperor Penguins make in the Antarctic in order to breed. Some do not finish the journey, find a mate, or manage to guard their chicks, so the film has periods of fairly awful suspense. The struggle to survive has such anthropomorphic resonances that for some the film exemplified "family values." Apparently, the French version had a set of voices speaking as if for the penguins (which sounds truly awful). More conventionally the English version uses the omniscient, voice-over narration dear to National Geographic, which coproduced. Gripping and worth studying for its editing alone, the film orchestrates much mass action and movement culled from a year of shooting. Luckily penguins do similar things and all look alike, so you get extraordinarily detailed coverage of each stage during their long and arduous journey.

Jorge Furtado's 13-minute *Isle of Flowers* (Brazil, 1989, Figure 18-16), once voted a most important short film of the twentieth century, follows the brief life of a tomato as it starts at the growing site, follows it being made into sauce, and then watches its dregs finishing up in the municipal dump. The film has virtuoso montage sequences, and as you can guess, tomatoes become metaphors for human beings. The film shocks its audiences by suggesting how despicably an industrial society treats the powerless.

FIGURE 18-15

Shooting *The March of the Penguins*. (Photo courtesy of the Kobal Collection/Bonne Pioche/Buena Vista/ APC/Jerome Maison.)

FIGURE 18-16

The municipal dump in *Isle of Flowers* where the tomato we have followed is flung out to die amid the trash.

In Lars Johannson's *The German Secret* (Denmark, 2005, Figure 18-17) the filmmaker chronicles his wife Kirsten Blohm crossing Europe in search of the Nazi father whose identity her mother refused to divulge until near death. Amazingly, there are still people alive 50 years later along the route who remember the beautiful, haughty blonde with the strangely neglected child. Piece by piece, Johannson and Blohm establish the truth, which shapes up to be very far from what they expected. In this tender and masterful film that is replete with intimate reflection and intense, sustained encounters, Kirsten's painful journey delivers only partial liberation from a legacy of doubt and anger.

THE HISTORICAL FILM

Strictly speaking, all film is history since every frame, no sooner recorded, becomes a preservation of the past. Film ought to be a good medium for historical films, but is not always so. More than most story forms, histories must often digress to build their tributary chains of cause and effect. Imagine a film about a plane crash in which all six of an airliner's safety features failed. You have a known outcome, but your film must spend most of its time explaining what each safety feature is supposed to do, how it failed, and what its breakdown contributed to the disaster. Here, in a tale of causality, time becomes of minor importance.

FIGURE 18-17 ————————————————

Mother and daughter in *The German Secret*. Who was my father? Why won't you tell me? *(Photo courtesy of Lars Johansson.)*

Even the makers of screen history themselves aren't always satisfied, as Donald Watt and Jerry Kuehl have pointed out.[6] Many history films, as they assert,

- Bite off more than they can chew.
- Commandeer specific images as backdrops for generalizations.
- Are inherently unbalanced whenever there is no archive footage for important events.
- Fail to recognize that the screen is different from literature or an academic lecture.
- Are often dominated by unverifiable interpretations.
- Try to sidestep controversy as school textbooks do.
- Fail to enlighten their audience about strings attached to funding.
- Suffer because their makers wanted to build a monument.
- Fail to acknowledge that historians find what they look for.
- Suggest consensus opinion, and gloss over vital disagreements.

FIGURE 18-18

American sports as a rehearsal for war teamwork in *Hearts and Minds*.

To this we can add that, by its realism and ineluctable forward movement, the screen history discourages contemplation and tends to glide over what it can't illustrate. Historical meanings are in any case abstractions, and the screen is inherently better at dealing with what is materially audible and visible.

We should be skeptical when a film uses omniscience to obscure its sources. The all-knowing narrator guiding us through tracts of history is worrisome, especially in those History Channel series that use archive footage to cover vast thematic and factual territory. In Britain, Thames Television's 26-episode *The World at War* (GB, 1973–4) and in the USA WGBH's *Vietnam: A Television History* in the 1980s each echo a textbook emphasis on facts. How much more relevant they would now seem, had they tackled the thorny issues of the time, which are now more pronounced than ever with the lapse of time. Even Ken Burns' *The Civil War* (USA, 1990), which counterpoints contemporary accounts and photographs, overwhelms the viewer with the repetitive minutia of its period when the viewer longs for larger dimensions of understanding.

Some screen histories succeed in this. An openly critical one-off film like Peter Davis' *Hearts and Minds* (USA, 1974, Figure 18-18) argues by analogy that the American obsession with sports provided a tragically misleading metaphor for the US involvement in Southeast Asia. Here the viewer is on a clearer footing and can engage with the film's propositions rather than go numb under a deluge of uninflected information.

Eyes on the Prize (USA, 1990), a PBS series from Blackside, Inc., provided a highly effective historical perspective which chronicled the development of the American civil rights movement. It managed to tread a fine line between historical omniscience and personal testimonies that were imbued with commitment. Though crew members were carefully chosen for racial balance, you are never in doubt that the film speaks on behalf of black people, so egregiously wronged in equality-proclaiming America.

The War (USA, 2007, Figure 18-19), directed by Ken Burns and Lynn Novick, is an oral history whose excellently chosen witness/participants each tell their stories in what adds up to multiple viewpoints. Unlike Burns' earlier, seemingly more linear and event-bound histories, its voice is free of patriotic hubris, and presents a forcefully non-nationalistic, anti-war perspective that is hauntingly tragic. This comes as a timely corrective when embedded journalism has presented so many hapless American soldiers as heroes fighting foreign evil in the Middle East. Even if World War II

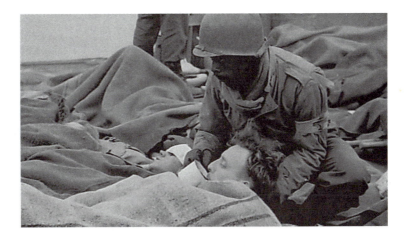

FIGURE 18-19

Warfare shorn of idealizing nationalism in *The War*.

was the nearest thing to a just war, *The War* makes it clear that all parties committed crimes against humanity, because inflamed or terrified soldiers commit atrocities as part of their bid to survive.

THE BIOGRAPHICAL FILM

Following a single character through time is a variation on the hero's journey paradigm of the folklorist Joseph Campbell.[7] Point of view plays a significant part, since the central character's sense of events is often in tension with that of his or her contemporaries. Usually the main character meets a challenge, refuses it, meets a more urgent version, goes on the journey, and develops by meeting test after test.

Peter Berggren is a Swedish filmmaker resident in the USA who specializes in musical biography. His joyous observational documentary *Chick 'a' Bone Checkout* (USA/Sweden, 2007, Figure 18-20) follows the Swedish composer Christian Lundberg writing a trombone concerto for virtuoso Charlie Vernon of the Chicago Symphony Orchestra. The true biographical subject is their collaboration, and it culminates in a performance of the concerto itself and a memorable encore by soloist and composer dressed as Chicago gangsters.

In *My Name is Celibidache* (Sweden, 2013), Berggren takes a different approach. Elderly musicians of the Swedish Radio Symphony Orchestra recall the amazing development in their orchestra under Sergiu Celibidache, its moody, charismatic Romanian conductor. The film moves chronologically through the conductor's tenure using an effortless and lyrical layering of imagery in which interviews float over archival footage of rehearsals and concerts. The true subject of the film is the phenomenon of artistic leadership by a conductor, and we learn how Celibidache's methods and personality were the inspiration of a lifetime for some, and a long ordeal for others.

NON-CHRONOLOGICAL TIME

TIME REORDERED

A common break with chronological time is to show an event and then backtrack to analyze the interplay of forces that led up to it, as Joe Berlinger and Bruce Sinofsky do in *Paradise Lost: The Child Murders at Robin Hood Hills* (USA, 1996). The film opens with the tragic prospect of three

FIGURE 18-20

Biography of a musical collaboration in *Chick 'a' Bone Checkout*.

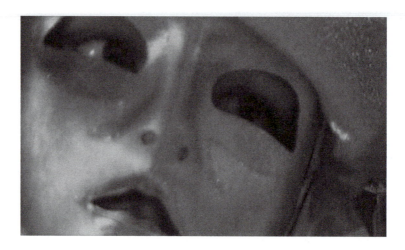

FIGURE 18-21

The Person of Leo N: Nature's cruel joke—to be a woman in a man's body.

murdered eight-year-old boys, and then focuses on the trial of the three local teenagers accused of killing them in a satanic ritual. The film casts doubt on the validity of the evidence, rather as the filmmakers did in their earlier *Brother's Keeper* (USA, 1992), which tells of some reclusive rural brothers accused of mercy-killing a sibling. Both films examine the arguments for and against each allegation by deconstructing the evidence, and then inviting us to draw likely conclusions like a jury. These are films interested not just in clarifying facts but in showing how poorly people separate reliability of character from stereotype. This takes their films deeper into social criticism than the conventional investigation.

A train journey is central to the operatic intensity driving Alberto Vendemmiati's *The Person de Leo N* (Italy, 2006, Figure 18-21), mentioned earlier. The journey proves to be the most fateful in Nico's life—it leads to the operating theatre where surgery will alter Nico's physical gender to fit a lifelong sense of identity as a woman. Along the way, there is a complex of flashbacks, including sequences of actors in masks, all associated with Nico's anxious and shifting preoccupations. What could possibly be more destabilizing than to be identified wrongly by gender, and to have to hide one's very essence? The flashbacks establish Nico's troubles in early life when treated as a boy, her loneliness as a misfit adult, and her patient love for her mother, who has never fully accepted that her son feels like a daughter. The handling of time matches the complexity of Nico's shifting consciousness while she gathers courage to gamble everything on the operation. The overriding questions that hang over the whole masterly narrative are Nico's own doubts: "Will my mother accept or reject me?" and "Will I find love at the end of all this?" The film finds an answer to both.

POETIC TIME

By exploring a mode of observation, mood, or belief, this category usually privileges imagery and metaphor over time. All the best documentaries have poetic elements, of course, but too few build laterally on the power and associations of imagery. Some are discussed in **Chapter 5: Story Elements and Film Grammar**, the most memorable being *Land Without Bread* (Spain, 1932), *Night Mail* (GB, 1936), *The Plow That Broke the Plains* (USA, 1936), and *The River* (USA, 1937). Humphrey Jennings, "the only real poet that British cinema has yet produced,"[8] made memorable documentaries during World War II while his country was under siege, notably *Listen to Britain* (GB, 1942), *Fires Were Started* (GB, 1943, Figure 18-22), and *Diary for Timothy* (GB, 1945, Figure 18-23). Their emotively loaded imagery and evocative sound design spoke deeply to the generation that lived through the events. In *Fires Were Started* Jennings alternates appallingly vivid

FIGURE 18-22

Making *Fires Were Started*, an early dramadoc that united horrific firefighting footage with improvised dialogue scenes among the firemen. *(Photo courtesy of The Kobal Collection/Crown Film Unit.)*

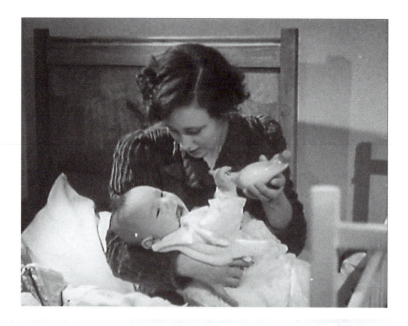

FIGURE 18-23

In *Diary for Timothy* a wounded pilot writes a journal for his baby son's eyes when peace returns.

actuality footage of London in flames with improvised firehouse scenes that use conspicuously stilted dialogue.

Some biographical films I specially admire are hard to find. Orod Attapour's *Parnian* (Iran, 2002, Figure 18-24) profiles an ill-fated family of Teheran archeologists. Both mother and son suffer from an incurable wasting disease that is visibly killing the mother. The father cares for them both while he and his son probe Iran's rich archeology with obsessive, desperate commitment. Every sequence carries richly poetic overtones, and every image reverberates in metaphorical relationship to others. Like the Persian poetry plainly influencing it, the film draws out a tragic vision of life as a wheel whose spiraling patterns bind us to those who lived and suffered before us—a message about the cyclical nature of existence similar to that in a famous Iranian novel, *The Blind Owl*.[9] Both works assert that we dwellers in the present must live and suffer as our ancestors did, and yet lead the way for those who follow. Miraculously compressed into *Parnian*'s austere half-hour is a whole vista of time, repeated destiny, decay, and renewal.

The common, perhaps highly significant, denominator is that all these filmmakers shot silent, concentrating on a logic of imagery first, and composing sound separately and later. The message? The order in which you do things absolutely determines where you end up.

THE JOURNEY OF INQUIRY

Two distinguished films probe family secrets and find surprises and heartache behind "successful" lives. Each film eschews chronological time in favor of the order in which significant new information surfaced. Andrew Jarecki's controversial *Capturing the Friedmans* (USA, 2003, Figure 18-25) follows up the arrest of a respectable Long Island teacher and one of his sons for alleged sexual crimes against children. The film gathers all available family perspectives, looks at the 8 mm home

FIGURE 18-24

A young archeologist suffering a wasting disease taunts destiny in *Parnian*.

FIGURE 18-25

A family harboring molesters in *Capturing the Friedmans*, or a miscarriage of justice? *(Photo courtesy of The Kobal Collection/HBO Documentary/Notorious Pictures.)*

movies of the archetypal suburban family at happy play, and finds in the end that nothing adds up and all is mystery. As so often, family members remain strangers to each other.

In Doug Block's *51 Birch Street* (USA, 2005), a son goes in search of the truth behind his parents' long but blighted marriage, hoping to reach his father after his mother dies. In the writing she left behind, Block is astonished to discover that the mother he thought he knew had maintained a secret love life. His father, who always seemed remote, suddenly marries his secretary of 40 years ago, and emerges as warmer and far more understanding of his dead wife than Block had ever imagined possible. Truth does indeed set you free.

Each of these biographies begins from some basic questions that, pursued through a labyrinth of ambiguous discovery, unfold like a detective story. Following clues and pursuing hypotheses, their protagonists lance at layers of protective myth and stereotype. It is however association and the hierarchy of discovery that determine the films' structures. Both pursue a crooked course, but high intelligence and sophistication make each seem to have taken the only path possible.

THE WALLED-CITY FILM

Societies, institutions, and tribal entities define their boundaries, close in upon themselves, and develop self-perpetuating codes. Films that profile them are often impressionistic and shot with multiple cameras since their boundaries often enclose many simultaneous activities. Juxtaposing these by theme, mood, or meaning can imply polemic by using the light hand of montage. The 10-hour PBS special *Carrier* (USA, 2008, Figure 18-26) aspires to be the mother of all such endeavors, though its subtitle ("One ship, five thousand stories") may seem more like a warning. Conceived by Mitchell Block and its director Maro Chermayeff, it draws on 1,600 hours of superb handheld filming during six months' residence aboard the nuclear-powered US aircraft carrier

FIGURE 18-26

Filming *Carrier*, an encyclopedia of military culture and a compendium of advanced documentary techniques and situations.

Nimitz. Each hour-long episode handles a theme ("controlled chaos," "show of force," "rites of passage") and each is bookended with title sequences that are unfortunately redolent of recruiting films. Do not be put off, even though most episodes are diffuse, high on testosterone (the average age aboard is 19), and punctuated with upbeat songs that seem suspiciously like narrative aids. The series is worth seeing from beginning to end as a thorough study of a military society riddled with contradictions and conflicts. Sailors of both sexes and all ranks are remarkably candid, and the unfolding stories of the 15 central characters become the series' connective tissue. We come to see a rare camaraderie that compensates for the turmoil and pain often lurking in the sailors' dysfunctional family origins. Most suffer excessively because of long periods of separation from their loved ones, as do the families they leave behind on land.

The sheer enormity of the series in relation to its enlightenment leaves you feeling ambiguous. Unintentionally, I think, it glamorizes military life and celebrates the gunboat diplomacy for which vessels like the Nimitz were created. The unspoken issues—why America chooses military might over domestic social justice, healthcare, and effective public education, and why military might makes ideological enemies rather than beats them—remain outside the film's sphere of attention. As with many documentaries, you are left wondering what restrictions the filmmakers accepted—or imposed on themselves—as the price of filming.

Most of Frederick Wiseman's documentaries—at long last available on DVD—are walled-city films, most notably two of his earliest—*Titicut Follies* (USA, 1967) and *High School* (USA, 1968). The Titicut Follies is a revue presented by the staff and inmates in a Massachusetts prison for the criminally insane. Wiseman makes it function both as a spine for the film and a grimly nihilistic metaphor. When you make films without to-camera interviews or narration you cannot retreat from scenes that are grippingly horrific. What we see might be retrieved from the eighteenth century, for in stark, Daumier black-and-white imagery we see the inmates' degrading spectrum of daily experience—from induction, psychiatric evaluation, nakedness, forced feeding, to burial. In one sequence, a seemingly sane Hungarian tries desperately to extricate himself from the institution's nightmarish embrace. In another, a psychiatric doctor with an ash-laden cigarette quivering on his lower lip rams a feeding pipe down a half-dead prisoner's nose. Each digression from the ongoing revue is so engrossing that the revue itself becomes a mocking commentary. Wiseman and his cameraman Bill Brayne lead us into a living hell, and at the same time define for all time what observational documentary can accomplish.

Two films by Nick Broomfield—*Soldier Girls* (USA/GB, 1981, with Joan Churchill) and *Chicken Ranch* (USA/GB, 1982, with Sandi Sissel, Figure 18-27)—qualify as walled-city films but differ significantly in approach from either narrated or observational approaches. *Soldier Girls* looks at women soldiers in basic training while *Chicken Ranch* is about the women, their relationships, and their customers in a brothel. Both explore social ghettoes and find their structure in a series of events that occurred spontaneously during the filmmakers' residency. Both show how those in charge of institutions try to condition and control their inmates, and though neither pretends to be neutral or unaffected by what it finds, each leaves us more knowledgeable and critical. By letting us see a discharged woman soldier in *Soldier Girls* embrace the camera operator, by including the brothel owner's tirade at the crew for filming what he wanted kept confidential, each admits where the filmmakers' sympathies lie and hints at the liaisons and even manipulation that went into their shooting. Broomfield has since made *Battle for Haditha* (GB, 2007, Figure 18-28), a documentary-style re-enactment of the 2005 killing of a marine by a roadside bomb in Iraq. When his colleagues fanned out to find the perpetrators, they killed 24 Iraqi civilians in a frenzy that the military tried to conceal.

Over time, a director's own themes emerge, and Broomfield—coming as he does from a monarchist society with long traditions of colonial domination—is perennially fascinated by the ways that those at the bottom of the social pyramid are coerced into fulfilling their masters' agendas.

FIGURE 18-27

The ladies in Nick Broomfield's *Chicken Ranch* pose with their Madame. The documentary led to a musical. *(Photo courtesy of First Run Features.)*

FIGURE 18-28

Battle for Haditha: docudrama can sometimes say what documentary cannot. *(Photo courtesy of The Kobal Collection/Channel 4 Films/Barney Broomfield.)*

THE THESIS FILM

This is any film using the essay form to educate, analyze, or elaborate on a thesis. Exposés, agitprop, experimental, or activist films are often structured upon the stages of an argument or extended process, and often use montage to display ideas for the audience to consider. Let's suppose you want to convince the audience that poor immigrants, far from draining the local economy, add economic value to a large American city. You must establish how and why the immigrants came, what work they do, what city services they do or don't use, what their enemies say about them, and so on. You must build an argument and advance the stages of a polemic in order to overcome the skeptics among your audience.

Of the films mentioned in **Chapter 3: Documentary History**, Buñuel's *Land without Bread* and Resnais' *Night and Fog* both present impassioned views of how human cruelty works. The Pare Lorentz ecology duo, *The Plow that Broke the Plains* and *The River*, convey strong messages about greed and the rape of the land. Michael Moore's *Fahrenheit 9/11* (USA, 2004) argues that the Bush administration, upborn after 9/11 by corporate media and embedded journalists, rode the wave of public feeling to further a prior agenda for invading Iraq and Afghanistan.

Hubert Sauper's *Darwin's Nightmare* (Austria/Belgium/France, 2004, Figure 18-29) draws chilling connections between the export of fish from Lake Victoria, the neglect and starvation of its native Tanzanian population, and the import of munitions used to fuel wars over Africa's mineral resources. Alex Gibney's *Enron: The Smartest Guys in the Room* (USA, 2005, Figure 18-30) built on work by *Fortune* reporters. It explains how the geniuses in the energy company kept double books in building their house of cards, and why it collapsed.

These are independent minds endeavoring to shine light into exceptionally dark places. Their freedom to argue rests squarely on the growth of accessible digital equipment, but remains limited by the fact that most film archives are corporately controlled and very expensive to quote. Meanwhile the Internet is developing as an uncontrolled arena for the exchange of information and opinion. History will probably judge public discourse to have changed radically at this time.

FIGURE 18-29

Poor fishermen in *Darwin's Nightmare* watch the planes that took their fish to Europe return bearing guns.

FIGURE 18-30

A day of reckoning in *Enron: The Smartest Guys in the Room.* *(Photo courtesy of The Kobal Collection/HD Net Films/Jigsaw Films.)*

TIME AS NON-RELEVANT

THE CATALOGUE FILM

This category's main and enthusiastic purpose is to examine comprehensively rather than critically. A film about harpsichords, steam locomotives, or dinosaurs might organize their appearance by size, age, structure, or other classification. Unless the film takes the stages of a restoration or archeological dig as its backbone, time probably won't play a centrally organizing role.

Joris Ivens' *Rain* (Netherlands, 1929, Figure 18-31) is a silent, highly atmospheric 12-minute film shot over two years in Amsterdam. It reveals the sheer beauty of rain in a cityscape. A year earlier Ivens had shot another equally lyrical 11-minute classic, *The Bridge*. Both films explore a sequence of powerful moods, and will stand for all time as defining portraits of city life in 1920s Holland. With *Borinage* (Belgium, 1932), Ivens and Henri Storck turned to social justice in which concern for the misery of exploited miners replaced Ivens' earlier interest in aesthetics. By showing how the men and their families lived from day to day, the film exposed to the rest of the world how a hidden and desperate part of European society existed.

Les Blank's films, usually described as celebrations of Americana, are really catalogue films. There is *Garlic Is as Good as Ten Mothers* (USA, 1977), *In Heaven There Is No Beer* (USA, 1984), and that delightful examination of resourceful women who happen to have a space between their front teeth, *Gap-Toothed Women* (USA, 1987). All are good-natured forays into special worlds, and might seem voyeuristic were they not so kindly. The travelogue, diary film, and city symphony are frequently montage-based catalogue types.

WHEN NO TIME STRUCTURE PREDOMINATES

There may initially be no obvious time structure. A film about stained glass windows may have none inherent in the footage. You could however posit a structure by dating particular windows, or arranging technical developments in glass manufacture, or dealing in turn with the region of the

FIGURE 18-31

Amsterdam under umbrellas in *Rain. (© European Foundation, Joris Ivens Archives.)*

artifacts, or the origin and idiosyncrasies of the glassmakers. Which option you take depends on what you want to say and what your material best supports. Anthology films that chronicle a particular year sometimes take this approach.

STRUCTURE QUESTIONNAIRE

Whether you are planning a film or confronting the dailies of one just shot, the structure you choose must accommodate some central concerns, so your options may not be as unlimited as you fear. Try answering these questions:

- How soon can your film gain momentum?
- How little exposition can you get away with, to get the film moving?
- Should you bunch the exposition (risky) or can you mete it out gradually? (Lack of essential information can be frustrating, or if well judged, prolong dramatic tension.)
- Does your film have a naturally inbuilt chronology?
  - According to an event or process?
  - Elapse of time?
  - Journey?
  - Other?
- What do you gain, and what do you lose, by sticking to that chronology?
- Does maintaining chronological order dissipate or focus the main issue?
- What stakes are your participants playing for?
- What can you do to raise them?

- Can you hold back your major sequences, or must you expend them early?
- What other aspects might structure your film?
  - Catalogue order (by physical size, age, complexity, color, etc.)?
  - By significance (in complexity, consequences, energy, etc.)?
  - By significance to a main character (the order of recall, effect, consequence, etc.)?
  - Narration (which might come from a character in the film)?
- What is the film's likely turning point, or climax?
- Where can you place the film's climactic scene(s) on the dramatic arc? Can it happen,
  - At the beginning, so the film becomes an analysis of its major event?
  - At the end, so the film builds toward its major event?
  - Two-thirds through, as happens most often?
- What proportion of your movie's screen time should you ideally devote to
  - Getting to the resolution?
  - Dealing with all the consequences that make up the resolution?
- How do you want your film to act on its audience?
  - Mostly inform them?
  - Take them through an intense experience whose outcome is unimportant?
  - Make them think about causes rather than effects?
  - Keep them guessing as long as possible?
  - How else?
- Whose POV is the film channeled through, and how might this help you move away from the obvious structural solution?
  - The main character?
  - A subsidiary character?
  - Multiple characters?
  - The storyteller?
- Who or what changes and develops during your film?
  - The POV character?
  - Someone else?
  - A situation?
- Where will this change probably happen?
  - Is it gradual and in the background?
  - Is it sudden, precipitous, and in the foreground?
  - Is it the film's climax?
- Where will your film's dramatic tension come from?
  - An overall situation that is long in developing?
  - A volcanic, climactic moment? (Can you delay it and raise the stakes?)
  - An impending change or crisis (such as a heart operation, say)?

Answering these questions probably won't lead to ready solutions, but will get you thinking hard about your story's essentials, which is the spade-work of creativity.

HANDS-ON LEARNING

To log the contents of a documentary, write about the way its structure and style deliver its content, and describe what thematic statement it makes, use **AP-7 Analyze Structure and Style**. To experiment with the counterpoint of language and imagery, why not make your own short essay film using **SP-9 Essay Film?**

NOTES

1. Michael Roemer, *Telling Stories: Postmodernism and the Invalidation of Traditional Narrative* (Rowman & Littlefield, 1995).
2. See "The Tradition of the Victim in Griersonian Documentary" by Brian Winston in Alan Rosenthal, ed., *New Challenges for Documentary* (University of California Press, 1988).
3. Heraclitus, c.540–c.480 BC.
4. Wilkie Collins (1824–1889) best known for *The Moonstone* and *The Woman in White.*
5. At the time I was unaware how central migration would be to my own family's history: of 30 members, 25 have changed countries.
6. Donald Watt and Jerry Kuehl, "History on the Public Screen I & II," in Alan Rosenthal, ed., *New Challenges for Documentary* (University of California Press, 1988), pp. 4318–453.
7. For the best, movie-oriented explanation, see Christopher Vogler's *The Writer's Journey: Mythic Structure for Storytellers and Screenwriters* (Michael Wiese, 1992).
8. According to the British director Lindsay Anderson.
9. Sadegh Hedayat, *The Blind Owl* (1937).

CHAPTER 19

FORM, CONTROL, AND STYLE

The word *style* often gets interchanged confusingly with *form*. Both express concern with the way you present a film's content, but form is the configuration and logic of the narrative, while style describes the ways in which the work allies itself with artistic precedent. This involves the telltale references and conventions by which audiences recognize a type of film and its purposes. Form is the structuring by which the film's content becomes a story.

Form and style seem symbiotic in the finished work, but during the film's inception you should try to see them as separate concerns. If, for instance, you have a body of filmed material about homelessness, you could conceivably edit it either as a societal problem to be solved by local government, or perhaps from a seven-year-old's viewpoint as a nightmarish loss of everything familiar. The overall content might be similar, but their forms—one a settled and logical discourse, the other a subjective journey of loss—are quite different.

The *genre* (category or type of documentary) of the two films would be different too: one would belong with social study essay films, and the other with subjective biography. Their differences would emerge from different styles achieved through selective editing, different rhythms and points of view, and perhaps a different use of effects and music.

FORM

Documentaries do not fall into categories as readily as fiction films, and the components you have to work with largely determine your range of possibility. Flaherty invented the genre of documentary because he recognized that nonfiction would fail to engage audiences unless it drew upon storytelling techniques from fiction like having central characters, narrative compression, and dramatic tension. He saw too that, like any mature narrative, documentary needed an overarching theme. All this was and is disturbing to the ethnographer, or to any purist suspicious of authorial manipulation. But films made for a wide audience cannot escape the expectations we carry from our viewing history, expectations aroused by a film's style and the *contract* it sets with its audience. Sometimes called the *hook*, this is the promise the Storyteller implies in a film's opening moments to take us on a particular type of journey. We enter the film with the pleasant expectation that the story will deliver on its promise.

Only you the director can decide how to do this, but the nature of your subject is a powerfully deciding force. Since a documentary is usually an improvised collaboration with its subjects, every project has useful inbuilt limitations. Pervasive are those that ration time, personnel, equipment, travel, shooting days, and resources. These restrictions help you define what you're doing, and often what you are *not* doing. Digital shooting and editing bring truncated production schedules so the new realities make filming a practical and challenging business. Ultimately whether you can work fruitfully within professional boundaries decides whether you survive—professionally, financially, and artistically.

The limitations you choose to work within are fruitful because they give you *something meaningful to push against*, and force you to find creative solutions. Let's briefly examine how setting their own aesthetic rules galvanized a couple of visual movements.

SETTING LIMITS

In the early 1930s some American photographers calling themselves Group f/64 banded together. They were frustrated that photographers were emulating the "high-art" form of painting and did not yet consider photography an art form. Group f/64 decided that photography could only realize its potential by concentrating on what was unique to photography. From this elemental clarification came the ground-breaking work of Edward Weston, Imogen Cunningham, Ansel Adams, and Willard Van Dyke.

In Denmark of the mid-1990s the founding members of the Dogme 95 cinema group came to similar conclusions and went on to produce landmark fiction. Their starting point was a playful manifesto explicitly rejecting the industrial embrace of Hollywood. Like documentaries, *The Celebration* (Thomas Vinterberg, Denmark, 1998, Figure 19-1), *Breaking the Waves* (Lars von Trier, Denmark, 1999, Figure 19-2), and *The Idiots* (Lars von Trier, Denmark, 1999) were all fiction films shot handheld using digital handicams. Their object was to make use of the fluidity and other-centeredness of observational documentary. Dogme's playfully critical manifesto appears in various versions and translations, so I have taken the liberty of putting it in vernacular English:

FIGURE 19-1

The Celebration: a Dogme fiction film using informal and immediate shooting techniques. (*Photo courtesy of The Kobal Collection/Nimbus Film Productions.*)

FIGURE 19-2

Improvisation, fine performances, and a documentary stylistic approach give *Breaking the Waves* an impassioned urgency. (*Photo courtesy of The Kobal Collection/Zentropa.*)

A Vow of Chastity

- *Shooting must be done on location. Props and sets must not be brought in, but shooting must go where that set or prop can be found.*
- *Sound must never be produced separately from the images or vice versa. Music must not be used unless it occurs where the scene is shot.*
- *The camera must be hand-held. Any movement or immobility attainable by handholding is permitted. The action cannot be organized for the camera; instead the camera must go to the action.*
- *The film must be in color. Special lighting is not acceptable and if there is too little light for exposure, the scene must be cut, or a single lamp may be attached to the camera.*
- *Camera filters and other optical work are forbidden.*
- *The film must not contain any superficial action such as murders, weapons, explosions and so on.*
- *No displacement is permitted in time or space: the film takes place here and now.*
- *Genre movies are not acceptable.*
- *Film format is Academy 35 mm.*
- *The director must not be credited.*

Furthermore I swear as a director to refrain from personal taste. I am no longer an artist. I swear to refrain from creating a 'work', as I regard the instant as more important than the whole. My supreme goal is to force the truth out of my characters and settings. I swear to do so by all the means available and at the cost of any good taste and any aesthetic considerations.

Signed_____ (member's name)

By rejecting a leadership hierarchy and even personal taste, the manifesto strikes at the narcissism of ego. About writing their manifesto, Thomas Vinterberg said,

> We did the "Vow of Chastity" in half an hour and we had great fun. Yet, at the same time, we felt that in order to avoid the mediocrity of filmmaking not only in the whole community, but in our own filmmaking as well, we had to do something different. We wanted to undress film, turn it back to where it came from and remove the layers of make-up between the audience and the actors. We felt it was a good idea to concentrate on the moment, on the actors and of course, on the story that they were acting, which are the only aspects left when everything else is stripped away. Also, artistically it has created a very good place for us to be as artists or filmmakers because having obstacles like these means you have something to play against.
>
> (Interview by Elif Cercel for *Director's World*. See http://stage.directorsworld.com)

The Dogme group liberated their creative energies by rejecting what they found destructive in current cinema practices, much as the Russian cinema had rejected Hollywood after the Revolution, and as the Free Cinema Movement rejected the safe mediocrity of British cinema in the 1950s. Each group set out to generate bold guiding values, and these helped catapult their work into public notice. Dogme, de-emphasizing leadership and dethroning film techniques, helped hand their actors a rich slice of creative control, to which they responded handsomely.

In documentary, certain limitations come with the subject, but others you must choose in order to challenge your inventiveness. So, what creative limitations will you set yourself?

CONTENT INFLUENCES FORM

Most who work in the arts—musicians, writers, painters, novelists, say—can control the content and form of their work. The documentarian, however, is more like a mosaic artist who gets perverse pleasure from working with the idiosyncratic, chance-influenced nature of found materials. In the end, each documentary depends on acts, words, and images plucked from life—all of them elements that occur spontaneously in various kinds of actuality, and which were perhaps chosen because what they materialized, thanks to the gods of chance, were *not* under the author's control.

Fiction films create characters and situations in the service of ideas, while documentary tries to discover ideas and meanings hiding out within real people and their lived reality. In documentary you are trying to discover the world as it is, rather than create a facsimile in order to say something about a theme or belief.

STYLE

You can choose some aspects of style, but not all.

STYLE YOU CAN'T CHOOSE

Unless your film is of the highly malleable essay type, its source materials already point the way and narrow your options. Your ethics, interests, and convictions about the work your documentary should do also disqualify some aspects of style. If this seems a little foggy for an art that is so collaborative, you can still recognize the authorship in a Michael Moore or a Werner Herzog documentary, even if you don't particularly care for their films. Contributing to this are,

- Choices of subject.
- Camera handling.
- Forms that each director favors.
- Marks of personality and taste.
- Influences from cinema they admire.
- Methods and messages from their thematic range.

A film's genre, voice, meanings, and style interact and overlap during production, and are difficult to separate afterwards. If you overreach during production you can upset the balance so that stylizing actuality (that is, intensifying its essential nature) turns into *stylized* actuality. The ultra-fragmented, MTV camera-waving style of Daniel Myrick and Eduardo Sánchez in their fake documentary *The Blair Witch Project* (USA, 1999), and the over-composed look of Errol Morris' biography of Stephen Hawking, *A Brief History of Time* (USA, 1991, Figure 19-3), both suffer in my view from an over-emphasis on a stylistic "statement." The film on Hawking, while arguing his complex theories brilliantly, uses specially constructed sets rather than authentic surroundings.

So what to do? Working simply, sincerely, and intelligently is most likely to connect an audience emotionally with your work. Simplicity is wise anyway, since you have a long developmental curve ahead as you acquire the necessary technical and conceptual skills to serve what you will

FIGURE 19-3

A Brief History of Time approaches the life and ideas of the paralyzed theoretical physicist Stephen Hawking with a dizzyingly stylized treatment. (*Photo courtesy of The Kobal Collection/Triton Films.*)

eventually have to say. Since you can't choose your identity, some of your film's style will take care of itself. Audiences and critics may even tell you what your style is. Beware! You'll then be tempted to imitate and enhance your reputation.

STYLE YOU CAN CHOOSE

A film's subject suggests appropriate styles. Films about a children's author, a tree disease, or early submarines all take place in very different worlds, belong in different documentary genres, and call for different approaches. A film about a Talmudic scholar should look very different from one about a skateboarder simply because each lives in an utterly different physical and mental realm. One might call for *low key lighting* (large areas of shadow), rock-steady indoor compositions, and a Vermeer palette of dark colors. The other is more likely to be *high key lighting* (mainly bright), and shot outdoors with an adventurous handheld camera.

All the conventions of the cinema are at your service as you intensify actuality to make it a story with style, point of view, and meanings. Every film, however, treads a fine line between the lax, prosaic realism of unmediated life on the one hand, and on the other, too much order and imposed meaning as seen in MTV nonfiction. You navigate between extremes: stamp your work too heavily and you crush the personalities, events, and subtexts subtly present in the dailies. Withdraw all interpretive effort from the tale, and the point of telling it evaporates.

Apart from rejecting what is false or superfluous, it is wise to question all your assumptions at the outset, in order to flush out options that you may not otherwise recognize. Use the Form and Style worksheet below (Table 19-1) as a set of prompts, and don't hesitate to rewrite it if you can make it better to serve your growing experience.

TABLE 19-1 Form and Style Worksheet (Project DP-11 on the book's website, www.directingthedocumentary.com)

DP-11 Form and Style Worksheet

These prompts are by no means exhaustive, and not all will be relevant. For grammatical simplicity I have assumed you have a single main character.

Limitations I will impose on myself while making this film are ...
The **main character** is trying to get, do, or accomplish ...
The **main conflict** my film handles (between ... and ...) suggests that contrasting or complementing visual and aural elements might be ...
The **environments** in this film
    Are composed of ... and suggest ...
    The main character belongs in ... but contrasts with ... because of ...
    I will therefore try to show each environment as ...
Different **rhythms** my film will contain are determined by ...
The film's **theme** calls for,
    Warm, close, intimate photography for ...
    Cool and distanced views for ...
    Static frames with action choreographed within them for ...
    Contained, measured movement for ...
    Fast, unstable, or subjective movement during ...
    Other_____
Changes and developments I expect in my film are in,
    Landscape or place characterization
    Pace or rhythm
    Season or country
    Other_____
Palette characteristics ...
    Predominant colors and tonality for each sequence ...
    Their progression through the film should suggest ...
Editing in my film should aim to be,
    Slow, deliberate, unhurrying
    Alternating between ... and ...
    Fast, glancing, and impressionistic
    Other_____
Stylized time treatment via slow or fast motion, freeze frames and other optical treatments would achieve ... in my film
Narration in my film might come from ... (character or type of narrator)
Sound design in my film should include ... and emphasize . . .

HANDS-ON LEARNING

To analyze a particular film, use Table 19-1 Form and Style Worksheet and perhaps **DP-8 Dramatic Form** too, to help you write about the relationship between dramatic form and style. Where does the film's authorial voice arise? What gives it substance and meaning?

CHAPTER 20

RE-ENACTMENT, RECONSTRUCTION, AND DOCUDRAMA

RE-ENACTMENTS

A key aspect of documentary is its ability to provoke discussion. A film does this by posing questions, exposing contradictions, or juxtaposing opposites—all of which challenge audience members to reconcile the contradictions and tensions that have emerged. Conjecture on a larger scale might require reconstructing bygone situations, such as a crucial career interview for a job that your reformed criminal main character has in fact already begun. The company decided to take a chance and hire him, and this has changed his life. The encounter was so pivotal a moment in his life that you decide you must reconstruct it for your film. Your participants are quite willing to re-enact the scene, but can you—should you—film it? To pass the scene off, conjectural as its contents are, as the real thing could be misleading. Will your audience need to know it's a reconstruction? If so, how do you let them know? You would rightly be accused of faking, and this could seriously damage your credibility—even your career. Some films run a "Scene re-enacted" subtitle, but this seems like overkill if narration or voice-over can imply this with a distancing past tense.

Errol Morris has written about his use of re-enactment to scrutinize witness testimony in *The Thin Blue Line* (USA, 1988).[1] The film shows six different re-enactments of the way a Texas traffic cop died, each illustrating a different witness's account in the trial (Figure 20-1). The intention is to show just how unreliable witnesses' memories are, and to prove—as it does conclusively—that not one of their accounts was accurate. In his article, Morris comments on the misuse of re-enactment and archive footage, pointing out that there is, for instance, only one set of shots showing Jews being put on a train to the death camps, yet the same footage is used for any film (including one of my own) about Jewish deportation. Those familiar with a period's archives find it distressing to see footage repeatedly transposed in time and place to serve a multitude of historical narratives. Today, cropping or altering images is only a mouse-click away, and offers a seductive solution for problems of missing narrative or absent coverage. When done in plain sight to serve the spirit of the truth, this may be no problem. But if the audience is deceived into accepting what it sees as reliable evidence, then it will be treated as deception. The dividing line is one of

FIGURE 20-1

Different witness versions re-enacted in *The Thin Blue Line*.

good faith; there is nothing controversial about showing that a participant got caught shoplifting, if factually this happened. But if he maintains that the store police entrapped him, it matters very much whether we see the actual arrest or a re-enactment.

TRUTHFUL LABELING

In Amsterdam in the 1990s some talented film students made an explosive documentary about dropout kids playing a deadly game of laying their arms between the wheels of railroad wagons. As the engine started in the distance, they would wait as long as possible while the clink-clink-clink of the couplings got nearer before jumping clear. The film culminates with a horrific hospital scene in which the smallest boy has lost both arms. Lodewijk Crijns' *Kutzooi* (Netherlands, 1995, Figure 20-2) turned out to have been wholly and masterfully fabricated—indeed, not a documentary at all, but a *mockumentary*. Like those with whom I saw it (mostly documentary teachers), I was irate with the film for bamboozling us, as I think any audience would be.[2] We were mugs who had trusted what it seemed to be—recorded actuality. In fact Crijns had been true to his own youth, and to boys' risky games, but the film was sailing under false colors. The point is that when someone swaps the labels we feel manipulated—indeed, Otto Schuurman showed the film to make this very point. Ironically, we would have praised it to the sky had the makers shown it as a Ken Loach type of fiction film taken, as it truly was, from Dutch working class life.

USING ACTORS

Some documentaries use actors to recreate biographical material, or even create someone representative but imaginary. Historical biographies routinely use actors when no archive footage exists of their subject, but this is still an acceptable way to explore history if identified as such. Eric Stange, himself a producer of history films, wrote:

> *Documentary reenactments are almost always shot without dialogue, through fog or haze, or in a shadowy half-light. The camera often focuses only on close-up details—a hand on a quill; feet running through the woods; a sword being buckled on—and almost never on an actor's face...*

These visual clues send several important messages: that the reenactment is not fictional (if it were, there would be dialogue); that the reenactment is only a "suggestion" of what happened (signified by the ambiguous fog or haze); and that the actors are not portraying specific people so much as representing them.

(from "Shooting Back," Common-Place, April 2001, see www.common-place.org/vol-01/no-03/stange)

Such material can stimulate the audience's imagination or fill significant gaps in the narrative. It can also, as the article goes on to say, rapidly lapse into money-saving cliché. For plentiful examples, see any episode of the PBS series *Secrets of the Dead* (USA, 2001–2004). The producers deserve plaudits for tackling riddles of history, but they often repeat their visual material many times, so it is stretched perilously thin.

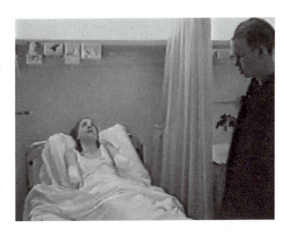

FIGURE 20-2

The youngest boy loses both arms in the mockumentary *Kutzooi*.

WHOLESALE RECONSTRUCTION

When reconstruction involves several scenes or even a whole film, the sources on which their veracity rests can be eyewitness memories, documents, transcripts, photographs, or hearsay. British television once showed an acted reconstruction directed by Stuart Hood of the trial of the anarchists Sacco and Vanzetti. Adapted from court transcripts of the famous 1920s trial, it proved intelligent, restrained, and austerely memorable. Because actors portraying the accused, the lawyers, and the judge used only the words and ideas of these people preserved in court records, one could accept it as trustworthy and documentary in spirit. Large-scale reconstruction should carefully identify its sources, or risk alienating its audience.

Usually included with the documentary genre is Peter Watkins' imaginative reconstruction *Culloden* (GB, 1964)—a beginning-to-end reproduction of the 1746 battle in the Scottish Highlands. It shows how feudally Bonnie Prince Charlie's supporters raised their army, and how brutally the British crushed his Jacobite cause. Apart from the costumes, tactics, and location there's little other pretence of historical accuracy since what the officers and foot soldiers say in Watkins' "interviews" are a modernist guess at what they might have expressed. The film nevertheless respects the distant historical actuality, and conveys much empathy for its unlucky participants. Yes, it deals with politics and the abuse of power, but its visceral sympathies lie with the humble folk so easily made into cannon fodder by their warlord masters. Those serving recently in Iraq, Afghanistan, Syria, and Egypt will understand its preoccupations intimately.

THE DOCUDRAMA

There is a use of the real that is yet more imaginative—some would say fanciful—called *docudrama* or *dramadoc*. This is a hybrid straddling two genres that is seen most commonly, for some reason, in Britain. Two examples from history must suffice, one successful and one not. Jeremy Sandford's *Cathy Come Home* (GB, 1966) dramatized the plight of Britain's homelessness at a time when, sad to think, it was new and shocking. Working from case histories, Sandford and his wife Nell Dunn constructed a "typical" blue-collar couple who overspend, encounter bad luck, and plunge down the social scale until the welfare state dismembers the family "for the good of the children." Coming on the heels of the Conservative re-election slogan, "You never had it so good," the British public was appalled to discover that in all its particulars the film was true to life. Its effectiveness lay in superb acting and a documentary presentation, and the furor it aroused caused a change in the law—rare for a film of any kind.

Another docudrama backfired rather badly. Anthony Thomas' *Death of a Princess* (GB, 1980) set out to show how a Saudi princess had been publicly humiliated and executed for a sexual offense. Instead it raised a storm of critical reaction on all sides, though less for using actors and reconstruction than for taking factual liberties. The truth was insufficiently determinable, and the portrayal of Islamic culture and assumptions were plainly outside the producers' realm of sympathy or expertise. Linking the film's inquiry, and further undercutting its trustworthiness, was a romanticized journalist figure serving as a proxy for Thomas's own journey of investigation. Undoubtedly he had researched among weird and sinister characters, but transmuting his role to that of a suave, James Bond-ish investigator made the film seem irritatingly self-involved, and implied that the rest of *Death of a Princess* was similarly contrived. It was docudrama with too much drama and not enough doc.

SUBJECTIVE RECONSTRUCTION

From Flaherty onward, documentary and reconstruction were inseparable. Today, someone recounting how he had found an unexploded bomb in a ploughed field as a boy might be filmed returning as an elderly man to the very spot where he found it. You might half-bury a bomb casing for him to find, and shoot his actions as he remembers them, laying his voice over the actions. The audience would know from its viewing history that the sequence represents the uncertainties of memory. Alternatively he could tell the camera what he remembers as he relives the actions of finding the bomb. Especially when memory is unclear, and a person must run through several versions in search of the most likely one, there are fertile possibilities for such techniques. Plainly you are not only exploring what happened, but the instability of human memory itself, as Alain Resnais did on a massive scale in his baroque fiction epic, *Last Year in Marienbad* (France, 1961).

Documentary is an equally good tool for investigating the psychology of memory. Lars Johansson's *Traveler's Tale* (Denmark, 1994,) accomplishes this masterfully: a fictitious old man looks back during the middle of the twenty-first century on film and video he shot just after the walls of Communism had fallen in Central Europe, and outsiders could make their first visits. Its vantage seen from old age sometime in the future, the film is a meditation looking on the socially ossified world that Johansson himself had recently captured while making a similar journey. At the heart of the film is pain at the beauty and illusory nature of experience, and nostalgia for the evanescence of memory. Suggesting this is a mysterious, *leitmotif* shot (shot repeated to accentuate its symbolic or other meaning) of a partially opened window that frames a field of brilliant yellow flowers (Figure 20-3). This shot, like so much in the film, resists explanation because it is an intuitive rather than expositional narrative. The window opening on the field of flowers somehow suggests the fertile, lost domain of memory and the past.

Occasionally a complete reconstruction is notable for persuading us to accept the authenticity of its central subject. A lovely BBC biographical documentary is Chris Durlacher's *George Orwell: A Life in Pictures* (GB, 2003, Figure 20-4). No voice recording or archive footage exists of Orwell, so the producers used the actor Chris Langham to create a facsimile. Looking like Orwell, he speaks words culled from Orwell's letters, diaries, novels, and essays. Drawing plentifully on period archive footage, the film takes "interviews" with Orwell (played by Langham) and intercuts them with interviews conducted with people who knew him. The effect is eerily authentic, for you go on a major personal retrospective with the great anti-authoritarian author. Mixed in, and not

FIGURE 20-3

Lars Johansson's *Traveler's Tale* (Denmark, 1994) explores the psychology of memory, so partial and evanescent.

at all intrusive, is a library of 8 mm home movie footage recreated in authentic places—again with Langham and other actors. Strictly speaking, much of its material is fake but the film adds up to a sustained, sympathetic, and imaginative portrait that one feels is trustworthy.

The authority on docudrama, and tireless champion of its merits, is the distinguished political filmmaker and documentary historian Alan Rosenthal. His *Why Docudrama? Fact-Fiction on Film and TV* (Southern Illinois Press, 1999) is a comprehensive survey of docudrama's history and possibilities.

FIGURE 20-4

An actor plays Orwell consummately well in *George Orwell: A Life in Pictures.*

FAKE DOCUMENTARIES OR MOCKUMENTARIES

Mitchell Block's renowned short film about a female rape victim, *No Lies* (USA, 1973, Figure 20-5), sets out to show how dangerous documentary becomes in amoral hands. The pressure we see the director apply to the raped woman is disturbing, yet we go along with it because her revelations are luridly fascinating. Then the film turns on its heel to confront us with the fact that both are actors. The exploitative relationship is a calculated performance, one made to,

> cinematically...demonstrate and commit rape—and [do] so in such a way as to make the experience of being the unwary, unprepared victim of an aggressive assault on one's person, on one's pride, and on one's expectations of and security in familiar activity in familiar surroundings a very real experience accessible to anyone of either sex who views the film.[3]

FIGURE 20-5

Rape and the documentary process in *No Lies*. *(Photo courtesy of Mitchell Block.)*

First we voyeuristically enjoy the fruit of exploitation, then the film rubs our noses in our prurience. Gotcha.

Ken Featherstone's *Babakiueria* (Australia, 1987) works differently. It reports how Aboriginal colonists discovered Australia back when the country was thinly peopled by primitive whites whose ritual was to cook flesh in places they called barbecue areas (hence the film's title). When the black colonizers send social workers, a nervously compliant white family tries to cooperate by giving up their children for their own good. By inverting Australian racial values, and farcically reversing white people's treatment of blacks, the film rams home what it feels like to have liberal paternalism forced on you by another race.

In Larry Charles' *Borat: Cultural Learnings of America for Make Benefit Glorious Nation of Kazakhstan* (USA, 2006), the inimitable Sacha Baron Cohen travels around America making people think he is an outrageously crass Kazakh journalist. Made from improvised situations based on a journey framework, this *Candid Camera* offshoot rejoices in springing practical jokes on the unwary. *Borat* aims to be murderously funny—and in scenes that defy belief, it truly is. It's not a documentary, but it borrows documentary methods to capture many spontaneous encounters as they are catalyzed by a highly skilled comedian. If it levels any critique, it is that too many Americans are alarmingly credulous. As a caveat, see Wikipedia for an account of the lawsuits that followed.

If you are working with satire, you must reproduce the form you are lampooning with masterly authority, and your audience will laugh and applaud. If however you mock their trust, then you are attacking the very foundations of audience participation, and will need a compelling reason to do so.

HANDS-ON LEARNING

If you are interested in reconstruction, or actively thinking of doing it, try using the **DP-9 Reconstruction Worksheet** (Table 20-1). It is the kind of provocative questionnaire that one

TABLE 20-1 Reconstruction Worksheet (Project DP-9 on the book's website, www.directingthedocumentary.com)

DP-9 Reconstruction Worksheet

Reconstruction:

- What are you really trying to get across to the audience?
- Could you make your point another way and avoid reconstruction?
- What, from the audience's point of view, makes a reconstruction permissible?
- Are you implying that what you show is typical, or that it is particular and pivotal? (Typical is probably OK, but reconstructing a pivotal moment could backfire.)
- Are you using the original participants, or actors playing them? Will the audience know this?
- What do the participants feel about re-enacting something bygone?
- How should you cover the scene to avoid injecting histrionics?

Docudrama:

- What is the film's premise and why does it need to be a docudrama?
- Why not make a fiction film avowedly based on real events?
- How will you justify "faking it" to the audience?
- What additional values will you put in play to justify taking so much control?

Mockumentary:

- Is the target of your satire (if that's what it is) some practice, custom, event, etc.? Or is it the documentary genre itself?
- If you are lampooning documentary (which can always use some house-cleaning), do you have enough knowledge, ideas, and material?
- How can your piece develop? (Many ideas for this form are one-liners, and not adequate for an extended piece.)
- What is your purpose, if you mean to deceive your audience and then undeceive them?

gradually internalizes as one works with a chosen *genre* (type, family) of film. The multidisciplinary nature of film means one must usually give consideration to a great many facets, which is what makes film such a fascinating and challenging language to use well.

NOTES

1. *New York Times* (http://morris.blogs.nytimes.com/2008/04/03/play-it-again-sam-re-enactments-part-one).
2. I am indebted to enlightening discussions of docudrama and false documentaries led by Otto Schuurman and Elaine Charnov at the "Sights of the Turn of the Century" documentary conference at the Centro de Capacitación Cinematográfica in Mexico City, 1996.
3. Vivian C. Sobchack, "*No Lies*: Direct Cinema as Rape," in Alan Rosenthal, ed., *New Challenges for Documentary* (University of California Press, 1988), p. 332.

CHAPTER 21

VALUES, ETHICS, AND CHOICES

ART AND TEMPERAMENT

Documentaries usually assert their truthfulness in one of two ways. In "fly on the wall" *observational filmmaking*, we see truth in cinema that is supposedly free of the observer's intrusion. The film tries to be honest to the spirit of its makers' best perceptions and to earn the audience's trust. However, it takes considerable artifice to maintain the illusion that truth is unfolding free of the recording process.

In *participatory filmmaking* the film team's work and thoughts can become part of the film's discourse, and in *reflexive filmmaking* the process reaches farther since the film can examine the act of perception as well as what is perceived.

To sum up, this spectrum of philosophies allows the camera to document aspects of the real world in the following ways:

- As though there is no mediating presence by crew and camera (transparent cinema).
- As events recorded by a camera and crew who visibly catalyze some of the events (participatory filmmaking).
- As events captured using a cinema process whose methods, personalities, and contradictions become part of the film's purview (reflexive cinema).
- As events captured and serving as a mirror that reflects the author's interface with the world in his or her cinema process (self-reflexive cinema).

In *Zen and the Art of Motorcycle Maintenance*,[1] Robert M. Pirsig writes about the metaphysics of quality, and about the importance of temperamental differences to attitudes about art and living. The book explores the implications of a 17-day journey by two motorcycles across America, driven by the narrator and a friend, and each carrying a pillion passenger. The narrator loves his motorcycle and teaches his son how to maintain it in good order, but his jazz drummer friend owns his motorcycle for the sheer exhilaration of motorcycling with his wife.

Pirsig calls himself a classicist and his friend a romantic, because the other man cares nothing for his machine's intrinsic qualities and strikes it petulantly when his neglect causes it to break down. The classical approach to art aspires to objectivity and values order, harmony, rationality, and form. The classicist strives for what is essence, eternal and ideal, while the romantic is often concerned with the darker passions. Dissatisfied with the existing social order, the romantic focuses more subjectively on their own transient sensations, emotions, and feelings.

You can honorably occupy any part of this spectrum, so long as you recognize your make-up, purposes, and priorities from the outset. What is your temperament like? Do you know what you believe? How will your beliefs guide and inform the way you see the world through filming it? What parts of film history, what particular works, have drawn you to them?

FORM FOLLOWS FUNCTION

The lens of temperament through which you see is something you determine while you explore your subject. Finding the right approach may be a question of emphasis and of how, temperamentally, you need to function as a storyteller. As you use your "history box," you will need to justify the process of recording and interpreting to your participants, who must trust the picture you are building of them. Will the complexities of this relationship affect important truths, and will you have to acknowledge this implicitly or explicitly? The recording process may be too intrusive to document some intimate occasions, or will seem so to the audience. Can you draw a line, and if so, where?

These all seem like theoretical questions until you encounter them in life and see the consequences that may follow. Luckily, it is the real world that helps us decide—not only what to do, but in what to become as we do it.

MORAL RESPONSIBILITIES

Making a documentary is modeling a vision of the world as it is, so we bear a moral responsibility for all we put on the screen. The consequences can be material and even dangerous, since screenworks of all kinds, even video games, alter the threshold of what's acceptable—for good or bad. Imagine that action movie heroes, instead of finding catharsis using assault weapons, instead began driving all-terrain vehicles over everyone who ignored them. There would soon be a rash of copy-cat massacres everywhere. Filmmaking is entertainment, and it leads by example. Filmmakers bear responsibility for the ethical and moral implications of their work.

EVIDENCE AND ETHICS

Your main ethical concern will always be with the integrity of the arguments you use. A documentary is usually more powerful when its ideas and themes arise from a visibly unfolding train of events, rather than when you selectively illustrate a narrated thesis—which in principle is not unlike a TV commercial. The same can be said of fiction films; it is the difference between "signifying" a situation versus showing it in the act of being. Once again, drama and the documentary share fundamentals.

Quantitative evidence, where justified, is easier to accept than qualitative. If known actions hinge on the credibility of a particular person, as so often happens in CBS' *48 Hours* true crime investigations, then you will need to build that person's character carefully from all the evidence you collect. From your research you may know all sorts of things about your contact, but your audience only knows what you put on the screen. In that sense, you are building a character no less deliberately than a playwright or screenwriter will do.

You may have to take special care to demonstrate that a point in your film is not contrived. In a documentary I made long ago about an English country estate, *A Remnant of a Feudal Society*

FIGURE 21-1

Evidence: a man demonstrates the price he believes he paid for doing his job. *(Frames from* A Remnant of a Feudal Society.*)*

(BBC "Yesterday's Witness" series, GB, 1970, Figure 21-1), a head groom spontaneously held out his deformed hand to demonstrate what happened (as he thought) to horsemen forced to ride in all winds and weather. In the wide shot it was unclear what was wrong with the hand, so the cameraman made a slightly wobbly zoom in close. In editing I kept the zoom because removing it to make a cut between long shot and close shot, though more elegant onscreen, would have made the groom's action look prearranged. One simple cut in the footage would have demoted its credibility!

Showing the origin and authenticity of evidence wherever you can helps maintain a good-faith relationship with your audience. Occasionally the filmmaker employs artistic license to serve a larger purpose—as Michael Moore did with chronology in *Roger and Me* (USA, 1989, Figure 21-2). By simplifying and transposing some causes and effects, Moore handed ammunition to his many enemies, and found his methods returning to haunt him. His later work *Bowling for Columbine* (USA, 2002), which targets the lethal inanities of gun culture in America, is more careful—and as a result hits harder.

BEHALFERS: SPEAKING FOR OTHERS

Speaking on behalf of others is almost a disease among documentarians, and (as I learned through Henry Breitrose, a fine writer on the documentary) they have a special name: *behalfers*. These folks make it their business to speak for those without a voice, which ultimately is everyone unable to make their own films. For decades Europeans filmed indigenous peoples like small children or zoo creatures incapable of articulating anything for themselves. Missionaries ran roughshod over native populations because they could not imagine that Africans or Aztecs were equipped to hold spiritual philosophies. Colonial history alone should remind us how charity gets dispensed by the privileged, how it can feel to the recipients, and how self-serving it can be to imagine one is promoting someone else's interests.

So whenever you get the impulse to do good, be awfully clear with yourself about its basis and its practical difficulties. Beneficiaries need accountability when you elect to speak for them, and

FIGURE 21-2

Roger and Me—the first Michael Moore film, and maybe the first to go for the managerial jugular using satire. *(Photo courtesy of The Kobal Collection/Warner Bros.)*

agreement about who has the right to control their image. Offering your participants a share in authorship may be the only way to overcome the distrust that poisons relations between the religions or the races, say, or between feminists and well-meaning males.

EMBEDDED VALUES

Look back a few decades to see how the fiction screen represents particular people, roles, and relationships. Criminals or gangsters are "ethnic" types; women are secretaries, nurses, teachers, and mothers. People of color are buffoon servants, vagrants, or objects of pity with little to say for themselves—and so on. All this is too familiar for comment. Well, three writers from the University of Southern California film school think differently. They call these regressive assumptions *embedded values*, that is, values so natural to the makers of a film that they pass below the radar of awareness. It follows that we are liable to overlook today's equally unsupportable assumptions.

In their book *Creative Filmmaking from the Inside Out: Five Keys to the Art of Making Inspired Movies and Television* (Simon & Schuster, 2003), Jed Dannenbaum, Carroll Hodge, and Doe Mayer of USC's School of Cinema and Television demonstrate the traps in making art. Their examination of ethics in practice is especially pertinent to documentary, where unexamined assumptions silently guide a film's outcome. The book, which is mostly aimed at fiction filmmakers, poses some fascinating questions that I have adapted below. The central question is, Will the world in your film reinforce received truths, or will it question them? Consider how your intended documentary represents these factors:

Participants:

* *Class*—What class or classes do they come from? How will you show differences? Will other classes be represented, and if so, how?
* *Wealth*—Do they have money? How is it regarded? How do they handle it? What does the film take for granted? Are things as they should be, and if not, how will the film express this?
* *Appearances*—Are appearances reliable or misleading? How important are appearances? Do the characters have difficulty reading each other's appearances?
* *Background*—Is there any diversity of race or other background and how will you handle this? Will other races or ethnicities have minor or major parts?
* *Belongings*—Will we see them work or know how they sustain their lifestyle? What do their belongings say about their tastes and values? Is anyone in the film critical of this?
* *Emblems*—Do they own or use important objects, and what is their significance?
* *Work*—Is their work shown? What does it convey about them?
* *Valuation*—For what do characters value other characters? Will the film question this or cast uncertainty on the inter-character values?
* *Speech*—What do you learn from the vocabulary of each? What makes the way each thinks and talks different from the others? What does it signify?
* *Roles*—What roles do participants fall into, and will they emerge as complex enough to challenge any stereotypes?
* *Sexuality*—If sexuality is present, is there a range of expression, and will you portray it? Is it allied with affection, tenderness, love?
* *Volition*—Who is able to change their situation and who seems unable to take action? What are the patterns behind this?
* *Competence*—Who is competent and who not? What determines this?

Environment:

* *Place*—Will we know where characters come from, and what values are associated with their origins?
* *Settings*—Will they look credible, and add to what we know about the characters?
* *Time*—What values are associated with the period chosen for the setting?
* *Home*—Do the characters seem at home? What do they have around them to signify any journeys or accomplishments they have made?
* *Work*—Do they seem to belong there, and how will you portray the workplace? What will it say about the characters?

Family dynamics:

- *Structure*—What family structure emerges? Do characters treat it as normal or abnormal? Is anyone critical of the family structure?
- *Relationships*—How are relationships between members and between generations going to be portrayed?
- *Roles*—Are family roles fixed or do they develop? Are they healthy or unhealthy? Who in the family is critical? Who does the family brand "good" or "successful," and who "bad" or "a failure"?
- *Power*—Could there be another structure? Do protagonists handle authority in a healthy or unhealthy way? What is the relationship of earning money to power in the family?

Authority:

- *Gender*—Which gender seems to have the most authority? Does one gender predominate, and if so, why?
- Initiation—Who will initiate the events in the film, and why? Who is likely to resolve them?
- Respect—How are figures with power depicted? How will you show institutions and institutional power? Are they simple or complex, and does what you can show reflect your experience of the real thing?
- Conflict—How do characters negotiate conflicts? What will the film say about conflict and its resolution? Who usually wins, and why?
- Aggression—Who is being aggressive and who is being assertive, and why? Who are you supporting in this, and whom do you tend to censure?

In total:

- Criticism—How critical is the film going to be towards what its characters do, or don't do? How much will it tell us about what's wrong? Can we hope to see one of the characters coming to grips with this?
- Approval/Disapproval—What will the film approve of, and is there anything risky and unusual in what it defends? Is the film challenging its audience's assumptions and expectations, or just feeding into them?
- World View—If this is a microcosm, what will it say about the balance of forces in the larger world?
- Moral Stance—What stance will the intended film's belief system take in relation to privilege, willpower, tradition, inheritance, power, initiative, God, luck, coincidence, etc.? Is this what you want?

ETHICAL CONFLICTS IN THE FIELD

Seldom will you make aesthetic and ethical decisions from a position of cool intellectual neutrality. Most questions arise from intruding into people's lives and learning from the consequences. Many issues and aspects of personality—yours as well as those of your participants—remain latent and invisible until the "history box" is running, and this of course is part of documentary's dangerous fascination. Once committed, you may have to defend your rights as chronicler and critic. Some will attack you for daring to make interpretive criticisms, while others will harangue you for failing to do so. So, what do you believe, and how will you justify your values?

Usually we only struggle with conflicting moral obligations when their material embodiment forces it upon us. We owe allegiance to people who trust us on the one hand, and to truths we hold dear on the other. When does obligation to a moral truth allow you to violate someone's trust or legitimize turncoat behavior? Can you let go of a conviction and make a different film if new evidence shows that you were wrong? Sometimes you are in trouble no matter which way you turn. In such circumstances it helps to remind oneself that one's movie is just one little person's view at one little moment in time. Freedom of speech does not mean freedom from friction.

FILM IS COLLABORATIVE, SO IS RESPONSIBILITY

Film's strength and authority come not from supermen or superwomen, but from the essentially collaborative nature of the medium. We work together, debate issues together, help and support each other's projects, and help each other live by values that may not be popular. Choose your team wisely, and seek their support whenever you need it. In an ethical issue, try to put all decisions on hold until you can confer with those you respect. Out of your conversations will come arguments and positions that can greatly help you uphold your own.

ART AS DISPLACED AUTOBIOGRAPHY

Luckily each of us probably carries only one or two strong convictions taught by life—an important message purposely explored at the very beginning of this book. Recognizing this, you can say, "*This* my life has shown me, so *this* is what I must explore, and *this* is what I stand for." Of course, different or more profound truths may emerge along the road.

Films, especially transparent ones aiming to present life in a rather authorless way, often mask the roots they have in their maker's psyche. I am convinced that most documentary—indeed most art—is displaced autobiography. If such a generalization seems outrageous, ask where you got the understanding that allows you to portray another person. Surely, from your own close engagement with life, from the energy generated by your own knocks and bruises. You need this energy because documentaries take months or years to complete.

By finding what you need to say being lived by other people, you put your convictions under test. It's no longer yourself-as-subject, but whether you can spot the rules of the universe at work. This you do best by finding the counterparts to your own needs and experience floating in life's stream. By catching and tethering them in a structured statement, you help them mirror the hard truths that life has taught you. Seeking your enduring preoccupations at work in others will lead toward filmmaking with overtones of universality. The discipline of such a process brings its own rewards: with growing maturity you can identify the surrogates to your own values and temperament, and watch them achieving a fully mysterious life of their own in your film. Your work quietly alters how you see the fundamentals of your own life—the very source from which your artistic process sprang. In this way, each project is midwife to the next.

This is the artistic process at work, the wellspring of life itself.

GIVING, NOT JUST TAKING

Luckily you don't just take from others: you also give. Your film examination often helps transform the very lives you thought you were capturing intact. Since filming can compromise, subvert, improve, or even create the end result in your film, you face a conundrum. The solution may be to share the paradoxes with your audience rather than mask them. Today's audiences are sophisticated and very interested in what filming does to the situation under study.

HANDS-ON LEARNING

Try making a participatory documentary by using **SP-13 Participatory Film**. Your charge is to "gather a core sample of attitudes and feelings from a range of interviewees on a contemporary issue, interview the best two in depth, then shoot illustrative material to flesh out the narrative that emerges from your questioning. The resulting investigative documentary should use multiple participants and a range of techniques" in which the director's path through the investigation is evident.

NOTE

1. Robert M. Pirsig, *Zen and the Art of Motorcycle Maintenance* (William Morrow, 1974). Before it became a bestseller, the book was first rejected by 121 publishers.

PART 7

ADVANCED PRODUCTION ISSUES

Sustaining an audience's interest through the extended and complicated issues found in longer documentaries takes imagination, planning, and experimentation. Story lines are more convoluted, and more rests on the credibility of what an extended chain of participants might say and do, something that you can only guess.

You will need additional technical resources for larger and more complicated productions, which means developing relationships with funds and foundations. You also find yourself responsible for more controlled and sophisticated filming if your filming is to meet professional expectations. The editing period, when you finish shooting, is usually much longer and involves seeking feedback from multiple trial audiences.

Part 7 expands on the three main stages of filmmaking to become Part 7A Advanced Preproduction, Part 7B Advanced Production, and Part 7C Advanced Postproduction.

PART 7A

ADVANCED PREPRODUCTION

The detailed proposal is your major tool in applying to funding organizations. This Part takes the proposal process farther to include defining a point of view. It includes genre, film dialectics, and developing the all-important Storyteller approach by which you establish a film's individual "voice." Since your ethical choices are important to the value system driving the heart of your filmmaking, there is a discussion of what makes evidence persuasive. Part 7A concludes with a round-up of the logistical preparations for a well-organized shoot.

CHAPTER 22

ADVANCED RESEARCH

The more complex the film, the more likely the subject is to alter and develop during the research period. Expect, therefore, a circular pattern of endeavor in which you are researching, rewriting your working hypothesis, and working on a changing proposal all at the same time. The object is seldom to develop a script, but to explore everything relevant so that one is fully prepared. Before using this chapter, you might want to review the fundamentals again in **Chapter 7: Research**.

RESEARCHING FOR INFORMATION

Quantitative and qualitative research are each categories of information you will seek in the field, library, or Internet. Each represents a different type of evidence that you will seek—either to support or to challenge the assertions participants make, or perhaps in support of claims you want your film to make.

Quantitative research means gathering data for anything you can count or measure. This might be facts and figures for populations, incomes, crime figures, percentages of people in a particular occupation, or the average age at marriage. Making valid numerical comparisons allows you to assert, for instance, that many accountants take early retirement, or to dismiss arguments for crime being an inherited trait. If birth complication figures rise after a county has dismissed all its midwives, but remain stable in those counties that retained their services, you can argue persuasively that midwives are useful and should be reinstated.

Your credibility always rests on information that can't be discredited. When you get a fact wrong, the whole fabric of your argument falls under suspicion, so check facts carefully and skeptically. When several credible figures are in circulation, use the least extreme. *Crosscheck* all important information using at least two authoritative sources: you'll be surprised how frequently "historical facts" have acquired respectability through exchange and repetition, which is the basis of prejudice. The Internet is replete with dubious facts, incorrect spellings, and wild assertions of all kinds.

Qualitative research involves asking broad questions about what cannot be quantified such as attitudes, aspects of character, motives, methods, goals, outlooks, presumed backgrounds, and so on. Much research for documentaries is of this nature, and involves making subjective judgments and using your intuition to look for patterns. As a safeguard, crosscheck attitudes or perceived outcomes, and pay careful attention to your teammates' differing impressions and reservations. The more closely you work with partners, the more you can double-check your ideas and impressions against the life-experience of other reliable minds. You should even discreetly cross-check opinions and feelings among knowledgeable participants. If, for instance, you are doing a town hall story, and someone tells you in confidence that the mayor "is very authoritarian," certain questions should reflexively pop up in your mind:

- *What agenda might the teller have*? If you believed him and then found out later that the mayor fired him for incompetence, you'd look really dumb.
- *How reliable is the informant's source?*
- *Was this assessment made first-hand from dealings?*
- Or *is it hearsay* from, say, TV reporting that was itself recycled from newspaper articles?

It is human to be subjective, so expect everything and everyone (yourself included) to be biased. Prolong the conversation with your informant to flush out all the information you can. Tap his views on unrelated issues to see how perceptive and fair he seems across the board, and perhaps what his attitudes to authority are in general. Talk to other knowledgeable people, to see whether, without revealing the target of your interest, you can validate or invalidate something potentially crucial that you've been told.

To make the strongest possible case, qualitative research that you use in your film must be juxtaposed with the right kind of visual or testamentary evidence, which may endorse or question someone's assertion. The reason you build pictures of each participant's character is to help us know about that person's agenda, to expect certain ambivalences (say), and to know how to interpret what he or she feels about something. His attitudes may rest on prejudices held as truths, so you must sometimes check whether a generalization is supportable or ought to be exposed as a fallacy.

ARCHIVAL MATERIAL

Film you want may be in government, state, local, or private hands and is often very expensive. You shouldn't assume that material you saw on television is available for you to use. Much history is in the copyright of the company that shot it, or that bought it.

Rick Prelinger of the New York Prelinger Archives (https://archive.org/details/prelinger) says that when your film depends on archive footage, be sure that (a) what should exist, does exist, and (b) that you can use it for a payment your production can afford. Negotiate early—never, ever wait till later. Be sure to declare the media, markets, and rights territory correctly and in their entirety because you will be at a huge disadvantage if you try to amend them later. Clear any music rights if music is integral to the footage you want. Anticipate all the extras the library may charge (duplication, research, etc.). Be sure to order the duplication in a format that will integrate with your production's workflow. If your film depends on a lot of material from a number of archives, consider hiring experienced archival researchers whose expertise will save you time and money. Prelinger's article contains much further useful detail.

FAIR USE AND BEST PRACTICES

Just as you can make "fair use" of limited literary material in a publication that discusses or critiques someone else's writing, there is a *fair use doctrine* that can serve as an advisory for what you can and can't do with segments of screen material taken without seeking permission. It is "advisory" because it has yet to be tested in court. If you want to avoid becoming a test-case, check latest developments in these two websites. One is the Stanford Copyright and Fair

Use Center at http://fairuse.stanford.edu and the other is via Pat Aufderheide at The Center for Media & Social Impact, School of Communications, American University, http://cmsimpact.org. By the way, her *Documentary Film: A Very Short Introduction* (Oxford University Press, 2007) is first-rate.

IN RELATION TO PARTICIPANTS

When you start research, you have little idea what your film will say or what part any individual might play in it. Be clear that you are talking with people to gain an understanding from those in the know, and that filming will emerge from what you learn over time. Be clear, too, that a documentary is a mosaic that comes together during editing, not the realization of a script. We shoot ten times more than we use, and this should remove people's fears that you want them to "perform." It also forewarns them that you may or may not use their contribution.

OBSERVATION AND ACCESS

Wherever possible, gain access through someone trusted by the individual or community. Being an unknown at a union meeting, for instance, can be extremely uncomfortable since your goals will be suspect. Be ready to explain yourself repeatedly in broad terms until everybody seems satisfied. Do be sociable and communicative, since this lowers tension. Do join in group activities if invited and be ready to make a fool of yourself as part of your entry test. Becoming accepted by a settled group can be a much longer process. In some European villages, for instance, a family can remain "newcomers" for two or three generations!

KEEPING NOTES

Usually it won't feel right to make audio or video recordings during your earliest research because it puts people on guard. If however you hang out with a local sports team, they will probably accept you and your aims over time. Better is to note key phrases and sayings that will jog your memory in relation to particular people. Afterwards, expand your notes to make them intelligible before your memory fades, and write out any important thoughts, impressions, and intuitions. These will be helpful when you want to pursue particular issues.

Exploratory writing is a vital structuring activity that enables you to develop your initial ideas. Do such interpretative writing alone, somewhere private, and not in sight of possible participants, who may grow uneasy about what you are cooking up. Should a court ever subpoena your notes, your lawyer will advise you to produce notes that people saw you writing, but may let you withhold speculative writing made in private.

OBSERVING CHARACTER

Wherever you must reveal character, and especially if yours is a character-driven film, you must incisively observe the main participants. This you will have to do in private, so you can summon up your memory-impressions and write candidly. The idea is not to make an exhaustive catalogue but to note down whatever is particular and telling, and to capture those fugitive impressions picked up by your intuition. Your aim is to make powerful thumbnail portraits of the main characters as a way of priming your camera operator. Most useful is a set of behaviors to capture on film.

Dramatists and psychologists have struggled over the millennia to create embracing charts of personality types and traits, so you might want to glance at a summation online[1] for ideas that appeal to you. Here are categories I use as my antenna seeks out the particular:

- **Physical**
  - *Environment*, chosen or unchosen (country, area, home, workplace, furniture, accessories, pictures, decor, anything incongruous, etc.).
  - *Appearance and condition* (gender, age, ethnicity, body type, clothing, social class, energy, strength, etc.).
  - *Quality of interactions* (with people, environment, animals, tools, materials, etc.).
  - *Mannerisms* (expressiveness, bodily confidence, communicativeness, repeated mannerism, etc.).
  - *Vocal characteristics* (vocal range, timbre, associations).

- **Psychological**
  - *Roles*, willing and unwilling (job, self-concept, perception of and by others, role conferred by family or workmates, etc.).
  - *Goals*, long-term and short-term (that he/she is trying to get, do, or accomplish are_____).
  - *Obstacles* (that blocked and impeded him/her),
    - Internal forces he/she is struggling with are_____.
    - External forces he/she is struggling with are_____.
  - *Major conflict* (main, prevailing collision of forces in this person, and the paradigm for everything else, is the struggle between_____ and_____).
  - *Attitudes* (confident or unconfident, active or reactive, honest or manipulative, knowing or gullible, self-dramatizing or self-concealing, optimistic or pessimistic, extroverted or introverted, trusting or distrusting, etc.).
  - *"Voice."* (How he or she acts on, or presents him- or herself to others. This may vary revealingly, according to the situation.)
  - *Development* (What does the person need to learn, become, attain? Will they do so, and in what time-frame?)

- **Ideological**
  - *Philosophy of life* (credo, why we are alive, what we are here for, etc.).
  - *Affiliations* (religious, social, or political beliefs underlying his/her actions).
  - *Spiritual outlook* (sense of kinship, religious, or other spiritual beliefs, etc.).
  - *Contradictions* (beliefs that you see contradict his/her actions).

These categories seek the rough edges, disparities, and contradictions that can make people so vital, unpredictable, and fascinating. For every quality you want to include in your film, note the evidence that persuaded you, since it won't exist onscreen unless you can pick it up during filming. You will work extensively with these qualities in the next chapter, **Chapter 23: Advanced Story Development and Proposal**.

OPEN QUESTIONS AND LEADING QUESTIONS

Most important while you research is to avoid *leading questions*. An example would be, "Do you think the mayor is authoritarian?" Instead ask *open questions* that give no hint of what you expect such as "What kind of person is the mayor?" One person may call him "principled, firm, and a little humorless" while another says he's "loyal to supporters, a bit austere, and not the best listener." A third thinks he's "a rough diamond" and "has done quite a bit of good for the town."

From these differing, subjective experiences comes a more rounded profile that is significant for what it omits: nobody says the mayor is corrupt, a bad manager, or unpopular.

When you want to test a controversial opinion, be sure to preface it with, "*Some people say that* the mayor runs a patronage setup, so what would you say to them?" "*The Nightly Sentinel's op-ed column said that* the mayor listens mostly to his wealthy business associates..." The italicized openings displace the opinion away from yourself, leaving you as the open-minded researcher trying to understand a spectrum of attitude, and seeking the listener's help. Never forget that enemies of your film will seize on any inaccuracy to discredit you and all your works.

TRUST

Documentarians have occasionally abused the trust placed in them by participants. A woman factory worker once spoke candidly and trustingly to a colleague's camera about sexual morals among her female coworkers. The (male) director apparently knew this was a risk but did not discuss it with her, and effectively gambled with her safety for the sake of a more sensational film. When the film went out over the air, her colleagues were so incensed that they beat her up. Usually nothing comparable is at risk, so there's no need to alarm participants by warning of all imaginable consequences, since this would scare most people away from filming at all.

When you are in doubt, however, take pains to secure "informed consent" (below). In the case of investigative filmmaking, the nature of the investigation itself should be fair warning for those of mature age and judgment.

Informed consent is the permission that a participant (or their guardian, if they are underage) gives you in writing after you duly warn them of foreseeable consequences. To those deserving of a fair warning, such as the youthful, immature, or those who are emotionally or intellectually unprepared, you explain the possible negative consequences of their contribution, which might include physical or legal danger, or damage to a person's reputation.

You will probably feel like a doctor advising patients about the benefits of an operation with its offsetting complications and consequences. Some people listen carefully, some over-react, and some may be inattentive or too unsophisticated to absorb the implications. Only if they have understood the relevant facts and risks can you consider using their material, and even then it may be wise to err on the side of caution.

In America during the 1970s, the Loud family consented to have their lives filmed (*An American Family*, Alan and Susan Raymond, USA, 1973, PBS 12 hour-long episodes). The exposure—first to the camera, and then to savage criticism in the press, which treated them as performers—placed the unfortunate family under intolerable pressure. Afterwards they claimed that Alan and Susan Raymond had not explained the consequences. Maybe so, but the open-ended nature of any such undertaking would make comprehensive explanation virtually impossible. Who could have foretold that Bill would leave Pat, or that Lance would come out of the closet?

THE CASE FOR SUBTERFUGE

In seeking (or not seeking) permission, outright subterfuge is sometimes justified. When someone has collaborated in the gassing of defenseless people, you are amply justified in using deception to get their testimony, as Claude Lanzmann did in *Shoah* (France, 1985, Figure 22-1). By presenting himself as a historian wanting to "restore the balance of truth" to the historical record, he got the unguarded testimony of a Nazi officer from Treblinka extermination camp and of a German guard at Chelmno, where Jews were killed in mobile gassing vans. In the light of what these men had

Someone said "the final
solution of the Jewish question".

FIGURE 22-1

Secret video recording of Franz Schalling describing how Jews were systematically killed using van engine exhaust fumes.

done, few would have scruples about deceiving them. Such clarity is rare; usually the issues are not so black and white.

COMPROMISING YOURSELF

The loyalties and obligations that develop between yourself and your participants can lead to thickets of ethical dilemma. A single example: You are planning a film about the victims of a housing scam whom you get to know and like. You also gain the confidence of the perpetrators, wealthy property developers, who offer you hospitality. Refusing might tip them off to your disapproval of their practices, so you go out, eat an expensive dinner, and laugh at their jokes. When you next visit their victims, you feel compromised from sleeping with the enemy. Even if you let this be known, it would be unwise to confide more than a sketchy idea of what you learned, or you will turn into a double agent.

HANDS-ON LEARNING

Here you should build a foundation for advanced filming in **DP-4 Full Working Hypothesis**, and also perhaps take advantage of **DP-6 Advanced Proposal** to develop the many significant aspects that an audience expects of a professional-level documentary. By making use of **DP-2 Style and Content Questionnaire**, you can explore your intended material's meaning. You can also examine its potential for shooting and stylistic differences when you plan how to shoot.

NOTE

1. See Wikipedia under "Personality Psychology," and for more ideas follow any links that resonate to the person you have under study.

CHAPTER 23

ADVANCED STORY DEVELOPMENT AND PROPOSAL

USING THE WORKING HYPOTHESIS TO THE FULL

You can now use all the hypothesis prompts in Table 23-1, first seen in abbreviated form in **Chapter 7: Research**. The remaining prompts embrace point of view, style, and Storyteller voice, and will help you put into effect what has been discussed in **Part 6: Documentary Aesthetics**.

TABLE 23-1 Prompts for a Full Working Hypothesis (for help see Project DP-4 on the book's website, www.directingthedocumentary.com)

DP-4 Full Working Hypothesis prompts

Steps
1. In life I believe that … (your life-principle concerning this subject)
2. My film will show this in action by exploring … (situations)
3. My central characters are … (names, role, characteristics, etc.)
4. What he/she/they are trying to get, do, or accomplish is …
5. The main conflict in my film is between … and …
6. My film's POV, or its POV character, will be …
7. I expect my film's structure to be determined by …
8. The subject and POV suggest a style that is …
9. The theme my film explores is …
10. The premise of my film is …
11. The Storyteller's characteristics are …
12. Possible resolutions to my film are …
13. Ultimately I want my audience to feel …
14. … and to understand that …

The prompts not used in **Chapter 7: Research** are:

6. Point of view: Explain and justify whether POV is: Omniscient? A narrator's? A character within the film? Multiple POVs? Director's or other central character's? And if so, is it a performative POV? Do POVs change, and if so, why? How does POV relate to #11 Storyteller Characteristics?

8. Style: Explain what genre (family or type of documentary) your film belongs in, and in what ways your film purposefully subverts the norms. How does style relate to #11 Storyteller Characteristics?

10. Premise: This is a sentence or two that defines the fundamental, driving idea behind the film, such as, "a resourceful Inuit leads his family through the vital acts of survival in the Arctic." How does the premise unite with #11 Storyteller Characteristics?

11. Storyteller characteristics: The concept of a definable personality and a set of attitudes driving the storytelling is crucial if the "voice" of your film is to surpass whatever emerges haphazard and by default. Try to characterize the Storyteller telling the tale as a strong, clear personality, one that may be earnest, sardonic, disbelieving, world-weary, excited, detached, rigorously scientific, naively learning, stoically refusing to be moved, or whatever else. Any storytelling voice you adopt is one you can influence and regulate from the beginning, but also one you probably need to keep out of sight during production. In the film itself, it becomes the posture a novelist, comedian, or actor adopts in relation to a given narrative or role. Necessarily it underlies and unites most of the other choices you have made while fashioning your working hypothesis.

Your storyteller's characteristics may be part of who you are in relation to the world, or they may emerge from the details of the story you are about to tell. Research will confirm what you are dealing with, and what attitude you can or should eventually take in the telling. Your Storyteller will be in formation all the way through research, and right up to the first day of filming.

EVIDENCE, EXPOSITION, AND DRAMATIC TENSION

Words used about documentary, such as "chronicles," "witnesses," "follows," "records," are all words suggesting that the documentary makes a case to its audience rather as evidence is presented to a jury.

EXPOSITION

As a filmmaker you are going to lead the jury through a narrative exposing them to the essentials of a situation. You might use any means in the documentary arsenal to do this. Perhaps your film is about an accident among workers in a scientific laboratory, one requiring complex safety protocols. Giving too much information (exposition) before it becomes relevant will numb the jury, but providing too little will leave them unable to make the right connections. So during research try considering:

- What world are we in and what does it feel like?
- What is this world's main condition, activity, or purpose?
- How does this world operate under normal conditions?
- What basic information does a first-time audience need in order to engage with the main issues?

- What has gone wrong?
- What is at issue?
- Who represents what here?

THE PROBLEM AND DRAMATIC CONFLICT

You film's participants and their issues will always need careful framing if your audience is to become fully involved with what is at issue in your film. This is true whether a man is trying to get off death row, as in Errol Morris's *Thin Blue Line* (USA, 1988), or whether he is an artist making ephemeral artworks that Nature will quietly destroy, as in Thomas Riedelsheimer's *Rivers and Tides: Andy Goldsworthy Working with Time* (Germany, 2002, Figure 23-1). Court trials make great drama because they openly deal with conflict, but all of life is made of tensions, and a drama always has a dramatic issue, called the "problem." It is fatally easy to mistake it, mis-identify it, or somehow ignore its importance.

VOLITION

Anyone involved in momentous actions operates under *volition*, which involves will, planning, and expending energy. It means confronting obstacles, struggling, and adapting to overcome obstructions. It applies as much to a shy five-year-old enduring her first day at school as it does to a Special Forces unit combating an insurgency. Information, atmosphere, novelty, and beauty are all important to documentaries, but the audience's cultural conditioning leads it to look for people whose will is at stake and who have principles at issue. So,

- What is each main person's role?
- What are their issues (that is, what is each trying to get, do, or accomplish)?
- Who or what is stopping them, and why?
- Who supports or opposes whom?
- What does each represent?
- What stages of the story have already happened, and what have yet to happen?

FIGURE 23-1

Rivers and Tides: Andy Goldsworthy Working with Time: what Man creates, time and Nature erase. (*Photo by Andy Goldsworthy.*)

CHALLENGING THE AUDIENCE TO MAKE JUDGMENTS

By assuming the audience is skeptical you can place participants' credibility under examination and raise our awareness of flaws and inconsistencies in their aims. By capturing strong, contradictory actions from your different factions, you will help maintain dramatic tension and assure momentum. Everything you can do to make your audience wonder, fear, think, judge, foresee, or hope involves them in using their emotional judgment and hypothesizing. Good art leads us to live vicariously, since we crave this kind of emotional workout. It also helps us rehearse our resources for handling similar situations.

CREDIBILITY OF EVIDENCE, WITNESSES, AND TESTIMONY

What you provide by way of images, actions, atmosphere, and speech will provide the *evidence* for your film's ideas and arguments. Since the audience cannot ask for elaboration, the filmmaker must anticipate when it needs context, confirmation, or interpretation—which is why you show your film repeatedly to trial audiences. The audience, like any jury, can assess people's motives from conflicting accounts, and enjoys judging what "really happened." In the investigative documentary, we frequently see testimony by a range of witnesses to support or undermine key allegations. The audience will need to know:

- What qualifies each person to give evidence?
- Is testimony derived from direct experience or only from hearsay?
- Is this person's testimony primary (witnessed by themselves) or secondary (a report of someone else's experience)?
- How credibly do they convey what they know?
- Do facts or other accounts support or undermine this account?
- What loyalties, prejudice, or self-interest may be skewing their viewpoints?
- What other evidence might alter, prove, or disprove their testimony?
- What do I (the audience member) know from experience that is relevant to what's at issue?
- Is there anything demonstrable from the witness's background that puts their motives, preparation, knowledge, and identity in a new light?
- Can an opponent interpret key testimony differently?
- How authentic and credible are the documents, pictures, memories, or records used in evidence (for instance, are documents originals or copies)?

Testimony is strong when,

- It conveys compelling facts or information.
- It is *primary evidence* (opinions and inferences based on firsthand perceptions).
- Witnesses use reliable principles or methods to interpret those facts.

Testimony is weak when,

- It involves hearsay.
- The witness has heard the testimony of other witnesses.
- It involves specialization that exceeds the witness's competency.

Witnesses,

- Should be open to challenge by others involved in the issue.
- May not get real questions until they are on-camera. This can be explosive but also ethically dubious.

CREDIBILITY OF DOCUMENTARY SOURCES

Texts, archives, and filmed material each provide testimony of varying reliability. What they demonstrate can be persuasive, enigmatic, or misleading. Each is an authored construct that you should question:

- Under what circumstances was the footage or document compiled?
- What proof is there that it is genuine?
- What intention or sponsorship lay behind its authorship?
- Is there more than one hand behind the materials, and if so, do significant differences or inconsistencies exist?
- What are its intended, unintended, and received meanings?
- What does it exclude?
- How will a contemporary audience receive it?
- What assumptions lie behind its making, of which its makers may have been aware or unaware?
- Has original material been edited, or reused, in a way that alters its meaning?
- Can you rely on the translation if the materials originate in another language?

MAKING A DATABASE AND MARSHALING EVIDENCE

With a long and involved film, you may need to enter key information in a database. This will allow you to,

- Find all material associated with a word, phrase, date, or other remembered determinant (concerning "rhododendrons" or "Cape Verde," say).
- Selectively remove, arrange, or juxtapose material using pertinent filters (time periods, characters, locations, shooting dates, say).
- Organize proof by its credibility or other criteria (by giving important items a rating).

When the time comes to film, ask yourself:

- What will you have to arrange, say, or do to put a participant under pressure to reveal the next levels of truth?
- How can you raise the pressure so there is more at stake?
- Can you add verbal or written testimony to existing visual archives?
- Will you need to demonstrate unreliability in a participant to ensure your audience watches critically?

DECIDING CENTRAL CHARACTERS

With a good idea of the story you want to tell, you can now think about choosing your central characters. Whom you choose will make a big difference to your story contents and the way it develops, so it is usual to think hard and delay as long as possible.

DEFER CHOOSING PARTICIPANTS

Mistaken "casting" can conceivably land you with someone who evades, distorts, or even manipulates the process to their advantage. If you do not recognize this until shooting is under way, it will be very difficult to extricate yourself. To make the wisest casting decisions, *defer as long as possible*. The longer you can watch people in action, the less chance you will miscalculate. To avoid choices you regret, beware those who,

- Are over-anxious to participate and try too hard to interest you.
- Have an ax to grind and want to use your film as a platform (unless that aligns with your purposes, of course).
- Think you are going to profit from using them and want money for their participation.

At the other end of the spectrum is the anxious personality who,

- Fantasizes calamitous consequences from participating.
- Is over-dependent on the good opinion of others.
- Is fearful of appearing critical about anything or anybody.

Choose people for their characteristics, interest in cooperating, and for what they know. Documentaries must often present conflicting accounts and conflicting agendas, so you want people who will be interesting, revealing, and persuasive.

WHEN IN DOUBT, MAKE A RECORDING

If choosing is difficult, shoot trial material of those under consideration and show the material in private to people you trust. Ask whom they find most interesting and why. Quite apart from what they say, it will lead you to see your participants with new eyes. If you still cannot choose, close your eyes and listen to participants' voices. Vocal qualities are important and often overlooked.

STORY DEVELOPMENT

What follows is purposely different from a conventional approach, in which you would research to form ideas and themes, then look for the visual or interview material to illustrate them. Instead, try listing all the observational material you can come up with, as if studying a foreign people whose language you cannot understand. The aim is to firmly and consciously privilege the camera over the microphone.

LIST YOUR ACTION MATERIAL

List all possible scenes that could study people trying to get, do, or accomplish things. This will involve you in studying action, character, and purpose. Before you shoot, explore the implications of your action/behavioral resources by ruling three columns on pieces of paper, and fill them in to resemble the specimen Table 23-2. The first column details the sequence's subject; the second explores what the sequence might establish, which might be expository information, character revelation, mood, feeling, or thematic development. The third column lists how you might film the sequence to enhance its intrinsic atmosphere and meaning, and invest it with mood and subtext.

If you are nervous about covering your subject, plan to shoot all the interview material you can think of—but after, not concurrently with, your main shooting. Even if you don't use the talking heads, you may need interview material as voice-over.

Extemporizing your ideas and expectations like this helps develop potential lying unseen in the material, and leads toward a film founded on observation rather than narration, always the

TABLE 23-2 Action/evidence/coverage style roundup helps make sequences tell their own tale through the visual language of cinema (Project DP-4 on the book's website, www .directingthedocumentary.com)

DP-7 Action/Evidence/Coverage Worksheet

Action	Evidence	Coverage style
1. CAFE: Sharon waitressing many tables where people mostly stare at computers and ignore her.	That she is overworked and unappreciated. Silent customers and feral roar of espresso machine are the only sound.	Hurried handheld camera carried low, contrasty picture, action mechanical in tone, masses of repetitive walking.
2. MUSIC SCHOOL: Sharon at her cello practice in rehearsal room.	Alone, she is a disciplined perfectionist, repeating phrases until she is satisfied. Someone knocks on the door.	Tripod mounted camera, low-key lighting, mostly long shots. Action poised, concentrated, composed.
3. HOME VISIT to mother in her cluttered flat. They discuss the family pet's illness.	She draws comfort from her mom but finds her disorder irritating. The TV is on all the time in the background.	High tripod-mounted camera; reddish evening light through window. Lots of shots through cluttered shelves, etc.
4. AUDITION: Sharon tries out for an orchestra position but feels under immense pressure.	Everything in professional music rides on public performance, which she fears terribly. The place sounds hollow and empty.	Under orchestral hall working lights. Alternating big close-ups with long shots so that Sharon looks sadly vulnerable in the huge space.

litmus test for cinematic storytelling. Why not wait till it's time to shoot? The problem is, once you roll the camera, you will be fully occupied supervising the scene, and can *only see opportunities for which you have prepared yourself.* This means that most directing takes place in preproduction!

DEVELOP EACH SCENE'S DRAMATIC CONTENT

To place each intended scene's potential under a magnifying glass, use the Dramatic Content Worksheet in Chapter 7, Table 7-3. Shake out whatever can be implied in each scene and you waste no opportunity to find dramatic potential.

ALTERNATIVE STRUCTURES FROM A CARD GAME

Another way to explore your material is to mount individual scene descriptions on card, and lay them out on a table like playing cards. Now experiment with possible sequences and structures, moving blocks around to see what different films emerge. Consolidate progress by corraling a colleague, and narrating how you see the film. He or she will have questions and suggestions that you can debate together by moving the cards around. This technique is especially fruitful late in editing, when terminal fatigue is near.

TRY YOUR MATERIALS AGAINST THE DRAMATIC CURVE

See if you have something to put in every category of the Dramatic Form Worksheet (Table 23-3). Don't worry what angle or point of view the film takes at this time—leave that for later. Notice that the story begins with a *hook* (something intriguing that grabs the audience's attention and promises fulfillment later).

DEVELOPING A PROPOSAL

Writing a coherent proposal is always a struggle, but it forces you to scrutinize every detail of your intentions. Most importantly, a first rate proposal demonstrates your understanding of the documentary genre, and proves that you have authorial, thematic, and organizational issues under control so you can *direct*, not just shoot well-intentioned documentation.

Each foundation, fund, or series exists to promote particular kinds of work and particular kinds of subject and there are, says Tod Lending, "different types of proposals depending on whom you are pitching to. A proposal for a broadcaster is quite different from a proposal for a foundation, NGO, corporation, or not-for-profit. It is very important for the filmmaker to know who their audience is for the proposal, and *what they expect*." You can also, as he says, "request to see other successful proposals that the potential funder/client/broadcaster funded."

Depending on the subject and style of documentary you are making, be clear about its content and strategies. Your writing should persuade the reader that your film has,

- A first rate story to tell that will move and inform its audience.
- Compelling characters with important issues underlying their motivations.
- First rate interviewees (if your film is necessarily structured around interviews) whose stories will add up to an interesting and dramatic narrative.
- The means to make human truths (if the film is primarily observational) emerge from behavioral evidence.
- Strategies for foreseeable practical and logistical problems.
- A valid and critical perspective on some aspect of the human condition.

Be sure to show why you are specially qualified to handle this subject. Proof might include your prior work as a filmmaker or other specialist, personal experience with the subject, or access that you alone have been granted. Like gripping fiction, the successful documentary incorporates:

- Well-placed exposition of necessary information (facts or context placed neither too early nor too late).
- Interesting characters who are actively trying to get, do, or accomplish something.
- Events emerging from the characters' intrinsic needs.
- Dramatic tension and conflict between opposing forces.
- Suspense—not people hanging off cliffs necessarily, but intriguing situations that lead the audience to anticipate, wonder, compare, and decide.
- Confrontation between the key persons, factions, or elements that are in opposition.
- A resolution (happy or sad, good or bad, satisfying or not).
- Change in at least one main character or situation. He or she *learns* something, and can therefore develop in some degree.

TABLE 23-3 The Dramatic Form Worksheet helps you visualize your film as a dramatic entity, and helps you spot whatever it lacks as a fully viable story (Project DP-8 on the book's website, www.directingthedocumentary.com)

DP-8 Dramatic Form Worksheet (for the film as a whole)

1. **Structure** (A well-structured story gives a sense of movement and purpose)

a) **Hook**	How will you seize your audience's attention?
b) **Contract**	How will you signify the "contract" that suggests what the film is going to deal with?
c) **Structure**. What will organize your sequences and drive your film forward from start to finish?	The steps of a process, event, or journey? The emotional order of someone remembering? The needs of a main character in a character-driven film? A series of orchestrated contrasts? A series of graduated moods? Other_____?
d) **Handling of time**. How will you show the order and passage of time?	According to the original events' chronology? As someone recalls the events? According to a storytelling logic for telling the events (for instance showing a court case conclusion before reconstructing all the steps to get there)? Other_____?
e) **Apex or crisis**	Can you see a pivotal event, moment, scene, situation as your film's likely high point? (You may not, yet.)

2. **Change, growth, and resolution** (A satisfying story reflects change and growth)

a) Who has the potential for **change**?	Who or what is under pressure? Who or what might grow? Who is taking risks? Who or what needs to change? Can you legitimately help that growth (by positive intercession)? Who or what is really stopping that change?
b) **Confrontation**	How will your audience see the main, conflicting forces meet and collide? How to ensure this happens onscreen?
c) **Resolution**	What outcomes seem possible? Which is most likely? How could you handle each so that your film ends meaningfully?

3. **Audience, impact, theme**

a) **Target audience**. Who in particular are you addressing?	A kind of person in the film? An authority or institution? A section of the public, and if so, which? Other_____?
b) My **audience must feel**...	What emotions must you awaken in your audience?
c) My **audience must think about**...	What issue, idea, contradiction, conflict, etc. should your audience be left thinking about?
d) The **theme** of my film will be...	Recall your "In life I believe that..." statement and restate the theme your film will establish.

If these criteria seem much like fiction, analyze some of your favorite documentaries scene by scene, and decide what their dramatic ingredients really are.

Unless you are thoroughly established, it is rare to get funding at the conceptual stage. More often you must have the film substantially "in the can" and be applying for completion money.

THE DEMO REEL

Any application should be accompanied by a 3–5 minute, specially edited trailer that shows the characters, settings, shooting style, and anything else that is fundamental to your proposal. It should have fine cinematography, an attractive and pertinent style, and characters one wants to know. This is your chance to make the screen argue for the strength and attractiveness of your proposal, and if your reel is outstanding it may clinch who gets the money. Package it attractively, include an overview list so users can easily navigate, and be sure the disk plays faultlessly from beginning to end.

BE SPECIFIC TO THE FUND

Angle your proposal toward the particular aims, goals, and values of the fund, foundation, or television channel to which you are applying. Be sure to state why this particular fund (series, channel, program) is the right place for your film. Every successful appeal for funds is the beginning of a lengthy relationship with them, so you must get off on the right foot.

Each funding institution has its own proposal forms, expects you to write about specific information in a specific way, and wants a specified number of copies with everything properly labeled. A weary foundation reader, sifting through hundreds of applications, will view any departures from the norm not as charming originality but as crass indifference to the jury's task.

WRITING QUALITY

Use compact, evocative prose in short, declarative sentences and colorful language that makes the reader see and hear. Eliminate all digressions and circularity, and describe each step so the reader can easily relate it to the whole. Funding juries know from experience that a sloppy writer is unlikely to be an orderly and conscientious filmmaker. Only a craft-conscious, clearly expressed proposal is likely to produce a film with similar qualities.

CATEGORIZED INFORMATION

Your goal is to present your film's content, argument, and materials as categorized information. The prompts in the Advanced Proposal Checklist (Table 23-4) are reminders of what a full proposal might need, but *you must present the information in the fund's preferred format*. Include photographs, colorful graphics, and a scintillating sample reel so the reader can fully visualize the film's essentials.

TREATMENT

If a *treatment* is required, it is not categorized information but a present-tense, short-story narrative written to evoke how an audience will experience your film on the screen. It must convince a sponsor, fund, or broadcasting organization that you can tell a good story, and make a cinematic film of impact and significance. Include no philosophical or directorial intentions. To write a treatment,

- Write an active-voice, present-tense summary of what an audience watching the film will see and hear from the screen, allotting one paragraph per sequence.
- Write colorfully so the reader can readily visualize what you see in your mind's eye. Convey information and evoke your characters by using their own words in brief, pithy quotations.

TABLE 23-4 Advanced Proposal Helper (Project DP-6 on the book's website, www
.directingthedocumentary.com)

PROJECT DP-6 Advanced Proposal Helper

1. **TITLE**_____
2. **SITUATION** My film's "corner of nature" and the situation or predicament of its main characters) are as follows_____
3. **TARGET AUDIENCE** (be specific, don't write "Everyone!")_____
   a) My film is intended particularly for (audience)_____
   b) I can expect the audience to know_____ but not to know_____
   c) My film will extend, subvert, or endorse the audience's expectations by_____
   _____
4. Countervailing facts, ideas, and feelings I want to get across to my audience are_____
   _____
5. **MAIN CHARACTERS**
   a) Name, age, special qualities, relationship to others in film_____
   b) Direct speech quotations that convey this person's essence are_____
   c) What he/she is trying to get, do, or accomplish_____
   d) Contribution I expect him/her to make to my film's story_____
   e) Metaphoric role I imagine for each person is_____
6. **LIST OF ACTION SEQUENCES** (see Style and Content Checklist following)
7. **CONFLICT AND CONFRONTATION.** Define,
   a) Conflicts the characters think they have are_____
   b) Main conflict that I see them playing out (and of which they may be unaware) are_____
   _____
   c) I will ensure the two major conflicting forces come into confrontation with each another
   by_____
8. **TO-CAMERA INTERVIEWS.** Interviewee list:
   a) Name, age, gender_____
   b) Job, profession, or role_____
   c) Main elements my interview will seek to establish_____
9. **FILM STYLE**
   a) **Genre** of your documentary will be_____, and you will see this in the film's style bec
   ause_____
   b) The film's lighting, camerawork, and editing will create a prevailing tone
   of_____and a_____ progression of moods.
   c) Camera and editing rhythms are likely to be_____
   d) I expect to use_____ intercutting or parallel storytelling to
   create_____(comparison, ironic tension, etc.)
10. **POINT OF VIEW AND STRUCTURE**
    a) **Point of view:** the consciousness through which we see the story will mainly be_____
    _____
    b) **Narration** will be by_____(narrator, director, one of the characters, etc.)
    c) **Structure:** elements that might structure the film are_____ (a process,
    journey, turn of the seasons, etc.)
    d) The film will handle the **progression of time** by showing_____
    e) I expect the **crisis** or climactic sequence to be_____, and for it to occur_____
    (approximate place in film)

(Continued)

TABLE 23-4 (Continued)

PROJECT DP-6 Advanced Proposal Helper

11. RESOLUTION AND ENDING
    a) The likely **resolution** (or falling action) after the crisis will be_____
    b) Possible endings are_____
    c) Likely meanings each ending might contribute are_____
12. SOCIAL SIGNIFICANCE. My film,
    a) Will make the audience feel_____ about_____(the lives or situations it portrays)
    b) Will imply that the social significance of its contents is_____
13. I MUST MAKE THIS FILM BECAUSE_____ (Why only you have the **energy, passion, and commitment** to make this an outstanding film)
14. THEME. The documentary's **theme** is_____
15. PREMISE. My film's **premise** is_____ (film's content and purpose summed up in a single sentence such as you'd see in a TV listing)
16. WHY SHOULD THE AUDIENCE CARE? My film is expressly designed to catch and hold its **audience** because_____

- Supply brief supporting material on your DVD "reel."
- Never write anything you can't produce.
- Keep within the specified page count.
- Check that you have implied everything in the proposal in your treatment.

MODEL APPLICATION

Study any model application available, and follow the funding agency's conditions to the letter, especially since your complete proposal may be limited to a very few pages. Typically a fund will expect you to supply most of the following:

- **Cover sheet** (one page).
- **Film description** (three pages).
- **Synopsis** of the project, in perhaps 25 words or less.
- **Treatment** explaining background information, structure, theme, style, voice, point-of-view, and format (16 mm film, HD, etc.).
- **Contributors.** Who you have lined up to participate and why they are interesting and necessary.
- **Funding already in place,** including the "in kind" contributions that you or others are making.
- **Target communities** for program, and why this audience is presently unserved (funds and foundations usually try to fill gaps). Say how you are known to, are trusted by, and have access to the community in which you propose filming.
- **Current status** of the project.
- **Applicants' resumés** (the initiators of the project).
- **Key production personnel** (names, positions, special experience and awards, short biography).

- **Sample work** (reel of previously completed film—see fund guidelines).
- **Work-in-progress** (WIP) demo reel of perhaps 5 minutes (see fund guidelines).
- Written **descriptions of prior work**, applicants' creative contribution to it, its relevance to WIP, and what the WIP represents (rough cut, trailer, selects, or a clip).

Keep reworking your proposal until every sentence is succinct, free of redundancy, and the project jumps off the page, crying out to be filmed.

Before you send your proposal off, check and recheck it for compliance, and have a couple of literate colleagues check it for typos or misspellings. Check that the DVD copy of your demo reel plays faultlessly from beginning to end.

HANDS-ON LEARNING

Depending on what stage of a proposal you are working on, any of the following may be helpful to your work: **DP-1 Dramatic Content Helper, DP-2 Style & Content Questionnaire, DP-4 Full Working Hypothesis, DP-6 Advanced Proposal, DP-8 Dramatic Form.**

CHAPTER 24

ADVANCED TECHNOLOGY AND BUDGETING

Budgeting and fundraising are a chicken and egg situation: you can't work without funds and you can't raise funds without a budgeted plan for your work. Deciding on the equipment and shooting schedule is the prelude since different levels of technology involve very different levels of cost. For a truly fascinating PBS survey of the most-used equipment by their documentarians, see www.pbs.org/pov/filmmakers/2013-documentary-equipment-survey.php#.UoT9B5Tk9bs. Their relative years of experience is also interesting.

For the workflow and technology information that follows, I am indebted to Mick Hurbis-Cherrier, my esteemed co-author of *Directing: Film Techniques and Aesthetics*, fifth edition, whose knowledge of digital technology (and most else) far exceeds mine. For more about the technologies surveyed below, consult his *Voice & Vision: A Creative Approach to Narrative Film and DV Production* (Focal Press, 2012).

WORKFLOW AND EQUIPMENT

Because digital electronics are in such rapid evolution, expect at the outset of each new project to research every aspect of *workflow*, which, as described in "Codecs and Workflow", **Chapter 12: Cameras**, is the format path, codecs, and technological processes that your project must follow. Those who lose their way, having begun in happy oblivion, usually fetch up against very expensive consequences. The only safeguard is rigorous research and crosschecking from the beginning. Workflow includes the technology for,

- Image shooting.
- Sound gathering.
- Editorial processes.
- Incorporating archive materials.
- Finishing processes, including sound.
- Mastering and distribution formats.

Preproduction meetings with your cinematographer, recordist/production sound mixer, editor, and postproduction lab (if you require lab services like color grading) are the forum for discussing what formats to adopt when you record both sound and image. Everyone in the crew *must be on the same technical page before a single frame has been shot.*

Whether you aim for release on television, Webcast, DVD, or a theatrical Digital Cinema venue, you must know your workflow from beginning to end, checking its viability by consulting with others who followed a similar path. There are four basic workflow questions:

1. *What is the shooting format?* Film, HD video (720p, 1080i), uncompressed or RAW video?

2. *How are we editing?* Format, codecs, frame rate, resolution?

3. *How do we want to finish and master the movie?* Film, HD video (720p, 1080i), uncompressed media files (2 K, 4 K)?

4. *How do we want to exhibit and distribute the project?* Broadcast HD format (720p, 1080i), Blu-ray, DVD, web, or a combination? Or high-end theatrical projection like 35 mm film, or Digital Cinema?

Within these general questions are many arcane details to reconcile if you are not to waste inordinate time, money, and energy later. Most directors need considerable education in these ever-evolving areas, so a cinematographer, sound mixer, and editor are more than creative collaborators—they must be technologically up to date or your project won't make it through to completion successfully. For up to date best practices in tapeless workflow, go to the Keycode Media site: www.keycodemedia.com/Tapeless-Workflow.

CHOOSING FILM OR DIGITAL ACQUISITION

Directors generally choose their cinematographers by the quality of their previous work, their creative judgment, and their ideas about the project at hand—but at some point you will need to have "the discussion" about shooting technology. What are you going to shoot on? Whether to shoot film or digitally has two major aspects: the first is creative—what look can I get from each production format? The second is budgetary—what will each format cost me? Both then involve additional choices: film shooting can be 35 mm or Super 16 mm format, and digital shooting can be done in HD broadcast standards (720p, 1080i) or at the uncompressed video file resolutions of 2 K or 4 K.

To shoot a scripted, acted history documentary digitally is not inherently cheaper than shooting film. However, the far higher *shooting ratio* of an observational documentary will almost certainly compel the use of video on cost grounds, and it can in any case produce aesthetically beautiful, professionally polished documentaries for far less than using film. Recent developments in RAW and uncompressed video shooting, enlarged image sensors, and a full range of superior, interchangeable lenses now give you a very sophisticated medium. Digital cameras like the RED Epic and Arri Alexa make digital video quite as expressive as any 35 mm film production.

The major expense with film shooting, apart from cost of the film stock, is the unavoidable involvement with a film lab and the expense of its services for processing, transferring, intermediate prints, effects, optical track masters, and possibly distribution copies too. A digital camera, on the other hand, uses reusable recording media like SD or S×S cards or hard drives, and computers handle all of its output.

Using film for documentaries is virtually obsolete because of cost and the inconvenience of frequent reloading. Consequentially 16 mm film labs are practically obsolete, though film will continue in use for the occasional specialized project. What film camera equipment you use depends on your chosen format, such as 35 mm or Super 16 mm (16 mm widescreen). Superior image quality is associated with 35 mm film because it: has finer grain (greater sharpness, or acuity); uses lenses with a usefully limited DOF; and can be shown in any cinema in the world. Furthermore, you can transfer it to any video format—at a hefty price.

Shooting on film takes heavy funding up front to buy stock, and is vastly expensive to process and print. Anybody experienced enough to light and shoot it will know where to get the equipment and how much it will cost. A film acquisition feature with a $2 million budget is considered cheap. Comparing the two film formats,

Super 16 mm shoot: This widescreen format is a less expensive and more mobile way to shoot on film, but get advice from someone who has successfully (and recently) completed your preferred chain of production.

35 mm shoot: You will need the appropriate camera support systems and a dolly on rails, especially if you shoot Panavision. Any handheld shots will need either a shoulder-mounted, short-run 35 mm camera or, if you intend a more gliding motion, a Steadicam™ operated by someone very strong and very experienced at using it.

The workflow from 16 mm or 35 mm film acquisition to a HD or D-Cinema master is complex, expensive, and requires careful research and consultation with a film lab.

BROADCAST HD, FORMATS, AND SCANNING

In the United States, *high definition* (HD) broadcast resolution conforms to the frame rate, aspect ratio, and resolution standards established by the consortium of engineers, communication companies, and policy makers of the ATSC (Advanced Television Systems Committee).[1] Of principle interest to filmmakers are the HD formats:

- *1080i HD* records 1,920 pixels × 1,080 lines at a frame rate of 30 interlaced frames per second.
- *720p HD* records 1,280 pixels × 720 lines at 30 or 60 progressively scanned frames per second.
- *1080/24p HD* records 1,920 pixels × 1,080 lines at a frame rate of 24p (resembling film).

Aspect ratio expresses the width of the frame in relation to its height, and is 16:9 for all the above standards (see Chapter 12). HD thus approximates the cinema format of 1.85:1, and is now the preferred aspect ratio internationally for HD television. Older archive material will probably be in 4:3, the original cinema screen format inherited by television in its early days.

FRAME RATES AND SCANNING

Because of differing electrical supplies, American frame rate standards are based on 30 fps (frames per second), while the European PAL system shoots at 25 fps. Which you use depends on where you live or where your film will be shown.

ATSC standards create the frames in each of its 30 fps formats using one of two strategies. One uses *progressive scanning*, meaning that the entire 720 horizontal lines of video information making up the image are scanned (drawn on your image sensor or monitor screen), from top to bottom, 30 times per second. Progressive scan formats are indicated with the designation "p" while the alternative "i" designation stands for *interlaced scanning*. A complete video frame results from two partial scans called *fields*. In one the odd lines of information are scanned from top to bottom (lines 1, 3, 5, 7, etc.) and in the other the even lines of information are scanned (lines 2, 4, 6, 8, 10, etc.). These two fields (the odd field and even field) are interlaced to create a full frame.

A (odd-line field)   +   B (even-line field)   =   C (eye perceives complete image)

FIGURE 24-1

Two frames, one with even lines and one with odd, interlace to make an "i" (interlace) frame. A "p" or progressive frame writes the complete frame from top to bottom.

The interlace system takes a 60th of a second to scan each field but achieves the full frame of two interlaced fields every 30th of a second (Figure 24-1).

Resolution determines image quality and is of paramount importance to director and cinematographer alike. It refers to the format's ability to reproduce visual detail, sharpness of line, subtlety and degrees of luminance, and accuracy of color. Several factors determine this: scanning type, lens quality, the number of sensor pixels, sampling bit rates, chroma subsampling, and data compression. Of principal interest is the *pixel count*. A "pixel" (short for *picture element*) refers to one of the hundreds of thousands or even millions of tiny capacitors that line the face of a video sensor, commonly a CCD or CMOS chip. Pixels are like the photoreceptor rods and cones in the retina of the human eye. They receive focused light from the camera lens, and translate the image's light values into digital information. In your *video monitor* this process happens in reverse: digital information becomes little points of light at each monitor pixel. Here again, the more pixels, the better they render image detail, light, and color.

The number of pixels in each of the ATSC standards (such as 720 and 1080) determine picture resolution. You calculate this by multiplying the vertical lines by the horizontal pixels. Thus the 720 format contains 921,600 pixels per frame, and 1080 contains 2,073,600 pixels per frame—more than twice the information, which means resolution that is twice as fine.

PICTURE AND AUDIO COMPRESSION

With so many pixels capturing so much detail and generating so much data, the camera, postproduction equipment, and television transmitters must all process a torrent of digital information. However, since each frame repeats much information from that preceding it, engineers have invented compression *codecs* (short for compression/decompression), which are like shorthand and reduce what must be "written" to the recording medium. A good codec is invisible, but a highcompression "lossy" codec will visibly intrude its economies onto the screen, particularly during image movement.

There are many different codecs, most proprietary by manufacturer. Sony HD cameras for example use MPEG-2 long GoP and Panasonic uses AVC-Intra. In many digital single-lens reflex (DSLR) cameras that shoot video, the H.264 codec is popular. All you need know at this juncture—not to disappear down the rabbit hole of formats and codecs—is that your shooting format and codec must be supported (a) by your editing system and (b) by your postproduction lab—should you need their services. Thus, in preproduction your DP, editor, and lab must all talk with each other.

SENSOR SIZE

Your camera's imaging sensor greatly affects the aesthetics of the final image, so size matters when you choose a camera (Figure 24-2). There are two issues in play: (a) larger sensors contain a greater pixel density (more or larger pixels) and can render finer detail, (b) lens *depth of field* (DOF) is involved because small video sensors render images with great depth of field, making it difficult to control this important compositional element.

Professional camcorders have long utilized large sensors (usually measuring 1/2″, or 2/3″—about the size of a 16mm film frame), and HD cameras often contain sensors approaching a 35mm film frame in size. Allowing interchangeable lenses, these cameras achieve the same quality, perspective, and DOF control as 35mm film. See **Chapter 26 Optics** for detailed information about depth of field and the creative impact of lenses.

FIGURE 24-2

CMOS video sensors, the heart of camera performance. (*Courtesy Samsung.*)

HIGH-END DIGITAL SHOOTING—UNCOMPRESSED AND RAW

Broadcast-quality HD is always recorded and transmitted compressed, then decompressed for display. For cinema projection, however, ultra-high-end digital cameras like the Arri Alexa, Aaton Penelope Δ, and RED Epic now record full resolution, 12-bit uncompressed video (or RAW files). They have light sensitivity and image quality easily matching 35mm negative film. Known as *2K* (2048 × 1080) and *4K* (4096 × 2304) after their approximate number of horizontal pixels, these ultra-high resolutions far exceed the ATSC HD standards because they're intended for the *Digital Cinema (D-Cinema)* standard, a high-resolution digital theatrical projection format established by the *Digital Cinema Initiative* (DCI). Camera sensors for these formats are of exceptional quality and size, and most have a single CCD or CMOS sensor the size of a 35mm negative frame, and shoot at 24 frames per second, the standard cinema projection frame-rate for motion picture film and the D-Cinema formats.[2]

CONSUMER CAMERAS

By comparison, low-end consumer camcorders have poor quality factory lenses, notoriously small imaging chips (which produce an unmanageably large DOF), lack of manual controls for focus, exposure, and so on. They are not considered viable for professional filmmaking, which demands manual control over all visual aspects of the image, but picture aesthetics can always take a back seat to the exigencies of documenting anything potentially fascinating. What equipment people in fact use is fascinating. David Tamés' documentary website Kino-Eye.com recommends items for a budget documentary shooting outfit, and lists seven American documentaries made with an iPhone, most of which can be seen on Vimeo or YouTube. They are listed here from short to long: *Kevin Sweet: Intervals* (1:19, David Tamés, 2012), *Flying iPhone 4 (HD Aerial Video)* (1:29, Brandon J Laatsch, 2010), *Coffee Branch iPhone Documentary* (3:00, Stephen de Villiers, 2012), *156 Turns* (3:24, Seth Schaeffer and Greg Tracy, 2010), *iSolation* (5:07, Daniel Hume, 2012), and *Syria: Songs of Defiance (24:52, Al Jazeera).*

Emad Burnat used a succession of consumer cameras while shooting his *Five Broken Cameras* (Palestine/Israel/France/Netherlands, 2013, Figure 24-3). During his valiant fight to document a

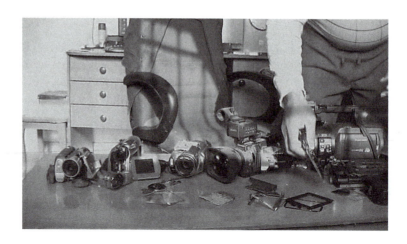

FIGURE 24-3

Emad Burnat looking over his wrecked gear in *Five Broken Cameras*.

FIGURE 24-4

Sound recorder for double system filming. (*Courtesy Zoom.*)

Palestinian village trying to hold on to its land, Burnat lost camera after camera. That each was of limited technical scope seems unimportant when they were in the hands of a powerful filmmaker, and especially so when documentary often incorporates archival sources of varying quality. Some filmmakers, however, have specifically used consumer cameras for their small size and low-tech aesthetic to creative advantage in fiction filmmaking, notably Thomas Vinterberg with *The Celebration* (Denmark, 1998), Spike Lee with *Bamboozled* (USA, 2000), and Rebecca Miller in *Personal Velocity: Three Portraits* (USA, 2002).

DIGITAL SOUND

Address all questions about sound to the sound recordist (on larger productions often called the *production sound mixer*). He or she heads the field sound team, which usually includes a *boom operator*. Choose equipment by deciding first whether sound will (a) be recorded *single system* through the camera and on the same recording media as the picture, or (b) *double system* using a separate, dedicated recorder that records on its own digital media (Figure 24-4).

Professional projects often shoot double system for two good reasons: (a) the audio aspects of digital cameras are generally inferior to those in a professional digital sound recorder, and (b) since field sound recordists must constantly monitor and adjust audio levels, they cannot keep intruding on the camera operator to do so.

DOUBLE SYSTEM SYNC

Since picture and sound in professional production are on separate media, they must be synchronized (*synced up*) during postproduction. Vital to this is the *slate* or *clapperboard* (Figure 24-5) which,

- Visually identifies the head of every take (including scene, shot, take, and sound number), but sometimes at the tail as a "tail slate."
- Verbally identifies the shot and take for whoever syncs sound to picture in the cutting room. In documentary, files can be very long so all identification is important.
- Creates a one-frame, easily identifiable "reference moment" by which to align picture with its accompanying sound.

FIGURE 24-5

Clapperboard—necessary whenever you use double system recording and must synchronize sound to picture.

That reference moment is either the sharp snap of the clapsticks recorded by both camera and audio recorder at the beginning of every take, or it can be a timecode reference on picture and sound when using a "smart slate." This generates visible timecode numbers (see "Smart Slates" under **Chapter 28: Advanced Location Sound**). With material correctly identified and logged, either system should make syncing sound to picture a straightforward procedure during postproduction.

Planning to shoot location sound poses these budgetary questions:

- Single system or double system?
- How many channels will you need to record?
- Will you need a portable mixer?
- How will you mike each different situation? (Boom? Planted mics? Radio lavaliers?)
- If you are using radio mikes, will you carry wired mikes as backup? (You should.)
- If shooting double system, what kind of slate will you use (regular or timecode)?
- What effects or ambient sounds should be recorded during location shooting?

Your sound recordist should be able answer your questions, and provide all the information you need to make an accurate estimate for the budget.

POSTPRODUCTION

Whatever acquisition medium you use, you will need an appropriate postproduction setup, from a $2,000 Mac computer equipped with $900 Final Cut Pro at the low end (Figure 24-6), to an

FIGURE 24-6

Mac computer equipped with $900 Final Cut Pro at the low end.

Avid|DS HD postproduction rig costing ten times as much at the high end (Figure 24-7). Some salient issues, all affecting the postproduction schedule, equipment choice, and budget, are,

- The length of the intended documentary.
- Likely shooting ratio, and magnitude of hard drive storage required.
- Whether special effects require extensive rendering (computer processing).
- Whether you will need film or digital lab services.

BUDGETING

In a broad sense, the *budget* of a film is essentially how much money (and other resources) one expects to have available. Budgeting is primarily the domain of the producer, but has profound consequences for the director's ability to function. A detailed budget includes a price line for every item or service, and lays out how much your film will cost and where the money will go. Allow for plentiful hard drive storage, including for the audio phase when you mix the final track using a Pro Tools™ software suite, and be realistic about the time you'll waste if you decide you can get by with a limited computer. Take advice so you budget for the sound mix, project mastering, music rights, color grading, pressing DVDs, and for otherwise making distributable copies.

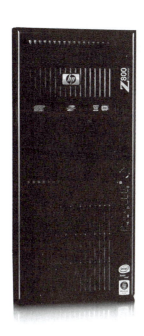

FIGURE 24-7

The heart of a high-end Avid|DS HD postproduction rig.

Use pessimistic figures because the real total for a film can be a mortal shock, and you don't want to get a reputation for naivety or (worse) outright deception when you have to find more money to finish. Approaching production, you and your production crew must consider:

- How much does the production have in the bank?
- What is still to come?
- What "in kind" resources are available?
- What will the film cost using the projected shooting schedule?
- Are there enough funds to cover projected costs?
- Are more funds needed?
- Where can savings be made?
- What shooting could be delayed until funds have been assembled?

ABOVE AND BELOW THE LINE

Broadly speaking, budget expenses divide into above-the-line and below-the-line costs. The line itself is the division between preproduction and beginning production. Thus:

Above-the-line costs:

Research costs

Any story rights involved (if you work with the author of a book on the subject, for instance)

Producer's fee

Director's fee

Costs for any tests necessary

_____ "The Line"

Below-the-line costs:

Production unit salaries

Location rentals

Film stock or media

Camera, electric, sound, and other equipment (purchase and rental)

Laboratory fees (processing and transfers)

Catering, hotel, and living expenses

Travel and transportation

Legal costs and production insurance

Miscellaneous expenses

Music rights and composition

Postproduction expenses (sound mix, color grading, mastering, and other services)

Distribution copies and publicity materials

Festival entry fees and travel to festivals

All movie budgets should also include a contingency percentage, usually 4 percent or more of the total budget. This is your Murphy's Law surcharge; it allows for equipment failure, bad weather, reshooting, and other hidden costs.

INSURANCES

A large line item that novices tend to avoid is production insurance, which should be a necessity for all film shoots, regardless of size, scale, and budget. Accidents happen: a participant falls and breaks an arm, a car is in an accident on the way to the set, a $10,000 lens lands on the side-walk… Without production insurance, any of these scenarios could easily shut you down. Most equipment rental houses require proof of insurance, and if your crew are union members, their union will stipulate what coverage is necessary when they are hired.

Insurance is complicated territory, so be sure to research exactly what kind of policies your project requires. If you're an independent filmmaker, The Independent Feature Project (IFP) website (www.ifp.org) is a good place to find advice on affordable insurance. Depending on the expense and sophistication of your production, you may need to carry any of the following:

- Preproduction indemnity
- Workers' compensation
- Film producer's indemnity
- Consequential loss

- Errors and omissions
- Negative insurance
- Employer's liability
- Public, or third-party, liability
- Third-party property damage
- Equipment insurance
- Sets, wardrobe, props insurance (for re-enacted scenes)
- Vehicles
- Fidelity guarantee
- Union and other insurances

Special insurances are also generally necessary when working abroad under unusual health or other conditions.

BUDGETING AND SCHEDULING SOFTWARE

For short film projects download the budget form from this book's companion website (www .directingthedocumentary.com). If you mean to approach anyone in the professional filmmaking world, all paperwork must use recognized budget and scheduling software, two facets of filmmaking inseparably linked. The industry

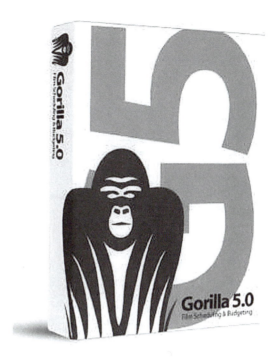

FIGURE 24-8

Gorilla™ budgeting software from Jungle Software.

favorite is Movie Magic™, an expensive but all-encompassing software package. Less pricey, and fine for the lean, mean independent, is Gorilla™ from Jungle Software (Figure 24-8), who like many software manufacturers offer a cut-rate "academic edition" for bona fide students. Either will help you break down the script (if one exists), turn it into a schedule, and arrive at a detailed, properly laid out budget based on all the variables you anticipate.

The beauty of dedicated relational databases is that whatever budget, coverage, or scheduling changes you enter will immediately ripple through the entire set of documents, showing up like magic everywhere it matters. In the case of re-enactment scenes, the software will also help you generate scene breakdowns, call sheets, contact lists, and organize locations and storyboards.

Most new users will need training to make full use of their purchase, but properly used, the software even monitors daily cash flow, so there need be no ghastly surprises lurking in the accounts department.

DRAWING UP AN EQUIPMENT LIST

KEEP IT SIMPLE

Early in your directing career, you and your crew will be hard put to stay on top of basic conceptual and control issues, so it's wise to foreswear advanced equipment and the time it takes to master it. Safety is involved too: a film production is no place for on-the-job training in potentially harmful equipment, especially any that involves high voltages. I once saw a wrongly tied-in electrical ballast transform a metal gate into a lightning generator. Thankfully nobody got hurt.

Brainstorm with your team in a production meeting and figure what equipment you will need for each situation. Expect an experienced sound department to want a rather large inventory. Often they must adapt to unforeseen lighting or other circumstances, and cannot comply without reserve equipment.

OVER-ELABORATE EQUIPMENT

It is tempting for the technician trying to forestall problems to insist on the "proper" equipment—always, of course, the most complicated and expensive. In experienced hands, sophisticated equipment saves time and money, but not in those of novices. Beware, too, of strong-minded cinematographers trying to pad their sample reel using exotic lenses, cranes, and dollies at your expense. Keep it simple wherever possible, but listen to experience.

SCHEDULING THE SHOOT

Software, as discussed above, will help you schedule and re-schedule participants, locations, crew, and other necessities. Aim to set the shortest practicable schedule because the number of working days translates directly into costs (see below, "Under- or Over-scheduling"). Take into account,

- Availability of crew and participants.
- Availability of locations.
- Travel and accommodation.
- Any special equipment, or facilities.
- Complexity of each lighting setup and power requirements.
- Time of day, so available light comes from the expected direction. (Take a compass when location scouting!)

Remember to factor in the expenses and delays imposed by travel between locations, time to set up and strike lighting setups, and some contingency time to allow for bad weather, illness, or equipment breakdowns.

LOCATIONS AND SHOOTING ORDER

Normally you shoot in convenience order according to the logistics of locations and the availability of participants and crew. Since lighting setups and changes take the most time during a shoot, a compact schedule avoids relighting the same set. Scenes at a common location are shot on the same day(s) regardless of their order in the eventual film.

If you are shooting to a script, schedule wide shots first because they establish the spatial relationships and layout, and often take all your lighting resources. Subsequent lighting for closer shots must match the master shot. Then if time runs out, you might get away with not shooting a close up or a detail. Master shots are usually indispensable because they cover so much of a scene's action. Shoot cutaways and inserts last because they can be shot separately and later, if need be.

SHOOTING IN CHRONOLOGICAL ORDER

If your film documents a process, such as surgery after an accident followed by lengthy physical therapy, you would need to shoot in event order. In other films you may be able to shoot for convenience, and imply the order and time progression in editing.

SCHEDULING FOR KEY SCENES

Occasionally a scene you plan is a mainstay, and should it fail, the film itself collapses. This might be a confrontation in the workplace, or a performance at a party political conference. If so, shoot the obligatory scene early, in case no scene means no film.

Another problem arises when you are shooting competitive processes, and don't know who will win. Perhaps you want to follow a young actor in a demanding Shakespeare part, but don't know until casting who will become your central character. Scheduling should allow you to follow three hopefuls, then the audition. Once the part is cast, you can plan the rest of the coverage.

EMOTIONAL DEMAND ORDER

If you have freedom in the order you shoot, it is wise to cover those that are factual and least emotionally demanding early in the schedule. Documentary participants take a while to grow into their new role because at first they have to struggle with feelings of strangeness while acting the part of themselves. If you can, hold back on any emotionally demanding scenes until later, when they have begun to relax and enjoy their role.

WEATHER AND OTHER CONTINGENCY COVERAGE

Make alternative shooting plans whenever you face disabling uncertainties. Schedule exteriors early in case unsuitable weather causes a delay, and arrange for *cover sets*, that is, interior scenes on standby as alternatives. This way you will not fall behind schedule.

ALLOCATION OF SHOOTING TIME PER SCENE

Depending on length and intensity of the scene, the amount of coverage, and the reliability of participants and crew, you might expect to shoot anywhere between one and three scenes per day. Traveling between locations, elaborate setups, or relighting the same location may greatly slow the pace.

UNDER- OR OVER-SCHEDULING

You can sabotage a promising film with misplaced optimism. Consider the following:

- Work may be alarmingly slow at first because the crew is figuring out efficient working relationships. Schedule the first two or three days of any shoot lightly.
- You can always shorten a long schedule, but it may be impossible to lengthen one too brief because key people have scheduled other jobs.
- Most nonprofessional (and some professional) units often expect to shoot too much screen time in too short a schedule. Be realistic.
- The standard turnaround for a crew (the time between the end of one shooting day and the start of another) is 12 hours, and 10 hours is the minimum.
- An average working day should be around 8–10 hours. Occasionally, you may need to schedule longer days. Beyond that, the law of diminishing returns kicks in—an exhausted crew working 14-hour days begins making serious errors.
- Dog-tired crew and participants tend to work progressively slower. Tempers and morale deteriorate, artistic commitment evaporates, and fatigue compromises safety.
- A normally cared-for crew will go all-out to help when there's an emergency.

THE CALL SHEET

The production manager is responsible for translating the shooting schedule into day-by-day *call sheets*. These, distributed to the crew (and posted on the project's Facebook page), detail:

- What portion of the documentary is being shot on a specific day.
- Who needs to be on the set.
- Any special equipment, props, or costuming.
- What time each person needs to be there.
- How to get to the set.
- Emergency contact phone numbers.

You can generate your own call sheets using one of the popular film scheduling software packages that integrate all scheduling functions.

HANDS-ON LEARNING

At the advanced level you should do your budgeting and production organizing by making use of industry-approved software, such as Movie Magic™ or Gorilla™. Not only will it make professionally presented budget information, it will make all necessary changes should a single item or schedule change, saving hours of computational labor. To assemble the information you need to enter in the software, use **BP-2 Advanced Budget**.

NOTES

1. Unfortunately, there are currently three other digital TV standards around the globe. DVB-T Digital Video Broadcasting-Terrestrial) is used throughout western and eastern Europe, Russia, Australia, and many nations throughout Asia and Africa; ISDB-T (Integrated Services Digital Broadcasting-Terrestrial) is used in Japan, Brazil, and most of South America; and DTMB (Digital Terrestrial Multimedia Broadcast) is used by China and Hong Kong.
2. During the writing of this edition there was much chatter in the industry about achieving resolutions of 5 K and 6 K ... so stay tuned.

CHAPTER 25

PREPARATIONS BEFORE DIRECTING

Documentaries frequently seem improvised, which may make a directing plan seem pointless. Think of it instead as an important plank in your all-important development work before you leap into the fray. Much of your true directing will result directly from your preproduction preparation.

THE DIRECTING PLAN

Plan multiple coverage of anything vital, such as expository information crucial to the coherence and impact of your story. Some reminders:

CASTING

Have you decided,

- Who you will film, have you secured their agreement, and is "informed consent" required?
- Who will be your *central character*(s) and why?
- What *metaphoric role* best fits each member of your cast?

REMINDERS FOR EACH SEQUENCE

Have you listed,
Drama and Dialectics: This is the key to giving your film definition and clarity, and is easy to get wrong. Question your choices rigorously!

- Your story's progression and meaning?
- The forces in opposition that your film is handling?
- *Expository information* the audience must have?
- Who and what is central to your story's *conflict?*
- Have you ensured a *confrontation?* Once you know the main oppositional forces in your film, you must ensure they meet.

- *What is at stake* for the main character or characters and should you do anything to *raise the stakes?*
- Typical and atypical action?

Imagery such as cityscapes, landscapes, workplaces that are emblematic of,

- Your participants' type, place, or condition.
- What are the points and counterpoints of your film's *argument*, so you can be sure to collect all the materials you need?

Point of view:

- Who must we specially understand and sympathize with, and why?
- How will you make us empathize with him/her/them (through secondary characters' points of view, perhaps)?
- Whose POV will you favor for
  - each sequence?
  - the film as a whole?

Development:

- Who ideally should grow and change?
- What are the chances this will or won't happen?
- What changes in thinking and feeling do you want us to experience as we follow the story?
- What should we feel and think by the end?

Thematic or other goals. What is your expected theme for,

- Each sequence?
- The film as a whole?

Aesthetic concerns: Define,

- What *form* and *style* best serve each sequence.
- The *style* you want for the film as a whole.
- What your film can borrow from other forms or from specific films.
- How the prevailing *point of view* in each sequence can affect its style.
- Anything to avoid (negative definition is also creative).

The genre your film fits into. Is it, for instance,

- A small town tragedy?
- A "Frankie and Johnnie ballad"?
- A "defeat snatched from the jaws of victory" type of story?
- A tragedy, farce, tall story, cautionary tale, or action documentary?

Storyteller POV. Most importantly,

- What *storytelling role* will you adopt, so your tale emerges with style, panache, and gusto?
- How will you shoot and edit your story to give it a clear, exciting identity as a *type* of story?

TEST YOUR ASSUMPTIONS

Check your intentions with trusted colleagues. That is,

- *Pitch* your project to anyone who will listen and give you feedback. Do so with different listeners until you get a consistently positive audience response.
- *Ask people to read the proposal* and comment on what it makes them expect. Are they seeing the film you see, and if not, why not?

OBTAINING PERMISSIONS

Forethought given to permissions, agreements, releases, and contracting can save you grief later:

People: Secure a commitment for agreed dates, amount of time, and involvement from those you intend to film.

Places: Secure written permissions from owners or administrators of non-public locations. Many cities require you to get a permit from the authorities to film in the streets or on public transportation.

Copyright: If music or other copyrighted material is necessary, now's the time to secure it.

Crew: If possible put them under contract.

Insurance: Do you need special coverage? (See **Chapter 24: Advanced Technology and Budgeting.**)

TRIAL SHOOTING

Do what is necessary to,

- "Audition" doubtful participants.
- Work out field communications with a new crew.
- Set standards for work you are going to do together.
- Test new or unfamiliar technology.

SCOUTING LOCATIONS

For the fundamentals, review **Chapter 11: Lighting** and **Chapter 12: Camera**. During preproduction, the DP, sound recordist, and director should check out locations for problems.

Camera:

- When is available light at its most useful? (Carry a compass so you can estimate the angle of the sun at different times of day.)
- What setups look promising?
- Is enough electricity available for lighting interiors?
- Can power cables pass under doors when you close windows during shooting?
- Where can you place lighting stands for maximum shooting freedom?
- How reflective are the walls and how high is the ceiling?
- Where might the camera go if it's a public event and you must shoot unobtrusively off a tripod using a long lens?

Sound:

- Can doors and windows be closed for sound isolation?
- Alignment of surfaces likely to cause *standing waves* (sound bouncing to and fro between opposing surfaces, augmenting and cross-modulating the source sound)?
- Are drapes, carpet, soft furniture available to break up the unwanted movement of sound within the space?
- Does the location space have intrusive resonances (mainly a problem with concrete or tile surfaces)?
- Can participants walk, and cameras be mobile, without the floor letting out tortured squeaks during dialogue scenes?
- Does ambient sound and noise penetrate from the outside?

   Intermittent sound intrusions might come from:

- Wildlife or domestic animals.
- An airport flight path.
- An expressway, railroad, or subway.
- Refrigeration, air conditioning, or other sound-generating equipment that runs intermittently and will cause problems unless you can turn it off while shooting.
- Construction sites. You scouted the location at a weekend, not realizing that come Monday morning, a pile driver and four jackhammers compete to greet the dawn. You have no hope of stopping them.
- A school. Expect hue and cry at set times of day.

LOGISTICS AND SCHEDULING

Estimating how long each type of scene takes to shoot comes with experience. A 30-minute documentary can take between three and eight working days to shoot, depending on

- *Distance of travel.* (Tearing down much equipment in the old location and setting it up anew is time consuming, so allow plenty of time for transport between the two. Also, a new film unit is slow at the start and faster ten days later). International travel needs careful planning as you probably need to comply with customs regulations concerning equipment—both going and returning.
- *Lighting* amount and complexity. Scenes with multiple key lights sometimes require walk-throughs and experiment in order to eliminate illogical shadow patterns.
- *Sound setup* amount and complexity. Scenes with multiple mikes and that require on-site audio mixing may take some time to set up.
- *Randomness of subject matter.* To film a postman delivering a particular letter may take no more than 10 minutes, but to film a spontaneous scuffle between schoolchildren during a lunch break, you may have to hang around for days.

   Avoid over-optimistic scheduling by making a best-case and a worst-case estimate and then allotting something in between. Whether your shooting is drawn-out or compact, make a draft schedule and solicit comment from the crew. In each schedule include,

- Everyone's mobile phone number.
- A phone contact for each location.

- Equipment or personnel required for such-and-such a time at each location.
- Maps marked with locations, phone numbers, and clear navigational instructions.
- Whenever the crew must converge at a prearranged place and time, ensure that each vehicle carries a mobile phone. This provides for a car getting lost or having trouble.

Expect trouble and you won't be disappointed. There's a reason why filmmaking is so often described in the language of military invasion.

LONGITUDINAL DEVELOPMENT

One luxury peculiar to the independent filmmaker (and there are few) is that you can shoot follow-up material over a long period. Independents often work as a group and on multiple projects, so occasionally deploying a crew for some follow-up may not be difficult. Returning at six-month intervals for a couple of years may capture real changes. Reality shows, which often use documentary techniques, have to accelerate change by artificially applying extreme tests of endurance, strength, or ingenuity.

LOCATION PERMITS

PERMISSION

You must secure permission to film in a location in writing *before* you start shooting. See the website www.directingthedocumentary.com to download a location permission form. A film of mine was once held up for a year after getting written permission to film an exhibition in a synagogue. I secured permission to film in the building, but the traveling exhibition's owner, after hugely enjoying himself presenting exhibition items to the camera, later denied he had given permission to film.

On private property (which may include a city transportation system) you must get written clearance by the relevant authority unless you care to risk being taken to court for invasion of privacy. The risk rises the more that you or your company look worth suing. Sometimes—and this is a great hazard to investigative journalism—a malicious party will initiate legal action just to get a court injunction so that your film cannot be shown.

Handheld cameras count as newsgathering and are generally protected under freedom of speech in the USA. Anything unrestrictedly open to public entry and view (such as the street, markets, public meetings) may be filmed without asking anyone's permission but there is often nobody around who cares.

TRIPOD OR OTHER CAMERA SUPPORT SYSTEMS

Cities often restrict street filming when you use a tripod or other camera support. Ostensibly this is because a film crew has the potential to become a spectacle blocking or disrupting traffic flow. Thus to film at any urban location you usually must work through a special division of the mayor's office or state film commission, who will require proof that you carry the relevant liability insurance. You may also need police permission and a cop to control traffic or to wave away troublesome bystanders.

GUERILLAS IN THE MIST

By tradition, documentary makers often shoot first and ask questions later, knowing that if somebody takes exception, the combination of ideals and poverty will probably lead to nothing more than an irritable dismissal. This gets risky in countries where the authorities regard cameras as engines of subversion. Moving images from a phone camera can provide powerful, instant, and worldwide evidence of wrongdoing, as governments discover when their agents can be seen beating up or killing people, only to appear damningly on YouTube within the hour.

THE PERSONAL RELEASE FORM

In the document called a *personal release* (see www.directingthedocumentary.com) the signatory releases to you the right to make public use of the material you have shot. Ask for the signature immediately *after* shooting, and to soften the predatory appearance of the request, you may want to offer a 24-hour window in which they can call you to discuss anything they might not want used.

Al Maysles asks people to sign, one after another, under a *common declaration* in an ordinary notebook. Signing seems less momentous when they can see that others have signed before them. Other documentarians—Fred Wiseman reputedly among them—secure a record of agreement by asking participants to give their name, address, and phone number on camera and to say that they give permission to be filmed. Participants know you can always play their verbal permission in court, but it offers little protection against someone who decides to pull out at a late hour, sending a whole project down the toilet with a whoosh. Neither a verbal release nor any signed document protects you against charges of slander or deception.

Whichever means you use, get personal releases signed in the euphoria immediately after the participant's filming. No signature is valid without the $1 minimum legal payment, which you solemnly hand over as symbolic payment. Minors cannot sign legal forms themselves and will need the clearance of a parent or legal guardian.

CROWD SCENE RELEASES

You can't get, nor do you need, releases from all the people who appear in a street shot, which contains what anyone in lawful transit might see. Normally you seek signed releases from speaking participants only.

LEGAL ISSUES

For all film-related legal matters, consult Lisa Allif and Michael C. Donaldson's highly readable and comprehensive *The American Bar Association's Legal Guide to Independent Filmmaking* (American Bar Association, 2011). The following are of particular interest to independent documentary-makers:

- Copyright and ideas
- Public domain
- Personal rights
- Hiring a scriptwriter and working with a partner
- Provisions common to most agreements
- Registering copyright of the script
- Chain of title
- Others who may have rights in your film
- Title clearance

- Errors and omissions insurance
- All the things that the camera sees
- Clearing music
- Hiring a composer
- Fair use doctrine
- Parody
- Clearing film clips
- Registering copyright of your completed film
- Copyright infringement
- Copyright on the Internet
- Legal referral services

PAYING PARTICIPANTS

Fiction filmmakers pay actors, but documentary-makers never normally pay their participants even when they have quite large budgets. To pay people would mean you were purchasing the truth you want to hear, which destroys your film's credibility. There are a couple of exceptions to this.

CELEBRITIES

If you engaged a history specialist like Harvard's Henry Louis Gates Jr., famed as the creator of multi-part series such as PBS' *African American Lives* (USA, 2006, Figure 25-1), you would be drawing on his time and expertise, and would of course need to compensate him for it. You'd probably also pay an honorarium to any celebrities he interviewed in order to reserve some of their precious time and respect their status. Some might do it free out of friendship for the host,

FIGURE 25-1 ——

Henry Louis Gates Jr. and his cousin John Gates at the Allegheny Courthouse looking over their ancestors' property records in *African American Lives*.

but any sums involved would all be decided through delicate negotiation during the proposal stage for the series.

PUBLIC SERVANTS

You emphatically do *not* pay a politician or other public servant. If in doubt, consider how your proposed action appears—do you endanger our trust in your film by paying or not paying? Could payments change what we learned? Are they appropriate in the circumstances?

PEOPLE IN DIRE NEED

If you film destitute tornado victims telling your camera what they have lost, or you show the desperate daily life of an AIDS sufferer who faces dying because he cannot afford medicine from Big Pharma, you'd have a heart of stone not to give something to help out as you left. If you are from the First World, and enhancing your career by showing suffering in the Third World, the least you can do is compensate those with so little to give, and who gave it anyway in a generous spirit. Ten dollars is little enough to you, but may be a week's income where you are filming. Give it freely afterwards; do not let it be a precondition for filming. In any community be careful to remain consistent with your giving, because people compare notes.

HANDS-ON LEARNING

For **Personal Release** and **Location Agreement** forms see under Miscellaneous at the book's website, www.directingthedocumentary.com.

PART 7B

ADVANCED PRODUCTION

This Part considers lenses in relation to the perceptions of space and perspective, which together do so much to shape the look and impact of photography. There is information on the principles governing the use of advanced camera and sound gear, but equipment that is more elaborate normally means you will be directing specialists rather than handling it yourself. Nonetheless, you need to know what they will be doing and why.

There is information about the extra personnel you need in a larger unit, and tips on leadership. Because a director must know how to catalyze telling scenes for the screen, there is a comparison between acting and being a documentary participant. There is also guidance on coverage and shooting with editing in mind, and, most importantly, a long chapter on interviewing—that vital key to opening people to the audience.

CHAPTER 26

OPTICS

SPACE AND PERCEPTION

Properly used, lenses complement your way of seeing. They do however take some basic under-standing, for though a camera lens functions like that in the human eye, the shortcomings of cam-era technology require you to make various adaptations. No art form is without its compromises, and all require the art that hides art. Painters, after all, have to render a three-dimensional world on a two-dimensional canvas. Likewise, camera and lens compromises result from most cameras recording in two dimensions instead of three, and from their field of vision being rather limited compared with that of the human eye. We compensate for this by arranging composition and lighting to create the illusion of depth, and cramming more than normal into screen space and screen time.

CAMERA EYE AND HUMAN EYE

The eye of the beholder is misleading, for the field of view (FOV) of the human eye is huge—approximately 160° horizontally, and 75° vertically (Figure 26-1). Try it for yourself by stretch-ing your arms ahead, wiggling your thumbs, then gradually stretching your arms sideways. You should still see your thumbs moving even though your arms are wide apart. No equivalency to this exists in camera optics: to replicate a human-eye sense of perspective in DSLR 35 mm photogra-phy you would use a 50 mm (standard) lens with a FOV of only 40° width and 27° height.

CHEATING SPACE

The significance is that even a wide-angle lens may cover less than a *quarter* of the eye's intake, with resounding consequences for dramatic composition. We therefore rearrange compositions to trick the spectator into seeing the eye's sensation of normal compositions, distances, and spatial relationships. Characters holding a conversation might stand closer than usual before the camera, yet pass as normally spaced onscreen; furniture placement and distances between objects are often *cheated*, that is, moved apart or together to produce the desired appearance onscreen. Even physi-cal movements need adjustment: someone walking past camera or picking up a glass of milk in close-up may have to carry out these actions one-third slower if it's to look natural onscreen.

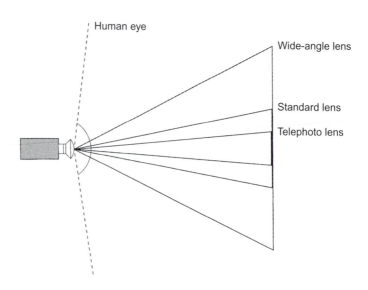

FIGURE 26-1

Field of vision of the human eye compared with greatly limited angle of acceptance for camera lenses. Vertical angles of acceptance (not shown) are even less, depending on aspect ratio.

Packing the frame, creating the illusion of depth, and arranging for balance and thematic significance in each composition are all routine compensations for the 2D screen's limited size and tendency to flatten space.

LENS CHARACTERISTICS

HOW WE USE PERSPECTIVE

We assess distances by comparing the size of things—say, a cat in the foreground and a sheepdog around 10 feet away in the background. Knowing their relative sizes lets us judge their distance apart. Figure 26-2, shot with a "normal" lens, allows you to make an accurate judgment of their distance apart by their relative sizes. Lenses other than normal alter this perception, and are classified as either wide angle or telephoto. Analogies from everyday life illustrate the differences:

Wide-angle lens	Normal lens	Telephoto lens
Door security spyglass (diminishes sizes, exaggerates foreground size in relation to background)	The human eye (renders perspective—foreground sizes relative to background sizes— as we consider normal)	Telescope (magnifies, brings everything closer, but compresses foreground and background together)

VARYING APPARENT SEPARATION

The same shot taken with a wide-angle lens (Figure 26-3) changes the apparent distance between foreground and background, making it appear greater. The telephoto lens (Figure 26-4) does just the opposite, squeezing foreground and background planes close together. If someone were to

FIGURE 26-2

Normal lens, where distances appear as the eye sees them.

FIGURE 26-3

Wide-angle lens.

walk from the background truck up to the foreground, the implications of their walk would be dramatically different in the three shots; all would have the same subject, all walks would last the same time, yet each lens would convey a different dramatic "feel."

MANIPULATING PERSPECTIVE

Using the magnifying or diminishing effect of different lenses allows us to produce three similar shots with very different feeling. By placing the camera differently (see Figure 26-5, Figure 26-6, and Figure 26-7) camera-to-subject distance changes, and with it, perspective too. Wide-angle lenses appear to increase distance; telephoto lenses appear to compress it.

FIGURE 26-4

Telephoto lens where the foreground to background distances appear different from those in Figures 26-2 and 26-3.

FOCAL LENGTH

Lenses are described by their *focal length* rating, which is the measurement in millimeters from the lens optical center to the film plane. Cameras have very different image receptors (such as 35 mm film, or ½ and ⅔ inch video), and each requires a certain degree of refraction. Thus to reproduce the look of normal perspective, each will need a focal length lens calculated for the image receptor size (see "Depth of Field" below).

PERSPECTIVE CHANGES WHEN CAMERA-TO-SUBJECT DISTANCE CHANGES

By repositioning the camera and using different lenses, as shown diagrammatically in Figure 26-5, we can standardize the size of the foreground truck, as seen in Figure 26-2, Figure 26-3, and

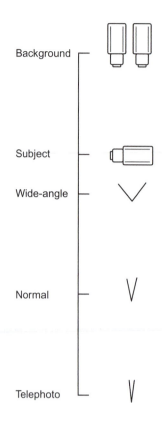

FIGURE 26-5

Different lenses from different distances in Figures 26-2, 26-3, and 26-4 produced the same size foreground truck but altered the apparent distance to its background. Perspective changes only when you alter the camera to subject distance, not because you change lenses.

Figure 26-4. Though foreground-to-background distances appear to have changed, the perspective changes we see result from changing the camera-to-subject distance, *not* from using different lenses.

To prove this, examine Figures 26-6, Figure 26-7, and Figure 26-8. Each shot is taken from the same camera position using a different lens, but in all three the proportion of the stop sign remains the same size in relation to the background portico. Perspective—size proportions between planes—has not changed, we simply have three different magnifications.

A lens change alone will alter the audience's *sense* of distances, but won't affect actual perspectives. The axiom is that you can only change perspective by changing the camera-to-subject distance. Changing lenses from a fixed camera position only enlarges or diminishes a given perspective, and shrinks or magnifies the apparent distances.

LENSES AND IMAGE TEXTURE

Compare Figures 26-6 and Figure 26-8. The backgrounds are very different in *texture*. The subject is in focus in both, but the telephoto version puts much of the image in soft focus, isolating and

FIGURE 26-6 ————————————

Wide-angle lens.

FIGURE 26-7 ————————————

Normal lens.

FIGURE 26-8 ————————————

Telephoto lens. This shot and Figures 26-6 and 26-7 are taken from a common camera position. Notice that the stop sign remains in the same proportion to its background throughout.

separating the subject from both foreground and background. This happens because the telephoto lens has a very limited *depth of field* (DOF). Its point of focus alone is truly sharp. Conversely, a wide-angle lens (Figure 26-3 and Figure 26-6) allows deep focus, useful if you want to hold someone in focus while he is walking between foreground and background. Deep focus may however drown its middle-ground subject in a plethora of irrelevantly sharp background and foreground detail. Isolating the subject by focus, rather than by lighting or framing alone, can be dramatically useful.

LENS SPEED

This deceptive term concerns a lens's ability to transmit light and has nothing to do with movement. A fast lens transmits much light, making it good for photography in a low-light situation while a slow lens transmits less light but may do so because it is a telephoto and has other advantages. Wide-angle lenses, by their inherent design, tend to be fast (with a widest aperture, say, of f1.4) while telephotos tend to be slow (perhaps f2.8). A wide-angle with a two-stop advantage might need only one-quarter the light of a telephoto, and so make night shooting viable.

Prime (that is, fixed) *lenses*, having few lens elements, tend to be faster than zooms, which are multi-element. Primes also have better acuity, because the image passes through fewer lens elements. The state-of-the-art RED modular digital camera (Figure 26-9, www.red.com) uses 35 mm prime or zoom lenses, and behaves like the feature film camera it really is, but with none of the bulk.

DEPTH

ZOOMING VERSUS DOLLYING

A zoom is a lens that is infinitely variable between its focal length extremes. A zoom of 10 to 100 mm focal length is said to have a ratio of 10:1, which means that zooming in on a subject magnifies it tenfold. As we have said, the proportion of foreground objects relative to their background does not alter. To produce a similar magnification with a fixed lens you would use a *dolly* movement (physically moving a camera toward the subject on a wheeled base). Here not only the size of the image is increased (due to closer camera-to-subject proximity) but *you see a continuous perspective change during the movement*. This reproduces the natural perspective changes our eye sees when we move around.

    Summing up, dollying gives movement with a perspective change, while zooming gives optical magnification without a change in perspective.

FIGURE 26-9 ―――――――――――――――――――

The RED modular camera fully equipped for handholding. (*Photo by courtesy of Red Digital Cinema.*)

GETTING A FILM LOOK

Until recently film stocks and video used to yield markedly different image aesthetics. As cameras have become more sophisticated it is increasingly difficult to identify the recording medium from the screen results. The latest postproduction software also gives a high degree of control over contrast, gamma (black levels), and color hue and saturation (color intensity). Differences between film and video images may show in other ways, however. In a 35 mm DSLR camera close-up of a man in a park, his face will be in sharp focus but the foliage in the background and foreground is agreeably soft-focus. The same close-up taken with a consumer video camera may have foreground, middle-ground, and background all in similar degrees of focus, subjecting the eye to a deluge of irrelevant detail. Why?

DEPTH OF FIELD

At the root of these differences is lens *depth of field* (DOF). The 35 mm DSLR camera image receptor has a larger area than many video imaging chips. The larger the image size, the greater the refraction (bending of light) by the lens, with the net result that there is less DOF. That is, less is acceptably in focus behind and in front of the plane of focus. A Victorian plate camera has a huge imaging area, and consequently DOF is so shallow that a portrait's eyes may be sharp while the tip of his nose is out of focus! Compare this with a family video camera, with its tiny ¼ inch chip image area: image refraction is so minimal that in daylight, hardly anything is ever out of focus.

    The optics of the larger format cameras, such as those in the Canon EOS line of DSLR cameras, allow you to isolate a given plane in focus and throw other planes into soft-focus (Figure 26-10). With a small-format camera you can achieve this effect only by using a telephoto lens, which means shooting off a tripod for steadiness. Another strategy is to open the f-stop wider to use a larger area of the lens. This increases the amount of lens refraction, giving a shallower DOF. Also affecting depth of field is distance from camera: close subjects have less depth of field than distant ones.

Summing up, the four variables that affect depth of field are,

1. Imaging sensor size (small = deep DOF, large = shallow DOF)

2. Lens aperture size (closed = deep DOF, open = shallow DOF)

3. Lens focal length (short = deep DOF, long = shallow DOF)

4. Focus point (close = shallow DOF, far = deep DOF)

COMPOSITION

In **Chapter 12: Camera**, "Composing the Shot," we considered the dynamics of operating in synchronicity with life as it unfolds and the basics of framing, including the Rule of Thirds. As a Storyteller, you aspire to inflect your camerawork with a spectrum of attitudes and ways of seeing—an authorial demand not easy to sustain when you are struggling to keep up with events. How well you and your camera operator function depends on three considerations.

- How thoroughly have you, as director, considered where you stand in relation to what you are about to film?

- How well have you prepared the camera operator in relation to your thinking?

- How well grounded is the operator in compositional principles?

FIGURE 26-10 —————————————

Selective focus places attention on the woman among these birdwatchers.

Composing images is a fascinating business. It revolves around the human eye's natural, inbuilt preferences and responses, and the way the eye suggests ideas and feelings to the mind. In return, the mind responds symbiotically by finding further proof in what the eye sees. This complements the expectations we have held all along for documentary—that there are meanings and designs in life for you to find and propagate. You have great latitude for artistry since there are multiple vantage points in most situations, and many ways to your audience's responses through framing, lighting, juxtaposition with background and foreground elements, and so on.

The visual composition that goes into *form* (which is how you present content) is more than embellishment; it is a force for communication. Form can interest and even delight the eye, but in purposeful hands it becomes *an organizing force that dramatizes relationships and germinates ideas* (Figure 26-11). As such, it makes the subject (or "content") accessible, heightens the viewer's perceptions, and stimulates critical involvement. The way most cinematographers study composition is through painting, a medium in which images are constructed with great deliberation.

FIGURE 26-11

The form of an image can be an organizing force that dramatizes relationships and germinates ideas.

STATIC COMPOSITION

A good way to discover the natural sensitivity and preferences of the human eye—yours and an audience's—involves making up a short slide display and exploring it with a few friends. Download 10–20 images of varied but striking design from a source like Google Images. Suggested artists:

(*Painters*) Mary Cassatt; Honoré Daumier; El Greco; Wassily Kandinsky; L.S. Lowry; Berthe Morisot; Edvard Munch; Alfred Sisley.

(*Photographers*) Ansell Adams; Diane Arbus; Henri Cartier-Bresson; Josef Koudelka; Vivian Maier, László Moholy-Nagy; Sebastião Salgado; Edward Weston.

Assemble your slideshow in random order, then show each picture for under 10 seconds. Avoid contemplating what story the picture tells, if any, but instead take turns to trace on the screen how your eye traveled around the picture from the moment of first seeing it. The aim is to reconstitute how your eye worked, what you noticed, and what you thought along the way. For the full exercise, see the picture analysis project at www.directingthedocumentary.com.

Typical thoughts:

- *What made my eye go to its particular starting point in the image?* Was it the brightest point; the darkest; an arresting color; a human face or a significant junction of lines creating a focal point? Something else?

- *What moved my eye away from its point of first attraction, and what drew it onward to each new place?*

- *If I trace out the route my eye took, what shape do I have?* A circular pattern; a triangle or ellipse; what else?

- *How do I classify this compositional movement?* Is it geometrical, repetitive textures, swirling, falling inwards, symmetrically divided down the middle, flowing diagonally…?

- *Are places along my eye's route charged with special energy?* Often these are sightlines, such as between two field workers, one of whom is facing away.
- *How are the individuality and mood of the human subjects expressed?* By making juxtapositions between person and person, person and surroundings, body language, facial expression?
- *How much movement did my eye make before returning to its starting point?*

ASPECTS OF VISUAL DESIGN

Visual design is an immensely complex business, and its rules and guidelines are not easy to understand, particularly from a book. Here are some initial categories and associations for you to consider, but your camera-operating will profit from a full study of compositional values if your eye and mind are to be ready. Camera operating also requires the operator to respond from a dramatic awareness. He or she should *see in terms of relatedness* and constantly use composition and juxtaposition to further the differing moods and dramatic potential of the filming. Table 26-1 features some of the elements and their associations that a trained eye will see.

The camera operator, particularly in improvisational situations, composes so that the audience sees and feels in particular ways. He or she must rapidly see, adapt to, and exploit the compositional potential of each new situation. The operator must take decisions in real time about framing, camera vantage, or movement while occupying the double role of audience and creator. He or she relies on intuition, knowledge of your story and its intentions, and compositional and dramaturgical values so internalized that he or she recognizes them as opportunities take shape. Very few camera operators rise to these heights of self-education and intuition.

VISUAL RHYTHM AND IMAGES IN SUCCESSION

The film spectator must interpret each shot within its given time. This is like reading an advertisement on a passing bus; if you don't get the words and images in the given time, the bus drives on leaving the message unabsorbed. If however the bus crawls past in traffic, you see its message to excess and may become bored and rejecting.

The analogy suggests there is *an optimum duration for each shot*, which you judge according to its content, meaning, and complexity (Figure 26-12). How much time the audience gets to "read" the shot depends not only on its content, but also on the cutting pace of those preceding. The innate principle the editor uses to determine each shot's duration—by content, form, and audience expectation—is called *visual rhythm*. The pace can be relaxed or intensified according to how you want to develop the audience's relationship to the film.

DYNAMIC COMPOSITION

A balanced composition can become disturbingly unbalanced if someone moves or leaves the frame. Even a movement by someone's head in the foreground may posit a new sightline and a new scene axis, and thus demand a compositional rebalance. This might involve not only reframing, but moving the camera to a new vantage point. A zoom into close shot usually demands reframing, for though the subject remains the same, the compositional content changes, sometimes drastically.

When you operate a camera, you might need to,

- *Reframe because the subject moved.* Wait to see if they move back or whether you should reframe.
- *Reframe because something/someone left the frame.* Will they/it return?

TABLE 26-1 Composition elements and associations

Element	Type	Typical association
Lines	Straight	Man-made, purposeful, of the mind and intellect, designed, intentional, divisional. Lines may be actual or implied.
	Curved or round	Organic, flowing, soft, pliable, adaptable, undulating, enveloping.
	Vertical	Rising, falling, contesting, bisecting, dividing.
	Horizontal	Space, broadness, depth, calmness, limpidity, serenity, bisection above and below.
	Diagonal	Purpose, dynamism, movement, descending or ascending.
	Converging	Fulfillment, destination, completion, unification.
	Diverging	Separation, profusion, multiplication.
	Between people or objects	Tension; will; intention; potential for communication, antagonism, attraction, questioning.
	Eyeline	Implied sightline that we are drawn to sharing.
Shapes	Organic	Profusion, welcoming, fruitful, invasive, multiplying.
	Angular	Orderly, defensive, purposeful, watchful.
Textures	Soft surfaces	Springy, welcoming, resilient, disordered, comfortable, light absorbing, fluid.
	Hard surfaces	Definite, contained, defended, ordered, light reflecting, rigid.
Colors	Hue	Colors hold innumerable natural and cultural associations. The most obvious are red for blood and danger, and green for safety and nature, white for purity, etc.
	Saturation (degree of purity or of dilution with white)	Degree of saturation has its associations and symbolic meanings, possibly connected with energy, assertiveness, boldness, etc.
	Brightness	Lightness might suggest assertive, outgoing energy; darkness could mean withdrawal, subservience, or gloom.
	Juxtaposition	What colors are juxtaposed to special effect?
	Dominant	What colors predominate in the frame?
Spaces	Positive space (objects that constitute a picture's subject)	Space occupied by the subject and its surrounding objects.
	Negative space (space around and between objects)	Space around and between objects that will often assume a shape, compositional weight, and meaning in its own right.

(Continued)

TABLE 26-1 (Continued)

Element	Type	Typical association
Juxtaposition	Balance or imbalance	Balanced or unbalanced subject within the frame may suggest a harmony or disharmony that might be thematic or associated with one of the characters.
	Contrast	Strong or ironic contrasts can make a telling authorial comment about the characters' environment, or authorial point of view.
	Repetition	Patterns, repetitive compositional elements, and mirroring can also strongly convey a mood or point of view.
Depth	Background plane Middleground plane Foreground plane	Sensation of depth can arise from dimensional lighting, perspective, or selective focus. Subject is normally focused in middleground, with foreground and background in lesser focus. Racking focus between planes can shift our attention to a new subject without reframing.
Framing	Closed	The frame contains the necessary narrative; information is arranged and enclosed within it. Framing often suggests meaning or subtext.
	Open	A necessary narrative element is either obscured or is outside the frame; the frame may look partial or unarranged. Half a face may look out of frame, causing the viewer to imagine the rest.
	Balanced	Elements are harmoniously arranged suggesting order and balance.
	Unbalanced	May be intended to create unease, or may anticipate new element entering the frame, such as someone appearing out of a door.
	Frame within a frame	A subframing, such as a room through whose window one sees outdoor activity framed by the window.
	Lead space	Space ahead of someone facing across screen.

- *Reframe in anticipation of something/someone entering the frame.* You hear steps approaching a door, and reframe to anticipate the door opening.
- *Change the point of focus to move the attention from the background to foreground or vice versa.* This changes the texture of significant areas of the composition.
- *Move within an otherwise static composition.* Any camera movement (across subject, diagonally, from the background to foreground, from the foreground to background, up frame, down frame) benefits from a motivation, either authorial, or by movement within the frame, such as a car passing or a character whose state of mind calls for closer study.

FIGURE 26-12

Two shots of old cities—one more organized and easy to assimilate than the other.

- *Decide who or what you feel close to.* This concerns point of view and is tricky, but, in general, the nearer one is to the axis of a movement, the more subjective one's sense of involvement, and the farther you are from the axis, the more objective, sociological, or historic is the viewpoint.

- *Decide how to adjust to a figure who moves to another place in frame.* Ideally subject movement and the camera's compositional change are synchronous, as they are in fiction films. In documentary, the camera move looks logical if it lags a little behind the movement, but inept if it anticipates it.

- *Decide how to angle composition in relation to sightlines.* Should you get close to their axis, or should you let them extend across the screen. Altering from one to the other often marks a shift between subjective and more objective points of view, or vice versa. Properly calculated, this can come as a relief or a welcome intensification.

- *Decide what a change of angle, or of composition, would make you feel toward the characters.* Maybe more or less involved, or more or less objective?

- *Look for a composition that more forcefully suggests depth.* In 2D photography this is the missing dimension that constantly needs reinforcing. Action taking place across the screen flattens space, while action that takes place in the screen's depth extends it.

- *Compose to include background detail that comments on, or counterpoints, foreground subject.* The aware camera operator sees dramatic ironies and tensions inherent in visual components, and consciously juxtaposes them.

INTERNAL AND EXTERNAL COMPOSITION

Beyond *internal composition*, that is, composition internal to each shot, there is *external composition*. This is the compositional relationship at cutting points between an outgoing image and the next or incoming shot. Seldom do we notice how much it influences our judgments and expectations. Take a favorite film and use your slow-scan facility to help you assess compositional relationships at cutting points. Find aspects of internal and external composition by asking,

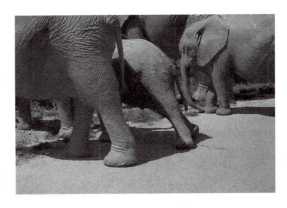

FIGURE 26-13

Using the Rule of Thirds in composing helps the eye decide meaning efficiently.

- *Where was your point of concentration at the end of the shot?* Trace where your eye travels through the shot with your finger on the monitor's face. Its last point as the shot ends is where the eye enters the incoming shot composition. Interestingly, the length of a shot determines how far the eye gets in exploring it—so shot length influences external composition.

- *Are complementary shots symmetrical?* Some shots—two people facing each other for instance, with lead space for each—should be complementary (designed to intercut) and their compositions should reflect this.

- *What is the relationship between two same-subject but different-sized shots that are designed to cut together?* This is revealing; the inexperienced camera operator often produces medium and close shots that cut together poorly because proportions and compositional placing of the subject are incompatible. The Rule of Thirds can help you stay compositionally consistent (Figure 26-13).

- *Does a match cut, run very slowly, show several frames of overlap in its action?* Especially in fast action, a match cut (one made between two different size images during a strong action) needs *two or three frames of the action repeated* in the incoming shot to look smooth, because the eye does not register the first two or three frames of any new image. Think of this as accommodating a built-in perceptual lag. The only way to cut on the beat of music is thus to place all cuts two or three frames in advance of the literal beat point.

- *Do external compositions make a juxtapositional comment?* Examples: cutting from a pair of eyes to car headlights approaching at night; cutting from a dockside crane to a man feeding birds, arm outstretched.

CHAPTER 27

ADVANCED CAMERAS AND EQUIPMENT

PRELIMINARIES

How your film looks depends on how you shoot it, and at what cost. This means choosing equipment carefully. Multiple standards of digital technology, and a bewildering array of excellent equipment make this a challenge, to say the least.

Generally speaking, the higher your recording quality, the costlier will be production—but the more marketable over time your work may become—if the subject and your treatment warrant it. Anything spectacular and durable such as *Winged Migration* merits the best imaginable quality because of its unlimited future life. You can however make significant work inexpensively—so long as you make a match between the medium, material, and market. You could for instance shoot the inside story on military college hazing rituals with a consumer handicam, because the audience understands the need to shoot undercover.

ARCHIVING ISSUES

The only moving-image medium to have physically endured for 100 years is 35 mm film. That doesn't mean film negatives have endured well: over time, the early acetate-based films turn to dust (when they didn't explode), and modern film stocks, though no longer inflammable, shrink and their color dyes fade. Paradoxically the only medium in which the original color is recoverable is the long-defunct, three-strip dye-transfer Technicolor. Media stored on high quality magnetic tape or hard disk have a relatively long life, perhaps 30–50 years, while optical media like DVD and Blu-ray are unproven and even unpromising. Pressed disks have a longer life than those you burn, which are deteriorating even before you use them, and may only remain readable for 2–5 years. The chemical surfaces of discount disks are often so unstable that they can become unreadable within weeks or months.

So use the best-rated media, and recopy anything that you mean to store over time every few years. Given the speed of technological change, you will probably also be updating to a new recording standard. Follow the discussions online for up-to-date opinions.

COMPATIBILITY

When a software or camera manufacturer recommends particular associated equipment, follow instructions assiduously. Some suggestions:

- Stay with a single manufacturer's gear wherever possible, so equipment will interface as desired.
- Understand the process and technical workflow of each production stage and know what formats and codecs your equipment can handle. Don't assume compatibility.
- Before you commit to using particular equipment and methods, crosscheck for definitive answers.
- Do not reinvent the wheel: seek those who have done what you propose doing, and follow their advice closely.

HIRING EQUIPMENT

To hire anything you will need to pre-arrange credit, which unless you are an established company is not simple. So visit the rental house in an off-peak time to get a guided tour and set up financial arrangements. They are usually happy to show you their holdings, and to share the relative merits of what they carry. Start building relationships by learning people's names, titles, and specialties. Knowing who does what will be most important should anything break down.

Part of the hire business is to avoid being scammed, so extended business conversations help them find out who you are, whom you have in common, and what you are planning to do. They also know plenty about common mistakes, and can give you tips to help your shoot go well.

SHOOTING ABROAD

Using native equipment abroad can spring some surprises. An American-standard camera shooting at 30 frames per second (fps) under European 50 hertz (Hz) fluorescent lighting will lead to a slow, pulsing illumination-effect onscreen. A European 25 fps camera shooting under 60 Hz American fluorescents will do the same. The pulsing results when the camera frame rate and the lighting power supply frequency are slightly out of step. You should see this in the video viewfinder, unlike those who shoot film, who find out only when it is too late. Altering the camera shutter-speed settings can sometimes cure the problem.

If you plan to shoot in non-native format (say PAL in America, or NTSC in Europe) run tests. You want to prove that everything, including battery chargers and your editing software, can function in all likely situations.

WORKFLOW

Most cameras record their files in a range of formats on removable solid-state memory cards, using one of many competing formats and compression codecs. To make wise choices, look ahead to your editing and distribution phases, asking what markets your final product is aimed at, and whether you mean to include Internet and Blu-Ray distribution versions. Make sure that,

- All of your preferred production formats (picture and sound) are supported by your editing system.
- Your editing system can output whatever files are necessary for sound mix, mastering, and distribution formats, as necessary.

Make a roundup of all the equipment, materials, and processes you can possibly need in your production and postproduction workflow. Rely on no link, such as a transcoding program, that you have not first thoroughly tested, because integrating the different frame rates, aspect ratios, and video compression codecs can spring massive problems upon the unwary.

If your technical grasp is shaky (and whose isn't?), Google key words to bring up explanations on the Internet and keep reading until you understand the guiding principles. In general, Wikipedia is a good source for clear technical explanations, and a good jumping off point for other reference works and information sites.

Particularly if you move between working with American standards and those elsewhere in the world, watch out that you don't end up with, say, 25 fps sound that is supposed to sync to 30 fps camera material.

CAMERA SUPPORT

TRIPOD AND PAN/TILT HEAD

Arri, Sachtler, and O'Connor make excellent tripods but there are others less expensive. If you plan to use a long lens, be sure the tripod has spikes, not rubber feet alone, since you cannot afford a spongy engagement with the ground (Figure 27-1). For a superior tripod, look for one that,

- Is made of carbon fiber—lighter than metal if you are trekking in the wilds.
- Can handle a camera 30 percent heavier than the one you plan to use.
- Has a tilt head with ball leveling, which allows you to instantly adjust the head according to a bubble level (Figure 27-2).
- Is equipped with a fluid drag for its pan and tilt head functions, not a friction substitute.
- Has a quick-release plate attachable to the underside of your camera (Figure 27-3). This will let you instantly dismount the camera and go handheld.
- Has a carry case and a spreader to go under your "legs," or tripod (Figure 27-4).
- Comes with a baby legs (low tripod, Figure 27-5), and hi hat or sandbag for low-angle camera support.

FIGURE 27-1

Spike feet on a Bogen® tripod ensure a positive engagement with the ground. Rubber feet are kind to floors but allow a sponginess that compromises telephoto shots.

FIGURE 27-2

Leveling is quick when your tripod has a ball head.

FIGURE 27-3

Quick-release plate mounted on underside of camera.

FIGURE 27-4

A light carbon fiber tripod and spreader. For quick relocations pick up the whole unit, camera and all. (*Photo courtesy of Vinten, a Vitec Group brand.*)

FIGURE 27-5

Baby legs for low-angle shots. (*Photo courtesy of Vinten, a Vitec Group brand.*)

FIGURE 27-6

Shoulder rig for DSLR camera. (*Photo courtesy of the Ikan Corporation.*)

FIGURE 27-7

Small camera stabilizer. (*Photo courtesy of the Ikan Corporation.*)

SHOULDER RIGS

These prosthetics come in a profusion of designs, each promising relief and control like none other. The operator may need one to survive long handheld takes if the camera is heavy and of awkward design, or if you are using a diminutive DSLR camera in video mode (Figure 27-6). Other types support the camera by bracing downward to the chest or stomach (Figure 27-7), but you may have to breathe carefully so the camera doesn't undulate. Rigs of any kind make it difficult to transition between low and high camera angles, and can either facilitate or impede following focus, adjusting the aperture, or performing any of the other agility tests expected of observational

FIGURE 27-8

A professional ENG camera is designed to sit comfortably on its operator's shoulder. (*Photo courtesy of Nomadic Pictures, Inc.*)

cinema. Really, there is no substitute for a camera designed for the human hands, eye, body, and shoulder that will be using it (Figure 27-8).

STABILIZERS

To see what a rich field exists for exotic camera supports you have only to look under "stabilizers" in B&H's listing (www.bhphotovideo.com). This cottage industry developed in the wake of the first Steadicam rigs, made for the heavy 35 mm cameras used in feature film production. Their results can be truly lyrical, as you can see in Wim Wenders' beautiful fiction feature, *Wings of Desire* (Germany, 1987). In documentary, Rachel Grady and Heidi Ewing apparently used a stabilizer to great effect in the "talking in tongues" sequence of their *Jesus Camp* (USA, 2006, Figure 27-9). If your film requires a great deal of controlled movement (ballroom dancing, drum majorettes, hunting, contact sports, etc.) certainly consider a stabilizer. With some practice they can produce wonderfully smooth camera movement, but they can make transitions to special angles quite difficult. Until you know what best fits your purpose, rent and don't own.

DOLLIES

Only a prestige documentary is likely to use a dolly, but with only a little rehearsal you can improvise the effect by shooting seated in a wheelchair or out of a car window. Improve smoothness by letting some air out of the wheelchair's tires.

SETTINGS AND OPTIONS

Any camera you use will come with many options and settings. They affect picture aspect ratio, shutter speed, exposure control, language, date/time/zone (for date stamping), frame rates for

FIGURE 27-9

Children seen agitated and possessed in *Jesus Camp* thanks to alert camerawork.

PAL/NTSC video system, black pedestal (useful for creating a common standard for black and colors when multiple cameras are used), manual/automatic focusing, which area auto-focus chooses to focus, and whether it should use face recognition. You must select ISO (sensitivity to light), pixel count, codec, and other things. Choices for sound will include sampling rate (normally 48 kHz) and adjustments depending on whether you are shooting at 25 fps (PAL) or 30 fps (NTSC). Within NTSC there is drop frame (DF) or non-drop frame (NDF), explained in the "Timecode" section below. For sound you will also have to choose between mono or stereo, and manual or automatic level control.

ASPECT RATIO

As explained in **Chapter 24: Advanced Technology and Budgeting**, aspect ratio refers to the width of the frame in relation to its height, which has changed during screen history (Figure 27-10). Cinema and TV ratios were formerly 4:3, that is, a screen of four units wide by three units high. In the 1950s cinema adopted various widescreen formats (1.85:1, 2.35:1, 2.39:1, 2.55:1). For a short illustrated history see www.dvdaust.com/aspect.htm. HD video at 16:9, which approximates the cinema format of 1.85:1, is now the internationally preferred aspect ratio for HD television. Inherently wide pictorial matter, such as landscape shots and anything in horizontal movement, fills the screen more satisfactorily (Figure 27-10). Vertical subjects such as head-shots and tall buildings are harder to accommodate, but most people feel that the wider screen allows for more interesting filming. The world's archives are mostly 4:3 (also expressed as 1.33:1), so postproduction must either show older material with black bands at the sides, or if the content permits, magnify the original and pare slices from top and bottom.

Shutter speed and motion: Shutter speed is a term left over from photography: it signifies the variable time a camera may take to record a single frame. If you see helicopter blades on the screen that are sharp and whirling in an odd, jerky movement, it's because the camera is using a fast shutter speed that "freezes" the blades. Interlaced video cannot normally shoot video with a shutter speed slower than 1/60th of a second, but you are free to use faster shutter speeds—up to 1/1000th of a second or faster. If you plan to slow down a racehorse or a pole-vaulter in postproduction, then you should use a fast shutter speed to get a crisp image.

FIGURE 27-10

Inherently wide pictorial matter fits today's aspect ratio most satisfactorily.

TIMECODE (TC)

In the American TV standard of NTSC you must make a choice concerning *timecode*, which is the unique time identity assigned to each video frame (Figure 27-11). In NTSC you must choose either *drop frame* (DF) or *non-drop frame* (NDF) timecode. Drop frame removes a digit every so often to keep timecode in step with clock time—useful when you are assembling footage to strict time requirements. Whether you choose DF or NDF doesn't usually matter so long as you stay consistent throughout production.

Try to use a camera with *addressable timecode* (meaning, you can set your own starting numbers and letters) so that every batch of material sails under its own unique timecode. Some cameras blindly reset to zero when you change recording media, so that every media item ends up with the same range of TC numbers, creating confusion during postproduction. With addressable TC you can avoid any such confusion.

Media Start	Media End
00:00:01;15	00:00:38;26
00:00:01;15	00:00:38;26
01:00:00;00	01:00:38;15

FIGURE 27-11

Timecode is the unique identity by which editing software handles each video frame. It is calibrated in hours: minutes: seconds: frames.

HIGH-END CAMERAS COMPARED

To see what state-of-the-art cameras offer, Table 27-1 shows a current list with their vital statistics, by kind permission of Fletcher Camera and Lenses. The cameras listed show what professionals currently prefer, the range of technological standards in use, and rental averages. Like nothing else, the fine print here should dramatize how vital it is to decide your workflow in advance. The Fletcher website (www.fletch.com) also shows the range of available lenses and accessories.

The shape and design of the camera body are decisive factors for documentary users. Only the Alexa, the Sony F5 and F55, and two of the Phantom cameras have their viewfinders placed

TABLE 27-1 The 2013 Fletcher camera comparison chart (by kind permission of Fletcher Camera and Lenses)

Imager (Actual Size)	Base ISO	Latitude	Frame Rates (Progressive Only)	Digital Sampling on Recorded Media	Recorded Bit Depth Format & Time	Data	Weight	Power	Highlighted Positives	Notable Credits	Average National Daily Rental BODY ONLY
CMOS 29.7mm Ø 23.8 × 17.8mm **4:3** ALEXA XT Studio & XT Plus	800	14+ Stops	**4:3 Mode** .75-90fps **16:9 Mode** .75-120 fps Mirror Shutter OFF .75-60 fps Shutter ON	3K 2880 × 2160 ARRIRAW 4:3 2K 1920x1080	12 Bit ARRIRAW Uncompressed 48 min - 512GB in 16:9 36 min - 512GB in 4:3 Optional (1) SxS Card Slot Records all **Classic ALEXA** formats (See Below)	9.4 GB per Minute	19.2 lbs Plus 23.1 lbs Studio	131w	Optical VF & Mirror Shutter(ST) True Anamorphic 4:3 Imager Wide Latitude Gently Rolls Off Highlights Proven Reliable, Post-Efficient Codex Workflow	Paddington Bear SkyFall * Life of Pi * The Avengers * Argo * * w/External Codex	$3000 XT Studio $2700 XT Plus $2500 XT
CMOS 27.9mm Ø 24.7 × 13.1mm **17:9** Sony F65 & SR-R4	800	14 Stops	1 to 120 fps Focial Plane Shutter OFF 1 to 60 fps Shutter ON	8K 8192 × 2160 2K 1920x1080	16 Bit F65RAW – LITE 60 min - 512GB 120 min - 1TB (Also Records SR-File Codec @ 10/12bit)	9 GB per Minute	12 lbs Body Only 16 lbs w/ SR-R4	62w Body Only 105w w/ SR-R4	8K, 6K, 4K De-mosaic Rotary Shutter 16 Bit Linear RAW IIF ACES Workflow & S-Gamut Wide Dynamic Range OLED Viewfinder	Oblivion After Earth Smurfs 2 Save Me Evil Dead Masters of Sex	$2500
CMOS 29.7mm Ø 23.8 × 17.8mm **4:3** Arri ALEXA XT M	800	14+ Stops	**4:3 Mode** .75-90fps **16:9 Mode** .75-120 fps	3K 2880 × 2160 ARRIRAW 4:3 2K 1920x1080	12 Bit ARRIRAW Uncompressed 48 min - 512GB in 16:9 36 min - 512GB in 4:3 Optional (1) SxS Card Slot Records all **Classic ALEXA** formats (See Below)	9.4 GB per Minute	12.8 lbs XT - M 12.1 lbs Classic M	35w Head 65w Body 131w XT System	Small Ideal for 3D & Cars True Anamorphic 4:3 Imager Low Light Performance Wide Latitude Pleasing Skin Tones Gently Rolls Off Highlights	Dawn of the Planet of the Apes [3] Black Sky SkyFall [2] X-Men: Days of Future Past [3]	$2500
CMOS 27.2mm Ø 23.8 × 13.4mm **16:9** ALEXA Classic EV/Plus	800	14+ Stops	.75-120 fps @ ProRes 4:2:2 .75-40 fps @ 2K ProRes or 4:4:4	2K 1920 × 1080	12 Bit ProRes 4:4:4 32GB SxS - 14 min 64GB SxS - 28 min	1.9 GB per Minute	19.2 lbs EV 23.1 lbs Plus	85w	Low Light Performance Wide Latitude Cost Effective Workflow Pleasing Skin Tones Gently Rolls Off Highlights	Game of Thrones Homeland Downton Abbey Bernie Random	$1800 Plus $1600 EV w/120fps $1400 EV
CMOS 27.1mmØ 24 × 12.7mm **17:9** Sony F55 w/R5	1250	14 Stops	24, 25, 30, 50, 60 1-60fps @ 4K[1] 1-180fps @ 2K[1] 1-180fps @ HD[1] 1-240fps @ 2K Raw[1]	4K 4096 × 2160 3840 × 2160[1] 2K[1] HD	16 Bit F55RAW @ 3.6:1 512GB AXSM - 60 min XAVC HD 2K 4K SR-SQ[1] & SR-Lite[1] 64GB SxS - 30 min	7.5GB per Minute	6.4 lbs F55 & R5 5 lbs Body Only	48w System 25w Body Only	Simultaneous records SxS & RAW F65 Color (S-Gamut) Global Shutter Records 4K Compressed Internally XAVC 4K is small HD Data Rate 2x Anamorphic De-Squeeze	Old School The Town That Dreaded Sundown Rake Bloodline Various National Spots	$1,250
CMOS 31.4mm Ø 27.7 × 14.6mm **1.90:1** Red Epic	800	12+ Stops 15-18+ w/ HDRx	1-96 fps @5K 1-120 fps @4K 1-160 fps @3K 1-300fps @2K 1-400fps @1K	5K, 4K 3K, 2K, 1K 1920 × 1080 1280x720	12 Bit REDCODE - 5K FF @ 7:1 128GB SSD - 33 min 256GB SSD - 66 min (HDRx cuts time in half)	3.7 GB per Minute	5 lbs Body Only 6 lbs Body & EVF	60w	Small Self Contained Ideal for 3D HDRx High Dynamic Range Established R3D workflow Modular Design High Frames per Second	Great Gatsby [3] Hobbit [3] Prometheus [3] Arrested Development House of Cards	$1,000
CMOS 27.3mm Ø 24.6 × 13.8mm **16:9** Canon EOS C500	850	12 Stops	24p, 25p, 30p, 50i, 60i @ HD 24, 25, 30, 50, 60, 120 @ 4K to External Recorder	1920x1080 Outputs 2K & 4K to External Recorder	8 Bit MPEG2-4:2:2 MXF 64GB CF - 160 min 10 Bit 4K RAW to External Recorder	0.4 GB per Minute	4 lbs Body Only	11.4w	4K Output w/ External Recorder PL or EF mount High Dynamic Range Small Self Contained Ideal for 3D	Various Independent Films Various National Spots	$900

Imager (Actual Size)	Base ISO	Latitude	Frame Rates (Progressive Only)	Digital Sampling on Recorded Media	Recorded Bit Depth Format & Time	Data	Weight	Power	Highlighted Positives	Notable Credits	Average National Daily Rental BODY ONLY
Canon EOS C300 CMOS 27.3mm Ø 24.6 x 13.8mm 16:9	850	12 Stops	24, 25, 30 fps @ 1080	1920 x 1080	8 Bit MPEG2-4:2:2 MXF 64GB CF - 160 min	0.4 GB per Minute	3.2 lbs Body Only	11.4w	Incredible Low Light Performance / Small Size / C-Log Workflow	Iron Man 3[2] / Community / La vie de'Adèle / Dirty People / Rush[2]	$450
Sony F5 CMOS 27.1mm Ø 24 x 12.7mm 17:9	2000	14 Stops	24, 25, 30, 50, 60 / 1-120fps @ 2K & HD[1] / 1-120fps @ 2 & 4KRaw[1]	2K 1920x1080 / Outputs 4K to External Recorder	10 Bit / XAVC & SR-SQ & Lite[1] / 128GB SxS - 60 min / 4K FSRAW to External Recorder	2.1 GB per Minute	5 lbs Body Only	25w	Choice of recording formats / Native FZ Mount allows wide range of lens to be used / Supports Lens Meta Data	Various / Independent Films / Various National Spots	$450
Red Scarlet CMOS 31.4mm Ø 27.7 x 14.6mm 1.90:1	800	12+ Stops / 15-18+ w/HDRx	1-30 fps @ 4K / 1-48 fps @ 3K / 1-60 fps @ 2K / 1-120 fps @ 1K	4K 3K / 1K 2K / 1920 x 1080 / 1280 x 720	12 Bit / REDCODE - 4K FF @ 7:1 / 128GB SSD - 51 min / 256GB SSD - 103 min	2.4 GB per Minute	5 lbs Body Only	60w	Cost vs. Performance / Small Self Contained Ideal for 3D / Established R3D RAW workflow / Interchangeable Lens Mounts	Love Puzzle / Maybe He Should Have Told Her Closer to Home	$400
Sony F3 CMOS 27.1mm Ø 23.6 x 13.3mm 16:9	800	11 Stops	1-30fps @ 1080 / 1-60 fps @ 720 / 1-60fps to an External Recorder	1920 x 1080	8 Bit / 32GB SxS - 100 min / 10 Bit / S-Log to External Recorder	.23 GB per Minute	5.3 lbs	24w	10 Bit Uncompressed / 4:4:4 S-Log Output / Low Power Consumption	Planet B Boy[3] / Plan 9 / Safety Not Guaranteed / Red Hook Summer / 60 Minutes[2]	$400
ARRICAM ST - 35mm Film _for comparison vs. the gold standard_ Full Aperture 31.1mm Ø 24.9x18.1mm	500	15-16 Stops	1-60fps	6K 4K 2K 1920x1080 Uncompressed (via Scanner)	16 Bit (Linear) / 10 Bit (Log) / 2P 22m12s 1000' / 3P 14m48s 1000' / 4P 11m06s 1000'	N/A	25 lbs 400' Load / 28 lbs 1000' Load	55w	4:4:4 Color Sampling / Established Workflow / Widest Available Latitude / Proven Archival Value	The Black Dahlia / Chicago / King's Speech / Quantum of Solace	$1000 w/Mags
Phantom Flex CMOS 30.1mm Ø 25.6 x 16mm	1200	10 Stops	1-1617 fps @ 2560x1440 / 1-2564 fps @ 1920x1080	2560 x 1440 Uncompressed RAW / 1920x1080	12 Bit - RAW / 32G Internal RAM / 4.5s@2500fps / 512G CineMags / 1m14s@2500fps	170 GB per Minute @ 1000fps	12 lbs / 14 lbs w/ CineMag	100w	Efficient Professional Workflow / Industry Standard / Low Light Performance / Uncompressed RAW / 4:4:4 Output	Final Destination 5[2] / Sherlock Holmes 2[2] / Numerous Spots	$5500 w/ CineMags (1TB) / $3000 Camera Only (32GB)
Phantom HD Gold CMOS 36mm Ø 25.6 x 25.6mm	250	10 Stops	5-1052 fps @ 1920x1080	2048 x 2048 Uncompressed RAW / 1920 x 1080	14 Bit - RAW / 32G Internal RAM / 8.9s@1000fps / 512G CineMags / 3m14s @ 1000fps	216 GB per Minute @ 1000fps	12 lbs / 14 lbs w/ CineMag	80w	Big Image for Repositioning / Uncompressed 14 Bit RAW / Efficient Professional Workflow / Ideal for Anamorphic Lenses / Expended Color Range	Sherlock Holmes[2] / Inception[2] / Tron: Legacy[2] / Numerous National Spots	$4500 w/ CineMags (1TB) / $1900 Camera Only (32GB)
Phantom Miro CMOS 22.6m 19.2 x 12mm	1100	10 Stops	1-1540 fps @ 1920x1080	1920x1080 Uncompressed RAW / 1920 x 1080	14 Bit - RAW / 12GB Internal RAM / 3.2s@1000fps / 240GB CineFlash / 78s @ 1000fps	225 GB per Minute @ 1000fps	3 lbs Body Only	30w	Small Size / Economical / Low Cost RAW Memory	Shark Week[2] / Stay[1] / X-Games[2] / Assorted National & Regional Spots[2]	$1400 w/ CineFlash (60GB) Mags

[1]Future Update   [2]Select Shots   [3]3D   Camera Must For Sale and Rent | Data based on 24fps and highest internal record.| Sorted by Price

forward of the camera so that they can sit—albeit ponderously—on the operator's shoulder for handheld shooting. Other cameras need a camera support such as a stabilizer, tripod, or dolly. For documentary this would compel you to work in the manner of a bygone era.

The lighter Canon EOS models and high-speed Phantom Miro, all using highly developed stills camera technology, can be held ahead of one's face—for a while. The Canons allow manual control of aperture and focus, and today's auto focusing and image stabilization are nothing short of miraculous. Included for comparison is the Arricam ST, the gold standard for 35 mm fiction features. From its design, weight, and top-mounted film magazine, you can see it requires a beefy tripod or dolly.

Each column in the chart carries information whose significance you should at least know about. Note that it is based on 24p performance (24 frames per second, progressive scan):

Imager: High-end image sensors, occasionally CCD (charge-coupled device) chips, but mostly now CMOS (complementary metal–oxide semiconductor). The imager aspect ratio, such as 16:9, tells you the shape of the chip's imaging surface. In the chart this is indicated as a rectangle with the imager shape given in millimeters. Each has a special distance from the lens flange to the focal plane (symbol Φ). Any imager above 2 K pixels will produce cinema-quality images.

Base ISO, like the older ASA film speed ratings, is an index of light sensitivity. See Wikipedia for a comparison.

Latitude is the difference in photographic stops between the least and the most light within which the imaging system can still register detail. The Arri film camera, whose film stock has 15–16 stops of latitude, now has a clutch of uppity digital brethren snapping at its heels.

Frame rates: Many HD digital cameras offer variable speed filming, so you can speed up clouds passing, or slow down colliding vehicles. See **Chapter 24: Advanced Technology and Budgeting** for frame rate, aspect ratio, scanning rates, and other technical information.

Digital sampling on recorded media is the amount of digital information recorded per frame. The more there is, the greater the detail. A number of the cameras produce RAW files, which are free of any compression codec. They take enormous storage capacity and need very fast computing. Check the compatibility of your editing system if you decide to work with RAW files.

Recorded bit depth format and time: Bit depth refers to an image's color information. The higher this is, the more colors it can store, which affects color subtlety and fidelity. Format refers to whether information is RAW or subjected to a specific (often proprietary) compression codec. Time refers to maximum storage using the recommended media.

Data refers to the amount of data output per minute. Shooting a subject with a lot of movement and at higher frame rates greatly increases the data amount.

Weight: This is a minimum figure. Camera weight increases as you load it up with matte box, monitor, radio mike receivers, and other peripherals.

Power: From wattage consumption you can calculate how many batteries you will need for a day's work. Err on the side of caution.

Highlighted positives are useful for deciding the camera's strengths and special uses.

Notable credits lists movies made with this camera, so you can see its performance in extreme lighting conditions, always the litmus test of camera technology.

Average national daily rental: This figure is for the camera body only—lenses and camera support, etc. are extra. Usually you can hire a basic shooting package. Read the hire house's terms very carefully and well in advance of hiring, since you'll need to satisfy their credit conditions and set up equipment insurance cover—both of which take time to arrange. The good news is that a week's hire is normally computed at three times the daily rate.

For a full range of cameras and accessories, go to B&H Photo, a New York supplier with highly competitive pricing (www.bhphotovideo.com). Their website also contains much information and instructional help. Another great resource for equipment and pricing is Abel Cine, especially if you want to research rental prices for budgeting (http://www.abelcine.com/store/Rental-Equipment). Whatever you plan to buy, check its reputation extensively with users familiar with its strengths and drawbacks.

CAMERA ACCESSORIES

MATTE BOX AND FILTERS

Chrosziel and other manufacturers make *matte box* kits for popular cameras. Mounted in front of the lens, a matte box lets you slot in a range of standard-size filters (Figure 27-12). You might find yourself needing any of the following:

- Common color conversion filters such as #85 and #80A. These allow you to quickly adapt to shooting under a different color temperature.
- 1 and 2 stop ND filters (.3 and .6). Good for reducing overall light transmission so that you can restrict DOF by working at a larger aperture.
- A graduated ND filter for cooling a "hot" sky. Be careful that camera movements don't reveal the filtering.
- Graduated color filters. Use these to color the sky or (say) the sea.
- Fog filter—creates a misty or downright foggy look. These come in various strengths and are tricky to use believably.
- Diffusion filter—also comes in various degrees. Its effect is to mix a modicum of white light with the picture's shadow areas. The effect is to lower contrast at the cost of some sharpness.
- Polarizing filter. Rotate it to tune out surface glare when shooting through windows, over water, or certain other reflective surfaces.

FIGURE 27-12

A matte box is an accessory that lets you slot in a range of filters in front of your camera's lens. (*Photo courtesy of Chrosziel GmbH.*)

- Close-up diopters—additional lenses that alter the characteristics of your main lens so you can (say) focus in closer.
- Split diopter. Lets you photograph a close object in focus through one half of the diopter, and a distant background, also in focus, in the other half.

LENS HOOD

These prevent strong, off-axis light (such as sunlight) from obliquely striking the front lens element and causing *halation* (light reflecting between the lens's interior elements). A lens hood may mount on the front of the lens, or come as part of the matte box assembly. Check wide-angle images for vignetting (dark in the corners) that can result from an incorrect size or shape of lens hood.

CAMERA AESTHETICS

CAMERA HEIGHT

Directors often uncritically use the camera at eye-level. This not only becomes predictable and dull, but there is a psychological reason to avoid it. At eye-level, the audience feels itself intruding in the action, rather like standing in the path of a duel. Being a little above or below eye-level positions gets us out of the firing line. If you can motivate high or low angles, or Dutch angles (camera tilted), consider using them to reduce the banality of naturalism.

Of course, the old adage says that a high-down camera position suggests domination, and a low angle, subjugation, but there are plenty of other, less colonial reasons to vary camera height.

ADAPTING TO LOCATION EXIGENCIES

There are no reliable rules for camera positioning and movement because every situation brings its own conditions. Limitations are usually physical: there may be windows or pillars in an interior that restrict shooting in one direction, or an exterior has an incongruity you must avoid. A Victorian house turns out to have a background of aerial power lines, forcing you to film from a high angle. Often you must shelve your expectations and redirect energy into solving the unforeseen. For the rigid, linear personality, this constant adaptation is frustrating, but for others it poses interesting, never-ending challenges. Nonetheless, you must plan, and sometimes plans even work out.

BACKGROUNDS

Deciding what part background plays in relation to foreground means being conscious of lens choices and camera positioning. For a depressed and hungry character there is a nice irony in showing a lurid Ronald McDonald watching her from behind a bus stop. The composition highlights her dilemma and suggests she might blow her bus money on a large fries.

The composition subject is often in the middle ground, as with the figures on the beach in Figure 27-13. The fringe of foreground palm roofing, the receding footsteps in the sand, and the glittering horizon help create the different planes. Depth, the third dimension, is often missing from two-dimensional imagery unless you take advantage of composition, lighting, and perspective to enhance the illusion of it (Figure 27-14).

REVEALING SUBTEXTS

Each shot has a subject, and its composition helps suggest a subtext. Looking down on the subject, looking up at it, or peering between tree trunks all suggest different contexts, contrasts, and

FIGURE 27-13

The subject is often in the middle ground, as here in a beachscape.

FIGURE 27-14

Unless you use composition, lighting, and perspective to create depth, it is often absent from two-dimensional imagery.

different ways of seeing. This means experiencing the action differently according to the juxtapositions you have arranged. You could use dialectical editing to make us see the irony of riot police lined up in front of a nice bed of tulips, but how much more effective to make the point in a single well-composed frame, especially as red flowers might even foreshadow the bloodshed to come.

Aim to make every framing contain significant juxtapositions, and try to build irony and dramatic tension into every aspect of your camerawork. Make each location a meaningful environment, and respond with your camera to the actions and sightlines of participants to help the scene's unfolding dynamics. Thus you endow us, your audience, with the consciousness of someone intelligent and intuitive who picks up all the contextual tensions and ironies.

COMPROMISES FOR THE CAMERA

Because movement within a frame can look 20–30 percent faster than in life, you may need to ask participants to slow their movements when shooting action sequences, especially in close-shot. No camera operator can keep a profile in tight framing if the person moves too fast. How much should you compromise participants' spontaneity to achieve a visually and choreographically polished result? This of course depends on the comfort of those you are filming. Sometimes you can ask for changes, other times you may have to loosen the shot (that is, go wider).

STROBING

Occasionally, when panning across a repetitive pattern such as a picket fence, you must vary the speed of the camera movement to stop the subject *strobing*. This happens when the frequency of the pattern interacts with the camera's frame rate (ever wonder how they won the West with wagon wheels turning backwards?) Film camera operators could not see the strobing, but anyone using today's video cameras can. Occasionally stripes or checks in clothing cause similar stroboscopic effects during camera movement. They are distracting and an aware camera operator will take steps to avoid the situation—by going wider, or slowing a panning movement.

CARE OF PEOPLE AND EQUIPMENT

TRAVEL IN WILD OR HAZARDOUS AREAS

Well before going abroad, make a safety check with US Department of State www.usembassy.gov or your own country's embassy website. Take particular note of hazard warnings, and if in doubt, call your embassy in that country for on-the-spot advice and contacts. Also,

- Check specialized guidebooks for medical information.
- Try to set up a friendly contact in case you need an interpreter, go-between, or other assistance requiring local knowledge.
- Get injections to guard against local parasites, diseases, etc.
- Research water safety and availability of electricity, cell phone, and Internet services.
- Research how to handle bribery demands.
- Leave detailed travel plans and contact numbers with those at home.
- Do the same with your embassy on arrival, and keep them apprised of all changes so they can take action should it become necessary.
- Carry toilet paper.

EMERGENCIES

Someone or something is bound to need mending on location, especially if you are abroad, so bring,

- Phrasebook.
- Information on nearest medical facilities in case of accidents.

- First aid kit including,
  - First aid manual
  - Bandages, tourniquet to inhibit severe bleeding, band-aids, disinfectant, tweezers, scissors, etc. for dressing small wounds.
  - Sun-block cream for working outdoors
  - Mosquito repellent
  - Water-purification tablets
  - Diarrhea and pain medicines
- Equipment manuals.
- Information on nearest equipment hire or repair center.
- Basic repair kit including,
  - Flashlight
  - Different types and sizes of screwdrivers, adjustable wrench, and pliers
  - Hex key and socket sets
  - Electrical wire, electrical tape, solder, and soldering iron
  - An electrical test meter for resistance, continuity, voltage, and other testing
- Compass to check the sun's orientation during location spotting.
- Radio or phone to check weather reports and news.
- Spare batteries for everything that uses them.
- Spare sound and power cables.

CHAPTER 28

ADVANCED LOCATION SOUND

This chapter summarizes some of the sound equipment, skills, and approaches required for advanced sound production, but you may first want to review the basics in **Chapter 10: Capturing Sound**. Fortunately, a great deal of advice is now available on the Internet. For cost-conscious reviews and practical articles on all aspects of sound, go to Fred Ginsburg's articles at FilmTVSound (http://filmtvsound.co). For an outstanding 72-page article on sound theory and practice, see "Location Sound: The Basics and Beyond" by Dan Brockett, published under the Ken Stone Index at www.kenstone.net/fcp_homepage/location_sound.html (an offshoot of Final Cut Pro). For a wide range of up-to-date sound equipment, go to (www.locationsound.com/proaudio/ls/index.html). The Broadcast Shop at www.thebroadcastshop.com is good for professional equipment, and the Digital Information Network at www.dvinfo.net has up-to-date information on various aspects of digital filmmaking. You can Google many instructional videos online via Vimeo and others.

Sound equipment evolves less rapidly than cameras, so I have mentioned some industry favorites in the discussions below. Planning sound coverage poses a number of questions:

- Will you record sound using the camera alone, or use a separate digital recorder?
- What sound rate should you use (normally it is 48 kHz)?
- Are you shooting to sync 24 fps, 25 fps PAL, or 30 fps NTSC? If the latter, will you use drop frame (DF) timecode or non-drop frame (NDF)?
- If you mean to shoot double system (using a separate camera and sound recorder), which kind of sync marker system will you use?
- How many types of sound setup can you expect and what will you need to mike each?
- What is the maximum number of sound channels you will need to record?
- How many channels does your camera afford, and will you need to incorporate a multichannel mixer?
- Do you plan to take advantage of the mobility of radio mikes?
- For economy, should you rent sound equipment, or purchase your own?

SHOOTING SINGLE OR DOUBLE SYSTEM

Single system shooting (camera recording both picture and sound) is common in low budget documentary work, but hazardous for run-and-gun shooting since the camera and *fishpole* (microphone boom) operator are linked together by cables, which take careful management.

Double system shooting means using a separate audio recorder, so sound and camera can operate freely and unattached (Figure 28-1). This lets you,

- Move together or separately at will.
- Record better quality sound.
- Get easier and more representative headphone monitoring by the recordist.
- Shoot wild tracks as you need them.

However,

- Someone, probably the director, will need to operate a clapperboard (as a sync marker).
- You may need extra personnel to operate more elaborate equipment, and keep records. Without logs, syncing sound and picture in postproduction can turn into a nightmare.
- Using a clapperboard will make your operation more visible and intrusive, but you can use mike-taps and low voice announcements instead.

CREEPING SYNC

Over time, recorder and camera may drift out of sync. You may detect creeping sync in the computer after 5 minutes running time, or it may only be discernible after an hour or two. *Creeping sync* is apparent to the eye once sound and action are more than two frames apart, which means only $1/15^{th}$ of a second out of sync. Only by advance testing can you know whether you are susceptible. Find out by shooting a 30-minute take; place a clapper front and end, then sync sound and picture and see whether the second clapper is still in sync 30 minutes later.

FIGURE 28-1

Using double system shooting, the sound operator is self-contained with her own recorder, and can operate near or far from the camera. (*Camille Zurcher/Colectivo Nomada.*)

USING THE CAMERA TO RECORD SOUND

Unless you use a professional-level camcorder with sturdy XLR connector inputs and businesslike VU meters, be ready for the following from lesser cameras:

- Flimsy input sockets.
- Inaccessible controls for changing input level while shooting.
- Input metering that is indefinite or misleading.
- Poor signal-to-noise ratio.
- "Hunting" for level when set to automatic level and mike input is low.
- Headphone output auto level, underpowered, or poor quality.

SOUND RECORDERS

Documentary often operates in marginal situations, and substandard sound can tip the balance into unintelligibility, so where possible, use double system recording.

LOCATION RECORDERS

Using a separate recorder puts the whole job in the hands of someone who is concentrating on sound, where it belongs. Digital audio, like video, can either record raw (uncompressed information, which takes up a lot of hard drive or memory card space) or use a codec to condense the files into less recording space. Your recorder must let you monitor through ear-enclosing headphones, and offer a choice of codecs so you can output files compatible with your editing system. Here's a link to an article comparing the different audio codecs and the operating systems that handle them: http://en.wikipedia.org/wiki/Comparison_of_audio_codecs.

For reliability and high quality recording, the Nagra VI is from the long established, top of the line Nagra range (Figure 28-2, www.nagraaudio.com). Lower-budget productions might use the 4-track Sound Devices 744T which records on to a hard disk or flash card (Figure 28-3 www.sounddevices.com/products/744t.htm). There is also the highly capable stereo Tascam range www.tascam.com which records to flash cards, and locks to external timecode for inter-machine syncing. Those on stringent budgets can use the Zoom H6 which offers six channels of recording and four XLR microphone inputs (Figure 28-4). Sound recorders feature extensively in radio and music recording, so there is a good range on offer. If you buy your own, comparison-shop for features, and put ruggedness, XLR connectors, and a choice of output codecs high on your list. Film equipment takes a beating, so a light plastic housing won't last long.

Three backup measures that may save you:

a) Any material shot on flash cards or hard drives should be quickly backed up on to a computer hard drive array in case the recording medium fails, gets lost, or recorded over.

b) When shooting with a mono mike feeding into a 2-channel recording system, use a "Y" connector to split its input across both channels. Then adjust one channel to peak at, say, −6 dB, and the other to under-record somewhat. Should your main channel overload, the second track stands ready as an undistorted alternative.

c) When shooting double system, let the camera's deck mike record *scratch* (catch-as-catch-can) sound too. You then have (a) a fallback track in case your main audio recorder fails, and (b) a guide-track as reference when syncing up poorly identified track material from the main recorder.

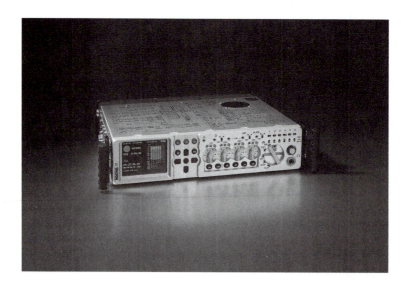

FIGURE 28-2 ———————————————————————————————————

Nagra VI, an outstanding sound recorder. (*Photo courtesy of Nagra, a Kudelski Group Company.*)

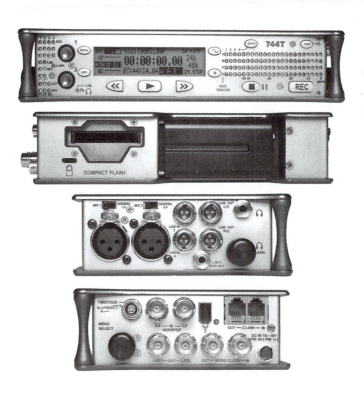

FIGURE 28-3 ———————————————————————————————————

The 4-track Sound Devices 744T records to a hard disk or flash card. (*Copyright Sound Devices, LLC—used with permission.*)

FIGURE 28-4

The Zoom H6 offers four XLR microphone inputs and six channels of recording total. An H6 is being used in Figure 28-1.

SOUND CODECS

Digital sound recording uses a variety of *codecs* and *sampling rates*. Sampling refers to the refresh rate the system uses as it draws sound waveforms. For sound fidelity, set your sound sampling rate to 48K or above (48,000 waveform re-draws per second). Stay consistent throughout your shoot because some editing software will gag if you feed it mixed sample rates.

SOUND MIXERS

If you are shooting a conference or concert, and need to combine and balance several mike inputs, you'll need a location mixer. This is because most cameras are limited to two sound channels. Choose a battery-powered mixer that you can sling over your shoulder, but remember that you become far less mobile as you cobble more sound equipment together. Professional Sound Corporation (PSC) makes excellent 4- and 8-channel portable mixers, as do Wendt (www.wendtinc.net/index.htm) and Shure www.shure.com/ProAudio/index.htm). In value for money, look at Mackie www.mackie.com or Sound Excellence http://soundexcellence.com whose ENG-44A is a modestly priced, serviceable battery-powered portable mixer with four inputs and two outputs (Figure 28-5).

EQ AND ROLL-OFF

It is not a good practice to adjust equalization (EQ) as you record. You may however *roll-off* (reduce in advance) the excessive bass of traffic, since this can mis-register in the level meter and lead to distortion. Many microphones and sound mixers have a bass roll-off or low-cut switch for this very purpose. If in doubt, record "flat" (all frequencies equally) and defer EQ to the postproduction stage.

FIGURE 28-5

Sound Excellence's ENG-44A is a modestly priced portable mixer with four inputs and two outputs. (*Photo courtesy of Sound Excellence, LLC.*)

VOLUME UNIT (VU) METERS

As we said in **Chapter 10: Capturing Sound**, most VU meters are *averaging* meters, that is, they display average sound levels with a slight time lag, which approximates the way the human ear registers sound. They do not reflect peaks accurately, where the killer distortion sets in, so look for a supplementary red LED light that gives an immediate readout of peaking. Alternatively you may have a whole bar of LEDs in a display, with sound levels beginning in green, transitioning through the caution area of orange, and peaking dangerously in red. Play back anything dubious on the spot.

WHEN THE MIXER FEEDS INTO THE CAMERA

Calibrating a supplementary mixer can be tricky, so read the manual. Generally you use the mixer's inbuilt tone-generator to set a saturation recording level of 0 dB on its VU meter. Next feed the mixer output signal into the camera's line level input. Manually adjust the camera's manual input levels to also register a 0 dB reading. Record a minute of tone, then check the recording with your editing program's playback to verify that saturation recording is indeed 0 dB. If it's off, lower the camera input until 0 db at the mixer VU meter will handle a peak of any frequency without distorting.

PEAK TESTS

In mike recording tests, adjust mixer input levels so normal speech registers at −6 dB on the VU meter, and peaks don't stray into the red area. Using editing software, listen back to your tracks to check speech quality, footsteps, door slams, etc. Experiment with deliberate overloads (peaking beyond 0 dB) to discover where audible distortion sets in and which frequencies seem most vulnerable. If absolutely necessary, *ride gain* (that is, adjust recording level during recording) to keep from peaking into the red. This is usually difficult or impossible with camera-only recording.

MULTIPLE MIKE INPUTS

If you cover several speakers with several mikes and leave all mixer channels equally open, all the mikes' ambiences sum together to create a dull roar. To minimize this, hold every channel low if nobody is using it, and raise and lower each mike as the person assigned to it speaks. If, however, you can record each mike into its own channel of a multichannel recorder, you can set all channels to record at full level, mixing them selectively later as needed.

PHASING

Multiple mikes whose inputs combine into a common recording channel can create *phasing*. This shows as recorded sound pulsing rather than holding steady as it should. This is caused by further and nearer mikes picking up the same source but in different phase relationships, so that one periodically cancels out the other. Try reducing the number of mikes involved in pickup.

RECORDING STEREO

Unless you have studied the engineering parameters for stereo or 5.1 recording, don't even attempt setting up multiple mikes. There's even one deadly setup in which one channel cancels out the other, and stereo is reduced to mono!

PHANTOM POWER

If a mike mysteriously refuses to work, suspect there is no phantom power present to activate the mike (see **Chapter 10: Capturing Sound**).

FIGURE 28-6

The Denecke smart slate electronic clapper system. The timecode numbers are in hours, minutes, seconds, and frames. (*Photo courtesy of Denecke, Inc.*)

SMART SLATES

A smart slate is a clapperboard containing a crystal-controlled timecode display (Figure 28-6). The numbers move when you raise the slate bar, and freeze when you close it. For double system shooting this makes syncing sound to its timecoded picture easy, but (a) the camera and the recorder must be compatible with the smart slate, and (b) their operators must remember to *jam sync* (synchronize) their timecode generators every morning, since they drift apart over time. Carry a traditional clapperboard in case the electronic wizardry goes on strike.

SOUND MONITORING

Professional quality, ear-enclosing headphones that isolate the user from the surrounding world are a necessity for monitoring your work. Headphones made by Sony and Sennheiser are popular with professionals (Figure 28-7). Be aware that,

FIGURE 28-7

Sennheiser® HD-25 ear-enclosing headphones. (*Photo courtesy of Sennheiser Electronic Corp.*)

- Camera outputs to headphones can be inadequate in level.
- You are probably only able to monitor sound as it enters the recorder, and cannot hear overload distortion, which happens during the recording process.
- Some professional equipment lets you verify recording quality by letting you monitor the actual recording, but with a slight playback delay.

- Headphone circuitry may include a compressor circuit that gives a false impression of the recording dynamics.
- Use headphones only to monitor audio content. Use the level meters (VU or Peak) to monitor the strength of the incoming sound levels.

MICROPHONE TYPES

Most documentary sound shooting uses cardioid and hyper-cardioid directional mikes, as well as lavalier omni-directional body mikes. They are made by a range of manufacturers such as Neumann, Sennheiser, AKG, Audio Technica, Beyer Dynamic, ElectroVoice, Schoeps, and Shure. Each mike type has a different *pickup pattern*, which determines how much off-axis sound it accepts.

CARDIOID

This kind of mike, as we saw in Figure 10-13 in **Chapter 10: Capturing Sound**, gets its name from its heart-shaped response pattern. Cardioid mikes are thus directional and have quite a broad angle of acceptance. Dynamic cardioids are an older design that—unlike sensitive, battery-powered electret condenser mikes—are completely sound-powered. Though less sensitive, they are rugged and will endure very loud transients, rough handling, and temperature or moisture extremes that would disable their more delicate cousins.

SHOTGUN

The hyper-cardioid or *shotgun* mike is ultra-directional and achieves this by discriminating strongly against off-axis sound. Named for their rifle appearance, shotguns like the Neumann KMR-82i or the Sennheiser MKH-70 (an industry favorite) use interference tube serrations to suppress off-axis sound. The polar pattern for a Sennheiser MKH-70 (Figure 28-8) reveals that its off-axis discrimination varies sightly according to frequency, a feature common to most mikes.

Shotguns, like telephoto lenses, tend to squeeze background and foreground together, so you must watch for sound originating from behind the subject. However, by angling the mike downward, you might be able to lower that idling truck motor, once it is out of the mike's "line of sight."

Use a hyper-cardioid to favor a sound source over others competing from other axes, such as a group of speakers in a noisy street. Since the fall-off between on-axis and off-axis sound is considerable for hyper-cardioids, you must pan the mike quickly to any new speaker in a group. Ultra-directional miking can become a handicap if people in a group are speaking unpredictably and from multiple directions. It that case, try a regular cardioid or even an omni-directional mike. Expect shorter hyper-cardioids to have a wider angle of acceptance than their longer brethren.

LAVALIER

The omni-directional lavalier is normally a miniature electret condenser mike that clips to a lapel or dress front (Figure 28-9). They are highly sensitive, full spectrum, and sometimes physically tiny, occasionally no more than a match-head. With each lavalier comes a small globular foam windscreen that fits over the mike to inhibit popping on speech plosives. If air currents become troublesome, wrap the "lav" in cheesecloth or bury it in the wearer's clothing. You can plug a "lav" into a microphone input, but for full mobility, it will have its own wireless transmitter (Figure 28-10). For easy disconnection between bouts of filming, tape the lav's XLR connector to the wearer's ankle.

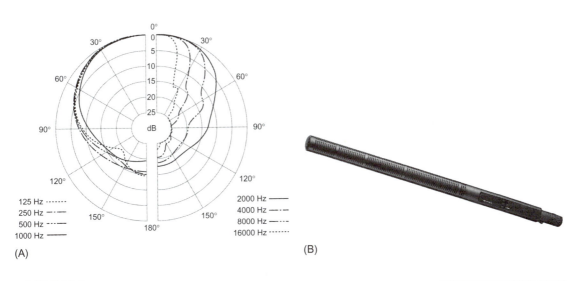

FIGURE 28-8

The polar pattern for the Sennheiser MKH-70 reveals off-axis discrimination that varies slightly according to frequency, a feature common to all mikes. (*Images courtesy of Sennheiser Electronic Corp.*)

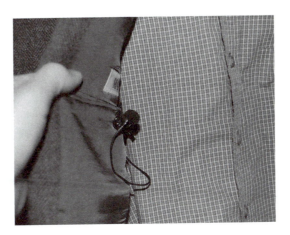

FIGURE 28-9

The omni-directional lavalier clips to clothing and can remain out of view.

WIRELESS MIKES

If several participants each have a wireless lavalier being picked up by a receiver plugged into a mixing desk, you should be able to confidently record several people on the move. Well, yes and no. Wireless mikes, like mobile phones, are occasionally vulnerable to radio frequency interference, emergency service transmitters, dead spots, and so on. They also take setup time, gobble batteries, and need channel changes, all taking time and expertise. So think of them as useful but occasionally treacherous. Check experienced users' comments on the Internet concerning pros and cons of particular models—for instance, how many radio channel alternatives a system should have, and how automatically and seamlessly it changes channels when encountering transmission difficulties.

MICROPHONE PLACEMENT

LAVALIER

Fix a lavalier out of sight in a speaker's clothing, if you can. Don't mount it too close to the speaker's mouth, because head-turns will register as drastic shifts in loudness. Sometimes when you must cover a group of individuals speaking unpredictably, hang a lavalier above them and make use of its omni-directional properties.

USING THE FISHPOLE

Your choice of microphone boom or fishpole is between aluminum and carbon fiber. The latter is less resonant and lighter, which will mean a lot to its handler (Figure 28-11). Expect to pay more for the convenience of having the cable pass through the pole's interior. Wherever the cable goes, guard against it tapping the pole during movement, since the mike will pick this up.

When lighting and composition allow, mike from above, as discussed in **Chapter 10: Capturing Sound**. It gives a nice sense of changing sound perspectives, and speech levels will be high in relation to footsteps, and movements by body and hands. You can also mike from either side of the frame, or from below. In the latter case, body movements may be disturbingly loud in relation to speech.

WHAT TO RENT AND WHAT TO OWN

If you are filming intensively and over a long period, it may pay you to purchase sound equipment rather than rent it. Owning your own editing setup is mandatory, and if you must shoot at short notice, owning your own camera may be unavoidable too. Something better in the sound world isn't going to suddenly appear—as happens with heartbreaking frequency with cameras.

FIGURE 28-10

A lavalier mike, its transmitter and receiver.

FIGURE 28-11

A K-Tek boom pole. Its five carbon fiber sections extend to 16 feet. (*Photo courtesy of K-Tek.*)

Thus, having your own set of basic mikes, mixer, and tripod may all make economic sense too. Anything else that you will use infrequently, such as wireless mikes, exotic lighting, or expensive camera supports, is better rented.

CHAPTER 29

ORGANIZATION, CREW, AND PROCEDURES FOR THE LARGER PRODUCTION

Successful small groups are apt to grow into larger organizations whose shooting requires the traditional divisions of labor. At the very least you will need a production department able to manage your logistics and finances, and additional crew members to assist the sound recordist and camera operator/director of photography. Series co-production for international markets, however, is now big business and every aspect of filmmaking has had to expand. Ambitious history or science productions can be as elaborate and costly to mount as fiction feature films, and a series or feature-length documentary may use actors, scripts, and a specialized crew. Now you need a whole production department.

OUTREACH

International production usually involves elaborate support from foundations, advance commitments by television or cable providers, and publicity, festival, international showings, and "outreach" after it. Funding agencies will expect your film or film series to lead an active after-life with supplementary publications and special showings that serve special interest groups.

PRODUCTION DEPARTMENT

Good production staff are organized, compulsive list keepers, socially adept and businesslike, and able to scan and correlate a number of activities. They can juggle priorities; make decisions involving time, effort, and money; and are unintimidated by officialdom.

PRODUCER

The effective producer is socially adept and a highly articulate salesperson. He or she presents film ideas and sample films, and makes pitches at documentary marketplaces such as the Amsterdam International Documentary Festival or the IFP (Independent Feature Project) Market in New York.

The producer makes deals with the commissioning editors from cable and television channels at such gatherings, something many filmmakers are diffident about doing. Television representatives, hunting new ideas and talent-scouting for promising filmmakers, then compete to develop co-financing deals for the products they want. An independent producer might work in an urban area with a number of directors. With ten directors, say, there might be upward of 30 viable documentary ideas to shop around at any given time.

The ideal producer combines the abilities of agent, salesperson, production manager (if he or she works closely with productions), and accountant. She or he knows the changing world of documentary and its audiences, can estimate and monitor costs during production, and can confidently discuss all aspects of proposals and co-financing. A producer ensures that the finished product gets full publicity, since without a determined effort publicizing their existence, films can sink without a trace.

All this takes a special temperament, and a producer should never be a wannabe director. He or she should love public service and nurturing production. Anyone with good taste and a stable of impressive production groups will, like a literary agent, become trusted and sought after by overworked commissioning editors, who in their search for original work look to the best producers.

In a large organization producers are often senior administrators. In the field, you may work with assistant producers, a *line producer* (assigned only to the production and who probably manages the budget and negotiates with vendors), as well as a *unit production manager* or UPM. While producers have creative input and even creative control, the rest of their staff contribute logistical assistance and financial management.

UNIT PRODUCTION MANAGER (UPM)

A necessity for any complex project, he or she lightens the load on the director by managing all the production arrangements. The UPM monitors cash flow, has contingency plans when bad weather stymies exterior shooting, and chases progress. Arrangements they make might include locating overnight accommodations, booking rented equipment at the best prices, securing location or other permissions, making up a shooting schedule (with the director), making travel arrangements, and locating food and accommodation near the shoot. In a large organization the UPM may cover several productions and be represented in your production unit by a *line producer*. A UPM acquires the best experience to become a producer.

SOUND AND CAMERA ASSISTANCE

SOUND ASSISTANTS

More sound personnel become necessary once you shoot double system or cover complex situations such as scripted re-enactments or large group activities (see **Chapter 28: Advanced Location Sound**). If production is to be efficient there is more gear to handle, greater complexity in the setups, and more records to keep. If you shoot on a stage, then a boom operator will be necessary—someone able to follow a script and precisely move the mike in time for each incoming line—a highly skilled operation.

CAMERA ASSISTANT

Particularly if you are shooting on film, there may be one or two camera assistants, whose jobs involve setup, follow focusing, marking takes, and transporting equipment ready for setup again.

They are responsible too for keeping the camera aperture and its lenses clean, and keeping logs on material shot.

GRIP

Grips fetch, carry, set up (mostly electrical and camera equipment), and when the camera uses a dolly or crane to take mobile shots they have the highly skilled and coordinated job of moving the camera support to precisely worked-out positions. Grips need to be strong, practical, organized, and willing. On the minimal crew, they help rig lighting or sound equipment.

GAFFER

The gaffer is an expert in rigging and maintaining lighting equipment, and knows how to split electrical loads so lighting runs off light-duty household supplies without starting fires or plunging neighbors into darkness. Good gaffers carry a bewildering assortment of clamps, gadgets, and small tools. Resourceful by nature, they sometimes emerge as mainstays of the unit. During a BBC night shooting sequence in England, I once saw a boy stumble behind the lights and hurt his knee. Having been told to stay silent during shooting, he doubled over, clutching his knee in mute agony. The kindly electrician (as the gaffer is called in Britain) swooped silently out of the gloom and cradled him in his arms until the shot was finished.

Usually the director of photography (DP) has a favorite gaffer, and the two work symbiotically, sometimes for life. Experienced gaffers know their DP's style and preferences, and can prelight ahead of a unit's arrival. Teams of long association gradually dispense with spoken language.

INTERNS

Organizations of all sizes often take *interns* (unpaid or low paid assistants) from a nearby film school—which is a great way for students to get experience, but also a way for the unscrupulous to get cheap labor. Most internships arise from a laudable desire to teach "the business" to the next generation. This can provide a capstone to your education, an immersion in professional procedures and etiquette, and a way to become known to local professionals. If they like you and your work, this can turn into your first job. A reputable film school in a large city will place its best students in internships.

PROCEDURES

Some of the procedures below will be beyond the capacities of a one- or two-person shoot, but necessary for a larger unit that verges on feature film production and uses double system shooting, elaborate lighting, and a dolly or other camera support. Scripted docudrama or historical reconstruction using actors will need the most technical support of all.

SYNC USING A CLAPPERBOARD

The traditional sync marking system is the archetypal wooden *slate*, or *clapperboard*, with a closing bar on top (Figure 29-1). With its piece of chalk and only a hinge to go wrong, it is exquisitely low-tech. The clapperboard rite serves various functions:

Picture. The inscription identifies the production name and shot numbers as they enter the industrial pipeline called *workflow*. In addition to the postproduction operation, this may include a film laboratory or animation studio. On complex productions, the slate carries

FIGURE 29-1

The traditional film clapperboard with not much to go wrong.

information for image quality-control experts in film labs or video studios, such as a *gray scale*, white and black as a contrast reference, and a *standard color chart*.

Sound. The operator's voice announcement "Shot 64 take 2" identifies the track for the sound transfer or digitizing personnel, and the snap of the clapper closing becomes the all-important sync reference.

SHOT IDENTIFICATION

Keep logs of important information as you shoot. Digital cameras generate the Society of Motion Picture and Television Engineers (SMPTE) electronic color chart, called *color bars*, often recorded as a reference at the head of each memory storage. The amount and type of written records vary according to how elaborate your sound recording is:

Single system: For single system video production, when it uses a slate at all, only a camera log is necessary to keep track of sound and picture, since both are recorded together on the same media. The camera assistant (if there is one) keeps a master log recording timecode readings, camera setup information, and content. Often no log is possible, so you simply shoot, then log content and timecode later.

Double system: Here you treat the operation like film and use the full clapperboard procedure to identify both sound and picture. This means keeping camera and sound logs. Sound being recorded separately, the recordist also compiles wild tracks, sound effects, or atmosphere recordings. Camera and sound recorder thus consume memory media at different rates and get out of numerical step. On the camera side, material is sometimes shot silent for convenience.

ALTERNATIVE NUMBERING SYSTEMS

There are two philosophies in use for numbering camera and sound setups:

Scene/Setup/Take system. This system, favored in Hollywood, might apply to a scripted docu-drama. Large organizations, using many people to make complex productions, need lengthy factory part numbers. Every slate number refers to a scene number in a written script—for example: "Scene 104A, shot 16, take 3." For the small, flexible production, this is overkill.

Cumulative Setup/Take system. This system, used universally in documentaries, also prevails in much European feature filmmaking. Shooting simply begins at slate 1-1. Each new camera setup or lens change merits a new setup number, and each new attempt gets a new take number (for example: "1 take 2," written "1-2"). For the overstretched small crew this is ideal since nobody needs to coordinate numbers with a script, or wrestle with renumbering the inevitable script departures.

SYNCING UP DAILIES

A clapperboard serves several functions, but its most important is to provide a sync reference. In double system shooting, sound and picture are shot by separate equipment and their products are not united until the editing stage. To sync sound with picture, the editor aligns the "snap" sound of the slate closing with the picture frame where the bar has just closed.

SHOOTING LOGS

Documentation helps to direct the material to the right place in the workflow chain, and to inform everyone concerned what to expect or do. A less obvious log function is to record (by its serial number) which piece of equipment made which recording. Should you hear a strange hum, or see a picture hue problem, you can quickly withdraw the offending equipment and have it tested. Shooting of any elaboration requires two kinds of log (see blanks at the website www.directingthe-documentary.com):

Camera log: Kept by the *assistant cinematographer* (AC), the log records each take's contents by slate, take, and timecode readings for each new unit of recording medium (P2 memory, hard disk, etc.). Its number and information will provide a vital overview during editing.

Sound log: Kept by the *sound recordist*, this log records slate and take numbers, and whether each track is sync or *wild track* (non-sync voice or effects recording). The sound log is important to whoever digitizes from the original storage materials (flash memory, hard disk, etc.) since some material will sync to picture, and some not.

THE COUNTDOWN TO SHOOTING

When you shoot double system, and use a clapperboard marking system, there is an unvarying ritual at the beginning of each take.

1. The director calls "Stand by to roll camera."
2. The clapper operator holds the clapperboard (aka clap-sticks) in front of the subject, positioned to be clearly visible to the camera.
3. The camera operator turns on the camera, says "Camera rolling" and calls out "Roll sound."
4. The sound recordist turns on the recorder, waits a moment for it to stabilize, then calls out "Speed."

5. The camera operator calls, "Mark it."

6. The clapper operator announces the scene and take number, closes the clapper with a bang, and immediately exits frame.

7. The director can now say, "Action."

STARTING WITHOUT A CLAPPER

If you shoot bird mating dances, or drug dealers working covertly on a street corner, you don't want to advertize what your camera is doing. You simply whisper or give a hand signal signifying "start rolling" and then, once the action is complete, your crew can make a sync reference in one of two ways:

Mike taps: The recordist puts the mike into frame, says "end slate," speaks the slate and take number, and taps the mike more than once so the impact of finger meeting mike is clearly visible to the camera.

Board on end (BOE): The camera assistant presents the clapperboard, but upside down, and calls out the scene number, adding "Board on end" or "End slate." The assistant then claps the bar, after which the director can call "Cut!"

When it comes to syncing up end-clapped sound material with its action, there may only be the mike tap, or end clapper, to identify what it is. You end-sync the take, then back up to define its beginning. If there is much end-clap material, there can be plentiful opportunity for confusion.

HANDS-ON LEARNING

For **Personal Release** and **Location Agreement** forms, as well **as Camera** and **Sound Logs**, see under Miscellaneous at the book's website.

CHAPTER 30

ADVANCED DIRECTING

The word "directing" suggests ordering people around, and is particularly misleading for documentary since you guide or lead the process, rather than command it. Your job is to know what motivates people, what psychological blocs you must remove, and what subtle pressures you can exert to catalyze behavior, or uncover hidden narratives. As leadership, this is very indirect. How best to prepare yourself?

Acting experience of any kind, particularly improvisation, is most valuable because it gives you firsthand experience of doing things in front of others, and in response to them. This is what your documentary participants will have to do for you. To understand them, it helps to be familiar with the ideas of the Russian acting and drama theorist Constantin Stanislavski (1863–1938). His work clarifies the psychological difficulties that bedevil anyone under intense scrutiny, and makes apparent what practical steps exist—whether you are an actor, director, or documentary participant—to alleviate the paralyzing curse of self-consciousness.

WHAT MAKES US FEEL NORMAL

THE MIND–BODY CONNECTION

The relative comfort we feel in everyday life depends on assumptions about our function, identity, and worth in the eyes of others. In unfamiliar social situations our psychological equilibrium is apt to suddenly depart, as everyone has experienced. Through his study of acting, Stanislavski discovered aspects of human psychology that are very helpful to nonfiction film directors.

Certain actors excelled because they had invented ways to ward off the self-doubt that is apt to cripple anyone in the public eye. From questioning them, Stanislavski discovered that each had found particular work to occupy their minds and bodies, and as a result could put all their mental energy into pursuing their character's actions, mental processes, and interactions with others. By stilling the judgmental self, they could play their parts naturally and believably, and function as normally as if they were alone. Today, actors are trained to sustain psychological *focus* by maintaining an inner dialogue "in character," and, most importantly, by keeping up a stream of their character's physical and mental tasks. Paradoxically, these actions awaken genuine feeling, whereas an actor who tries to reach directly for feeling hits a wall. Stanislavski realized that emotions arise out of actions, and that going through certain actions awakens accompanying emotions.

What impedes the free movement of this psychic interplay is the neurotic ego, always ready to judge how one is doing. In new or unexpected situations it pops up like a jack-in-the-box, creating insecurity of all kinds, and disrupting the normality of relaxed concentration. When we are being watched, any opportunity for unstructured thought, even the fear of losing focus, allows the ever-anxious, ever critical mind and judging mind to rush in. Immediately the unlucky actor loses conviction in everything he says and does, and since no inner state is without an outer manifestation—another Stanislavski observation—the audience straightaway notices something is amiss. The fiction director is there to help remove whatever is breaking the actor's focus.

Your function as a documentary director is similar. Apply these simple human principles to directing documentary, and,

- A person's body language tells you whether they are unified and focused, or divided and troubled. Is the filming situation causing it, or something else?
- You can lower participants' self-consciousness by giving them familiar mental or physical work to do.
- The most intense focus for an actor or documentary participant—and thus the greatest relaxation—comes from pursuing something compelling, since this shuts out other forms of consciousness.

DOING WHAT COMES NATURALLY

To help participants take part naturally and spontaneously, you must reiterate trustworthy reasons for making the film. You must ensure that the participant is doing something comfortably routine, or something that involves him or her with its special meaning. A sheltered middle-aged couple, for example, will happily fall into a recurring discussion about which food is best for the dog's arthritis. A self-conscious construction foreman, asked to supervise the loading of a heavy steel beam, will immediately fall naturally back into his officious everyday self.

In quite a short time, participants become used to working with you, and come to enjoy being who they are in the presence of your camera and your crew. I once filmed elderly miners discussing the bitter days of a strike, one in which they had derailed a train manned by "scabs" or strikebreakers. We shot them outside their old mine, and because they were reliving the deepest, most divisive issues in their lives, they were completely oblivious of the camera even though it came within feet of their faces.

SELF-IMAGE AND SELF-CONSCIOUSNESS

The easiest people to work with are those unmindful of their effect on others. Old people and small children can be naturally themselves because there is no ego, no internal censor at work. Knowing this, you can predict who lies at the other end of the scale, and will need help to get over their self-consciousness. Those with nervous mannerisms who are compulsively careful of their appearance won't settle easily in front of a camera. During a street interview with an elderly lady, I saw her completely lose focus. I was puzzled until I saw how, in mid-sentence, she began removing the hair net she realized she was still wearing.

The more "proper" someone feels they must look, the less flexible, impulsive, and openly communicative they will be. But care and circumspection were this lady's stamp, so her action was so wonderfully representative that her friends would have smiled in recognition. Notice that the pressure of the camera's presence did *not* make her behave uncharacteristically.

"Doesn't the camera change people?" people often ask. Yes, it does, but only in aspect or degree. This can go either way—toward self-consciousness or toward self-revelation. Indeed the camera may catalyze an honesty and depth of feeling never before seen by a participant's closest friends and family. Often when the "history box" fulfills the human craving for recognition, the floodgates open. The implications are most important:

- You don't need to be unduly protective of participants. People know their boundaries and seldom ever go beyond their capacities.
- Somewhere, lurking in everyone, is the urge to confess, to come clean, to tell all.
- Filming a revelation doesn't mean you must use it. You and your advisers can thoroughly consider the consequences of using (or not using) the footage later.

Some exceptions:

- Consider erasing anything that would be damaging to a participant if it fell into the wrong hands. To keep it and use it, you need the participant's *informed consent* (that is, you fully and carefully explain the likely consequences and ask the participant whether he/she is willing to give you permission to use it).
- If someone else, not you, has editorial control of your material, keep nothing that can potentially do damage. If it's taken out of your hands, used, and causes your participant harm, you will be held responsible, not the executive who decided to use it.
- Some people even say, if you shoot it, you'll use it. So, if you don't trust yourself to abstain, don't shoot it!

HABITS OF BEING

Particular jobs attract particular kinds of personality, and some employment instills mannerisms and self-awarenesses that can be a liability in filmmaking. Lecturers address invisible multitudes instead of talking personably and one-on-one, as they did during research. Officials unused to making public statements suddenly go in dread of crossing their superiors, and become excruciatingly circular and tentative. This is fine if that is what you want to show, but if it's not, then you must estimate what is deeply ingrained habit, and what is a misperception about filming. A common notion is that one must project the voice. If so, move the camera closer and ask for a more intimate mode of conversation. You can also try saying, "There is only one person, me, listening to you. Talk only to me."

If the participant cannot respond to direction, a little playback may do the trick. People seeing and hearing themselves for the first time are usually shocked, so only ever expose an unsatisfactory "performance" supportively, in private, and as a last resort.

Sometimes you will get someone whose concept of being in film makes them valiantly project *personality*. If you are making a film about stage mothers, you could hardly ask for anything more revealing.

KEYS TO DIRECTING PEOPLE

The skills used to direct actors in fiction, and those in a documentary (whom Bill Nichols calls "social actors"), are not radically different:

- Don't ask them to *be* anything (be natural, be normal, etc.). Asking someone to "just be yourself" sets anxious people worrying. What did he really mean? How does she see me? And which self does he want?
- Make sure that anyone on camera has appropriate tasks to occupy them in mind and body.

FIGURE 30-1

A mother and daughter put at ease in *Au Pair to Paris*.

- Ask people to do only what is organic to their normal life.
- If you plan to cut from location to location, you may need to remind participants where we last saw them, and what they were doing and saying before the new scene.

One cannot choose what to be, only what to do. Once when filming a mother and daughter in the kitchen together at night, I saw they were camera-conscious. In a moment of inspiration, I asked them to resume a recent disagreement. They went straight into a friendly argument, and became visibly at ease. I realized they were *enjoying* the sensation of re-enacting their habitual roles (Figure 30-1).

When making a "transparent" film (one designed to look as though there is no observing camera or crew) tell participants to,

- Ignore the camera and crew's presence.
- Not to worry about mistakes or silences since we shoot far more than we use, and edit everything down.

Both requests relieve participants from feeling they must "play to the audience." The crew helps by avoiding eye contact, concentrating on their jobs, and giving no facial or verbal feedback.

When making a reflexive film, tell participants that,

- You are filming to catch things as they happen.
- They can talk to you or to the camera as they wish.
- They can go wherever they need to go, do whatever they need to do, while filming.
- Nothing is off limits, and no thought or subject of conversation is disallowed.

FIGURE 30-2

Nick Broomfield chastised as an upstart by the Leader

In Nick Broomfield's *The Leader, His Driver and the Driver's Wife* (GB, 1991, Figure 30-2) the director uses boyish disingenuousness to draw out the South African white supremacist leader. Eugene Terre'blanche (sic) is such an egomaniac that he falls for Broomfield's provocation, with hilariously revealing consequences when he acts like a general chastising a mere upstart.

Directorial manipulation must be justified and well judged, or the audience becomes uneasy. There are moments of this discomfort in Ross McElwee's otherwise very sophisticated and highly influential *Sherman's March* (USA, 1989), an autobiographical film about searching for a wife. The director's self-presentation plays up his innocence, but merely holding a camera confers power, so we sometimes worry on behalf of the young women he courts (Figure 30-3).

SOCIAL AND FORMAL ISSUES

ADVANTAGES OF THE SMALL CREW

Aided by compact digital equipment that needs little lighting, we are back in the intimate shooting conditions of the early twentieth century, which is perhaps why documentaries keep getting more effective. The smaller, more human scale lets us make films in a quirkier, more individual way—surely a major development. Fewer crewmembers, however, means that the qualities of those who remain are vital. Nothing affects your fortunes more than choosing collaborators wisely.

HAVING OR LOSING AUTHORITY

A major anxiety when you start directing is feeling you lack the clout to do so. Authority is not, after all, something you can switch on when you need it, especially if you sense a hostility in those

FIGURE 30-3

Holding a camera gives a power advantage in *Sherman's March*.

you presume to lead. How you collaborate with differing personalities is always a sensitive matter, but never an insurmountable one among those who love their work. Most who choose to work in documentary are mature and dedicated people, so it is unwise to try to fool them or make claims beyond your knowledge.

Directing in a large organization you may realize, as I once did, that you are the outsider leading resentful insiders. As the leader and parental figure, you may deliberately be made to feel inadequate. Every human situation has its pecking order: a young director should expect veiled hostility from older crewmembers; a woman should be ready for patronizing behavior from male subordinates, as should a foreigner from the locals. This is bound to happen sometime, so know your rights and insist on them whenever you sense your crew is testing you. All tiresomely human, but watch your back!

Counter these threats—real or imagined—by choosing coworkers carefully whenever you can, and consulting them as respected partners. Particularly when you lead a new unit, start coolly and formally. This implies that everyone is professional and knows the boundaries of their responsibilities. Later, you can gradually relax and bring everyone closer during the intense, shared experience of filmmaking.

If instead you start informally, and then discover that someone in the unit is lax or subtly undermining your authority, it will be difficult to tighten up without generating resentment.

To have authority really means being respected; it means behaving as though you felt confident ("fake it until you make it"). You, not your coworkers, are responsible for your confidence issues. It means having the humility to ask for help or advice when you need it, and sometime it will mean standing by tough decisions or warning intuitions. Your crew depends on your judgment, and needs to feel that though you may bend under load, you won't break. Stay abreast of their concerns and problems, and be sure to make your own organizational work impeccable.

USING SOCIAL TIMES AND BREAKS

A shared intensity of purpose usually binds everyone together during a shoot. Try to maintain this during meals or rest periods by keeping crew and participants together when everyone is relaxing. This is often the time when ideas, memories, and associations emerge. Conserved and encouraged, this fellowship increases humor and intimate communication, and energizes even a weary crew. Make a point of asking questions of your crew: it helps make them feel connected and respected. They notice things through the camera, or through the sound person's headphones because they are monitoring different planes of reality from you, and pick up different nuances.

SHARING IN ALL THINGS

Ideally, the crew attends all major postproduction screenings. This is when the growth and internal complexity of the film emerges, and it is here that the comprehensiveness of your work begins to show. Crewmembers learn not only about the nature of their contributions, but about the larger organism of documentary itself, which is not necessarily taught during a craft education and is not apparent during routine shooting. In a crew that respects each other, everyone supports and learns from everyone else. All for one, and one for all.

CAMERA ISSUES AND POINT OF VIEW

COMPROMISES FOR THE CAMERA

When shooting action sequences, you may need to ask people to slow down or control their movements, since tightly framed movement looks 20 percent to 30 percent faster than it really is. Worse, the operator's fanciest footwork cannot keep a hand framed and in focus if its owner moves too fast. Documentary participants can often modify their actions without a trace of self-consciousness once they begin enjoying their collaboration with the filming. You see this enjoyment radiating from Nanook, who seems nothing if not authentic as he acts the part of an Inuit from an earlier generation.

How willing are you to intrude to get a result that is visually and choreographically accomplished? The ethnographer shuns such intrusion, and most documentarians have some of the ethnographer in them. But, as Jean-Luc Godard observed, "You can either start with fiction, or with documentary. But whichever you start with, you will inevitably find the other."[1]

CAMERA AS PASSPORT

People in public places often defer to anyone holding a camera, especially when it looks professional. Thus, when you shoot in crowds, don't fear going where you would not normally enter. The camera is your passport: let its needs draw you to the front of a crowd, or make you squeeze between people looking in a shop window, or cross police lines. In most countries, this is part of the freedom of the press. This may not work in all cultures: a colleague went to film in Nigeria and learned (through having stones flung at him) that taking a person's image without asking is theft. In some political climates, holding a camera is seen as holding a weapon. See this in action in Emad Burnat and Guy Davidi's *Five Broken Cameras* (Palestine/Israel/France, 2011), an extraordinary firsthand record by a brave and sophisticated Palestine farmer who became a crusading journalist. Around the time his son was born, his village founded a nonviolent movement to resist the annexation of their land for settlers' apartment blocks, and Burnat began documenting the village's turbulent resistance with a video camera (Figure 30-4). As peasants trying to block the annexation of their land, they face increasingly violent confrontations with the Israeli Army, who sometimes fire live ammunition. Narrated with deadpan factual neutrality, the film is a unique

FIGURE 30-4

The son for whom *Five Broken Cameras* is meant as a record of resistance.

record of humor, persecution, and random death. Angry soldiers react by breaking or shooting at Burnat's cameras, and one camera saves his life by blocking a bullet aimed at his head. Most remarkable is the restraint in Burnat's voice-over, which returns often to the awful cost of continuing, and yet the impossibility of giving up.

POINT OF VIEW AND MOTIVATING THE CAMERA'S MOVEMENTS

There are no universal laws for camera positioning since every situation has its inherent limitations and its inherent meanings. Obstacles are usually physical: perhaps the view from a window restricts you to shooting an interior from one direction only, or you must shoot around an incongruity. You use a low framing on a genuine settler's log cabin in order to avoid seeing, above the ancient trees, an ominous revolving sausage over the neighborhood hot-dog stand. Making documentaries is astonishingly serendipitous; so often you must alter plans to accommodate the unforeseen. Such limitations shape film art to a degree undreamed of by film theorists, who overestimate the director's control, and underestimate the parts played by chance and improvisation.

Ideas on how to place your camera, and what movements it should make, will come to you naturally if you let it mirror the stages of revelation by which your consciousness registered unfolding events. Much of this comes from *inhabiting* the POV of others. Your camera can relay,

- A character in the film's POV.
- Multiple characters' POVs.
- The director's POV.
- An omniscient storytelling POV.

EXPLAINING MULTIPLE ANGLES ON THE SAME ACTION

If film language mimics perception, why cover an action from multiple angles? Imagine cutting from long to close shot, and then back to long shot again. By so doing, you are suggesting an observer's concentration intensifying, then relaxing. Now imagine a tense family meal in which the cutting draws on five different camera positions. It's a familiar enough film convention, and draws on the tradition in literature where the author implies multiple viewpoints through the use of language. The reader understands *shifts in psychological viewpoint*, not changes of physical point of view, and the same holds true when you cut multiple views together for the screen. Though film seems to give us "real" events, what it really gives us is a "seeming." We see not the events themselves, but a *construct* that implies multiple, humanly motivated ways of perceiving them.

Compare this with your experience as a bystander at a major disagreement. You got so absorbed that you forgot all about yourself. Instead, you were sucked into a series of involuntary agreements and disagreements, seeing first one person's viewpoint, then another's. So much were you involved that your sense of self vanished, leaving you inside the protagonists' heated realities, one after another. Screen language mimics this heightened state of subjectivity by relaying events as a series of psychologically privileged views. They lead you to identify with one person after another as the situation unfolds—sympathy and fascination, distaste and anxiety... Each inner state moves you to search for clues to underlying meanings—that is, for the subtexts. Cutting from angle to angle thus mimics this familiar psychic experience, but it will fail unless the tempos in the scene, the shooting, and editing all feel "right."

That state of heightened and embracing concentration is not one we normally maintain for long. It feels "right" and "works" when the *shifts in POV arise from an empathic observing sensibility*—either that of a character, or that of the invisible Storyteller. Without this invisible grounding, the different angles won't feel integrated.

ABSTRACTION AND SYMBOLISM

We cannot keep up a probing emotional inquiry (close shots) for long since it is very draining. Often we withdraw into mental stocktaking or even detachment (long shots). In this condition our eyes may zero in on something distractingly neutral (cutaway) or we may move our examination from a part of the scene to the whole, or from the whole to a significant part. When you find yourself observing in similar circumstances, study your own shifts of attention and see how you sometimes escape into a private realm where you can speculate, contemplate, remember, or imagine. Detail that catches your attention often turns out to have symbolic meaning.

As you direct or shoot, keep your eyes open for anything expressive or symbolic. It might be a column of ants suggesting tireless persistence, or a butterfly in an empty lot that suggests renewal. Abstraction can signify inward pondering in search of a recent event's significance. A pictorial device often used to suggest this state is *rack focus* (focus moving selectively between planes in a composition). When an object is isolated on the screen, and its foreground and background are thrown out of focus, it strongly suggests abstracted vision, as does abnormal motion (slow or fast) in some contexts.

These are some of the ways to represent how we penetrate, then dismantle reality, and distance ourselves from the psychic overload. We may be searching for meaning, or simply refreshing ourselves through imaginative play, but falling into a state of abstraction fulfills our need for some contemplative time out.

SERENDIPITY

Chance can work in eerie ways. The British miners mentioned in an earlier chapter had sabotaged a coal train manned by strike-breakers. The evening before we came to film them, an express train derailed close to the original site. For me and my crew, this felt like the hand of fate, and it was not the only occasion when something paranormal happened. After some queasy soul-searching

FIGURE 30-5

Be ready for the unexpected—a train wreck that occurred nearby while filming *The Cramlington Train-Wreckers*.

FIGURE 30-6

The doctor, a former strike-breaker in *The Cramlington Train-Wreckers*.

about voyeurism, I altered our plans to film the wreckage. It brought home, like nothing else, the destruction the saboteurs had risked by their demonstration, and the depth of alienation that had caused them to take such a risk (Figure 30-5). The next morning I interviewed an aging doctor who had been a student "scab" (strike-breaker) 40 years earlier in the original incident (Figure 30-6). Knowing we were coming to interview him, he thought he was dreaming when called out in the night to attend to casualties in a train crash.

For some, all this adapting to the unexpected is frustrating, but others take it as a challenge to their inventiveness and insight. In pursuit of spontaneity, you may be tempted to make no plans, but plan you must, since plans quite often work out.

FIGURE 30-7

Searching for the history of the universe. The observatory in *Nostalgia for the Light* capturing light transmitted billions of years ago.

SUBJECTIVITY VERSUS OBJECTIVITY

The world we know is full of dualities, oppositions, and ironic contrasts. For instance, you drive your car very fast at night, and then, stopping to look at the stars, experience your own insignificance under those little points of light that took millions of years to reach earth. Patricio Guzman's masterpiece *Nostalgia for the Light* (Chile, 2010, Figure 30-7) evokes this wonder by introducing us to astronomers in an Atacama Desert observatory that is capturing light transmitted billions of years ago. They are looking for the origins of the universe, but Guzman uses their dedication as a metaphor for his own as he searches to comprehend the brute cruelty that decimated his generation of young intellectuals. When a CIA-backed coup deposed the elected President Allende, General Pinochet seized the reins of power and took revenge by letting his police and military liquidate thousands of young dissidents. Those we see digging in the desert sands near the Observatory are their parents, siblings, and lovers who are still tragically looking for their remains, hastily scattered by the regime during its dying days (Figure 30-8).

Guzman's film is a harrowing work of beauty that ponders how a nation can so deliberately discard its own history, how the past and the future can be allowed to coexist so deceptively in a nation's consciousness.

SPECIAL MEANING THROUGH FRAMING

Screen language exists to frame and juxtapose every aspect of what a keen Observer notices, and to give a purposeful Storyteller materials with which to tell a story. Framing alone can change meanings since isolating people in separate close shots, for instance, and intercutting them, will have a very different feel than cutting between two over-the-shoulder (OS) shots or showing the whole scene in medium long shot (MLS).

In the single shots, the spectator is always alone with one of the contenders, a relationship nurtured by editing. In the OS and MLS shots, however, we always see one person *in relation to* the other, and our involvement is with them as a pair, not with each separately. This feels different, but

FIGURE 30-8

The bereaved, searching for their loved-ones' remains hidden by the Chilean military regime in its dying days.

there is nothing obscure here. Your guide to how an audience will respond always lies in using the lexicon of cinema to translate aspects of your own emotional experience. By becoming intensely aware of *how* you experience, you involve yourself in fabricating the cinematic equivalencies.

USING CONTEXT

How do different backgrounds work with a particular foreground action? If a participant is in a wheelchair, and you angle the shot to contain a window with a vista of people in the street, the composition unobtrusively juxtaposes her with the freedom of movement she so poignantly lacks. This is James Stewart's perspective in Hitchcock's *Rear Window* (USA, 1954) as he waits in his wheelchair for his broken leg to repair.

Looking down on the subject, looking up at the subject, or looking at it between the bars of a railing can all suggest ways of seeing *and therefore, of experiencing* the action that makes the scene. True, you can manufacture this relationship through editing, but it's labored and open to distrust. You accomplish far more by capturing whatever visual relationships already exist, and by building pithy observation and juxtaposition into each frame.

As you operate the camera, make yourself respond physically to each location's particularities; make your camera respond to how participants' movements and actions convey the scene's subtext. When you need to make a camera movement, try to use the movement of a character or vehicle to motivate shift in the camera's gaze to a new composition.

It makes a big difference to the audience to be seeing through an intelligence that resonates to an event's movements and underlying tensions. The audience always prefers to share the consciousness of someone intelligent and intuitive, not that of a mechanical eye swiveling toward whatever moves its body or lips.

Handheld or tripod-mounted camera? Camera handling options can suggest either the steadiness of a settled, historically informed human view, or the unsettled movement associated with quest, uncertainty, excitement, or flight. These two kinds of camera-presence—one studied, composed, and controlled, and the other mobile, spontaneous, and physically reactive to change—alter the film's storytelling "voice," and project different perceptual relationships to the action, especially when they are juxtaposed. Usually practical matters will influence your choices:

The tripod-mounted camera can zoom in to hold a steady close shot when the camera is distant, but may not be able to migrate quickly to a new vantage point, should the action call for it. Mount the camera on a quick-release plate, and you can release it and go handheld in the twinkling of an eye.

Spatially a tripod-mounted camera always sees from a fixed point, no matter whether the camera pans, tilts, or zooms. Its perspective (size of foreground in relation to background) remains the same, reiterating to our subconscious that the observation is rooted in an assigned place. This feeling would be appropriate for a courtroom, because the positions of judge, jury, witness box, and audience are all ritually preordained and symbolic. No court would tolerate a wandering audience member, so it is logical that the camera/observer also be fixed.

The handheld camera gives great mobility but with some unsteadiness and a feeling of human impulse and vulnerability. In the right context, these qualities become highly appropriate and expressive. In *Five Broken Cameras* mentioned earlier, the vantage is repeatedly that of non-violent protesters facing soldiers firing tear-gas and bullets, and the vulnerable and reactive camera handling is perfectly appropriate to the experience.

When used to cover a spontaneous interaction like a conversation, a handheld camera can reframe, reposition itself, and change image size to produce all the shots you would expect in an edited version: long shot, medium two-shots, complementary over-the-shoulder shots, and big close ups. Capturing a well-balanced succession of such shots is a rare skill and calls for the sensibility of editor, director, photographer, and dramatist—all in one camera operator. Luckily human interactions generate much redundancy, so you can usually edit intelligently shot handheld footage to yield an approximation of the feature film's access to its characters. However, make the cutting too elegant, and your technique may undermine the spontaneity of the scene. When you cannot predict the action or know only that it will take place somewhere in a given area, going handheld may be the only solution. Some cameras are equipped with image stabilizers that compensate (sometimes very successfully) for the kind of handheld unsteadiness that comes from, say, the occasional need to breathe.

Great camerawork is a matter of utter concentration and astute sensitivity to underlying issues. For a recent lexicon of handheld shooting, see the work of Axel Baumann, Ulli Bonnekamp, Mark Brice, Robert Hanna, and Wolfgang Held in any episode of Mitchell Block and Maro Chermayeff's extraordinary ten-episode miniseries *Carrier* (USA, 2008). For other classic North American handheld work, see that by,

- John Marshall in *Titicut Follies* (Frederick Wiseman, USA, 1967)
- William Brayne in *Warrendale* (Allen King, Canada, 1967)
- Slawomir Grünberg in *Omar and Pete* (Tod Lending, USA, 2005)
- Mira Chang and Jenna Rosha in *Jesus Camp* (Heidi Ewing and Rachel Grady, USA, 2006) which makes creative use of a Steadicam camera mount.

COVERAGE

SCENE BREAKDOWN AND CRIB NOTES

When filming a scene, you should have clear ideas about what you want it to establish or contribute to your intended film. List your goals so you overlook nothing in the heat of battle. If, for

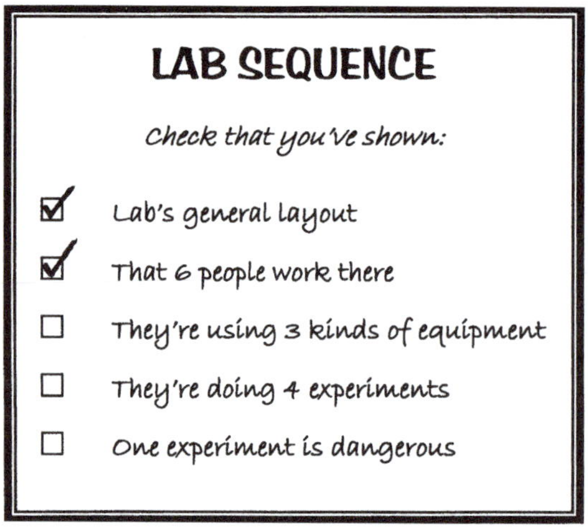

```
┌─────────────────────────────────────────┐
│  ┌───────────────────────────────────┐  │
│  │                                   │  │
│  │          LAB SEQUENCE             │  │
│  │                                   │  │
│  │       Check that you've shown:    │  │
│  │                                   │  │
│  │   ☑  Lab's general layout         │  │
│  │                                   │  │
│  │   ☑  That 6 people work there     │  │
│  │                                   │  │
│  │   ☐  They're using 3 kinds of equipment │
│  │                                   │  │
│  │   ☐  They're doing 4 experiments  │  │
│  │                                   │  │
│  │   ☐  One experiment is dangerous  │  │
│  │                                   │  │
│  └───────────────────────────────────┘  │
└─────────────────────────────────────────┘
```

FIGURE 30-9

Director's crib notes.

instance, you are shooting in a laboratory, you might make *crib notes* (reminders) on an index card (Figure 30-9). If your audience needs to see the lab workers' dedication, you must get shots to establish these things. Then, treating the camera as an observing consciousness, you imagine in detail *how you want the scene to be experienced*. If for instance you were shooting a boozy wedding, you might want the camera to adopt a tipsy guest's point of view. Going handheld, peering into circles of chattering people, it could legitimately bump into raucous revelers, quiz the principals, and even join in the dancing. If however you were shooting in a ballroom dance studio, with its elaborate ritualized performances, you might use a Steadicam, or use a tripod placing and handling of the camera that is formal and grounded.

So, how to show lab workers as heroic? The answer might lie in studied shots emphasizing the danger and painstaking rigor of the work they do, and thus the human vulnerability of each worker. Perhaps you show a face near a retort of boiling acid. You make us see that each person has his own world, and must coexist with danger in order to investigate on behalf of humanity. You begin to see the calm, concentrated eyes above the masks, the expertly used elaborate equipment, the dedication.

Whatever the shooting situation, ask yourself,

- What factual or physical details must I shoot to imply the whole?
- What will be each essential stage of development that I must cover?
- What signals the start and end of each developmental stage?
- Is elapsed time important, and if so how do I imply it?
- Where does the majority of the telling action lie? (In the courtroom, for example, does it lie with judge, plaintiff, prosecutor, or the jury?)
- Who is the central character and how does he/she act upon the situation?
- When is this likely to change, and what makes the next person become central?
- Who or what develops during this scene? How will I show it?

EYELINE SHIFTS MOTIVATE CUTS

Frequently someone you are shooting will hold out a picture, refer to an object in the room, or look offscreen at someone or something. In each case, his action and *eyeline shift* directs our attention to something we want to see. You gratify this need with an insert or cutaway. The corollary is that, in order to use a cut, insert, or cutaway legitimately, an editor must find its *motivation* (justification) within the scene—whether emanating from a character or from the needs of the narrative.

Sometimes a cutaway or insert conveys a Storyteller attitude. For example, a faucet drips incessantly in the kitchen of a neglected elderly man. You film a close shot of it, including the dusty, yellowing photographs in the background. Neglected faucet and photos speak volumes about long-standing disregard. Such shots, drawing the viewer's eye to significant detail, arise from (and are motivated by) the Storyteller's intentions. They express an authorial conviction about this man and his life that the audience does well to notice, since it will surely have consequences in the story later.

REACTION SHOTS AND EYELINE CHANGES

After you have covered two or more people in conversation, make your editor happy by asking them to prolong their conversation while your camera gathers *safety coverage*. It now concentrates on close-ups of each individual listening, watching, reacting, and shifting their gaze between the other speakers. These shots can later be intercut with speakers and act as a highly motivated cutaway. Spontaneous eyeline shifts are worth their weight in gold to the editor, but you cannot ask participants to make them, since people usually become very self-conscious.

COVER ALTERNATIVE VERSIONS OF IMPORTANT ISSUES

Try to *cover each important issue in more than one way* so you have alternative narrative possibilities later. You could for example cover a political demonstration with footage showing how the demonstration begins, shoot close shots of faces and banners, the police lines, the arrests, and so on. But you might also acquire coverage through photographs, a TV news show, participant interviews, or street interviews. This would produce a multiplicity of attitudes about the purpose of the march and a number of faces to intercut (and thus abbreviate) the stages of the demonstration footage. You now have multiple and conflicting viewpoints, and materials that allow you to intensify yet greatly compress the narrative through parallel storytelling.

PRODUCTION STILLS

Good production stills are incredibly important when it comes to publicizing your film. During production, carry a high-resolution digital stills camera so that someone can shoot the high points. Decide beforehand what compositions will best represent the thematic issues in the film. How to reveal the participants' personalities? And what exotic or alluring situations might help draw an audience? Stills should epitomize the film's subject and approach, and thematic issues. Compositions should capture the important relationships and personality traits of the participants.

NOTE

1. Richard Roud, *Godard* (Martin Secker and Warburg, 1967), p. 55.

CHAPTER 31

CONDUCTING AND SHOOTING INTERVIEWS

The documentary interviewer wants to draw people's stories from them, and the interviewee usually wants to comply, but interviewing takes skill. In life, every exchange with a new interlocutor unlocks different facets and potential, and sometimes takes both in unforeseeable directions. This is because we do not have a finite story and identity waiting to be uncovered, but instead, aspects within us that are fluid and unforeseen. Ray Carney, writing about John Cassavetes' approach to characterization in his improvised fiction films, argues rightly that human identity is not fixed, but something constantly negotiated through interaction with others.[1]

Few other realizations will be more significant to your filmmaking. Choosing what approach to take during an interview, and where to shoot it, can release quite different facets of your interviewee. How you engage with people onscreen is only an extension of how you have engaged with them from the very beginning. Work on becoming a better interviewer is therefore work on becoming a better director.

FIRST CONTACT

INITIAL RESEARCH

When you explain the project to potential interviewees, describe it in broad generalizations only. This lets you keep your options open at a time when you have little certitude about your film's substance, and prevents you creating impressions that could prove misleading or even paint you into a corner. Early conversations are mostly an exercise in sustained listening. Often you hear something that makes you think, "I must have this in the film." Note it down. Later you'll prepare questions to elicit as naturally as possible a full version of what you've just heard. Do not press any questions at this stage! Often, indeed, you'll have to stop someone by saying, "Don't tell me! Hold on to that thought for later when we have the camera."

After "auditioning" several possible interviewees, your instincts usually tell you who has the best experiences and who talks most coherently and engagingly. If in doubt, make some audio recordings and decide from listening to them. Voice quality can be an important factor.

DECIDING ABOUT LOCATION

You can shoot an interview anywhere significant to the participant, but try to estimate what each location may contribute. The interviewee may be more at ease at home, in their workplace, or at the home of a friend, and will likely give responses that are more intimate. In public places, such as streets, parks, or the beach, the participant might feel either more exposed or like one of many, depending on his or her history and temperament. Settings such as an old battlefield, childhood home, or first workplace may shake loose many emotion-laden memories. Other settings could make the same person feel exposed. So, get an idea of your interviewee's life, then suggest salient spots for an interview and see how he or she reacts.

WHO INTERVIEWS

Busy directors sometimes rely on a researcher, who runs ahead digging up facts and locating likely participants. Researchers become trusted creative colleagues and when it's time to shoot, the question arises: Should the researcher or the director conduct the interview? Each may have advantages. The researcher is continuing a relationship already established, and this might put a hesitant participant at ease. When the director interviews, however, the interviewee is addressing a fresh listener, and may be more spontaneous and comprehensive.

ONE CAMERA OR MORE?

When you interview someone for whom you have no cutaway footage, you can shoot the interviewer as safety coverage using a second camera. This of course makes the interviewer into a featured player in the film, but you can get round this by using participants to converse with each other, coaching them beforehand as necessary. You can also assure yourself of being able to cut around the interview by employing two cameras (carefully color-matched) on the subject, one in medium shot and one in close shot. You should also try to get one long shot distant enough to make lip movements indeterminate and that can serve as an all-purpose long shot, or as an establishing shot.

WHEN OTHERS ARE PRESENT

Whoever is present will affect an interview. A second person can encourage and challenge, inhibit and discourage. Imagine you are interviewing a gentle, older woman whose peppery husband is forever correcting her. You wisely arrange for the husband to do something in another room so she feels free to tell her own story. If the inequality of their relationship was important, then you would shoot them together. I once shot an interview with a farm manager sitting next to his wife, and as he spoke, she interrupted and modified everything he said to make it "nice" (Figure 31-1). This was revealing and funny. Try to see each situation through the subjects' eyes so you can perhaps foresee what to expect.

INTERVIEWING GROUPS

Interviewing need not be one-on-one. A married couple, separately inarticulate through shyness, may goad each other into action-and-reaction very well. Putting two people together who disagree, and then interviewing them, can be a highly productive strategy because their inhibitions disappear as they become combative. Often they will turn to each other and forget all about you, which is ideal.

FIGURE 31-1

A husband interrupted and corrected by his wife in *A Remnant of a Feudal Society*.

To interview a whole group, try one of two ways:

- "Recognize" each new speaker from among those whose body language shows they want to speak.
- Encourage people to begin speaking to each other rather than to you.

When you bring a camera and talk to anyone in a public place—say, at a school gate—others will gather to listen and join in. By not imposing control, the conversation often turns into a spirited exchange or dispute. The interviewer, now on the sidelines, can always interpose a new question or make a request, such as, "Could the lady in the red jacket talk about the company's attitude toward safety?" And talk she will. You can remain happily silent because your mission—to catalyze people's thoughts and feelings—needs no further action.

VOX POPS (*VOX POPULI*, LATIN FOR "VOICE OF THE PEOPLE")

Person-in-the-street interviews can be very useful. You put the same few questions to a range of people, and their replies strung together become a rapid and instructive flow. This is an entertaining technique for manufacturing a Greek chorus of opinion. You can orchestrate diversity or homogeneity, thesis or antithesis. Sections of vox pop can lighten something essentially sober and intense, such as a film about political developments, and they can function as legitimate parallel action. I once used them as parallel storytelling to help compress a 3-hour peace speech into less than 12 minutes. They served as a dialectical counterpoint between the man on the podium and the man (and woman) in the street. Each gave piquancy to the other—and virtue came of necessity.

PREPARATION AND BASIC SKILLS

POLITELY SETTING LIMITS

Before you interview, decide how each interviewee fits in with your film's central purpose. That way you can politely set limits on what each should contribute. I don't mean prepare a script or anticipate specific statements, since that would turn participants into actors. Just be ready to say what areas you do and don't want to explore. This way, you legitimize any interruptions to redirect the conversation.

METAPHORIC THINKING

Turning your film into a story usually means delineating a set of antagonistic forces, each championed by one of your film's personalities. Your job is to elicit the material that will articulate these archetypal forces. Is this a good versus evil situation? The one against the many? The righteous against the doubters? Decide what archetypal situation you are handling, and what role each "actor" might be seen playing in your film. Without revealing any of this to your participants, you set out to catalyze the antithetical components for assembly later. You should not be manipulating reality, just catalyzing the main elements of the inherent drama.

Earlier we said that "plot" represents the rules of the universe, and that the protagonist is often someone challenging those rules. Anywhere there is a protagonist, there is an antagonist too, and thus a conflict. Decide whether the struggle is against timeless universal law, or against societal norms that shift from generation to generation. Who or what is the opposition?

HUMAN CONSTANTS

All human situations tend toward the kind of constants articulated in myths, folk-tales, fables, and ballads whose modern equivalencies march onward in contemporary films, books, stories, and celebrities. Such sources, when you find the equivalent for your story, help you spot what may be missing from your story.

Generating the right analogies, and finding apt metaphors for your characters and their situations, greatly helps you recognize what archetypal role each player occupies in your story's growing framework. For obvious reasons, this naming and analysis is something you share with nobody other than your artistic collaborators.

JUST BEFORE THE INTERVIEW

REHEARSE ALONE

When alone and before you interview,

- Phrase your questions to make them simple, direct, active-voice, and unambiguous.
- Speak each aloud and listen to your voice. Is the question direct and natural?
- Is there any latitude whatever for the question to be misinterpreted? If so, keep altering the wording until only the intended understanding is possible.
- Listen to your questioning again for signs of manipulation, and eradicate it.

FREE YOURSELF TO LISTEN

Avoid burying your face in notes during the interview. Better is to maintain eye contact and give facial (*not* verbal) reactions to keep your side of the conversation silently alive. To free yourself for this, list your questions on an index card and keep it on your knee for security. With it near, you won't be afraid of "drying up" and you'll probably cover everything without needing the prompts. At the end, before you let the participant go, check to ensure you covered everything.

PREPARE THE CAMERA OPERATOR FOR TOUCH-DIRECTIONS

Some notes on camera placement appear in **Chapter 30: Advanced Directing**. Now you're going to set up a signaling method with the operator so you can determine when to zoom between shot sizes. If you have plenty of pictorial material to edit in parallel, then you can do as Errol Morris does, and shoot the whole interview in a one-size shot. Other directors incorporate different sizes of shot according to the speaker's intensity. Varying the shot sizes offers a greater prospect for seamless *ellipsis* (abbreviation) of the results. To prepare for this, you'll need to develop signals with your camera operator about when to zoom in and out. Varying an interview image size allows you to,

- Cut between different sized shots and thus a good chance of abbreviation, though with some loss of credibility because of the cutting.
- Restructure an interview.
- Remove what's redundant.
- Eliminate the interviewer's questions.
- Run longer stretches of uncut interview on the screen since the camera intensifies and relaxes its scrutiny, and answers the spectator's need for variation.

WHEN TWO MATCHING SHOTS MUST CUT TOGETHER

As we said in **Chapter 12: Camera**, "Composing the Shot," any wide, medium, and close shots intended to cut together must have their *compositional centers similar in each composition* if cutting between them is to feel smooth. In an interview, the compositional center is usually the subject's eyes, but the same principle affects long and medium shots of a house on a hillside, or any other image with size variations.

AGREE ON IMAGE SIZE-CHANGES

While you are lining up, look through the camera viewfinder and agree with your operator on three standard image sizes and framings. Be clear if you want the operator to make all camera movements usable for speed and composition.

From your interviewing position under or next to the camera, you are going to signal when and how you want each shot to change. I do it by pressing different parts of the operator's foot:

- Press the ankle for wide shot (to cover each question).
- Press top of foot for medium shot (used after the answer has got under way).
- Press the toe for close shot (for anything intense or revealing).

During lengthy answers, alternate shot size between medium and close shots. Whenever you are going to pose a new question, however, drop back to wide shot. I try to change image size whenever a speaker shows signs of repeating something. Such repetition is normal, and subsequent versions are often more succinct. If the repeat is in a different image size, you can cut between the two versions. Once the operator gets the hang of your strategy, he or she should be able to carry it out without instruction.

VARY ZOOM SPEEDS

Ask the operator to match the speed of zoom-ins and zoom-outs to the speaker's current rhythm. Only under specially agreed circumstances should movements be long and lingering. Cutting into a slow-moving zoom can look hideous, so movements should either be usably elegant, or made fast and functional during a throw-away moment—such as when you are asking a new question. If you sense this is happening, draw out your question to give the operator time to settle.

PREPARING THE INTERVIEWEE

SAY WHAT YOU NEED

You have the right and even the obligation to tell the interviewee what aspects interest you for the film. You can, after all, only cover what fits your film, so remember to reiterate *the general subject areas you want to cover, and those you don't*. Knowing this helps put the interviewee at ease and guards against digression. Even though you feel apologetic, make your limitations sound reasonable—because they are.

ESTABLISH YOUR RIGHT TO INTERRUPT

Another way to lower the interviewee's anxiety is by explaining that you may occasionally need to interrupt or redirect the conversation. I usually say,

> This is a documentary and we always shoot ten times as much as we use. So don't worry if you get anything wrong because we can always edit it out. Also, if I feel we're getting away from the subject, I may rudely interrupt, if that's all right with you?

Nobody ever objects; indeed, inexperienced interviewees seem reassured that you take responsibility for where the conversation will go. This will only work if you have oriented the interviewee to the overall purpose of the film in the first place.

Put the interviewee at ease: When the camera rolls, remain relaxed and unhurried. Don't change your manner, since this signals rising tension. Give interviewees initial work in areas that interest them but are non-threatening. While they are speaking, give them your undivided attention and imply whatever permission the interviewee seems to need by nodding, smiling, raising an eyebrow, shaking your head in disbelief, etc.

Only rarely does this fail to work. In an interview I began with the famous pediatrician Dr. Benjamin Spock,[2] he became visibly uncomfortable, though he had been fine throughout the previous days of shooting him in political action. I was concerned, because I needed a long interview for potential voice-over as narration to all the footage we'd shot, and I was returning to the UK. His to-camera manner was now so strangely stiff and inhibited that we stopped the camera to find out what was wrong. He admitted rather sheepishly that he was only used to talking to women. Someone suggested we put our production assistant, Rosalie Worthington, in my position under the camera lens. So, I posed the questions, and Spock gave his answers to Rosalie, his manner now relaxed and avuncular. Had reflexivity been an option (and had I possessed the imagination to use it), I could have included this oddly revealing information in the film.

CAMERA AND EDITING CONSIDERATIONS

INTERVIEWER AND CAMERA PLACEMENT

You can set up the relationship between camera and interviewee in two ways and with two different results. Either the speaker talks to the audience in an *on-axis* interview, or they talk to a third party next to the camera in an *off-axis* interview. Each approach carries a different implication and reflects a different philosophy:

On-axis interview: The interviewer's role, as I see it, is to *ask questions the audience would ask if it could*. Once the interviewee is talking, anything signifying the interviewer is irrelevant and distracting. Since I always edit out interviewing questions, I use this approach. It places the audience in direct relationship with the interviewee (Figure 31-2).

To interview on-axis, sit on a low box with your head right below, and almost touching, the camera lens. The interviewee who talks to you, talks directly with the audience.

Off-axis interview: This approach is favored by reporters and diarists, who make a feature of catalyzing interviews. The interviewer sits either in or out of frame and usually to the left of the camera (Figure 31-3). Even when you remove all trace of the interviewer and their questions, the interviewee's off-axis eyeline signifies the presence of an invisible interlocutor unmistakably. The farther the interviewer is from the camera-to-subject axis, the more persistent this impression becomes.

FIGURE 31-2 —————————————————

On-axis interviewee talking direct to the audience.

FIGURE 31-3 —————————————————

Off-axis interviewee talking to an interviewer beside the camera.

WHEN THE INTERVIEWER SHOULD BE ON-CAMERA

If the questioner's presence, pressure, and reactions are integral to the exchange, you may need his/her presence on camera with the interviewee. Many television interviewers are masterly at this, and so the off-axis interview complements the interviewer's function, especially when they create pressure by interjecting reactions and questions.

PREPARING TO EDIT OUT THE INTERVIEWER

INCLUDING THE QUESTION IN THE ANSWER

If you mean to edit out your questions, ask interviewees to give free-standing answers that do not depend on your question to make sense. An interview briefing might go like this:

If I ask, "When did you first arrive in America?," you might answer "1989," but the answer "1989" wouldn't stand on its own, so I'd be forced to include my question. However, if you said, "I arrived in the United States in 1989," it's a whole and complete statement and that's what I need.

Everyone understands, but most forget. So, while you interview, listen critically to how every answer begins. Is it freestanding or does it depend on the question to make sense? Typical replies:

"My first job was sweeping out the stockroom..."
"My brother, I suppose, he was always the favorite..."
"If I had my life over, would I do the same again? I suppose so..."
"It was six feet above normal...."

If you get freestanding openings, as in the first three examples, you are fine. If however you get an unusable opening sentence, interject and ask your interviewee to restart the sentence. Sometimes you will have to feed appropriate opening words, such as, "Try beginning, 'When I first left home'..." This usually solves it.

VOICE OVERLAPS

Note that *you cannot edit out the questioner if any voices overlap*. As an interviewer, then, you must listen to ensure that each new answer starts clean, and you must be extra careful not to trample on your interviewee's last words with your next question. Either will produce a voice overlap that makes clean editing impossible. If you have an overlap, tell the interviewee what happened and ask to re-do that section.

VOX POPULI INTERVIEWS

When you shoot *vox populi* (voice of the people) street interviews, the camera is mobile and hand-held, and is not something you can sit under. This means you can only do off-axis interviewing. Remember therefore to *alternate the sides from which you interview*, since a series of replies all from one side is tedious and even a little strange.

SOLVING THE NEED FOR ELLIPSIS

If you shoot intending to abridge interviews later in editing, you must shoot with *ellipsis* in mind. You have several possible solutions:

JUMP CUTS

If you shoot all your interviews in a single size (as Errol Morris does), then you can only bridge different sections together by jump cutting. This is fine if you abridge boldly and consistently as a style, since the jump cut signals "a piece of time was cut out here." Used only intermittently, jump cuts become disconcerting; a subject's face suddenly changes expression, or a head jumps to a slightly different position (Figure 31-4). Particularly in a transparent film—that is, one hiding editorial processes under the guise of continuity—the odd jump cut completely ruptures the illusion.

CUTAWAYS

You can eliminate potential jump cuts by cutting away to something pictorially relevant, but unless it adds something, and unless you use this consistently as a rhetorical device, the lone cutaway reeks of expediency. Cutaways of a nodding interviewer (shot afterwards and looking inane) or shots of the speaker's clasped hands will seem even more bogus.

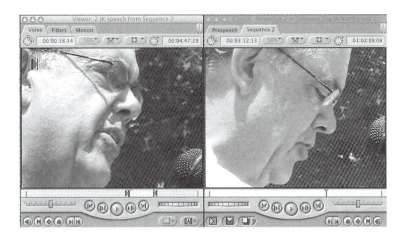

FIGURE 31-4

A jump cut occurs when two similar images mismatch, making it plain that footage has been removed between them.

PARALLEL STORYTELLING

An elegant solution to ellipsis is to run multiple story strands in parallel, cutting between them and abbreviating each as you go. If it helps sustain story momentum too, this works very well.

VARYING SHOT SIZES

You can also vary shot sizes during the interview, as mentioned above, and hope that your chosen sections will cut together. Often they are indeed different shot sizes, and cut well together. To allow for this, the camera operator makes periodic image size-changes (see "Just Before the Interview" above). Screen conventions allow you to cut them together, providing,

- There is a bold change of image size, either larger or smaller.
- The subject is in a roughly similar physical attitude in the two shots.
- The framing of each size shot is proportionally similar.
- Speech and movement rhythms flow uninterrupted across the cut.

So long as there are large differences in subject size or angle between your camera positions, minor mismatches will pass unnoticed.

THE INTERVIEW BEGINS

INTERVIEWING AND DIRECTING

To face another human being while making a documentary means to probe, listen, and obliquely reveal oneself and one's purposes with follow-up questions. Often, by challenging someone to delve into an experience for the "history box," you catalyze realizations in your participant that lead to real change.

Thus interviewing subtly *supports and directs*—quite a responsibility. This should never mean manipulating the interviewee into exhibitionism, but rather, by providing a sense of occasion, of giving even-handed and neutral assistance, and of providing creative resistance, you invite the interviewee to explore pathways truly their own, and often for the first time. When this happens it is very apparent, and quite magical.

LEAD BY EXAMPLE

If you are formal and uptight, your interviewee will be more so. You'll get spontaneity by being relaxed and natural yourself. I try to lower the perception of pressure by making my first questions deliberately slow and bumbling. That way I signal that my expectations are totally unlike the manic brightness of the live television show, where hosts chivvy people into performing.

LEADING QUESTIONS AND OPEN QUESTIONS

Either through anxiety or the need to control, an interviewer will sometimes signify the reply he or she wants with a *leading question*. Look at the difference:

> *Leading question*: "Do you think early education is really a good thing?"
> *Open question*: "What do you feel about early education?"

The leading question corrals the interviewee into a particular response. As the participant deals with it, he is embarrassed to find himself answering to prescription, and his resulting staginess and self-consciousness devalue the answer. An open question would be, "Talk some more about the feelings you mentioned when you came home as a kid to an empty house." You are asking him to elaborate on something already mentioned—maybe in private. Open questions ask only for a sincere reply and hand control to the interviewee.

FOCUSING QUESTIONS

Novice interviewers sometimes go fishing with catch-all questions: "What is the most exciting experience you've ever had?" Devoid of preparation or focus, they fling out a big, shapeless net. Another habit, rampant in town hall meetings, is the rambling, multipart question. The person answering can usually only remember the last item in the list. So, lead your interviewee into a chosen area, make your questions specific, and take just one issue at a time.

THE RIGHT ORDER FOR YOUR QUESTIONS

Posing questions in the order you need for your film is unnecessary, since you will reorganize everything in editing. You should put them in the order that is least threatening to your participant. Make a gradual start by asking for information. Facts are safe while opinions or feelings take a more confident, relaxed state of mind that usually comes only when the first apprehensions have melted away. Once your subject has become used to the situation and even enjoying it, you can move on to the more probing and personal stuff.

Listen to your instincts so you maintain the appropriate pressure and flow. Highly sensitive issues can still be difficult. Once, researching for a film I made about Alexandra Tolstoy (Figure 31-5), the twelfth and most controversial child of the great novelist, I read in her autobiography that she had been an unwanted child. Worse, she had learned in childhood that her mother had tried to abort her. I hoped to touch on this without offending her, so I nervously delayed broaching this to the end of the interview. Her reply came from the heart, and was full of dignity and honesty. I had hardly supposed that a lady of 86 could still feel the anguish of childhood.

Whatever emerges about a person's private pain usually leads to deeper appreciation of their strengths, and so in editing I placed her reply early in the film. There, it illuminates everything she says subsequently.

MAINTAIN EYE CONTACT AND GIVE BEHAVIORAL FEEDBACK

During the interview, maintain eye contact with your subject, and give visual (never vocal!) feedback while the interviewee talks. Nodding, smiling, looking puzzled, and facially signifying agreement or doubt, all provide the kind of feedback we normally give vocally. They sustain the

FIGURE 31-5

Alexandra Tolstoy in *Tolstoy Remembered by his Daughter*.

interviewee through what otherwise might feel like an egocentric monologue. Errol Morris however claims to get his extraordinary interviews by keeping expectantly silent and just letting the camera roll.

AIM TO ELICIT FEELINGS

If an interviewee gives you objective fact or measured opinion when it is his feelings you need, he may be afraid to appear self-indulgent. People will often give a general answer, for instance,

Q: What was your experience in the submarine service like?
A: Oh it was all right, you know, nothing great.

An older man, he belongs to the School of No Complaints where seeking attention and admitting your needs are contemptible. You must draw this speaker out by *asking for the specific*. Maybe he answers, "Well, it was hard, and I didn't much like the leadership in my company." Now you need some color. By asking "Can you tell me a story about that?" he produces something you can see and feel. Success!

Turn interviews toward feelings and stories every time. A question like "You said you had strong feelings about the fears suffered by latchkey kids?" works well because it signals your interest in how she *feels*. Narratives need specifics. Many people (men in particular, I have to say) produce not the stuff of experience but an arid wad of conclusions. The emotions attached to their memories were long ago buried deep in a mental filing cabinet marked "sissy stuff." It is always the buttoned-up interviewee who gives you the summary rather than the more experiential stuff within. If there's any way to break into the saferoom, it's by gently sidelining generalizations and asking for specifics or an illustrative story.

GOING WHERE ANGELS FEAR TO TREAD

Making documentary faces us with a precarious duality: we can create a liberating arena for discovery and growth, or we can manipulate and exploit. This is an ever-present temptation since you can only make documentaries by intruding into other people's lives. Much documentary interaction happens, thank goodness, at a light-hearted level, but in this chapter we must examine the most demanding end of the spectrum.

TEMPTATIONS WHEN INTERVIEWING

The thrill of the righteous chase can delude you into trampling someone's defenses, and although you have opportunities during editing to recognize and prevent this becoming public, the damage to your relationship with your subject (and your coworkers) may remain. A really dangerous situation is when you don't have final editorial control. Your superiors may decide to use something over your objections, something you deeply regret shooting.

Here is another interviewing dilemma. You take a participant up to an important, perhaps unperceived, threshold in his life. In a revealing moment, the interviewee crosses into new territory and you see what the French anthropologist Jean Rouch calls a "privileged moment," where for participant and audience alike all notion of film as an artificial environment ceases. It is a wonderful moment, but it hinges on the revelation of some fact whose consequences could become damaging if made public.

Do you now lean on the person to permit its inclusion in the film? And what if the participant is so trusting that you alone can make the decision whether or not it will do damage? Here, wise and responsible colleagues can help you carry the burden of decision. Only you, however well guided by advisers, can finally decide.

HAVING POWER

The interviewer has the upper hand simply by arriving with that instrument of history called a camera. You can use it to intimidate or liberate, depending on how you handle your role. Your best safeguard is to find participants who appreciate your values and aims, and are ready or even eager to make a journey of exploration with you. In return, you make yourself emotionally accessible and ready to give as well as take.

WITNESSING

You aspire to create a partnership with your interviewee like the "poet as witness" that Seamus Heaney describes in his discussion of World War I poets.[3] To Heaney, those who wrote about the appalling carnage and losses of that war came to represent "poetry's solidarity with the doomed, the deprived, the victimized, the underprivileged." The witness, he says, "Is any figure in whom the truth-telling urge and the compulsion to identify with the oppressed becomes necessarily integral with the act of writing itself." Those heroic souls who faced tanks in Tianenmen Square, who stood in solidarity with Palestinian villagers in the Occupied Territories, or who, as members of Voices in the Wilderness, made themselves into human shields during their country's bombing of Iraq in 2003, were brave enough to live their convictions to the ultimate.

Once I met such people among World War I conscientious objectors, of whom one who was a Quaker said, "We felt very strongly that we would rather be killed than kill other people" (Figure 31-6). Half a century later, this statement of belief—uttered so quietly and matter-of-factly—still gives me the shivers. What love and reverence for humanity, to hold such a belief and live by it! And what a privilege to record for posterity what he and others had done.

As documentary makers, we try to find ordinary people living extraordinary lives, and then to act as witnesses to what is special. That I believe is the witnessing of which Heaney wrote.

FIGURE 31-6

Frank Merrick, a World War I conscientious objector in *Prisoners of Conscience*: "We would rather be killed than kill other people."

THE INTERVIEWER'S NIGHTMARE

Every interviewer dreads the person who can't or won't talk.

Q: "You weren't satisfied when you moved into this apartment?"
A: "Yep."

Try asking, "Tell me how that happened." If he doesn't respond, it may be wise to abandon the attempt. He may be stonewalling, or resolved not to speak about this or about any upsetting experience. An old and dear colleague, formerly a World War II pilot who had crashed and suffered innumerable hospital operations, told me almost with pride that he had never spoken about his fighter pilot experiences, and never would. When I tried pressing him to give details for history's sake, he sent me an (excellent) autobiography—written by someone else! Some people simply can't or won't relive emotions. Their experiences have left terrible marks which they can't imagine revisiting. Because of this, many Holocaust survivors took their stories to the grave.

DUMMY RUN

Very occasionally it happens that you need to stop an interview because the interviewee proves hopelessly unsatisfactory for some reason. Every crew will sometimes pretend the camera is running in order to avoid hurting the participant's feelings.

INTERVIEWING IN DEPTH

CROSSING THRESHOLDS

In a memorable interview you will see someone cross an emotional threshold and break new ground. This gives what all stories need—a central character who is visibly in movement and developing—and it delivers the emotional content or even shock that we hope for in dramatic art. Let's say that you challenge a caretaker daughter with some negative feelings toward her elderly mother, and before our eyes she admits to despising aspects of the mother she thought she only loved. A man crossing a similar threshold might admit that he all along felt unequal to a job from which he suffered a humiliating demotion.

Both times the interviewee *is experiencing an important realization for the first time*. This is a breakthrough, a *beat*, and the suspense and sense of sharing is electrifying. Under such circumstances, your job is to remain expectantly silent. Wait and wait, if you need to—the silence will be full of drama onscreen.

SILENCE IS YOUR MOST POWERFUL INSTRUMENT

Moments occur in interviewing when you sense there is more to tell, but the person is wondering whether to risk telling it. A gentle "And?" or simply "Yes, go on" signals your support in continuing. After this, stay silent and wait. That silence becomes gripping because imaginatively we enter the interviewee's mind as she visibly and dramatically grapples with a vital issue.

To the insensitive or inexperienced interviewer, silence is failure. So they come crashing in with new questions. The underlying cause is *not listening for the subtext and not trusting intuition*. But making documentary is not live television and there's no risk in waiting. You are going to edit your material: you take no risks by backing your hunches and keeping silent.

DON'T CATCH THEM WHEN THEY FALL

Neil Sandell of *Outfront* (see end of this chapter) warns not to break out of your role and comfort someone who becomes emotional or distraught during an interview. To stem suffering is commendable, but it turns the interviewing relationship into something different. Often the reflex to console comes from embarrassment and wanting to guiltily slam a door on what you've precipitated. But people simply don't go where they can't cope. Provided you have only used light pressure, anyone who breaks down and weeps needs to cross a Rubicon of some kind. Let them handle it, Sandell advises, and just remain quietly present and supportive.

PRIVILEGED MOMENTS AND BEATS

The most impressive windows on human life come as detonations of truth—Jean Rouch's "privileged moments"—when someone on camera suddenly manifests a new awareness. You see these moments during everyday interactions, and sometimes during a one-on-one interview. In a film of mine it was a father realizing that, for all his patriotic love of country, he would rather leave America than allow his sons to risk losing their lives in a pointless war. This had happened in Vietnam to his brother—a loss that left his whole family convulsed in mute, inexpressible grief for decades.

A privileged moment is really a *beat*, a moment of irrevocable change that we saw being resisted, fought for, fought against, dreaded, and then finally accepted. Alleluia!

BEING ADVERSARIAL WITHOUT GIVING OFFENSE

Here are a couple of non-threatening ways to open up a delicate area:

THE DEVIL'S ADVOCATE APPROACH

If you say, "*Some people would say* it's not frightening for a kid to get home before his mother," then you are playing the devil's advocate role. The italicized words invite the interviewee to discharge his feelings at all those too crass to realize how scary it is for a young kid to enter an empty house. Tim Russert used this approach on President Bush: "How do you respond to critics who say you brought the nation to war under false pretenses?"

STARTING FROM GENERALIZED COMMENT

You want an interviewee to say on camera what she's told you in private: that she chose to dutifully nurse an ungrateful father instead of getting married. You'd like to ask, "Didn't you resent your father's expectations when you saw the love of your life marry someone else?" But this is too brutally direct, so you start at a safe distance: "Our society seems to expect daughters more than sons to make sacrifices for their parents, doesn't it?" She nods and starts talking about her parents' generation. This is an easier place to start than asking her to flaunt a sense of personal victimization. Whenever she ventures an opinion, you ask for an example. By mutual and unspoken agreement, the two of you steer toward the poignant testimony that both of you want to put on record. At the end you have helped her frame the sad injustice that overcomes women unprepared for a societal trap.

These approaches work because the interviewer's ego is removed from the equation, and because they start from the general and work toward the particular. Many who have too much pride to admit pain will do so if it might save someone else from a similar fate. Without this beautiful and generous human impulse to save others, much documentary would be impossible.

SEEKING BRIEFER VERSIONS

Facing an unexpected task or question, the human memory usually yields its contents in untidy, associative fragments. When it's a matter of getting a few facts in order, this can be tiresomely slow, and as if sensing this, many people spontaneously repeat their explanation in a quicker and more orderly form. With emotionally difficult material, your interviewee will search and struggle against inhibitions to explain. For emotionally loaded events this is patently sincere, spontaneous, and full of dramatic tension. Probably she will go back to explain, question herself, form a firmer picture, and then tell the whole episode again.

When you would like this to happen but it doesn't, you can ask, "Maybe you'd just like to go over that once more and give me a shorter version." Often the interviewee is grateful, and you get a nice short version. In editing you can now choose or even combine the best of each version.

TRIGGERING UNFINISHED BUSINESS

As you work with a central character in a documentary, you often sense what their *unfinished business* is. In drama this is like standing at the steep part of the dramatic curve a little before the crisis in their life's dramatic arc, where you find the *complications* and *rising action* part of the particular *problem* that is central to your film. It is that area of life where the traveler encounters test after test. Each confirms the direction he or she must take in order to find the El Dorado of final crisis and the liberty of release.

Novice directors are often hesitant, fearful of rebuff, or too self-conscious to act when they have an intuitive sense of their complicity in such a journey. Yet it takes no mystical powers to sense which way a person leans, only sustained and careful observation. It's far easier, in fact, to see other people's unfinished business than it is to see your own.

If you elect to play a director's role, you are helping overcome an obstacle course of challenges by which participants discover their issues and their strengths. You are investigating, making a record, and accompanying people on what is potentially the most important journey of their life. In choosing to make documentary film, you have assumed a certain responsibility to help seek truth, and as we said earlier in the book, you are not a catalyst walking away unchanged, but a vulnerable reagent evolving with others in a mutually chosen experiment.

CONCLUDING THE INTERVIEW

INVITATION TO ADD ANYTHING NOT COVERED

Before ending the interview, check your topic list. Is there anything on it that you overlooked? No? Good. Now, *while the camera is still running*, ask "Is there anything else you want to add, anything we forgot to cover?" Not only do you hand the last word to the participant, but you are putting this fact on record in case any dispute should arise later. After you cut the camera, thank your participants and briefly appreciate whatever was successful about the exchange. Keep everyone in place so the recordist can shoot a minute or two of presence track. Next day, you may want to phone the interviewee to see if there was anything important that he or she has thought of since.

THE RELEASE

When everyone rises to start dismantling equipment, give each participant a token sum (often the minimum $1) and ask them to sign the *individual release form* (see forms at www.directingthedocumentary.com). This is the permission form that each participant signs and which explicitly allows you to use the material publicly—a vital document that you must keep safe. Getting the signature is always an uncomfortable moment, and I confess that whenever I could, I gave this ghastly ritual to an assistant with instructions to carry it out as a necessary formality. As we have said, it is normal and even mandatory in many organizations *not* to pay for participation in a documentary. To do otherwise would open you to charges of checkbook journalism.

INTERVIEWING SELF-ASSESSMENT

To assess your interviewing, try the Assessing Yourself as an Interviewer project (Table 31-1). What did you forget? What do you need to work on? It is usual to find spontaneous moments of humor, inspired questions, and well-judged pauses, but also self-consciousness, persuasion tilting into manipulation, haste disguised as enthusiasm, and timidity masquerading as respect. What a rendezvous with the ego! To improve on the blind spots, stress, and artificiality in your performance will help you in your next experience of interviewing.

GOING FURTHER: "INWARD JOURNEY" MONOLOGUES

Most interviewees speak in the past tense about events already concluded. They face an interviewer and give—or resist, or deny—what the interviewer tries to get. The inference is that the relationship is inherently interviewer-centered, and to some degree inherently adversarial. Once I tried to break out by asking an interviewee to see a scene in her mind's eye and describe in the present tense what she saw. It failed because she kept reverting to the past tense. As a survivor of Auschwitz, she had the strongest imaginable justification for thrusting memories back into

TABLE 31-1 Interviewer Performance Checklist (Project PP-1 on the book's website, www.directingthedocumentary.com)

Project PP-1 Assessing Yourself as an Interviewer

	Did you…	Score 0–5
Preparation	Question in order to evoke responses in specific areas? Tell interviewee what you do and don't want to cover?	
Getting expository information	Get information to comprehensively set the scene? Get it from more than one person, so you have options? Keep a checklist so you forgot nothing vital?	
Directing and interacting	Maintain eye contact? Shape and direct the interview by questioning? Let the interview proceed informally and by association? Exert control over the substance of the interview? (It's your film and what it says is your responsibility.) Let the interviewee take control if your intuition told you it would lead to something important? Did you press for clarification? (If you don't know what the interviewee meant, your audience won't either.) Encourage your interviewee to stay with a significant subject until you felt it was fully explored? Keep exploring until you reached complete factual and emotional understanding? Refuse to settle for abstractions or generalities?	
Listening	Listen as if hearing everything for the first time and thus monitor what a first-time audience hears? Listen to ensure the answer starts comprehensively, and if not, have the interviewee start over? (Answers shouldn't depend on information in the question.) Not think about your next question (since it stops you listening)? Listen and catch subtexts, those unspoken meanings lying beneath the surface?	
Steering	Direct interviewee by saying, "Could you talk about (subject)…"? Summarize what you understand so far, and ask the participant to continue? Courteously change subject by saying, "Could we move to … (new subject)"?	

(Continued)

TABLE 31-1 (Continued)

Project PP-1 Assessing Yourself as an Interviewer

	Did you ...	Score 0–5
Follow-up	Follow up all intuitions and instincts? Store further points as you listen, and eventually bring the interviewee back to them? Expand on something by saying, "Can we return to ...?" Encourage going farther by quoting interviewee's significant words in a questioning tone? Open an emotional area by saying, "I got the impression that you have strong feelings about ...?" Repeat the interviewee's last words in a questioning tone when he/she stopped and needed encouragement? Name the impression you're getting, for example, "You seem hesitant to tell me something" or "You seem amused", etc.?	
Silences	Correctly interpret an "I'm finished" kind of silence? Keep the camera running during a silence until he or she carried on? Were you right to interject and move on?	
Interviewing people in crisis and "doing damage"	Overcome your fear of intruding? (People know instinctively what they can handle. Just go carefully.) Did you act on the knowledge that crises are when people most need to talk? Did you act on the idea that giving testimony is healing, and being a good listener is part of it?	
Closure	Find that a good interview left a sense of catharsis? Remember to say, "Is there anything you'd like to add?" before concluding the interview? Thank the interviewee at the end? Check back next day to see what afterthoughts the interviewee has had since? Maintain humility by acknowledging your failures?	

the distance. However, my instinct wasn't completely misguided since the Canadian Broadcast Corporation's radio story program *Outfront* (www.cbc.ca/outfront) does something similar, and gets superlative results. Of themselves they say, with winning moxy, "***Outfront*** is where we hand *you* the microphone. You make a radio documentary, with our help. Then CBC broadcasts it—and you'll even get paid!" In the National Public Radio (NPR) Third Coast Audio Festival broadcast of February 2, 2008, producer Neil Sandell described the methods they use (http://thirdcoastfestival.org/library/609-re-sound-81-the-outfront-show). "Ironing Man" and "One Blue Canoe" are examples that will leave you with a lump in your throat. To catalyze such naked memoir, an *Outfront* producer might say,

"Close your eyes so you can begin seeing things in your mind's eye"
"Use this sentence to begin…" (interviewer gives a *prompt*—see below)
"Describe in the present tense what you see. Wait for the pictures to form and take as long as you need."

The radio producer's *prompts*, spoken as necessary, might sound like this:

"I am in my bedroom choosing what to wear…"
"I am driving on the highway and there's a large white van coming toward me…"
"As I return to consciousness, the first things I hear and see in the hospital emergency room are…"

The *Outfront* approach is a wonderful way to generate film narration or voice-over. From this freestanding monologue an editor can extract a spontaneous inner journey—quite different from the conventional interview.

Radio documentary is resurgent in America and elsewhere, and showing the way forward with mind-journeys. NPR's Third Coast Audio Festival puts out wonderful work drawn from worldwide. Try the Australian work on Show #57 at www.thirdcoastfestival.org/re-sound.asp (rebroadcast February 23, 2008). For depth of social comment listen to Claudia Taranto's *A Tale of Two Townsvilles*; and for unforgettable sound design and sheer gut-wrenching emotion listen to Kyla Brettle's *000 Ambulance*.

For adventurous radio work and offbeat treatments, listen to Ira Glass and his National Public Radio team in *This American Life* at www.thislife.org. They excel at funny, quirky, and intimate first-person shows that take in-depth looks at aspects of popular culture. One called "Testosterone" told of people getting more testosterone and coming to regret it, and of other people losing testosterone, and coming to appreciate life without it. The pros and cons of the hormone of desire are at www.thisamericanlife.org/radio-archives/episode/220/testosterone.

HANDS-ON LEARNING

As preparation for interviewing, try out **SP-11 Advanced Interview, Three Shot Sizes** and then assess your work using **PP-1 Assessing Yourself as an Interviewer**.

NOTES

1. Ray Carney, *The Films of John Cassavetes* (Cambridge University Press, 1994), pp. 21–22.
2. *Dr. Spock: We're Sliding towards Destruction* (USA/GB, 1969), BBC "One Pair of Eyes" series.
3. Seamus Heaney, *The Government of the Tongue* (Faber, 1988), p. xvi.

PART 7C

ADVANCED POSTPRODUCTION

If you make a film containing many interviews, you will almost certainly work from transcripts. **In Chapter 32: From Transcript to Assembly** there is a way to quite quickly make them into an initial script for assembly by the editor. Long projects are procedurally similar to short ones, but naturally pose more problems of structure, length, and dramatic balance. They are also more likely to need a narrator, so **Chapter 33: Creating Narration** describes various methods of developing them. For films in need of music, there is **Chapter 34: Using Music and Working with a Composer.** Then, to balance your story and test its effect on audiences, there is **Chapter 35: Editing Refinements and Structural Solutions.**

CHAPTER 32

FROM TRANSCRIPT TO ASSEMBLY

The more interviews, events, and elements you must orchestrate in your documentary, the more experiment you will need to fully explore your material's potential. Initially this means making the shots and topics labeled and thoroughly accessible. Take time to figure out how best to develop any indexes, graphics, guides, and color-coding you think will help, since this saves time and energy for creative matters. This I learned as an editor for the soccer World Cup documentary *Goal* (Ross Devenish and Abidin Dino, UK, 1967), when hired to edit the final game between England and West Germany. It comprised 70,000 feet (13 hours) of 35 mm film shot mostly silent from 17 camera positions. The only orientation was a shot of a clock face at the beginning of each 1,000-foot roll.

Before I cut anything, my assistant Robert Giles and I spent a week up to our armpits in film, making a diagram of the stadium and coding each major event as it appeared in the various angles. The game went into overtime due to a foul, and it was eventually my luck to establish that, during this most decisive of moments, *not one* of the 17 cameras was rolling. So, using sports reports and Robert's masterly grasp of the game, we used an assortment of close shots to manufacture a facsimile of the missing foul. Luckily, nobody guessed we'd had to fake it. That project was an editor's deathtrap, and without my feature film training in making a good retrieval system, the men in white coats would have carted us away in the legendary rubber bus. Filing and indexing digital material is the modern equivalency, and just as important.

Following is how to carve up transcript copies so you can narrow your choices and make a workable blueprint called a *paper edit*. Figure 32-1 is a flow chart illustrating the procedure, designed to minimize your effort in quickly producing a long first cut. As with all filing systems, *stick with one system for the duration of the project*, and make improvements only when you start a new project.

WHAT YOU NEED FOR TRANSCRIPTS

ACCURATE TRANSCRIPTIONS

These should be made verbatim, including all the ums, wells, you-knows, and other verbal curlicues that people use while their mind assembles what they want to say. Punctuation should follow the way a person speaks, and never be adapted to make his presumed intentions clearer on paper.

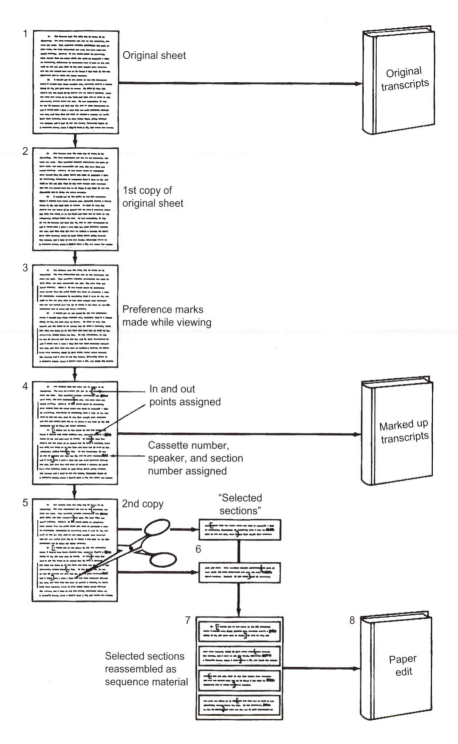

FIGURE 32-1

Flow chart illustrating the paper edit procedure.

Whenever a speaker plainly starts a new line of thought, start a new paragraph; otherwise keep typing in long paragraphs. Remember, it is not literature, and you aren't laying it out for easy reading. You are trying to record verbatim what someone said. The temptation to edit and clarify as you transcribe is ever-present, so resist, because making a passage clearer on paper than it really is will only make more work later for the film editor.

TIMECODE (TC)

Every frame of video you shoot will have its own timecode, which is like each frame's street address on a road called Time. In transcriptions you only need interpolate a timecode occasionally, and even then only in minutes and approximate seconds. A TC reference is useful at:

- The beginning and end of each interview.
- Questions, because they often initiate a new topic.
- Every half-minute or so in lengthy material, to help the editor navigate the text.

LINE NUMBERING

Word processing can provide a legal line-numbering feature that might be valuable when you have many speakers. I once made a film with over 20 characters telling the convoluted story of the conscientious objector movement in World War I.[1] Had each interview transcript been line-numbered, the origin of even the smallest sections would have been far easier to track—a lifesaver on a really big project.

USING A DATABASE

If you're working with a modest amount of source material, you may get by with nothing more technical than a yellow highlighter and Post-It® notes. For a series like the Michael Apted *Up* series that draws on a gargantuan base of common transcript and archive material, you would need to customize an all-purpose database program such as Filemaker Pro. By defining your chosen fields, and filing your information in them, you can then search with incredible speed, making your priority perhaps person, period, location, or key words. You can display the results of your search as a list, a table, or as index cards—however you set up the system. Of course, data entry takes time and effort, but there's nothing like it for helping you to internalize your resources. As you transfer the details, you gestate creative ideas, and can put them into effect efficiently and thoroughly because any of your material is at your fingertips.

SELECTING AND ASSEMBLING TRANSCRIPT MATERIALS

Now you can make a *paper edit*, a blueprint from which the editor constructs a first, loose assembly. The flexibility of the paper edit system lets you move slips of paper around like the raw materials for a mosaic. Each round of experimental juxtapositioning sets you thinking and gives you ideas. To avoid your film becoming wall-to-wall talking, handle the process in two stages: (1) choose and assemble the action and behavioral material to establish the temporal spine of your film, and then (2) choose interview "rib" material that will illuminate and expand on the spine where necessary.

Stage 1: Make an action assembly: that is,

Prepare a list of action sequences and code them for easy identification. The sequences in college for a woman called Jane might look something like this:

1/Jane/1 Jane's graduation speech
1/Jane/2 Jane has dinner with boyfriend's family

```
Q:  What do you remember about the farmer?

Ted:  What do I....?  Oh, well, you know, [he
was all right if you kept your place.  But if
you got smart, or asked too many questions,
he'd be after you.  "Where's that wagon load of
straw?  Why ain't them cattle fed yet?"  And
then he'd say there were plenty of men walking
the streets looking for work if I didn't want
to work.  The only thing you could do was be
silent, 'cos he meant what he said.]  Now his
wife was different.  She was a nice soul, you
know what I mean?  Couldn't see how she came
to marry him in the first place....
```

6/Ted/3
'Ted's descript. of Farmer Wills.'

FIGURE 32-2

A selected section showing in and out brackets, media origin ID, and tag description.

1/Jane/3 Conversation between Jane and English teacher
2/Jane/1 Conversation, Jane and Dad

Now loosely edit them so each has a beginning, middle, and end, and assemble them in chronological order so they move logically through time.

View the action or behavioral assembly several times to establish its narrative possibilities and its deficiencies firmly in your mind.

Stage 2: Mark up the interview transcripts:

Step A: Place a complete printout of the transcript files (Frame 1) in a binder titled *Original Transcripts*. This represents the as-is transcription from the original recording.

Step B: Take a second printout (Frame 2) and read it while playing its interview. Put a quick, rough vertical *preference mark* in the margin of any section you find effective (Frame 3). Don't analyze your reactions, *respond* with a mark, and keep listening.

Step C: As in Frame 4, (a) designate good in- and out-points to bracket each *preferred section*, then (b) give each a *section ID* consisting of original reel number, character's name, and section number ('6/Ted/3' say), and (c) add a handwritten *tag description*, such as "Ted's descript. of Farmer Wills." Tags let you sort and structure slips of paper when you face dozens or hundreds of them, and the section IDs tell you where to find the material in the video files (Figure 32-2).

Step D: Make a photocopy of the fully marked-up preferred section sheets (Frame 5), filing the uncut parent copy (Frame 4) for future reference in a binder titled *Marked-Up Transcripts*.

Step E: Scissor the marked sections (Frame 5) into individual slips of paper (Frame 6), ready for sorting and grouping. Each carries an ID, so you know at a glance what it is, what it can do, and where it came from.

Step F: Match your chosen interview sections with your assembly of action material (Frame 7) without worrying about length or redundancy. Your object is to get likely material in roughly the right place, since future judgments can only be made by repeatedly screening the material, not from anything on paper. Your paper files and searchable database remain on hand as tools for mining your resources.

Step G: Staple all your material to sequentially numbered sheets of paper, dividing them into sequences. Place all this in a third binder (Frame 8) called the *Paper Edit*, ready for rapid execution on the computer as the first rough assembly of chosen materials.

Now you have a rudimentary story, and can rule lines between sequences and even group the sequences into scenes and acts.

FROM PAPER EDIT TO FIRST ASSEMBLY

From this approximate master plan you begin making a loose, baggy monster of an assembly. Until you retrieve each selected section you won't know whether you can execute the chosen in- and out-points. Maybe you can't lose all those verbal warm-ups before the in-point; maybe your out-point leaves Ted on a rising voice inflection so that his statement sounds strange and unfinished. Don't worry if it is all vastly too long and repetitious. This is normal; refined decisions can only come from screening the material during editing proper.

Be cautious and conservative with your first structure. If your film is about a rural girl going to the big city to become a college student, stay true to the events' chronology rather than, say, making the events unfold according to their importance to her. At this early stage, that would be a leap in the dark.

As a rule when editing, only fix the top layer of problems in any one pass. Expect to make repeated passes, each tackling a more subtle level of disorder. Make the crown first, cut and polish the jewels later.

LITERAL AND NON-LITERAL COMMENTS

Certain pieces of interview or conversational exchange gravitate toward certain pieces of action, either because the location is the same or because one comments on the other. This "comment" may be literally a spoken comment, or better, implied nonverbally through ironic juxtaposition (of action or speech) that makes its own point in the viewer's mind.

An example would be a scene in which our student Jane faces having to make a graduation speech before the whole school, a prospect she admits scares her. A literal comment would simply interject some of the interview shot later in which she confesses how nervous she felt. A non-literal comment might take the same rehearsal and intercut her mother saying how calm and confident she usually is. A visual comment during the rehearsal might show that she is flustered when the microphone is the wrong height and that her hands shake when she turns the pages of her speech. What's the difference? The literal comment is show-and-tell, since it merely illustrates what Jane tells us. The non-literal comment is far more interesting because it supplies us with conflicting information and asks us to make a judgment. Her mother enviously imagines that Jane can handle anything, but we notice signs that the poor girl is under strain. Either the mother is overrating the girl's confidence or she is out of touch with her child's inner life. This privileged insight, discreetly shared with the audience, gives us behavioral evidence that all is not well, that the girl is suffering, and makes us scrutinize the family dynamics more critically. The guiding philosophy is that human life is a cover for the struggle and turmoil beneath. Too often we deceive ourselves and each other, and a sympathetic dramatist's job is to hint at the hidden complexities.

TREATING YOUR AUDIENCE AS EQUALS

The order and juxtaposition of materials have potent consequences. How you eventually present and use your material reveals your ideas about the people and the premise you are exploring, but it also signals how you intend to relate to your audience as their Storyteller. Here you can juxtapose mismatching *pieces of evidence* like a lawyer piquing the interest and involvement of the jury, your audience. Good evidentiary juxtaposition provides sharp impressions, challenges the jury's judgment, and removes much of the need to explain.

When you can better see how the material plays, you might intercut her high school graduation, conversations with a teacher, discussions with her father, and leaving home along with the development of her first semester as a college drama student. You would then have two parallel stories to tell, one in the "present" and one in the "past." It is still too risky to do all this yet.

GIVE ACTION PREFERENCE OVER WORDS

Notice that instead of first developing a narrative wordplay and illustrating it with action material—which is the instinct of the teacher and journalist—we created the best possible narrative from pure action, and then used speech to fill out its deficiencies. The difference onscreen will be highly significant because we made full use of the cinema as a medium.

NOTE

1. *Prisoners of Conscience* ("Yesterday's Witness" series, GB, 1969).

CHAPTER 33

CREATING NARRATION

Many filmmakers shy away from narration because of its association with the voice-of-God discourses of yesteryear. This is a shame, since there is nothing more satisfying than knowing you have written some really effective narration. Usually it is indispensable in films about natural history, science, government, history, as well as in films that are avowedly journalistic or in diary form. You will assuredly have to write narration sometime in your career, so keep in mind that narration plays a vital role in three masterly documentaries praised in earlier chapters. I refer to Alain Resnais' *Night and Fog*, Patricio Guzman's *Nostalgia for the Light*, and Emad Burat and Guy Davidi's *Five Broken Cameras*. In each, a master Storyteller creates a gripping counterpoint between imagery and an interior monologue. Each demonstrates how sensitively a narration can conduct us through humanity's darker regions.

NARRATION PROS AND CONS

Narration is a lifesaver when used to rapidly and effectively introduce a new character, summarize intervening developments, or concisely supply a few vital facts. Especially when a film must fit much into a short duration, time saved in exposition is time gained elsewhere. Good narration,

- Supplies brief factual information.
- Uses the direct, active-voice language of speech.
- Uses the simplest words for the job.
- Is free of cliché.
- Gets the most meaning from the fewest syllables.
- Feels balanced and potent to the ear.
- Avoids emotional manipulation.
- Avoids value judgments, unless first established by pictorial evidence.
- Prepares us to notice evidence we might otherwise miss.
- Helps us when necessary to draw conclusions from the evidence.

Bad narration, however,

- Describes what is already evident from the picture.
- Is condescending.
- Uses the pseudo-scientific passive voice.
- Uses convoluted sentences, and sonorous, ready-made phrases and clichés.
- Uses jargon or corporate-speak rather than workaday speech.
- Over-informs, leaving the audience no time to imagine or contemplate.

VOICE

A narration can adopt any appropriate tradition of "voice" already established in other narrative forms such as theatre, literature, song, and poetry. Documentaries may therefore,

- Use a character's voice-over as narration because he or she has insider knowledge and a right to an opinion.
- Take an omniscient or historical view, as do films that survey immigration, war, slavery, etc.
- Adopt the guise of a naively inquisitive visitor (as in films by Nicholas Broomfield, Michael Moore, and Morgan Spurlock).
- Take a what-if, suppositional voice, as in Cayrol's commentary for *Night and Fog* (Alain Resnais, France, 1955, Figure 33-1), whose authority probably arises from Cayrol having been a Holocaust survivor himself.
- Express a poetic and musical identification with the subject, as in Basil Wright and Harry Watt's *Night Mail* (GB, 1936, Figure 33-2).
- Radicalize the audience by using a bland or understated way of looking at an appalling situation, as in Luis Buñuel's *Land without Bread* (Spain, 1932) or Burnat and Davidi's *Five Broken Cameras* (Palestine/Israel/France/Netherlands, 2013).

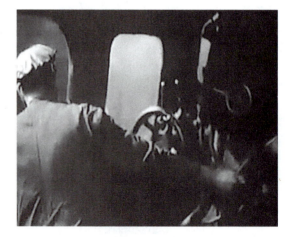

FIGURE 33-1 ——————————————

A what-if, suppositional voice narrates *Night and Fog.*

FIGURE 33-2 ——————————————

Celebrating the dignity of the ordinary person's labor in *Night Mail.*

- Use a letter- or diary-writing voice, as in the authentic war journals and correspondence from which Ken Burns builds much of the narration for *The Civil War* series (USA, 1990, Figure 33-3).
- Write a diary for the next generation, as Humphrey Jennings imagined a war pilot doing for his baby son in *A Diary for Timothy* (GB, 1946, Figure 33-4). The narration, by the novelist E.M. Forster, expresses a war-weary generation's hope of resuming family life.

DRAWBACKS

Viewers will assume that the narration is *the voice of the film itself* unless you establish that it is that of the filmmaker or one of the film's characters. They will be influenced not only by what the narrator says, but disproportionately by the quality and associations of the narrator's physical voice. The deep male "radio voice," for instance, represents Authority with all its connotations of condescension and paternalism. The need to avoid stereotyping one's own work makes finding an appropriate voice excruciatingly difficult. You will help yourself if you use narration sparingly and neutrally, leaving the audience as free as possible to develop its own judgment, values, and discrimination.

PROBLEMS NARRATION CAN SOLVE

Perhaps you have a personal or anthropological film and need to provide factual links or set context. Maybe expositional material is lacking and the film's story line needs simplifying. In each case, narration will probably emerge as the only practical answer. After you have assembled your movie, see how it stands on its own feet and whether it has any of these common problems:

- Difficulty getting the film started (convoluted and confusing setup).
- Origin and therefore authenticity of materials unclear (there might be some reconstruction, for instance).

FIGURE 33-3

A narration made from correspondence and war journals in *The Civil War* series.

FIGURE 33-4

In *A Diary for Timothy* the narration develops a war-weary generation's hopes of eventually resuming normal life again.

- Audience needs more information on a participant's thoughts, feelings, choices.
- Overcomplicated storyline needs simplifying.
- Getting from one good sequence to the next takes too much explaining by the participants.
- Film's final issues lack focus so film fails to resolve satisfyingly.

When a lukewarm trial audience grows more enthusiastic after you added some off the cuff comments, you know that your film has problems, and narration may be the only way to supply the missing information succinctly.

COMPARING WAYS TO CREATE NARRATION

Below are two common ways to create a narration, each with pros and cons.

METHOD A—READING FROM A SCRIPT

The traditional method can work well if you base your film's verbal narrative on a *bona fide* text such as letters or a diary, because the formality present in anyone's reading will feel authentic. But if you want spontaneity or a one-to-one tone of intimacy, written narration nearly always fails, no matter how professional everyone is. Think how often the narration is what makes a film dull or dated. Common faults:

- Verbosity (a writing problem).
- Doubt over who or what the narrator represents (a question of the narrator's authority).

- Something inauthentic or thespian in the narrator's voice. It may be dull, condescending, egotistic, projecting, trying to entertain, trying to ingratiate, or have other distracting associations (a performance and/or casting problem).

METHOD B—IMPROVISATION

Improvised narration can rather easily strike an informal, "one-on-one" relationship with the audience. It works because the speaker is having to create what he or she says on the spot, just as we do in daily life. Improvisation is good,

- When a participant serves as narrator.
- When you use your own voice in a "diary" film that must sound spontaneous and not scripted.

   Below is what to do for each generative method.

METHOD A: CREATING THE SCRIPTED NARRATION

WRITING

It will help to write and record scratch (temporary) narration during editing. Then, by reading your words aloud against each film section, keep simplifying and refining your wording in search of the power of simplicity. It is normal to go through dozens of drafts before everything feels right and falls into place. When it comes time to record, the narrator will have a well-tried text.

   Good writing must,

- Be consistent in tone, since it is now an additional "character" in the film.
- Pick up its sense and rhythm from the words of the last speaker and feed into those of the next.
- Be the right length so the narrator doesn't have to speed up or slow down to fill the space.
- Allow your audience to notice things in picture *before* the narration comments on them. Narration that leads or accompanies what we notice turns your film into a slide-lecture.

TIMING AND SYNTAX

Narration should follow the order in which the audience notices things. Sometimes you will have to adjust syntax by inverting the sentence structure. If, for instance, you have a shot of a big, rising sun with a small figure toiling across the landscape, you might first write, "She goes out before anyone else is about." But the viewer notices the sun long before the human being, so your syntax is violating the order of perception. The viewer, unaware at first of any "she," simply loses the rest of the sentence. However, reconfigure the syntax as "Before anyone else is up, she goes out" and the problem is solved. It works because you have complemented the order of perception (sun, landscape, woman) instead of blocking it.

ACCOMMODATING SOUND FEATURES

Sometimes you must alter phrasing or break sentences apart to allow space for featured sound effects, such as a car door closing or a phone beginning to ring. Effects can create a powerful mood that helps drive the narrative forward, so don't obscure them. They also help reduce the bane of documentary—*verbal diarrhea* (film industry shorthand for "too much loose talk.")

COMPLEMENT, DON'T DUPLICATE

When you write for film, never describe what we can already see. Narration must *add* information, never duplicate it. You would not say that the child is wearing a red raincoat (blatantly obvious from the shot) or that she is hesitant (subtly evident), but you can say she has just had her sixth birthday. This is legitimate additional information because it is not what we can see or infer.

TRYING IT OUT: THE SCRATCH RECORDING

Once you have written your narration, record a scratch (quick, trial) narration using any handy reader's voice, including your own. Lay in the scratch narration (see "Secrets of Fitting Narration" below) and view your work several times dispassionately. Improved versions will jump out at you. You'll see where you need pacing and emotional coloration changes, and that you must thin out the narration where the narrator is forced to hurry. Elsewhere the narration may seem perfunctory because it needs developing.

Now you can more easily imagine what kind of voice you'd prefer. Keep writing and rewriting until you've got every sentence and syllable just right. Now you are ready to think about auditioning and recording the final narrator.

NARRATION: AUDITIONING AND RECORDING

A SCRIPT FOR THE NARRATOR

The script you prepare should be a simple, double-spaced typescript, containing only what the narrator will read. Set blocks of narration apart on the page and number them for easy location. Try not to split a block across two pages, because the narrator may turn pages audibly during the recording. Where this is unavoidable, make pages rattle-proof by putting them inside plastic page protectors, or lay them flat so no handling is required while recording.

If you write a contract for the narrator, stipulate a proportion of call-back time in case you need additions at a later stage.

CONVERSING AND READING ALOUD ARE DIFFERENT

When you speak to a listener, your mind is occupied in finding the right words. Reading from a script however turns you into an audience for your own voice. A few highly experienced actors can overcome this, but they are rare. Documentary participants speaking from a script are going to have more difficulty still, even though the words and ideas were originally their own.

VOICE AUDITIONS

Directing a reader so that he or she sounds natural turns out to be the hardest thing in the world. Few readers can make a written narration sound remotely natural, not even highly trained actors. To guard against disappointment, start the process well in advance, record to picture (described later), and never assume all will be OK on the night, because it never is.

To test native ability, give each person something representative to read. Then ask for a different reading of the same material, to see how well each narrator responds to directions, which may involve meaning or tone. One reader focuses effectively on the new interpretation but relinquishes what was previously successful. Another reader may be anxious to please, can carry out instructions, but lacks a grasp of the larger picture. This is common with actors of limited experience.

Choosing an omniscient narrator is, as we have said, tantamount to choosing a personality for your film itself, and most voices will have disconcerting associations. For any number of reasons, most will simply sound horrendously wrong. As with any situation of choice, you should record several, even when you believe you have stumbled on perfection. After you make audition recordings, thank each person and give a date by which you will make a decision.

Make your final selection by trying speakers' voices against the film until you are satisfied. Your final choice must be independent of personal liking or obligation. Make it solely on what you and your counselors agree is the best narration voice.

RECORDING AND DIRECTING THE NARRATOR

Show your chosen narrator the whole film and listen to his or her ideas about what it communicates and what the narration adds. Encouraging the narrator to find the right attitude and state of mind will do much to get written words sounding right. This is because we speak from thoughts, experiences, memories, and feelings. Invoking the whole person of the narrator gets better results than imagining that everything is already on the page and can be coached, sentence by sentence.

Record in a professional fashion, that is, with the picture running so that the narrator (listening on headphones) can key into the rhythms and intonation of adjacent voices in the film. As you go to record each section, the narrator should cease watching the picture (that is the job of the editor and director) and his or her headphones should be cut off from track in- and out-points, which would be distracting. No access to a studio? Set up your own rig with video playback and original sound made available to the artist via headphones. It will be more than worth the trouble.

Large organizations sometimes have access to landlines, conferencing facilities, and so forth which make it feasible to record a narrator from a distant location. This may work for history, science, or journalism, but a narrator in a remote location is difficult to engage emotionally for films that require a personal tone. No fiction director would choose to work miles apart from their actors, and nor should you.

ACOUSTIC SETTING

Your best voice recording will probably come from having the speaker between 1 to 2 feet from the microphone. Surroundings should be acoustically dead (not enclosed or echoey), and there should be no background noise. Listen through *good* headphones or through a quality speaker in another room. It is critically important to get the best out of your narrator's voice. Watch out for the voice trailing away at ends of sentences, for "popping" on plosive sounds, or distortion from overloading. Careful mike positioning and monitoring sound levels are vital.

READING

The narrator should read each block of narration and wait for a cue (a gentle tap on the shoulder or a cue-light flash) before beginning the next. Rehearse first and give directions; phrase these positively and practically, giving instructions on what feeling to aim for rather than why. Stick to essentials, such as "Make the last part a little warmer" or "I'd like you to try that a bit more formally." Name the quality or emotion you are after. After rehearsing each block, record it and move on to rehearsing the next.

Sometimes you will want to alter the word stressed in a sentence, or change the amount of projection the speaker is using ("Could you give me the same intensity but use less voice?" or "Use more voice and keep it up at the ends of sentences"). Occasionally a narrator will have some insurmountable problem with phrasing. Invite him or her to reword it while retaining the sense, but be on guard if this starts happening a lot. Sometimes narrators want to take over the writing. Let this happen only if you hear definite improvement.

Once you have recorded all the narration, play all the chosen parts back against the film so you can check that it all works. If you have any doubtful readings, make additional variants before letting the narrator go. These you audition later and use the best.

METHOD B: CREATING THE IMPROVISED NARRATION

A spontaneous and informal narration is one that sounds like person-to-person conversation, and you can easily create this through interviewing. Under these circumstances the speaker's mind is naturally engaged in finding words to act back on you, the interviewer—a familiar situation that unfailingly elicits normal speech. The drawback is that it may be hard to get the precision and compression possible through writing a narration. Ways to create an improvised narration follow.

SIMPLE INTERVIEW

This method lets you extract a highly spontaneous-sounding narration in the cutting room. Commonly, the director interviews the documentary's "point of view" character carefully and extensively. Probably it is best done in spare moments during shooting while the chase is on, but do it in a really quiet place. When you interview, *make sure the replies stand on their own as statements* because you must eliminate your voice asking questions. Replies that overlap the question or lack self-contained starts won't make sense unless you retain your question, which defeats the object of creating interior monologue material. For instance,

Q: "Tell us about how you make your catch in the bay"

A: "With pots, and a boat"

Remove the question, and "With pots, and a boat" is meaningless. So amend your question and ask again:

Q: "Tell us what your work is, what you catch, and how you go about it."

A: "Well, I'm a lobster fisherman and we use lobster pots, and a boat to get from one ground to the next."

Remove the "Well" and now you have a nice, affirmative statement that makes a serviceable first-person narration. As you interview, listen carefully to make sure you cover all your bases. Keep a list handy of what information you must elicit so nothing gets forgotten, and for anything at all important make sure you get more than one version from more than one person so you have options in the cutting room later.

Sync interviews can be used as sound-only voice over, cutting to the speaker's image only at critical moments. Overused, however, this is the slippery slope to a talking head picture. You can also get people to talk to the camera while they go about their normal activities. *The House*, a 1996 British TV documentary series about London's deteriorating Royal Opera, had wigmakers and set designers talking to the camera about the management's failings while they powdered wigs or arranged props.

Today you aren't bound to make transparent films—that is, ones that pretend we are seeing real life with no camera crew present. Nowadays we happily share the whole reality of filmmaking with the audience.

If you need to narrate your own film, get a trusted and demanding friend to interview you.

IMPROVISING FROM A ROUGH SCRIPT

In this relatively structured method, you supply your narrator with a text that he or she reads, then gives back. When you ask interview questions, he or she replies in character, paraphrasing the information in the first or third person, as necessary. Finding the words to express the narration's content reflects what happens in life; we know what we want to say, but must find the words to say it.

IMPROVISING FROM AN ASSUMED IDENTITY

This method is good for creating, say, a historical character's voice-over. It develops from a character or type of person the narrator has "become." Together you go over who the narrator is and what this character wants the listener to know. Then you interview him, perhaps taking on a character role yourself so you can ask pertinent and leading questions. Replying from a defined role helps the narrator lock into a focused relationship.

RECORDING PRESENCE TRACK

Whenever you record a voice track, record some recording studio *presence track* or *location atmosphere*. As we have said earlier, this provides the editor with the right quality of "silence" to extend a pause or to add to the head of a narration block. Even in the same recording studio, and using the same mike, no two presence tracks (also called *buzz track* or *room tone*) are ever exactly alike.

SECRETS OF FITTING NARRATION

However you generated narration, the same principles to fit it to picture apply. Following are little-known principles that greatly increase your narration's effectiveness, and which will give your audience a strong sense of security and confidence in your film's narrative voice.

USING THE FIRST WORD'S POWER ON A NEW IMAGE

Skillful writing and sensitive word placement gives you not just a tool of communication but an exquisitely accurate scalpel. For instance, if we cut shots together as in Figure 33-5; the outgoing shot is a still photo showing an artist at work at his easel, and the incoming shot shows a painting of a woman. The narration says, "Spencer used as a model first his wife and later the daughter of a friend." By juxtaposing the words and images differently we can imply three quite different meanings. The crux lies in which word hits the incoming shot, as illustrated in the diagram. Using a single, unchanging section of narration, and the same three shots, we can in fact identify the person in the portrait as wife, daughter, or friend.

In another situation, illustrated in Figure 33-6, a simple shift in word positioning may alter, not an image's meaning but its emotional shading. For instance, you see two shots, each of a piece of sculpture, and you hear the narrator say, "His later work was provocatively different." Alter the relationship of narration to incoming image by a single word, and the second sculpture becomes either just "different" or "*provocatively* different." Something you should know: during a flow of words and accompanying images, *the first word to coincide with each new image greatly influences how the audience interprets it.*

OPERATIVE WORDS

Sometimes you put words to images, sometimes images against given dialogue or narration. A little-known secret to doing this well is to make use of the fact that speech has strong and weak points against which to position a picture cut. You can spot the strong points simply by treating

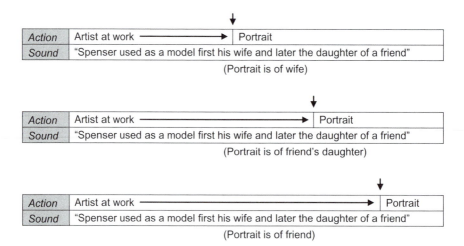

FIGURE 33-5

Different cutting points imply different identities for the portrait's subject.

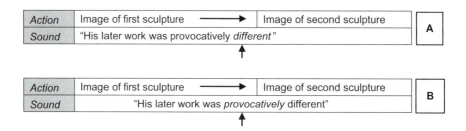

FIGURE 33-6

The first word on each new image affects how we interpret its meaning. Such "operative" words are italicized to demonstrate how emphasis can change. In (A) the later sculpture seems like a departure in the artist's work, while in (B) the second sculpture evoked an excited reaction.

it like music, so you hear patterns in the speaker's language. In order to stress meaning, we inflect key syllables with a slightly louder volume or higher note. A mother might say to her recalcitrant teenager: "I want you to wait right here and don't move. I'll talk to you later."

Different readings imply different subtexts, but a likely one is: "I want you to **wait** right here and don't **move**. I'll talk to you **later**. Stressed syllables encode the dominant intention, so I call them *operative words*. Using a *split-page script* form, we could design images to cut like this:

Picture	Sound
Wide shot, woman and son.	"I want you to …
Close shot, boy's mutinous face.	wait right here and …
Close shot, her hand on his shoulder.	don't move. (pause) I'll …
Close shot, mother's determined face.	talk to you later."

By cutting to a new image on operative words, you punch home the mother's determination and imply the boy's stubborn resistance. In any well-edited fiction film, the rhythms intrinsic to this principle permeate the editing of dialogue scenes. You cannot preplan this, because the editing has to respond to the rhythms in the players and their physical movement. These subtly lead the audience's expectations, and the editor, by orchestrating them, can exploit all the colorations of their *subtexts* (larger meanings hidden from sight).

When you edit, try to imagine you are a foreigner seeking meaning through people's verbal music and body language. This is deeply ingrained in the psyche since that's how we strained to understand the world as small children. Within a single sentence you hear rising and sinking tonal changes, rhythmic patterns like percussion in the stream of syllables, and dynamic variations of loud and soft. Working from this sensibility, your editing, shot selection, and placement now take place inside an essentially musical structure, and form a new, larger set of patterns. Here film, music, and dance joyfully link arms.

By paying attention to *operative words* and their potential, you will see patterns of pictures and words becoming receptive to each other, and falling into mutually responsive patterns. Magically effective, they drive the film along with an exhilarating sense of inevitability. Good editing is the compositional art that disguises art.

To bring this cinematic music to fruition when laying narration to picture, you will often have to make small picture-cutting changes, though sometimes altering the natural pauses in the narration will stretch or compress a section to produce the right lengths. Be very careful, however, not to disrupt the natural rhythms of the narrator or of a participant.

CHAPTER 34

USING MUSIC AND WORKING WITH A COMPOSER

WHERE TO USE MUSIC

USING MUSIC TO REVEAL HIDDEN DIMENSIONS

Documentaries, like fiction films, often use music to build tension, facilitate a transition, or enliven material that is lackluster. In fact, music can *suggest what cannot be seen*, and this might be a character's interior mood, expectations, or withheld feelings. Such a character is the 82-year-old central character in Pernilla Rose Grønkjær's lyrical and delicate *The Monastery: Mr Vig and the Nun* (Denmark, 2006). The retired parish priest Mr. Vig remarks poignantly that, during all his long life, he has never known love. He is now trying to donate his decrepit rural castle as a future monastery, and arriving to claim it is a Russian Orthodox nun from Moscow who wants to arrange extensive repairs. Though she is fifty years younger, and they are formal and undemonstrative with each other, she begins to look after him (Figure 34-1). It is Johan Söderqvist's music that suggests a mutual affection developing inside these two tough and reserved characters. His guitar and string orchestra score has been described as "exquisite and … a living, breathing character all on its own."[1] Hear it at www.themonasterymovie.com/monastery.html and try to see the film, which has sequence after sequence of gorgeous imagery.

Today, less is more. A rhythm alone without melody or harmony can sometimes supply the uncluttered accompaniment that a sequence needs. Music can supply an underlying mood, and in a story with fine shading, a good score can hint at the integrity or melancholy in one character, and the emotional impulsiveness directing the actions of another. Music can enhance not just the "givens" of a character (what we already know about him or her) but the hidden interior developments that culminate in a particular action, thus implying moods, motives, or interior processes that are otherwise inaccessible.

MUSIC MISUSED

Music, sad to say, sometimes duplicates or even upstages what's already evident on the screen. Walt Disney was infamous for "Mickey Mousing" his films—the industry term for clamping musical strait-jackets around the minutia of action. The first of his "true life adventures," *The Living Desert*

FIGURE 34-1

Pernilla Rose Grønkjær's lyrical and delicate *The Monastery: Mr Vig and the Nun.*

(directed by James Algar, USA, 1953), was full of extraordinary documentary footage but disfigured by making scorpions square-dance and supplying a different note, trill, or percussion roll for everything that dared move. Used like this, music becomes a smothering form of control that blocks the audience from making any of its own emotional judgments.

HELPING TO INDICATE NARRATIVE STRUCTURE

Music can unify a thematic identity in several separated scenes, or strengthen dramatic structure by heralding the transition to a new act. Short *stings* or fragments of melody—a well-established convention in fiction film—can work in documentary when they belong to a larger musical picture, but use them cautiously unless the style of the film and its sound design have been boldly prepared for it.

HELPING TO INDICATE EMOTIONAL DEPTHS

Good music can prompt the audience to investigate emotional dimensions to the film that otherwise would pass unnoticed. Errol Morris does this masterfully in *The Thin Blue Line* (USA, 1989, Figure 34-2), in which the bleak, beautiful repetition in Philip Glass's minimalist score underlines a nightmarish conundrum. A man trapped on death row for a crime he claims not to have done must eternally relive the fateful events that led to his entrapment. Morris is quite justified in calling his film a "documentary *noir*."

Films provide their own clues about where music is needed. Often it seems natural during periods of tension, exhilaration, and in journeys or other bridging activities—a montage of a character driving across country to a new home, for instance. Transitions of any kind usually benefit from music, especially when the mood changes with the location. Music can enhance an emotional change when, for instance, an aspiring football player learns he can join the team, or when someone newly homeless must lie down in shame for her first night in a doorway.

Music can summon the spirit of an age, heighten the residual emotion in a landscape or city vista, or suggest an exotic ethnic or cultural atmosphere. Ethnic scenes in documentary pose problems of authenticity, however, and a poor facsimile of Thai music is no solution for a film set in Bangkok. With the aid of music, a film can modulate from realism to a more prophetic vision, as

FIGURE 34-2

Philip Glass's music in *The Thin Blue Line* alerts the audience to obsessive emotional dimensions in all the characters.

Godfrey Reggio does in his long, grandiloquent parable about man's rape of the natural world, *Koyaanisqatsi* (USA, 1983). Music can supply ironic comment, or suggest alternative worlds, as in Alain Resnais' matchless Holocaust documentary, *Night and Fog* (France, 1955), in which Hanns Eisler's score plays a major part. Instead of picture-pointing the deportation trains, or playing an emotionally loaded accompaniment to the mountains of human hair and tangled eyeglasses, Eisler's score pierces our defenses with a delicate, ghoulish dance or a sustained and unresolved interrogation between woodwind instruments.

MUSIC AS STORYTELLER VOICE

Now documentaries are more ready to be subjective and lyrical, music is ready to assist the Storyteller's "voice." The best examples seem to give expression to nascent feelings and an emotional point of view, either that of a character or of the Storyteller. Music can even function like a Storyteller's aside by implying something we cannot see or interpreting what is visible but apparently neutral.

STARTING AND STOPPING MUSIC

Film music, like debt and smoking, is easier to start than stop, and ending a section of music without giving the audience withdrawal pains can be difficult. The panacea is to supply a substitute, and this can either be a commanding effects track (a rich train-station atmosphere, for example, really a composition in its own right) or a new scene's dialogue. The diversion might also be behavioral rather than sonic—an inciting moment of action that lugs the spectator's attention forward into a new phase of the narrative, for instance.

STOCK MUSIC

When using music not composed to fit your film, section-ends can either be faded out or, better, come to a natural finish. In the latter mode, you would back-lay the music from the picture finish point, either arranging to fade music up at the picture start, or lengthening the scene to fit the music from composer's start to composer's finish. When music is over-long, you can frequently cut out repeated phrases. Most music is replete with repeated segments.

If you need something from the recorded classical repertoire, enlist the advice of a knowledgeable enthusiast. Be careful not to select something overused or fraught with existing film associations, like Vivaldi's *Four Seasons*, or Strauss's *Also Sprach Zarathustra*. You can never know if a piece works until you play it against the sequence in question.

SPOTTING SESSION

Spotting for music is the process of director and editor viewing the fine cut, and discussing a framework for a music cue list. For this you will need a start and stop for each proposed section, and a description of how you want the music to function. It might be to suggest release or change, foreshadow danger, or even suggest the maturing of a central character in years and judgment. Taken together, the notes you make at this stage will be helpful for developing an overall musical structure.

You must also decide where music should come from. Some might be popular music or orchestral music of a particular era used for atmosphere, for which you will need copyright clearance, which may be troublesome to acquire. You won't need clearance, however, if the music is a legitimate part of a scene, coming from a radio in a store, say, or made by a visible street musician.

Part of your process now will be to experimentally throw in *temp music*, because you often cannot judge what music of any kind will do until you try it.

For the rest you will need a film composer.

LIBRARIES AND COPYRIGHT

Music libraries will license a range of music at affordable prices and with a minimum of difficulty. I am assured that their offerings have improved in the last decade. To get the right to use other previously recorded music is more complicated, and requires fees and clearances that involve any or all of the following: composer, artist(s), publishers, and the record company. Students can often get written clearance for a manageable fee but only for use in festivals and competitions. If you then sell your film or receive rentals for showings, you may find yourself at the sharp end of a lawsuit.

Find out about clearing music for your film from Lisa Allif and Michael C. Donaldson's *The American Bar Association's Legal Guide to Independent Filmmaking* (American Bar Association, 2011), or Phillip Miller's *Media Law for Producers* (Focal, 2003). Never, ever assume that recorded music will be available when you get around to inquiring.

WORKING WITH A COMPOSER

Commissioning original music has two big advantages: it solves the clearance problem and gives you music unique to your film. Film composers are usually hired last in the creative chain, and are expected to work fast and efficiently under pressured circumstances. That said, the more time you can give them, the better.

For most of what follows I am indebted to my son Paul Rabiger of Cologne, Germany, who makes music for film there—largely documentaries (http://paulrabiger.com/en/index.html). Like many involved in producing music economically, he works largely with sampling technology and virtual instruments, but likes to use live instrumentalists when the budget allows. Favored software includes Digital Performer, Steinberg Cubase, and Logic Pro. Such programs permit many tracks, integrate MIDI with live recording, and support video in Quicktime format so that the composer can build music to an accurate video version of the film. MIDI is short for Musical Instrument Digital Interface, a communications protocol that connects computers and electronic musical instruments.

CHOOSING A COMPOSER

Generally, each composer has their own range of preferred sound, texture of instruments, and musical genres. You should certainly approach those whose musical style already fits your film. Writing for film is an interesting challenge, but a composer new to the process should be warned film composing nearly always happens under the gun.

People who make interesting music are often actively developing, and may jump at the chance to work in a genre that is new to them. A good way to protect yourself, yet see if their ideas work, is to *pitch* a given scene to two or three composers and invite a musical treatment from each. You can usually arrange this process for no fee, or one that is minimal. Its advantages are that short-listed composers can show you their work, and you see how the discussion and development process goes with each. You may get some pleasant surprises.

Any composer under consideration should see the whole film and discuss their reactions and initial ideas for music with you. To make an investment of hard work in your film, they need to like and respect it. You want to see what connections they have made with your work, and thus whether their musical ideas are likely to complement your film. The composer gets the prize of having their music accompany a film—usually highly desirable for anyone not yet a household name.

Upfront you should be very explicit about what your budget and schedule allow, since you will probably be asking for a lot of work in a short time, and for not much money.

WHEN THE COMPOSER COMES ON BOARD

The composer who joins you early will see the latest available film version, and mull over the characters, settings, and the film's overall content. If the music must reflect a particular era or ethnicity, research will sometimes be necessary. Let the composer take a copy of the film home, so that ideas can develop from multiple viewings. With time in which to develop basic melodic themes and decide what instrumental texture works best within the budget, he or she will probably see particular characters or situations, each deserving of their own musical treatment or *leitmotif* (pronounced "light-motif," which means recurring themes). Recurring sounds or sound textures in the sound track may also have a thematic subtext, and may at the composer's suggestion become leitmotifs in their own right, possibly integrated with the music.

WHEN THERE IS A TEMP TRACK

Often while editing, the editor drops in *temp* (temporary) or *scratch track* music because it helps establish a particular sequence's potential. It is wise to warn the composer ahead of time that temp music exists, and to offer to omit it if they prefer, since they may be thrown by a Beatles song or a soul-stirring passage from Shostakovich's *Leningrad Symphony*.

Many composers take the temp music as a useful demonstration of the rhythm, orchestration, texture, or mood you have in mind. It obviates the awkwardness of discussions in which filmmakers know what they like, but have zero command of a musical vocabulary in which to describe it.

Temp music can be an important tool of communication that shows the tempo driving the cutting, say, or how music should act as a counterweight to a fast action scene. This leaves nothing up to theoretical discussion, since what you want is of proven viability. Paul Rabiger adds: "Music is often dictated by the sounds that are already inherent in a scene: there should be some sense of this going on: for example, horses' hooves on cobble stones require perhaps a careful rhythmic handling by the composer. Or the elongated sounds of water—fountains, traffic, the sea—these tend to merge with long sustain sounds that can be good, but can also create problems." He believes temp music can point to sonic solutions that might take far too long to find by discussion and experiment alone.

DISCUSSING A MUSIC CUE LIST

Once you are near a *picture lock* (pictorially complete version), it is time to screen the film formally so that the composer, director, editor, and producer can break the film into acts, noting where they transition along the film's time line. You discuss where music seems desirable, what it should achieve, and what kind of instrumentation, tempo, mood, and musical texture seem best. Start-points may begin from particular cues in the imagery or dialogue, and discussion typically centers on how time is supposed to pass, and whether you want music to shore up a weak scene, as often it must.

When music's job is to set a mood, it should do its work, then get out of the way, perhaps returning to comment later. Since the rhythms of action, camera movement, montage, and dialogue are themselves a kind of music, they may need no enhancement, and the composer will sometimes point out just how effective, even loaded, a silence can be.

Knowing where each music section starts and stops, the composer aims to depart the discussion session with a music cue list in hand, notes as to the music's function, and beginnings and endings defined as timecode in- and out-points. The DVD or other version of the film you give to the composer must carry a cumulative timecode identical to that in your editing software, or you won't have a common reference.

COMPILING MUSIC CUES

Log sections from point to point in the cumulative timecode, and for tightly fitting sections log them to the nearest half second. Figure 34-3 shows what this looks like. Ending cues will take careful planning, and the rule of thumb is to conclude (or fade out) music under cover of something more commanding. You might take music out during the first seconds of a noisy street scene, or just before the dialogue in a new scene. For best-practice examples, study fiction films that successfully integrate music with your film's type of action. The computer-savvy composer then takes a download copy, and either writes a traditional score to be performed and recorded, or creates music sections directly using computers and MIDI-controlled synthesizers.

UNIFYING THROUGH TIME

The longitudinal relationships in a complex film's progression often need clarifying and strengthening, so your composer may use special coding to help group scenes, characters, or situations into musically related families. In a 90-minute film there may be many music cues, from a *sting* or short punctuation to long and elaborate passages that build, say, foreboding or melancholy. The composer may develop a theme for a main plot, then employ other themes for two subplots. Keeping these from clashing during cross-cutting can be problematical, so their relationship in key is important. Using a coding system keeps the composer aware of the logical connections and continuity that the music must underpin.

```
                          Music Section 4

      00:59:43    Begin music over long shot of Drottningholm Palace

      00:59:59    Medium shot actors crossing courtyard and entering
                  theatre building

      01:00:22    Interior theatre, long shot

      01:00:31    Backstage, actors enter

      01:00:40    Stage manager tests primitive wind machine (make
                  space in music here)

      01:00:51    Actors getting into costumes (bring music up
                  between 00:54 and 01:05)

      01:01:24    Curtains opening on dress rehearsal

      01:01:34    Lose music under first lines from cast
```

FIGURE 34-3

Typical scene measurements for a music cue segment.

Music can also function as a key to the viewer's memory. By repeating a theme or musical texture, music can unite a discussion with the mood of its original event, and reinforce the drama in human states of emotion.

Given the sophistication that music brings, it is evidently important to have concluded editing. The composer's recurring nightmare, especially in documentary, is creating music for a film whose final form is still in debate.

KEYS IN DIEGETIC AND NON-DIEGETIC MUSIC

In the planning stage the composer decides, based on the emotional logic of the story itself, what progression of keys to use through the film. You will recall that any sound that is a part of the film characters' world is called *diegetic* sound, but since the characters can neither hear nor react to the film's own music, this counts as *non-diegetic* sound. That, in fact, is addressed to the audience as part of the film's authorial commentary. When non-diagetic composed music takes over from diagetic music coming from a radio, say, the keys between the two usually must not clash. This is true for all adjacent music sections, not original scoring alone.

CONFLICTS AND COMPOSING TO SYNC POINTS

An experienced musician composing for a recording session will write to very precise timings, paying attention to track features such as dialogue lines and spot effects such as a door slam or a bird call. Instrumentation must not fight dialogue, nor can the arrangement be too busy at points where it might compete with dialogue or effects. Music can successfully displace an overloaded diegetic track. That is, in place of a welter of naturalistic sound, a musical comment may be far more impressionistic and effective.

To work around dialogue and spot effects, the composer should have an advanced version of the sound track rather than the simple dialogue-only track available during editing.

CONDUCTOR NEEDS

When you record a written score to picture—the recommended recording practice, by the way—the score is marked with cumulative timings so the conductor can see that sync points are lining up during recording.

Low budget film scores are more likely to use MIDI computerized composing techniques, and because the composer builds the music to a Quicktime scratch version of the film, music fitting is done at source.

How long does it take? An experienced composer likes to take upward of six weeks to compose, say, 15 minutes of music for a 90-minute feature film, but may have to do it in three weeks or less, with a flurry of music copyist work at the end if musicians are to play from scores.

LIVE MUSIC SESSION

With higher budget productions, the editing crew prepares for a live music recording session which is done to picture under the supervision of the composer, director, and editor. Only the editor can say for sure whether a shot can be lengthened to accommodate the slight mis-timings that always appear during live recording. Be prepared anyway for conductor, composer, and soloists to pursue a degree of perfection indistinguishable to ordinary mortals.

MUSIC IN POSTPRODUCTION
FITTING MUSIC

After a live recording session, the editor lays in each music section, adjusting picture and dialogue tracks as necessary. If the music is appropriate, the film takes a quantum leap forward in effectiveness. In the feature film world, there are music editors who specialize in cutting and fitting music.

THE SOUND MIX

The composer may want to be present at the final mix session if it affects the functionality of the music. If the music results from using MIDI, the composer can sometimes return to the musical elements with minimal delay and fashion a new version incorporating necessary changes.

NOTE

1. Kirby Dick interview with the director in *Still in Motion*, May 14, 2007 at http://stillinmotion.typepad.com/still_in_motion/2007/05/interview_perni.html.

CHAPTER 35

EDITING REFINEMENTS AND STRUCTURAL SOLUTIONS

Long and complex films present two main kinds of problem in editing. One is the familiar task of achieving integrity and flow in individual sequences, and the other is the more intangible difficulty of getting the film's architecture right. This matters because it is the support structure upholding the audience through a mass of related issues, and it should lead to a rewarding conclusion. Let's first explore some analogues illustrating how things work at the scene level.

EDITING RHYTHMS: AN ANALOGY IN MUSIC

If we imagine an edited conversation between child and grandparent, music makes a helpful analogy. We have two different but interlocked rhythms going: the rhythmic pattern of their voices in a series of sentences that ebb and flow, speed up, slow down, halt, restart, fade, and so on. Set against this, and taking its rhythmic cue from speech rhythms, is the visual tempo set up by the interplay of cutting, image compositions, and camera movement. The two streams, visual and aural, proceed independently yet in rhythmic relationship, like the music and the physical movements in a modern dance performance.

HARMONY

When you hear a speaker and see his face, sound and vision are in an alliance like musical harmony. We could, however, break the literalness of always hearing and seeing the same thing *(harmony)* by making the transition from scene to scene into a temporary puzzle.

COUNTERPOINT

Suppose we have a shot of a man talking in picture about unemployment and while he continues talking we cut to a somber cityscape, letting his remaining words play out over it. This functions as if one had glanced out of the window and seen all the houses spread below, the empty parking lots, and cold workshops of closed factories. The editing reproduces the instinctual glancing outside while listening. The speaker's words powerfully *counterpoint* the image, and send us imagining all the other people in this predicament. It is not a mere juxtaposition, nor is it an illustration: it is a new idea planted visually. This counterpoint of a sound or words against an incongruous image has its variations. One usage is nearer illustrating the actuality of what words can only describe. We might for instance cut from a bakery worker talking about fatigue to long shots of a bread factory taken through shimmering summer heat.

DISSONANCE

Another usage might create discrepancies and tension that force the viewer into making judgments. For instance, we hear an architect describing an enlightened and attractive philosophy of architecture, but see the man's work as a series of disappointing, nondescript boxes. This discrepancy is like a *dissonance* that spurs the viewer to crave a resolution. Comparing the man's beliefs with his practice, the viewer resolves the discrepancy by deciding he is an idealogue who is out of touch with the common person's reactions.

USING YOUR INSTINCTS WHILE EDITING

As you watched your inner process of inquiry and empathy toward a couple conversing, so you can now monitor your audience reactions to a piece of editing. Where is the dream state of high consciousness broken? What breaks it? What is missing, or too long, or too short? What else is needed?

Your instincts will tell you what the film needs, if you ask them and wait for your thoughts to coalesce. You are trying to construct an *authentic stream of consciousness*, and just as you would recognize a wrong note or wrong chord in a musical composition, so your instincts, trained by thousands of hours of screen works, recognize where things go awry in a piece of editing. It may still take considerable inquiry to find the false note.

USING TRIAL AUDIENCES

You know what the audience should see and feel, and it's easy to assume that this is happening. But nobody working on the production makes a good critic any more. By this stage, everyone associated with the film, particularly the director and editor, is feeling fatigued and encumbered. Your audience will all be newcomers with a fresh eye, so now you need to round up a few newcomers as a trial audience, out of whom you can squeeze the all-important feedback.

Sitting at the back through each viewing, and sensing shifts of attention from the audience's body language, you come out knowing which sections are gripping and which are not. You'll have a lot of questions to ask, but focus first on the parts where the audience shows signs of restlessness.

SUBTEXTS AND MAKING THE VISIBLE SIGNIFICANT

A baffling problem that often emerges during editing is that for some reason, nobody *gets* the underlying reason for something. They don't understand that a bank official feels bad when he can't give the small business owner a loan. You know him to be expressionless but sympathetic, while audiences see him as the heartless arm of capitalism. The problem is one of subtext: for some reason they don't notice what you notice. Why?

In *Literature and Film*, Robert Richardson goes to the heart of the filmmaker's problem:

> Literature often has the problem of making the significant somehow visible, while film often finds itself trying to make the visible significant.[1]

It is seldom easy to drive the film audience's awareness beyond what is literally and materially in front of the camera. For instance, we may accept a scene of a mother making lunch for her children as simply that. So what, you ask, mothers make lunch for kids all the time. But there are nuances: one child has persistent difficulty choosing what she wants and the mother is trying to master the irritation she feels. Looking closely, you see that the child is manipulating the situation. Food and eating have become their battleground, their frontier in a struggle for control. The mother's moral authority comes from telling her daughter she must eat right to stay healthy, while the child asserts her authority over her own body by a maddening noncompliance.

If the audience had first seen child and mother in some other, more overt conflict over control, they would know what to look for in this scene. There may, of course, be several other ways to channel the audience's attention, but without the proper structural or contextual support, the significance and universality of this scene could easily pass unnoticed. What you began to see on your fourth and subsequent viewings won't necessarily strike even the most perceptive among your first-time viewers. They lack the expanded insight that comes from your behind-the-scenes knowledge and repeated exposure.

However your knowledge evolved, you must do the same with your audience's. You may have to restructure the film, or add shots or scenes that alert the audience to that power struggle. You may have to show an additional scene with the bank manager to show that he is a compassionate man.

WHEN INSTINCTS AREN'T ENOUGH

Long-form films are frequently alarming in their earliest cut versions because they can utterly fail to deliver. Sequences that work at a local, immediate level add up to a totality that is a disappointment. You are baffled by the film's anti-climactic feeling, or, you miss a certain character who leaves the film early. Instincts tell you many things, and you try to act on them. But once you've done all that, you will need new strategies if you are to assess the cumulative effect of the film's parts. You need some special tools to help you figure out the how and why.

USING THE DIAGNOSTICS AGAIN

DIAGNOSTIC LOG

To diagnose story structure problems we make use of Diagnosing a Narrative (Table 35-1), last seen being used as a planning tool in Chapter 15. It is especially potent for unraveling structural problems during editing. You can find blank forms with the Analysis Projects at www.directingthe-documentary.com under **AP-5 Diagnosing a Narrative**. Log your film, sequence by sequence, then identify each by a content tag-title such as "Terry's first confrontation with his supervisor." Under "Contribution" name what the sequence contributes, such as "Terry's old problem with authority figures reappears." Allot each sequence an impact rating between 1–5 stars, number the sequences sequentially, and if you wish, use the elapsed-time facility in your editing software to log each sequence's duration. Now you can decide from your log:

- Each sequence's identity—because you had to name it (the tag-title).
- What it contributes to the audience's stream of consciousness in terms of experience, events, facts, impressions, etc.
- Whether its length and impact rating are consonant. Lengthy sequences that contribute little are prime candidates for the chop.

TABLE 35-1 Project AP-5 Diagnosing a Narrative is a first-rate tool for digging out the structural problems in a problematic edited version

Project AP-5 Narrative Diagnostic Worksheet	
Production title_____ Length_____	
Editor_____Date_____ Page #_____	
Sequence Content Tag-Title	**Contribution to Film's "Argument"**
_____ _____ _____ Seq #_____ Ends at TC ___:___:___	_____ _____ _____ Impact ✶ ✶ ✶ ✶ Length ___:___:___
_____ _____ _____ Seq#_____ Ends at TC ___:___:____	_____ _____ _____ Impact ✶ ✶ ✶ ✶ Length ___:___:___
_____ _____ _____ Seq #_____ Ends at TC ___:___:____	_____ _____ _____ Impact ✶ ✶ ✶ ✶ Length ___:___:___
_____ _____ _____ Seq #_____ Ends at TC ___:___:____	_____ _____ _____ Impact ✶ ✶ ✶ ✶ Length ___:___:___

- What the progression of impact ratings looks like, from the film's beginning to its end. Plotting them horizontally gives you a characteristic curve for the entire film. Does it peak early, or sag in places?
- Note that placing a sequence somewhere new won't change its content, but may drastically change its function because of its changed context.

Now divide your film into Acts and rule lines between Acts.

- Is all material in its right Act?
- Does the length and complexity of each Act look proportionate? (Act II is normally longer and more complex than Acts I and III)
- Does the film quickly imply a "contract" so the audience can decide to stay with what lies ahead?
- Does the film's introduction and development proceed logically? (Often there are back doubles or repetitions, or sequences that seem long-delayed)
- Can you see redundancy? (Showing the same basic situation twice is redundant unless the second raises the stakes)
- Are there any significant holes in the film's argument?
- Is there too much exposition before there's any action? (Explanation is sometimes better *after* the mystery of the action)
- Can the film's exposition be better apportioned?
- Do the characters appear when you are ready for them?
- Do characters disappear for long periods?
- Did a new and important character appear late? (You should somehow introduce him/her earlier.)
- Looking at the argument, whose POV does the film favor?
- Does the film's resolution fall in the right place and occupy the right amount of time?

Aspects of your film will be limited to a particular position by their evident chronology, but other material may be moveable and deliver a better impact in a different position. Here's how.

TURNING YOUR FILM INTO PLAYING CARDS

Photocopy your completed form, and scissor the copies into discrete sequences. Gum them on numbered index cards, and you have made a set of playing cards that you can group into Acts I, II, and III.

Move material around on a table to see the potential in using the material differently. This is good to do in a group discussion, because participants can argue for changes and illustrate their ideas by moving sequence cards around, narrating the new order, and describing the impressions and advantages created.

In playing-card form, everyone has an overview of what the film holds, and can take a bird's eye view of its potential. If the sequences you eliminate carry a note of their lengths you can quickly estimate time saved. And since the cards are numbered, you can quickly reset them at any stage to the film's existing form.

The longer and more convoluted the work in hand, the more essential a distancing method like this becomes. Without such an overview, and without discussing the film as a set of movable parts, it is much harder to decide alternative forms. This is because films always hold you in the iron grip of their present. The card-making process lets you oversee the film's whole dramatic development, and allows you to guess where it gets hung up, goes in circles, or otherwise shoots itself in the extremities.

DEALING WITH MULTIPLE ENDINGS

A film with multiple endings nearly always has the same problem: you haven't decided what your film is really about. You are hanging on to multiple intentions and hoping to cover them all. Face it: you can't. To escape the labyrinth, write an updated Working Hypothesis and revise the Premise. Once you have clarified your priorities, jettison the outriders. Grit your teeth and kill your darlings...

MORE TRIAL AUDIENCES

Particularly with a long film, you will need several different trial audiences to gauge the effect of each round of changes. You will know better with each viewing what specific feedback you're seeking, and can structure the Q & A accordingly.

LENGTH

Is your film really holding up at its present length? A common mistake is to set a desirable length and then resist trimming the film because you "always intended" that it be, say, feature length (90 minutes), or an hour (57 minutes). Yes, it's disappointing when your film doesn't stand up, but if your trial audiences keep finding it too long, you must bite the bullet and make a good film from a yawningly long one. You won't regret it. Shorter films find more favor at festivals than even the quite decent long ones.

FEAR OF FAILURE

If you are reading this in a funk, remember that every film you'll ever make is a crap shoot. Everyone has successes and failures, and probably more of the latter than the former. Both are equally important to your growth. For an inspiring and touching primer on the importance of failure, watch J.K. Rowling's address to the Harvard graduating class at http://harvardmagazine.com/go/jkrowling.html. She, of course, is the single mom who was on the verge of homelessness, but put her energy into writing because that's what she loved and could do well. Her *Harry Potter* books subsequently got a whole generation of kids to discover the joy of reading, but before that she got down to rock bottom.

> So why do I talk about the benefits of failure? Simply because failure meant a stripping away of the inessential. I stopped pretending to myself that I was anything other than what I was, and began to direct all my energy into finishing the only work that mattered to me. Had I really succeeded at anything else, I might never have found the determination to succeed in the one arena I believed I truly belonged. I was set free, because my greatest fear had been realized, and I was still alive, and I still had a daughter whom I adored, and I had an old typewriter and a big idea. And so rock bottom became the solid foundation on which I rebuilt my life.

Her long and impassioned speech describes how one must go all the way in doing one's own work if one is to become truly oneself. The subtext is, "You have one life; how are you using it?"

NOTE

1. Robert Richardson, *Literature and Film* (Indiana University Press, 1969), Ch. 5, p. 68.

PART 8

WORK

After your training period you have to make the difficult transition into paid employment. Even if you have established a top-notch reputation for craftsmanship and reliability, you will probably have to struggle for a subsistence living while you get established, like most people in the arts.

For these two final chapters I consulted the career development specialist Dirk Matthews of Columbia College Chicago, and Tod Lending, Academy-nominated director of many PBS films (www.nomadicpix.com). He is an old hand at writing proposals for grants, foundations, and broadcasters.

During Dirk's decades of placement counseling, he has tracked thousands of arts students setting out to find professional employment. He stresses the need for patience and realism: "Those seeking employment need to understand their strengths and weaknesses, and by leveraging these, can find a rich and rewarding career… There are a multitude of options in work and careers for those who study documentary." The first step is to "have students complete a variation of a SWOT analysis, an evaluation of Strengths, Weaknesses, Opportunities, and Threats" (see www.businessballs.com/swotanalysisfreetemplate.htm). For the beginner there are "many differences between employment and a career. A job can be the big break, or just a means to an end, to pay bills." In other words, expect to zig-zag through related work to eventually get where you want to go. "In film school, students tend to be limited by the concentrations they are taught (cinematography, post-production, etc.) and lose sight of the fact that there are wider assortments of secondary and tertiary careers to those tracts of study … Areas where they are successful are actually the areas where they are using their strengths in an authentic way … Given the rapid growth of technology and social networking, students graduating today may be working in careers that haven't even been created… Only a few years ago the idea of someone being hired to primarily work on social media would have been unheard of. Now, the title of Social Media Manager, or something similar, is a fairly common job in areas of film, marketing, and even journalism."

CHAPTER 36

DEVELOPING A CAREER

Establishing yourself as a documentary director begins with the work you have to show from your education period, as well as the networking and forward planning you have accomplished. You will need to be in love with the filmmaking process, so that you eat, sleep, dream the search for subjects and for unique treatments for them. You will need to keep seeing and making films, and to read, think, study, and argue your way into possessing a combative and original mind.

WILL I FIND WORK TO PAY MY BILLS?

ON GRADUATING

With good skills and some effective short films to show for it, we can fast-forward, perhaps to the point where you have gained an award or two. By now people in the local film industry may know you, especially if some have been your teachers in film school. To earn a living, you will need to have established a solid gold reputation for (a) reliability and professionalism, and (b) professional competency and dedication as a craftsperson in one or more of the key documentary areas:

- *Camera* (DP, operating, lighting, or gaffer skills)
- *Sound* (recordist and/or microphone operator, or sound design)
- *Postproduction* (editor or sound postproduction)
- *Production* (producer, production manager, production secretary, or assistant director)

You should be able to earn money at crewing, or in some associated craft, while you deploy a long-range plan to equip yourself for directing. Expect to learn hugely from friends and associates while you amass life experience in the field.

NETWORKING

The film industry, of which documentaries are just a part, is a set of linked villages. You get work by *networking* through personal connections with friends, associates, and professional contacts acquired during schooling and internships. Established film schools have alumni associations or other, less formalized networks in the major film centers. Through warm recommendations by teachers and contemporaries, you should be able to plug into these networks and get interviews and advice.

All film work is intensely social, and documentary in particular is not for shrinking violets. You have to go out, meet people, and get to know your way around. Finding work is much like researching a subject: it requires you to waylay people, tell them what you do, ask for help and advice, and offer your services. There is nothing inherently cheap or dishonorable in this, but most of us start out shy and fixated on avoiding rejection. If you think this is tough, ask a few actors what they go through at casting sessions.

CRAFTSPERSON

There are regional and national differences in the film and television industries, but developing as a freelancer is similar everywhere. A long time ago, some interesting facts emerged at a colloquium given at Columbia College Chicago by former film students. All were working professionally, and all,

- Took about the same (long) time to get established and to begin earning reasonable money.
- Had moved up the ladder of responsibility at roughly the same (slow) pace.
- Found that greater responsibility came (suddenly) without warning.
- Were scared stiff when it came, feeling they were conning their way into an area beyond their competence.
- All grew into their new levels of responsibility.
- All loved their jobs and felt privileged to work in an important area of public life.

Unless you can count on family help, your paid work may for a long time lie in fulfilling mundane commercial needs. That is, you will expend lots of imagination and effort crewing for industrial, training, or medical films; or shooting conferences, graduations, and weddings. Society always needs craftspeople that can make things and provide services of value.

Consider the nonfiction offerings of the Internet streaming service Hulu: sports, design, real estate, food, pets, children's shows, news and information, cars, how-to, how it works, mechanics, history, intervention (people confronting their worst demons), arts and culture, comedy (clubs and open mike nights), LGBT community interest material, and on and on. Someone has to dream up fresh ideas for that growing cornucopia of human interests. Someone has to form the entrepreneurial alliances, groups, companies, and film units that generate and sell the content. Why not you?

Developing the ability to complete all kinds of projects reliably, inventively, and to high standards will give you satisfaction, higher-level skills, and confidence and pride in your capacities. Each new level of accomplishment brings recognition, so that you and your associates can seek ever more interesting and demanding work. A similar training, after all, served Robert Altman and many another director very well.

YOUR DEMO REEL FOR GETTING WORK

From your best and most applicable work, custom-build a reel for each different job application, and include a descriptive hand-list. A wide range of pertinent work is a showcase for your experience and flexibility. Your reel should show your professionalism and include both work initiated by you, and work done for others—each identified for what it is. Always be sure to give credit to others where it is due. "To start building a reel," says Dirk Matthews, "review each project you have worked on and choose the strongest scene. What best showcases your talent in each project? Maybe it is your best camerawork, or the moment where all elements of the film gelled together. After you have a few scenes, these can be cut together, starting with best work."

UPLOADING

"YouTube is not the only place to upload a reel. While it is a great platform for social networking, there are many, many distractions in the design. Someone may be watching your reel, get distracted, and click on the video of a cat riding a dog, or the latest movie trailer that pops up in the sidebar. Vimeo is a platform with better online compression and far fewer distractions. It is good to have your reel on both, but think of where on the internet to hang your shingle so that people can find you and view your work." Dirk believes one should start promoting one's next film in preproduction, "through social media, press releases, building a website for your film, etc. Ideally, you would have some festival, market or distribution interests in the works while you are shooting. This is where a marketing person or a publicist is well worth an investment. There is also a whole new market for online distribution. Snag Films is just one example (www.snagfilms.com)."

YOU, ON THE WEB

Dirk says, "You will be Googled when you apply for opportunities, promote a film, or seek distribution." So,

- You want more than just Facebook and social media links to show up in the search results.
- The more professional your links and sites, and the better you update them, the better your online presence supports your professional endeavors.
- Purchasing a custom URL is a great way to assemble information and links about yourself. Its address should be on every business card, résumé, or cover letter you send out professionally.

Once you are on the web, self-reflection is important. If you use it irresponsibly, readers may think you hate your work and care more about food and drinking. Using the various platforms responsibly, on the other hand, can demonstrate your ability to network and build relationships. Knowing who you are, what types of opportunities you want, and articulating this concisely will help you get the results you want. For potential collaborators or employers searching among your records on the web, there are many ways to establish your identity:

- Social networks (Facebook, Google + , Twitter, Instagram, etc.)
- Professional networks (LinkedIn, or see a list at http://www.sitepoint.com/social-networking-sites-for-business)
- Online profiles (these are more about a static view of your résumé)
- Online portfolios (reels, websites, etc.)

MAKING A JOB FOR YOURSELF

The film and television industries are downsizing permanent staffs and employing freelancers. This means opportunities for small, self-starter companies, but—wouldn't you know it?—work usually goes to those with a record of accomplishment. For the novice this is catch-22. Your investment in your future is the films you made at school, or have made since then at your own expense. If you have a passion for stained glass, for science, for alternative power systems, or for medieval farming, then your work and self-promotion should clearly evidence your enthusiasms. Your areas of passionate interest can lie anywhere—ornithology, teaching, ghosts, or the politics of water supply in the Third World. Use the work you've done to introduce yourself to individuals or organizations with interests that parallel your own. Almost certainly they will recognize you as one of their own, and sometimes before you know it, you're in another country doing the kind of useful work you

FIGURE 36-1

Morgan Spurlock experimenting with a diet of McDonald's in *Supersize Me.*

always dreamed of. Okay, you're working for expenses only, but you're racking up demonstrable experience for your résumé and demo reel, which in the early stages is what counts most.

Along the way, expect to meet hard times, lose jobs, encounter discouragement, and live on the edge. You may find you are inordinately good at sound, and stay with it. Or that you have a penchant for the more studious and solitary life of the editor (my passion). Perhaps directing is something you find you can gladly put off till the future.

However hard the life is, you will never have to wonder why you go to work every day. In what other profession could the activist Morgan Spurlock (*Supersize Me*, USA, 2004, Figure 36-1) take on the McDonald Corporation and convulse the world with horrified laughter? Where else could he go looking for America's "biggest enemy" equipped only with a "hasty round of survival training, a camera, and his trademark mustache"? (*Where in the World is Osama bin Laden?*, USA, 2008).

THE SEARCH FOR SUBJECTS

While crewing you must develop ideas for your own documentaries, which means looking for subjects and treatments that will demonstrably attract a sizable audience. Documentary markets are evolving, and audience appreciation for the genre is maturing. TV and cable networks now show independently produced documentaries, but rely increasingly on international co-productions to share the high cost of any series with worldwide appeal.

STUDY THE COMPETITION

Check out your particular areas of interest at film sales and rental websites. Make a study to see where gaps exist in the existing commercial structure, gaps you could fill. Make yourself current by seeing everyone else's work, especially at festivals, which are really job-fairs for filmmakers. Much of what you will see acts like aversion therapy—it tells you the subjects and treatments that are overused and clichéd. College-age filmmaking, for example, seldom thinks beyond a college-enclosed audience. Instead, study how experienced filmmakers present themselves to see what you can learn.

PRACTICE YOUR PITCH

The vast majority of proposals are imitative and stereotypical because their writers think no further than a "good subject." They fail to develop individual approaches, original and critical thematic ideas, or to question what makes pertinent and arresting film art at this moment in history. These come only from the actively original mind, and tend to win immediate recognition, both by funding committees and audiences.

On your way to developing high abilities, seek colleagues or doc makers at large who are willing to exchange pitches via Skype. One learns the most from critiquing other people's performances, and getting them to respond to yours. You don't need to physically meet, only to have a pitch and a demo reel with which to practice via YouTube (see "BBC documentary pitch demo").

THE DEMO REEL FOR A PARTICULAR PROPOSAL

With each pitch and grant application, have ready an edited demonstration reel *of around 3–5 minutes maximum* that shows the most attractive and intriguing aspects of your proposed project. A good reel can often clinch a jury decision in your favor because it argues powerfully *and briefly* for both the foundations of your project and for your proficiency. It is the taster morsel that shows the best you have shot. If it has great landscapes, or a gritty industrial setting, include a montage of the best shots. If your film is character-driven, assemble material to establish in a minute or so how attractively interesting and unusual your central characters are. Make certain your demo reel is accessible, and plays faultlessly from beginning to end, online or offline.

DOCUMENTARY PROPOSALS

Study up on everything available on grants, funds, and grantwriting. Think of it not as tin-cup begging, but as your best shot at communicating your vision and originality. Remember, *you are what you write*, so develop the very best proposals you can produce, equip yourself with a first-rate demo reel, then try your luck—and keep trying. Stellar performance never happens by luck or "talent"—it happens through practice, application, and heart-and-soul involvement. Remember, you are not competing with colleagues, but aiding and abetting them—and they, you. Give and seek critical feedback, and build on each other's critical acumen. Really good, fresh proposals are rare because so few people really work at it. If you propose excellent, unusually realized projects with a clear dramatic form, they will stand out from the crowd.

The long established Independent Feature Project (IFP) has good funding ideas and information on its website (www.ifp.org). Each year, public television in the USA throws out The Doc Challenge in which filmmakers from around the world have five days to make a short nonfiction film. The top 12 films, determined by a panel of judges, premiere at Hot Docs in Toronto, the largest doc film festival in North America. This competition allows film students, emerging filmmakers, and seasoned pros the opportunity to make a great documentary and to win cash prizes, free services, and the chance to screen at festivals (www.pbs.org/pov). Undoubtedly other national broadcasting organizations are making similar offers as they reach out for the talented work being made on the periphery.

USING FESTIVALS

At documentary festivals, you may be able to win funds and encouragement by coming armed with interesting approaches and ideas. If you have cornered the rights to a "hot" subject, you might get offers of partnership from established concerns, which can also be a good deal. Get legal advice in creating partnership agreements[1] and be very careful not to get swallowed up.

See what TV networks and distributors advise in relation to proposing "your" kind of films. The Independent Feature Project website has much good information on all aspects of producing as an "indie" (www.ifp.org), especially the financial aspects. It even advertises job openings and publishes requests for specialized partnerships.

Go to pitching sessions and get a feel for what it is like. At those held most famously by the International Documentary Film Festival in Amsterdam, Hot Docs in Toronto, Points North Pitch in Maine, and Op Docs in New York, hopeful producers pitch ideas and undergo a public grilling by a panel of commissioning editors, who may or may not subsequently buy into the project. Pitch an idea of your own if you can.

Sessions are popping up everywhere, and TV organizations that show or fund documentaries—such as PBS, ITVS, BBC, BritDoc Foundation (Channel 4), CBC, Al Jazeera—each have their own support website with examples and advice to help attract good proposals, which they insist are forever in short supply.

THE IMPORTANCE OF SHORT FILMS

Festivals *adore* good short films, and can never get enough. It takes style, originality, and discipline to say a lot in a short compass, yet most documentary beginners try to hole-in-one (to borrow a golf simile) with documentary of stupifying length and ambition. It takes forever to finish, uses up all their resources and optimism, and is nearly always a huge, costly, and dispiriting mistake.

Why waste years making a 90-minute monster, when you could use the same resources to make nine crisp, funny, searing, and thoughtful 10-minute films? Each will have a new cast of characters, and each will improve on the last since you learn so much from finishing cycles of production.

SEEKING JOB INFORMATION

The Internet ought to be a good labor exchange, and at least one film job site is open for searches (www.media-match.com). Services like this exist primarily to make money for their organizers, and are by no means a passport to employment. But if you are the only filmmaking primatologist in your area, you may have the very skills that someone needs. Tim Curran's FAQ, which speaks autobiographically, may also be helpful (www.timcurran.com). I found it, and a great deal more, by entering "documentary" and "career" in Google. Two other good sites are Indeed (www.indeed.com) and Mandy (www.mandy.com).

Information about the non-Hollywood film industry and expectations for independents can be found at the IFP (Independent Film Project, www.ifp.org). The Salt Institute (www.salt.edu) specializes in documentary stills and sound work for sociologists, and you may find diary and blog items there to stimulate your ideas. Ethnography, sociology, ecology, and many other disciplines are sometimes interested in co-production. Go to their conferences, and network like crazy. Almost certainly you can emerge with partnerships in the making.

INFORMATIONAL INTERVIEWS

Dirk adds that, "students can sometimes call or email a company or professional individual and ask for some time to find out more about the industry. They should not ask for a job or whether they are hiring, but instead ask along the lines of, 'what is the ideal employee' or 'what type of entry level positions do you hire?' ... It can be a good way for students to put themselves in front of a professional without asking for job. The result is a connection, more information, and a possible professional mentor."

ON GETTING A WORK INTERVIEW

If you mean to approach anyone in an organization, first learn all you can about the individuals in it and their business. When you send your résumé, send it to a named individual with a brief, carefully composed, *individual* cover letter describing your goals. Be sure to say in what ways you might be an asset to their business, group, or company. After a few days, call to ask if you can have a brief chat "just in case something opens up in the future." If you are invited for a chat or formal interview,

- Dress conservatively.
- Be punctual to the minute.
- Let the interviewer ask the questions.
- Be brief and to the point when you reply.
- Say concisely what skills and qualities you have to offer. This is where you can demonstrate your knowledge of (and therefore commitment to) the interviewer's business.
- Never inflate your abilities or experience.
- Know what you want, and show you are willing to do any kind of work to get there.
- Leave an up-to-date résumé with a link to an online demo reel.

People who deal with job seekers can tell the hardworking realist from the dreamer. They know this from how you present yourself—on paper and in person. Interviews often conclude by asking if you have any questions, so have two or three good ones ready that demonstrate your knowledge of, and interest in, the interviewer's company, group, or enterprise.

If shyness is holding you back, do something about it. Time will not liberate you. Get assertiveness training, join a theatre group, or sign on for an improv comedy class and die a thousand deaths making a fool of yourself.

NOTE

1. See Lisa Callif and Michael C. Donaldson, *The American Bar Association's Legal Guide to Independent Filmmaking* (American Bar Association, 2011), and Philip Miller, *Media Law for Producers* (Focal Press, 2003).

CHAPTER 37

STARTING UP ON YOUR OWN

Everyone hungry to make films wants to know the "secret of how you got the money" for a particular project, but each process is different. It is particular to the project, to you the producer, and to the organization to which you are applying. Getting funds is key to making documentaries for a living.

STARTING A BUSINESS

If you begin to make films of your own, you will have to decide whether to incorporate or apply for fiscal sponsorship. By making film for money, you are for legal purposes "sole proprietor" of a business. This is straightforward enough from a tax and bookkeeping point of view, but has its risks. Should you face a legal claim, a court will make no separation between your business liabilities and your personal assets, even those you hold in common with a spouse or family members.

INCORPORATING

You can build a legal firewall between your business and your private assets by *incorporating*. This requires registering with the appropriate governmental office, paying a fee, listing your business entity's name, purpose, place of business, and other information. To set this up, and get your taxation and record-keeping liabilities straight, engage an arts lawyer, for whom it will be a straightforward undertaking.

FOR-PROFIT OR NONPROFIT?

Now you must decide whether your business is For-Profit or Nonprofit. You can, by the way, pay yourself a salary under either model. As a Nonprofit—by far the most likely case—you set out to create works for the public good more on a charity model, while the For-Profit model involves developing a profit-based business plan, with shares offered to shareholders and investors. For expert advice on the basic choices, see Cianna Stewart's International Documentary Association (IDA) article (at www.documentary.org/content/documentaries-are-businessesor-should-be).

FISCAL SPONSORSHIP

The nonprofit option further involves choosing between setting up your own arrangement with the Internal Revenue Service (IRS) as a nonprofit, or of arranging *fiscal sponsorship* through an existing nonprofit organization, such as the International Documentary Association (IDA), which says:

> Fiscal sponsorship is a formal arrangement in which a 501(c)(3) public charity, such as the IDA, agrees to sponsor a project that furthers our mission, for the purpose of fundraising through grants and donations. This alternative to starting your own nonprofit allows you to seek grants and solicit tax-deductible donations for your documentary, with the oversight, support and endorsement of IDA.

In return for this service, the nonprofit organization takes a small percentage of funds raised. Key to seeking funds in this way is that donors can claim their contributions as a tax-deductible donation. Many nonprofit organizations run this service, and Chicago Filmmakers, for example, has a long record of helping fund narrative and documentary films (http://chicagofilmmakers.org/cf/content/fiscal-sponsorship).

SEEKING FUNDS

CURRENT INFORMATION

Since the advent of social media, funding documentaries (and much else) has become a fast-evolving situation. For up-to-date information, search the Internet using salient words such as *documentary, fund, festival, pitching, proposal, investors,* etc. Remain skeptical about what you find until you establish reliable trends and patterns from multiple sources. Preeminent among help websites for serious documentarians is the D-Word (www.d-word.com) founded by Doug Block, which says about itself,

> The D-Word hosts discussions about the art, craft, business, and social impact of documentary film. Our Public Topics are open to all. Documentary professionals can apply for free access to a wide range of industry discussions in our Business, Creative, Social, and Technical Topics. Founded in 1999, The D-Word has become the leading documentary community with more than 10,300 members, including over 4,700 documentary professionals from around the world.

New funding methods have come about because the traditional agencies and foundations make applications so lengthy and so biassed toward those already established. This discriminates against newcomers and against contemporary subjects needing an immediate response, so social media have come up with the crowdfunding concept.

Crowdfunding uses a dedicated website portal to attract many supporters or backers who, for a variety of motivations, are ready to subscribe on the spot to an invention, experiment, business, or other project. Known also as *platforms*, there are over 250 organizations that offer crowd-funding services, many dedicated to particular geographic areas. Their service conditions vary significantly (see Wikipedia's "Comparison of crowd funding sources"). Backers decide whether or not to subscribe on the merit of the pitch, demo reel, information, and special assurances. Those who do subscribe become potential supporters and publicists throughout your film's completion in their locality, so crowdfunding can serve more than one purpose.

Typically a film project will need a given sum to complete a particular stage—perhaps $20,000 to buy library picture rights, do a sound mix, and make distribution DVDs. There are various alternative funding options:

- In an *All or Nothing* platform, pledges return to the subscribers if the total falls short of the target amount.

- In a *Keep It All* platform, the project receives whatever money was raised.
- In *Bounty* funding, whoever completes the project claims the funds raised as a bounty.

Your success still depends on the same factors you need when selling your wares more traditionally: you will need a first-class pitch, a relevant and eye-catching demo reel, and good accountancy to demonstrate why you need the money and how you intend using it. Above all, you need a project whose subject and treatment are so compelling that people instinctively fumble for their credit cards.

KICKSTARTER

In the USA, the best-known arts project portal is currently Kickstarter (www.kickstarter.com/hello). Though it handles only US, UK, and Canadian projects, the platform is open to backers from anywhere in the world. Donors' pledges are collected via Amazon Payments, with Kickstarter retaining 5 percent of the funds raised and Amazon an additional 3–5 percent. Unlike many fund-raising forums, Kickstarter does not retain ownership of projects, nor does it interfere in the project in any way. Most usefully, after funding is complete, Kickstarter leaves the web pages of its previous projects open to the public. Projects and media that remain on the site cannot be edited or removed.

Backers learn to exercise caution since Kickstarter cannot guarantee that people posting projects will use the money as promised. If, however, they take the money and fail to deliver the project, backers can sue for legal damages. Projects sometimes fail after successfully raising funds because the creators underestimated the costs and difficulties of completion.

CAVEATS

Crowdfunding is not a magic bullet for fundraising, and given its newness and rapidly evolving practices, you should regard it as a work-in-progress. Carefully check your chosen portal's website for all you must do when using it, and be aware that somebody's innovative approach today, copied by hundreds of applicants, will have lost all its novelty by tomorrow. Check out recent documentary crowdfunding experiences at The D-Word (www.d-word.com), an excellent (and free) source of information on all aspects of making documentaries.

FUNDS AND FOUNDATIONS

The United States has a complex and shifting system of *federal, state, and private funding agencies*, each with its own guidelines and a record of funding particular types of film and subject. Funding organizations usually grant no more than a percentage of the budget, leaving the filmmaker, now usefully armed with the promise of partial funding, to find the further partnerships that will make up the balance. As a rule, private grant foundations prefer to give *completion money* to films that are self-evidently promising, while government agencies, if they fund research and preproduction, give only to those with an established track-record. If they stipulate that you work with a board of academics, stop and think. A camel, they say, is a horse designed by a committee.

SURVEY ORGANIZATIONS

Two US organizations exist to help people find the appropriate private fund or charity. There is the Donors Forum, a clearinghouse in Chicago that periodically publishes local information (www.donorsforum.org), while New York has the Foundation Center (http://foundationcenter.org) as its nationwide source of donors and donor organizations. Many people compete for their support, so expect to jump through many hoops.

TOD LENDING ON PROPOSALS

The following is Tod Lending's view on proposals:

Almost all documentaries, no matter what genre, are made in the cutting room, not in the proposal stage. The purpose of the proposal is not to create a script that you must follow once you're in the field. Its purpose is to sell the project so that you can get to the field and/or editing room in order to *find* the story you've proposed, tell the story you imagined, or tell a new story that you had initially never imagined.

There are two major types of proposals, and all kinds of variations in between. One is the proposal for foundations, including broadcasting and government entities such as PBS, CPB, NEA, NEH, etc., and these I will call "grant proposals." The second proposal is for commercial broadcasters—cable and network. That is an entirely different little beast— two pages maximum—and it must have a 5–10 minute reel attached.

All proposals should have a demo reel attached. A good one presents compelling characters, either actual drama or the clear potential for drama to develop, an interesting story, strong visuals, and evident command of the craft. A good demo reel can get an average to below-average proposal funded, whereas the opposite is not true. A below-average demo reel will kill a good proposal because it raises serious questions about the proposal.

When deciding what headings and sections should be in the proposal, consider first what structure will best sell the project. You are trying to raise money and so you need to put on two hats, that of a salesman and that of an attorney/expert. The latter needs to be worn especially when pitching to foundations. In a proposal let the reader know what the foundation is looking for, and do the same in a pitch/meeting. If they're interested in your project, they'll call you in and you'll need to be prepared. Let the reader know that your understanding of the issues embodied within your story are of the utmost importance to the program officer. This is the opposite of pitching to a broadcaster, who is primarily interested in character, dramatic content of the story, and that you have access. Unique access to a story is a *huge* selling point to both broadcasters and foundations, so highlight this in the proposal as well as the pitch.

My typical categories for grant funding:

1. **Executive Summary**
2. **Introduction**
3. **Story and Content**
4. **Structure and Style**
5. **Themes and Issues**
6. **Project Need** (Argue why this film should be made. In this well-researched section the filmmaker demonstrates that he knows which media have already addressed the issue he's pitching. Put on the lawyer/expert hat and make the case for why your film should be made, and what kind of gap it will fill. Mention some personal connection, but more important is the contribution the film will make toward public discourse on a particular issue. Addressing the needs of underserved populations is obviously primary here.)
7. **Community Engagement Plan** (extremely important)
8. **Distribution Plan**

9. **Promotional Plan**

10. **Project Advisors** (unimportant to broadcasters, but extremely important for any type of grant proposal)

11. **Budget and Financial Support** (This is a short narrative description of what time-frame and what activities the budget covers. It may also contain information on what funds have been raised to date, in-kind contributions, and how funds have been spent.)

12. **Projected Time Frame**

13. **Production Personnel**

Also important to include are letters of commitment from broadcasters and funders, and letters of endorsement from experts in the field. Other sections that I sometimes include: Historical Background, Audience, Additional Narrative Elements. If music is an important element in the film then it probably needs to have its own section.

FUNDING ORGANIZATIONS

BROADCAST ORGANIZATIONS

The Independent Television Service (ITVS) website is a mine of information on recently funded independent productions (see www.itvs.org, see "For Producers"). This site gives valuable hints on writing a better application. The Public Broadcasting Service (PBS) also gives similar information for their important series *POV* at www.pbs.org/pov/utils/aboutpov_faq.html and their call-for-entries website is www.pbs.org/pov/utils/callforentries.html#callforentriesk. These organizations expect makers to initiate films and to seek funding only at the completion stage. They facilitate many important American independent documentaries, and so are inundated with applications. ITVS (www.itvs.org/funding/open-call/how) and *POV* both ask independent producers to apply with a substantial amount of the footage, or better, a long edited version.

Documentary sites like these all over the world are immensely helpful when you are making documentaries for television, which is still the main forum. Many who apply to them, however, make abysmal applications, so their advice is intended to parry the commonest mistakes and misunderstandings. An ITVS regional jury on which I once sat for three days found only six applications promising out of 140. This experience made it plain that a person's organization and vision are visible on paper, and even more so in a demo reel. Two of those we chose (which ITVS in the end failed to support) went on by other means to become quite famous independent films.

GOVERNMENT AGENCIES

If your record of accomplishment is slender (perhaps a short film that has won some festival awards), and you are seeking preproduction, production, or completion money, investigate your *state or city arts council*. Each state in the US has a *state humanities committee* and yours may, as part of its support for the arts, give grants to documentaries on a competitive basis (see http://www.prairie.org/humanities-resources/documentary-films). Your local or state authority may do so too, and this is a good place to start. The *National Endowment for the Humanities* (NEH) works to fund groups of accredited individuals (usually academics) producing work in the humanities. Guidelines can be obtained from The National Endowment for the Humanities (www.neh.gov) whose website has much good information.

Many states and big cities have a *film commission* or *film bureau* that exists to encourage and facilitate fiction filmmaking because it's good business for the region. They exist to develop formal and informal relationships with visiting film productions. See www.studio1productions.com/

Articles/FilmCommission.htm for a list of film offices. Like most, my state is a good information source for festivals, locations, personnel, equipment, and so on (http://www.illinois.gov/dceo/whyillinois/Film/Pages/default.aspx).

MARKETING AND DISTRIBUTION

To find out about the markets you might enter, there is a wealth of documentary-related information and a useful month-by-month festival calendar available through the International Documentary Association (IDA, www.documentary.org/about-us).

Check out AIVF (Association of Independent Video and Filmmakers, www.aivf.org), an organization dedicated to supporting the independent filmmaker. There documentary folk can see what independent fiction-makers are producing and vice versa. Fiction and documentary should be symbiotic, not Balkanized. Acquaint yourself with the mandate of the Corporation for Public Broadcasting (www.cpb.org) which distributes money to a number of funds, including ITVS (the Independent Television Service, www.itvs.org), but be ready for Byzantine funding requirements and relationships.

If you are located in the Los Angeles area, the IDA (International Documentary Association, www.documentary.org) has a strong program of local events at which you can learn and network. For those further afield, it publishes *International Documentary*, an important quarterly with articles on new films, filmmakers, trends, festivals, and technology. The IDA website contains directories of festivals and competitions, funding, jobs and opportunities, classes/seminars/workshops, distributors looking for new films, new publications, and so on.

Other countries have comparable organizations which you can locate using a search engine. Today there are vibrant documentary communities in almost all countries, with Australia, New Zealand, Canada, Britain, Denmark, the USA, and India foremost among English-speaking countries. Documentarians are an opinionated, voluble, sociable lot, and nobody with a computer ever needs to feel isolated. No matter what language you speak, you will find rivers of discussion, criticism, and technological review on the Internet. Search and thou shalt find!

If you plan to live by camerawork, consider taking out a subscription to *American Cinematographer*, a monthly publication for feature fiction workers that publishes occasional articles on high visibility documentaries. More importantly, it will keep you abreast of state-of-the art methods and innovations in camera technology and lighting. The journal includes news, interviews, and a lot of "who's doing what" information (see www.theasc.com). Like most contemporary organizations, AC also sends out material online.

Videomaker magazine reviews new equipment in the "prosumer" range (that is, high-end consumer, low-end professional), and has accessible explanations and videos explaining techniques and technical principles. Its website (www.videomaker.com) is a mine of technical, workshop, and instructional information. Also look to your local equipment rental houses as a source of information. They often host workshops, conferences, and demonstrations as a way to introduce the community to their offerings and personnel.

A PERSONAL MESSAGE

Documentary is a lovely and evolving field in which the levels of inventiveness, humor, courage, and productivity are all rising. I believe this is because documentary people are remarkable for their conviviality and helpfulness. They have chosen documentary film—be it ecological, activist, humanitarian, poetic, or historical—as the work that matters to them most in all the world.

I hope that you, dear reader, decide to join this community, and that your work contributes to a better world for our children. Thank you most sincerely for using this book, and if you have any comments to help make the next edition better, email me at mrabiger@aol.com. I will try to reply. Please don't send unsolicited proposals or films—I simply don't have time to review them (or to do lots of other good things).

May you have good luck, good filming, and good friendships.

INDEX

Titles of films are indicated in *italics*.
Other publications are indicated by *title* (author or publication type).
Page numbers in *italic* refer to illustrations.
Page numbers in **bold** refer to tables.